MW01195851

Seekers of the Face

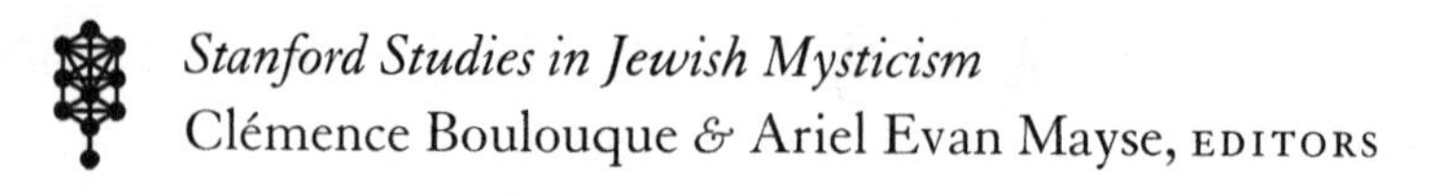

Stanford Studies in Jewish Mysticism
Clémence Boulouque & Ariel Evan Mayse, EDITORS

SEEKERS OF THE FACE

Secrets of the Idra Rabba
(The Great Assembly) of the Zohar

Melila Hellner-Eshed

Translated by Raphael Dascalu

Stanford University
Stanford, California

STANFORD UNIVERSITY PRESS
Stanford, California

Seekers of the Face was originally published in Hebrew in 2017 under the title *Mevakshe ha-panim: mi-sodot ha-Idra raba shebe-Sefer ha-Zohar* ©2017, Rishon LeZion: Yedioth Ahronoth Books and Chemed Books.

Printed in the United States of America on acid-free, archival-quality paper

Library of Congress Cataloging-in-Publication Data
Names: Hellner-Eshed, Melila, author. | Dascalu, Raphael, translator.
Title: Seekers of the face : secrets of the Idra rabba (the Great Assembly) of the Zohar / Melila Hellner-Eshed ; translated by Raphael Dascalu.
Other titles: Mevakshe ha-panim. English
Description: Stanford, California : Stanford University Press, 2021. | Originally published in Hebrew in 2017 under the title Mevakshe ha-panim. | Includes bibliographical references and index.
Identifiers: LCCN 2020051463 (print) | LCCN 2020051464 (ebook) | ISBN 9781503628427 (cloth) | ISBN 9781503628588 (epub)
Subjects: LCSH: Idra rabba. | Zohar. | Cabala.
Classification: LCC BM525.A6 I374513 2021 (print) | LCC BM525.A6 (ebook) | DDC 296.1/62—dc23
LC record available at https://lccn.loc.gov/2020051463
LC ebook record available at https://lccn.loc.gov/2020051464

Cover design: Kevin Barrett Kane

Text design: Kevin Barrett Kane

Typeset at Stanford University Press in 11/15 Granjon LT Std

In loving memory of the healing countenance
of my beloved Dror.

Erekh Appin—Healing Countenance. For there is no healing in the world except when gazing face-to-face.

Idra Zuta, Zohar 3:292b

Contents

PART 2

Seekers of the Face

Introduction

The work known as the Idra Rabba—the Great Assembly—is a grand story, perhaps the greatest story in the Zohar. The Idra Rabba tells of an emergency assembly convened by Rabbi Shim'on bar Yoḥai, the Zohar's hero, to which he summons his disciples, the *ḥavrayya* (Companions). The gathering takes place in a field, among the trees, at a time beyond time and in a place beyond place. The assembly's mission is an audacious one: to heal the face of God, and thereby transform and heal the face of the Jewish religion. This is to be done by invoking and manifesting three distinct faces of the Divine, reconfiguring them and realigning them in order to ensure the flow of abundant blessing into the world.

The story of the Idra Rabba—which begins with the dramatic call *Time to act for YHVH!* (Psalms 119:126)—is inlaid throughout with revelations of profound secrets concerning the Divine, spoken by the teacher and his disciples. The Idra Rabba portrays the Divine with daring anthropomorphic images and descriptions. The various dimensions of the Divine are conceived and interpreted in the language of "faces" (*partsufim*), as well as boldly embodied and detailed descriptions of the male and female bodies within the Divine, bodies that manifest an erotic and sexual relationship.

A daring myth emerges from the work as a whole, setting forth the development of the various faces of the Divine, which human beings encounter in a revealed or concealed manner, in thought, imagination, and experience.

Simultaneously, the gathering is an initiation ceremony for the disciples of Rabbi Shim'on bar Yoḥai, who are summoned to join their teacher and become "pillars," mystically upholding and sustaining all existence.

Alongside the Idra Rabba in zoharic literature is the Idra Zuṭa—the Small Gathering—which relates the events of the day of Rabbi Shim'on bar Yoḥai's death, and records the secrets that he reveals to his disciples before departing this world. These two works, along with some other fragments scattered throughout the Zohar, are unique in their conceptual, religious, linguistic, and literary characteristics, setting them apart as a distinct stratum within the zoharic corpus: the stratum of the Idras. Among the many religious-mystical-revelatory languages we find in zoharic literature, the language of the Idras probes particularly deep layers of the psyche.

These two assembly narratives occupy a unique and sacred position within the Zohar—a status that has become only more exalted as the Zohar's reception and canonization has progressed. Through the generations, the Idras attracted commentaries and interpretations from some of the greatest and most creative kabbalists. These two magnificent compositions broadened the horizons of Jewish mystical and esoteric thought, enriching it and adding new layers of complexity.

The Idra Rabba sits at the heart of my book. Despite its formidable density, the Idra Rabba is coherent in its concepts, language, and style, and possesses narrative continuity and a complex and sophisticated literary structure. In this book, I seek to mediate between the text and the reader: describing and illuminating this classical work, whose daring theology and dense literary style render it inaccessible to most readers today, even those well versed in Jewish literature.

This book aims to clarify and shed light on numerous dimensions of the Idra Rabba: the narrative of the assembly with its various characters; the theology and mystical language that distinguish the work; possible motivations for its authorship; the religious-spiritual principles that emerge from it; and the components that make it transformative, intoxicating, and both attractive and threatening. Throughout, these investigations are accompanied by my attention to the Idra's great call for the transformation and healing of religion. This call captivated me from my very first reading of the work, awakening me to the inspiration that it may hold for contemporary spiritual seekers.

My Path to the Idra and to Writing This Book

Once I began to read the Zohar and to immerse myself in it, I found that its diverse ideas, figures, forms, and textures captured me—echoing central aspects of my own life at different periods. It was as if I were constantly wandering in the same field, yet with each season certain flowers would stand out in their beauty, often very different from previous ones. Perhaps this is the experience of studying any great classic work that we encounter time and again throughout our lives, or at least any work in which we have immersed ourselves for an extended period. Such is the way of Torah (teaching).

For many years, the world of the zoharic Companions and their great teacher Rabbi Shim'on bar Yoḥai was the central focus of my study, teaching, and writing. The mystical and experiential world—both divine and human—that unfolds in the stories of their escapades and scriptural interpretations, with the profound mysticism and eroticism that they generate, filled my heart, mind, and imagination. These stories are the distillery for the unique zoharic spirit, sweet and spicy and flowing like honey, that illuminates the eyes of those who taste it. This unique spiritual flavor of the zoharic stories changed my life.

In the first year of my studies at the Hebrew University, I read my beloved teacher Yehuda Liebes' article "The Messiah of the Zohar," which is dedicated entirely to an exploration of the Idras, and in particular to the Idra Rabba. The article astounded and moved me. Never before had I encountered an academic article of this kind: dense with ideas, associative, full of inspiration and creativity. I wanted more, and of course I immediately wanted to read the Idra literature that was the focus of his study.

I remember my initial readings of the Idra Rabba as an experience shrouded in wonder and mystery, and almost entirely inscrutable. In recent years, the Idra literature has once again captivated me. This time, I returned to it after decades of immersion in the Zohar, its language, and world. Now I felt ready to enter the inner sanctum of this magnificent composition.

There is something scandalous, astonishing, fascinating, and terrifying in the encounter with a sacred Jewish text that is primarily concerned with the various faces of the Divine, and with the hyperrealistic fine details of those faces, from the eyes to the curls of the beard. One's bewilderment at being exposed to the Idra's face terminology only grows as one encounters descriptions of the emanation of the divine body, and its distinctly sexual development into masculine and feminine bodies.

How can we understand the language of God having a face in the context of Judaism—a religious civilization that has often tended toward avoiding, if not outright rejecting, anthropomorphizing of the Divine? How might one grasp a deity portrayed as multifaceted—with a face, body, and sexuality? How might one read this great call to transform the face of the Jewish religion? How might one decipher the theology that emerges from a discourse that is so richly imaginative and mythological?

My encounter with the Idra Rabba—with the divine faces as they are gradually woven with words into living sacred images, with the courage to get up and demand a change in religious worldview, with the expanding states of consciousness of the participants in the gathering, and with the multiple dimensions of reality that are present and occurring simultaneously—has influenced my consciousness, its borders growing flexible and its horizons ever-widening.

As my reading progressed, the inscrutable density of the language came alive and started speaking to me in ways that I could comprehend with growing excitement and delight. The divine images, at first schematic and rigid, became fluid, taking on various guises. Very slowly, I found my way through the pathways of the Idra's world. I have no doubt that part of my attraction to the Idra stems from the very effort it demands of us to open the eye of the spirit, so as to perceive its images and become acquainted with its religious and mystical language.

In addition, I was attracted by the remarkable shift from the discourse of levels, lights, and *sefirot* prevalent throughout the Zohar to the discourse of faces and bodies in the Idras. There was something at once thrilling and frightening in the experience of relinquishing a safe foothold in order to encounter the surreal—even psychedelic—imagery of the Idras, without knowing where or how exactly I might return to ordinary reality. For me, engaging with the Idra Rabba was akin to diving into the depths of a vast ocean, gradually and excitedly discovering its treasures.

To write this book, I needed to grasp the conceptual depth and exegetical imagination that lie at the foundations of the Idra's project of transforming and healing religion, Divinity, and all realms of reality. To this end, I had to become intimately acquainted with the Idra's terminology of faces, and to sit with its opaque and paradoxical modes of expression. In addition, the Idra Rabba required me to experience different states of consciousness, and to internalize a mythical language with a unique syntax, grammar, and inner landscapes. All of this was necessary in order to make sense of a religious language that speaks of Divinity in terms of "expansion of the face," "relaxation of the face," "healing" or "sweetening the face," "filling the face with fragrance," and "illuminating one face with another."

In the course of researching this book and writing it, I had to seek out the tools best suited to convey something of the Idra's world—in terms of language, imagination, thought, and consciousness. I discovered that I had to let go of my need to answer and explain. Rather, I needed to identify the right questions to ask—questions that would enable me to understand better the nature of this classic work.

Further, I confess that the desire to write has led me to confront my great fear of entering the Holy of Holies of the Zohar, lest I err or cause harm by trespassing on sacred ground. In order to enter, I felt that I had to gain Rabbi Shim'on bar Yoḥai's approval. When faced with the choice between fear or love, I followed the example of the Idra Rabba: I chose to write out of love. My intention is to delicately unveil the essence of this work that I so admire, while taking great care to reveal its secrets in an appropriate manner, avoiding crude exposure, and doing my best not to diminish this unique cultural treasure. I hope that I have succeeded in this task.

On the Idra in Our Contemporary World

For contemporary readers, studying the Idra Rabba provides an encounter with one of the classics of Jewish esoteric literature and Jewish literature in general, and a work of great importance within the mystical literature of the world. Studying it enables us to enter into an intellectual-mythical-mystical composition that intensively investigates questions concerning the origins of being beyond space and time, and illuminates the processes of human consciousness and development.

This is an encounter with one of the most marvelous human attempts to imagine, perceive, and express the Divine in order to establish a living connection with it. Far from being a philosophical treatise, the Idra Rabba is a work of religious art. It is a testament to the creative power of a protest against the increasing rigidity of religion—one that produced an exceptionally daring and creative religious alternative, born from the recesses of the soul.

Studying the Idra reveals the unique charm of a text that in its very fabric embraces both the abstract and the concrete, the unconscious and the conscious, the transcendent and the personal, the ideational and the sexual, all somehow infused into one another. These qualities demand that the reader's consciousness becomes flexible in order to contain modes of apprehension that are not dualistic, binary, schematic, or modular. To one who makes the effort to become familiar with its world, the Idra Rabba offers a wealth of myth, mysticism, and theology, in a uniquely Jewish language. Reading it is an adventure, a journey through multidimensional expanses to the face of God.

We live in a period in which many voices are calling for a renewal of religion, in an effort to maintain its vitality and relevance. There is no doubt that my wish to write this book was strengthened by my sense that in the Idra Rabba there flow rare wellsprings of inspiration for this quest. I perceive cultural attitudes that enable a growing openness to and appreciation of different aspects of the language of the Idras emerging in these first decades of the 21st century. This openness is connected to a deep thirst for an amplified religious language that can contemplate a God more expansive than the traditional metaphors of king, father, and master allow.

Alongside the traditional imagery of God as a masculine creator and king, the Idra Rabba introduces two additional divine figures of central importance: the non-dual Divinity in its ultimate oneness, and the feminine Divine in her various guises.

Some elements of the Idras' archaic imagery may remain foreign, incomprehensible, even off-putting to many contemporary readers. Nevertheless, in certain circles today, there are aspects of religious-spiritual consciousness that are more open to many of the concepts expressed in the Idras. The following two sections briefly describe some of the reasons for this.

On Oneness

Intellectual, theological, and spiritual trends of the 21st century offer a variety of conceptions of God's unity. Contemporary conceptions of divine oneness are primarily a product of a confluence of distinct cultural, intellectual, and spiritual traditions: the spiritual traditions of the East, neo-Hasidic discourse (which is kabbalistic in origin), the syncretism of New Age thought, as well as various psychological theories, Jungian among others. The dissemination of these concepts has also been accelerated due to the growing popularity of various meditative practices (especially from the Hindu and Buddhist traditions) that explicitly aim to cultivate a quieting of the dualistic and active mind, in order to connect to a still consciousness and a sense of oneness that lies at the source of all manifestations.

I can personally attest to the sheer surprise and joy at encountering the Idra's language of oneness within my own religious tradition. So there is indeed a concept of a dimension of divine oneness in Judaism, coexisting with the particularistic language of the God of Israel! However, in the Idra, this dimension of being is not described in static terms of abstract perfection (as in the philosophical tradition), but rather with lively dynamism.[1]

Reclaiming the Feminine Divine

Concepts of the Divine as a feminine being are also resurfacing in contemporary Jewish cultural consciousness, which is gradually rediscovering the figure of the *Shekhinah*. The *Shekhinah*—the divine presence that dwells in our world, understood as a feminine aspect of God—had been a living force in the religious language of Kabbalah and Hasidism. This figure received a near-mortal blow in the wake of the widespread popularity and influence of the Haskalah (Jewish Enlightenment) movement. In the 20th century, poets such as Hayyim Nahman Bialik, mystics such as Hillel Zeitlin, and writers such as Shai Agnon were among the few who lamented that the *Shekhinah* "has been exiled from every corner," as Bialik put it in his poem "Alone" ("Levaddi").[2]

In recent decades in Jewish culture, especially in North America, the feminist struggle on the part of Jewish women and men has sought to express and acknowledge the feminine and motherly aspects of the Divine in the language of prayer and in the texts of ritual blessings (*berakhot*). In addition to the spiritual-religious aspiration to raise the *Shekhinah* from the dust and allow her to attain her former stature in Jewish religious culture, one can detect the influence of the goddess culture that has emerged from the study of myth, New Age feminism, and neo-paganism.

These distinct intellectual currents have a common aspiration, namely, to make religious language more flexible and inclusive, so that it may accommodate new-ancient feminine formulations, for those seeking a connection with these aspects of the Divine. Within Judaism, these approaches—holistic, feminist-theological, Jungian, New Age, and so forth—have brought into stark relief the heavy toll of the loss and neglect of the feminine in Jewish theological language.

The foundational quality of the call to the Idra Rabba's gathering is one of emergency. To write about this work, I needed to recognize that I too feel a sense of urgency in the impulse to write about the world that opened before me when I read the Idra. I had to impart the call to transform and heal religion to those around me, and to share the startling experience of encountering the faces of the Divine as they move from abstraction to living presence.

In the Jewish world in which I live—just as in Muslim, Christian, and Hindu societies—ideologically narrow agendas and fundamentalist tendencies are now growing stronger. In response to these agendas, I felt a need to incline my ear in a more attentive way to the manifesto offered by the Idra Rabba for the religious world, calling for reform, and offering healing and expansion. In the Idra, I have searched for inspiration for those confronting the religious confusion that has come to characterize our world. I have tried to put my heart and mind to depicting accurately the radical broadening of legitimate religious language that one finds in zoharic literature in general, and in the Idras in particular. This expansion of religious language comes to refresh the religious world and enliven it.

Tools and Supplies for the Journey

Thinking about the appropriate tools for deciphering the Idra Rabba's dense and multilayered text is bound up with the question of what the work is and how to read it: Should it be read as the most highly developed and complex story in the zoharic collection? As a theological-political manifesto in the guise of a story? As a myth? As a mystical revelation—the climactic event in the human encounter with the various faces of the Divine? As a polemic against the conception of God that Maimonides presented in *The Guide for the Perplexed*? In my reading, I have found the Idra Rabba to be all of these things, and more. Out of the many tools that might shed light on such a complex work, I chose those that were at my disposal, and those in which I have a personal interest.

My teachers have taught me to read each and every sentence very slowly, to try first to understand what I was reading within the conceptual and linguistic context of the work itself and then within the wider context of the Idras and zoharic literature in general. And finally, to explore the text against the background of associations from Jewish sources that predate the Zohar: Jewish philosophy, ancient Hekhalot literature, classical rabbinic literature, and of course the Hebrew Bible, whose language rests at the very foundation of the Idra's creative midrash.

This exploration has taught me that, in order to understand the language and imagery of the Idra, one must be wary of the temptation to think systematically according to the familiar map of the ten *sefirot* as we know it from kabbalistic literature and its appearances throughout the Zohar. I also learned that I had to refrain from a technical or allegorical reading, and from overreliance on later commentators.

Additionally, I found that the intensity of contemporary notions and ideologies regarding gender and sexuality had the potential to create a barrier between the reader and the text itself. In order to have an appreciation of the idraic world and encounter it in its fullness, I needed to be mindful in deciding when to use this contemporary lens and when to try to temporarily set it aside.

Another lens through which I considered the Idra Rabba, and which provided central inspiration to me, was the assumption that its authorship emerged from personal and experiential contemplation of human consciousness in its various states. The Idra is a daring attempt to describe consciousness in its encounter with the divine realm, and it is a testament to the richness of human consciousness in depicting various dimensions of Divinity. The tools that served me for this purpose are various conceptions concerning human consciousness borrowed from depth psychology, and from the language of archetypes from the school of Carl Gustav Jung and his student Erich Neumann, whose highly original and creative research explored the emergence and stages of development of human consciousness. In addition, new insights into human consciousness have been furnished by the mystical psychologies of Sufism, Hinduism, and Buddhism. Finally, openness is perhaps not something that we are accustomed to viewing as a tool, but I would suggest that openness of mind, imagination, and heart to the Idra Rabba's multidimensionality and simultaneity is a necessary condition for a grounded and insightful reading of this work.

Acknowledgments

The time has come to send this book out into the world, and I am overwhelmed with gratitude for the many people who enabled the various aspects of this work.

I thank my teacher and beloved friend Yehuda Liebes. When I first encountered the Zohar, reading his seminal article on the Idra Rabba, "The Messiah of the Zohar," was a formative experience for me. The article, along with its footnotes, appendices, and the poem accompanying it, provided the fundamental language for this entire book, which might be read as an ongoing conversation with Yehuda and all that he has taught his students about the Zohar and the Idras over the past decades. Yehuda taught me the delight of slow reading, and imparted to me the boundless curiosity to explore layer after layer of zoharic writing. He taught me to open myself to the Zohar's depth, humor, dialectic, and paradox. He taught me to delight in the search for the myriad sources out of which the Zohar's language is woven. And on top of all of this, he taught me love. The sparks of Yehuda Liebes' Zohar and of his students, and the many things that I have learned from them over the years, are present within the pages of this book. *Happy is the generation that hears your words of Torah! Happy is my portion, that I attained this!*

I thank my friend and dear teacher Avraham Leader. Together, over three years, we translated the Idra Rabba's Aramaic into Hebrew. In our weekly meetings, we investigated its each and every word in an attempt to unlock the text's meanings. These meetings were an extraordinary experience of deciphering obscure passages, growing clarification, and uncovering surprises and insights concealed throughout the Idra's every page. For me, studying with Avraham afforded me a fascinating encounter with his tremendous knowledge of the full range of kabbalistic literature, with the demand for a precise explication of the Idra Rabba's statements as they emerge from its own world, and with the courage to search and seek out possible meanings of these matters in our own world. Time and again, we stopped in wonderment, faced with a new interpretive possibility in this dense text, having arrived at it only after long and loving labor. At such times, we found it amusing that no one but us would understand the delight of this journey.

I thank my teacher and friend Danny Matt, the scholar and wonderful translator who has headed the great project of translating the Zohar into English. Collaborating with him as he translated the Idra into English was truly enriching, an experience that gleamed with zoharic radiance, as befits all Zohar lovers.

I am filled with gratitude to Raphael Dascalu, sitting in faraway Melbourne, Australia, who took upon himself the daunting task of translating this book into English. As each chapter arrived in my inbox, I could discern the ongoing development of his nuanced attentiveness to the Hebrew of the original text as well as to my own intentions. This sensitivity to language, along with his thoughtful comments on the book's content, have refined this book and attuned it to the English reader.

My deep gratitude to my dear friend Minna Bromberg. Together, and with delight, we honed each word, sentence, and paragraph of the English text so that my personal voice would be audible throughout this translation. Our weekly sessions were a pure pleasure, and we didn't want the project to come to an end.

I wish to thank Alan Harvey, Caroline McKusick, Jessica Ling, Elspeth MacHattie, and the entire Stanford University Press team. Their kindness and professionalism made the various stages of production a pleasure.

I thank the participants in all the study groups in which I taught and studied the Zohar over the years. Ideas, images, and reflections from those meetings made their way into the pages before you.

I thank my many friends who read, commented upon, and edited various chapters of the book as I was writing it: first and foremost, my friend and teacher Art Green, my soul friend Tirzah Firestone, and my friend David Ferleger.

I thank the Shalom Hartman Institute—my intellectual home—in which I have been conducting research, studying, and teaching for many years. Thanks also to the researchers in the institute, who offered their thoughts and wise counsel.

I thank the Institute for Jewish Spirituality (IJS), which has given me ample opportunity to teach Zohar to rabbis, cantors, and lay leaders in North America for almost two decades. I wish to remember with great love and admiration my dear friend and mentor Rabbi Rachel Cowan, founder and long-time director of IJS, who continuously encouraged me in this work. May her memory be a blessing.

As the Hebrew edition of this work was being completed, my beloved husband, Dror, passed away after a year-long battle with cancer. He accompanied the production of this book with encouragement, laughter, and patience. I am filled with gratitude for having had the opportunity to share years of joy and love with him. And finally, with love—for, as the Idra says, *the matter depends upon love*—to my children, Hallel and Yotam, I say, thank you for your love.

I am truly filled with gratitude.

The Structure of This Book

Part 1 of this book may be viewed as a broad introduction to the Idra Rabba. It deals with the terminology of faces that makes the Idra unique and with the fundamental subjects at the Idra's core. The first four chapters in this part introduce the various divine faces that feature in the Idra's lexicon, constituting a gateway for those who wish to enter into its unique and otherwise inaccessible world.

The last three chapters (Chapters 5, 6, and 7) in this part are concerned with fundamental issues that emerge from studying the Idra, such as the relationship between various divine entities and the work's stylistic and literary distinctiveness, its mystical character, and its overarching themes. Part 1 concludes with these central questions: What is the Idra trying to say? What meaning might lie concealed within it for us, its readers?

Part 2 of this book follows the textual order of the Idra Rabba as it presents a study and analysis of the work. Thus, this part matches the structure of the Idra: moving from the highly impressive opening scene (Chapter 8) through the processes of configuring the divine *partsufim, Arikh Anpin* and *Ze'eir Anpin* (Chapters 9 through 17), and the description of the sexual union of the male and female bodies of the Divine (Chapters 18 through 21) to the dramatic closing scene (Chapter 22). This part is characterized by analyses of extensive selections from the text of the Idra, and discussions of the themes arising from those selections. From time to time, I elaborate on a specific theme or provide the necessary background for the interpretive discussion.

This book's two parts thus present various levels of treatment of the work, with different resolutions: in the first part, I consider the Idra from a bird's-eye view and examine its general themes; in the second part, I attempt to mediate between the text and the reader, presenting a close analysis of selections from the work—indeed, this section is something of a personal conversation with the Idra Rabba.

Some Notes on Translation

When citing the Zohar in translation, I have relied upon Daniel Matt's English translation as presented in *The Zohar: Pritzker Edition*. Specific references to both the Aramaic text and Matt's translation are provided (for example: Zohar 2:176a; trans. Matt 5:531). Matt's translation is based on an Aramaic text of the Zohar that he compiled from multiple manuscripts and printed editions. Stanford University Press has made this Aramaic text available online (for the link, please see the entry for Daniel Matt in the Bibliography). In cases where my interpretation of a passage differs from Matt's translation, I state that the translation has been "emended."

Translations of verses in the Hebrew Bible—when those verses are not translated in Matt's edition of the Zohar—are generally based on the Jewish Publication Society's 1985 translation, with some emendations.

I have made an effort to leave in the text some central zoharic Aramaic terms that appear throughout the Idra Rabba. These include the names of the divine faces (*Arikh Anpin* and *Ze'eir Anpin*), as well as important concepts and divine qualities such as *Din* (Judgment) and *bissum* (aromatizing, sweetening). I hope this allows some of the fragrance of the original terminology to linger.

May you enter in peace, and emerge in peace.

PART I

I

Introduction to the Idra Rabba

Idra Literature in the Zohar

The Book of the Zohar contains a rich collection of stories that make it unique among the kabbalistic works of the medieval period.[1] They fracture our conventional perception of reality, and open a window into the divine wonder that lies within that reality. These stories introduce the reader to the adventures of Rabbi Shim'on bar Yoḥai, the great teacher, and his circle of disciples, known as the *ḥavrayya* (Companions). The narratives take place on various planes of earthly and divine existence, and manifest a variety of states of consciousness and awareness. In these stories, the verses, words, and letters of the Torah constitute the fundamental language of the midrashic and mystical discourse that develops among the characters. Together, the tales present the *ḥavrayya*'s untiring quest to access and unveil a stratum of mystic reality lying within and beyond the verses of Torah, gushing with vitality and alive with divinity.

Within the great collection of the Zohar's stories, two shine in their uniqueness: the Idra Rabba and the Idra Zuṭa, "The Great Gathering" and "The Small Gathering."[2] In most of the Zohar's stories, two or three members of Rabbi Shim'on bar Yoḥai's circle are the central characters, and their stories transpire while they are walking on their way or studying by night. In contrast, the Idras tell of two occasions when Rabbi Shim'on gathered the *entire* group of his close disciples for a specific task. The literal meaning of the term *idra* in Aramaic is "threshing-floor" or "room," and here, it refers to this group's gathering place.[3]

As the great scholar of the Zohar Yehuda Liebes concludes, the stories of these gatherings are "the literary, narrative, and conceptual apex of *The Book of the Zohar*."[4] They are characterized by a particularly dramatic and exalted literary style and by a theology, myth, mysticism, and a religious language that make them unique and distinguish them from the rest of the zoharic corpus.

The Idra Rabba (Zohar 3:127b–145a) describes an emergency gathering convened by the master, Rabbi Shim'on bar Yoḥai, focused on reconfiguring and restoring the whole of divine, cosmic, human, and religious existence. The Idra Rabba describes a divine being composed of three fundamental components, namely, the three divine faces (*partsufim*): *Arikh Anpin*—the "Long-Faced One" or "Slow to Anger"; *Ze'eir Anpin*—the "Small-Faced One" or "Short-Tempered"; and *Nuqba*—the feminine aspect of the Divine.[5]

The Idra is constructed as a mosaic of innovative interpretations, presented by all the gathered members of the circle. This structure is a testament to one of the most important aspects of the Idra: the disciples' transformation from Rabbi Shim'on bar Yoḥai's admiring novices into independent creators, or as the Idra puts it, into "pillars" upon which the world may rest. The events in the Idra Rabba constitute the disciples' initiation ceremony, obliging them to take their rightful place as creative interpreters of Scripture—a potent yet dangerous role. According to the Zohar's conception, it is the words spoken by the participants in the gathering that configure and repair the divine dimensions of being, in mythic "real time." Invoking and reconfiguring the various faces of Divinity and aligning these faces with one another, the *ḥavrayya* clear an illumined and open pathway for the divine flow. Their sacred speech ensures that the streams of cosmic emanation are properly aligned, flowing from their source in the divine One into differentiated and finite human existence. The Idra Rabba, sublime and dramatic, also claims a dear price in human life. At the end of the scene, three out of the nine disciples who participate in the Idra depart this world in ecstatic death.

The Idra Zuṭa (Zohar 3:287b–296b) describes the last day of Rabbi Shim'on bar Yoḥai, about to depart this world and enter the realm of divine life. In this work, Rabbi Shim'on bar Yoḥai is the sole speaker; while his disciples, gathered around him, receive an outpouring of Torah before his death. Carefully arranging his words, the great teacher divulges secrets to his close disciples pertaining to the various aspects of the Divine. These mysteries have been concealed deep within his heart awaiting this day. He describes and configures the divine *partsufim*, actively stimulating the divine emanation to flow into the world, through his speech. At the climax of this process, Rabbi Shim'on bar Yoḥai's soul departs, in rapturous union with the *Shekhinah*.

In the Idra Zuṭa, five divine *partsufim* are described: in addition to *Arikh Anpin*, *Ze'eir Anpin*, and the *Nuqba* of the Idra Rabba, we are introduced to the *Abba* (Father) and *Imma* (Mother). These five *partsufim* form a kind of "inner" divine "family" within the Godhead.

The Idra Zuṭa explicitly recollects the great gathering at which all were present—the Idra Rabba—and both Idras are characterized by great pathos and a sense of urgency. The Idra Rabba emphatically identifies itself as an emergency gathering, and it carries a sense of the moment's fatefulness. The call for total concentration of all aspects of the participants' personalities into their mission fills the opening lines of the Idra.[6] And as was mentioned, the drama culminates with the deaths of three of the Companions before the end of the gathering.

The Idra Zuṭa is also full of emotion and drama, stemming from the certain knowledge that this is Rabbi Shim'on bar Yoḥai's last day on earth. The master gathers his disciples with a heightened sense of mission. He hopes to bequeath to them mysteries that he has not yet revealed, and to leave them in possession of the necessary tools to continue the task of mystical reparation (*tiqqun*). The drama in the Idra Zuṭa reaches its climax in the ecstatic moments during which Rabbi Shim'on bar Yoḥai's soul departs this world, as a direct result of the erotic union between him—in his transpersonal aspect as the *sefirah* of *Yesod*—and the *Shekhinah*.

In addition to the Idra Rabba and the Idra Zuṭa, another work that discusses the secrets of the *partsufim* is the Idra Raza de-Razin (The Assembly of Mystery of Mysteries; Zohar 2:122b–123b). The zoharic literature also speaks of the existence of yet another Idra, the Idra de-Vei Mashkena, meaning the Idra that is concerned with the secrets of the Tabernacle (*mishkan*). However, it is not entirely clear to which of the extant zoharic works this title might refer, if it refers to any at all.[7] From the viewpoint of narrative coherence, the Idra literature may be arranged as follows: Idra de-Vei Mashkena, Idra Rabba, Idra Zuṭa, and Idra Raza de-Razin.[8]

In addition to all these, there is a short work, Sifra di-Tsni'uta, a kind of ancient Mishnah, that constitutes the basis for the Idras' language. Also referred to as Tsni'uta de-Sifra (Zohar 2:176b–179a), it is perhaps the most cryptic and enigmatic work in all of zoharic literature. One might translate this title as "Book of Concealment," "Secret Scroll," "Hidden Book of Creation," or "Book of Secrets." This impressive and moving work is characterized by a uniquely poetic and hymn-like rhythm and an enigmatic and exalted style. Its subject is the secret of the emanation of divine and cosmic being. This work is entirely devoid of a narrative frame, context, or mention of time or place, conveying its content as an eternal, objective truth.

Sifra di-Tsni'uta is arranged in five chapters that are composed of short sentences and are extremely cryptic and full of archaic imagery. It weaves together interpretations concerning "The Work of Creation" (the first chapters of the Book of Genesis), interpretations of letters—particularly the letters *yod*, *he*, and *vav* of the Tetragrammaton—and primordial images. All of these are directed toward describing the ancient processes of the formation of the divine faces, down to the creation of human beings. It presents a conception of cosmic cycles in which each cycle results from an exhalation of divine breath and ends as that breath is drawn back into the Divine. One can see Sifra di-Tsni'uta as a kind of *yantra* (mystical diagram) or *mandala*—a multidimensional picture of divine existence that invites mystical contemplation.

Sifra di-Tsni'uta has a unique status within zoharic literature:

> What is Concealment of the Book [Tsni'uta de-Sifra]? Rabbi Shim'on said, "There are five chapters contained in a great palace and filling the whole earth." (Zohar 2:176a; trans. Matt 5:531)

It is the "story of everything," epitomized, encrypted, and shrouded in mystery. The Idra Rabba builds upon the short and cryptic Mishnah of Sifra di-Tsni'uta, interpreting and expounding upon selections from it in great detail.[9]

Curiously, even while reading "standard" zoharic passages, one at times suddenly encounters statements bearing distinctly Idra-like terminology. It is as if the text had suddenly transported us to another land, or as if it had slipped into a foreign language with no warning. This literary phenomenon calls for investigation into the manner in which the zoharic text was composed, and the relationship between the strata of the body of the Zohar and of the Idras.[10]

Finally, it is worth noting that in the same region and during the same period that the zoharic corpus was being composed, other works were created whose theological terminology, style, or content point to a close relationship with the Idra literature; this similarity occurs primarily in the writings of David ben Judah he-Ḥasid and Joseph of Hamadan.[11] However, none of these works share the Idras' dramatic literary framework and style.

The Divine Faces (*Partsufim*)

The Idra Rabba focuses upon the description of the various "faces" of the Divine, and upon invoking and configuring their various aspects. Here is a brief account of each of these aspects, as they appear in the Idra:

> The Holy Ancient One (*ʿAttiqa Qaddisha*), or The Long-Faced One (*Arikh Anpin*). This is the archaic, primordial, and hoary face of the Divine, radiating whiteness. This is the face of God that personifies oneness, the Source of all things, the life-force itself, and absolute Compassion.
>
> The Small-Faced One (*Zeʿeir Anpin*). This is the divine face in its dualistic dimension. It is the young, small, and short-tempered face of God; the face of the God of religion, the God of Israel, YHVH; the face of the masculine God, that represents order, logic, normativity, and law. This is God as the Just King. This face radiates beauty and compassion, but its most prominent trait is impatience and an inherent inclination toward strict judgment.
>
> *Adam*, Male and Female (*Dekhar ve-Nuqba*): From the head of *Zeʿeir Anpin*, the Divine expands into a fully developed figure, containing within it a masculine body and a feminine body. This is the Divine in its fully differentiated and developed manifestation, in which there exists a distinction between the masculine and the feminine. When they are conjoined in sexual union, an alignment between the divine faces becomes possible, allowing the mysterious spirit of *ʿAttiqa Qaddisha* to

penetrate and fill up both the male and female aspects of *Adam*. Adam, the first human being, was created in the image of the Divine, as were his descendants, the terrestrial humans. As mentioned above, this aspect of the Divine possesses a complete body, and not merely a head and face. Within this divine body, the *partsuf* known as *Nuqba* (the Female) stands out uniquely, containing within it the feminine face and body. It is common in commentaries on the Idra Rabba to regard the Godhead as made up of three aspects constituting a trinity of divine faces: *Arikh Anpin*, *Ze'eir Anpin*, and *Nuqba*. I have however, refined and nuanced this description by regarding the embodied masculine and feminine aspects of God as distinct from *Ze'eir Anpin*.

The Idra Rabba not only describes the way these three faces come to be, but also tells how Rabbi Shim'on and his disciples initiate a dynamic reconfiguration of these three facets of the Divine. The purpose of all this is to align and restore balance to the relationship between them.

The opening of the Idra summons the *ḥavrayya*, those who know the secrets of the Divine, to examine the blemishes and problems in the layout of the divine faces. To the Idra's mind, these blemishes are reflected in religious life on earth. The Companions' task, under their master's direction, is to find appropriate ways to heal them. The Companions' mission is critical because healing and reconfiguration enable the uninterrupted flow of divine bounty from its primordial and unified Source, through the filters of a dual Divinity in its masculine and feminine aspects, into our very own world. Without this healing, all reality faces the disastrous consequence of being cut off from the life-giving plenty of the Source.

Summary of the Idra Rabba's Structure

In order to orient ourselves to the Idra Rabba's world, it is, first, important to understand its general structure. The following summary of this complex and dense narrative is merely an initial account of the work's surface. Still more complicated is the attempt to understand the exegetical material from which the Idra is constructed, and to offer viable interpretations of passages that might seem at first to be impenetrable. Thus, the second part of this book, as noted in the introduction, focuses on mediating between the reader and the text itself. Through a close reading of select passages of the Idra, I will attempt to shed light on its most interesting, perplexing, and surprising aspects.

The beginning of the Idra is constructed of a series of proclamations, rituals, and ceremonial gestures that together constitute the invitation to the gathering, and create the conditions for its propitious fulfillment. Rabbi Shim'on, the great teacher, opens with an announcement declaring the divine and earthly emergency that calls for this gathering. The opening passage establishes the spiritual stature of the teacher and also of the circle of participants. A dramatic ritual oath binds them together.

Following the opening passage is an account of the undifferentiated Divinity, which precedes all forms and faces of the Godhead. Here we also read of the failed preliminary attempts to bring about differentiated existence. These inchoate entities that emerged into being and immediately ceased to exist, are represented in the archaic figures of ancient kings who appeared, reigned, and died. Their story is a mythical rendering of the Edomite kings listed in Genesis 36:31–39. Just as the Edomite kings ruled "before a king ruled in Israel," so did these forces rule before the emergence of the divine cosmic order.

The myth of the Edomite kings appears three times in the Idra Rabba, in three variations. Each one symbolizes a particular stage in the differentiation of divine being. Following this is a detailed account of the first divine *partsuf, Arikh Anpin* (the Long-Faced, Patient, or Long-Suffering One) or *'Attiqa Qaddisha* (the Holy Ancient One). The Idra describes the various parts of this face (forehead, eyes, nose, and so on), their configuration and formation, each one expressing a specific quality of *'Attiqa Qaddisha*.

The description of this face reaches its most elaborate form with the thirteen *tiqqunim*. These constitute thirteen divine adornments or garments that configure the various parts of the Ancient One's white beard. Each part of the beard represents one of the Thirteen Attributes of Mercy[12] ascribed to this aspect of the Divine. These descriptions of the thirteen *tiqqunim* are not merely descriptive or theoretical; rather, they are performative and theurgical, meaning that they activate and transform the human and divine realms of existence.

The creative interpretations, uttered by each and every one of the disciples, stimulate the life-force and radiance that flow from the ancient face of God, and enable humans to experience them. Once the configuration of

Arikh Anpin's face is complete, the master summarizes the events up to this point, and offers his encouragement for the next phase of the Idra; namely, the configuration of the face of *Ze'eir Anpin*.

The face of *Ze'eir Anpin* comes into being out of some quality or life-force that is emitted from *Arikh Anpin*. First comes a description of the way in which this figure's amorphous head and skull are fashioned, after which the facial features are described and configured, becoming a fully formed human face. It is the handsome face of a young warrior, endowed with dynamic expressiveness, in which the qualities of Justice (*Din*) and Compassion (*Ḥesed*)[13] are in endless interplay. Just as in the description of *Arikh Anpin*, here too the most mysterious and profound element of this account of the divine face lies in the nine adornments (*tiqqunim*) of *Ze'eir Anpin*'s black beard, corresponding to the Attributes of Mercy in this face. The configuration and repair of *Ze'eir Anpin*'s face and beard focus time and again on the relative abundance of harsh Judgment (*Din*) in the personality of *Ze'eir Anpin*, as compared with the absolute and bounteous Mercy of *Arikh Anpin*'s attributes.

The manifestation of this face is not the final stage in the process, for the Divine cannot be fully expressed and perfected without a body. Thus, the next portion of the Idra is a description of God's development into a full human figure, as *Adam*. The generation of the divine body occurs through the simultaneous and intertwined development of masculine and feminine bodies that emanate from the head of *Ze'eir Anpin*. This androgynous figure has two heads and two bodies, joined at the back. This Adamic figure continues to evolve, developing male and female genitalia. Once the two conjoined bodies have attained completion and sexual maturity, a polarization of qualities occurs within them: Compassion (*Ḥesed*) and whiteness are concentrated in the male body; while Justice (*Din*) and redness are drained into the female body. At this point, once the bodies have become distinct, the Idra Rabba describes how *'Attiqa*, the primordial Divinity, causes the androgynous body to split in two, separating the male and female bodies so that they can reunite face to face. The climax of this passage lies in its description of the encounter between the masculine and the feminine, full of love and desire. This encounter is the realization and embodiment of the divine image as *Adam*, a being composed of male and female bodies conjoined in union.

The attainment of harmonious coupling between the masculine and feminine balances the qualities of Justice and Compassion, and brings a flow of blessings into the world, enabling the production of generations in the Adamic image of God. However, it is a process that is full of obstacles. Into the masculine and feminine realm of being enters a powerful force of harsh Judgment: the Serpent. From this point until the end of the work, we find an exegetical development of the biblical narratives of Adam and Eve in the Garden of Eden, and their descendants up until the story of Noah, all in the typical style of the Idra. The Idra understands these primordial creation myths as occurring within the Godhead, expressing a mode of existence that has not yet attained balance and stability. The Idra's interpretations conclude with an overview of the whole of history, up to the vision that appears in the Book of Daniel, in which an ideal human being, the Messiah of the End of Days, appears and draws near to God, the Ancient of Days (*'Attiq Yomin*).

The final portion of the Idra describes the exit from the Great Assembly. This passage presents a number of scenes, including the deaths of three of the Companions, who are carried off to heaven by angels. The work ultimately ends with an interpretation of those shocking deaths, with the reassertion of Rabbi Shim'on bar Yoḥai's status as the teacher and master of the remaining six disciples, and with a renewed and reinforced sense of intimacy and interconnectedness.

Interpreters of the Idra

Throughout the generations, the Idra has been interpreted thoroughly, comprehensively, and creatively by some of the greatest kabbalists. Within the vibrant community of kabbalists in 16th-century Safed, two intellectual giants studied the Idras in depth: Isaac Luria, known as the Ari (1534–1572), and Moses Cordovero (1522–1570). These two figures devoted creative, systematic, comprehensive, and probing thought to the Idra literature.

Cordovero saw a single theological, metaphysical, and mystical language in both the Idra Rabba and Idra Zuṭa. In contrast with his usual method in *Or Yaqar*, his comprehensive commentary on the Zohar, in which he interprets the text in a running fashion, he chose to take apart the literary wholeness of the two Idras, weaving their themes into a single synthetic and systematic treatment. Cordovero's understanding of the nature of the various divine figures emerges from an attempt, at times forced, to harmonize these two works, with a view to presenting a unified theosophical system. His commentary on the Idras, expansive and conceptually rich, was published in Volumes 21, 22, and 23 of *Or Yaqar*, as part of a section titled *Ḥesheq*, an acronym for *Ḥeleq Shiʿur Qomah* (The portion on the stature of Divinity). There are also important interpretations of the Idras in his great work *Elimah*. His last work, *Tomer Devorah* (Deborah's date palm), reworks the parts of the Idra Rabba that discuss *Arikh Anpin*'s face and the Thirteen Attributes of Mercy, turning them into a psychospiritual practice of moral refinement (*tiqqun middot*). The Idras also occupy a central place in Cordovero's programmatic work *Or Neʿerav* (Part 4), in which he seeks to demonstrate the superiority of Kabbalah over all other branches of Torah study.[14]

As is well known, Isaac Luria did not commit his teachings to writing. Despite this, it is clear from the various recensions of his teachings in the works of his disciples that he saw himself as an interpreter of the Idras, and that his new teachings are built upon his reading of these works. Lurianic Kabbalah is thus intensively reliant on the religious-mystical language of the Idras, which he read with exceptional depth and sensitivity. Luria even sought to reenact the events described in these works, gathering his disciples together at Meron for a renewed Idra.[15]

Moses Ḥayyim Luzzatto, known as the Ramḥal (1707–1746), also composed a commentary on the Idra Rabba, titled *Sefer Adir Ba-Marom*. His admiration for the Idra Rabba may be observed in his words of wonder in the commentary's opening tribute: "This Idra, by which [Rabbi Shimʿon bar Yoḥai] attained the greatest perfection yet—for himself, his Companions, and for the entire world."[16] Luzzatto even composed a new work after the fashion of the Idra Rabba, and established a circle of companions in 17th-century Italy based on that of the Idras.[17]

The present work will approach understanding the Idra Rabba and illuminating its contents mainly by reading it as an independent work, establishing its relationship to the Idra Zuṭa, and situating it in its broader zoharic context. In general, this means that we will not approach the Idra according to these later kabbalistic interpretations, despite the importance and profundity of the kabbalists' work, and despite the fact that their overarching ideas (particularly those of Luria and Cordovero) had a major impact on my own thinking.

Critical Idra Scholarship

Academic studies of the Idras have also been written over the years, forming a branch of general zoharic scholarship. In the following paragraphs, as I close this chapter, I note the major milestones of Idra scholarship, emphasizing the approaches that form the basis of my own reading of the work.

Gershom Scholem, who laid the foundations for critical scholarship of the Kabbalah in the 20th century, understands the Idras as a zoharic version of the ancient *Shi'ur Qomah* tradition, which focuses upon the existence of a mythical divine form in human likeness.[18] In his view, Sifra di-Tsni'uta and the two Idras were composed by Moses de León, whom he takes to be the sole author of the Zohar. He assumes that the presentation of the Idras as a commentary upon an ancient and obscure work—namely, Sifra di-Tsni'uta—is a literary conceit of the author.[19]

Yehuda Liebes, one of the greatest scholars of zoharic literature in our generation, devotes his seminal article "The Messiah of the Zohar" to investigating the Idras and examining the character of Rabbi Shim'on bar Yoḥai as the Zohar's messianic hero.[20] This article is a treasure trove of foundational insights concerning the Idra, a close analysis of selections from it, bold hypotheses concerning parts of it, and references to interpretations from the full span of zoharic and kabbalistic literature and scholarship, illuminating diverse aspects of the Idra literature.

In his ground-breaking study "How the Zohar Was Written," Liebes reopens the question of how zoharic literature was composed, and suggests that it was the product of a circle of kabbalists rather than a single author.[21] (In keeping with Liebes' view, I use "author" and "authors" interchangeably in the rest of this book.) In this historical circle, whose potential participants Liebes attempts to identify and trace, older kabbalistic material was reworked in various ways according to the inclinations and conceptions of the authors. Within this framework, Liebes explores the conceptual foundations of the Idras, and their unique qualities, distinct as they are from the religious and intellectual discourse of the main body of the Zohar.[22] In addition, he points to a lack of conceptual correspondence between Sifra di-Tsni'uta and the Idras in the Zohar, and suggests that we should not consider them to be the product of a single author.

Similarly, he notes the presence of different layers of redaction in the Idras, which one may detect based on distinct "drafts" of the Idras and related works that have been preserved in the Zohar and in contemporaneous kabbalistic works (such as the writings of Joseph Gikatilla, Joseph of Hamadan, David ben Judah he-Ḥasid, Moses of Burgos, and others). According to this view, the Idras as we know them are only one particular reworking of this literature—one of many versions that were redacted and edited in 13th-century Castille. The author of the Idra Rabba, as it is known to us, added the dramatic narrative of the gathering involving Rabbi Shimʿon bar Yoḥai and his Companions. The author fashioned this literary aspect of the work after the likeness of the circle in which he was active, modeling it on his own experiences. The sense of imminent redemption and cosmic healing that was palpable in that circle lent the Idras a dramatic and messianic dimension.

Moshe Idel, my teacher and one of this generation's greatest Kabbalah scholars, treats the Idras primarily in the context of his discussions of the forces of Justice (*Din*), of anthropomorphism, and of the gendered quality of the divine faces in the Idras.[23]

Elliot Wolfson, one of the preeminent Kabbalah scholars in the United States, delves deeply and in great detail into matters concerning vision and imagination in Jewish traditions of the medieval period and earlier. His works considerably expanded my understanding of these elements in religious consciousness and terminology. His numerous books and articles offer many references to various aspects of the Idra literature. His studies of the kabbalistic imagination, anthropomorphism in Kabbalah, the status of the feminine in theosophical Kabbalah, and the relationship between revelation and concealment have been of considerable assistance to me.[24]

Neta Sobol has analyzed manuscripts to examine the way in which the Idra Rabba was conceived and composed, and she discusses some of the fundamental issues in the Idra literature in the light of parallels in the Zohar, earlier kabbalistic sources, and the various manuscripts.[25] She also points to the eclectic quality of the text, and presents hypotheses concerning the evolution of the Idra's ideas at various stages of the production of its final text.

Shifra Asulin has thoroughly researched the feminine figure of the Divine in the Idra Rabba and Idra Zuṭa. She understands the divergent presentations of this figure in the two Idras as pointing to theological, psychological, and mystical differences between the two works.[26]

Avishar Har-Shefi has studied and elucidated the myth of the primordial kings in the Idra Rabba, pointing to differences between the various attestations of this myth in the Idras, and to its sources in literature predating the Zohar.[27] Similarly, he has examined the Idra Zuṭa and its relationship with the Idra Rabba.[28] His studies, too, have been of great value to my research.

In his comprehensive book on the Zohar, Pinchas Giller devotes two chapters to a study of the Idras, including their literary and conceptual aspects. This book also offers his translations of selections from the Idras and from Sifra di-Tsniʿuta.[29]

Daniel Matt's translation of the Idra Rabba was recently published as part of the monumental project of the Pritzker translation of the Zohar into English. This translation along with the many illuminating notes accompanying it is an exceptional reference tool for researchers of zoharic literature, and it has been of great assistance to me.[30]

I have drawn considerably on the scholarship outlined here, and it was of continual use to me in approaching the Idra. As the reader will see, I also have occasion to refer to these studies throughout the present book.[31]

2

The Language of Divine Faces

The Idras exhibit a unique mode of mythical and mystical discourse, quite distinct from that of the rest of the zoharic corpus. The main body of the Zohar discusses the divine realm of being in kabbalistic terminology that is based on a structure of ten modes of divine being and action (*sefirot*). These are referred to as levels, attributes, lights, hues, or names, and together they constitute the Divinity that acts upon the world and is known within it.[1] While it is true that the Zohar chooses not to employ the usual kabbalistic terminology of *sefirot*, there is no doubt that the conceptual, imaginative, and symbolic edifice of the Zohar is built upon kabbalistic discourse and the paradigm of ten *sefirot* as it had developed by the time the Zohar was composed. The ten *sefirot* are abstract qualities, such as Wisdom (*Ḥokhmah*), Understanding (*Binah*), and Splendor (*Hod*), and the Zohar relates to them as hypostases—fundamental dimensions of reality—that differ from one another in quality and gender. These divine attributes that the Zohar discusses in conceptual and experiential terms are in a state of flux, of dynamic motion. They are in a relationship with one another, exhibiting nearness or distance, alienation or intimacy. This motion is reflected in the world, in the Torah, and in human beings.

In contrast with this discourse based on the ten *sefirot*, the Idras choose to speak in terms of *partsufim* (faces). *Partsuf* is a loanword in rabbinic Hebrew, adopted from the Greek term *prosōpon* (face);[2] the Aramaic equivalent of the Hebrew term *panim* (face) is *appin* or *anpin*. Echoing their biblical, midrashic, and targumic sources, the Idras employ the terms *appin* and *partsuf* interchangeably.[3]

Like human faces, the divine faces discussed in the Idras are full of expression, revealing rich and varied qualities. On the one hand, the choice to speak of the Divine in terms of faces—as opposed to more abstract attributes, such as Wisdom (*Ḥokhmah*) or Compassion (*Ḥesed*)—is a choice to represent the Divine in a particularly personal, mythical, and concrete fashion. On the other hand, and from a dialectical point of view, one conceives of and experiences the divine realm in a more complex fashion when one thinks in terms of faces than when one employs sefirotic terminology. It is tremendously difficult to formulate what one senses in a glance at the face of another human being in linear terms, to translate it into a continuum of words or statements. Speaking of the Divine in terms of faces thus generates an experience of simultaneity, much like a hologram, or the multitude of impressions we receive on even glancing at another's face that can only be translated into speech by assembling a great volume of parenthetical statements. In addition, by choosing faces over *sefirot* as the fundamental building blocks of its discourse, the Idra Rabba places the conscious, rational, and verbal aspects of the human encounter with faces alongside the unconscious layers of such an encounter.[4]

The choice of such a personal language emerges from a deep awareness of the need to reclaim and redeem personal aspects of theological discourse. Jewish theology had become increasingly abstract under the influence of the rational and critical force of Aristotelian philosophy in its various Jewish formulations, the most prominent representative of which was Maimonides, with his tremendous literary and intellectual project, *The Guide for the Perplexed*. There is no doubt that a fear of theological abstraction—to the point that the living God vanishes—is a major motivating and generating force in the Idra. Nonetheless, the text does not express a nostalgic or regressive yearning to return to an understanding of God as it existed at earlier stages in the development of Jewish tradition. Rather, it articulates the desire for a world that is complex and can contain contradictions, holding together both the abstract and the personal.

The Idra Rabba discusses three divine *partsufim*: *Arikh Anpin*, or *ʿAttiqa Qaddisha*—the Long-Faced or Patient One, the Holy Ancient One—the ancient and archaic face of God, elderly and crowned with white hair, abundant with love and life; *Zeʿeir Anpin*—the Small-Faced, Young-Faced, or Short-Tempered One—a face that ranges between redness and whiteness, whose expression fluctuates between Judgment and Compassion. From the head of *Zeʿeir Anpin* the semblance of *Adam* emerges, developing into an androgynous human figure, comprising two conjoined bodies, one masculine and one feminine. *Nuqba*—the feminine—a *partsuf* that comes into being as the Adamic divine body emerges, is described as having a whole female face and body, including accentuated sexual organs. Interpretations of the Idra generally treat this third *partsuf* as the female divine figure in and of itself, with the masculine aspect being subsumed into *Zeʿeir Anpin*.

The Idra Rabba discusses the three *partsufim* extensively, and is particularly concerned with the dynamic relationship among them. The first section of the Idra Rabba focuses on the relationship between *Arikh Anpin* and *Zeʿeir Anpin*; that is, the large and the small, the One and the dual, the old and the young. Next, it treats the relationship between the divine masculine and feminine, and their various states as they face one another. The fundamental idea throughout the Idra is that the correct alignment of the *partsufim* with one another is the key to divine and cosmic healing.

The Idra Rabba thus builds the divine realm upon three fundamental aspects, and upon the complex and dynamic relationships among them: the undivided, the masculine, and the feminine. This tripartite structure has some interesting parallels. For example, there are the various ways in which the midrashim in the body of the Zohar interpret the verse *A river flows from Eden to water the garden* (Genesis 2:10). The Zohar understands this verse as an account of the dynamic relationship between three aspects of divine being: Eden, the River, and the Garden. This furnishes us with a close parallel to the Idra Rabba's terminology of *partsufim*, but in naturalistic terms.[5]

If we were to translate the *partsufim* into sefirotic language, we might say that *Arikh Anpin* refers to the qualities of the *sefirah* Crown (*Keter*), or to the *sefirot* Crown-Wisdom-Understanding (*Keter-Ḥokhmah-Binah*); *Zeʿeir Anpin* refers to the *sefirot* beneath Understanding, or according to Cordovero, from Wisdom to Foundation (*Yesod*); finally, the feminine (*Nuqba*) is related to those *sefirot* that are connected to Judgment (*Din*), and more specifically to the final, feminine *sefirah*, Sovereignty (*Malkhut*). However, identifications of the *partsufim* with specific *sefirot* must always be qualified. Although it is possible to see an expression of certain *sefirot* in the various *partsufim*, it is clear that in the Idra Rabba there is no attempt to fully harmonize these two paradigms or to bring them into alignment.[6] To a degree, the Idra's tripartite conception also parallels the three fundamental components of Neoplatonic discourse (albeit in structure rather than content): the One, the Intellect, and the Soul. Of course, the Idra's three faces also bring to mind the Christian Trinity.[7]

In the Idra Zuṭa, two additional *partsufim* join those discussed in the Idra Rabba: *Abba* (the Father), which refers to the *sefirah* of Wisdom (*Ḥokhmah*); and *Imma* (the Mother), which refers to the *sefirah* of Understanding (*Binah*). Thus, in this Idra we have an account of a more "familial" cosmic Divinity, including a grandfather (*Arikh Anpin*), a mother and father, a son (*Ze'eir Anpin*) and daughter (*Nuqba*). The connections and interrelations among the *partsufim* in the Idra Zuṭa thus differ considerably from those described in the Idra Rabba.[8]

In the following chapters, we shall become more closely acquainted with the three *partsufim* of the Idra Rabba, and explore elements of their relationship with one another.

On the Qualities of Face Terminology

Beyond the desire to restore a face to the Divine, thereby reaffirming a divine personality, face terminology conveys unique qualities. Through these qualities, the Idra imparts its unique mode of religious discourse, and expands the ways in which human beings can connect with the Divine.

The Face as a Fundamental Human Experience

With their innumerable expressions, our faces succinctly disclose essential aspects of our personalities. We know this as an existential experience that accompanies us from birth to death. Scrutinizing and interpreting faces is a quintessential human experience. Psychoanalysts such as Donald Winnicott and Wilfred Bion have observed that a mother's face nourishes a child as much as do her breasts. The face satiates the baby with its presence, or starves her with its absence. We can turn our face to another attentively or lovingly, or turn it away in an expression of alienation, apathy, or antipathy. The feeling we have looking into the face of an elderly man or woman, the experience of lovers gazing at each other face to face, the sense of personal redemption that we might experience if we dare to show our face to another human being without obscuring or veiling it—such moments can illustrate the fundamental and essential place that the face occupies in human existence. It is the face that enables each of us to turn to another with the will and desire to connect and communicate.[9]

The Idra's choice to portray God in terms of various faces and the glances and gazes exchanged between them touches upon a fundamental human experience. In the Idra, the experience of faces and facing becomes a central characteristic, both within the divine world and in the relationship between humans and the Divine.

The Face as a Living Presence

As noted earlier, in the Idra Rabba, we are presented with a seemingly impossible task, an effort to turn the most abstract into something human: to give God a face. Perhaps this demonstrates an awareness that one can experience the abstract and the godly only through its human garb, as it arises in the consciousness and imagination.[10] In contradistinction to the impulse to provide an account of divine transcendence and ever-increasing abstraction, the Idra focuses on clothing and embodying the Divine in a human face. In this context, Liebes writes: "The human face (*partsuf*) is similar to the heavenly face, insofar as it emanates from it, *for in His image did God make man* (Genesis 9:6). [. . .] With respect to the heavenly face, we discern it primarily as it is reflected in the face of flesh and blood."[11]

The Idra's central activity—namely, configuring the divine faces—facilitates a connection between human beings and those faces. This is an entirely different act from iconic portrayal, still photography, or a sketch of a face. The Idra does not seek to make a static (re)presentation of a deity, but rather to invoke the Divine as a living face in the consciousness and experience of the reader, to call into that reader's own mind the face of the living God. According to the Idra, the *partsufim* enable the hidden Divine to address or turn to something outside of itself. This turning, this address, is a prerequisite for establishing a relationship between human beings and God.

This insight received unique expression in the theological thought of Jean-Luc Marion, who makes a distinction between the *idol* and the *icon*.[12] The idol, the statue or molten image, represents the invisible as visible. The human eye longs to rest its gaze upon the visible, the conceivable—yet this very desire makes the idol an object that only reflects the viewer back to herself, like a mirror. In contrast, the icon expands one's vision beyond the concrete depiction perceived by the eye. The icon presents the invisible as it is. It does not seek to fix the viewer's gaze upon something visible; rather, it enables the experience of the invisible through the visible. Thus, the icon represents a departure from a narcissistic conception of religion, in which one sees only oneself. Returning to the Idra, the divine faces that the Companions configure are neither a boundary nor a screen upon which the gaze rests or is fixed; they are a symbolic and imaginal space through which consciousness may pass into invisible dimensions. The Idra's configuration of the *partsufim* is not a theoretical exercise in mythical theology. Rabbi Shim'on emphasizes that the invocation of the divine faces is not a one-time emergency measure; he wishes for them to accompany his disciples continuously, as a living presence.

The Face as a Conduit and Filter of Light

To my understanding, the detailed discussion of divine faces entails the construction of a selection of filters for the divine light, or for the hidden God, which cannot be known or revealed directly. The face is a complex filtering mechanism, an edifice of fine latticework through which the light contained within may pass outward in different ways and with varying intensity. Each feature of the divine face transmits the inner divine quality passing through it in its own unique and distinctive way. As we shall see, the eyes, nostrils, and mouth in *Arikh Anpin* are openings through which light and life pass in an unmediated and unregulated fashion. Adjacent to these features are expanses of skin that are not covered by hair: the parting of the hair, the forehead, and the cheeks. These surfaces may be likened to riverbeds of varying breadth, through which light passes at various intensities. There are also the hairs of the head and beard, which function as channels and streams, transmitting the bounteous flow of divine light in an even more highly regulated manner.

The *partsufim* thus transmit and regulate the infinite divine light, thereby enabling us to experience it in a softened or dimmed form. If God were to have no face, how could we stand in the presence of the brilliant and boundless white light that gushes from the inner depths of the Divine? We could never endure the overexposure, disappearing before we even came into existence.

Indeed, some passages in the body of the Zohar present God's emanation of the world and into it as a pure light that then creates a complex framework of veils or screens for itself. These veils are intended to conceal, regulate, and dim the brilliant light within them. The veils themselves are made from light, but a duller or coarser light. They thus enable the existence of a reality distinct from the Divine, nourished by the light, but without being obliterated by it:

> The concealed primordial light created by the blessed Holy One shone until worlds could not bear it. What did the Blessed Holy One do? He made a light for His light, clothing one in the other; and so for the other lights, until all worlds endured vitally—and can bear it. (Zohar 3:204b; trans. Matt 9:321)

The Idra's uniqueness lies in its choice not to discuss the emanation of ten veils, screens, or vessels that contain and regulate the divine light in abstract terms, but rather to replace this discourse with a bold mythical account of the same functions being performed by the living face of God.

The Idra's formulation of these processes also suggests a stimulating insight regarding the face's role in interpersonal relationships: we need a face to regulate the transmission of ourselves to another, so that our whole inner being will not spill out, and so that another human being can bear the potency that lies within us. Our faces allow us to encounter another human being directly, but to retain our own distinct sense of self.

The Face as a Tiqqun

The term *tiqqun* (plural, *tiqqunim*) is central to the language of the Idra Rabba. The Idra employs the concept of *tiqqun* in a unique sense, applying it specifically to the discourse of divine faces. In the Zohar in general, and in the Idra in particular, the term *tiqqun* (literally, "repair") does not merely signify the opposite of destruction, as it often does in rabbinic Hebrew. Rather, it is multivalent, referring to the acts of configuring, arraying, establishing, clothing, beautifying, adorning, enhancing, or even embodying (in the sense of generating or configuring a body).[13] The task of *tiqqun*, configuring the various divine faces, refers to the ability to clothe a divine quality in words, images, or ideas, and to discuss it via the face and body. In the Idra, the *tiqqunim* form the mechanism that enables the unveiling of the concealed Divine.

The *tiqqun* enacted by each of the Companions in his act of creative exegesis is no mere intellectual or artistic enterprise. Rabbi Shim'on describes how each *tiqqun* that emerges from their mouths ascends and enters the specific part of the divine face that they are discussing, framing the process in visionary terms:

> I saw these enhancements [*tiqqunim*] shining upon it, awaiting the words of our mouths—to be crowned, each ascending to its place. As it was arranged by our mouths, every single one ascended and was crowned, arrayed in the arrangement bestowed here by each of our mouths. As each of us opened his mouth to arrange a certain enhancement, that enhancement sat waiting for the word to issue from your mouth, and then it was crowned, ascending to its place to be adorned. (Zohar 3:135a; trans. Matt 8:378)

The divine face awaits and anticipates the unique mode of speech that takes place in the Idra Rabba. When the *tiqqunim* settle within the divine face and beard, those parts of the face grow luminous, flowing with divine bounty. Human speech invokes and summons the divine face, stimulating the flow of divine Mercy (*raḥamim*) that emerges from within it.[14]

At the same time, the term *tiqqun* also refers to the restoration of something that has become corrupted or damaged. The *tiqqunim* construct the foundations upon which a harmonious relationship among the divine faces may take place. The precise alignment of the *partsufim* with one another carries profound importance for all levels of cosmic reality. Indeed, it ensures the uninterrupted flow of the divine life-force from its hidden sources, through all the layers of the divine dimensions, and ultimately into our world.

In academic scholarship, the activity of influencing or affecting the heavenly worlds and divine beings is called *theurgy*. The Idra thus describes a theurgic process, in which humans aspire to activate the Divine, bringing an outpouring of blessings upon the world.

The Face of God in Jewish Tradition

The Idra Rabba did not develop its anthropomorphic discourse of divine faces in a vacuum. Conceptions of the Divine in human form or of human beings in the likeness of God have deep roots in the Hebrew Bible, in classical rabbinic theological discourse, and in esoteric traditions such as *Shi'ur Qomah* and Hekhalot literature. These traditions provide the key to understanding how the Idra's theology—which at first glance seems so radical—could be accepted by so many in the Jewish world, who came to see it as reflecting a sacred tradition by which one should live.

A number of studies have been dedicated to the topic of divine faces as it appears in Jewish literature, and also to exploring the connection between the human face and the face(s) of God.[15] The following paragraphs briefly note some of the major stages in the development of these concepts, from the Hebrew Bible up until the Zohar.

In biblical sources, "God's face" is a fundamental mode of divine revelation in the human world. The Bible describes the human need for the divine face. Divine favor toward humans, described as an illuminated face, is life; if God turns His back, or conceals His face, the consequence is perdition, darkness, physical and spiritual death. The revelation of God's face may be particularly propitious, an expression of divine favor, as in the Priestly Blessing *May YHVH make His face shine upon you and be gracious to you! May YHVH lift up His countenance to you, and grant you peace!* (Numbers 6:25–26). Alternatively, the face of God may denote terrifying anger or rage: *I will set My face against that man, and I will cut him off from among his people* (Leviticus 20:3). Thus, in the Bible, there is a tension between two competing conceptions: one according to which the face of God should not be seen, represented in God's words to Moses, *You cannot see My face, for a human being may not see Me and live* (Exodus 33:20); and another that presents accounts of affection and intimacy between God and the Israelites, and in particular the dialogue between God and Moses, in terms of a "face to face" encounter: *Face to face YHVH spoke to you on the mountain, out of the fire* (Deuteronomy 5:4); *YHVH would speak to Moses face to face, as one man speaks to another* (Exodus 33:11).

In the Apocrypha, we find accounts of human beings standing before the Divine in Enochic literature, which describes the heavenly ascent of Enoch.

In Slavonic Enoch (also known as the Second Book of Enoch), one finds the first account of two faces—one small and one large—that are created on earth in the divine image.[16]

Later rabbinic literature develops a new discourse concerning the divine face and the ways in which it is revealed to humans. A number of rabbinic midrashim describe the human encounter with God in terms of the perception of a human figure, and they point to the unity underlying the changing faces of the Divine, a conception based in the authors' own distinctive religious world view:

> For the Blessed Holy One appeared to them at the sea as a warrior, at Sinai as a scribe teaching Torah, in Daniel's time as an elder teaching Torah, in Solomon's time as a young man. The Blessed Holy One said to them: You see me in many likenesses, but I am the one at the sea, I am the one at Sinai. *I am YHVH your God* (Ex. 20:2).[17]

The reciprocal face-to-face relationship, described in the Bible as one of fellowship and love, was sexualized in rabbinic discussions of the cherubs in the Tabernacle and Temple. The biblical image of two cherubs standing face to face in the Tabernacle was interpreted as a representation of loving union or coupling, exemplifying God's love for Israel.[18]

The Song of Songs, describing the erotic relationship between a man and a woman, also underwent a dramatic transformation in rabbinic thought. The rabbis interpreted this work allegorically and symbolically as a depiction of the relationship between God and Israel. They thereby opened up new possibilities for understanding the detailed account of the beloved's face and body as a description of the Divine.

Invoking and summoning the divine form and face constitutes a central aspect of the religious quest in the Jewish esoteric literature of late antiquity known as Hekhalot (Palaces, Temples) or Merkavah (Chariot) literature. In this tradition, the ultimate goal of the mystical practitioner's arduous and dangerous journey was to see the form of God sitting upon the celestial throne. The visionary hoped ultimately to enter the seventh celestial palace or temple, and to be granted a glimpse of the King in all His beauty and splendor.[19]

In one work in this tradition, Hekhalot Rabbati, we find an account of a daily occurrence of central significance, when the eyes of God and Israel meet. This moment is described as one of particular love and intimacy:

> My only pleasure in the worldly home that I created is when your eyes are lifted to Mine, and My eyes are lifted to yours, when you recite before Me: *Holy, holy, holy* (Isaiah 6:3).[20]

The continuation of the passage presents an even more striking image, full of love and affection: God kisses and caresses an iconic likeness of Jacob, the patriarch of Israel, which is inscribed upon His throne:

> [Testify to them,] what I do to the visage of Jacob your Father's face, which is engraved on My glorious throne: For when you recite *Holy, holy, holy* (Isaiah 6:3) before me, I bend down over it and kiss it, stroking and caressing it, my hands upon my arms—when you recite before Me: *Holy, holy, holy* (Isaiah 6:3).[21]

The nature of the human-Divine relationship in these passages, and the strikingly embodied and sensuous ways in which God is described, directly inform the conception of the divine body in the Idras.

The Hekhalot literature also developed upon rabbinic exegesis of the Song of Songs. In this context, and for our present purpose, the *Shi'ur Qomah* literature is particularly important. These works emerged from the Hekhalot and Merkavah circles, and intensively developed the connection between the verses of the Song of Songs and the body of God. Here, one encounters elaborate and detailed descriptions of the dimensions of God's body and face.[22]

The German Pietists (Ḥaside Ashkenaz of the late 12th to mid-13th centuries) also continued this project. In their discussions of the divine glory (*ḳavod*), a concept that represents the experienced and visible aspect of God in their theology, we find references to the existence of a face within this entity—a face that may be glimpsed by human beings.[23] These circles produced the *Hymn of Glory* (*Shir ha-Kavod*)—also known by its first line, *An'im Zemirot* ("I shall sweetly sing")—which was integrated into the liturgy. In this composition, there is a palpable tension between an abstract conception of the Divine and depictions of God's body and face.[24]

Another milestone in the development of Jewish discourse on the divine face is in the Zohar itself. In the body of the Zohar —that is, in passages that do not belong to the Idras—we find a number of expressions of a conception of divine faces. Some of these conceptions are mystical and mythical paraphrases of rabbinic midrashim that discuss the faces of God. For example, in Pesiqta Rabbati, Rabbi Levi is credited with saying that "the Blessed Holy One appeared to them with many faces at Sinai: With a stern face, with a raging face, with a sallow face, with a joyful face, with a smiling face, with a patient face."[25] This formulation is amplified mystically in the Zohar:

> It has been taught: How many faces upon faces has the blessed Holy One! Shining faces, dim faces; high faces, low faces; distant faces, near faces; inner faces, outer faces; right faces, left faces.
>
> Come and see: Happy are Israel before the blessed Holy One, for they are united with high faces of the King—faces with which He and His Name are united, faces that are He and His Name! Other nations are united with those distant faces, with those low faces; so they are distant from the body of the King. (Zohar 2:86b–87a; trans. Matt 4:490)

In this context, it might have been possible to understand the term "face" in an abstract sense, referring to distinct facets of the Divinity or different aspects of divine governance. However, the emphasis on both the *face* and the *body* point to the Zohar's deliberate choice to embrace corporeal elements in its theological discourse. The Deity is a king with a body, and His face takes on different expressions: shining or dim, near or far. The people of Israel's unique merit is expressed in their nearness to the King's supernal and essential face and body.

Another passage in the Zohar raises the subject of the Divine's desire for its faces to be perceived. Only the mystic knows how to enable these faces to break through the divine darkness in which they are immersed, and to shine forth. The hidden Divinity needs human beings to bring these hidden faces out of their concealment:

> All those faces of the King are concealed in the depth behind darkness, and all those who know how to unify the Holy Name fittingly split all those walls of darkness, and the faces of the King appear, illuminating everything. (Zohar 2:57a; trans. Matt 4:300, emended)

In this passage, the association of face imagery with light terminology in the context of the divine realm is informative, alerting us to another textual tradition from which the Zohar draws: the Neoplatonic world of imagination and thought. The influence of such discourse is detectable in kabbalistic works that predate the Zohar, as well as in the Zohar itself.[26] Plotinus (3rd century CE), the founding figure of the Neoplatonic tradition, describes the emanation of the Intellect—and thereby the emergence of a unified multiplicity—from the One, as follows:

> And so, if one likens it to a living richly varied sphere, or imagines it as a thing all faces, shining with living faces, or as all the pure souls running together into the same place, with no deficiencies but having all that is their own, and universal Intellect seated on their summits so that the region is illuminated by intellectual light—if one imagined it like this one would be seeing it somehow as one sees another from outside; but one must become that, and make oneself the contemplation.[27]

In his account of the divine realm, Plotinus combines face and light imagery in a way that will come to characterize later Neoplatonic writing. In addition, this passage calls on the reader to identify and attain union with the object of contemplation, rather than seeing such an activity as merely a theoretical exercise. Indeed, both the fundamental impulses and the terminology of Neoplatonic thought may be identified in the Zohar, as translated and assimilated into a medieval Jewish intellectual milieu.[28]

Jewish Philosophy and the Idra Literature: Between Abstraction and Anthropomorphism

Of course, alongside religious traditions that encouraged their adherents to immerse themselves in contemplation of the divine face and body, there were Jewish thinkers who directly opposed such tendencies. This was particularly true of philosophically inclined Jews of both an Aristotelian and Neoplatonic orientation, who aimed to render the concept of God increasingly abstract, and utterly rejected the attribution of any corporeal form to the Divine. The crowning achievement of this project is Maimonides' *Guide for the Perplexed*, in which anthropomorphic verses from the Bible are systematically interpreted in a metaphorical vein. In the words of Moshe Halbertal, the *Guide* presents a kind of "therapy for religious discourse," purifying it of human dross.[29]

It seems that the authors of the Idras were not in denial of such traditions, nor did they seek simply to ignore them and return to a naïve conception of rabbinic thought, or to the Hekhalot models of late antiquity. On the contrary, to make sense of the detailed and intensive treatment of the divine *partsufim* in the Idras, one must acknowledge the authors' familiarity with the philosophical tradition, and with Maimonides in particular. Indeed, their work is in many ways a response to Maimonides, framed in a dialectical and sometimes sarcastic engagement with his ideas, while also drawing boldly and unapologetically from Jewish anthropomorphic discourse. The Zohar, and the Idras in an even more striking way, attempt to steer Jewish religious language away from the path of over-abstraction and intellectualization of the Divine—lest the Divine should lose its vital connection with the rich and multifaceted human experience.

The Idra Rabba is thus a response of appropriate scale to Maimonides' vast project. It not only declares that God has a nose, forehead, and eyes—it describes them hyperrealistically, in fine detail, sometimes crossing over into the territory of the surreal. In other words, it is precisely Maimonides' profound influence in articulating a radically abstract theology, and it is precisely a complex and conflicted stance toward that conception, that led the authors of the Idra to formulate such a bold refutation, with such personal and fantastical accounts of the Divine.

My teacher Yehuda Liebes described the purpose of the Idras' face terminology as an attempt "to give the God of Israel back His face," after medieval Jewish theological discourse had grown too abstract and transcendental.[30] Indeed, the Idras consistently demand that we not relinquish the mythical God of the Bible, the divine face as a central aspect of the human encounter with God, or the *Shiʿur Qomah* tradition with its insistence upon divine embodiment. As Elliot Wolfson put it: "The internalization of anthropomorphic likeness is one of the most innovative and distinctive phenomena in the Zohar, and in Sifra di-Tsniʿuta and the Idras in particular."[31]

It is particularly notable that the Idra Rabba does not *reject* Maimonidean abstraction but rather attempts to *integrate* it. Thus the authors insist that God's eyes as they are described in the Bible are first and foremost eyes, but these eyes are also divine providence; God's forehead is indeed a forehead, but it is also the stream of divine Will.[32] The authors of the Idra thus want a God who is present, with whom one can establish the kind of emotional and sensory connection that can only exist in the face-to-face encounter of seeing and being seen, at the very same time as they recognize the mysterious and sublime Divinity that dwells deep within—behind the face, beneath the surface. They borrow liberally from biblical and rabbinic sources, *Shi'ur Qomah*, and of course Maimonidean discourse. They thereby forge new alternatives, creative and radical, in which transcendent abstraction and embodiment are intimately intertwined with one another. Thus, it might be said that the Idra's face terminology integrates the most abstract registers of theological discourse with the most intimate and personal. In the words of Moses Cordovero in the opening passage of his commentary on the Idras: these works are "[d]rawing those things that are figuratively described in corporeal terms, raising them into their spiritual dimension [. . .] and entering into the spiritual from within the physical, and the physical from the spiritual, so that the reader's mind may dwell on two planes at once."[33]

One of the most stunning expressions of mystical theology may be found in the works of Muḥyi al-Dīn Ibn al-ʿArabī (1165–1240). One of the greatest Muslim mystics, he too proposes an integration of the sensory and personal with the abstract and transcendental. In his book *Fuṣūṣ al-Ḥikam* (The bezels of wisdom), Ibn al-ʿArabī articulates an integrative and holistic approach, uniting the abstract, the imaginative, and the sensory. Any true conception of God must engage both the intellect and the imagination, applying them together to grasp divine immanence and transcendence:

> "By the 'imagination' [*khayāl*] they liken Him by making Him transcendent; and by the Intellect [*'aql*], they make Him transcendent by means of likening Him. Each is [inextricably] bound up with the other, so that transcendence cannot be unaffected by likening, and vice versa. One who focuses exclusively on intellectual contemplation of the Divine in the transcendent and abstract sense attains only half the gnosis of God. That is because the intellect, by itself, absorbing knowledge in its own way, knows only the transcendent and nothing of what is immanent."[34]

Arikh Anpin: The Long-Faced, Patient One

Arikh Anpin—the Long-Faced or Patient One—is the name of the most ancient and undifferentiated of the divine faces.[35] Another frequent name for this aspect of the Divine in the Idra Rabba is *'Attiqa Qaddisha*, the Holy Ancient One. This face is also sometimes called *'Attiq Yomin*, the Ancient of Days—a formulation originating in the Book of Daniel, where God is described in these terms.

'Attiqa is not associated with the details of the creation narrative of Genesis, with the establishment of law and order, or with individual divine providence. This is the Divine as the great wellspring of life, love, and forgiveness. This *partsuf* radiates light, floods over its banks, abounds with vitality, and sustains all things that come into contact with it. In its luminescence, being itself becomes possible. *'Attiqa Qaddisha* is unique insofar as it doesn't *act*, it simply *is*. That is to say, this is not a deity in the sense of performing acts or imposing order, but rather in the sense that it is Being or the Source of Being. In this *partsuf*, the most fundamental aspects of existence are emphasized: nourishment, love, mercy, forgiveness, wakefulness, and unending presence.

Although the Idra Rabba employs the terms *'Attiqa Qaddisha* and *Arikh Anpin* interchangeably, they emphasize different qualities in this aspect of the Godhead. Whereas the term *'Attiqa* alludes to the primordial and archaic quality of this Divinity, *Arikh Anpin* refers to other attributes: on a theological level, the quality of this Divinity is patience, forgiveness, and absolute mercy and compassion, which is why it is called the Patient or Long-Suffering One (*Erekh Appayim*)—one of the divine attributes mentioned in Exodus 34:6. In addition, the Idra appeals to the literal sense of the term *anpin* as "nose." The term *af* (nose) may refer to "anger" in biblical Hebrew—as in "flaring the nose" (*ḥaron af*)—so that *Erekh Appayim* comes to mean the Long-Nosed One or the Long-Breathed One: namely, the Patient One. On the continuum between anger and long deep breathing and patience, the nose thus represents the locus of emotional sustenance in the breath. Similarly, *Arikh Anpin* implies certain facial characteristics: the Long-Nosed One, the Long-Faced or Relaxed-Faced One. When *Ze'eir Anpin*, the Small-Faced or Short-Tempered One, gazes up at this primordial face, he is healed.[36]

We might have thought that the authors of the Idras would choose to describe this undifferentiated and primordial dimension of the Divine in exalted and impersonal terms: rivers or springs, or the celestial realm of light and its phenomena. But this proves not to be the case. Instead, we encounter pages upon pages of surrealistic images of an actual, elderly face, described in the finest detail: a skull, forehead, eyes, nose, cheeks, head, and beard hairs.

Let us look at an example:

> It has been taught in the Concealment of the Book: The Ancient of Ancients, Hidden of Hidden, was arrayed and prepared—that is, He existed and did not exist, did not actually exist yet was arrayed. No one knows Him, for He is more ancient than the ancients, but in His arrayal He is known—like an elder of elders, more ancient than the ancients, more concealed than the concealed—known by His signs yet unknown.
>
> Master of white—His garment and sparkling countenance. Seated on a throne of flames, to subdue them.
>
> Through 400,000 worlds the whiteness of the skull of His head spreads; and from the radiance of this white the righteous inherit 400 worlds in the world that is coming.[37] (Zohar 3:128a–b; trans. Matt 8:327–328)

The Idra purposely pushes language to its limits, working at the overlapping fault line between abstract and concrete, and overflowing with paradoxical language.

Approaching and understanding *'Attiqa* requires great patience. One must read very slowly, cultivating a state of consciousness that can contain both strangeness and familiarity, concreteness and abstraction, and an array of biblical citations and allusions. The reader must open the eye of the spirit, to see the vast and intricate pictures that are gradually woven in the lines of the text and between them—for this is not a matter of ordinary language, of the familiar symbolic order, or of the law. Only with the eye of the spirit, the heart's discernment, and the images perceived in dreams can one grasp something of *'Attiqa*.

I must pause here to emphasize the difficulty of translating the complex *partsuf* of *Arikh Anpin* into commonly used theological and philosophical terms regarding Divinity. In contemplating the terms available—oneness, unified, unitive, undifferentiated, nondual, unitary, monistic, pre-differentiated—I and those I have studied and worked with have found that while *'Attiqa* shares in different aspects of each of these terms, none of them encompasses the complexity of *Arikh Anpin*. *'Attiqa* does not have the perfect, static, and monolithic quality of the Jewish Aristotelian oneness of the Divine, nor does it partake of the abstract Neoplatonic sense of the One. While sharing some attributes of the Brahma in Hindu tradition, the Being aspects of *'Attiqa* are mingled with emotion, will, and sometimes even archaic action. Other terms, such as those central to Christian mystical theologies, carry historical baggage that might obscure the uniqueness of the Idras. The main reason that no single term offers a perfect fit is that *Arikh Anpin* is an intense and paradoxical mixture of the abstract and the personal.

Nevertheless, I have been comfortable with using the terms *oneness* and *undifferentiated* throughout this book. Undifferentiated refers specifically to that aspect of the Divine that is entirely characterized by life and *Ḥesed*, yet is prior to the emergence of the tension between *Ḥesed* and *Din* (and is in that sense pre-differentiated). From this perspective, undifferentiated can fittingly be applied to *'Attiqa*. Oneness as the Source of all, holding in potential all that will become differentiated reality, also resonates particularly with a Jewish sensibility and language that imagines God as One.[38]

Let us turn from theological terminology to images. Where might we find a parallel to the rich and surreal images of *Arikh Anpin*'s skull, dripping with life-giving dew? While they are not anthropomorphic, and despite the imperfect fit noted earlier, Neoplatonic sources do feature descriptions of the unceasing and eternal process of emanation that resonate with this idraic image. In these works, the One—the Source of all being—emanates forth the cosmos, simply by virtue of its perfect existence. As Plotinus states in the *Enneads*:

> The One, perfect because it seeks nothing, has nothing, and needs nothing, overflows, as it were, and its superabundance makes something other than itself.[39]

Similarly, parallels to *'Attiqa*'s white and luminous head may be found in Gnostic Neoplatonic accounts of the One, the Source of all things. For example, the Secret Book of John, apparently composed in the 2nd century CE in Alexandria, contains the following passage, in which the One is described as the

> Unity [existing as] pure light, into which it is not possible for any light of the eye to gaze. [. . .] It is eternal, it does not need anything [. . .] all

> it asks for is Itself alone within the perfect light [. . .] it is the light who gives light, the life who gives life [. . .] his aeon is indestructible, being in a state of tranquillity, at rest in silence. [It is] the one that exists before the All, for it is the head of the aeons.[40]

Despite its commonalities with this discourse of sublime luminosity and transcendence, the Idra differs from these sources considerably in its inclination to depict the origination of existence in strikingly personal terms, such as *'Attiqa*'s white skull as the genesis of the divine being. Like the authors of Neoplatonic literature, the authors of the Idra are interested in the question of the origins of being; but the latter address this topic while embracing their visual and mythical imagination. They move away from abstraction, and insist on returning to the head (Hebrew *rosh*, ראש) implicit in the Hebrew phrase *In the beginning* (*be-reshit*, בראשית), describing the appearance of God's head in its state prior to the emergence of all things from it.

The head of *'Attiqa Qaddisha* is crowned with white hair, the face adorned with a white beard. The hair of this face, as well as that of *Ze'eir Anpin*, is discussed in great detail and depth in the Idra Rabba. *'Attiqa*'s hairs are conceived as the channels that transmit the divine life-force inhabiting its skull. The head and beard hairs each possess a distinct character, transmitting different divine qualities or modalities through themselves, as if these qualities were flowing down a stream or a river.

'Attiqa's beard is the personal and visual representation of the luminous stream of Mercy (*raḥamim*) that flows from within this divine face. The beard is conceived of as a quality emerging from within the face, a radiant aura of sorts that imbues the face with beauty. The secrets of the divine beards comprise some of the most profound insights into the Divine, not belonging at all to the familiar reality of the senses but rather to the realm of spiritual perception:

> The beard that is most concealed and precious of all His array, the beard not known by those above or those below, the beard that is the praise of all praises, the beard that no human prophet or saint has ever approached to see, the beard that hangs by its hair to the navel of the heart, white as snow, most glorious of all, concealed of all, faith of all faith! (Zohar 3:130b; trans. Matt 8:346)

Rabbi Shim'on declares that the beard and its mysteries are revealed only to those who are deserving of such revelations, who possess the necessary attributes, and know God's attributes and the secrets of the structure of the divine world.[41]

The beard is divided into thirteen sections: the hair of the temples, of the mustache, of the beard hanging down to the navel of the heart, and so on. Each part represents one of the Thirteen Attributes of Mercy, derived from Micah 7:18–20:

> Who is a God like You, removing iniquity and passing over the transgression of the remnant of His people? He does not retain His wrath forever, for He delights in love. He will return and have compassion upon us; He will subdue our iniquities; and You will cast all their sins in the depths of the sea. You will grant truth to Jacob, love to Abraham, as You swore to our fathers from days of old.

The thirteen sections of the beard are configured by the Companions' *tiqqunim*. Each disciple is summoned in turn, and given an extremely complex and difficult mission: to describe one segment of the beard, and connect it exegetically to the Attribute of Mercy that corresponds with it. This task requires the exegete to engage a range of cognitive capabilities, and to access particular modes of consciousness, ultimately producing a multidimensional *tiqqun*. Connecting the formal manifestation of each part of the beard with a particular quality of God's Mercy (*raḥamim*), is a demonstration of the disciple's exegetical virtuosity, and of his ability to fulfil the mission on several cosmic planes. Once the thirteen segments of the beard have been properly configured, they shine brilliantly with *Arikh Anpin*'s distinctive qualities of boundless Mercy.

The experience of reading the *tiqqunim* of the supernal beard is particularly surreal and fantastical: surreal in the sense that the picture it presents is strange and curious, both attractive and frightening—responses that arise specifically out of its realism and the detailed portrayal of a human face or beard. It is fantastical insofar as it expands our consciousness, exposing it to that which lies beyond its usual, habitual states. These accounts of the divine beard focus on their subject in a manner that is highly unusual when considering the face of another human being. The reader is not presented with a clearly defined organ, such as an eye or a nose, but rather with a description of a particular segment of a beard, sometimes in hyperrealistic terms, at extremely close range. There is a hypnotic quality to the cadences and images in the Idra in general and in the *tiqqunim* of the beard in particular, guiding the reader into a realm of heightened surrealism, laying bare a fluid and dynamic reality that lies beyond the conscious mind.

It is worth noting here that the meaning of *tiqqun* in the Idra is "to clothe," "align," "complete," or "beautify." However, when applied to the beard, the term conveys an additional meaning: to style, comb, or curl.[42] Thus, the thirteen *tiqqunim* of the beard presented by the Companions should also be understood as a means of combing and curling it. Indeed, when Rabbi Isaac is called to offer the first *tiqqun* of the beard, Rabbi Shim'on addresses him as follows: "Stand erect and twirl the curls of the Holy King's enhancements!"[43]

Ze'eir Anpin: The Small-Faced, Short-Tempered One

Ze'eir Anpin—the Small-Faced, Young Faced, or Short-Tempered One—is the name of the second divine *partsuf* to be configured in the Idra Rabba. This aspect of the Divine distinguishes, examines, and analyzes, responding to the existence of the world in which humans live and act. This divine face reflects our reality, and it is in turn reflected in it. *Ze'eir Anpin* belongs to a differentiated mode of being, a world of multiplicity and polarities. Thus, it possesses a dynamic and ever-changing expression: it can express love or fury, it can shower us with compassion, or burn with blazing rage. This is the aspect of God identified with the law, and the religious and ethical system. This is YHVH, the God of Israel.

Visually, the head of *Ze'eir Anpin*, which is gradually revealed throughout the course of the second part of the Idra Rabba, is a representation of the majestic face of the male lover in the Song of Songs: the black-haired and black-bearded man, a warrior. *Ze'eir Anpin* is associated with redness, the color of Justice (*Din*), the latter being a foundational aspect of this figure's very existence. *Ze'eir Anpin*'s red Justice is diluted or tempered by *Arikh Anpin*'s white light of Compassion (*Ḥesed*), which pours down upon *Ze'eir Anpin* at times. The secret of the beauty of *Ze'eir Anpin* lies in this mixture of whiteness and redness—*My beloved is white and ruddy* (Song of Songs 5:10)—but he has a distinct tendency toward red Justice, manifesting in anger and impatience. As the Idra continues, the androgynous divine body will emerge from his head. Having within it masculine and feminine sides, this body will become progressively more complete and refined, ultimately separating into two distinct bodies, and then attaining wholeness and balance in a renewed union of those bodies.

The opposition between *Ze'eir Anpin*'s duality and tendency toward Justice and *'Attiqa*'s oneness and Compassion constitutes a fundamental dichotomy—an axis of sorts—within the Idra. Indeed, the very first time that *Ze'eir Anpin* is mentioned, it is in opposition to *Arikh Anpin*:[44]

> This Ancient of Ancients is called *Arikha de-Anpin*, Elongated Countenance, and the exterior one, *Ze'eir Anpin*, Small Countenance, compared to the Ancient One, the Elder, Holy of Holies. (Zohar, 3:128b; trans. Matt 8:330)

This preliminary and minimalistic account is disconcerting, despite (or perhaps because of) its brevity: the figure of *Ze'eir Anpin* is not described in its own terms but in relation to *Arikh Anpin*. It is called *the exterior one*, an entity lying outside the primordial, vital, and merciful *Arikh Anpin*.

The duality of *Ze'eir Anpin*'s face—ranging between Justice and Mercy, left and right—reappears throughout the Idra in various formulations:[45]

> Upon this depend right and left, radiance and darkness, Compassion and Judgment. All right and left depend upon this, not upon the Ancient One. (Zohar 3:136a; trans. Matt 8:388)

A fundamental aspect of coming to know and understand *Ze'eir Anpin* is that this face is characterized by differentiation, by dynamic relationships between its different sides and competing impulses.

As with *Arikh Anpin*'s features, *Ze'eir Anpin*'s facial features are gradually configured and adorned in the Idra Rabba: the forehead, the eyes, nose, and so on. We might expect a balanced treatment of the hues of Justice and Mercy in this face, but in fact *Ze'eir Anpin*'s threatening and frightening aspects receive greater emphasis. Here we have a judging forehead, flashing eyes, a nose flaring in anger. Thus, in the *tiqqunim* of the nose, we read:[46]

> From one nostril issues fiery smoke, subsiding into the Hollow of the Great Abyss. From the other nostril issue flames of fire, flaring into four thousand worlds on the left side. (Zohar 3:138a; trans. Matt 8:402)

Reading the *tiqqunim* of *Ze'eir Anpin* is not easy. The reader must let go of rigid conceptions of the God in which she or he believes (or disbelieves) and become receptive to the Divine as described by the Idra, where God is a being that is formed and generated, undergoing processes of evolution and regression. *Ze'eir Anpin* is not a transcendent and unchanging aspect of the Divine, but the precise opposite. This is a personal and emotional figure, whose chief mode of behavior is reactive.

In addition, the Idra Rabba scandalously applies the myth of the creation of the earthly Adam in Genesis to the Divine itself. According to the Idra, expressions of divine anthropomorphism are no mere projections of our limited imaginations upon a formless God. On the contrary, in the Idra, *Adam, the Human Being par excellence*, refers first and foremost to God. All earthly human beings, both male and female, are created in the image and likeness of this divine *Adam*. As readers, our consciousness must become flexible and receptive enough to imagine the Idra's God as androgynous, with a body both male and female. Reading through the *tiqqunim* of *Ze'eir Anpin* brings the extent to which transcendental theologies have been internalized in contemporary religious culture (often unconsciously) into much sharper relief; indeed, the Idra, time and again, challenges such conceptions in the most striking terms.

However, the Idra's theology is more complex still, for as I noted in the first chapter, the work does not simply reject all forms of abstraction and return to an ancient mythical conception of God. The Idra saturates the reader's consciousness with visual, mythical, sensory, and erotic terminology, but at the same time, it embraces an abstract theology. The reader must affirm images, representations, and corporeality, yet also adopt a subtle and complex conception of the Divine, one that is in dialogue with medieval Jewish philosophy and has internalized certain elements of it.

Another challenge for the reader who is just becoming acquainted with the figure of *Ze'eir Anpin* stems from its alternating depiction as the omnipotent God of the Hebrew Bible and as a distressed figure, a deficient and diminished deity. *Ze'eir Anpin* indeed needs assistance, both from *Arikh Anpin*, who showers compassion upon him, restoring him to a state of balance, and from human beings, who configure, groom, and adorn his face and body, bringing him to a harmonious state of conciliation and placation. Indeed, this section of the Idra Rabba is most significant for its articulation of conflicting perspectives: a vibrant, vital, and admiring description of the central figure of the Jewish religion, the God of Israel; a critique of certain characteristics of that deity; and a vision of how that figure might be reframed and healed.[47]

After completing the *tiqqunim* of *Ze'eir Anpin*'s face, the Idra turns to his beard, as it did in depicting *Arikh Anpin*. Unlike *Arikh Anpin's* white, smooth beard, this beard is black and curly, with coarse and uneven hair. It is *Ze'eir Anpin*'s most active facial feature, through which his attributes and modalities flow into the world. In contrast with the thirteen *tiqqunim* of *'Attiqa*'s beard, here there are only nine, the nine attributes of a warrior, engaged in fierce battle against mighty forces of Judgment (*Din*). The nine *tiqqunim* are derived from Psalm 118, which describes a warrior facing his enemies, summoning God's might to assist him. *Ze'eir Anpin* is a Divinity characterized by strength and activity, and the configuration of these attributes expresses a human desire to summon the presence of an active, forceful, and victorious deity. For example, the following lines appear in the ninth *tiqqun* of *Ze'eir Anpin*'s beard:[48]

> Ninth enhancement (*tiqqun*): Hairs join, all evenly, until the hair that hangs—all in beautiful symmetry, like a mighty hero victorious in battles. [. . .] All is drawn to this, as it is written: *The beauty* (*tif'eret*) *of young men is their strength* (Proverbs 20:29). He appeared at the Sea like a fine young man, as is written: *a young man like the cedars* (Song of Songs 5:15)—like a hero performing mighty deeds. This is *Tif'eret*, Beauty—power, might, and compassion. (Zohar 3:141a; trans. Matt 8:425)

But just as divine wrath may be directed against the forces of evil or the enemies of Israel, it may be turned against Israel, if they do not behave as required. Israel can cause this terrifying anger to subside by stimulating the

Thirteen Attributes of Mercy within *'Attiqa* to pour down into *Ze'eir Anpin*. *Arikh Anpin*'s Attributes of Mercy then soften and heal *Ze'eir Anpin*, filling him with whiteness and compassion. It is only through the power of these attributes that humans may continue to exist.

The Divine Body: Male and Female

Another theme treated in the Idra is the double body of God, with its male and female aspects. Once the reader's consciousness has acclimated to the detailed descriptions of divine heads and faces, and the reader's imagination has further expanded to encompass an account of the cosmic beards that grow from these faces, a new development lies in wait for the reader, requiring a yet greater expansion of consciousness. From the head and beard of *Ze'eir Anpin* a male body begins to emerge, beside which there develops a female head and body. Yet again, the Idra challenges the philosophical theology of which Maimonides is the main representative, a theology that forcefully proclaims that God has neither body nor corporeal form.

In the Idra Rabba, the divine body comes into being simultaneously with male and female aspects—alternating, traversing from male to female and back again. This body develops masculine and feminine backs, genitals, hands, and feet, joined together back to back. Now, a new head joins the white head of *'Attiqa* and the black-haired head of *Ze'eir Anpin*: the head of the feminine Divine (*Nuqba*) with her multicolored hair.

This two-faced androgyne has a long history in Jewish thought:[49]

> Rabbi Jeremiah b. Eleazar said: When the Blessed Holy One created the first Adam, He created him an androgyne. This is as it is written: *male and female He created them*. (Gen. 5:2)
>
> Rabbi Samuel b. Naḥman said: When the Blessed Holy One created the first Adam, He created him two-faced (*du partsufin, diproso-pon*; Greek *diprosōpon*). Then He sawed [Adam] in two, and made him into two bodies [lit., two backs]—one here and one here.[50]

This midrash is responding to the problem posed by Genesis 5:2: How may one describe the figure of *Adam* who is created as "male and female"? How may one imagine such a simultaneous act of creation? This interpretation also harmonizes the account of the creation of human beings as "male and female" in Genesis 1 with that of the creation of a woman from a man's rib or side in Genesis 2.

The Idra Rabba appropriates the androgynous figure of *Adam* from the midrashim, and applies it to the divine world in its own account of the emergence of God in a human likeness. In addition, the Idra follows the midrash in intuiting a deficiency in this androgynous state: because there is no clear separation between the male and female bodies, establishing a relationship of face-to-face intimacy and coupling is impossible. The potential for such a connection does indeed exist, but while positioned back to back, they remain sterile in a relational and procreative sense. Elaborating upon the midrash's account, in which the primordial androgyne is sawn in two, the Idra details the separation of the conjoined bodies, which is necessary so that they may encounter each other face to face.

Two processes precede the separation of the divine bodies. First, all the redness and Judgment (*Din*) on the masculine side of the body settle in the male's back, before passing into the female. The masculine body thus loses its color, turning white and becoming full of Compassion (*Ḥesed*), while the feminine side fills with redness and Judgment (*Din*). There are two purposes to this polarization. On the one hand, in almost chemical terms, it creates the possibility of separation; on the other hand, it forms the basis for the attraction between the two figures once they have been separated.

The second process is the formation of male genitals (*ammah*, the penis) and female genitals (*'ervah*, the vulva), reaching maximal sexual maturity just before the separation of the conjoined bodies. The genitals, called "covering" (*kesut*) in the Idra, are of cosmic dimensions.[51] They develop in tandem in the conjoined bodies: as the penis grows and lengthens, a hollow forms in the female body in response, which will match the male genitalia when the time comes for it to be penetrated:

> It has been taught in the Concealment of the Book: The Male extended and was arrayed in His enhancements. The enhancement of His covering was arrayed, and this is His phallus. The length of that phallus is 248 worlds, all of them suspended from the mouth of his phallus, called *yod*. [. . .]

> Once this phallus extended, the side of *Gevurah* extended [. . .] on the left side of the Female. It sank into the Female in a certain place and was designated as nakedness—covering the whole Female body. That place is considered total nakedness—to conceal the site of that phallus called *Ḥesed*, in order to assuage this *Gevurah*. (Zohar 3:142a; trans. Matt 8:430, 432)

Like ancient figurines in which the male and female genitals protrude dramatically while the rest of the body is represented in a schematic fashion, the genitals are treated so extensively in the Idra that one might suggest that the body as a whole merely provides the foundation for its sexual aspect.

Rather than an account of the origins of "man and woman," the theme that emerges from these passages is that the masculine and feminine are fundamental existential principles whose union is a necessary precondition for any continuity, generation, and birth. The genitals are said to generate tremendous mutual attraction. The way in which they are formed, and their back-to-back state at this stage, awaken a desire to separate in order to conjoin once more and complete the figure of *Adam*. The shifting relational states between the Male and the Female—separation, attraction, coupling—are expressed in the wide range of symbolic language used to describe the female genitalia. On one end of this spectrum, we find terminology derived from the ominous and archaic "Land of Edom," the "place of redness [*adom*]."[52] On the other end of the spectrum, we find the female sexual organs described as the "Holy of Holies," the locus of sublime desire and sanctity into which the phallus as high priest enters on the most sacred day of the year.

In general, reading the Idra's mythology of masculinity and femininity raises fascinating questions regarding gender. If one views the matter through the lens of gender theory, there is much to explore and analyze in these accounts of the origins of the divine masculine and feminine, and the essential difference and lack of equality between them. However, we need to be careful when selecting methodological and theoretical tools to help us understand the Idra's myth. In my own view, sociological methods may sometimes lead to overly reductionist interpretations of these myths.[53] I have found, however, the study of mythology and dream interpretation to be of tremendous value when attempting to read these accounts accurately and fully and striving to appreciate just how daring they are. In order to make sense of the accounts of the male sexual organ as a cosmic channel surging with Compassion, and the female genitalia as a burning red cavern, it helps to be open and sensitized to myths of origination and creation. These accounts reflect an attempt to return to the most fundamental and primal images that convey the elemental possibility of life. At this stage in the unfolding of the Divine, as it flows into corporeal forms, the genitals represent the most archaic mode in which these bodily forms encounter one another.

It is *'Attiqa Qaddisha* who actually initiates the separation between the male and female divine bodies. After this, the Male and the Female are able to attain union. The intoxicatingly fragrant connection between the two figures is powerful; indeed, it is through this encounter that the greatest *tiqqun* of all existence takes place:[54]

> The Ancient of Ancients, concealed of all, separated one from the other, and united them to be sweetened as one.
>
> When He separated them, He cast *dormita*, a deep slumber, upon *Ze'eir Anpin* and separated the Female from His back, arraying all Her adornments and concealing Her for His day, to bring Her to the Male. As is written: *YHVH Elohim cast a deep slumber on the Adam, and he slept* (Genesis 2:21). [. . .]
>
> *And He took one of his sides* (Genesis 2:21). What is meant by *one*? This is the Female. She ascended and was adorned. [. . .]
>
> As Sabbath was about to enter, He was creating spirits, demons, and whirlwinds, and before He completed them, *Matronita* came in Her adornments and sat before Him. When She did so, He left those creatures and they were not completed. Since *Matronita* was sitting with the King, and they joined face-to-face, who would dare to come between them? Who would approach them? [. . .]
>
> When they united, they were sweetened by one another—a day on which all are sweetened. Consequently, judgments were sweetened by one another, and those above and those below were harmoniously arranged. (Zohar 3:142b–143a; trans. Matt 8:438–440)

But the coupling that is meant to inaugurate cosmic harmony is not successful. A potent and destructive force of Judgment (*Din*), opposing the harmonious union, penetrates into the story in the figure of the primordial and seductive Serpent. The Idra describes the Serpent's relationship with the Female, the latter being connected both to the Male and the potent force of Judgment. The conclusion of the Idra details the various attempts at enabling a balanced and sweet coupling between the Male and the Female, presented as a midrash on the opening chapters of Genesis: the Adam and Eve narrative, the birth of Cain and Abel, Cain's murder of Abel, and the coupling from which Seth is born. Thus, the final portion of the Idra Rabba presents a dense myth dealing with questions of physicality, sexuality, femininity, the origins of evil in the world, motherhood, and the enigmatic connection between women and the powers of evil.

The description of God in human form, as a male and female coupling, impresses an insight upon the consciousness of the reader that carries profound implications. The two heads of God, the undivided and the dual aspects, do not fully encompass or exhaust the divine existence. Something else is required. God needs a body that will reflect divine life and being in a fuller and more variegated fashion. Indeed, even embodiment in a single body, androgynous though it may be, is not sufficient. The divine Male and Female must undergo individuation and develop into separate entities, distinct and complementary. Put differently, the splitting of the image of *Ze'eir Anpin*'s body into distinct male and female bodies reflects the insight that the unity created in the relationship between two—the connection of one to the Other—is the state in which even greater harmony might be attained. In the Zohar, the coupling of the Male and the Female is described as *bissum*—a "sweetening" or "aromatizing" or "filling with fragrance." Through *bissum*, the Female retains her aspects of Judgment, but these destructive forces are now perfused with desire, blessing, and fecundity.

This theology carries fascinating anthropological and psychological implications. Here, true oneness is to be sought not in solitude, but in togetherness, in the encounter with another human being. Eros, attraction, connection, completion, desire, joy in another person—who is always other but who also completes us after being separated from us in the primordial past—this is human wholeness. This is a human vessel worthy of being filled with the divine spirit and life-force.

In the passages of the Idra that treat the generation of the male and female bodies within the Godhead, the Female is depicted in a highly schematic fashion: only her head, hair, and sexually arousing parts are discussed, and in particular, her genitals.[55] This raises the question: why does the Idra Rabba lack a detailed description of the female torso?

First of all, it should be noted that the Idra does not provide a full and detailed description of the whole masculine body either. The account here has none of the beauty and splendor of the Song of Songs, which scans the body of the male lover from his locks to his feet. It also seems that the lack of detail here is not anchored in concerns about modesty, for it is the genitals—of both the Male and the Female—that are described completely unapologetically and in extensive detail. In my opinion, the focus on the Female's genitals is motivated by the Idra's core passion: the connection and alignment between the differing entities. The opening sections of the Idra are primarily concerned with the alignment of the relational gaze between the undivided and the dual aspects of the Divine; while this latter portion of the work is focused on the relationship generated by the coupling of the Male and Female face to face. Thus, the emphasis in the early portion of the Idra is on facial features and on the hair, which is understood to be the most basic channel of communication between the faces. Once the initial body is generated, however, the descriptions shift to the genitals, the organs that enable the Male and the Female to achieve a body-to-body connection through coitus with one another.

Another fundamental issue that arises from reading these passages touches upon the nature of *Ze'eir Anpin* in the stages following the formation of the Adamic figure; that is, the Male and Female bodies with their respective *tiqqunim*. Indeed, we shall see that once the Male and Female are separated, the Idra makes virtually no references to the term *Ze'eir Anpin* but refers instead to "Adam" or "Male and Female" (*Dekhar ve-Nuqba*). This could be read as a developmental depiction of the Divine, in which *Ze'eir Anpin* transforms into the divine figure of the androgynous *Adam* and then into the two separate bodies.

However, it seems that even after the formation of the Male and the Female bodies, *Ze'eir Anpin* remains present. As it approaches its end, the Idra Rabba returns to an account of the relationship between *Ze'eir Anpin* and

ʿAttiqa Qaddisha, despite the fact that the Divine has already manifested itself in the Adamic figure.[56] It thus seems that the Idra is describing a process in which each successive stage of development does not eliminate that which precedes it. Indeed, these passages provide a good example of the dangers of rigid and linear thinking when reading this work. The archetypal divine figures continue to exist side by side simultaneously. Despite the distinction between *Zeʿeir Anpin* and the figure of *Adam*, they continue to inhere in one another in a mysterious way that evades neat definition.

The Chain of Divine Faces

In a fascinating passage, appearing in the main body of the Zohar but exhibiting terminology characteristic of the Idra, there appears an image that enigmatically and schematically represents a reality in which the various aspects of the Divine are interconnected, and also bound to the human realm. According to this passage, the dew of life trickling from *ʿAttiqa* into the lower dimensions is not an event that happened at some point in the primordial past; rather, this process is ever-present, continuously sustaining all existence throughout time:

> Every single day, dew trickles from the Holy Ancient One to the Short-Tempered One, and the whole Orchard of Holy Apples is blessed. Some of that dew is drawn to those below, and holy angels are nourished by it. [. . .] Of that food, Israel ate in the wilderness. (Zohar 2:61b; trans. Matt 4:331, emended)

In this passage, the literary style conveys its content. This is not a turbulent or dramatic event, rather, the dew drips continuously, gradually, accumulating bit by bit. This dew, this light, this life-force seeps through the filters of undivided *ʿAttiqa*, into the head of *Zeʿeir Anpin*, the dual aspect of the Divine. From *Zeʿeir Anpin*, it drips into the Orchard of Holy Apples—a symbol of the female body of the Divine. From there, life trickles into the human realm, manifesting as manna, the miraculous sustenance that appears in the desert, luminous and subtle.[57]

All aspects of reality, all faces of God, are thus interconnected by the primordial divine emanation that comes to all of them in a unified chain of being. Here, the conception of God as the Source of all being is no mere theoretical abstraction, divorced from the world; rather, something of the Divine passes through all layers of the cosmos; it is ever-present, and can be experienced in human life. The very structure of reality enables the presence of the most sublime and mysterious to be present throughout all its dimensions and, in particular, in human beings.[58]

3

The Gaze

One theme that greatly preoccupies the Idra Rabba is the relationship between two of the *partsufim*: *Arikh Anpin* and *Ze'eir Anpin*. Many of the scriptural interpretations in this work are dedicated to comparing these two aspects of the Divine: patience versus impatience; the undifferentiated versus the dual; boundless mercy versus stern judgment; whiteness versus the multicolored; a white eye versus eyes shot with red; an open mouth from which the breath of forgiveness perpetually issues versus a red mouth pronouncing authoritative decrees; a nose from which the spirit of the life-force of all life blows versus one that smolders with fire and smoke. Each of these images becomes a specific point of comparison between the two figures.

These comparisons develop our understanding of both the possible solutions to *Ze'eir Anpin*'s distress and ways to enact these solutions; they also address our basic interest in the relationship between the various aspects of the Divine. In abstract theoretical terms, one might say that the Idra Rabba uses these two *partsufim* to explore the characteristics of the undifferentiated Divine—calm, stable, and benevolent—in contrast with the binary, discerning, and (re)active God. Discussion of these distinct depictions of the Divine brings into sharper relief the distress, imbalance, and vacillation that inhere structurally within the dualistic consciousness of *Ze'eir Anpin* as this figure manifests within the human realm.

Establishing a healing relationship between these two *partsufim* reconfigures and heals the cosmos. This restorative relationship between *'Attiqa* and *Ze'eir Anpin* is expressed primarily in the correct alignment between their faces, so that *Ze'eir Anpin*'s gaze is brought to meet that of *'Attiqa*. Whenever *Ze'eir Anpin* reacts to the evil and sinful state of human affairs with a constricted face and wrinkled brow, exhaling angrily from his nose, his eyes turning red, and pronouncing harsh decrees from his mouth—he may, by turning his face toward the luminous countenance of *Arikh Anpin*, be healed and calmed. This is described with breathtaking beauty in the Idra Zuṭa:

> What is meant by *Erekh Appin*? Healing Countenance. For there is no healing in the world except when they gaze face-to-face. (Zohar 3:292b; trans. Matt 9:811)

Here, the term *erekh* (length) is interpreted to mean *arukhah* (healing), as in the biblical verse, *Behold, I will bring her healing* (*arukhah*) *and cure* (Jeremiah 33:6). This face-to-face gaze heals both *Ze'eir Anpin* and the cosmos.

When *Ze'eir Anpin*'s gaze is directed toward *Arikh Anpin*, two events occur simultaneously in different dimensions of being: the face of *Ze'eir Anpin* grows wider and larger, and all that exists within the domain of *Ze'eir Anpin* falls into place—balance is restored and all is reconfigured and healed:

> When *Ze'eir Anpin* gazes at this one, all below is restored and His face expands and lengthens (*mitpasheṭin va-arikhin*) at that time—but not constantly like the Ancient One. (Zohar 3:128b; trans. Matt 8:330, emended)

The lengthening of *Ze'eir Anpin*'s face thus refers to its transformation into a Long-Faced or Patient One (*Erekh Appayim*). It expresses the patience and calm that flow from within *Ze'eir Anpin* as a consequence of that gaze. What transpires in this state that widens, expands, and heals all things? What happens as *Ze'eir Anpin* beholds *Arikh Anpin*, and is beheld by him? What is this gaze, and what are the authors of the Idra trying to communicate to their readers? These questions occupy a central place in the present book; indeed, they inspired me to write it.

Psychoanalytic thought has devoted much attention to the face in general, and the gaze in particular. Donald Winnicott, Wilfred Bion, and Heinz Kohut studied the role of the face and gaze in mother-baby relationships (or relationships between any nurturing caregiver and a child) in an attempt to understand what transpires in the mutual gaze between infant and mother. All three came to the conclusion that the mother's face contains and creates order in the emotional world of the infant. Whether constructive or destructive, the infant's relationship with the mother, predicated upon this gaze, forms the ground out of which grow the child's conception of self (a sense of distinctness and separation) and of the world around her or him. Winnicott noted the way in which contemplation of the mother's face shapes the infant as a subject. Through this gaze, the infant learns to identify the emotional world that alters and shapes facial expressions, and is reflected back in the mother's countenance.

Michael Eigen, a prominent psychoanalyst based in New York, has studied a range of aspects of the face-to-face gaze. He notes that "[t]he centrality of the human face as symbolic of personality permeates the fabric of human experience. It is often observed that a full face-to-face sexual encounter is unique to human beings, an event profoundly linked with an earlier structural correlate—the rapt stare of the human infant at the mother's face during feeding."[1] He points out that staring into the face of another encompasses both the experience of distinctness between subject and object and the experience of identification and coalescence of the two. The elements of separation and union that coexist in such a gaze enable each other, and together constitute a basic structure of human subjectivity.[2]

We find further parallels to these insights when we read the Idra Rabba's accounts of the role of the face and gaze in the relationships between *Ze'eir Anpin* and *'Attiqa* and between the divine Male and Female. Indeed, they enable us to form a deeper understanding of the Idra's choice to adopt a discourse of divine faces, rather than one of abstract qualities.

'Attiqa's Gaze

'Attiqa's gaze is a world unto itself. By means of this gaze, *Arikh Anpin* communicates a stable and constant flow of whiteness, light that is life and love. The facial expression of *Arikh Anpin* is unchanging: "This eye, the eye of watchfulness, is constantly open, constantly smiling, constantly joyous."[3] Despite

the Idra's philosophically colored unwillingness to ascribe agency and intent to *'Attiqa*, the most sublime aspect of the Divine, this *partsuf* does express will (*ratson*) and unconditional love. Light streams from his gaze, ever-open and ever-attentive, and his facial expression conveys the generous flow of divine bounty. If this flow does not reach us or *Ze'eir Anpin*, this is not because the facial expression is subject to change but because it is obscured from us. *'Attiqa*'s gaze is attentive and providential, but not in a judgmental or scrutinizing sense, for his mode of vision is not distinct or dualistic; indeed, it transcends the dichotomy between good and evil. *Arikh Anpin*'s field of vision is described as broad and peripheral, an unfocused gaze; neither invasive nor trained individually on the object of contemplation. Despite this, it is far from indifferent. It accepts, invigorates, and sustains all that falls within it.[4] As we shall explore in greater depth later, the idraic language of the Zohar compares the experience of being held in *'Attiqa*'s gaze to the experience of being bathed in milk flowing from the breasts of the divine Mother. *'Attiqa*'s gaze, in this sense, does not belong to the realm of human drama. The consciousness that flows out of it is prior to all divine and human designs.[5]

We can find similarities between *'Attiqa*'s gaze and the Mother archetype as described by Jung, and particularly as formulated by his disciple Erich Neumann in his profound and exhaustive study of the myth of the Great Mother across cultures. According to Neumann, the Great Mother, experienced as a life-giving and nourishing presence, represents an early phase in the development of human consciousness. In this phase of its development, individual consciousness is immersed in an even more primal consciousness and permeated by it. Here, masculinity and femininity still exist in a unified and indistinct manner; impulses that enable and support creation and order exist alongside those that oppose and negate them, as well as the primordial seeds of good and evil.[6] This indistinct mode of being is represented by the *uroboros*, a symbol depicting a mythical serpent with its tail in its mouth. *'Attiqa*'s gaze, in an archaic fashion, contains some of these qualities of the mother's face—or perhaps the mother's breasts, as described later—the face that provides the ever-flowing wellspring of life for the newborn.[7]

Another distinction that can shed light on *'Attiqa*'s facial expression may be found in Tibetan Buddhism. This culture is intensely focused on exploring the structure, processes, abilities, and limitations of human consciousness, alongside the broad development of techniques that might enable human beings to contemplate the dynamics of their own minds. In this context, we find a distinction between two states of consciousness, called *great space* and *limited space*. Great space represents an expansive and open consciousness, corresponding closely with the Idra Rabba's account of *Arikh Anpin*. In contrast, limited space refers to a crowded, particularly tense, and overly focused state of consciousness, corresponding with the Idra's descriptions of *Ze'eir Anpin*.[8]

The gaze is perhaps the most distinctive expression of a face-to-face relationship. In the Zohar, this phrase "face-to-face" most often occurs when describing the erotic coupling of the Male and Female. Connection via the face should therefore be understood as a cognate mode of coupling, occurring in a primordial state in which the Divine is represented as two bodiless heads. Despite this, the authors of the Idra Rabba made a deliberate and conscious decision not to describe these relations in sexual terms. This approach becomes all the more apparent when one considers that in earlier stages of the development of Idra literature, which may be reconstructed using a range of zoharic and extra-zoharic texts, *Ze'eir Anpin* appears to have been a female figure. The relationship between the two *partsufim* was one of union between the male *Arikh Anpin* and the smaller female face, the *Shekhinah*.[9] The Idra's choice, as reflected in the complete text in its present form, to present both of the initial divine faces as masculine in gender, rather than as the divine Male and Female, creates a representation of a very specific emotion: male-female eros is replaced with the feeling existing between an older man and a youth. Here, the gaze represents emotional sustenance and connection rather than sexual union.[10] Whereas coupling entails intermingling, this connection between the faces is not mutual, much less egalitarian: here, one side is filled with light and life by the other's gaze, like a child suckling from its mother's breast while staring into her face.

The Face's Healing

The central task of the Idra's participants may be described as the attempt to shift the head of *Ze'eir Anpin*, so that he might direct his gaze toward *Arikh Anpin*'s face. *Ze'eir Anpin* scrutinizes and supervises the world. All deeds and intentions, good and evil, are examined by him, and his facial expressions are shaped in response to the events in the lower worlds. When overly focused on worldly affairs, the divine face becomes constricted, and harsh Judgment (*Din*) begins to overcome the face's Mercy (*raḥamim*). The process of healing for this state of excessive divine attention upon the world begins when *Ze'eir Anpin*'s face releases and relaxes its all-penetrating scrutiny. Complete healing occurs only when *Ze'eir Anpin* turns to face the Source of all, which is also the Source of the binary and structured Divine, namely, *Ze'eir Anpin* himself. While contemplating *'Attiqa*'s face, *Ze'eir Anpin* can allow his gaze to be less tightly focused. His gaze broadens, his expression is open, ready to be washed in the flowing and gushing whiteness from *'Attiqa*'s eye, to be revivified by the breath of pure forgiveness that issues from his mouth, by the life-breath of his nostrils, by the unconditional love emanating from his forehead. In a certain sense, *Ze'eir Anpin* returns to his former self, an open and receptive face.

In this vein, we find an account of *Ze'eir Anpin*'s eyes when his eyelids are lifted so that his eyes may meet the eye of *'Attiqa*. *Ze'eir Anpin*'s eyes, full of anger, are cleansed of redness as they bathe in the white of *'Attiqa*'s eye, imagined here as milk flowing from a mother's breasts:

> Eyes of the head are different from other eyes. [. . .] In the cover of the eyes flash fourteen million, adhering to the eyelids, which are the cover, and the providential eye of the Ancient One is above them.
>
> When that cover lifts, He appears as one who awakens from sleep. His eyes open and see the open eye, and are bathed in one whiteness of the good eye, as is written: *bathing in milk* (Song of Songs 5:12). What is meant by *in milk*? In the white of the primordial eye [the eye of *'Attiqa*]. During that time compassionate providence prevails. Therefore David prays: *Awake! Why do you sleep, O YHVH? Rouse yourself!* (Psalms 44:24)—so that He may open His eyes, to be bathed in this whiteness. (Zohar 3:136b; trans. Matt 8:392, emended)

In another Idra-like passage of the Zohar that describes the divine King's face, bathing in the white of *'Attiqa*'s eye is described explicitly in terms of washing in motherly breastmilk:[11]

> Eyes of the King—supervising all [. . .] Eyebrows [. . .] —a place drawing from that river, to bathe in the whiteness of the Ancient One, from the milk flowing from Mother. For when *Gevurah* extends and

> eyes flash in red, the Holy Ancient One shines its whiteness and kindles Mother, who is filled with milk and suckles all, and all the eyes bathe in that mother's milk, flowing forth constantly, as is written: *Bathing in milk* (Song of Songs 5:12)—in Mother's milk, flowing constantly, ceaselessly. (Zohar 2:122b; trans. Matt 5:152)

One may well ask why it is the Companions who are responsible for shifting *Ze'eir Anpin*'s head, for restoring its flexibility. Why is it not natural for the youthful head, the Deity as warrior king, to contemplate the face of *Arikh Anpin*? Part of the answer, anchored in zoharic theology, is that the position of the head is a result of human error and transgression. Human beings cause *Ze'eir Anpin* to fix his gaze upon the world, and therefore to identify and play out his role as cosmic Judge.

An alternative answer to these questions may emerge from the work of Erich Neumann. In his book *The Origins and History of Consciousness*, Neumann presents his understanding of the emergence of consciousness, based on his study of a range of mythologies and his many years working as a therapist. Neumann argues that before a distinct "I"—the Ego—develops, an infant's consciousness exists in a state of identification undifferentiated from the fundamental and original nature of all things, the source of all things, which he calls the Self. This is an expression of a deep, universal "I."

From the moment that the Ego becomes cognizant of its distinctness from the Self, it begins an ongoing process of differentiation and separation from it. The Ego's process of individuation and separation from the Self continues until the middle years of a person's life. In the second half of life, a change takes place: the separate and autonomous existence of the Ego begins to fracture, and the possibility of—and interest in—returning once more to the Self is awakened. This renewed and reoriented focus is enabled by the healing and strengthening of the axis that initially joined the Ego to the Self, an axis that was damaged and distorted in the process of the Ego's development and aspiration to distance itself from its source. In the process of healing this axis of communication and connectedness, the Ego expands. However, this growth is no longer motivated by the Ego's desire for autonomous power in its own right, but by the process of drawing near and connecting to the Self. Now an entirely new living connection becomes possible between the Ego and the ocean of life, the depth and creativity that exists within the Self. Total overlap between the Ego and the Self occurs only in death, as the Ego is completely swallowed up in its source.[12]

Neumann's fascinating conception finds an echo in the Idra, at the base of which lies the project of turning the attention of the young, small, differentiated face of *Ze'eir Anpin* away from the human world, and redirecting it to its source in *Arikh Anpin*. Initially, the Idra describes how *Ze'eir Anpin*, the God-King (Ego), emerges from *Arikh Anpin*—the undifferentiated Divine—and becomes increasingly distinct as King of the cosmos and the God of Israel. He forges his own path, weaving a myth all his own, while at the same time forgetting his source and wandering far from it. But something goes wrong. Failing to maintain a connection with the undifferentiated Divine, the developmental process produces a surplus of harsh Judgment (*Din*), which becomes visible in *Ze'eir Anpin*'s face and subsequently in the human realm. Neumann describes two possible situations of distortion or illness in the connection between the Ego and the Self: in one situation, the Self floods and overwhelms the Ego entirely, the latter losing all sense of its distinctness; in the other, the Ego becomes inflated, identifying itself wrongly as a manifestation of the All, replacing the Self. The latter distortion is closely reflected in the Idra: *Ze'eir Anpin* fills up with himself, with his role, with his cosmic persona as King, while losing His connection with the primordial Ancient One. Drawing further away from *'Attiqa* and moving from the state of undifferentiated unity of the source to a dualistic consciousness that perceives the multiplicity of reality—in all its tensions, distinctions, and endless variety— is completely natural in and of itself. As we have seen, this is simply the trajectory of being as it emerges. The problem arises when the nourishing relationship with the source is lost. This relationship, like suckling, is subtle and delicate, and must be maintained even as distinct being becomes manifold.

One can translate the failure of the Divine, here described in mythical terms, into an account of the problematic quality of the Jewish religion itself. This religion devoted great energy to developing its dualistic, legal, systematic, and ethical aspects; but in the process, those elements that are anchored in a basic experience of the Divine as a primordial and undifferentiated being were weakened.

Returning to the question of why the connection between *Ze'eir Anpin* and *Arikh Anpin* is not simply natural, we might, in light of Neumann's conception, suggest that a complex and balanced relationship between the various aspects of religion was never properly established—these aspects being a precondition for its vitality. This situation arose because *Ze'eir Anpin*'s energy and focus were directed toward his own coming-into-being, his differentiation from the Source, and the vitality of his divine Ego and its maturation.

The Idra Rabba, the Great Assembly, is convened precisely to address the disconnection between *Ze'eir Anpin* and *Arikh Anpin*, with Rabbi Shim'on bar Yoḥai declaring, *Time to act for YHVH!* (Psalms 119:126) The human intervention that is required is to manifest the possibility of turning *Ze'eir Anpin*'s gaze back toward its Source, of returning to the Divine as an infinite ocean of love and oneness. It must be emphasized that the Idra does not contain any of the characteristically Gnostic hostility toward the God of the world, *Ze'eir Anpin*, as an ignorant and aggressive demiurge. According to the Idra's conception, YHVH is our God, and we are created in His image.[13]

In addition, the Idra Rabba emphasizes that *Ze'eir Anpin*'s contemplation of *Arikh Anpin* occurs only occasionally: "When the need arises, [*Ze'eir Anpin*'s] face expands and lengthens, for He gazes upon the face of the Ancient of Ancients, and He has compassion on the world."[14] The participants in the gathering are thus not aiming to bring about *Ze'eir Anpin*'s constant and continuous gaze upon *'Attiqa*. In fact, such a situation would signify nothing less than a surrender of the God of religion, law, and justice—and in some sense, a rejection of the manifold reality in which we live. In the body of the Zohar too, the only portrayal of a continuous and constant state of face-to-face gazing is in the relationship between the Father (*Abba*) and Mother (*Imma*), representing the *sefirot* of Wisdom (*Ḥokhmah*) and Understanding (*Binah*). The constant gaze between these two entities, existing as they do in a state of perpetual coupling, enables and ensures the continuation of existence. However, the relationship among the divine potencies below these two higher *sefirot* is characterized by dynamism and change. This applies to the relationship between Compassion (*Ḥesed*) and Judgment (*Din*) and, in particular, between Beauty (*Tif'eret*) and Sovereignty (*Malkhut*). These relationships have a structure of dual consciousness; they are in a constant state of motion and "happening." As we have seen, this applies to *Ze'eir Anpin* as well, when his face is turned toward the world.

In any event, the world cannot exist solely on a foundation of Compassion. Thus, the gaze that expands *Ze'eir Anpin*, conferring upon him the traits of patience and forbearance, must occur only when necessary. From this point of view, the Idra Rabba presents a mysticism that does not flee from the world, or renounce it in favor of some other reality. Unlike various strands of Neoplatonism or Gnosticism, the Idra does not reject this world with all its problems. The Idra explicitly affirms the multiplicity and diversity of reality; the occasional redirecting of the gaze toward the undifferentiated Divine seeks to bring about a harmonious balance in this reality.

Descriptions of the Gaze

The face, as we recognize it from our own experience, is much more complex than the sum of its parts, their configuration and relationship to one another. The face is dynamic. Countless gestures and miniscule motions are constantly occurring, informing the observer of the internal life of the individual. In this sense, the gaze is a considerably more complex form of communication than speech.

In the Idras we encounter a complex and extended description of *Ze'eir Anpin* turning his face toward the face of *Arikh Anpin* and contemplating it. The Idra Rabba employs a wide array of images in its attempt to convey something of this gaze.[15] Stage by stage, this work describes how the face of *Ze'eir Anpin* expands from its state of constriction, filling with the love that flows to it from all parts of *Arikh Anpin*'s face. *Ze'eir Anpin*'s forehead turns to face the forehead of *Arikh Anpin*, which flows with unconditional love, and it sheds its light upon *Ze'eir Anpin*, causing his redness and fury to abate. *Ze'eir Anpin*'s eyes look directly into the calm and stable gaze of *Arikh Anpin*'s eyes, which remain always open, smiling, and joyful. *Ze'eir Anpin* receives a loving gaze from those eyes, entirely unveiled—for *'Attiqa* has no eyelids. *'Attiqa*'s gaze has no harmful intent, so there is no need for *Ze'eir Anpin* to be on his guard. From this gaze, there issues a river of the white light of life that flows into the eyes of *Ze'eir Anpin*, washing them with milk, and cleansing them of their redness. *Ze'eir Anpin*'s nose, which exhales the winds of anger, receives a sweet gust of the very life-force of life itself from *Arikh*

Anpin's nose, a comforting and healing breeze. *Ze'eir Anpin*'s face fills with the joy of life from the joyous light that shines from the apples of *'Attiqa*'s cheeks. *Ze'eir Anpin* is granted infinite forgiveness from the open mouth of the Holy Ancient One.

A central account of the unfolding of this gaze, and of the process by which *Ze'eir Anpin* is filled up with *'Attiqa*'s light, appears in Rabbi Abba's description of *Ze'eir Anpin*'s beard. This interpretation evokes *Ze'eir Anpin* as a bearded man, King, and warrior. This state is potent, but unsweetened by a connection with *Arikh Anpin*:

> Rabbi Abba rose. He opened, saying, "When the array of this beard is arranged in royal enhancements—like a mighty hero, handsome to behold, noble and dominant, as is written: *Great is our Lord and mighty in power* (Psalms 147:5)—and when He is assuaged by the enhancements of the precious holy beard, gazing upon Him, then He is called, by virtue of His radiance, *A compassionate* [. . .] *God* (Exodus 34:6). [. . .] When He shines with the radiance of the Ancient of Days, He is called *abounding in kindness* (*ibid.*). And when they gaze upon one another, it is called by another enhancement: *and truth* (*ibid.*), for faces shine." (Zohar 3:140b; trans. Matt 8:420, emended)

Bissum (the process of "sweetening," "aromatizing," or "filling with fragrance") begins when *'Attiqa* sets his sight upon *Ze'eir Anpin*, and continues with the illumination of *Ze'eir Anpin*'s beard by that of *'Attiqa*. The stages of this process parallel the Attributes of Mercy recounted in Exodus 34:6–7: *a God compassionate and gracious, slow to anger, abounding in kindness and truth*. Ultimately, *Ze'eir Anpin*'s face is entirely illuminated with the word *emet* (truth).

Rabbi Abba's interpretation reflects an acutely mythical understanding of the events that transpire within the divine *pleroma* (Godhead) when Moses turns to God, who is furious with Israel because of their transgressions, and recites the Attributes of Mercy. It is important to remember that *Ze'eir Anpin* represents the dual consciousness of God, distinguishing between justice and injustice. Thus, it is only natural that *Ze'eir Anpin* should be filled with the rage of harsh Judgment as he looks down upon the Israelites, dancing around the Golden Calf only moments earlier. But then *Ze'eir Anpin* lets his gaze upon the world slacken for a moment, and allows that gaze to be lifted toward *'Attiqa*.

Each of the Attributes of Mercy that Moses recites further stimulates and increases the flow of Compassion from *'Attiqa* to *Ze'eir Anpin*. Finally, *Ze'eir Anpin* turns fully toward *Arikh Anpin*, coming face to face with him—or, as the Idra describes it, beard to beard—and being illuminated. The word *emet* in the verse does not represent a divine attribute in this interpretation, but rather describes the state of complete union between the divine gazes.

As we have already seen, the powerful impact of the Idra Rabba lies largely in the interweaving of physical and highly anthropomorphic descriptions of the Divine with abstract and light-infused Neoplatonic language regarding the emergence of the cosmos and the relationship between the One, Source of all being, and the Intellect (*nous*), the latter being the secondary primordial entity that emanates from the One. Indeed, in Plotinus' works we find accounts of the relationship between the Intellect and the One that are highly reminiscent of the dynamic between the divine gazes of *Ze'eir Anpin* and *Arikh Anpin* in the Idra. Thus, Plotinus describes the Intellect as "seeing" the One and knowing it. This knowledge arouses thought, love, and the will to become like the One and draw near to it. By its very nature, the One does not *do* anything other than overflow; but in being seen by the Intellect, it is known without knowing, becoming a source of motion.[16] These formulations reflect a discernible endeavor to portray the One as non-active, and an effort to transfer all activity to the Intellect, which is already a distinct consciousness.

There is no doubt that the Idra Rabba, even though diverging considerably, mythologizes the conceptual world of Neoplatonism by ascribing personal, attentive, and providential qualities to *Arikh Anpin*, and attributes of dynamism and changeability to *Ze'eir Anpin*. These ideas are interwoven with the fundamental human experience of gazing, and enriched by the Idra's profound readings of scriptural verses, speaking as they do of the divine countenance and the human desire to receive its merciful gaze. Philosophical concepts, striking imagery, and poetic language are woven together here, creating one of the Idra's defining qualities.

The Human Gaze

Alongside its mythical and metaphysical study of the mutual gaze between the divine faces, the Idra also discusses ways in which human beings may properly align their own minds, cultivating a refined mode of consciousness in order to connect with the primordial and healing face of God. From the very beginning of the Idra, *Ze'eir Anpin*'s desire to turn toward *'Attiqa* is also applied to the perfected human being—the zoharic saint or *tsaddiq*. This seeker's consciousness, which reflects that of *Ze'eir Anpin*, brings about the aspiration to connect with the divine life-force as it flows through the enhancements (*tiqqunim*) of *'Attiqa Qaddisha*:

> The desire and joy of the righteous, who are in *Ze'eir Anpin*, is to see and cleave to the arrayal of the Ancient One, concealed of all. (Zohar 3:129a; trans. Matt 8:334, emended)

Gazing at *'Attiqa*'s face, washing in the brilliant whiteness of Compassion streaming from his entire face and beard, *Ze'eir Anpin* expands and relaxes. According to Rabbi Shim'on, such an experience also awaits the righteous in this world, with the help of "the spirit of wisdom":[17]

> Their whiteness is like the white of the eyes when they are bathed in the white of the supernal eye. This the righteous are destined to see in the spirit of wisdom, as it is said: *For eye-to-eye they will see.* (Isaiah 52:8) (Zohar 3:137a; trans. Matt 8:394–395, emended)

The idea of consciousness as a reflection, on a human scale, of *Ze'eir Anpin*'s consciousness clarifies that the call to healing put forth by the Idra relates not only to the divine world and its sacred faces (*partsufim*) but also to the religious and spiritual experience of human beings. The connection established by *Ze'eir Anpin*'s contemplation of *Arikh Anpin*'s face is not merely an inner-divine event but a viable practice for healing and calming the dual and tempestuous human consciousness by connecting to the face of undifferentiated but ever-compassionate Divinity. The mystic's profound longing to attain *'Attiqa*'s gaze thus testifies to a recognition of the need to heal constricted and dualistic states of human consciousness through relaxation, expansion, and reconnecting the mind to the deepest reaches of its Source.

4

Reflections on *Ze'eir Anpin*

We have already become acquainted with the primordial God, ancient, grandfatherly, and white; with the face of the young warrior with his black locks; and with *Adam*, the Male and Female divine body. Against the background of the intensive treatment devoted to these figures, it is perhaps surprising that an account of God as a settled and balanced personality—a king, judge, loving father or husband, so familiar in depictions of the Divine in rabbinic literature—is almost entirely absent from the Idra. In the body of the Zohar, in contrast, this familiar characterization of God is clearly and prominently present in depictions of the *sefirah* of Beauty (*Tif'eret*). This *sefirah*, which represents the masculine God YHVH, contains the qualities of resplendence, equilibrium, and calm. In Jungian terms, one might say that the masculine archetype in the Idra Rabba possesses no figure who might occupy a middle position between the wise old man (*senex*) and the young warrior (*puer*).[1] This fatherly figure is simply absent from the Idra's conception of the Divine.[2]

One might suppose that such aspects of the Divine would be incorporated into the figure of *Ze'eir Anpin*, the God of Israel. But this is not the case. Accounts of *Ze'eir Anpin* emphasize the surplus of Judgment (*Din*) in this figure, and the polarity and the split between it and the merciful and compassionate *'Attiqa*. The character of *Ze'eir Anpin* raises fundamental questions about the figure of the Divine in the Idra, questions that I explore further in the present chapter.

Ze'eir Anpin, the God of Judgment

A cumulative reading of the passages of the Idra describing *Ze'eir Anpin* reveals a portrait of a divine figure brimming with Judgment (*Din*). This figure's predisposition and fundamental nature appear to be red Judgment. The Judgment meted out by *Ze'eir Anpin* is neither arbitrary nor capricious but a response to evil deeds on the part of humanity. Its purpose is to ensure the continued reign of order and justice in the world. Furthermore, Judgment is a necessary aspect within the warrior God's face, as he battles aspects of Judgment on three fronts. On the cosmic plane, he confronts the fragments of the primordial kings of Edom, while on the earthly plane he battles against human evil in general, while also taking up the cause of Israel as a nation against its oppressors. Nevertheless, there is no doubt that a greater emphasis is placed on the threatening aspects of Judgment than on the rich spectrum between the poles of white Compassion and red Judgment. *Ze'eir Anpin*'s reactions are generally not depicted as complex, measured, or varied. In the face of sin, evil, or injustice, the divine forehead immediately fills with the forces of Judgment, who are summarily dispatched into the world.

Excessive Judgment within *Ze'eir Anpin* is not a given. As he is the first representation of a discerning and dual consciousness within the Divine, we might have expected to meet the more attractive and fascinating aspects of this figure, the erotic aspects that form a bridge between oneness and dazzling multifariousness. Indeed, passages elsewhere in the Zohar describe the variegation, dynamism, *eros*, and mutability that accompany the movement from a stable and constant consciousness of oneness to a dualistic and binary consciousness.[3] But in the Idra Rabba, the reader's overall impression is that *Ze'eir Anpin* is manifestly dominated by Judgment, and that the presence of Compassion within this figure is enabled only by his connection with *'Attiqa*. For example, in the description of *Ze'eir Anpin*'s forehead, which symbolizes divine supervision and providence, it is emphasized that his forehead is composed entirely of Judgment except when it is illuminated by *'Attiqa*'s forehead, the supreme *Rava d'ravin*:[4]

> When this forehead is revealed, all Masters of Judgment are aroused, and the whole world is delivered to Judgment—except at the time

> when prayers of Israel ascend before the Ancient of Days, and He wishes to have compassion upon His children: He reveals the forehead of the Will of Wills (*Rava d'ravin*) and illumines that of *Ze'eir Anpin*, and Judgment is soothed. (Zohar 3:136a–b; trans. Matt 8:389, emended)

In *Ze'eir Anpin*'s forehead, no qualities of love or merciful providence are present alongside red Judgment. He is thus unable to assuage the force of his Judgment from within Himself. Only the illumination of *Arikh Anpin*'s resplendent white forehead can calm *Ze'eir Anpin*'s destructive fury.

Another factor that contributes to the strangeness of this judgmental figure is that *Ze'eir Anpin* is not described as, for example, *Arikh Anpin*'s beloved son but rather as a mere emanation from the latter's nature—a kind of garment, body, or even armor that *'Attiqa* generates to cloak his radiant essence. *Ze'eir Anpin* thus remains an external manifestation of *Arikh Anpin*, "the exterior one" in the Idra's terminology. What are we to make of the Idra's choice to present *Ze'eir Anpin* in such a fashion?

First of all, we must recall that as readers, we must be daring and read the passages as they appear, and accept that this frightening character is indeed how the Idra's authors experienced the presence of the Divine. The character of *Ze'eir Anpin* as depicted by their quills is not the product of a philosophical or theological symposium; it emerges from the depths of the conscious and unconscious minds of religious artists.

The choice of such a divine figure may also express the authors' stance on the nature of human beings and the world. Humanity is full of judgment, impatience, and anger, and in this it must reflect the Divinity in whose image it was created. Or perhaps the reverse is true. The wicked, judgmental, and unjust state of human beings engenders the image of an angry and punishing God-Father-Ruler as a divine persona that must govern and function within such a reality.

Another possibility for explaining the character of *Ze'eir Anpin* is grounded in theology, and relates to the process-oriented conception of the Divine in the Idra Rabba. The character of *Ze'eir Anpin*, brimming with Judgment, is described mainly in his primordial state, that is, only as a head. According to the "economy of Judgment" in the Idra, this is excessive Judgment, an unfitting and imbalanced state, but one that can become sweetened and equilibrated at a later stage as it expands out and develops into a male and female body. It is thus precisely the reactive, angry, and imbalanced character of *Ze'eir Anpin* that provides the mythical impetus to continue and develop or refine this divine figure into a further manifestation as Male and Female. One might say that the restlessness and discomfort caused by *Ze'eir Anpin*'s excessive Judgment is at the root of the divine motion toward a more balanced expression of Judgment and Compassion.

In yet another sense, from the point of view of the task presented to the Idra's participants, the judgmental character of *Ze'eir Anpin* constitutes the basis of their theurgic praxis. It may be that the work's very description of *Ze'eir Anpin* is part of the attempt to heal and restore balance to him. That is to say that the authors chose to present this figure in an extreme fashion, in the fullest expression of his Judgment, so that they could direct their healing theurgic activities toward that excessiveness, thus bringing the state of balance into sharper relief against the background of *Ze'eir Anpin*'s fierce and forceful Judgment. However, such an explanation has apologetic aspects, for it presupposes that this cannot be the *true* figure of God but merely a show put on by the authors for theurgical purposes.

A more reflective possibility is to understand the presentation of *Ze'eir Anpin* as a kind of critique or even parody of Jewish religion, a caricature of sorts. The authors of the Idra are expressing in mythical terms a critique of the exclusive focus of certain Jewish circles upon dualistic aspects of religion—Jewish law (*halakhah*), the forbidden and the permitted—without any connection to the undifferentiated Divine, and without any wider conception of the reality, language, and ethics that emerge from that mode of being. It is worth recalling that it is precisely the danger inherent in a limited conception of the Divine that causes the Great Assembly to be convened in the first place, and that underlies the great effort to renew the face of religion and to heal it.

Ze'eir Anpin and Gnosticism: Between Splitting and Healing

Aside from the problematic nature of the figure of *Ze'eir Anpin*, it is virtually impossible to overlook the Gnostic overtones of the descriptions of *Ze'eir Anpin* and *Arikh Anpin*. This is particularly true once we become acquainted with the polarity between the two divine *partsufim* that represent destructive Judgment and absolute Compassion, respectively.

Gnosticism is a general term for a number of religious movements that emerged during late antiquity in the Hellenistic world among pagans, Jews, and Christians. As a rule, Gnostic theology is characterized by a hard dualism, articulated in mythical accounts of the battle between good and evil. In these narratives, we encounter a splitting between the good deity, who is absolute goodness, and the evil deity, who is called the *demiurge*—the creator of the world. The good deity is transcendent, the source of souls, and external to the world created by the evil deity. In contrast, the demiurge and his denizens oppress souls and cause them to fall into a deep slumber, forgetting their origins in the good, higher deity. The various Gnostic schools offered their adherents a range of methods to avoid and evade the control of the demiurge and find refuge with the good and loving deity. It is possible that these conceptions were born of powerlessness in the face of the sheer wickedness of the world, from a religious and emotional viewpoint. The clear split between the good deity and the demiurge allows one to resolve the tension between the evil of the world and the existence of a good and forgiving God, who contains no trace of evil. Gnostic theology continued to exist even in the medieval period, and Gnostic intuitions and impulses, together with the mythical and metaphysical struggle between good and evil, persist in contemporary culture—in, for example, New Age movements and fantasy literature and film.[5]

The many points of correspondence between Gnostic elements and kabbalistic sources have been noted by Gershom Scholem. He describes the emergence of Kabbalah in the medieval period as a bursting forth of mythic and Gnostic elements in the heart of rabbinic Judaism. In fact, Scholem views Kabbalah as "Jewish Gnosticism," and even attempts to identify the historical channels that enabled contact between Christian Gnostic groups and the first circles of Kabbalists.[6] Scholars of the Kabbalah have critiqued Scholem's views on this matter over the past few decades. For example, Moshe Idel attempts to demonstrate the existence of ancient Jewish streams of Gnosticism, claiming that it is these that made their way into medieval kabbalistic sources.[7] Whatever the case may be, it is impossible to ignore the powerful scent of Gnosticism that rises from the Idra Rabba's account of the two divine faces—*Arikh Anpin* and *Ze'eir Anpin*. It seems that the Idra is unable, or at least unwilling, to contain its full complexity within a single divine figure, and so it divides the Divine into two opposing figures.[8] *Arikh Anpin* represents absolute goodness, complete Mercy; while all Judgment in the world is drained into the figure of *Ze'eir Anpin* and, later, the Female. The strongest impression left upon a reader of the Idra Rabba is that of the difference, emphasized time and time again in myriad ways, between *Arikh Anpin* and *Ze'eir Anpin*—the brilliant whiteness of Compassion versus the redness of Judgment.

The question of the relationship between Kabbalah and Gnosticism is a fascinating one with regard to the Kabbalah and the Zohar in general and Idra literature in particular. However, a deeper reading of the Idra reveals that the elements that seem at first blush to be Gnostic reflect a more complex understanding of the world, which I will now try to articulate, cautiously.

First of all, it must be noted that notwithstanding the distinction between the two *partsufim* and the many passages that discuss the differences between them, the Idra emphasizes that these differences are contrasting aspects of a single and unified entity: "The principle of all: The Ancient of Ancients and *Ze'eir Anpin*, are all one."[9] According to the Idra, the difference between these faces is primarily epistemological rather than ontological; which is to say that it is a product of human consciousness rather than the state of the Divine itself. As readers, we must surely pay close attention to these declarations, expressing as they do the religious conceptions of the Idra's authors in the most profound terms.[10]

In addition, despite the Idra's emphasis on the distinctness and polarity between the *partsufim*, the work differs from Gnosticism in its emotional stance toward this dichotomous portrayal, and in the "spiritual activism" that it encourages. Whereas Gnosticism expresses profound hostility toward the demiurge and the material world created by it, this is by no means the Idra's attitude.

The authors of the Idra Rabba value and empathize with the figure of *Ze'eir Anpin*. They are aware of his problematic stance toward the world and the distress that arises from it, and they fear him, but they do not hate him or wish to overthrow him. Furthermore, they understand Judgment to be a fundamental condition for the differentiation that enables diversity, transformation, and *eros*, all of which they cherish deeply. They seek out difference and change in a positive sense, as motion along the continuum between the attributes of Judgment and Mercy.

In light of this, it might be said that the Idra actually presents us with a decidedly *anti*-Gnostic perspective. The Idra's heroes—and, one assumes, its authors—do not see themselves as victims of an evil god but rather as children coming to the aid of their Father. This religious and existential stance, of human beings who must come to the aid of God, was dramatically expressed in classical rabbinic literature,[11] but it is most fully expressed in theosophical Kabbalah and the Zohar. In the Idra, we encounter the most mature and radical formulation of such a concept.

The Idra Rabba, therefore, does not wish to invoke and summon a God whose face expresses only Compassion; rather, it wishes to establish a more balanced and viable mode of being, a balanced state, in which *Ze'eir Anpin* turns his face to the world in a richer and more varied manner. Indeed, the theological and mystical task of the gathering described in the Idra Rabba is to generate diversity and transformation within *Ze'eir Anpin* himself. Its purpose is to ensure that, when necessary, his personality will be able to receive into it the Attributes of Mercy, so that he may be present in the world not as scorching Judgment but rather as a balanced integration of the potencies of Judgment *and* Mercy emanating from *'Attiqa*. This *tiqqun* is enabled in a number of ways: by the human being who performs it, by *'Attiqa*'s luminous whiteness that shines upon *Ze'eir Anpin*, and by the *bissum* (aromatization) generated by the coupling of the divine Male and Female.

A Prayer for *Ze'eir Anpin*'s Life

The passage that may best express the Idra's anti-Gnostic stance appears among the *tiqqunim* of *Ze'eir Anpin*, in the context of an account of God's ears and hearing. This passage opens a window into the authors' attitude toward the two *partsufim* and their interconnectedness.

The text that forms the basis of the exegesis in this passage is the opening verses of the visionary chapter of Habakkuk:

> A prayer of the prophet Habakkuk, in the mode of Shigyonot.
> YHVH, I have heard Your hearing;[12] I am afraid.
> YHVH, Your deed, in the midst of years revive it;
> In the midst of years make it known.
> In wrath remember compassion. (Habakkuk 3:1–2)

The Idra reads this passage as an account of the prophet's experience of a state of *shigayon* (ecstasy or mystical contemplation). In this state, the prophet oscillates between experiencing God as *Ze'eir Anpin* and experiencing him as *Arikh Anpin*. Employing a radical mode of midrash by splitting the verse in two and seeing it as a process, the Idra reads only the first part of the verse—*YHVH, I have heard Your hearing; I am afraid*—as relating to *Ze'eir Anpin*. The second part of the verse—*Your deed, in the midst of years revive it* [. . .]—is now understood as addressing *Arikh Anpin*:

> Come and see what is written: YHVH, I have heard Your hearing; I am afraid. YHVH, Your deed, in the midst of years revive it; in the midst of years make it known. In wrath remember compassion (Habakkuk 3:2). This verse is well known, for when the holy prophet heard, contemplated, and knew—fathoming these configurations—it is written I am afraid, for it is fitting to fear and be shattered in His presence. This applies to *Ze'eir Anpin*.

The Idra interprets the expression *I have heard* to signify understanding and apprehension. Habakkuk declares that his experience of "hearing" the aspect of *Ze'eir Anpin* fills him with fear: *I have heard Your hearing; I am afraid*. In addition, here, the Zohar is putting a creative twist on the more basic understanding and translation of this verse—*I have heard of your renown*—and is reading it instead, as Daniel Matt has observed, as, "I have perceived the entire auditory process of *Ze'eir Anpin* [. . .] so [I am] fittingly afraid."[13] The Idra continues:

> When [Habakkuk] contemplated and knew, what is written? *YHVH, Your deed, in the midst of years revive it*, This was spoken to the Ancient of Days. [. . .]
>
> Your deed—what is meant by Your deed? *Ze'eir Anpin*.

After understanding the distress and imbalance within *Ze'eir Anpin*, the prophet now turns to the Ancient of Days, *Arikh Anpin*. Expressing his own deepening grasp of the divine essence of *Arikh Anpin*, the prophet beseeches *Arikh Anpin* to ensure life, vitality, illumination, and bounty for *Ze'eir Anpin*. *Ze'eir Anpin* is understood here as *Your deed*, that is, the creation and charge of *Arikh Anpin*. The Idra goes on:

> *In the midst of years* (*revive him*)—Primordial Years (*shanim qadmoniyyot*), called *days of old* (*yemei qedem*; Micah 7:20), and they are not called Years of the World (*shenot 'olam*). Primordial Years are *days of old*; Years of the World are *days of the world* (*yemei 'olam*; Malachi 3:4). Here, *in the midst of years*. Who are *years*? Primordial Years.
>
> *Revive him*. Whom? *Ze'eir Anpin*, all of whose radiance is sustained by those *years*. Therefore he said, *Revive him*!

This passage presents two orders of reality and time, and they are in opposition to each other: "Primordial Years" (*shanim qadmoniyyot*) or *days of old* (*yemei qedem*), versus "Years of the World" (*shenot 'olam*) or *days of the world* (*yemei 'olam*). *Ze'eir Anpin* belongs to the dimension of time called "Years of the World"—that is to say, he is the God who acts within time as it is familiar to us, within the chronology of the world, in history and epic.[14] In contrast, *Arikh Anpin* is associated with "Primordial Years," or "the days of old," that is to say, archaic time, prior to "Years of the World."[15]

In order for the God of "Years of the World" (*Ze'eir Anpin*, the God of Israel) to continue to be a *living* God, he must be connected to the atemporal Source from which he emanates, that is, to *Arikh Anpin*, the personification of "the days of old." *Ze'eir Anpin* must be revitalized *in the midst of years*: that is, cradled in the intimacy of *Arikh Anpin*. According to the Idra's interpretation, the prophet's words are to be understood as a prayer directed to the depths of the most ancient and primordial reaches of Divinity, entreating *Arikh Anpin* to ensure the ongoing survival of *Ze'eir Anpin*.

In a certain sense, this prayer is also addressed to *Ze'eir Anpin* himself, so that during times of world-consuming anger, he may recall and reconnect to *'Attiqa*'s Mercy, which is the source of his own Mercy:[16]

> *In wrath remember compassion*—that supernal *Ḥesed* of the Ancient of Ancients, by which Compassion is aroused for all: for whoever needs Compassion and whoever deserves Compassion. (Zohar 3:138b; trans. Matt 8:406–407, emended)

This richly emotional plea also echoes the human blessing to God that appears in a well-known narrative from the Babylonian Talmud.[17] The passage describes how, on Yom Kippur, in the Holy of Holies, Rabbi Ishmael

b. Elisha, the High Priest, encounters the Deity seated upon His throne (described in terms very similar to those used for *Ze'eir Anpin* in the Idra). God asks Rabbi Ishmael to bless Him, and the blessing that is pronounced is the great request: "May it be Your will that Your mercy will overcome Your anger, and may Your mercy prevail over Your attributes, and may You conduct yourself toward Your children with the attribute of mercy, and may You enter before them [in Judgment] while stopping short of strict Justice."[18] The prayer is that life, human life, may continue. Divine anger untempered by Mercy, and judgment of the world in accordance with "strict Justice," essentially means the negation of the continued existence of humanity.

The power and magic of this passage in the Idra Rabba rests mainly in its artistic use of midrash. The conceptual content of the passage—the relationship between the undifferentiated and the dual—could have been summarized in abstract theological terms in just a few short lines. But what makes the Idra Rabba a classic work of literature is its conscious rejection of abstraction, its affirmation of art. We can see here how the Idra's theological and theosophical paradigm shapes the way in which the exegete reads and artfully interprets the biblical verses. The opening verses of the chapter "in the mode of Shigyonot" in Habakkuk, some of the most ancient in the Bible, become an archetypal narrative about the human search for God, about the deepening consciousness as this search progresses, and the expansion of that consciousness so that it may encompass additional dimensions of the Divine. Perhaps the most moving aspect of this interpretation is the shift in emotional hues as the experience of *shigayon* progresses: moving from fear to mercy, from mercy to mystical praxis and prayer.

This interpretation of Habakkuk in the Idra reflects the attitude of the Idra's authors toward *Ze'eir Anpin* and *'Attiqa* in a most fascinating way. In a certain sense, this passage encapsulates the essence of the entire Idra. Habakkuk, the hero of the passage, becomes the prototypical mystic, while the zoharic exegete (perhaps Rabbi Shim'on) starts out with the exact words of the prophet and creatively continues them. The interpretation captures the process through which the mystic enters the mysteries of the divine realm. He learns how to align the undifferentiated and dual faces so they face one another, whiteness facing the varicolored, absolute Mercy facing the fluctuation between Compassion and Judgment, good and evil. From all this rises a passionate prayer and plea for the well-being of *Adam*, meaning *Ze'eir Anpin*, who constitutes a prototype for flesh-and-blood human beings.

Despite the fundamental terror we experience in the presence of *Ze'eir Anpin* in his wrath and fury, here we have a heartfelt prayer that seeks to sustain that figure, an entreaty to fill him with the "Life of Life" itself, with the complete Mercy of *'Attiqa*. The zoharic exegete's prayer is that *'Attiqa*'s outpouring of life to *Ze'eir Anpin* should never cease, that the timeless and undifferentiated One should bestow life upon the time-bound and dual Divine, that these two modes of consciousness should never become severed from one another. Here one witnesses the creative and uplifting effort to affirm and support *Ze'eir Anpin* and the dual consciousness that He represents. This is an expression of the Idra Rabba's unique tone—profound criticism for the Divine in its manifestation as *Ze'eir Anpin*, alongside a fierce will to temper and heal that very aspect of the Godhead in order to ensure its continued existence and presence in a way that best benefits the world.

There is no doubt that in the Idra Rabba there exists a "Desire for White," as the poet Allen Afterman called it, a desire for a more nourishing connection with *'Attiqa Qaddisha*—the Holy Ancient One, the divine being that is the Source of all.[19] But there is no thoroughgoing protest against reality, no negation of the discerning mind's categories, as one finds in the *Advaita* schools of Hinduism, for example. The Idra's project is to configure and heal *Ze'eir Anpin*'s Adamic face—whether through his illumination by *'Attiqa* or by coupling with the Female—and not to obliterate it by subsuming it into the limitless and indistinct expanses of whiteness.

5

Literature, Mysticism, Praxis

Up to this point, we have delved mainly into the conceptual, theological, and mythical aspects of the Idra's face discourse, which make the work unique. This chapter identifies further characteristics of the Idra Rabba that make it distinctive and that explain something of the secret of its charm and its reception as a canonical work. Some of these aspects are literary; others touch upon the mystical character of the Idra, the mode of consciousness that it induces, and the praxis that it enables.

Divine Secrets and the Literary Plot

The choice to embed the revelation of the many mysteries of the divine faces within a literary narrative about an emergency gathering to which the great master Rabbi Shim'on bar Yoḥai summons a circle of his disciples is quite astounding, and it lends the Idra Rabba singular power and allure. The sense of urgency and danger, the narrative tension around the enmeshment of the upper and lower worlds, the master's mode of addressing his disciples, the heightened vigilance in the disciples' responses and biblical interpretations, the personal blessings that the master addresses to his disciples—these are among the factors that inspire excitement, awe, and surprise in the Idra Rabba's characters, and in its readers throughout the generations. These qualities motivated Isaac Luria and Moses Ḥayyim Luzzatto to attempt to replicate the Idra Rabba, convening their own circles of disciples to enact Idra-like episodes.

Works contemporary with the Zohar—whether presenting the emanation of worlds as an abstract metaphysical teaching or even discussing the divine faces—possess none of the dramatic power and mystical tension that pervades the Idra, and that leaves such an indelible impression upon the reader. Indeed, in contrast with philosophical approaches that accord greater value to texts that present their ideas systematically and in abstract terms, and whose pronouncements stand independently, universally, and atemporally, the authors and editors of the Idra chose a genre that tightly entwines conceptual discourse with a literary narrative and with all the drama and emotion that unfolds within that narrative.[1]

This unique synthesis ensures that the Idra's mysteries do not remain mere abstractions but become a mode of knowledge that remains closely associated with, and even inseparable from, those who utter them. They are set within the specific location of the speakers, within the flow of the narrative. They retain the emotional expression of the speaker and listeners, reflect the master-disciple relationship, and echo the human and cosmic events that precede and follow the teaching. In this sense, the Idra Rabba may be said to be a distinctly deictic text, which is to say that it is a text that is not neutral or universal but rather points to a specific object, time, or addressee. When Rabbi Shim'on bar Yoḥai says, "Now then!" he emphasizes that we are not located in a neutral or undefined time but at a moment that is particular, fateful, and constituting an important stage in the process of redemption. The term "now" (*'attah*) generates a homiletical atmosphere that applies closely to the specific moment, event, and speaker. This deictic quality—locating the abstract and general mystery or knowledge within a spatial and temporal context and among specific addressees—deeply impresses the content of both the narrative and the scriptural interpretation upon the reader, in a manner that is simultaneously discursive and non-discursive. In addition, the Idra's construction of a literary world is precisely what enables readers of every generation to feel drawn into it, and to feel that they are participating in it emotionally.

The Idra's synthesis of narrative and divine secrets also has a mystical purpose. It binds the human and divine realms together. Through their scriptural interpretations, the Companions drive the process of divine configuration and healing. Thus, the divine realm influences and is in turn influenced by the narrative; it is bound up and enmeshed with it. It is not merely the work's background but an active participant in the narrative.

In addition, the synthesis between the descriptions of the divine faces and relationships and the narrative of the Companions is what ultimately generates the tension between revelation and concealment of the many secrets that are revealed or formulated in the Idra Rabba. The narrative layer provides the drama and thrill in the motion between exposure and concealment, and in the experience of revelation as it transpires. This tension is present throughout the entire work, from Rabbi Shimʿon bar Yoḥai's call at the beginning of the narrative—"Woe if I reveal! Woe if I do not reveal"—declared through tears of excitement and trepidation, through his entertaining the prospect that the whole circle of Companions would do better to vanish after the revelation of the divine mysteries, to his shocking contemplation of the possibility that the deaths of three of the Companions at the end might be a punishment for divulging too much.

In light of these thoughts, it is worth noting that two of the Idra's greatest interpreters, Moses Cordovero and Isaac Luria, chose to separate the scriptural interpretations from their speakers and their context, focusing instead on the "Treatise on Divinity" that is embedded within the work.[2] Cordovero virtually removed the binding of the Idra Rabba and the Idra Zuṭa, collating them and structuring his commentary on the text as a continuous reading of the common themes that arise from the two works. He thereby blurs the narrative character of each of the Idras, virtually to the point of erasure. Luria focused on the Idras' theological discourse, delving into it deeply, and building layer upon layer of new conceptual structures on it—but without paying any attention to the works' narrative frame. However, I do not believe that this exegetical choice points to Cordovero's or Luria's devaluing of the text's narrative aspects. There is no doubt that these two great exegetes ascribed tremendous value to the story of the Companions in the Idras, to the point that they attempted to revive and reenact it within their own kabbalistic circles.

Oral and Written Torah

The Idra Rabba's choice to weave its discourse on the divine faces into narrative form is connected to another important aspect of the work: its emphasis on speech, or orality. The aim of the Idra's authors was not to leave behind a systematically theoretical or mystical work that would circulate as the work of an individual author or mystic, but rather to transmit a living memory of the episode and the mysteries revealed therein, a kind of reenactment of a past event. Of course, this literary emphasis aligns with one of the fundamental principles of the Idra, that the interpretations *recited* by the Companions are the basic means by which reality is made manifest, configured, and repaired—*recited*, not *written*.[3] This principle appears time and again in the Zohar. An informative example may be found in the Zohar's discussion of Shavuot Eve.

The practice of *tiqqun leil shavu'ot*—staying up all night on Shavuot Eve and adorning the *Shekhinah* with jewels made of innovations in Torah in anticipation of her marriage to the masculine aspect of the Divine on Shavuot day—is an invention of the Zohar and has become, in modified forms, a central feature of Jewish observance of Shavuot.[4] Rabbi Shim'on invites all his disciples to come together for this nocturnal mystical event, inviting each of the assembled to elaborate on a biblical verse. Rabbi El'azar, his son, chooses to configure and adorn the *Shekhinah* with a verse from the Song of Songs: *Who is this that ascends from the wilderness* [. . .]? (Song of Songs 3:6) Rather than interpreting the term *midbar* (desert) as signifying the wilderness or a wasteland, he understands it to refer to the discursive (*medabber*) ability of human beings, to speech (*dibbur*). The passage describes the manner in which human speech enables the *Shekhinah* to rise into the inner reaches of the Divine, and how speech also draws her into the world, so that she might dwell in it:

> *Who is this that ascends from the wilderness* (*ha-midbar*) [. . .]? (Song of Songs 3:6) [. . .] By that מדבר (*midbar*)—by the whispering of lips—She ascends. [. . .] במדבר (*ba-midbar*) means בדבורא (*be-dibbura*), *by speech* [. . .] *She ascends from* המדבר (*ha-midbar*), indeed *from ha-midbar*! By that word of the mouth, She ascends. [. . .] Afterward through speech She descends, hovering over the heads of the holy people. (Zohar 1:10a–b; trans. Matt 1: 68–69)

The Zohar's emphasis on speech is a conscious and deliberate continuation of the self-conception of the rabbis as the bearers of Oral Torah, which develops and emerges dynamically in conversation with the written and eternal text:

the Written Torah. In addition to this rabbinic attitude, the Zohar identifies itself with the *Shekhinah*—called "the world of speech," the world of orality.

Returning to the Idra, and keeping this context in mind, we might be able to understand the curse that Rabbi Shim'on addresses to his disciples: *Cursed be the man who makes a carved or molten image* [. . .] *and sets it up in secret!* (Deuteronomy 27:15; Zohar 3:128a).[5] These words may be directed at those who would enshrine the oral in written form; that is to say, those who would seek to transform the quality of creative and dynamic speech into an abstract, well-ordered, and systematic theoretical treatise.

Nevertheless, the Idra is a written text, describing oral communication. Indeed, the work is explicitly conscious of its written quality.[6] The gifted artists who wrote and compiled the Idra created a magical sense of orality in the written text. On the one hand, this duality engenders a characteristically "oral" dynamism; on the other hand, it liberates the reader to explore the text freely, interpreting or even critiquing it, like any written text in Jewish tradition. The fictional narrative within the text allows us both to be swept up in the story and its magic and to stand outside it, the pages of the book lying open to scrutiny and critique before us. Indeed, as the great kabbalist Isaac the Blind wrote, objecting to the commitment of Kabbalah to writing: "The written word has no master."[7] That is, once their work is published, authors lose control of the use and reception of it.. But sometimes it is better that way, for then it becomes possible for the text to be endlessly interpreted and reinterpreted, each time through new eyes.

Simultaneity and Collapsing Polarities

Another unique characteristic of the Idra Rabba is the abundance of dichotomous characteristics to be found therein: language and image, the concrete and the abstract, the commonsensical and the psychedelic, realism and surrealism, the uncanny and the familiar, the semiotic and the symbolic, mythology and theology, innovation and tradition, and so on. The mere juxtaposition and simultaneity of these qualities, whether they complement or stand in tension with each other, generates the "idraic effect": a kind of experiential intoxication, as the reader's consciousness moves beyond its habitual state and is inundated with content that arouses wonder and surprise.

Language and Image The most intensive and pervasive mode of simultaneity in the Idra Rabba is that of language and image. The work shifts between these two dimensions with astounding litheness. On the one hand, the Idra possesses tremendous linguistic virtuosity, and its protagonists are true exegetical artists. They delve into the pool of biblical and midrashic sources, so rich in ideas and vocabulary, with great facility—delighting in it, drawing upon its rich denotative and symbolic possibilities, and exploiting it creatively. On the other hand, the language of the Idra is hypervisual. Indeed, the whole zoharic corpus is a highly visualized world composed of words, yet this quality is further intensified in the Idra. Its elaborate descriptions of the features of the divine faces and bodies offer rich and vibrant images, communicating content possessing a multidimensionality and simultaneity that eludes discursive language.

In contrast to certain Jewish approaches that are hostile toward any visual representation, the Idra found a way to express Jewish theological discourse through visual descriptions, in a kind of pictorial theology. The Idra's images penetrate deeply and provocatively, introducing semiotic, visual, emotional, and multivalent material into the symbolic stratum of the work's teachings and scriptural interpretations. This quality arouses the reader's imagination in a manner that both engages the reader and invites participation. For while language possesses a deconstructive quality, inherent in the very linearity of a sentence, images unify many elements simultaneously, binding them together as one. The images that we find in the Zohar and the Idra are a unique linguistic phenomenon, for although they are composed of words rather than colors or lines, they are extraordinarily potent in their ability to unify rather than deconstruct.[8]

The Concrete and the Abstract A striking characteristic of the Idra's discourse is the simultaneity of concreteness and abstractness, image and concept. For example, it is hard to imagine something more concrete than the Idra's description of the hairless "passage" between the nostrils and the mouth on *'Attiqa*'s face; however, it is through this account that we become aware of the profound theological concept of a God who forgives, "passing over transgression." There is nothing more concrete than the description of *Ze'eir Anpin*'s rose-red lips; yet it is this very account that experientially intensifies our understanding of the theological notion of the world's dependence upon the king's decree, issuing from these divine lips.

Much power and depth lie in this simultaneous quality, for the experience that emerges from it is neither superficial nor one dimensional, as in other forms of expression such as the parable, symbol, or illustration. The Idra's images broaden the ways in which we grasp matters, at the same time expanding the horizons of discursive apprehension.

Another mode of simultaneity connected to the concreteness-abstractness dyad occurs between *concrete substantiality* in the accounts of the parts of the face or body and *consciousness-expanding visuality*. Throughout the various *tiqqunim* of the divine faces in the Idra Rabba, the faces do not increase in their concreteness, resolution, or realism. On the contrary, through the process of close contemplation, the focus shifts—and within the close-up images, the faces become expanses of wellsprings and waterways, gushing rapids of light of varying qualities and intensities.

The Idra's accounts of the divine faces are wonderful and terrifying, attractive and alarming. The hyper-visual quality of the images—such as the crystalline dew trickling from *'Attiqa*'s skull to *Ze'eir Anpin*, or the contact between *Ze'eir Anpin*'s black locks and the Female's multicolored hair—broadens and extends the horizons of our visual and kinetic comprehension.[9] The tension between the strangeness and the familiarity of the faces described, the simultaneous experience of concreteness and extreme abstraction, together create an intensification of emotion, spirit, creative energy, imagination, and experience—all in a manner unattested in other parts of the Zohar.

Originality and Tradition The rabbinic expressions *tanna* ("we have learned"; "it is taught [or recited]") and *be-matnita dilan* ("in our mishnah") appear throughout zoharic literature, implying that the work is citing or paraphrasing an ancient source. There are various possible explanations for this phenomenon. It may be that the text is trying to create an impression of antiquity in a case of daring innovation, and to anchor the discussion in authoritative sources. Alternatively, it may attest to a well-developed fictional trope. Finally, it may actually be the case that these passages develop or rework earlier sources that were transmitted within kabbalistic circles.

Even a superficial consideration of the Idra reveals that the *tiqqun* of each aspect of the divine faces and bodies is composed of a series of statements that begin with the expression *tanna*. These traditions, presented as a mishnah or *barayta* (extra-mishnaic tradition), constitute chapters of some sort, ultimately forming a tractate describing the divine figure—much like the earlier work *Shi'ur Qomah*. In addition, the Idra itself begins with the expression *tanna*, presenting the entire work as a mishnah, as a received tradition that is now being recited, in which all the Idra's mishnayot are set.[10]

It seems that through its repeated use of the expression *tanna*, the Idra constructs a dialectic, a fruitful and engaging relationship, between tradition and innovation. It presents its innovative discourse on Divinity as exegesis or expansion of the mishnaic or extra-mishnaic material cited throughout the work. The form and terminology present the material as traditional, while at the same time the content is bursting with daring creativity. In this manner, the narrator and readers are spared a sense of scandalous transgression. Even if we don't know exactly where to find the mishnah that treats the divine forehead, the Idra assures us that somewhere such a tradition exists.

At the same time, we must consider the possibility that the Idra is indeed reworking older material. Yehuda Liebes points to such a possibility in his article "How Was the Zohar Composed?" Shifra Asulin further develops this theme, analyzing one of the "mishnaic" collections in the Idra, and attempting to identify the kabbalistic schools from which these sources emerged based on conceptual and stylistic criteria.[11]

In sum, the Idra's discourse encompasses detailed accounts of the divine faces; interpretations of the divine attributes; the experiences of the participants in the event; the description of the generation of reality; a deep engagement in the tactile in the finest detail; and the dialectic overlap of concreteness and abstraction. This embrace of striking simultaneity gives rise to the dizzying, overwhelming, and intense consciousness that is unique to the Idra.

Idraic Midrash

Another element that lends a unique flavor to the Idra Rabba is its midrashic quality, the manner in which it interprets Scripture. Here are some of the defining qualities of this aspect of the work. First, like other midrashim in theosophic-theurgic kabbalistic literature, the Idra's interpretations are structured like a mosaic, the collected verses and fragments of verses together forming a myth. These myths, called by Moshe Idel "intertextual myths," are built upon the assumption that the literary corpus being interpreted is unified, and that it is therefore possible to make connections between its various parts. The fabric of relations and internal literary allusions builds a myth that, apart from being coherent and unified, is exegetical, interpreting earlier texts.[12] Thus, for example, the mythical account of the eyes of *'Attiqa* and *Ze'eir Anpin* is gradually woven out of a collection of biblical verses that describe the eyes of God. The mosaic of verses, and the repeated emphasis on a selection of them, create the unique imagery of the whiteness of *'Attiqa*'s eyes versus the majestic, kohled, and multicolored eyes of *Ze'eir Anpin*. To some degree, the endpoint of these meandering interpretations is known in advance: they emphasize the difference between the non-dual and the dual aspects of the Divine. However, the specific way in which the images are constructed is anchored in a distinctly interpretive and exegetical manner by the eye verses in the Hebrew Bible.

A central characteristic of the Idra's exegesis, representing a kind of hermeneutical key to many of the interpretations, is a particular mode of analysis of single verses to refer to both *Ze'eir Anpin* and *Arikh Anpin*. Thus, many verses, whether they have explicit parallelism or not, are interpretively split, one half being applied to *'Attiqa* and the other alluding to *Ze'eir Anpin*. For example, this is how the Idra interprets the verse *Time to act for YHVH—They have violated Your Torah* (Psalms 119:126): *Time to act for YHVH* applies to *Ze'eir Anpin*, while *They have violated Your Torah* refers to *'Attiqa Qaddisha*.[13] In other cases, verses are "classified" based on their appropriateness or applicability to the various faces of the Divine.[14] This interpretive strategy is familiar from the main body of the Zohar, in which different parts within a biblical verse are interpreted as giving voice to the relationships between different *sefirot* (for example, *Malkhut* speaking to her beloved *Tif'eret*).[15] This strategy attains true virtuosity in the zoharic technique of interpreting a verse "according to *raza di-mehemnuta*" (the Mystery of Faith) in which each word in the verse being expounded is applied to a different *sefirah* in sequence, from highest to lowest. This technique is also mystical and theurgical in character; in addition to *describing* the flow of divine bounty from the sefirotic tree, it has the effect of *stimulating* that flow.[16] Uniquely, in the Idra, the focus of exegetical creativity is the divine faces and the relationships between them.

The mission-driven structure of the Idra Rabba and its vivid presentation of a dramatic initiation ceremony for Rabbi Shim'on's disciples also lend a unique character to the scriptural interpretations presented in the work. Throughout the narratives in the main corpus of the Zohar, there is an associative quality to the interpretations presented by the characters, generating a musicality that I have described in the past as similar to a jam session in jazz. One of the Companions begins interpreting a verse; then another joins in and responds with an interpretation of a further verse associatively connected with the first. This structure creates an unusual effect of surprise and playfulness—as readers, we wait in suspense to see what the next interpretative "riff" will be and from which biblical words it will emerge.[17]

The musicality of the scriptural interpretations in the Idra Rabba is very different. They do not have the same feeling as those throughout the rest of the Zohar: the joy of bubbling, fragrant, overflowing speech, spoken while strolling through the landscape; the delight of interpretations spoken in the wee hours of the night; the eroticism of the interpretations, stimulating the descent of the cosmic flow of divine bounty into the world.[18] Here, there is an overwhelming sense of tension and fatefulness. Delight, eroticism, and joy here give way to interpretations presented with awe in the presence of a tremendous moment. Here, each of the Companions' interpretations is intended to ensure the correct configuration of the divine faces, and their proper alignment with one another—thereby ensuring the harmony of the divine realm, and blessings and bounty for the human realm.

In the Idra Rabba, there is not a single Companion who begins his discourse freely or in an associative manner. The master summons and gathers his disciples; it is he who addresses each one, inviting them to rise and configure one of the *tiqqunim* of the divine beard. At times throughout the event, Rabbi Shim'on turns to one of his disciples and demands a response to a question that he poses. In addition, the interpretive improvisation in the Idra Rabba is more demanding than in other sections of the Zohar. Each of the Companions in the Idra is required to stand up in turn and configure and evoke one of the *tiqqunim* of the beard of *Arikh Anpin* or *Ze'eir Anpin*, employing as his tools the words of the verses concerning the Attributes of Mercy and the interpretation of those verses. There is no room to choose the subject of the interpretation, no choice but to respond to Rabbi Shim'on's call to expound. Each Companion called to the mission of *tiqqun* must bring the full range of his mental faculties and the full scope of his virtuosity to the task if he is to be successful. The seemingly impossible demand is that the interpretations will bring these two foci of attention—one physical and concrete, the other abstract and theological—together, forcing them to comingle, so that they might form a complete and harmonious interpretation.

Space, Time, Consciousness, Experience

Various dimensions of space and time and also diverse states of consciousness are highly important among the factors shaping the Idra. In this section, we shall try to understand the nature of these dimensions, to discern the states of consciousness from which, and in which, the Idra Rabba's characters function, and to determine the mode of mystical experience to which these states give rise.

Space The narrative, the narrator, and the words of the participants—Rabbi Shim'on and his Companions—all point to multiple planes of reality in which the events described in the Idra take place. On the revealed plane, the event occurs in this world, in a field among the trees. But while Rabbi Shim'on and his disciples may gather in the human realm, their activity is intended to transform the face of reality in both the human and the divine realms, and to effect changes in the connection between those dimensions, as the supernal worlds touch upon and participate in the lower world. In this sense, the Idra Rabba leaves us with the distinct impression that it is occurring beyond space, or more precisely, in a place belonging to a different order of reality. The rituals and gestures that mark the Companions' entry into the field, as well as Rabbi Shim'on's paradoxical and hypnotic language, together create an experience of passing into another dimension of reality, or into a unique and expansive state of consciousness, in which the participants will remain throughout the event. Thus, for example, the celestial angelic realm will constitute part of the scene from its very beginning, as we hear the beating of the wings of the heavenly host gathering to join the Companions, and will still be present near the end of the work, when Elijah the Prophet descends from his heavenly abode.

The Idra therefore unfolds in a space where there is no hermetically sealed boundary between the human and celestial realms. The *tiqqunim* themselves also transpire in various overlapping dimensions of existence, with Rabbi Shim'on emphasizing that the *tiqqunim* are "seen and not seen."[19] This paradoxical statement determines the peculiar mode of existence belonging to the *tiqqunim*: they are not visible to everyone's corporeal eyes; indeed, the privilege of seeing them is reserved for those "in possession of [the necessary] traits" (*ba'alei ha-middot*),[20] which is apparently an admiring reference to the Companions, who possess unique and unmediated knowledge of the divine attributes (*middot*).

Time Many zoharic narratives deal with the unique properties of time, and time plays an important role in those stories. The different phases of the day, and the transitions between them, often constitute a story in their own right: dawn, morning, the afternoon, dusk, night, midnight, and the hours before dawn. These are all significant elements of the story, as each phase of the day is bound up in a specific way with a particular divine modality. The progression of time often drives the narrative, which transpires while individuals are walking on the roads by day, or sitting together and engaging in Torah study after midnight. The Zohar's unique attentiveness to time and its properties calls for sensitivity and caution when ascribing a specific quality or character to any moment, and identifying the activities and intentions (*kavvanot*) that are appropriate for it.

In contrast with this, the Idra is set outside of time as we know it. As the scene unfolds, there is no indication of the progression or changing of time. There is no description of the alternation of day and night, light and darkness; there is no break or pause, no sense of the duration of the events described. From the moment that the Companions gather together for the Idra, time vanishes. While there are references to loss of the experience of time in other zoharic stories, attesting to entry into a particular state of consciousness or a mystical plane of experience,[21] this sense is amplified in the Idra, for as we enter the setting in which the object of contemplation is *'Attiqa Qaddisha*, existing beyond language and time, the dimension of time vanishes. It is as if time consciousness makes way for the eternality, permanence, and timelessness of the white dew constantly trickling from *'Attiqa*'s head.

Plane of Consciousness The Idra's plane of consciousness is uniquely characterized by the capacity it affords human beings to stand in the presence of the Divine. Yehuda Liebes described this as "mythic" reality, a dimension in which there exists a "direct reference to the divine entity itself, which is available on the same plane of awareness and meaning as are all other observable phenomena."[22]

In his commentary on the Idra Rabba, Moses Ḥayyim Luzzatto understands the Companions' gathering among the trees at the beginning of the work as an entry into the Garden of Eden, the realm of the *Shekhinah*. If we accept this interpretation, the field reflects distinctly female properties, representing in a sense the genitalia of the feminine Divine, the womb of the *Shekhinah*: "Thus [Rabbi Shim'on] said, *Gather, Companions, at the threshing chamber*—so that they might all gather as one, thereby ascending into the foundation of the Female (*yesod ha-nuqba*) that is the Garden of Eden."[23] This dimension is connected to the human realm, for all existence is inscribed in the *Shekhinah*'s womb. This is a place of creation, delight, and transformation; it is the gate through which one enters the divine realm above it. Indeed, the Idra Rabba's state of consciousness matches Moses Cordovero's description of the terrestrial Garden of Eden, in which the human and divine realms are coterminous:

> There is no doubt that there exists a terrestrial Garden of Eden. [. . .] In several passages, the Zohar indicates that the Garden of Eden contains trees, flowers, and spices. These things are physical, and it does not seem to be referring to the soul after its departure from the body. [. . .] This being the case, this whole turbid world has a soul and spirituality, called the Garden of Eden, and it is concealed and spiritual. [. . .] The only ones who conjoin with the deeper recesses [. . .] are those holy ones in the world, of pure vision. [. . .] So too the zoharic masters, who were of pure vision. [. . .]

> There may be conjunction between the physical and the spiritual, which is the ever-purifying physical point, unifying with the spiritual, at the end of the world in the East.[24]

The idea that being present in the Garden of Eden is a precondition for contemplating God, and for unmediated contact with the Divine, also emerges elsewhere in the Zohar itself:

> The Companions have already aroused the laws of the Garden of Eden [. . .] upon which no eye prevails aside from the souls of the righteous—to be engraved above and below, to contemplate from there the mystery of their Lord and supernal bliss. (Zohar 1:38a–b; trans. Wolski and Hecker 12:6)

Another image that well suits the Idra's plane of consciousness is the Orchard (*pardes*), an ancient description of the space in which the mystical encounter between human beings and the Divine occurs. According to the Talmud, the Orchard is the realm into which four great heroes of rabbinic literature entered; only one of them, Rabbi Akiva, entered in peace and emerged in peace.[25] The Orchard is a dimension that one must know how to enter and exit for it possesses a logic distinct and different from that of familiar and mundane reality. Indeed, the theme of entering and emerging is repeated many times in the Idra Rabba, and the ability to enter and emerge is a defining feature of those worthy to participate in the occasion.

The events described in the Idra therefore occur in a medial dimension, one that participates in terrestrial physicality and in the reality of divine beings. In this realm, both archetypal and mythical, human beings and divine faces occupy the same space or are in close proximity. They intermingle far more intimately than is familiar to us in our mundane reality. A deeply inspired account of such a dimension may be found in the writings of Ibn al-ʿArabī, who proposes the existence of a medial realm called a *barzakh* (lit., "boundary"), which mediates between the world of the senses and that of thought and ideas. In this dimension, the two worlds meet: the abstract is clothed in forms, and the sensuous becomes spiritually elevated. The spiritual must not remain abstract, lest it disappear, and the sensuous must not remain corporeal, lest it become fixed or is reduced to mere concreteness.[26] "It is the vast prairie where the theosophist-mystics feast their eyes. [. . .] For the mystics, this Earth is where theophanies and theophanic visions take place."[27]

An alternative presentation of this dimension of reality and consciousness, equally impressive, was formulated by Henry Corbin, one of the great scholars of mysticism in the 20th century.[28] Corbin, whose research focuses on medieval Islamic mysticism and mystical philosophy, claims that it is impossible to understand the world in which these mystical texts were composed without properly grasping the dimension of the imagination. In his view, the dominance accorded to rationality in the modern period has led to a devaluation of the imagination, restricting it to the world of artists, children, and the insane. We must therefore redirect our attention to the imaginal world and its connections with the mystical realm, and study it closely.[29]

Corbin thus focused on what he called *Mundus Imaginalis*, the "Imaginal World": that medial realm that sits between physical reality and the world of abstract ideas, discussed by Muslim mystics and Sufis in the medieval period.[30] This is the realm of sacred imagination, the production house for the religious imagination, in which a person who has refined his or her spiritual character can encounter beings who belong to various dimensions of divine reality rather than the world of our day-to-day consciousness. At the same time, the sacred imagination is not foreign to the system of normative religion. It is an essential and amplifying component of the "sacred theater" from which religious ritual frameworks are constructed. The uniqueness of mystical texts lies in the tremendous importance that they ascribe to this dimension, while attempting to train the mind and senses to enter into it and function within it.

As we have noted, Corbin asserts that in order to read the mystical sources with the seriousness that their authors ascribed to them, we must become familiar with the dimension of imaginal reality before analyzing and abstracting these texts. It seems that the Idra Rabba also unfolds in this realm. The texture of the reality in which the Idra is set is not physical in the usual sense, but it is also certainly not a world of conceptual abstraction alone. The entire circle of Companions enters this setting, which, as we have seen, Jewish mystical tradition identifies as "the terrestrial Garden of Eden." In this mythical and archetypal dimension, an encounter transpires between the Companions and the faces of the Divine. The Companions are initially nestled among the trees, but the field soon loses its physical contours and begins to transform, coming to resemble the mysterious land of the *Shekhinah*. They stand before the faces of God expounding Scripture, but they simultaneously remain conscious and communicative, seated in a circle upon the ground; they speak in verses, while at the same time they are entangled in the hairs of the divine beard.[31]

The *Mundus Imaginalis* therefore provides a language by means of which we may try to understand the nature of the plane on which the Idra takes place, thereby avoiding the reduction of the event to a mere metaphor or symbol. For according to the Idra itself, the events actually transpire: entities are created, the supernal descends, the terrestrial ascends, the faces of God are radiant and effusive. This is a mystical, shamanic, mythical, or archetypical reality—it is not merely symbolic.[32]

A striking example of this is the Idra's conception of speech, according to which words possess tremendous creative power. Against the familiar laws of physics, and similar to the effect of the creative speech of God in the Bible, when the Companions recite their *tiqqunim*, the *tiqqunim* occur in reality. The scriptural interpretations are not a theoretical encyclopedic compilation of theosophical concepts, or a literary description of divine reality; they are potent theurgical acts. We might say that the *tiqqunim* expounded by the Companions are hyper-theurgic, or performative. The interpretations evoke and activate *tiqqunim* within the expanse of the divine face in real time. Each layer of divine reality that is unveiled or garbed by the words of the interpretation becomes alive and present. In the state of consciousness in which the Idra transpires, language creates and generates reality.

From the outset of the gathering, an aperture to this alternate mode of consciousness is opened, and through it the Divine descends to the human and the human ascends to the Divine. The language of the Idra that is full of solemnity and pathos well suits this reality, as does its more grandiose visionary terminology. In the Idra, there is an explicit awareness that this is a unique plane of consciousness, and that it is evoked in the ceremony of the prologue and epilogue of the work, accentuating the importance of knowing how one might enter into it and emerge from it in an appropriate manner.

Mystical Experience Another component shaping the Idra Rabba is the quality of mystical experience it describes and the distinctive imprint that it bears.

In this sense, the Idra's opening scene is of great importance, determining to a large degree the emotional quality of the experiences that the participants will undergo throughout the work.[33]

The words, gestures, and ceremonies that feature in the opening scene of the Idra together create a tense anticipation of what is to come. Thus, even at the outset of the gathering, the Companions feel their knees trembling and knocking together at the sound of the heavenly host gathered above their heads, and the earth shakes as Rabbi Shim'on opens his mouth. The state of cosmic emergency conveyed by Rabbi Shim'on's words in the opening passage of the Idra determines the force and character of the work's discourse of mystical experience. Rabbi Shim'on emphasizes that the reason for the gathering, their mission, requires putting love at the center rather than fear; but in order to enter the realm of love, the participants—and indeed the entire terrain in which they now find themselves—must necessarily pass through a state of profound trembling. Perhaps it is this tremor that creates a fissure in their habitual experience of reality and enables them to enter an entirely different mode of consciousness. As we shall see, the disciples' interpretations are also defined by an extraordinary emotional intensity. The quality of mystical experience in the Idra Rabba is distinctive in its blend of excitement, fear, boldness, and creativity. It seems that the purpose of the detailed and demanding ceremonies in the opening scene is to create a container that will be able to withstand the energy and intensity of the participants' experiences.

In general, the language of mystical experience in the Idra Rabba is direct and intensive, proportional to the mission and sense of urgency that characterizes the entire episode. As in other fields that it treats, the Idra approaches the subject of mystical experience with characteristically high intensity. The terminology in which the features of the various divine faces are described overflows with a unique mystical quality. The language is fantastical and liquid—paradoxical, primordial, lofty, and sublime. The effect upon the reader is hypnotic. It moves in dizzying fashion between imagery and virtuosic linguistic exegesis, leaving the reader's mind dazzled. Even Rabbi Shim'on's words of encouragement to the disciples throughout the episode contribute to the mystical experience. The sublime language, visionary expressions, exaggeration, and praise of the master and the disciples all intensify the consciousness of the participants, elevating it to heights that transcend the boundaries of normal perception, so that they might remain within the trans-personal reality of the event and function within it.

The unmediated connection with the Divine reaches its climax toward the end of the work with the ecstatic deaths of three of the participants. Here, the boundary between the divine and human realms dissolves. The three can no longer resist the gravitational pull of the Divine, and their spirits soar upward to cling to the Divine. This intensity of mystical experience renders the Idra unique among zoharic narratives; in it the mystical experience glimmers, is delicate, even cautious, and as I have remarked in the past—is a contained experience with clearly delineated boundaries.[34]

The Figure of the Master and the Purpose of the Circle of Companions

The choice to present the Idra Rabba as an initiation rite for the disciples shines particular light on the status of Rabbi Shim'on bar Yoḥai, the mystical master and leader. The revered figure of Rabbi Shim'on is continually shaped and refined throughout zoharic literature; however, his dominant presence as a teacher, seer, mystic, and the light of the world and Torah comes to its climax in the Idra. Indeed, this is one of the work's distinctive aspects. Rabbi Shim'on, the great teacher and leader of the circle of Companions, is the one who convenes the gathering, sets its goals and content, and determines the manner in which it proceeds. He orchestrates the process of gathering and sets the appropriate emotional tone. In addition, Rabbi Shim'on provides the main testimony for the powerful mystical experiences, and it seems that the participants experience the divine world primarily through his mediation. He illuminates the events of the divine and human realms for his disciples and for the reader as the episode progresses, pointing out to the Companions the ever-widening cosmic plane in which they are participating. Rabbi Shim'on's role as the master teacher is to point out, to ascribe meaning to, and to experientially evoke and intensify events.

As we shall see, at the very outset of the Idra, the master indicates the goals of the assembly to the students, the most central of which is to establish additional "pillars" that might support reality. After his introductory words concerning the task ahead, the disciples all take their place in the scene and become "pillars of the world" before our eyes. This transition, from indicating a thing to entering into it experientially, is one of the qualities of mystical literature and great poetry.

Rabbi Shim'on is depicted as a leader and authoritative teacher. When he summons one of his disciples to arise and enact one of the divine *tiqqunim*, this is no mere suggestion but a moment of examination. The disciple must fulfil the mission with which he has been entrusted. The greatness of Rabbi Shim'on as a teacher comes through in his responses to the *tiqqunim* presented by his disciples. He understands that his disciples' emotional and intellectual effort requires encouragement and support, so he does not leave them dispirited after their words. He blesses each and every one of the exegetes with a special blessing that refers specifically to that person's interpretation, binding him to *'Attiqa*, who is the focus of the *tiqqun*.

Rabbi Shim'on chooses not to conceal his experience from his disciples but rather to share with them moments of exciting or frightening personal revelation. One example of this is his intense inner conflict after the deaths of three of the Companions.[35] Another is his highly personal, impassioned, and ecstatic response after the mystical-visionary interpretation of one of the participants:

> Rabbi Shim'on said, "All lamps—you Companions, who are in this holy ring—I call the highest heaven and the highest holy earth as witnesses that I see now what no human has seen since the day that Moses ascended Mount Sinai the second time. I see my face shining like the light of the powerful sun that is destined to radiate healing for the world, as is written: *For you who revere my name the sun of righteousness will shine, with healing in its wings* (Malachi 3:20).[36] (Zohar 3:132b; trans. Matt 8:359)

Rabbi Shim'on coordinates the task of crowning the various faces of God with the Attributes of Mercy, and he perceives the entire act of *tiqqun* in a visionary state, from beginning to end. From time to time, he interrupts an interpretation to provide a cosmic or divine perspective on the event, or to emphasize that the *tiqqun* is not merely theoretical but generates reality, now, in real time. As the master teacher he is responsible for orienting his disciples, elucidating for them the cosmic impact of their words on the divine realm.

Once again, the transformations occurring in the divine realm throughout the Idra are no mere product of our intuition as readers. Rabbi Shim'on, the great teacher, is the one who explicitly directs his students' gaze, and ours, to the widening cosmic horizons, revealing them and giving them validity. Throughout the work, he is the one who illuminates the meaning of the events, opening his disciples' spiritual eyes to matters that they do not yet know how to perceive, matters that language cannot yet articulate. The Companions experience the cosmic upheavals and emotional turmoil, but it is Rabbi Shim'on who gives these their meaning; indeed, to some degree, he shapes these processes by making them present in discursive reality. Alongside this, Rabbi Shim'on himself attains visionary, messianic, and ecstatic experiences during the event—experiences that he claims never to have had before.

A typical example of his role as a figure who points to expanded cosmic states and modes of consciousness, thereby inviting the Companions to participate in them, appears in the transitional passage between the *tiqqunim* of *Arikh Anpin* and those of *Ze'eir Anpin*. In a visionary revelation, Rabbi Shim'on testifies that he can perceive with his mystical vision how the words of the *tiqqun* that emerge from the mouths of the Companions actually bring the *tiqqun* into being. The *tiqqun* ascends to its place in the divine face, settling within it and growing luminous. Rabbi Shim'on's words here represent a climactic moment of profound mystical and visionary experience, characterized by a rich use of imagery, movement, and heightened emotion:

> Rabbi Shim'on said to the Companions, "When this canopy that you see over us was spread, I saw all these enhancements (*tiqqunin*) descending within it, illumining this place [. . .] awaiting the words of our mouths—to be crowned, each ascending to its place. [. . .] As each of us opened his mouth to arrange a certain enhancement, that enhancement sat waiting for the word to issue from your mouth, and then it was crowned, ascending to its place to be adorned.
>
> "All the columns on either side rejoice upon hearing what they do not know and they listen to your voices. How many chariots appear here for your sake! Happy are you in the world that is coming!" [37] (Zohar 3:134b–135a; trans. Matt 8:377–378)

Rabbi Shim'on's role as a teacher could never be actualized without students. Just as the disciples need a teacher, the master must have disciples. He divulges secrets; there must therefore be faithful souls who will receive these mysteries, and who will fulfil the mission of continuing to compose creative interpretations concerning the various faces of the Divine. The group must remain coherent and bound together by love, enabling the Companions to be bold as they arise and expound, as they step into their role as cosmic pillars and configure the divine *tiqqunim*. As in other zoharic narratives, it is the circle of disciples that creates and reinforces the figure of the master teacher so that he can fulfil his archetypal roles: as the one who perceives the *tiqqun* that the cosmos requires; as the one who indicates, unveils, and illuminates matters; and as the one who is able to bring together the disparate aspects of reality and the Companions in a single sacred whole. Therefore, the circle of Companions is, in itself, a precondition for the *tiqqun* of the Idra to take place. Without his students rising to the occasion and becoming pillars, Rabbi Shim'on could not resolve the question with which he opens the Idra: "How long will we sit on a single-based pillar?"[38]

Religious Praxis in the Idra

The interpretations of Rabbi Shim'on and the Companions configure and give utterance to the unique quality of each part of *Arikh Anpin*'s face and each segment of his beard, causing them to shine and gush forth their bounty. After the interpretations, Rabbi Shim'on blesses the individual who presents them, that he may have an enduring and vital connection with the Ancient of Days. The usual formulation of the traditional benediction—*Blessed are You, YHVH, Sovereign of the world*—is focused on human praise of YHVH, the king of the world, that is, *Ze'eir Anpin*. Indeed, the character of *Ze'eir Anpin* as portrayed in the Idra is certainly in need of blessings. Here, the blessing works in a reverse fashion—it is a request that human beings be blessed with the continued presence of the Ancient of Days, *'Attiq Yomin*, in their lives.

The formulation of the blessing in the Idra is thus a kind of translation and realization of its theology. It shifts that theology from the realm of theory, experience, and even ecstasy into the sphere of religious praxis, by articulating and evoking it in the religious language of real life. The Idra thus establishes a religious milieu that reflects and corresponds with its call for the transformation of religious life through the expansion of legitimate discourse concerning the Divine. Rabbi Shim'on's blessing refers to the part of the face or beard treated in the preceding scriptural interpretation. Now a personal connection is drawn between the facial features of *'Attiqa* and the individual speaker. For example, after the *tiqqun* of *Arikh Anpin*'s forehead, spoken by Rabbi Shim'on's son Rabbi El'azar, Rabbi Shim'on recites the following blessing: "Blessed are you, my son, by the Ancient of Days! You will find favor of the forehead when you have need of it."[39] After the *tiqqun* of the eyes, spoken by Rabbi Abba, Rabbi Shim'on says: "How fine! The Ancient of Days will open his eye upon you."[40] After Rabbi Yitsḥak's first *tiqqun* of the beard, he is blessed by the master in these words: "You are worthy of beholding the glory of the enhancements of the beard and the Countenance of Days of the Ancient of Ancients."[41]

The blessings formulated by Rabbi Shim'on emphasize the ongoing connection between speech *about* the sublime and transcendent *'Attiqa* and his living presence in the actual lives of human beings. The Companions, who configure the facial features of *'Attiqa*, merit the divine bounty that flows from this face into their lives.

The Idra thus seeks to make the face of the Ancient of Days a living presence in the lives of the Companions: to walk on the path, speaking *'Attiq Yomin*'s Torah, and experiencing his blessed presence when it is needed.[42] We must ask whether Rabbi Shim'on's invitation in the Idra Rabba to bring the God of oneness into the world of religion—liturgy, religious custom, poetry and language—was answered over the many hundreds of years since the Idra's appearance. Indeed, there is no doubt that the Idra had a profound effect on kabbalistic thought. Entire intellectual worlds were generated, relating to the undifferentiated divine realm. Nor can the Idra's influence on religious praxis be doubted; it is clearly attested in the Lurianic intentions (*kavvanot*) for prayer; in Isaac Luria's hymns (*piyyuṭim*) for the Sabbath; in Moses Cordovero's work *Tomer Devorah*, which invites people to model their lives on the divine attributes expressed in the thirteen *tiqqunim* of *'Attiqa*'s beard; and other works. The custom of *tashlich* (going to a body of water on the first day of Rosh HaShana), is a notable example. This ritual has enjoyed widespread popularity since the 16th century due to Luria's and, later, Ḥayyim Vital's constructing of it as a deeply idraic act in which we call the

Thirteen Attributes of *'Attiqa* forth into reality and cast our iniquities into the infinite supernal ocean of Mercy.[43]

However, if we consider whether *'Attiqa Qaddisha* is present in our prayers and rituals in our contemporary world, whether he is present in our religious language and imagination, whether contemporary Jewish religiosity has at all taken up the challenge posed by the Idra to expand legitimate religious discourse—it seems that we would have to admit that the figure of the undifferentiated God has not entered religious language in any meaningful way.[44] Imagining what our religious language could have gained from the presence of this primordial divine figure, emanating unconditional life and love, it is saddening that *'Attiqa Qaddisha* is hardly present at all in the normative and familiar spheres of Jewish religious life.

6

Overarching Themes in the Idra Rabba

Up to this point, we have focused primarily upon the Idra Rabba's languages—the languages of face, of gaze, and of coupling. Now we shall take a panoramic view of the picture that the Idra paints using these languages. From this vantage point, we may perceive the broader dynamic processes described in the Idra, and take note of three overarching themes: the formation of the Divine in its various aspects, the emergence of existence, and the various ways in which Judgment (*Din*) is modulated. Complementing these three themes, I will offer a fourth—my own interpretation of the work—arguing for a reading of the Idra as an experiential inquiry into the nature of human consciousness that draws on mythical and mystical discourse.

One can read the entire Idra through the prism of any of these four themes. However, no one of these themes, standing on its own, exhausts the work's meaning. Only an approach that brings together and synthesizes these overarching themes can allow a fuller and more complex understanding of the work.

A Mythic Account of the Emergence of the Many-Faced Divine

First and foremost, the Idra Rabba is a kind of theogony, a great myth concerning the birth of the Deity, or of the various manifestations of the Divine. This myth is recounted in deeply Jewish language, and its building blocks are interpretations of verses of Scripture. The Idra describes how a deity that might be captured by and addressed with language gradually emerges from the infinite Divine that exists far beyond the boundaries of any discursive speech and intellectual apprehension. The hidden and primordial God, beginningless and infinite, lacking directionality and without intention, is gradually distilled and woven into divine faces that possess directionality and will. The process begins with the formation of *'Attiqa Qaddisha*'s face, after which *Ze'eir Anpin* gradually emerges, and finally the Divine takes the form of a fully developed male and female figure. Through this process, the various faces of the Divine are born; these engage in a relationship between and among themselves and with the human realm. It is the emergence of the indistinct and infinite Divine into its manifestation in various aspects and faces that enables the creation of the world, emanating and unfolding as it does from within God. Zoharic literature in general is daringly innovative in asking previously "forbidden" questions about the origins of the Divinity itself, and many zoharic passages are mythical renderings of the process of emanation and articulation of the Godhead. What is unique to the Idra Rabba is addressing these questions of origin in the language of faces.

This divine evolution takes place within itself and emerges from itself; at the same time, it is aroused and stimulated by the mental processes of the participants in the Idra Rabba. It might be appropriate to call this process *autogenesis*: "self-birth."[1]

A fascinating characteristic of this theogonic myth is the developmental theology that it expresses. God is not understood as perfect and static but rather as a being that undergoes development and refinement. This Deity evolves from primordial and sublime oneness into a fully fashioned, variegated, humanized, and gendered Deity, within whom dynamic and erotic relations take place. This process is not described as a regression, as the loss of sublime oneness and its replacement with multiplicity, but rather as the opposite. It is described as progress and expansion. In practice, the differentiation and evolution of the Divine into a number of distinct figures enables the repair and resolution of certain deficiencies in the more primordial Deity, in particular by refining those systems that regulate the flow of Judgment and Compassion and maintain the balance between them.

It is particularly notable that the Idra's theogony describes partial and discordant processes of generation, in sharp contrast, for example, to the full and perfect description of creation in Genesis. For example: the connection between *Ze'eir Anpin* and *Arikh Anpin* is unstable, and *Ze'eir Anpin*'s face tends toward an excess of Judgment. The processes that strive toward the coupling of the Male and Female also exhibit polarization and separation. Seeing this unsettledness and disharmony allows us a better understanding of the central place occupied by human beings in the Idra: they are entrusted with the task of ongoing configuration, enhancement, and healing of the divine realm. The Companions, the enlightened "gnostics," possess *knowledge* of the unfolding of the divine reality; at the same time, they bear the responsibility for *maintaining* that realm through a renewed process of divine coronation, establishing and attuning the flow of bounty within the divine realm and from that realm into the realm of human beings. The "reboot" that the Companions create for the divine system, and the maintenance that they provide, ensure its proper function: the flow of divine bounty and blessing, the illumination of the various divine *partsufim*, and as a result, the illumination of the human realm.

Another characteristic of the Idra's theogony is that each and every phase of divine emanation and development is not a complete metamorphosis in which a new divine figure replaces, conceals, or annuls the previous one. Rather, this is a process of manifestation of various aspects of the Godhead even as they exist simultaneously and interact dynamically with one another. The Idra effectively describes how multiple complex and distinct manifestations of the Divine emerge from their undifferentiated and mysterious source. The divine modalities coexist at all times, yet their expression or presence in the world changes throughout time, according to the situation and need. Thus, for example, the illumination of *'Attiqa* manifests during prayer, Sabbath meals, in the glow of the new moon at its first appearance, and during seemingly inescapable moments of distress (for example, during the splitting of the Red Sea). *Ze'eir Anpin* continues to act within national history and mythology as the God of Israel, the warrior—this aspect of God is depicted in large portions of Scripture. The Divine as a conjoining and coupling of the Male and Female, as *Adam*, is present in contexts in which the world is blessed: during sexual intercourse on the Sabbath eve, during *kiddush* on the Sabbath day, on festivals, and every day at dawn.

Thus, the stages in the formation of the divine faces described in the Idra's theogonic myth are not only a singular event but might be better understood as cyclical, constantly ebbing and flowing. Isaac Luria, one of the most creative exegetes of the Idra literature, was of the opinion that the divine *partsufim* are constantly undergoing transformations—both linearly, or even eschatologically, and cyclically, in processes of evolution and regression (such as the separation and coupling of the Male and Female, which occur at certain points in the cycle of the calendar). However, it seems that the Idra itself is not explicitly concerned with cyclical progression and regression within the Godhead, nor with the ongoing occurrence of these divine processes. One gets the impression that the mysteries revealed in this work are the initial process of divine emanation, preceding the existence of time itself.[2] At the same time, the Idra's intense engagement with the coming-into-being of the Divine, extends forward, toward temporal existence, into the human realm and the ways in which humanity reflects the divine realm and exists in a relationship of mutual influence with it.

The Unfolding of Existence

One can also read the whole Idra Rabba as an attempt to trace the emergence of reality out of its hidden wellsprings. The perennial question of cosmogony, how existence emerged, is the fundamental riddle addressed by philosophers, mythmakers, theologians, and scientists in all periods. Whereas the biblical creation narrative opens with the words *In the beginning God created the heavens and the earth* (Genesis 1:1), according to the Idra Rabba the great story of the origin of being lies long before the opening verses of Genesis. The myth of the beginning of the concentration and contraction of the Divine into faces that may turn toward created existence occurs beyond space and time. In this sense, the entire Idra Rabba is an investigation into the beginnings that antedate the biblical beginning—the narrative in which God appears as the creator and artisan. It does not describe how God creates the world but rather how the conditions for the formation of any distinct existence at all are created, including the faces of God themselves. The Idra describes the unfolding of existence from the undifferentiated Divine, timeless and infinite, into complex and variegated reality. Only at a distance of eons, after the divine *partsufim* have come into being, and the Male and Female bodies have conjoined in sweet coupling, does the later narrative of the creation of the physical world begin, as recounted in the Book of Genesis.

The Idra's investigation of the coming-into-being and unfolding of existence is a daring act when considered in light of statements that limit the fields humans are permitted to investigate, such as the admonition of Ben Sira, as cited in the Talmud: *Seek not that which is too wondrous for you, and inquire not into that which is concealed from you; consider that which has been allowed you—you have no business seeking the hidden.*[3] Or, as the Mishnah puts it: *One who considers four things, it would be better had he never come into the world: What is above, what is below, what is before, and what is after.*[4] Indeed, the Idra Rabba is not naïve in its discussion of such topics but rather expresses an acute awareness of the tension between revealing and concealing the mysteries of the Divine and existence. The freedom and authority with which it delves into the mysteries of the creation—despite traditional limitations—stems both from the Idra's sense of urgency, according to which there is an obligation to unveil the divine mysteries in order to configure anew the faces of God in their relation to the world, and from its view that the revelation of these mysteries is preferable to a situation in which human beings will stray after foreign and misguided speculations. In addition, there is a practical implication to knowledge of these mysteries: such knowledge enables human beings to bring the flow of Compassion that shines forth from *'Attiqa*'s face into the world, along with the fragrant flow that issues from the coupling of the Male and the Female within the Divine. Similarly, the knowledge that is transmitted in the Idra is of a salvific character, for it assures the place of the "gnostics" in the divine realm after their deaths in the temporal world.[5]

At a later stage, from the moment the male and female bodies begin to form and the central topic shifts to the figure of *Adam*, the Idra follows the biblical and midrashic myth of the creation of Adam in Genesis. It interprets the biblical verses through a cosmic-divine prism, through which one might decipher the processes of the formation of reality. The creation of *Adam*, male and female; the Serpent's seduction; the birth of Cain and Abel; Cain's murder of Abel—all of these are interpreted as occurring in the "heavenly field,"[6] in the archetypal feminine Divine realm. Such an interpretation synthesizes Platonic and Neoplatonic elements: human physical existence and the earthly creation narrative are formed in the image of the divine drama. Even further, terrestrial existence is a dense and coarse materialization of the subtle and unified divine reality, which emanates and unfolds into the lower dimensions of being. But the stream of emanation does not flow calmly, and the passage from undifferentiation to the duality and multiplicity that we see in the world is characterized throughout by imbalance and an excess of Judgment. It is particularly notable that a stable and sustainable structure for reality becomes possible specifically at the more advanced stages of the unfolding of being, when existence has become more complex, with the development of distinct masculine and feminine aspects.

Another significant property of this chain of being is the interdependence of its various parts, and in particular the reciprocal relationship between its sublime upper link and its complex lower links. Earthly human beings, occupying a place far from their ultimate source, have the unique ability both to maintain and care for the well-being of reality in all of its dimensions and to enable the penetration of the most hidden divine spirit into their realm.

The Idra is thus concerned not only with describing the various stages of the unfolding of divine and human existence but also with the problems that arise from this process and with responding to those problems. Overcoming obstacles, along with the refinement and reconfiguration of the various divine manifestations, enables the continuation of the particularization of reality, and simultaneously ensures a mode of existence in which all parts of the divine and human realms remain interconnected.[7]

Ways of Attenuating the Power of Judgment

Taking a bird's-eye view, one can interpret the Idra Rabba from beginning to end as a description of various encounters with and responses to the quality known as *Din* (Judgment). The Idra describes the unfolding of progressively more detailed layers of existence, and *Din* is present in each and every one. At each stage, the entities associated with Judgment attempt to undo the balance of the system in which they are located. Moreover, the qualities of Judgment differ at each level of existence. In the opening of the Idra, they manifest as the primordial kings of Edom; later, in the description of the Garden of Eden, the power of *Din* appears in the figure of the Serpent—the evil and seductive force, present also in the human heart as the Evil Inclination (*yetser ha-ra'*). Judgment, or *Din*, operates in all dimensions of reality, thought, and imagination, and we may locate its various manifestations as an archaic, anti-cosmic, sacred, demonic, or erotic force. To ensure the possibility of establishing a worthy, vital, and stable divine and human existence, Judgment must be dealt with differently in each of its distinctive, primordial manifestations. Every stage of the coming-into-being and establishment of the divine *partsufim* marks a new chapter in the management of these forces of Judgment. The Idra has a unique vocabulary for describing the different management strategies: concealment, suppression, containment, battle, and sweetening (*bissum*), as well as draining, scattering, and transforming these potencies. Taken all together, these strategies constitute a grand myth about the eternal relationship between Compassion (*Ḥesed*) and Judgment (*Din*), forces that are fundamental to any given reality.

Let us survey the major stages of this theme in the Idra Rabba. The reader encounters the most primordial aspect of Judgment at the very beginning of the Idra Rabba, in the myth of the kings of Edom.[8] These are archaic forces of Judgment, which attempt to emerge into distinct being out of the infinite and indistinct divine ocean. However, this first appearance of primordial Judgment is unmediated and imbalanced, and in order for the creation or emanation of viable and lasting being, Compassion has to *store away* or *conceal* those forces.

Following this, once the *partsuf* of the Ancient One has been configured, we find that the mere presence of the white face of forgiveness and life *suppresses* Judgment. *'Attiqa*'s head, the force of white Compassion, is described as seated upon a flaming throne of Judgment and suppressing it. Only when white is seated upon red, Compassion upon Justice, can any process of creation begin.

As the process of divine individuation continues, with the emergence of *Ze'eir Anpin*, an attempt is made to deal with the forces of Judgment within him by *balancing* and *containing* them through the power of white Mercy that shines forth from *'Attiqa*'s face. We also see another way of confronting these forces. In his capacity as a warrior, *Ze'eir Anpin* engages in direct *battle* against the menacing forces of Judgment—here depicted as existing externally to him, rather than being contained within him.

Later still, with the formation of the divine male and female bodies, the dynamic process that Judgment undergoes is described in terms of *concentration* and *draining* from the male body into the female body. The Female herself, now full of *Din*, adopts still another surprising strategy in an attempt to attain a balance between these competing forces; she *draws* the forces of Compassion within the Male into herself, in order to temper the power of the Judgment within her. The Female achieves this by concentrating the force of Judgment within her into certain parts of her body, and into her genitals in particular, in order to draw the Male toward her for sexual coupling.

The next stage, which is extremely important, is the treatment of the harsh power of Judgment through the coupling of the Male and the Female. Intercourse itself neither eradicates nor expels Judgment but rather *sweetens* it and makes it fragrant.[9]

Yet the attempt to balance out the forces of Judgment does not end here. Now, in the figure of the primordial Serpent, these forces penetrate the Female. In this situation, the excess of Judgment must be treated through a process of potent *catharsis* in the form of *draining*, *extraction*, and *ejection*, which takes place with the birth of Cain and Abel.

The treatment of Cain (representing absolute *Din*) and Abel (who symbolizes *Din* as well, but not entirely) also reflects a process of *suppression*, *storing away*, and *concealment* of Judgment. These two avatars of Judgment are *exiled*, or *cooled*, in the liquid cosmic basins of the Great Abyss and the Great Sea, and the two brothers become a single body, sunken within the nether reaches of the abyss. This body becomes the source of the souls of the wicked, and of various classes of bodiless demons. At this stage, the treatment and adaptation of *Din* occurs by *scattering* it, in countless fragments, into souls and demons.

The process of expelling *Din* through the birth of Cain and Abel frees the Female from the potent Judgment of the Serpent, and she becomes ready and ripe for the third coupling. This introduces us to the *sweetening* (*bissum*) that is the Idra's most unusual way of dealing with Judgment. Sweetening does not nullify or repel the force of *Din* but rather changes its "aroma," transforming its energy from something dangerous and destructive into something erotic and sweet. This harmonious coupling, in which Judgment is sweetened, enables the birth of Seth and, from him, the production of generations of *Adam*'s descendants in the image of God.

Judgment in all its guises—from its roots in the depths of the Divine down to its emergence in the form of the Other Side (*Siṭra Aḥra*) and evil in the human realm—is one of the overarching themes of all zoharic literature, presenting us with a wide variety of ways to act in the face of these powers and to deal with them.[10] The Idra Rabba contributes its own unique language and myth to this vast topic. Indeed, the Idra may be read as a breathtaking myth about the emergence and unfolding of the powers of Judgment in its various manifestations at all levels of existence, and about the ongoing attempts to confront and withstand those powers.

Reading through the Lens of Consciousness: Oneness and the Dual, Male and Female

Alongside the idraic subjects I have discussed up to this point, a sustained and continuous reading of the Idra raises the possibility that this grand myth about the Divine actually represents an experiential exploration of human consciousness—its origins, development, and limits—using the tools of mythical narrative. According to such a reading, the engraving of the kings into *'Attiqa* himself, and the way in which his face in all its details is woven, may be understood as a visual and mythical account that traces the virtually unfathomable beginnings of the awakening of consciousness: how an inchoate intentionality arises within a consciousness closed within itself, broad and unselfconscious, and spatial orientation and focus begin to emerge. In like fashion, the configuration of *Ze'eir Anpin*'s face then represents the transition from a unified state of mind to a more complex and distinct condition, marked by reflection and discursivity.

In this interpretive possibility, the Idra is a mythical narrative that describes two modes of consciousness, oneness and duality. The Idra analyzes the similarities and differences of these two types of consciousness and the relationship between them. Thus the redirection of *Ze'eir Anpin*'s gaze toward *'Attiqa* represents the proper relationship between the refracted, binary or dual consciousness, and oneness. *Arikh Anpin* and *Ze'eir Anpin* do not stand in direct opposition to one another, nor are they hostile to one another. The Idra does not harbor the Gnostic antipathy toward the dual aspect, nor does it seek to refute the truth of a dualistic perspective, as does Hindu Advaita Vedanta philosophy, for example. According to the Idra, nondual consciousness contains within it the conditions for the emergence of dual consciousness, the former enabling the existence of the latter. The crystalline dew of *'Attiqa*, symbolizing the transparent light of unified consciousness, is a precondition for the emergence of the colorful and variegated: "The appearance of that dew is white, like a crystal stone in which all colors are seen."[11] The diversity within *Ze'eir Anpin*'s realm is enabled by the light gushing toward it from *'Attiqa*—the undifferentiated crystalline dew shines through the depths of dual consciousness. Indeed, the Idra Rabba is very much focused upon the tension and difference between these two *partsufim*, *Arikh Anpin* and *Ze'eir Anpin*. Nevertheless, according to the Idra, a dualistic mode of being cannot endure without the presence of oneness as well, radiating absolute and unconditional Mercy. Conversely. the formation of a dual consciousness is what enables the contemplation of oneness, and the creation of a relationship with it.

Reading the Idra as a study of the human consciousness, a dynamic mapping of it, also enables us to compare this study to parallel accounts in the main body of the Zohar, and to identify the distinct ways in which the subject is presented in these two strata of the zoharic corpus. Thus, if we consider the main body of the Zohar, we find that the binary consciousness that is subject to the law of time is identified with the feminine, the *sefirah* of Sovereignty (*Malkhut*), the ever-changing rose; whereas the unified and stable mode of consciousness that transcends time is identified with the Tree of Life, representing the masculine *sefirah* of Beauty (*Tif'eret*).[12] In contrast, in the Idra Rabba, duality is a characteristic of *Ze'eir Anpin*, the male God, the warrior, while the stable and enduring non-binary presence is that of *Arikh Anpin*, the elderly or ancient figure. That is, in contrast with the main body of the Zohar, the Idra does not represent a gendered binary but rather focuses on the dichotomy between the young and the old, the historical and the primordial, the small and the large, the contracted and the expansive.[13] Corresponding with this, in the main body of the Zohar, the ideal relationship between the eternal and the changing, the Male and the Female, is one of erotic coupling. In contrast, in the Idra Rabba the relationship between the binary and oneness is described in terms of *Ze'eir Anpin* appearing before *'Attiqa*—an act in which the former is bathed, relaxed, soothed, and filled with light and Compassion.

In the context of characterizing states of consciousness and the relationships between them, it is important to note that the Idra Rabba does not in any way suggest that all dualistic aspects should be expunged from the mind, or that we should embrace only a nondual consciousness at all times.

Dual consciousness is a precondition for all that makes us human: language, analysis, and the capacity to choose. It enables "spectacular difference," as the Israeli poetess Zelda puts it.[14] This awareness forms the basis of a developing, changing, and diverse reality; it is also the precondition for existing and acting within that reality. The Idra teaches that this dual consciousness must know itself, its limitations and essential characteristics. We should not seek to negate it, but rather to heal the connection between it and oneness. This connection deepens, opens up, and expands dual consciousness, allowing its fullest and most beneficial manifestation.

Such an understanding of the Idra Rabba poses the following challenge: How may one exist in a state of dual, discerning, temporal consciousness, and at the same time recognize the timeless? How may a mind characterized by duality and multiplicity attain some knowledge of oneness, of the existence of the resplendent dew, of the hidden and sublime dimension contained within the One? A state of consciousness that allows the One to be present in the dual is familiar to us from moments of deep contemplation, from heightened sensual and emotional states, or from the effects of mind-altering substances. A fundamental precondition for entering such a state is that one must break free, even if for a mere moment, from all-engulfing dual consciousness to a condition described in the Idra's richly visual language as the shifting of *Ze'eir Anpin*'s gaze away from the world and its redirection toward the face of *Arikh Anpin*.

Reading the Idra Rabba while paying close attention to aspects of human consciousness also points us to the final portion of the text, which is not focused on the relationship between oneness and dual consciousness, but rather works with the categories of Male and Female. In a sense, the dual mode of consciousness has undergone a process of embodiment, manifesting from this point onward in a body and sexuality. The disciplines of psychology and mythology provide us with helpful tools for understanding this portion of the work. Particularly useful are the methods bequeathed to us by depth psychology from the school of Jung and Neumann, who discuss the complex and complementary relationship between masculinity and femininity as archetypal structures of the psyche. Using these tools, we can read the male-female relations in the Idra as more process focused, developing relations between modes of consciousness and psychic structures. According to such a reading, the mythic narrative of the separation of the Male and the Female from each other, and their subsequent reunification, describes masculine and feminine consciousness as they pass from an initial and undifferentiated state into one in which they become distinct from one another to the point of diametrical opposition. Once the difference between them has been accentuated, the two modes of consciousness are joined once again in a more highly developed and mature manner, enabling them to comingle without losing their distinctiveness. Since the Idra employs sexual terminology when discussing the coupling of the Male and the Female, it is appropriate to apply the term *hieros gamos* to this account of commingling: that is, sacred coupling, or sacred marriage, as discussed by Jung.[15] In this context, particular note should be taken of the terminology of *bissum* (sweetening or aromatizing), which is repeated throughout the account of the development of consciousness, up to the state of harmonious coupling. Rather than posing a danger or threat to one another, the distinct components of human consciousness exist in a state of ambrosial fragrance and sweetness.

To my understanding, the precision exhibited by the Idra Rabba's analysis of the various aspects of the Divine points to the authors' deep, personal, experiential inquiry into their own mental processes. It is quite possible that it is this experiential aspect of the inquiry that lends the Idra's accounts such a sense of certitude. Alongside mythical and mystical readings of the Idra Rabba, a spiritual-psychological mode of interpretation can enrich our understanding of the work, and allow us to illuminate otherwise dense and inaccessible dimensions of it. For me, such a reading of the Idra opened a gate through which I was able to enter its symbolic world, so breathtaking yet inaccessible, and provided me with a major key to understanding the work.

7

What Is the Idra Rabba Trying to Communicate?

Having become familiar with the Idra's unique face terminology, and with the work's major themes, we can now ask the most fundamental question: What did the authors of the Idra want to communicate to their readers, and what meaning lies in the work for those of us who encounter it today?

In this closing chapter of the introductory section of this book, I offer my personal conclusions on the religious, theological, ideological, and spiritual insights that emerge from the Idra, framed as they are in the work's distinctive language. These insights are not communicated to the reader in an explicit or systematic fashion. Rather, they emerge from a slow and cumulative reading of the Idra, after having absorbed the work's many images and shifts of perspective and its rich array of concepts. In this context, it must be emphasized that the quest for the Idra Rabba's motivation is mandated by the very fact that it is *not* an ancient myth, not "innocent," but rather a mythical text authored in the medieval period, composed out of a sense of ideological urgency, and self-conscious of its own creative production. The fact that the Idra Rabba was produced by self-reflective artists of exceptional mythopoetic talent and skill renders the need to respond to this profound question all the more pressing: What is the Idra Rabba, and what is it trying to communicate?

First of all, I shall present the Idra Rabba's great manifesto: the call to heal and renew the face of Jewish religion. This is the primary key to deciphering the work. I shall then present a number of additional interconnected insights that emerge from the work. I encourage the reader to return to this chapter after finishing the second part of this book, which presents a close reading of the Idra Rabba.

The Idra Rabba's Manifesto: A Call to Heal and Renew the Face of Jewish Religion

First and foremost, we may understand the Idra Rabba as a great call to heal and renew the face of the Jewish religion. The work originates from a deep sense of urgency to renew a Judaism that was undergoing processes of increasing rigidification and abstraction. Born in the depths of the authors' souls, this sense of urgency brought forth a bold and creative religious alternative.

The healing transformation to which the Idra aspires entails an expansion of the boundaries of the legitimate religious language in which Jews can express their spiritual lives, forge a relationship with the divine realm, and become more deeply connected to it. The Idra is a manifesto, a complete platform comprising a critique of the state of the religion and proposals to remedy it, all enshrined in the discourses and exegeses of Rabbi Shim'on and his disciples. In its character, it bridges the mythical, the mystical, the exegetical, and the narrative.

In order to identify the components of this manifesto, I must once again offer a brief formulation of the Idra Rabba's mission, drawing on the work's face terminology, and then attempt to translate that terminology into more abstract terms. As I have said, the Idra points to disharmony and discord between the various aspects of the Divine. This deficiency in the mutual illumination of the divine faces (*partsufim*), this disconnectedness between them, causes *Ze'eir Anpin*—the God of Israel—to become constricted and inflexible, and to fill with Judgment (*Din*) to a degree beyond that which is necessary or desirable. The prescription that the work offers as a remedy for this problematic situation is expressed in two images: *Ze'eir Anpin* turning to face *'Attiqa*, and the divine Male and Female turning to face each other in fragrant coupling. The Idra employs the concept of *alignment*—which is to say that it formulates a mystical discourse that centers on aligning the divine *partsufim* with one another and with the human realm. The reader is encouraged to invoke the divine faces: to describe them, make them present, and transform them into an active reality. The proper configuration of these faces ensures a continuous and unobstructed flow of divine bounty—from its primordial depths (*'Attiqa*), via the dualistic aspect of Divinity as structure, language, religion, and law (*Ze'eir Anpin*), through the feminine Divine (*Nuqba*), and finally into the very fabric of our existence in the world. The reconfiguration (*tiqqun*) of the divine realm results in a situation in which all the faces shine, rejoice, and turn to face a beloved other. They abide in a mutual relationship, and fill with the flow of divine bounty. Conversely, if *Ze'eir Anpin* fails to meet *'Attiqa*'s gaze, or if the divine Male and Female fail to face each other, this becomes a source of alienation, harsh Judgment, destruction, and confusion in the divine and human realms.

The Idra's unique development is its call to the Companions—a circle of the most select human beings—to join their master on a fascinating and dangerous assignment, pregnant with fatefulness: to rectify the state of aspects of the Divine, through a precise and delicate process that influences and shapes the divine realm. The Idra's heroes are armed with the words and letters of the Torah, with intentions of the heart, and with a deeply creative exegetical imagination. The purpose of all this is a renewed establishment and positioning of God, a configuration and initialization of the divine faces.

If we strip the Idra of its mythical language, and attempt to cloak it in the language of discursive theology, we discover a penetrating critique of Jewish religion, as well as the proposal of a surprising and daring alternative. I shall attempt to translate the face terminology into a religious theological platform. According to my understanding, this manifesto is present throughout the Idra in various ways, and it conveys ideas that may be profoundly inspirational for our own time.

At the very foundation of the Idra Rabba lies a critical theological claim: in the process of developing the dualistic, legal, institutional, and ethical dimensions of the Jewish religion, other important aspects of religious life were deemphasized, and their presence waned. While not rejecting the value of ethics and morality in religious life, the Idra explores the fateful implications of investing tremendous effort in a religious consciousness that exclusively discerns and defines, constructing a conception of reality according to categories such as the permitted and the forbidden, the pure and the impure, the private and the public, the Jewish and the non-Jewish. Becoming overly concerned with these dualistic approaches, even though they are the building blocks of proper society and human conduct, can nonetheless keep human beings from connecting with reality's deeper oneness. The emphasis on these dualistic aspects contracted and constricted Judaism, making it narrow and filling it with Judgment.

In addition to this over-emphasis on the discursive, other trends within medieval Jewish thought promoted a transcendent and abstract theology, retaining a focus on oneness yet deemphasizing the personal elements of the Divine and the human connection with them. We find this in the reinterpretations of Judaism in the spirit of Aristotelian and Neoplatonic philosophy. The most outstanding and impressive representative of this trend was Moses Maimonides in his *Guide for the Perplexed* (written in the 12th century), in which he sought to rectify and reconfigure Judaism itself. Maimonides' project of selection, deconstruction, and reorganization of religious language, aimed at presenting an utterly transcendent and abstract God, was certainly ambitious and daring. Even the authors of the Idra would no doubt have recognized this. At the same time, they identified the great cost of such a religious worldview. The adoption of a totally abstract and transcendental theology through a new mode of scriptural hermeneutics erased God's face, and negated the personal and emotional presence of the Divine—a move that could endanger Judaism itself.[1]

According to the Idra, the remedy for this state of affairs is the expansion of Jewish religious discourse and its conceptions of God. This will come about through illuminating additional facets of the Divine, and invoking those elements of the Godhead in human experience. The broadening of religious discourse is a necessary and urgent project, aimed at ensuring the very vitality of Judaism. Judaism must discover ways to reopen channels of communication and nourishment with those divine dimensions from which it has become consciously or unconsciously estranged: the primordial Divine as **oneness**, the personal and **embodied** aspect of God as *Adam*, and the *masculine* and *feminine* aspects with their mutual erotic and sexual relationship. The living presence of these aspects of the Divine expands the imaginal range of normative Judaism—with its central image of the God of Israel (YHVH)—allowing it to be suffused with the plenitude of a deity flowing with boundless and unconditional kindness and love, as well as with the emotional and intellectual richness that comes with the idea of the divine Male and Female in erotic relationship with one another. These images all hold the potential to heal, broaden, deepen, and renew the Jewish faith. This expansion could also counteract the fear that Jews might leave the fold owing to their dissatisfaction with the overemphasis on discursive and binary elements on the one hand and the neglect of universal aspects and divine oneness on the other, or owing to the lack of any relation to those processes of *eros*, life, and fertility that touch upon the lived reality of human beings.

Aiming to bring about the rectification and healing of the Jewish religion, the Idra—profoundly aware of the role of language in shaping consciousness—invests tremendous creative energy in establishing terminology, images, parables, myths, and ritual practices that will transform the Idra's manifesto into a living reality in the human consciousness. In the following section of this chapter, as I continue my effort to understand and translate the mythical language of the Idra into a language of theology and a religious platform, I will note the major points that constitute the Idra's manifesto.

The Undifferentiated Divine—The Source of All Things.

Judaism must find the language to express a conception of God as the Source of all things, and make space for the idea of a unified mode of existence flowing with life and love into all existence. These are the characteristics of *'Attiqa Qaddisha*. This primordial Divinity stands beyond the boundaries of human speech, the symbolic order, and discursive reasoning. As we have seen, the figure of *'Attiqa* is composed both of primordial and mythical images of the Divine as deepest antiquity and of elements from the Aristotelian and Neoplatonic philosophies that exerted so powerful an attraction during the period in which the Zohar was written. These conceptions describe a deity that is the Source of all being, existing above and beyond the figure of YHVH, the God of law and of the nation. The undifferentiated God represented by *'Attiqa* exists beyond narrative and beyond nationhood, a deity whose care is universal and cosmic—not particular or particularistic. However, a careful review of earlier layers of Jewish esoteric teachings may also reveal the threads that connect the Jewish national narrative with these aspects of the Divine.

If no way is found to establish a connection with the primordial and undifferentiated Divine, this mode of being will disappear from human consciousness. Judaism will develop in a discursive and binary direction, unchecked and imbalanced, and it will lose its spirit and its ability to contain a multitude of dimensions of reality. Jewish law (*halakhah*) may rule over any kind of reality that is quantifiable or measurable, but other areas of life and their inner landscapes will remain bereft of a meaningful and suitable religious language.

As we have seen, amplifying the presence of the undifferentiated Divine in religion poses no threat to the continued existence of *Ze'eir Anpin* as a central aspect of God. The Idra's call to summon *'Attiqa* is not bound up in a rejection, hostility, or a desire to dispense with the central divine figure of Judaism, identified with YHVH. The Idra seeks to heal this aspect of the Godhead, to expand it and ensure its well-being, by connecting it with both the undifferentiated and the feminine aspects of the Divine, so that its orientation toward the world will be emotionally balanced. In other words, this is not a call to revolution, or to the violent destruction of earlier layers of the culture and religious discourse; rather, it is a desire to rectify and heal the faith, expressed by people who live fully within the realm of Torah, cherishing Judaism and concerned for its future. This aim does not make the Idra any less radical or daring. Instead, it reflects the work's organic approach, which seeks to contain the many layers of Jewish thought, and recast them in a new and more inclusive language. The existence of a Jewish language that acknowledges and invokes the Divine-as-oneness, revitalizes and deepens normative religious discourse, which is now marked by distinctions and duality. This discourse becomes enriched by a deep belief in the existence of a divine dimension that exists beyond the dichotomies of the permitted and the forbidden, the pure and the impure.

The Divine as Corporeality Judaism must reconnect with the conception of a Deity in human form, as described by the Idra. As we have seen, the sources of such a conception are biblical and post-biblical, and this idea is featured in the Jewish *Shi'ur Qomah* tradition. In contrast with other trends within Judaism, the Idra does not view anthropomorphism or a personal conception of the Divine as a threat to the religion; rather, these views represent an important aspect of its theology. It is through them that human beings come to know the Divine within themselves. Conceiving of God in corporeal terms enables human beings, replete with their humanness and their earthiness, to draw near to the God in whose image they were created.[2] In the first generation of Kabbalah, we find the 12th-century Rabbi Abraham ben David (the RaBad) openly disputing Maimonides' sweeping rejection of anyone who professes a belief in the Divine as anthropomorphic and embodied.[3] Maimonides saw such people as heretics who have no place in the World to Come. In his objection to this, the RaBad writes:

> Why has he called such a person a heretic? There are many people greater than and superior to him who adhere to such a belief on the basis of what they have seen in verses of scripture and, even more, in the words of [. . .] [the] aggadot.[4]

This critique acknowledging the existence of legitimate Jewish traditions that do attribute corporeality to the Divine has been a project of Kabbalah ever since these sharp words from the RaBad.

Eroticism and Sexuality, Masculinity and Femininity Judaism must find a language, gestures, rituals, myths, and thought that will invoke the presence of divine femininity in its religious life. It must shake the dust from the female aspect of the Divine, and invoke the feminine religious language that the rabbis developed around the figure of the Assembly of Israel (*Keneset Yisra'el*) and the *Shekhinah*. But it is not enough to summon and reconfigure. In order to experience the feminine Divine, there must be a creative effort to expand this figure into every possible facet of the religious world. A tangible and unsuppressed reality of God as the *Shekhinah* is necessary, as the Beloved and as the Great Mother, so that fundamental aspects of religious experience will not remain mute or invisible, bereft of language. Nor does this language threaten to displace YHVH, the God of Israel, his Torah and laws, from their central place in Judaism. The cultivation of the feminine Divine will enrich the masculine and personal figure of the God of Israel. God will no longer be understood as perfect and static, but as a developing and dynamic being.

Human beings, created in the image of God, are male and female; a fusion between these aspects in the Deity ensures a truer, fuller, and richer connection between human beings and elements of the Divine that have been denied, suppressed, or concealed. Thus, the language of relationship between the masculine and feminine Divine—full of emotion, *eros*, and sexuality—allows Jews to bring their religious lives together with the sensual and erotic aspect of their lives, rather than perceiving them as mutually exclusive or even hostile to one another. Coupling, the act of sexual love, is a momentous experience—positive, joyful, and creative—for all human beings, and it is a point of entry into the spiritual experience of human beings connecting with the Divine. Granting earthly coupling a sacred status—flesh, blood, and spirit—also carries implications for religious life, fulfilling the desire for a passionate encounter between the human and the sacred.

This call to emphasize the feminine as well as the erotic unification of the feminine with the masculine aspects of the Divine, through Jewish ritual practice and intention, is foundational to Kabbalah. The comeback of the feminine into legitimate religious language and imagination is central to kabbalistic thought both before and after the Zohar and reaches its apex in the 16th century.[5] I have no doubt that these innovative kabbalistic traditions can provide much inspiration for our own times.

The Unity of God The theological language of the Idras, and of the Zohar in general, seeks to develop and communicate the understanding that the concept of "the unity of God"—which is so central in Jewish tradition and religious discourse—does not refer to simple or monolithic unity but rather to a unity that is complex and dynamic. The principle of divine unity as formulated in the Idra Rabba does not stop with either the unity of the personal Deity of biblical literature, a male God, or with a philosophical conception of oneness, an abstraction with which it may be difficult to connect. The kind of unity that inspired and animated the kabbalists, the authors of the Idra Rabba, embraces and encompasses both abstract and personal components—transcendent, conceptual, and sensuous, all held together in a dynamic and vital manner. These propositions are not in conflict with the concept of divine unity but rather contribute to it and enrich it.

The Idra's proposal for rectification and healing, for *tiqqun*, is not limited to theory and theology but extends into the realm of personal religious experience. The work's narrative of the aid that the Companions extend to

God, configuring and aligning the divine *partsufim*, creates a paradigm for human conduct. In the religious, spiritual, and psychological language of the Idra, the purpose of humans on earth is to use the tools of knowledge, self-awareness, and concentration in order to properly align the human mind with the face of the Ancient One, full of healing. Already, in the opening passages of the Idra, it is explicitly stated that *Ze'eir Anpin*'s desire to gaze upon *'Attiqa* applies also to the cultivated and perfected human being, the *tsaddiq* (righteous or holy person) of the Zohar:

> The desire and joy of the righteous, who are in *Ze'eir Anpin*, is to see and cleave to the arrayal of the Ancient One, concealed of all. (Zohar 3:129a; trans. Matt 8:333–334)

The Idra describes a process of inner-divine healing that mirrors and is mirrored in a human effort toward *tiqqun*. The expansion and release that *Ze'eir Anpin* experiences while gazing at *'Attiqa*, the experience of his eyes being bathed in the whiteness of *Ḥesed* that flows from *'Attiqa*'s eye, is also attainable for the righteous in this world, according to Rabbi Shim'on.[6]

The Idra's mysteries are therefore intended to facilitate the establishment of a connection between earthly human beings and the highest aspects of the Divine. Far from being diminished, the realms of the commandments, prayer, Torah study, friendship, and companionship are all deepened, enriched, and diversified.

A deep belief in the divinity of human beings and in the possibility of a meaningful human connection with the Divine empowers the Idra to enact a daring project of reform in religious discourse. It is not the suppression of human emotion or eroticism that will lead to the exaltation of God and ensure a connection with the Divine; rather, it is the magnification of the human figure—drawing the human and the Divine near, and likening one to the other—that is the surest path to the continued vitality of religion.

From the Idra's manifesto there thus emerges a great call—perhaps even startling in its audacity—to reconfigure, heal, and refine the very face of Judaism. This is not a call to form a mass movement or to formalize a creed; rather, it is the creation of religious art, which can only be produced by artists of great mastery.

What Else Is the Idra Trying to Say?

Apart from its great manifesto, the Idra also seeks to convey to its readers a number of additional insights concerning human beings, the world, and the Divine. In concluding this chapter, I explore and elucidate three such insights. The first touches upon certain relationships—those within the divine realm and those between the divine and human realms—and the tremendous importance the Idra ascribes to them. The second concerns the appreciative and exalting attitude of the Idra toward human beings, the body, and *eros*. The final insight relates to the importance of *arikhut apayim*—patience and the cultivation of extended breath.

Relationships and Modes of Connection The relationships between the various facets of the Divine and between these and the human realm, and the different modes of connection among all of these, receive great attention throughout zoharic literature. In the Zohar in general, the accounts of the various *sefirot* serve as a backdrop for the drama of the different modes of interconnectedness and relationships between them, and of the kinds of reality that these interactions generate. The Idra Rabba enriches and expands upon this theme in its own distinct language. In describing the mythic relations between *ʿAttiqa* and *Zeʿeir Anpin* and between the divine Male and Female, the Idra focuses upon two archetypical modes of connection or communication: gazing and sexual coupling.

As we have seen, the gaze is one of the most fundamental components of face terminology, and it enables a face-to-face connection. Indeed, the configuration of the Ancient One's face, which is the focus of the Idra's opening passages, is the most basic condition of *ʿAttiqa*'s encounter with that which exists outside of him. At a later stage, the emergence of *Zeʿeir Anpin* will create the possibility for a face-to-face encounter and for the formation of a connection with the Other. The act of one face turning to face another creates a connection, a transmission, vitality, and healing. In effect, a considerable portion of the *tiqqunim* of the various parts of *ʿAttiqa*'s and *Zeʿeir Anpin*'s faces describes different modes of interconnection and transmission between these two *partsufim*: forehead to forehead, eye to eye, beard to beard, and so on. In other strata of the Zohar, the most common terminology for describing connection and conjoining is sexual or erotic coupling—embracing, kissing, sexual intercourse, delight, fertilization, and so on. One gets the impression that the Idra requires a different language in order to describe the relations transpiring between *Ze'eir Anpin* and *Arikh Anpin* because they occur deep inside the divine realm. For them, the authors created a language of relatedness and interconnection that does not immediately bring to mind the corporeality associated with physical love and the delightful but capricious drama of erotic desire. Rather, it might bring to mind the mystical importance of the relationship between master and disciple in the zoharic circle—as indeed in all circles of Jewish mystical teaching through the ages—relationships that are intense, passionate, non-sexual, yet highly erotic. The relations between *Ze'eir Anpin* and *Arikh Anpin* are described in terms of appearance, bathing, rinsing, illumination, and the maternal and nourishing imagery of suckling.[7]

Alongside this, the Idra offers its other mode of connection: coupling, which occurs between the divine Male and Female. The erotic and sexual connection between the bodily parts and genitals, the delight of the act, and the life that they engender, comprise a profoundly felicitous language of connection, as does the encounter between their faces.

The centrality of the theme of relationality and interconnectedness in the Idra explains the dominant focus on the divine face and genitals. These are the zones of contact that engender the very possibility of a relationship with another. The Idra thus places at its center the message that relationships and interconnectedness are a basic precondition for the emergence and evolution of being itself—whether divine or human. Furthermore, these modes of connection are primal, preverbal, primordial. In the gaze of the youth toward the elder there are infinite worlds, for the most part existing beyond the boundaries of speech. The gaze between the masculine and feminine faces at the time of coupling generates passion and joy, tension and release, and the desire to be included and enveloped in the other.

Alongside gazing and coupling between the divine *partsufim*, another channel of connection, more concealed but highly significant, must be acknowledged: relationships of human beings of flesh, blood, and spirit with the Divine in its human aspects. In the Idra, human beings do not form a link with an abstract God but rather with one with an image and likeness, one in whose image humans themselves were created. The Idra's identification of the righteous with *Ze'eir Anpin* indicates that, just as *Ze'eir Anpin* is able to establish a connection with *Arikh Anpin*, human consciousness is structured in such a way that it too can make the same connection. We are invited to mimic the activity of *Ze'eir Anpin*, who turns toward *'Attiqa* to be illuminated in his light. Thus, we too may be refined, and we too may attain a balance between the impulses of Love (*Ḥesed*) and Judgment (*Din*). In such a manner, we just might be able to encounter our fellow human beings and the world in a spirit of greater benevolence.

A Song of Praise to Adam: Humanity, the Body, and *Eros* In the Idra Rabba, we find a sublime song of praise, unparalleled in Jewish literature, to *Adam* and the human likeness, to the existence of the human within the Divine and the Divine within the human. At the conclusion of the *tiqqunim* of *Ze'eir Anpin*'s beard, Rabbi Shim'on makes the following proclamation:

> The principle of all: The Ancient of Ancients and *Ze'eir Anpin* are all one—He was all, is all, and will be all; He did not change, will not change, does not change. He is arrayed in these enhancements—an image comprising all images, an image comprising all names [. . .] when diadems and crowns conjoin in total perfection. Therefore the image of *Adam* is the image of those above and those below, who are included in him. Since this image includes above and below, the Holy Ancient One arrayed His adornments and those of *Ze'eir Anpin* in this image. (Zohar 3:141a–b; trans. Matt 8:426)

Adam is the comprehensive image, the depiction that contains all dimensions of the cosmos, both godly and human. Thus, when the Divine seeks to take on a form, to be configured and adorned, to enable existence and encounter it, *this* is the form that is chosen. The human figure is already present, concealed within the very beginnings of creation, within the head of the most Ancient and Hidden God. Despite its profound strangeness and primordiality, *'Attiqa*'s face is basically human. The Adamic or human quality gradually develops and unfolds into the face of *Ze'eir Anpin*, YHVH, whose face is still more human—containing both Love (*Ḥesed*) and Judgment (*Din*). This process comes to its ultimate fullness and refinement in the form of the divine

Male and Female, each now endowed with a complete body, who engage in face-to-face sexual coupling with one another.[8] In other words, as the Idra frames it, more than God is anthropomorphic (human in form), human beings are theomorphic (divine in form). Human beings were created in the image of God-in-the-image-of-Adam—this divine *anthropos* is the blueprint, the seal or mold of all of humanity.

It must be emphasized that the Idra Rabba does not refer to the qualities of *Adam* only in an abstract or conceptual sense, but also to the human form, the body and physicality of the Male and Female. The Idra considers the body to be something sublime, defining wholeness and holiness. The face and the body are the space in which the Divine realizes itself, and they precipitate the encounter and connection between the human and divine dimensions. Implicitly, whatever does not belong within the human body is distant, impure, and dangerous. In addition, this body is not neutral—it is sexual and erotic, thereby marking *eros* and sexuality as sanctified in the Idra Rabba. The Idra's choice of embodiment as a legitimate theological approach makes communication with the Divine possible, through various channels simultaneously: sensory, emotional, conceptual, imaginal, and/or abstract.

The Adamic image, encompassing all dimensions of reality, receives a heightened expression in a moment that is understood as one of the important aims of the unfolding of reality as presented in the Idra: the penetration of the supernal spirit, exhaled from the mouth and nose of *'Attiqa Qaddisha* into the very depths of *Adam*'s being. Not only does the divine *Adam*—that is, *Ze'eir Anpin*—have the distinction of containing *'Attiqa*'s spirit-breath, the human Adam also carries it within. The image in which human beings are created is that of God as Male and Female; thus, flesh-and-blood human beings, male and female, are the sanctuary of the hidden spirit that issues forth from *'Attiqa*. Implicitly, sexual coupling between human beings enables the conjoining of worlds and divine faces.

It would be impossible to overstate the power of the Idra's conception, according to which the wholeness of a human being—whether in the divine or human realm—is only fully realized in face-to-face sexual coupling between male and female. The language that is consistently applied to the sexual act, at every stage, is that of *bissum* (aromatizing), illumination, and blessing. In continuity with the tradition of the Song of Songs and its interpretive tradition, and alongside the erotic language of the main body of the Zohar, the Idra Rabba discusses sexuality and the sexual organs in an extremely daring and direct manner. In their ideal state, they are charged with the highest degree of sanctity.

This song of praise comes to its true climax only later, in the Idra Zuṭa. The Companions who gather in the Idra Rabba do so in order to begin a cosmic task of *tiqqun*, an alignment that moves from above to below: from the simple to the composite, from the sublime to the corporeal, from the conceptual to that which has a face, from the Divine to the human. The Idra Rabba begins with profound and hidden primordiality, and after a long process of unfolding and unfurling, concludes with the world of Adam. The product of the process of configuration and alignment is Adam, complete, the fruit of the fragrant coupling of the Male and Female—a being whose flow of Judgment is regulated, who contains the spirit of *'Attiqa Qaddisha*. But the ultimate conjunction between the divine and human worlds takes place in the moments of Rabbi Shim'on's death, at the conclusion of the Idra Zuṭa, as he undergoes a transformation, and in his transpersonal mode of being, he comes to personify the divine quality of the *sefira* of Foundation (*Yesod*). Rabbi Shim'on embodies the phallus, the final and critical link that enables the ultimate connection between the divine masculine and feminine, and between the human and divine realms. At the end of the Idra Zuṭa, the process of bringing together the many dimensions of reality thus comes to its conclusion. There is no doubt that from this point of view, one can identify the broad contours that bind the Idras together—from the opening passages of the Idra Rabba to the concluding lines of the Idra Zuṭa—like conscious and deliberate strokes of an artist's brush.

As we have seen, the Idra Rabba is a continuation and amplification of the Jewish tradition of anthropomorphism, and it stands in steadfast opposition to the competing Jewish cultural trends of abstraction and transcendentalism. Kabbalah developed and refined Jewish anthropomorphism by fashioning the divine figure as one that contained within its unity a male and female body, and by asserting that this principle of pairing exists already within the Godhead and that it is a vital component in ensuring the very stability of the cosmos.

Patience and Length-of-Breath An additional insight that arises from the Idra Rabba touches upon the centrality of patience and breath. The very being of *Zeʿeir Anpin*, and therefore the existence of human beings who are created in his image, is dependent upon the quality of patience: the ability to breathe, to let go, to fill with breath and forgiveness. The Idra describes at length the divine anger of the impatient God of Judgment. The task of the participants in the Idra is to transform the wrathful, quick-breathed face of *Zeʿeir Anpin*—to flood it with the healing length-of-breath that issues from *Arikh Anpin*, and fill it with mildness and Compassion. In this sense, the Idra's project of *tiqqun* is a development upon Moses' task, when he stood before the wrathful Deity bent on destroying the Israelites. Moses invokes God in the language of *erekh apayim* (length of breath), reminding God of his innate ability to let go of his anger and be filled with the slower breath of forgiveness. Now, in the Idra, with the heavenly Torah in danger of being annulled, and while divine impatience and anger are dominant, Rabbi Shimʿon and his Companions are charged with the task of using Love and Compassion to restore divine patience and length of breath. With fine psychological insight, the Idra teaches us that to attain and produce the extended, long breath of patience, one must cultivate a relationship with *Arikh Anpin*, allowing for a positive experience of being seen by that aspect of the Divine. The remedy for our own impatience may be the fostering of a connection with a Divinity whose very being is patience and breath.

Rabbi Moses Cordovero provides us with a striking example of a traditional kabbalist who understood the Idra in such a way. He dedicated the first section of his work *Tomer Devorah* (Deborah's date palm) to a spiritual practice derived from the Thirteen Attributes of Mercy in *Arikh Anpin*'s beard. Cordovero instructs people to emulate the divine attributes of *Arikh Anpin* in their interpersonal behavior and to learn the secret of patience from them.[9]

The Idra's insight on this point carries great psychological and spiritual significance on a human level. Human anger is presented here as being in clear opposition to wisdom, while patience is precisely that which creates the possibility of creation. I believe that one of the great lessons the Idra Rabba can teach us on a practical level is precisely this—internalizing the vital importance of patience.

In the last two chapters, I have examined the themes that recur throughout the Idra Rabba, providing the reader with a number of lenses through which to consider this text. It emerges as a great work of art that presents profound and complex themes, which it dares to address in visionary terms of narrative, image, hymn, and exegesis. Indeed, there is no doubt that as artists, the authors of the Idra deftly engage both hemispheres of the brain, left and right. Passages of tremendous exegetical and verbal virtuosity are integrally connected with images, sensations, and figures from the vast expanses of the subconscious. One can sense how much the authors of the Idra wanted to emphasize that human consciousness is neither mechanical nor rigid. The Idra's discourse points to human consciousness not as existing in a binary mode, in which the concrete and the abstract are mutually exclusive, but as characterized by spaciousness and flexibility. Various kinds of concrete, visual, and personal concepts dwell within it, alongside abstract thought that grasps existence and the Divine in terms of values and qualities. It is only the coexistence of these elements that enables the creation of great art.

During the first part of this book, we have explored the Idra from a panoramic and inclusive point of view. We are now prepared to enter the second part of the book and to approach the text, the scriptural interpretations, and the narrative and images that are woven from them, in order to become acquainted with the Idra Rabba itself, up close and unmediated.

PART 2

8

Entering the Idra Rabba

The fabric of the Idra Rabba is woven from scriptural interpretations that discuss the divine realms and from the narrative of Rabbi Shimʿon's circle. The work begins with a stirring scene in which Rabbi Shimʿon and his disciples gather to configure and heal the face of God.

The story is framed as an ancient mishnah, a classical rabbinic oral tradition. The opening lines describe Rabbi Shimʿon, the Zohar's hero, addressing a question to his disciples—a question that leaves more hidden than revealed:

> It has been taught: Rabbi Shimʿon said to the Companions, "How long will we sit on a single-based pillar?" (Zohar 3:127; trans. Matt 8:318)

The art of beginning is an important matter, and one can only make a first impression once. These puzzling opening words mark the beginning of a long exposition, in which the earthly and divine characters of the Idra Rabba will be introduced, as will the distress, the vision, and the motivation that led to the gathering. This exposition, the focus of the present chapter, tells us much about the authors and editors of the Idra and about what they wished to express in the words and images we encounter at the outset of the work. As this chapter reveals something of the mysteries of the prologue, we shall see that it is a key that ensures safe entry into the Idra Rabba, its scriptural interpretations, and the earth-shaking events that occur within it.

The opening scene of the Idra is constructed as a series of statements brimming with pathos, ritualistic gestures, and scriptural interpretations, layered upon one another. These all amplify the mystical and revelational tension, the sense of urgency and drama bound up with the gathering that is now taking place, and they thus establish its status as a sublime event. The opening scene prepares the readers' minds to recognize that, in the pages that follow, they will encounter the story of an event unlike any other that has ever transpired, and perhaps unlike any that *will* transpire until the messianic period. However, alongside its dramatic quality, for those with a firm grounding in the Zohar, the Idra's rallying cry is also marked by a degree of familiarity; the characters, and indeed, some of the events and scriptural interpretations, bear a clear affinity with the best of zoharic poetics.

The opening scene is impressive on its own, even without a full comprehension of its meanings, allusions, and mysteries. Indeed, its power may rest precisely on this. It fuses narrative, drama, midrash, ritual, and pathos into a splendid choreography. This inspires fear, but at the same time, it seduces the reader, tempting her to join the Companions and boldly enter the next stages of the ceremony. I shall present the opening scene as a whole, and only afterward will we examine its individual components, each of which contains fundamental themes of the Idra in condensed form. Each and every line of this rich and dense passage is in turn laden with meanings that operate on various levels, interwoven with one another and illuminating the scene from different angles.[1]

> It has been taught: Rabbi Shim'on said to the Companions, "How long will we sit on a single-based pillar? For it is written: *Time to act for YHVH—they have violated Your Torah* (Psalms 119:126). Days are few and the creditor is pressing. A herald proclaims every day, but Reapers of the Field are few and at the edges of the vineyard, not noticing or knowing properly where the place is.
>
> "Gather, Companions, at the threshing chamber, wearing coats of mail and lances! Arm yourselves with your equipment: with counsel, wisdom, understanding, knowledge, vision, hands, and feet. Proclaim as your king the one who has power of life and death, so that you may

decree words of truth, to which the holy ones of the Highest listen, which they delight to know and hear."

He sat down and wept. He said, "Woe if I reveal! Woe if I do not reveal!"

The Companions who were there kept silent. Rabbi Abba rose and said, "If it pleases my Master, behold what is written: *The secret of YHVH is for those who revere Him* (Psalms 25:14), and these Companions revere the blessed Holy One and they have already entered the Holy Assembly of the Dwelling, some of them entering and emerging."

It has been taught: The Companions were numbered in the presence of Rabbi Shim'on, and they were: Rabbi El'azar, his son, Rabbi Abba, Rabbi Yehudah, Rabbi Yose son of Ya'akov, Rabbi Yitsḥak, Rabbi Ḥizkiyah son of Rav, Rabbi Ḥiyya, Rabbi Yose, and Rabbi Yeisa. Extending hands to Rabbi Shim'on, raising fingers above, they entered the field among the trees and sat down.

Rabbi Shim'on rose and offered his prayer. He sat down among them, and said, "Let each one place his hands on my potent breast."

They placed their hands, and he grasped them.

He opened, saying, "*Cursed be the man who makes a carved or molten image—a craftsman's handwork—and sets it up in secret!*" And they all called out and said, "Amen."

Rabbi Shim'on opened, saying, "*Time to act for YHVH—they have violated Your Torah* (Psalms 119:126). Why is it *time to act for YHVH*? Because *they have violated Your Torah*. What is meant by *they have violated Your Torah*? Torah above, which is nullified if this Name is not actualized by its enhancements. This is addressed to the Ancient of Days. It is written: *Happy are you, O Israel! Who is like you?* (Deuteronomy 33:29), and it is written *Who is like You among the gods, O YHVH?* (Exodus 15:11)."

He called Rabbi El'azar, his son, and seated him in front of him, with Rabbi Abba on the other side. He said, "We are the sum of the whole. Now the pillars have been firmly established."

They were silent. They then heard a sound and their knees knocked together. What sound? The sound of the winged assembly on high assembling.

Rabbi Shimʿon rejoiced, and said, "*I have heard Your sound; I am afraid* (Habakkuk 3:2). There it was fitting to be afraid; for us the matter depends on love, as it is written: *Love your neighbor as yourself* (Leviticus 19:18),[2] *You shall love YHVH your God* (Deuteronomy 6:5), and it is written *'I have loved you,' says YHVH* (Malachi 1:2)."

Rabbi Shimʿon opened, saying, "*One who goes about gossiping reveals a secret, but the faithful of spirit conceals a matter* (Proverbs 11:13). *One who goes about gossiping*—this verse is difficult: since it says *gossiping*, why *one who goes about*? It should say, *a man who is gossiping*. What is meant by *one who goes about*? Well, if someone is unsettled in spirit and untrustworthy, whatever word he hears moves around inside him like a thorn in water, until he casts it out. Why? Because his spirit is unstable. But of one whose spirit is stable, it is written *but the faithful of spirit conceals a matter. The faithful of spirit*—of stable spirit. The matter depends on the spirit.

"It is written: *Do not let your mouth make your flesh sin* (Ecclesiastes 5:5), and the world endures only through secrecy (*raza*). Now, if in mundane matters secrecy is necessary, how much more so in the most mysterious matters of the Ancient of Ancients, which are not transmitted even to supernal angels!"

Rabbi Shimʿon said, "I will not tell the heavens to listen, nor will I tell the earth to hear, for we sustain the worlds."

It has been taught—mysteries of mysteries: When Rabbi Shimʿon opened, the earth quaked and the Companions trembled. He revealed in mystery, and opened, saying [. . .] (Zohar 3:127b–128a; trans. Matt 8:318–325, emended)

Sitting on a Single-Based Pillar

It has been taught: Rabbi Shimʿon said to the Companions, "How long will we sit on a single-based pillar (*be-qayma de-ḥad samkha*)? For it is written: *Time to act for YHVH—they have violated Your Torah* (Psalms 119:126). (Zohar 3:127b; trans. Matt 8:318)

The opening words of Rabbi Shimʿon, the great teacher summoning his disciples to assemble, are a question, a protest, and a proclamation. It is an enigmatic opening passage, but it is nonetheless clear that Rabbi Shim'on is pointing to the fact that there is something deeply troubling in the present reality, that things cannot continue as they are, and that the present state of affairs must be changed.[3] The choice to begin a manifesto such as the Idra with a question, with an expression of astonishment that opens up new avenues of response, is nothing short of fascinating. As we shall now see, the personal, national, earthly, and divine meanings of this question are many, and are deeply interconnected.

What, then, does it mean to exist "on a single-based pillar"?

Let us begin with the literary world of the Zohar's characters. Rabbi Shim'on may be saying that he cannot (or does not wish to) continue to be the sole teacher—one pillar—among his disciples and that additional teachers/pillars must be established alongside him.[4] From classical rabbinic literature, Rabbi Shim'on is familiar to us as a figure who considers himself superior, unique in his generation. The Zohar only deepens the singular aspects of his character.[5] His words here emphasize the deep loneliness inherent in such a state, in which he is the only one to receive and transmit the supernal mysteries. Rabbi Shim'on thus seeks to establish a relationship with the wise Companions, "the Reapers of the Field," whose existence will expand and broaden the foundations upon which the world stands. Indeed, in the continuation of the passage, Rabbi Shim'on will proclaim that *three* pillars have already been erected—himself, Rabbi Abba, and Rabbi El'azar —and that the members of his circle are the pillars of the world.

Beyond this, "a single-based pillar" refers to the world in its entirety. In the Talmud, there is a discussion about what the world stands upon, and following a string of answers, we reach the final response: "The world stands upon a single pillar, called Righteous (*tsaddiq*), as it is said: *The righteous is the pillar of the world* (Proverbs 10:25)."[6] This pillar is the righteous human being, who functions as an ethical foundation for the world. However, in *Sefer ha-Bahir* (Book of Brilliance), an early work that provided the framework for much of kabbalistic discourse, mythical and divine dimensions are attributed to this righteous human pillar:

> There is a single pillar from earth to the heavens, and its name is Righteous (*Tzaddik*), named for the righteous ones (*tzaddikim*).

> When there are righteous (*tzaddikim*) in the world it is strengthened and if not, it is weakened.
>
> And it bears the whole world, as it is written, "The Righteous One is the foundation of the world."
>
> And if it is weak, the world cannot endure. Therefore even if there is only one righteous person (*Tzaddik*) in the world, that one upholds the world.[7]

The Bahir's pillar is cosmic or divine; however, its fate depends upon earthly, righteous human beings. In kabbalistic literature following the Bahir, and in the intellectual milieu in which the Zohar was produced, the pillar became the primary representation of the *sefirah* of Foundation (*Yesod*), a divine quality of flowing bounty, transmission, and dissemination that is associated with male sexuality and *eros*, and that is symbolized by the phallus.[8] The phallic pillar of Foundation, the *axis mundi*, upholds and supports the spatial expanse of the world, ensuring that heaven and earth do not collapse into one another. At the same time, it functions as a channel between heaven and earth, enabling transmission and flow between them, sustaining and animating all existence.

In light of these traditions, Rabbi Shim'on's objection to a mode of existence founded upon a single pillar represents an attempt to reopen the question of the foundations upon which the world is based. It may be that he believes that existence is not sufficiently stable when it rests upon the pillar of Foundation. According to the kabbalistic conception reflected widely in the main body of the Zohar, the ideal functioning of the *sefirah* of *Yesod* is dependent on two important factors: the flow of divine bounty that descends to it from the higher *sefirot*, and the conduct of the feminine *sefirah* of Sovereignty (*Malkhut*), symbolized by "the Earth," which Foundation fertilizes and fructifies. However, this ideal erotic dynamic of a desirous and flowing connection between the *sefirot* does not reflect existence as it is familiar to us. Improper conduct on the part of human beings ruptures the connection between earth and the pillar. The pillar is not strengthened, divine bounty does not pass through it, coupling does not occur in the proper manner, and the Earth (Sovereignty or *Malkhut*) grows parched. Thus, Rabbi Shim'on's call may represent a desire to remedy this faltering erotic dynamic with the help of the Companions, and to establish a new structure that enables a vivifying and sustaining flow of divine bounty, ensuring the endurance of all existence.

Another perspective on the pillar's solitariness is highly personal, and touches upon the figure of Rabbi Shim'on himself. In the Zohar, Rabbi Shim'on is understood—both by himself and by his disciples—to be a human manifestation of the *sefirah* of Foundation (*Yesod*) in the world.[9] He is therefore the living pillar that establishes and upholds the world, ensuring that all divine influx is channeled into the human realm, and facilitating the transmission of divine mysteries to his disciples. The potency of the divine pillar of the world, as well as the potency of Rabbi Shim'on, the human being and master, are dependent on many factors. His introductory words reveal that the project of nourishing and sustaining existence places the Foundation in too isolated and solitary a position. It cannot be sustained. Something must change.

Reading Rabbi Shim'on's call in light of the Idra's own mythical-theological discourse raises another possible avenue of interpretation. Such an interpretation becomes clear only to a reader who reads the prologue of the Idra after having already become acquainted with its distinctive religious language, which describes the Divine through the paradigm of *partsufim* rather than *sefirot*. In light of this unique theology, Rabbi Shim'on's claim is that Judaism has come to rest upon God as *Ze'eir Anpin* alone, the small and impatient face that is associated with law and the creation, and lacks a vital connection with God as *'Attiqa*—the wellspring of all things, absolute Compassion—and with the feminine aspect of the Divine. An existence that rests upon only one aspect of the Godhead is fundamentally imbalanced, and lacks the bounteous flow that is generated only when the various divine faces are aligned with one another.

In a more inclusive sense, Rabbi Shim'on's words may refer to the inherent danger in any solitary mode of being that lacks a face-to-face relationship with the other. A lack of balanced and mutually complementary relationships—whether they are between fellow human beings, man and woman, male and female, or complementary qualities such as Compassion and Judgment—threatens stability, vitality, *eros*, and divine bounty. Indeed, immediately following the Idra's opening scene we encounter the myth of the kings of Edom, which will be discussed at length in the next chapter, describing the unsustainability of a solitary mode of being that lacks relationality.

Thus, the opening words of the Idra are a cry, a proclamation that a mode of being that rests upon a single pillar is fundamentally unsustainable. The full extent of the Idra's allusions, some of which we have discussed here, is gradually revealed to us as the work progresses. The fascinating thing about the Idra—indeed, about zoharic literature in general—is that the various planes on which the opening section can be interpreted are superimposed upon one another like transparent layers. The layers do not negate one another, but rather supplement each other, enriching and adding further complexity to the whole.

Time to Act for YHVH

Rabbi Shim'on's next statements draw a connection between his own words and the verses of the Hebrew Bible. Rabbi Shim'on is "the Light of the Torah," and his chief tool is the interpretive and creative reading of biblical verses.

He begins with the verse *Time to act for YHVH—they have violated Your Torah* (Psalms 119:126), which carries a rich set of cultural associations. Classical rabbinic literature presents two fundamental interpretive possibilities for this verse. The first possibility is to read the verse in its order, from beginning to end: Now is a time to act for YHVH, a time that demands a special mobilization for the sake of God. Why? Because people have violated his Torah. Desecration of the Divine, or denigration or violation of the Torah, obligates us to gird ourselves with might, and *to act* vigorously to fulfill God's word and law. According to the second possibility, the verse is read in reverse: *They have violated Your Torah* (*heferu toratekha*) is understood as a command (*haferu*, "violate!")—one must rise and act, even in formal violation of the Torah, in order to respond to the urgent need *to act* for the sake of God.[10] This exegetical possibility presents a radical interpretation of the verse, according to which—despite an awareness that changing the Torah is forbidden—in troubled circumstances one may perform acts that violate norms or traditions in order to rectify the situation or reassert God's place in the world.[11] In addition to these two readings, another concept appears elsewhere in the Talmud, in the name of Hillel the Elder, in association with this verse. According to this formulation, at times during which the connection between the Torah and human beings is ruptured, one must act—gathering the people together, standing in protest and rebuke, in order to reinforce that connection and endear the Torah to human beings:

> It is taught: Hillel the Elder says: When people gather in, scatter; when people scatter, gather in. [. . .] If you see a generation that does not cherish the Torah, gather. As it is said, *Time to act for YHVH—they have violated Your Torah* (Ps. 119:126).[12]

In what follows, Rabbi Shim'on will provide the verse with a new and daring meaning, but for the moment the verse resonates with the various rabbinic interpretations, thereby establishing the scene as one fraught with fatefulness, bearing upon the very connection between human beings, the Torah, and God.[13]

Summoning the Companions

After Rabbi Shim'on's initial proclamation (framed as a question), and the second (achieved through biblical citation), a third proclamation is issued. Paraphrasing a passage in the Mishnah,[14] it declares:

> Days are few and the creditor is pressing. A herald proclaims every day, but Reapers of the Field are few and at the edges of the vineyard, not noticing or knowing properly where the place is. (Zohar 3:127b; trans. Matt 8:318)

The measured and rhythmic words evoke a rich set of images, communicate a sense of urgency and pressure, and highlight the dearth of people properly equipped for the work. At first blush, we might think we are indeed dealing with an early rabbinic text from the cultural context of the Mishnah, addressed to agricultural laborers who work on the land, in the field and the vineyard. However, just like the realistic account in the original passage in the Mishnah (a short day, much work, slothful workers, a great reward, a pressing master), the opening passage of the Idra carries a religious valence. The field and the vineyard, the days, the creditor, and the herald—all these are symbols for a different mode of being, peering out from behind the agricultural scene.

Through a zoharic lens, the mishnaic terms may be translated as follows: there is no time; the prosecuting power of harsh Judgment is placing pressure on the world, as is the power of evil. Perhaps in the very term "days" there is a reference to the *sefirot*, sometimes called "days," as being in a state of contraction and constriction. Loud voices of warning respond to the problematic state of affairs: the blasting voice of the divine herald, the sound of the Torah's words, the reproving voice of the teacher. From these, there emerges a call for healing and repair in the religious, conceptual, and divine field.[15] The labor is imposing and intensive, and those capable of engaging in it are small in number. They are the "Reapers of the Field," a reference to the enlightened ones, the mystics, in zoharic literature. The field that they harvest—from which they reap spiritual fruits and nourishment—is the field *Shekhinah*. She is called Ḥaqal Tappuḥin Qaddishin, the Field of Sacred Apples.[16] These enlightened figures are few and far between, and they are scattered "at the edges of the vineyard"—at the margins of the culture, the religion, or mystical practice. These farmers of the spirit must be brought to the center if they are to generate truly transformative power.

The Idra's call to assemble therefore springs from a sense of emergency, arising from the existence of only one pillar and from the need to act for the sake of YHVH:

> Gather, Companions, at the threshing chamber, wearing coats of mail and lances! Arm yourselves with your equipment: with counsel, wisdom, understanding, knowledge, vision, hands, and feet. Proclaim as your king the one who has power of life and death, so that you may decree words of truth, to which the holy ones of the Highest listen, which they delight to know and hear. (Zohar 3:127b; trans. Matt 8:319–320)

Two images come to mind upon reading these lines. The first is a colorful medieval image: the call to the Order of Knights to come and swear fealty to their lord and king, for whom they will take on any mission, prepared to battle to the death. The second image is older, and belongs to inner-Jewish cultural discourse, and more specifically to the world of classical rabbinic literature: the creative students of the Oral Torah are described as warriors on a battlefield, waging the "war of Torah" and willing to die for its sake.[17] The motif of the heroes of the beit midrash (study house) at war, transforming from enemies to lovers through the course of the battle, is appropriated from rabbinic sources by the Zohar, which describes the Companions as the warriors of the Torah and the *Shekhinah*.[18]

The knights of this order carry the weapons and ammunition of their personalities—wise counsel, discernment, heart. They are summoned first and foremost to coronate their king and to declare their loyalty to him. The king is certainly God, but in this context it also represents the tongues in the mouths of those assembled, which have power over life and death, as stated in the Book of Proverbs.[19] Following in the footsteps of this verse in Proverbs, rabbinic statements, and Sefer Yetzirah (the Book of Creation), the Zohar repeats again and again the idea that the tongue (or speech) possesses the power to generate a blessed or destructive reality.[20] Speech is the primary mechanism for creation in the world of the Zohar. From this point of view, the tongue is the chief human organ in the Idra—after thought and the primal voice, it is the tongue that determines the speech that generates action in the world of deed.

The question and protestation with which Rabbi Shim'on begins his discourse, the proclamation of *Time to act for YHVH*, and the call to the Companions to gather for the mission with their fullest range of powers, together constitute the opening passage of the Idra Rabba. As we have seen, in the background of this dense passage sits a wide and varied range of sources. Perhaps the most striking is the Palestinian Talmud, wherein Hillel the Elder and Rabbi Shim'on are both quoted:

> It was taught: Rabbi Shim'on b. Yoḥai says: If you see that people have forsaken the Torah to a great extent, rise and hold fast to it, and you shall receive all of their reward.
>
> What is the basis for this? *They have violated your Torah; time to act for YHVH.* (Cf. Psalms 119:126)
>
> Hillel the Elder used to say: When they gather, scatter; when they scatter, gather.

> And so would Hillel say: If you see that the Torah is beloved to Israel, and everybody is rejoicing in it, scatter; if not, gather.[21]

This ancient rabbinic source provides a background to various parts of the Idra's opening passage: Rabbi Shim'on's call to arise and hold fast to the Torah in order to further strengthen it, the verse *Time to act for YHVH*, and Hillel the Elder's instruction to gather together when the Torah is not sufficiently cherished by Israel. All of these elements are echoed in Rabbi Shim'on's call to the Companions—the Reapers of the Field, lovers of the Torah—to come together from the periphery of the vineyard, to gather at this time of urgency in order to *act*, to reinforce and strengthen the Torah as it is in danger of vanishing from the world.

"Woe If I Reveal! Woe If I Do Not Reveal!"

After Rabbi Shim'on's dramatic pronouncements, the Idra describes the following scene:

> He sat down and wept. He said, "Woe if I reveal! Woe if I do not reveal!" (Zohar 3:127b; trans. Matt 8:320)

This is a dramatic moment in the life of the Zohar's hero. He sits and weeps. At first glance, it seems that Rabbi Shim'on's tears express his deep uncertainty about whether or not he should reveal these mysteries.[22] Woe if he reveals, for he well knows the enormity of the event at the threshold of which the Companions stand. Through his tears, it is as if he is posing a question about the fate of the gathering: Will the mission be a success? Who will enter in peace, and who will emerge in peace? Woe if he does not reveal, for then the opportunity for the necessary healing and *tiqqun* will be entirely blocked.

Rabbi Shim'on's call generates a tension between revelation and concealment that runs throughout the work from beginning to end. Indeed, the dynamic between the concealment of divine secrets and revealing them is one of the overarching themes of zoharic literature in general, undergirding the erotic poetics of the Zohar.[23] The mystical secret of the Zohar is generated—or revealed—when one enters into the hidden and profound expanses of divinity and humanity. The mysteries are extremely potent. When revealed in an appropriate fashion, they are full of joy, invigorating, and they bring a flow of divine bounty into the world; but when divulged improperly, they are like unveiling nakedness inappropriately, dangerous and destructive. Make no mistake: the intention of zoharic literature is not to promote the values of esotericism and secrecy but to encourage revelation and innovation in the language of religion and divinity.[24] Therefore, the question is not *whether* to reveal, but *how* to reveal.

The Idra begins and ends with the tension between revelation and concealment, with Rabbi Shimʿon ultimately left wondering whether it would not be better if all the Companions—who have undergone potent revelatory experiences and had divine secrets divulged to them—were to be hidden away from the world so that these mysteries will not fall into the hands of the unworthy. In addition, Rabbi Shimʿon entertains the terrifying and scandalous thought that the deaths of three of the Companions in the course of the assembly may be a divine punishment for revealing too much.

However, it must be emphasized that the tension between revelation and concealment is a deliberate and conscious literary component of the text. In order to create tension in the narrative and enthrall the reader, the highly skillful authors carefully selected the formulation *Woe if I reveal! Woe if I do not reveal!* This statement, taken together with the tension between revelation and concealment throughout the Idra, lends an intensity and a drama to the mysteries as they are being revealed that would most likely be lost were they transmitted merely as data, as a treatise composed of statements about the Divine, without a narrative frame.

Taking this line of thinking one step further, perhaps Rabbi Shimʿon's statement is a literary ploy: What kind of reader would not want to know something so enshrouded in mystery, presented with such emotional apprehensiveness? The protagonist's words serve to amplify the content that is about to be revealed; their purpose is to fill the moments leading up to the revelation with tension and pathos.

The hero of the narrative chooses to reveal, just as the authors of the work itself chose to commit it to writing rather than maintaining its secrecy. We can thus say that the opening passage is intended to reveal but also to set a tone of solemnity, heightened emotion, and fatefulness that colors the process of revelation as it unfolds. We, the readers, are invited to internalize this tension.

Based on context and on our familiarity with Rabbi Shimʿon as he appears in the Zohar, it appears that his weeping carries yet another dimension of meaning. He is aware that he is about to divulge profound secrets, and his tears bear witness to the intense emotion that characterizes the moments before revelation. It is as if this account holds within it an ancient biblical image—that of Joseph crying moments before revealing his true identity to his brothers.[25] Joseph's tears express the tension inherent in the knowledge that all that had been concealed and held within is about to burst forth into the open.

Joseph is identified in the Zohar as a figure who embodies the *sefirah* of Foundation (*Yesod*) in a paradigmatic sense. This is the divine quality of abundant bounty, bestowal, instruction, creativity, eroticism, and male sexuality. The peculiar dynamic that characterizes this *sefirah* is the movement, tension, and delight that exists in the space between restraint and flowing forth, between concealment and revelation. Fittingly then, the scene with Joseph and his brothers at the moment of revelation is understood by the Zohar to represent the erotic and sexual tension in the moments of restraint, in the moment before seminal release.[26] The other figure who is identified with the *sefirah* of Foundation in the Zohar is Rabbi Shimʿon himself; therefore his tears, and his ambivalence about whether or not to divulge, amplify the *eros*-filled tension that precedes the release of the secrets.

The master cries, and from this we may learn that crying is permitted, even desirable. The recesses of the heart are unlocked; the tears mark the beginning of the story's flow.

Those Who Enter and Emerge

> The Companions who were there kept silent. Rabbi Abba rose and said, "If it pleases my Master, behold what is written: *The secret of YHVH is for those who revere Him* (Psalms 25:14), and these Companions revere the blessed Holy One and they have already entered the Holy Assembly of the Dwelling, some of them entering and emerging." (Zohar 3:127b; trans. Matt 8:321)

Rabbi Abba, the most prominent of the disciples, addresses Rabbi Shim'on. He indicates that the master's ambivalence has been noted, but his main purpose is to encourage Rabbi Shim'on not to withhold the secret any longer, for the Companions are indeed worthy of hearing and receiving these profound mysteries. Rabbi Abba cites the biblical verse *The secret of YHVH is for those who revere Him* (Psalms 25:14), which was already understood in classical rabbinic sources to refer to non-discursive, revelational, or intuitive knowledge bestowed by the Divine as a gift to those who fear him.[27] One may assume that in addition to their literary context, these words are intended for readers of the Idra, who are like spectators, peering into the gathering over the Companions' shoulders. These words evoke fear, perhaps even trembling, in the reader. Perhaps we are unworthy of the secrets that follow. However, at the same time, they arouse our curiosity and a desire to be included in this extraordinary event.

Another claim that Rabbi Abba makes here in favor of receiving the mysteries is that the circle of Companions has already been tried and tested at a similar gathering: "they have already entered the Holy Assembly of the Dwelling, some of them entering and emerging." The mystical characterization of "entering and emerging" is familiar to us from zoharic literature as one of the many epithets of the circle of Companions.[28] This term links the Companions to the figure of Rabbi Akiva, the hero of the talmudic account of the four sages who entered the Orchard (*pardes*).[29] Out of the four who entered, three did not "emerge in peace": one died, one was "harmed," and one became an apostate. Only of Rabbi Akiva is it said that he "entered and emerged in peace." The Companions see themselves as Rabbi Akiva's heirs insofar as they enter the divine garden, the Orchard, yet also know how to emerge unharmed. Indeed, at the end of the Idra Rabbi Shim'on will praise those of the Companions who have managed to emerge in peace.[30]

This description also refers to the fact that the members of the group are married. Those who "entered and emerged" are those who know the sexual realm and hold its mysteries in their bodies and souls. The expression may also imply that these individuals have had an encounter with dangerous or negative sexuality and have emerged unharmed from this experience.

We may gain a deeper understanding of the nature of "emerging" from the mysterious allusion in Rabbi Abba's words to an earlier assembly focused on the secrets of the Tabernacle, from which not all the participants emerged unharmed. The details of this gathering are not provided in the zoharic corpus as it has reached us.[31] Beyond the question of the nature of that event, we might expect that Rabbi Abba would claim that *all* the participants had entered and emerged and are therefore worthy of participating in the present assembly of the Idra Rabba. What, then, are we to make of his statement that only some of the Companions emerged?

The solution to this mystery is to be found in the concluding passage of the Idra, in which it is related that the souls of three of the participants in the Idra left their bodies. Responding to the question of why these specific participants died, the Idra's narrator responds: "Because on a previous occasion they entered and did not emerge, whereas all the others entered and emerged."[32] It therefore becomes clear that of the Companions participating in the Idra, some had in the past entered and emerged in peace, while others had entered and not emerged in peace. It may be that those who "entered and did not emerge" left a part of their soul in the Orchard, in the expanded state of consciousness of the divine realms, and were no longer fully present in the physical world.[33] According to this explanation, these three Companions emerged from the earlier assembly alive, but their souls remained enmeshed with the supernal realms. Rabbi Abba's allusion to those who did not "emerge" therefore subtly anticipates the deaths of the three Companions at the end of the work.[34]

Another possible interpretation is that, if one is to enter and emerge from the Orchard unharmed, one must be able to transition from mystical words and concepts to the living essence that pulsates beyond them. According to this reading, those who failed to emerge had been exposed to *language* concerning the Divine without having been successfully guided to the unmediated reality to which this mode of discourse refers.[35] They were familiar with the map but not the territory.[36]

The Field and the Threshing Floor

> It has been taught: The Companions were numbered in the presence of Rabbi Shimʿon, and they were: Rabbi Elʿazar, his son, Rabbi Abba,

> Rabbi Yehudah, Rabbi Yose son of Ya'akov, Rabbi Yitsḥak, Rabbi Ḥizkiyah son of Rav, Rabbi Ḥiyya, Rabbi Yose, and Rabbi Yeisa. Extending hands to Rabbi Shim'on, raising fingers above, they entered the field among the trees and sat down. (Zohar 3:127b; trans. Matt 8:321)

The Companions are counted and number nine, and together with their teacher, they are ten, just like the *sefirot* or a *minyan* (a quorum for prayer). The ritual gesture that they make at this point is not entirely clear. They reach their hands toward Rabbi Shim'on, either all together or one by one, and extend their fingers, perhaps as is done during the Priestly Blessing.[37] They then enter and seat themselves in the field, among the trees. We do not know where the Companions have been until this point, perhaps in Rabbi Shim'on's house, but the scene itself takes place outside, in the field. The assembly may take place in the threshing floor of the field, for that is one meaning of the term Idra. Either way, the setting of the Idra is not a study house, a synagogue, or a ruin in the Land of Israel—it is a field, among the trees. This is typical of many zoharic narratives, which take place on roads, in fields, in caves, or by wells. There, in the outdoors, on the road, they may encounter their beloved, the *Shekhinah*; and there the surprises that await them as they journey arouse consciousness and the potential for renewal and creativity in Torah. In this choice, the Zohar patterns itself after the rabbinic stories that describe sages walking on the path. However, the total absence of the *yeshivah* from zoharic narratives seems to express—albeit implicitly—a biting criticism of the Jewish institutions and study houses of medieval Spain.[38]

In addition, the author's choice to locate the Idra in nature echoes two seminal events in Jewish historiography that occurred outside. The first is the revelation at Mount Sinai, at which the Torah was given to the Israelites—outside any human settlement, and outside the Land of Israel. The second is the Vineyard at Yavneh, where the early rabbinic sages gathered after the destruction of the Second Temple in order to decide upon the nature and character of Judaism after the loss of its center in Jerusalem. The gathering in the Vineyard at Yavneh is a symbol of the tremendous creativity of the early rabbinic sages, and of the potential to renew Judaism through daring and creative interpretation of the verses of the Torah. Thus, the foundations of the Written Torah, the Oral Torah, and the Esoteric Torah are all laid down outside the boundaries of human settlement: at the mountain, in the vineyard, in the field.

In addition to the terrestrial aspects of the field, entering into the field may represent a passage into a new expanse of consciousness. The "Reapers of the Field"—the mystics—are invited to enter into their "field," none other than the *sefirah* of Sovereignty (*Malkhut*), which is the field of the zoharic mystic's intention and activity.[39]

Indeed, in the Zohar, the field and the threshing floor (the *idra*) are distinct symbols of femininity. Staging the event in a setting that represents femininity, the *Shekhinah*, implies that the space that awakens to healing and reparation is the feminine, identified in the Zohar as this world, the realm of human beings. The feminine quality of terrestrial existence is expressed in the laws of change and time, and in the cycles of birth, maturation, and decay that characterize it. This is the place from which the call for *tiqqun* comes, and in the end, it will benefit from the bounteous flow of goodness that the event will produce. Here we find an expression of the zoharic law according to which "arousal below" (*it'aruta di-ltata*) precedes and precipitates "arousal above" (*it'aruta di-l'eila*), stimulating the flow of divine bounty from the upper reaches of the supernal realms.

Another possibility, following from this reading, is that the threshing floor represents the female genitalia, the organ within which coupling occurs. Indeed, the rabbinic sages figuratively liken a woman's sex organs to a threshing floor, in which the male threshes and winnows.[40] This is the locus of pleasure and fruition, and also birth into the physical world.[41] In this context we may refer to the Idra Zuṭa, at the end of which the character of Rabbi Shim'on takes on transpersonal and divine dimensions. As a manifestation of the *sefirah* of Foundation (*Yesod*), he actualizes the coupling of the divine Female and Male, and his soul departs at the ecstatic climax of this act of coupling. If we consider the narrative, mystical, and mythical continuity that connects the two Idras—beginning with the Idra Rabba and reaching its climax and conclusion in the Idra Zuṭa—we discover that its ultimate realization is rooted in this feminine dimension. The ultimate purpose of the act of configuration, healing, and reparation is the coupling of the divine Male and Female. This coupling is enabled by Rabbi Shimʿon bar Yoḥai as his soul departs, and it occurs deep within the Female's vagina, which the Idra Zuṭa calls the "point of Zion."

The Adjuration and the Curse

> Rabbi Shimʿon rose and offered his prayer. He sat down among them, and said, "Let each one place his hands on my potent breast."
>
> They placed their hands, and he grasped them.
>
> He opened, saying, "*Cursed be the man who makes a carved or molten image—a craftsman's handwork—and sets it up in secret!*" And they all called out and said, "Amen." (Zohar 3:127b–128a; trans. Matt 8:321–322)

After offering his prayer, Rabbi Shimʿon summons all of the Companions to a ritual that echoes biblical adjurations and covenants. The Companions place their hands on his breast, and he takes them.[42] Here we see the master forming a personal connection with each one of his disciples. We also witness the formation of a fellowship, in which the members are bound to one another through their common affiliation with their teacher.

Since Rabbi Shimʿon's adjuration appears immediately after the ritual hand gesture, we can propose an additional interpretation of the latter. According to the Jewish laws of oaths, one who makes a vow must hold an object before or while making it. It is thus possible that Rabbi Shimʿon takes his disciples' hands as part of his adjuration of them. If this is the case, the origins of this motif may lie in the ancient narrative of Abraham adjuring his servant while the latter places his hand beneath Abraham's thigh, that is, beside his genitals: "Put, I pray you, your hand under my thigh" (Genesis 24:2).[43]

Rabbi Shimʿon cites a verse from the biblical curses and blessings that Moses instructs the Israelites to recite upon Mount Gerizim and Mount Ebal when they enter the Land of Israel. The verse is invoked as if it applies to the present; those whom it forswears are the Companions gathered around Rabbi Shimʿon. Why is this specific verse selected in the present dramatic context? It seems that the injunction is not applied to making depictions or molten images of the Divine—if that were the case, it would have been more appropriate to cite the second of the Ten Commandments: "You shall not make for yourself an image, nor any manner of likeness, of anything that is in heaven above, or upon the earth below, or in the water beneath the earth" (Exodus 20:4). The curse invoked by Rabbi Shim'on is unique in its ceremonial character, which entails a dialogue between the speaker of the curse and the people, creating a firm bond between the participants.

Another element in this verse is the prohibition against keeping a carved or molten image *secretly*. What is the meaning of this clause? Does it imply a twofold transgression—fashioning an abominable idol and concealing it? Or perhaps the emphasis here is on the hypocrisy of establishing some manner of idolatry while concealing it from the community at large? And what might this statement mean in the context of the Idra? This question is sharper still for the experienced reader of the Idra, who knows that as soon as the introductory passage is complete the Companions will begin to expound the fine details of the divine faces (*partsufim*), in highly anthropomorphic terms—indeed, these accounts constitute the majority of the work, they are its centerpiece. The focus on the features of the divine faces and body stands in great tension with the fear of transgression inherent in producing a graven image, and with the curse expressed in the verse cited by Rabbi Shim'on. The reader might well wonder where the boundary lies between configuring or adorning the Divine and a sin that brings a curse upon the sinner.

One possibility for understanding the verse accords well with a passage appearing at the beginning of the Idra in some printed editions of the Zohar. Here, the proofreader who edited and prepared the text for print prefaced the Idra with a clarification, warning the reader not to take physical and anthropomorphic descriptions of God literally. Rather, they are to be understood as a metaphorical account of a deity who possesses no body or face:

> Abraham the Proofreader (*ha-magihah*) said, in order to remove the stumbling-block from the path of readers upon whom the light of the Kabbalah has not yet shone: Let the listener hear, and the discerning understand, that all the expressions cited by the godly Rabbi Shim'on bar Yoḥai in this holy book—such as *the forehead of the skull*, *hairs of the*

> *head, cranial cavities, nose of the Ancient One, ears, hands, feet* [. . .] certainly refer to attributes and *sefirot*, and to esoteric intellectual meanings, and all the body parts referred to by these sages are a similitude and sign for hidden and lofty matters, not [a description] of any corporeal or material thing, God forbid! For there is no similarity in any way whatsoever between [God] (blessed is He!) and us. [. . .] May God deliver us from error. Amen, so be His will.[44]

It thus seems that Abraham the Proofreader understood the biblical curse as a warning to the Idra's readers, urging them to avoid imagining the fine anatomical details in corporeal terms but rather to understand them as a verbal representation of "esoteric intellectual meanings."[45] However, the proofreader's words do not sit well with the Idra's own mode of religious discourse. In contradistinction to the Maimonidean assumption that "there is no similarity in any way whatsoever between [God] (blessed is He!) and us," the entire Idra is deeply concerned with the sanctity of precisely that similarity.[46]

Yehuda Liebes suggests that we read the verse as Rabbi Shim'on's warning to his disciples that they are not to innovate anything from their own minds that is not anchored in the mysteries that they received from him or through his inspiration. According to this interpretation, a *carved or molten image* refers to a thought that is without an authoritative source, without roots. Indeed, this is the general approach of the Zohar: to celebrate and sanctify the "new-ancient": that is, new matters that have never before come to light and yet are nonetheless simultaneously bound to cross-generational tradition and the authority of the master.[47] In a similar fashion, Neta Sobol offers an additional interpretation, suggesting that we see in the curse a warning against leaving the dimensions of the *corpus dei* (*Shi'ur Qomah*) or the limbs of the divine likeness without connection to the words of the Torah.[48]

My own view is that the curse renders the Idra's project more precise, specific, and sharply defined. As we have seen, the Idra seeks to configure or establish anew the personal figures of the Divine, by engaging the imagination and exegetical creativity. The call to religious activity of this sort poses a challenge to the philosophical exegesis of Maimonides, who fought to purify the human consciousness from the dross of anthropomorphism. The Idra seeks to restore these divine figures, whose radiance has dimmed as a result of this philosophical mode of exegesis, to the religious consciousness.[49] In this context, the purpose of Rabbi Shim'on's curse is to emphasize that the effort of the idraic project aims to manifest the *living* presence of the Divine personae, rather than rendering them a static *carved or molten image*—neither (of course) in matter nor in spirit or imagination.

In this sense, Rabbi Shim'on's warning echoes the Tosefta's interpretation concerning the dangers that await the individual who enters the Orchard (*pardes*): "They composed a parable. To what may the matter be likened? To a street passing between two paths, one of fire and the other of snow. If one turns this way, one is burnt [by fire]; if one turns that way, one is burnt [by snow]. What should one do? Walk in the middle, turning neither this way nor that."[50] Rabbi Shim'on, who convenes the gathering, is conscious of the dangers that lie in the path that he seeks to forge to the Divine—namely, the configuration of personal representations of God through living speech. To one side of this path is the pitfall of idolatrous concretization, freezing the living face of the Divine; on the other beckons the trap of philosophical abstraction. This is a dialectical path, which requires us to hold both extremes simultaneously, walking a thin line without falling into the traps that await on both sides.

The meaning of the verse's proscription of concealing an image—*and sets it up in secret*—also requires some investigation. It may be that, in addition to the injunction against rigidifying the unfolding events as a *carved or molten image*, the continuation of the verse warns the Companions against hiding their insights and experiences from the rest of the circle. Once the ring is closed around the participants, their role is to reveal, to innovate, to be daring—and not to conceal.[51] Here, we witness the Zohar's logic concerning the elusive dynamic between revelation and concealment. In contrast with other contexts, in which divulging mysteries is akin to forbidden sex, in the Idra, concealment is even more problematic—even bringing with it curses. If we combine our understanding of the proscription of making a *carved or molten image* with our understanding of the proscription of concealing insights, we may suggest that the Idra's use of this verse reflects a unique consciousness. Although it is virtually inevitable that certain moments will become a *carved or molten image* in the mind of a speaker or listener, as long as this is not concealed, the participants can remain on guard and ensure that whenever something becomes rigid or fixed, it is returned to fluidity.

Time to Act for YHVH—Deepening the Interpretation

> Rabbi Shimʿon opened, saying, "*Time to act for YHVH—they have violated Your Torah* (Psalms 119:126). Why is it *time to act for YHVH*? Because *they have violated Your Torah*. What is meant by *they have violated Your Torah*? Torah above, which is nullified if this Name is not actualized by its enhancements. This is addressed to the Ancient of Days. It is written: *Happy are you, O Israel! Who is like you?* (Deuteronomy 33:29), and it is written *Who is like You among the gods, O YHVH?* (Exodus 15:11)." (Zohar 3:128a; trans. Matt 8:322)

After issuing his warning, Rabbi Shimʿon returns to the verse that he cited when summoning the Companions, and offers his own novel and radical interpretation of it. As we have noted, the verse *Time to act for YHVH—they have violated Your Torah* became an urgent call for change. Apart from its appearance in a classical rabbinic context, as mentioned previously, it is worth noting the dramatic way that Maimonides employs the verse in his introduction to *The Guide for the Perplexed*, granting authority to his own daring project: divulging secrets that will shake and transform the very fabric of religion.[52] In the Zohar itself, in several places, we find a theurgical-kabbalistic interpretation of this verse. *Time to act for YHVH* (*ʿet laʿasot l'YHVH*) is read as follows:

> *ʿet*—read here as a symbol of the *sefirah* of Sovereignty, *Malkhut*;
> *laʿasot*—should be filled, made present, and activated;
> *l'YHVH*—for and with YHVH, the *sefirah* of Beauty, *Tifʾeret*.

The Zohar thus understands the verse as a call to enable the erotic union of Sovereignty and Beauty, who have been separated as a result of human violation of the Torah.[53]

It seems, at first, that Rabbi Shimʿon repeats the verse as it has been interpreted throughout the generations—whether in classical rabbinic literature or the Zohar. However, his words actually present a highly innovative reading. Rabbi Shimʿon suggests a different relationship between the two parts of the verse, relating respectively to *ʿAttiqa* and to *Zeʿeir Anpin*. His reading encapsulates the central purpose of the Idra's gathering, albeit in an encoded and condensed manner. The linguistic basis for this interpretation is the transition from relating to YHVH in the third person (*Time to act for YHVH*) to addressing Divinity in the second person (*they have violated* ***Your*** *Torah*), from which a distinction may be drawn between the objects of the verse. According to this reading, the verse is a call addressed to the Ancient of Days, the Holy Ancient One, and it may be paraphrased as follows: "Since your Torah, O Ancient One, is being violated or nullified, we must act for the sake of YHVH—that is, *Ze'eir Anpin*—so as to reestablish your presence."

The Torah of the Ancient of Days, or the presence of *'Attiqa*, is in danger of disappearing from the world. When such a thing happens, the world recognizes only the divine aspect of YHVH, generating a reality supported by "a single-based pillar." The dynamic connection that should exist between the Ancient of Days (the Divine as the Source of all things) and YHVH (God as king and commander) is disrupted. Religion itself is thereby impaired, for the Deity and our conception of it is reduced to one particular aspect of the Divine. Thus, the verse cries out to *'Attiqa* that something must be done for the sake of YHVH by amplifying *'Attiqa*'s presence through his configurations and adornments (*tiqqunim*).

What, then, is this "Torah above" mentioned in the passage? Immediately after Rabbi Shim'on's words in the opening passage of the Idra, an ancient Torah appears and counsels *'Attiqa* to adorn himself first, to configure and align his own face, and thereby to enable the creation of some existence external to himself.[54] The counsel of this primordial and wise Torah thus initiates the process of the configuration and arrayal of *'Attiqa*, and one might even say that God is configured and generated from this primordial Torah. "Violation" of this Torah would thus seem to be neglect of configuring *'Attiqa*, which obstructs a direct view between the various faces of the Divine, and blocks the bounteous flow emanating from the Holy Ancient One.

This interpretation is striking in its boldness: in the words of Scripture, which in their plain sense refer to YHVH, Rabbi Shim'on sees a direct address to the concealed aspect of the Divine—so concealed that it does not even appear explicitly in the Torah. Also interesting is Rabbi Shim'on's interpretation of the verse's call to "action," for in the course of the Idra it will become clear that *'Attiqa* performs no "acts" at all—indeed, the primordial Deity is not so much an *agent* as a *presence*. Those who *act for YHVH* are the human beings who participate in the gathering and who, through the power of their words, invoke the presence of *ʿAttiqa* with his *tiqqunim*. Furthermore, Yehuda Liebes has raised the possibility of understanding this passage as a call to the Companions to join together in *recreating the Divine itself*—so that the formulation *Time to act for YHVH* is interpreted to mean *Time to make YHVH*.[55]

When fully elucidated, Rabbi Shimʿon's interpretation thus epitomizes the entire Idra's great call concerning the transformation that Jewish religious discourse and experience must undergo. This interpretation is the general principle of the Idra as a whole, while the various parts of the gathering flesh out the details of this principle. However, we must keep in mind that to a reader encountering the text for the first time, knowing little or nothing about it, Rabbi Shimʿon's discussion remains puzzling and obscure (even if it is full of pathos and dramatic force). This new reader does not yet understand the significance of the danger that lies ahead or the magnitude of the process of *tiqqun*—these will become clear only as the Idra progresses, with the presentation of the Companions' scriptural interpretations and the configuration and adornment of the divine *partsufim*.

After interpreting Psalm 119:126, Rabbi Shimʿon recites two additional verses: *Happy are you, O Israel! Who is like you? A people saved by YHVH!* (Deuteronomy 33:29), and *Who is like You among the gods, O YHVH?* (Exodus 15:11). Both verses express wonderment (*Who is like you?*) at uniqueness: Israel's uniqueness among the nations in the first verse, and YHVH's uniqueness among the heavenly beings in the second verse. Rabbi Shimʿon offers no exegesis of the verses, nor does he explain why he chooses to recite them here. However, later in the work, he returns to these verses, explaining them as a testament to the deep connection between Israel and YHVH.[56] Perhaps the recitation of these verses constitutes some kind of response to the hidden question that surely bothers the reader throughout the opening passage of the work: How can Rabbi Shimʿon be so daring, arrogant, even brazen as to "configure" the face of God? The very juxtaposition of the verses to each other responds to this wonderment, albeit in an enigmatic fashion: the bravery and boldness to embark on such an imposing mission is anchored in the similarity, the parallel, the bond between Israel and YHVH. The divine faces depend upon human beings, while the uniqueness of Israel and of God—concerning both of whom it may be said, *Who is like you?*—generates a deep and essential bond between them. Perhaps we ourselves might be bold, and suggest that—just as in the case of the verse *Time to act for YHVH*—Israel is not merely *redeemed* by YHVH but *redeems* him.

Fear and Love

> He called Rabbi El'azar, his son, and seated him in front of him, with Rabbi Abba on the other side. He said, "We are the sum of the whole. Now the pillars have been firmly established." (Zohar 3:128a; trans. Matt 8:323)

After reciting these verses, Rabbi Shim'on seats Rabbi El'azar (his son) before him, and Rabbi Abba (the most senior of the disciples) behind him. Once they are seated, Rabbi Shim'on declares the process of *tiqqun* to have already commenced. Whereas Rabbi Shim'on's complaint at the outset of the Idra was that existence was poised on "a single-based pillar," here he announces that the world has already entered a more stable state, supported by three pillars. Furthermore, these three figures are "the sum of the whole," implying that the remaining Companions are the individual components of this whole. The sequential structure 1-3-10, expressed in the Idra's participants, corresponds with the divine dimensions that are to be configured and adorned: the ten *sefirot* are a kind of particularization of the three divine *partsufim* (*Arikh Anpin*, *Ze'eir Anpin*, and the Female), which themselves emerged from the unitary essence of God.[57]

> They were silent. They then heard a sound and their knees knocked together. What sound? The sound of the winged assembly on high assembling.
>
> Rabbi Shim'on rejoiced, and said, "*I have heard Your sound; I am afraid* (Habakkuk 3:2). There it was fitting to be afraid; for us the matter depends on love, as it is written: *Love your neighbor as yourself* (Leviticus 19:18), *You shall love YHVH your God* (Deuteronomy 6:5), and it is written *'I have loved you,' says YHVH* (Malachi 1:2)." (Zohar 3:128a; trans. Matt 8:323)

The moment of silence, free of speech or motion, is of great importance here. The stillness reveals something new. The Companions tremble at an unfamiliar sound, a sound informing them that the upper world is now rousing, responding to their preparations for the event. Now that the pillars have been erected, the host of supernal angels joins the Companions to listen to their words and participate in the gathering. While the others respond to the presence of the divine realm with fear and trembling, Rabbi Shim'on expresses joy, and thereby attempts to settle the terror that has taken hold of the Companions. His words are among the climactic moments of the Idra's opening passage, and perhaps of the work as a whole: "There it is fitting to be afraid; for us the matter depends on love!" Rabbi Shim'on frames this pronouncement as a grand manifesto, and it is of central importance in understanding the Idra's project and the self-perception of its participants.[58] Here, Rabbi Shim'on distinguishes between an emotional state in which the encounter between humans and the Divine causes great fear and awe, modeled here in the verse from Habakkuk, and an encounter that emerges from love and awakens love. Fear and awe are not rejected as a religious state of mind and spirit, but they belong "there" and in the past; here and now, while the Companions ("us") gather in the Idra, "the matter depends on love." It is as if Rabbi Shim'on is saying, "Here, our language is love. We love God, and God loves us; love is the vessel to reconfigure and heal God, the world, and human beings."

The relationship between fear and love in religious devotion is a familiar subject in various religious contexts, and Judaism is no exception. The God who comprises an aspect of devouring fire, who terrifies human beings, is depicted in the Hebrew Bible: for example, in the narrative of the death of Aaron's sons Nadab and Abihu, who make an offering on the day the Tabernacle is completed. In his work *The Idea of the Holy*, theologian Rudolf Otto distinguishes between human encounters with the Divine or holy that arouse fear (*mysterium tremendum*) and those that arouse attraction and love (*mysterium fascinans*).[59] The Idra Rabba marks a process by which fear, which is appropriate to other settings and times, here makes way for love. But to what is Rabbi Shim'on alluding when he refers to fear belonging "there"? As in other cases in the opening section of the Idra, there are several interpretive possibilities, all of which may be correct.

It is possible that "there" refers to the great historical event of God's revelation to the Israelites at Mount Sinai. This event, at which revelation was translated into law, is described in Scripture as full of fear and terror. In contrast, at the outset of the Idra, we are standing on the threshold of a new revelation, one that occurs with the active assistance of the Companions, the focus and purpose of which is love that will temper the great Judgment that inheres in divinity and in reality.

"There" may also refer to the ground-shaking experience of the prophet Habakkuk, the opening verse of whose ecstatic vision Rabbi Shim'on quotes. God's nearness, or hearing of and comprehending God's tremendous power, fills the prophet with fear. In kabbalistic literature—and in the Bahir and Zohar in particular—the figure of Habakkuk is further developed, and he is presented as an ecstatic mystic, who is occupied with the Work of the Chariot (*Ma'aseh Merkavah*). The verse cited in the Idra appears several times in the more developed myth of Habakkuk's origins and personality that the Zohar weaves, and it may be that Rabbi Shim'on is alluding to parts of this mythical mosaic when he refers to the fear that is appropriate "there."[60]

Another possibility, pointed out by Yehuda Liebes, is that this is a reference to an earlier gathering in which the Companions participated, one dominated by fear. Perhaps this is the earlier Idra alluded to in Rabbi Abba's reference to the Companions who "entered and emerged."

To these possibilities for understanding Rabbi Shim'on's enigmatic words, we may add the interpretation of the verse as it appears in the Idra itself—a kind of riddle posed at the outset of the narrative, which becomes clear only as the plot progresses. During the *tiqqun* of *Ze'eir Anpin*, there appears an interpretation of this verse that we have already encountered in the first part of this book. Here, Habakkuk's fear is understood as a consequence of his encounter with the face of *Ze'eir Anpin*, brimming with Judgment. Meanwhile, the second part of the verse—*YHVH, Your deed, in the midst of years revive it*—addresses the higher face of *Arikh Anpin*, full of Compassion, praying and entreating it to extend life to *Ze'eir Anpin*, thereby soothing the latter's anger.[61]

Thus, according to the Idra, love and fear are relational modes that correspond with the mystic's progressively developing levels of perception of the various aspects or faces of the Divine.

Alongside the loving relationship between humans and the Divine, Rabbi Shim'on's words also allude to the love between the fellow Companions. The gathering described in the Idra demands partnership, loyalty, and love between its participants. Love in general, and love between the Companions in particular, is a cornerstone in zoharic literature, appearing again and again in many different forms.[62] In many zoharic narratives, the intimacy and love between the members of Rabbi Shim'on's circle is richly described, with delight and *eros*.[63] In a quasi-idraic passage that appears in the Zohar (*Aḥarei Mot*), Rabbi Shim'on explicitly discusses the love between his disciples and seeks to encourage and reinforce it:

> And you, Companions who are here, just as you have been previously in love and affection, so from now on: do not part from one another. (Zohar 3:59b; trans. Matt 7:387, emended)[64]

Indeed, in the manuscript version of the Idra available to Moses Cordovero, after proclaiming that "the matter depends on love," Rabbi Shim'on cites the verse *Love your neighbor as yourself* (Leviticus 19:18).[65] According to that version, alongside the love of human beings for the Divine (*You shall love YHVH your God*), and of God for humans (*I have loved you*), love and affection (*ḥavivuta*) is expressed primarily in interpersonal love. In his commentary on this passage, Cordovero writes:

> *Love your neighbor as yourself*: Scripture states concerning one's fellow, *You shall love*; and it states concerning the love of God, *You shall love YHVH your God*. Just as love of one's fellow is love without fear, so one's love of God must of necessity be without fear. Thus, we should not fear, since "the matter depends on love."
>
> And it is written, *I have loved you*: Lest you might think that love of God and love of one's fellow are separate matters, it is written, *I have loved you*.
>
> The meaning of *I have loved* is not that we should fear [God], for the whole intention of one who loves another is that the beloved should love and not fear.[66]

According to this moving interpretation, both God's love of human beings and humans' love for God are derived from the first love: love of human beings for one another. Thus, the love between human companions is a necessary condition for other loving frameworks. And further, just as human love aims to conquer fear—"the whole intention of one who loves another is that the beloved should love and not fear"—the same is true of divine love for humanity.

However, it must be noted that there is a fundamental difference between the love of the Companions that is found in many other zoharic narratives and their love as expressed in the Idra Rabba. In the body of the Zohar, the Companions' love is free-flowing and delightful; in the Idra, it is a tense and restrained emotion. This difference is rooted in the Idra's sense of emergency and in the specific characteristics of its project that make this work so distinct from other zoharic narratives. While in many zoharic narratives we find the Companions meandering and walking about in a leisurely way, in the idraic narrative we find the protagonists on an ominous mission, where each is responsible for fulfilling a vital role.

Containing the Secret

> Rabbi Shim'on opened, saying, "One who goes about gossiping reveals a secret, but the faithful of spirit conceals a matter (Proverbs 11:13). One who goes about gossiping—this verse is difficult: since it says gossiping, why one who goes about? It should say, a man who is gossiping. What is meant by one who goes about? Well, if someone is unsettled in spirit and untrustworthy, whatever word he hears moves around inside him like a thorn in water, until he casts it out. Why? Because his spirit is unstable. But of one whose spirit is stable, it is written but the faithful of spirit conceals a matter. The faithful of spirit—of stable spirit. The matter depends on the spirit.
>
> "It is written: *Do not let your mouth make your flesh sin* (Ecclesiastes 5:5), and the world endures only through mystery." (Zohar 3:128a; trans. Matt 8:324)

In this passage, the master emphasizes the theme of steadfastness of spirit, and the value of keeping a secret, and the importance of grasping the centrality of these two concerns. The Companions are not knights whose mission it is to safeguard material treasures or secrets of state; they are about to receive from one another great spiritual secrets upon which all existence depends.[67] They must contain the unfolding events, speaking of them only within their own circle. To this demand for faithfulness of spirit and containment of secrets, Rabbi Shim'on adds the radical statement that "the world endures only through mystery (*raza*)." Here, the cosmological riddle that has fascinated all cultures—What is the foundation upon which the world rests?—receives a new answer, one that tells us much about the inner world of the Zohar: The root and foundation of all reality is mystery.

Indeed, mystery and the secret (*raza*) stand at the center of the Zohar's world: The secret of divinity, of the human being, of faith, of the soul, the body, Torah, evil. The characters in the Zohar are perpetually devoted to the difficult but delightful project of revealing and concealing, and even creating, the secret. But in the Zohar, the secret is not a concealed body of knowledge that is deemed secret merely because it is transmitted esoterically or orally. Nor is it a specific, static, or univocal understanding that lies beyond the revealed words of the Torah (such as a fixed astrological meaning or certain allegorical readings of biblical verses). Rather, in the Zohar, the "secret" is a fertile, living stratum of reality, pulsating deep beneath the surface of the world as we perceive it. It is gradually unveiled as we come to know, understand, and love the words of the Torah and prayer, and as we contemplate nature and human existence. The secret in the Zohar is made up of the threefold connection between the seeking soul, the object of inquiry (for example, a difficult verse or the dilemma of human suffering), and the conditions of reality (for example, the time of day or a specific festival). The secret disclosed to the kabbalist's mind at one moment is therefore not necessarily the same secret that would emerge at another moment, and the secret that pertains to the structure and character of one soul is not necessarily that which pertains to another. In their mode of living and behavior, the Companions are intently focused on perceiving this stratum of existence, experiencing it, and translating it into images and words.[68]

However, despite the fact that the Zohar's secret is a dynamic reality, it is not entirely malleable and not entirely inarticulable or undefined. The secret is mainly characterized by the connection between a word, verse, image, or event in the temporal realm and some dynamic within the divine realm. The Zohar's protagonists contemplate how human reality, on the one hand, and the Torah, on the other, reflect qualities of motion, obstruction, commingling, or separation within the Godhead. They become acquainted with the relationships between the divine *sefirot*, and with the way that they intersect with human existence, acting upon it and being acted upon by it in turn. In this sense, unveiling the secret reveals the great chain of being that connects all dimensions of existence: from the infinite God to the myriad hues of the distinct and transient world of human existence. Unveiling this secret is no mere theoretical activity. Since it connects the higher and lower worlds, this act of discovery enables the kabbalist to understand what is required in order to amplify the flow of divine bounty into the world. An intimate knowledge of the divine interconnection between all things directs the mystic toward the theurgical practice that will best improve and balance the state of the world.

This being the case, the Zohar does not conceal its secrets from the reader, and for the most part, it does not have an agenda of esotericism that might lead it to hide things from the reader. In the words of Joseph Gikatilla, the Zohar's secrets are "hidden mysteries that are visible to the eye."[69] The knowledge or description of the "esoteric teaching" is written explicitly upon the pages of the Zohar. However, this is merely a sign or a map, pointing the way to the true secret, which is the experiential dimension. The secret itself resides in the experience of standing face to face with the myriad dimensions that lie beyond the physical senses. Thus, for example, in the zoharic work that describes the celestial palaces (Hekhalot), the secrets that lie within them are described as "not capable of being revealed" (Zohar 2:253b [Hekhalot])—other than in an experiential sense. These secrets are thus not to remain hidden as the result of some kind of commandment or desire; rather, their secrecy is anchored in their very essence.[70] Thus, it might be best to describe the Zohar's understanding of the terms *sod* and *raz* as denoting mystery, rather than a body of knowledge that must remain secret.

As the Idra progresses, we learn that divulging these divine secrets brings those who communicate them joy, tears, visions, ecstasy—and it even leads to the deaths of three of these figures. Those who endure the process of revelation and emerge from the Idra in peace do so due to their spiritual and psychological stability, their steadfastness of spirit, and their ability to contain the mystery. Even at this early stage of the Idra, Rabbi Shim'on emphasizes the extraordinary power of the secrets that are to be revealed during this gathering, in comparison with other secrets of the cosmos:

> "Now, if in mundane matters secrecy is necessary, how much more so in the most mysterious matters of the Ancient of Ancients, which are not transmitted even to supernal angels!" (Zohar 3:128a; trans. Matt 8:324)

Heaven and Earth

> Rabbi Shim'on said, "I will not tell the heavens to listen, nor will I tell the earth to hear, for we sustain the worlds."
>
> It has been taught—mysteries of mysteries: When Rabbi Shim'on opened, the earth quaked and the Companions trembled. He revealed in mystery, and opened, saying . . . (Zohar 3:128a; trans. Matt 8:325)

Rabbi Shim'on's words here, which conclude the scene of entering the Idra, are almost unbelievable in their boldness. He presents a reverse paraphrase of Deuteronomy 32:1, in which Moses adjures the heaven and the earth to hearken to his words of rebuke: *Listen, O heavens, and I will speak! Let the earth hear the words of my mouth!* This invocation emphasizes the momentous significance of the events unfolding, but it also entails a warning: the elemental and everlasting entities that uphold the world are present, they are observing, and they will bear testimony in the event that human beings forget these words. Rabbi Shim'on entirely dismisses the need for such testimony. According to him, the world is not governed by the laws of nature; he does not follow the laws of heaven and earth but rather those of human beings, and more precisely, the *tsaddiq* and the Companions. In contrast to Moses, who was afraid and in need of calling upon heaven and earth, Rabbi Shim'on is an elite figure, a symbol of the *sefirah* of Foundation (*Yesod*), the Covenant that upholds the world.[71] This radical statement must be understood against the background of the comparison between Moses' figure and that of Rabbi Shim'on throughout the Zohar. In various ways—sometimes subtle and sometimes quite blunt—the Zohar places Rabbi Shim'on above Moses, the foremost of the prophets.[72]

It would seem that the exclusion of heaven and earth here reflects two distinct aspects. One is physical: Rabbi Shim'on is no longer concerned with the physical heaven and earth. He transcends the physical realm[73] in favor of the divine realm.[74] On another level, heaven and earth represent reality as we conventionally understand it, while the focus of this gathering is on a new covenant, a new heaven and earth, a new reality. Thus, he no longer needs the testimony of heaven and earth.

Conclusion

The opening scene of the Idra is a foundational text, dramatic and awe-inspiring. It contains within it a choreography, a performance, and a manifesto, it is full of mystery, secrecy, and enigma. Rabbi Shimʿon is simultaneously the scene's choreographer and main character: He sits, weeps, rises, prays, extends his hands to his disciples, takes their hands into his bosom, and seats the participants in their appropriate configuration.

The power of this passage lies in its cultivation of a sense of human and cosmic urgency pervading the gathering, using scriptural verses, midrashic sources, and imagery to create a multilayered experience. Given the diversity within this scene, woven as it is from many distinct components, let us briefly review its ritual dynamic: Rabbi Shimʿon's question concerning a reality that rests upon a single pillar; the summons to the mystical warriors to gather together; Rabbi Shimʿon's weeping, centered on the subject of revelation and disclosure; the Companions' extending of their hands to the master, raising their fingers, and becoming a true circle or brotherhood; the entry into the field and sitting within it; Rabbi Shimʿon's prayer; the seating of Rabbi Shimʿon at the center of the circle of Companions; a ceremony of interconnection and adjuration; a warning with a curse; the Idra's first distinctive scriptural interpretation, of the verse *Time to act for YHVH*; the positioning of Rabbi Elʿazar and Rabbi Abba, establishing the three pillars; an awesome experience of celestial sounds; Rabbi Shimʿon's joy at the arrival of the angels; his call to transition from fear to love; a request that the Companions keep the secrets that are to be revealed; and the closing proclamation that the Companions are the pillars or foundations of the world.

Within these constituents of the opening scene of the Idra, the primary themes of the work's entire narrative are contained in a germinal state. The enigmatic verses and puzzling statements that appear here will gradually become clearer as we progress in our close and attentive reading of the Idra.

The opening passage, as we see, presents itself neither as a philosophical treatise nor as an anonymous manifesto. It is written in a personal tone, intimately bound to its characters, to a particular time and place that together generate its powerful emotive quality and sense of urgency. It is an event that takes place between master and disciples, with every stage in the scene oriented toward consolidating a circle of Companions that is bold, absolutely devoted, willing to take risks, and spiritually ambitious. On an architectural and choreographic level, the ceremony presents a symbolic representation of a gradually increasing number of pillars supporting the world. It begins with a single pillar; then three pillars are erected; finally, all ten participants will become pillars of the world. Throughout, the Idra's trajectory may be seen as a dedication or initiation ceremony for these pillars. Each of the disciples will stand in turn and reveal his own uniqueness while fulfilling the mission assigned to him.[75]

9

The Kings of Edom

The First Appearance

After the opening scene, the main body of the Idra commences, replete with its scriptural interpretations and *tiqqunim*. Although we might expect Rabbi Shim'on's first scriptural interpretation to be focused on the Godhead or on the process of emanation, he instead introduces an obscure verse from Genesis that has no apparent connection to the mysteries of the Divine. His interpretation of this verse takes us back to a time that precedes time itself, before language, long before the creation as described in the Torah, and even before the *sefirot* came to be.

> When Rabbi Shim'on opened, the earth quaked and the Companions trembled. He revealed in mystery, and opened, saying, "*These are the kings who reigned in the land of Edom before a king reigned over the Children of Israel* (Genesis 36:31). Happy are you, O righteous ones, to whom are revealed mysteries of mysteries of Torah, which have not been revealed to holy ones of the Highest. Who will examine this? Who will be worthy of this? It is testimony to faith of total faith. May the prayer be accepted, that it may not be considered a sin to reveal this.
>
> "And what will the Companions say? For this verse is difficult, since it should not have been written so, because we see that there were numerous kings before the Children of Israel appeared and before they had a king, so what is intended here? Well, it is mystery of mysteries,

> which humans cannot know or perceive or arouse in their minds." (Zohar 3:128a; trans. Matt 8:325–326)

In this passage we learn that when Rabbi Shim'on began to reveal the mystery of mysteries, the very place quaked and the Companions trembled. Here we have the first appearance of the myth of the primordial kings of Edom, a myth also referred to as the Death of the Kings and, later, in Lurianic Kabbalah, as the Shattering of the Vessels. This motif will appear three times in the Idra Rabba. Rabbi Shim'on emphasizes that this myth is a testimony to faith, a secret that cannot be apprehended in an ordinary state of human consciousness, that cannot even manifest itself or be aroused in such a state of mind. It is such a hidden and concealed mystery that Rabbi Shim'on prefaces his discourse with an entreaty, a prayer that revealing this secret might not be considered a sin.

Before acquainting ourselves with this instance of the motif at the beginning of the Idra, we shall attempt to understand the nature of this myth, its sources, and how one may interpret its various appearances throughout the Idra.

The Kings of Edom: From Scripture to the Zohar

Within the narrative cycle of Jacob in the Book of Genesis, an entire chapter is devoted to an account of Esau's lineage, in the course of which we are told of eight kings who ruled in the Land of Edom before the establishment of an Israelite monarchy. The kings of Edom are listed by name, sometimes along with their cities or fragments of mythical narrative:

> These are the kings who reigned in the land of Edom before a king reigned over the Children of Israel.
>
> Bela the son of Be'or reigned in Edom; the name of his city was Dinhabah.
>
> Bela died, and Jobab the son of Zerah of Bozrah reigned in his stead.
>
> Jobab died, and Husham of the land of the Temanites reigned in his stead.
>
> Husham died, and Hadad the son of Bedad, who smote Midian in the field of Moab, reigned in his stead; the name of his city was Avith.

> Hadad died, and Samlah of Masrekah reigned in his stead.
> Samlah died, and Saul of Rehoboth by the River reigned in his stead.
> Saul died, and Baal-Hanan the son of Akhbor reigned in his stead.
> Baal-Hanan the son of Akhbor died, and Hadar reigned in his stead; the name of his city was Pau, and name of his wife was Mehetabel, the daughter of Matred, the daughter of Me-zahab. (Genesis 36:31–39)

Just as in one of Borges' fantastical stories, this list seems like a text from another reality, belonging to a different order of time, that has been inserted into the narrative flow of Genesis.[1] Indeed, the Idra literature uses these verses to recount a myth concerning primordial entities, prior to creation itself, who are honorably named "kings." This myth is centered around the efforts of these entities to emerge and endure in their existence, and their repeated failure. They fade, and are gathered back in without generating any continuity. The topic of the kings thus requires us to broaden our constricted state of consciousness in order to become receptive to inchoate movements that never attained full and enduring existence, rough drafts of creation that did not succeed, did not emerge into being.[2]

The myth of the kings appears a number of times in the Idras, with some diversity and variation in emphasis. Its "earliest" and most terse formulation is within the enigmatic work Sifra di-Tsni'uta, which will be discussed later. The motif also appears in the Idra Zuṭa, but it appears in its most central and fully developed form in the Idra Rabba—being addressed three times in that work.[3]

In the Idra Rabba, the myth of the kings of Edom initiates each stage of the unfolding of the Divine, appearing slightly differently in each stage, depending on the reality that is coming into being. Rabbi Shim'on first invokes the kings in the opening passages of the Idra Rabba, before the *tiqqun* of *Arikh Anpin*, the initial divine face from which all existence emanates. They are next mentioned before the configuration and adornment of *Ze'eir Anpin*, the dominant figure of God in Jewish consciousness and religious discourse. Finally, they are discussed a third time after the account of the emanation of the feminine aspect of the Divine, before her body is configured and adorned, and prepared for sexual coupling (*zivvug*).

Pre-Creation Processes

In Kabbalah scholarship in the past, there was a widely held view of the narrative of the kings of Edom as a foundational myth concerning the origins of evil in the world, one that describes a cathartic dynamic in which the Divine expunges refuse or evil from within itself. However, in a thorough and detailed study devoted to the various appearances of this motif in the Idra literature and the Zohar, Avishar Har-Shefi suggests a different focus for the myth.[4] He argues that its major focus is not the origin of evil, but rather the attempts at creation that always accompany the beginnings of great works. Thus, every appearance of this motif throughout the Idras depicts initial and unsuccessful attempts to establish existence. The myth of the kings clarifies what *cannot* sustain the world; from this, we learn what *can*.

Indeed, it would seem that the myth of the kings is an expression of the human attempt to inquire into origins, to ponder the question of what came before existence as we know it. It opens a door to inquire into what comes before the Beginning—whether we are referring to the origins of the cosmos or of the Godhead itself.

Within the Hebrew Bible too, one sees an impulse to consider the beginning of beginnings: to explore what preceded the creation of the world as described in Genesis, to imagine cosmogonic processes and inquire into primordial days. This impulse only grows stronger in talmudic and midrashic literature.[5] These matters are fraught with profound questions: Where did we come from? What lies at the foundations of our existence? What mythic-cosmic layers of being lie beyond the reaches of our consciousness? As a mythic response to these philosophical and proto-scientific riddles, the Idra literature offers the story of the Death of the Kings, seeking to enter a mode of reality that begins well before "In the beginning . . ." (the words that open the biblical account of creation). It seeks to inquire into the unfathomable question: What was the nature, the essence, of the Divine before the creation of any other being? What is the process of unfurling and unfolding that leads from absolute infinite being to the world of multiplicity and variegation that we see? And what do human beings stand to learn through becoming acquainted with the process of creation?

An additional way into understanding this myth and its imagery is the contemplation of processes of human consciousness. It seems that, alongside the quest for the origins of being, the authors of the Idra also set out in search of the initial moments in which unified and undifferentiated consciousness begins to become self-aware and to create from within itself.

A unique aspect of the story of the Death of the Kings is its boldly mythical way of describing the drafts of reality that never emerged into being. It would certainly have been possible to describe the primordial flashes of existence in less personal and mythical terms, as is done in other texts. Thus, for example, the Idra Zuṭa describes the processes of creation in a technical manner, as sparks generated by a hammer-blow: " like a blacksmith pounding an iron tool, scattering sparks in every direction; and those flying forth flash and scintillate and are immediately extinguished. These are called Primordial Worlds."[6]

Moses de León chose to describe these modes of existence in a more philosophical fashion:

> Know that before everything, and as the beginning of everything, Wisdom (*Ḥokhmah*) comes into being. For Supernal Crown (*Keter ʿelyon*) is a primordial [and] pure ether that can never be grasped, and there would thus be no existence, for none could comprehend it, for it can never be grasped. [. . .] For while the subtle primordial ether is at a level that cannot be grasped, nothing can endure. Therefore did they say, "creating worlds and destroying them." For all of them need the ether, but the ether cannot be grasped, so they could not grasp it. So all of them were destroyed, as they could not endure. Until the blessed Holy One fashioned a certain ether from that which cannot be grasped, an ether that can be grasped.[7]

This subtle and abstract formulation could not be further from the powerful and personal imagery of the myth of the primordial kings, their ascents and deaths, before the creation of all things.

From this perspective, the myth of the primordial kings represents another layer resting upon the classical rabbinic narratives of archaic creatures and their derivatives and descendants in kabbalistic literature.[8] According to the talmudic legend, the serpent-like Leviathans, primordial sea creatures, were so immense that the reverberations of their lovemaking in the vast oceans threatened to destroy the world. God therefore killed the female and castrated the male. This myth illustrates how, in order to establish an enduring creation, archaic forces such as these must be limited or repressed. So too, in our myth, the primordial kings are sacrificed in the process of moving from formlessness to order, from *chaos* to *cosmos*. They must die, be annulled, or hidden deep in the abyss. But in a timeless or spaceless dimension, death is not a complete or final annihilation. The kings, these fundamental archetypes, change in form, name, and place—but they continue to exist, lurking beyond the boundaries of conscious being.

The Kings of Edom in the Works of Cordovero and Luria

The Death of the Kings occupied a significant place in the kabbalistic literature of 16th-century Safed, particularly in the works of Moses Cordovero and Isaac Luria. These thinkers delved deeply into the myth and transformed it into a comprehensive language, in which one could give utterance to things that preceded our functional and stable reality.[9] These two spiritual giants interpreted the name of each and every king, and traced the contours of the mode of existence peculiar to that king, each in his own unique way. Isaiah Tishby[10] used the myth of the kings of Edom in the Zohar and its later reverberations in the Kabbalah of Cordovero and Luria as a test case through which to examine the dialectical interplay between tendencies toward systematic abstract thought and tendencies toward the mythic and the imaginative throughout the history of the Kabbalah.

Cordovero understood the kings, in their first appearance in the Idra Rabba in particular, not as primordial manifestations of evil but as primal and wondrous forces of creation, striving toward being. In his view, the concealment of the kings is a consequence of the tremendous light of God as *'Attiqa*, before it takes the form of a face that can create boundaries for that light and mediate its intensity.

Luria identified the kings as the shadow side of the *sefirot*, or as *sefirot* in an immature state. In his view, the kings are a kind of archaic and imbalanced prototype of entities that will later transform, in proper order, into the ten *sefirot*. Luria developed this mythical motif with exceptional insight, profoundly contemplating the question of how the remains of the fallen kings nonetheless fit into the stable and enduring reality of the *partsufim*.

According to his approach, the kings, their deaths, their dismemberment into particles or sparks, and the possibility of integrating them into the stable and orderly world—these are the very substance and drama of existence, from the creation until the coming of the Messiah. The better-known Lurianic myth of the Shattering of the Vessels and the human role in raising their sparks is a variant of Luria's understanding of the Death of the Kings. Ultimately, the process of sorting the sparks of the kings and integrating them into the figure of *Adam* will bring human history to its completion and conclusion.

The Kings in Sifra di-Tsniʿuta

As noted previously, the "earliest" attestation of the motif of the kings within the zoharic corpus is in Sifra di-Tsniʿuta. This densely mythical work describes—in its distinctive visionary poetry—the gradual formation of the divine faces, and the manner in which existence and its properties emerge. The Idra Rabba treats this work as an ancient source to be interpreted, and this also holds true of the myth of the kings.[11]

In the opening lines of the work, a primordial tradition (*mishna*) is transmitted, spoken in allusions and cloaked in mystery:

> It has been taught: The Book of Concealment, a book balanced on scales. For until there was a balance, they did not gaze face-to-face, and the primordial kings died and their adornments vanished and the earth was nullified. Until the head of Desire of all Desires arranged and bestowed garments of glory. (Zohar 2:176b; trans. Matt 5:535, emended)

From this dense and mysterious passage, we learn that at some point in primordial time all existence was in a state of imbalance. This is expressed in the lack of face-to-face relationships between entities. As a result, the primordial kings died, and their *ziyyuneihon* (adornments), a term that may be understood to refer either to their weapons or to their female partners, vanished. The imbalance, and the Death of the Kings, led to the annihilation of existence.

The "scales" are a key concept in this enigmatic text. Gershom Scholem finds that the scales are to be identified with "the *sefirah* of Wisdom, which establishes divine harmony, penetrating all worlds and all being." He also observes the link between the scales and "the balance between the masculine and the feminine."[12] Yehuda Liebes understands the scales as "the abstract principle of creation that precedes creation itself."[13] To these, I would add the observation that scales are associated with the very principle of duality and dialectic, the source of the tension between various things in the world—whether that tension is one of attraction or repulsion. Together, difference and attraction can serve as a basis for enduring creation, because they generate duality and enable resistance to the profound desire to be drawn once more into the Source, the great ocean of the Infinite. Thus, only harmonious scales can bring created being as it exists in the mind of God to full and enduring existence. The kings who existed before the scales had no such ability, so they simply could not survive. As Liebes puts it:

> The kings of Edom [. . .] died because of their singleness, they had no balance, no harmony of Male and Female, and they symbolise the primordial worlds of void that were destroyed before the stable and enduring world was created. In parallel, these kings play a poetic role: [the word *nimlakh* can mean both coronated and regretted; thus] "Kings" (*melakhim*) are also thoughts that arose in the mind of the Creator, who came to regret them (*nimlakh*).[14]

This primordial and unstable state shifts, making room for the beginning of an enduring reality, as "garments of glory" are prepared for the ancient supernal head—which we will soon learn is the head of *ʿAttiqa*. Thus emerges being, a new reality bursts forth, now with a "head" and "face." In this process, particles of those kings, sparks of those initial thoughts that were born and died, glimmered and faded, find their place within configured reality.[15]

This is the brief and enigmatic scene of the Death of the Kings as portrayed in Sifra di-Tsniʿuta. The Idra develops this myth in the most spectacular way. It dwells upon the processes that originate deep within the Beginning, where there is only undifferentiated Divinity, an infinite ocean within which no difference whatsoever is distinguishable.[16]

First Appearance in the Idra: Engraving and Concealing

Here we have the first appearance of the myth of the Death of the Kings in the Idra Rabba:

> "It has been taught: Before the Ancient of Ancients, Concealed of Concealed, had prepared adornments of the King and crowns of crowns, there was neither beginning nor end. He engraved and gauged within Himself, and spread before Himself one curtain, in which He engraved and gauged kings, but His adornments did not endure. As is written: *These are the kings who reigned in the land of Edom before a king reigned*—Primordial King—*over the Children of Israel*, the Primordial One (Genesis 36:31). All those who had been engraved were called by name, but they did not endure, so He eventually put them aside and concealed them. Afterward, He ascended in that curtain and was arrayed perfectly." (Zohar 3:128a; trans. Matt 8:326)

According to this account, the first movements that occur in the infinite divine consciousness are initial attempts at tracing a boundary, first drafts of an outline, efforts to enable something to come into being that is not simply the vast and undifferentiated ocean. It is an undirected motion of engraving and inscribing, occurring within the self-enclosed Divine, perhaps merely as pre-conscious fluctuations.

These processes occur within "the Ancient of Ancients, Concealed of Concealed," before he "had prepared adornments of the King and crowns of crowns." It is a divine dimension reminiscent of Jung's and Neumann's descriptions of the first stage of consciousness, referred to as the uroboric stage. The uroboros is an ancient symbol of a snake with its tail in its mouth, and in Jung's thought it serves as an archetype linked to undifferentiated, infinite consciousness—a consciousness satisfied in itself, containing all things and interlinked with all things. It is a state of consciousness that precedes the emergence of the ego into independent existence, and it precedes gender, sex, and all other binarity.

Next, a curtain or veil is spread, separate from the Divine itself, in which the kings are engraved.[17] Before the ancient divine consciousness has been configured and enclothed in a face with which it can turn toward existence, these kings are its initial and inchoate conjectures and engravings, striving toward being and power. The kings are the first manifestation of Judgment (*Din*) in the sense of a boundary within the expanse of the Infinite, and they are therefore connected to the kingdom of Edom and to redness (*adom*), a color that represents Judgment.

But the attempt fails. The kings are primordial, spectacular, terrifying, sparks glimmering from within the divine consciousness, blazing forth and fading back into the Infinite like fireworks. They are an attempt that cannot succeed because they are so unripe, one-dimensional; they are too near to the oceanic depths of the Divine, and their impulse after blazing out is to sink and dissolve back into that expanse as before, like flashing thoughts that arise in the mind and then sink back into the nether reaches of the unconscious. The kings do not have sufficient internal structure to endure independently outside the Infinite. They may be great and mighty, even wondrous, but their very strength and primordiality is their downfall. The primordial kings can only remain as they are; they are unable to adapt, transform, or accommodate. They are too immense, and unable to shrink into a systematic order. In a certain sense, the kings are too unformed and unprocessed, lacking the essential functions of flexibility and adaptability that allow primordiality to take its place within the cosmic order. Their primal existence cannot enable the creation and development of a human form, of Adam.

In the Idra's own terminology, the problem is that the kings are initial attempts at creation that precede the configuration and adornment of *'Attiqa*. In such a situation, all being is in a state of timelessness and placelessness. Before the configuration of *'Attiqa*, these primordial kings simply reign and die, glimmer and fade. Only after the kings are concealed or "die" can a more orderly attempt at creation take place, beginning with the configuration of the face of *'Attiqa*. Once this aspect or face of the Divine is configured, attempts at integrating the remains of the kings into existence may begin.

If we pay close attention to the first appearance of the myth of the kings in the Idra and the terse account in Sifra di-Tsni'uta', we may see that while in the latter the emphasis is on balance and coupling, that is not the focus in the former. The Idra emphasizes the inability of the kings to endure in their existence because the face of *'Attiqa* has not yet been established and configured. The kings are concealed until such time as a more orderly and stable creation is established. Only in subsequent appearances of this motif in the Idra will an emphasis be placed on the balance and companionship lacking in the kings. Filling these deficiencies is a prerequisite for *tiqqun* and the establishment of a stable existence.

The Idra's choice to weave the myth of the kings of Edom into the beginning of the process of configuring the divine faces is deeply impressive from a conceptual and spiritual perspective. Rabbi Shim'on begins with drafts, with possibilities of worlds that were not chosen, with miscarriages of the divine consciousness, with the primordial and ancient kings that could never belong within the world familiar to us. This choice teaches us not to dismiss or repress the primordiality that was never shaped into existence. Only by being conscious of its existence may we come to understand the creative effort involved in producing structured order. All order is built upon the foundations of rejected possibilities that never came to fruition, that were not suitable or satisfactory. In this formulation there is a statement about the value of discarded plans, of those thoughts that never became actions, of the beautiful musings that glimmered and faded into the ocean of the unconscious, with all of its ancient and mighty creatures. A comprehensive exploration of reality must necessarily devote some attention to these important aspects—the potential entities that never emerged into lasting existence. By becoming acquainted with them, we may explain both those processes that are prior to stable existence and the subsistence of such pre-cosmic elements within our own existence (even if they differ in name and form). Recognizing pre-cosmic reality is not to be perceived as a shortcoming, and there is no shame in mentioning it. The deep intuitions of the British psychoanalyst Wilfred Bion, which are discussed in relation to the second appearance of the kings of Edom in the Idra, are illuminating as we try to understand this dense myth.[18]

The first appearance of the myth of the kings in the Idra leaves many riddles unanswered: Where precisely were the kings concealed? Will they ever emerge from this state, and if so, when? Does their concealed presence have any effect on the reality that is now being configured? Some of these questions will be resolved as this motif reappears in the Idra. For the moment, their concealment clears the path for the configuration and adornment of the face of God: *Arikh Anpin*.

10

Arikh Anpin

Origins

Arikh Anpin, Elongated Countenance, the Patient One; *'Attiqa Qaddisha*, the Holy Ancient One; *'Attiq Yomin*, the Ancient of Days. These are the names of the divine face, the *partsuf*, on which the first section of the Idra is intently focused. In this stage, the Infinite, unbounded and undefined, is gradually configured, taking shape as the scriptural interpretations unfold. Rabbi Shim'on and the Companions invoke this aspect of the Godhead through their living account of the formation of his face. Only after this configuration is it possible for this manifestation of the Divine to have intentionality. This face, with its ability *to face*, thus inaugurates the creation and configuration of all dimensions of reality that exist outside of it.[1]

This Divinity is described in its manifestation both before being configured and thereafter, with its face. The most basic way in which the archaic imagination can grasp something of this divine reality is by describing it as existing without time, "without beginning or end." In this state, God's actions are framed as "engraving" and "gauging"—a description, or so it seems, of primal, undirected movement occurring deep within the very being of the Infinite. In a second stage, *'Attiqa* is described as engraving or gauging within an additional dimension: a veil or curtain (*parsa*). The existence that is inscribed upon that curtain is that of the kings that we encountered in the previous chapter. The mode of being depicted on the curtain turns out to be unsustainable, and the kings die:

> "It has been taught: Before the Ancient of Ancients, Concealed of Concealed, had prepared adornments of the King and crowns of crowns, there was neither beginning nor end. He engraved and gauged within Himself, and spread before Himself one curtain, in which He engraved and gauged kings, but His adornments did not endure. As is written: *There are the kings* (Genesis 36:31) [. . .] but they did not endure, so He eventually put them aside and concealed them. Afterward, He ascended in that curtain and was arrayed perfectly." (Zohar 3:128a; trans. Matt 8:326)

Suddenly, alongside what appeared to be a singular divine reality, the primordial Torah appears, providing wise counsel concerning the correct manner in which an enduring creation might occur:

> "And it has been taught: An impulse arose in the Will to create, the Torah had been concealed for two thousand years, and He brought her out. Immediately, she said before Him, 'He who wishes to arrange and form should first arrange His own array.'" (Zohar 3:128a; trans. Matt 8:326, emended)

Here, with the Divine described as having a will to create, no longer are we speaking about conjectural or playful impulses from within the mind of God that remain within it. The Torah, hidden for two thousand years, emerges from her concealment, stands before the Creator and provides her counsel. What is this primordial and wise Torah? It seems that the authors of the Idra took their inspiration from accounts of primordial Wisdom, God's advisor who takes pleasure in God's world, as described in Proverbs 8, together with classical rabbinic works that valorize Torah/Wisdom and believe it precedes the existence of the world.[2] Even before encountering the white face of *'Attiqa*, we hear the Torah's advice. It is didactic in tone, and perhaps even carries a hint of rebuke: "He who wishes to arrange and form should first arrange His own array"!

The Torah's words are reminiscent of political advice: one who wishes to rule a well-ordered state must first ensure that one's individual self is in order, for everything follows the head.[3] This applies both in the realm of human creativity and in a psychological context. Creation reflects its creator; its stability and balance depends upon that of the creator. The divine personality thus stands in need of a prior process of configuration and self-analysis. The screen or curtain, which provides the medium upon which the initial sketches of existence are made, must not be disconnected or alienated from the Divine.

It would seem that the ultimate success of this configuration—"Afterward, He ascended in that curtain and was arrayed perfectly"—reflects on the advice provided by the Torah. The Ancient of Ancients must enter the curtain. The latter is the expanse within which existence is first imagined—perhaps it is even an archaic symbol of the parchment of the Torah. There, on that screen, is the Divine configured in the form of the face of *'Attiqa*—and we can finally become acquainted with this face.[4]

The entry into this curtain constitutes a fateful moment in the timeless Beginning, for it testifies to God's willingness to participate in the creation of the world. I believe that this account represents a critique of the conception of God as the unmoved mover, a transcendent force existing outside the framework of that which it moves. That God, as described in the works of Aristotelian philosophers such as Maimonides, is not connected to the world or involved in it. In contradistinction, the Idra, from its very inception, seeks to establish a different understanding of the Divine. Embracing such a figure entails letting go of the transcendental disconnect between God and the world. Static and distant perfection is replaced by a Divinity that shares a deep connection with the world—a connection that entails involvement and vulnerability—a Divinity that wants to *face* the world.

The Ancient of Days

In the background of Rabbi Shim'on's account of *'Attiqa* are the verses describing Daniel's vision of a divine figure:

> I watched until thrones were placed, and Ancient of Days did sit. His raiment was as white snow, and the hair of his head was like pure wool; his throne flames of fire, its wheels burning fire. A river of fire flowed out before him, a thousand thousands serving him, and ten thousand times ten thousand standing before him. The judgment was set, and books were opened.[5] (Daniel 7:9–10)

As Gershom Scholem notes, the description of the Ancient of Days in Daniel's vision provided the Idra with a term "that unites [. . .] the visionary image of the hoary elder, the Ancient of Days, and the concept of God as superior to and transcending all things. However, the term *'Attiqa Qaddisha* also refers to the God who abandoned his transcendence and took on a [human] likeness."[6]

Rabbi Shim'on's discourse thus describes a divine figure who is near in some sense to our cultural imagination, on the human and individual level. However, his words are full of paradox, rendering all that seemed so familiar quite strange:

> "It has been taught in the Concealment of the Book (*bi-tseni'uta de-sifra*): The Ancient of Ancients, Hidden of the Hidden, was arrayed and prepared—that is, He existed and did not exist, did not actually exist yet was arrayed. No one knows Him, for He is more ancient than the ancients, but in His arrayal He is known—like an elder of elders, more ancient than the ancients, more concealed than the concealed—known by His signs yet unknown. Master of white—His garment and sparkling countenance. Seated on a throne of flames, to subdue them." (Zohar 3:128a–b; trans. Matt 8:327)

In this scene, a primordial and concealed figure becomes manifest, likened to a hoary elder. Only his white face merits a detailed description. The figure is entirely white, but seated on a throne of flames. That is to say that, outside this figure, there is a reality that bears some relationship to the color red. In contradistinction to the account in the Book of Daniel, in which the fire in the description of the throne, wheels, and river evokes the celestial realm, it seems that in the Idra, the fire is a manifestation of the forces of Judgment (*Din*) that must be harnessed: "Seated on a throne of flames, to subdue them." It seems that merely by sitting upon them, *'Attiqa*'s whiteness overpowers the flames. In a subsequent passage, the Idra will further develop this imagery:

> "It is written: *His throne, flames of fire* (Daniel 7:9), and the Ancient of Days sat upon this throne. Why? As it has been taught: If the Ancient of Days does not sit upon this throne, the world cannot endure that throne. When the Ancient of Days sits upon it, this is in order to subdue that throne, and whoever rides reigns." (Zohar 3:130a; trans. Matt 8:342)

The superlative quality of Rabbi Shim'on's words—"Ancient of Ancients, Hidden of the Hidden"—emphasizes the concealed nature of this figure.

Indeed, the paradoxical description "known yet unknown" applies even now, after his arrayal and configuration.

Skull and Brain

We now move to a psychedelic depiction of *'Attiqa*'s head: his skull, brimming with crystalline dew, from within which a white light shines in thirteen directions, sustaining countless worlds. The description, replete with whiteness, translucent and crystalline liquidity, evokes inestimable antiquity:

> "Through 400,000 worlds the whiteness of the skull of His head spreads. [. . .] In the skull dwell 120 million worlds, moving with it, supported by it. From this skull trickles dew to the exterior one, filling His head every day. [. . .] From that dew, holy ones of the Highest are sustained, and it is the manna ground for the righteous in the world that is coming.[7]
>
> "That dew trickles to the Holy Apple Orchard, as it is written: *The layer of dew lifted, and look, on the surface of the desert—something fine, flaky* (Exodus 16:14). The appearance of the dew is white, like a crystal stone in which all colors are seen, as is written: *Its appearance was like the appearance of crystal* (Numbers 11:7)." (Zohar 3:128b; trans. Matt 8:328–329)

If the readers could depend upon some degree of familiarity in the opening account of the hoary elder, they now find themselves in entirely unfamiliar territory. These are attempts to communicate something that lies beyond the bounds of language itself, images brought up from the abyss of the subconscious, from the depths of being.

The image is so archaic that even describing it is difficult: a white skull, radiating whiteness beyond compare; white illumination spreading from the white skull in all directions; the skull is not empty but full of worlds; it is full of dew, requiring no willful or directed action. This is a collection of images and movements that harks back to the Beginning, to the earliest moments of generation and coming-into-being: a sphere, whiteness, illumination, trickling. What of the depths of the human soul did the quill grasp in this passage?

The skull represents the sphere, a symbol of wholeness, without beginning or end. This image also conjures associations with death, as in the mishnaic passage of the skull floating on the water.[8] However, we would do well to recall that the biblical valence of the term used here—*gulgolet* or *gulgolta*—is "head": *Gather of it every man according to his eating, an omer a head (la-gulgolet), according to the number of your persons* (Exodus 16:16). It may well be that the Idra is referring to the head prior to the formation of a face, prior to life as we know it. Here too there is whiteness: it appears to be a whiteness of pre-eternality, of the Beginning and Source of life, prior to any color. In the words of Joseph Gikatilla, describing the whiteness of the *sefirah* of Crown (*Keter*): "The beginning of all appearances in the world is whiteness."[9]

As we have said, the skull brims and overflows with the most subtle of liquids, here called "dew." This dew dripping from the skull is life, or perhaps pure consciousness, and it is liquid and luminous in nature. The lights that shine forth from this skull give life to all things.

At this stage, the entity depicted before us has no clear intention or will. It is an archaic and impersonal account of an inchoate divine mode of being, bountiful, cascading, overflowing its banks.

Among the images of the skull, the following account of the radiation of white luminescence in thirteen directions is particularly striking:

> "The whiteness of this skull radiates in thirteen directions engraved: in four directions on one side, in four directions on the other side, in front; in four directions in the back; and one above the skull, that is, upward. From this the length of His face extends through 3,700,000 worlds, and that is called ארך אפיים (*Erekh Appayim*), Elongated Countenance, referring to the length of the face. This Ancient of Ancients is called *Arikha de-Anpin*, Elongated Countenance, and the exterior one, *Ze'eir Anpin*, Small Countenance, compared to the Ancient One, the Elder, Holy of Holies of Holies." (Zohar 3:128b; trans. Matt 8:330, emended)

The whiteness shines from within the skull in thirteen rays, bursting forth in four directions: four on each side of the skull, four behind, and one additional ray above the skull. These thirteen rays of light may be some kind of very primal roots for God's Thirteen Attributes of Mercy, which will become manifest as part of the verbalization and conceptualization that follows, in the context of the *tiqqunim* of the beard.

Even though the account of *'Attiqa*'s white skull and its crystalline contents is concerned with the very beginnings of being, prior to all things, the text has no qualms describing the skull in relation to existence outside it: "the exterior one" and "the Orchard of Holy Apples." That is to say, even before we have encountered *Ze'eir Anpin* and the Female, we know that their viability depends on the crystalline dew trickling from *'Attiqa*, permeating them with vital power.

The skull is the wellspring of life in all its purity. The white light gleaming within it is no mere terrestrial light but a divine light: Anything that comes into contact with it miraculously receives life itself, is blessed, flourishes. Each world that has received the white light of life also transmits white light back toward its source.[10]

Now the contents of the skull are described:

> "In the hollow of the skull, a membrane of air concealed supernal Wisdom, uninterrupted, and this is not to be found or opened. This membrane envelops the brain of supernal Wisdom, so this Wisdom is covered. [. . .] This brain, which is concealed Wisdom, is tranquil and quiescent in its place, like fine wine upon its lees." (Zohar 3:128b; trans. Matt 8:331)

Within the skull is a membrane of air covering and closing in concealed Wisdom. That brain membrane enables divine consciousness, here called "concealed Wisdom," to remain within its own deep, tranquil, and clear state of being, without disturbance.

This description of the enclosed and tranquil state of concealed Wisdom—the brain, or the contents of *'Attiqa*'s skull—is highly reminiscent of Plotinus' account of the serenity of the One, the primordial and undifferentiated principle, in its independent and unknowable essence: "he himself, staying still at the summit of the intelligible, rules over it; he does not thrust the outshining away from himself [. . .] but he irradiates forever, abiding unchanged over the intelligible."[11] This is connected to the Neoplatonic undercurrent (discussed previously) that informs the Idra's account of the trickling and luminescence from within *'Attiqa* as an unintentional flow, one that springs from the very existence of light and goodness. Just as the One naturally overflows from within itself, without conscious will or intent, so does Wisdom lie upon enduring being—just as wine upon lees, fermenting in and of itself, without any guiding hand.

In these opening descriptions of *'Attiq Yomin*, we find a mixture of Neoplatonic conceptions, mythic images, and language reminiscent of psychedelic experience. If we wish to employ Jungian terminology, we might suggest that undifferentiated consciousness closes in upon itself in uroboric fashion—however, it brims and spills over. This state is depicted throughout the Idra in a series of largely interchangeable archetypal images, all describing abundant whiteness: the hoary elder whose gaze is full of whiteness, an eye radiating a stream of light, semen emerging from the phallus, or milk gushing from the breast.

11

Arikh Anpin

Features of the Face

Upon the screen spread out by the concealed Ancient One, and in the lines of the book before us, the configured and arrayed face of *'Attiqa* now takes shape. It is gradually woven into being out of Rabbi Shim'on's words and those of his disciples. Now the luminous skull is also referred to as *Arikh Anpin*.

The majority of the account of *'Attiqa*'s face is provided by Rabbi Shim'on himself. In detail, he describes to his disciples (and to the reader) the face as it steadily takes shape: the skull is slowly covered in hair, a face emerges—and within it, a forehead, eyes, a nose. Each part of the head is described in close-up, in images that are simultaneously concrete and abstract, surreal and psychedelic. We observe here a consistent pairing between visuality and abstraction: the *tiqqunim* of *'Attiqa* evoke images that attempt to express abstract ideas (such as "beginning" or "unity") using visual terminology; but more than this, they point to a creative effort to locate highly tangible, mythical, and experiential images in the depths of the primordial imagination—images that are prior to abstract discourse. This is theology framed as a face, accompanied by a project of tying these images poetically into scriptural verses and fragments of verses, with their various midrashic associations. This literary matrix enriches and thickens the Jewish exegetical and homiletical dimension of the images evoked.

We might have imagined that the orifices of *'Attiqa*'s face (the eyes, the nostrils) would be identified with the divine bounty flowing forth from the skull, while the skin and surface of the head might constitute a veil of sorts, separating the luminous wellspring within from that which exists without. But the Idra's imagination is unlike ours: all of the facial features—orifices, protuberances, hair—represent a mode of *facing*, of directing the divine presence beyond, outward. The face is gradually scanned from top to bottom, from the hair of the head to the tip of the beard, and described as a network of channels for the transmission of light in various frequencies and intensities.

The face might be thought of as a kind of filter, regulating the outflow from within the hidden depths of the Divine. Features of the head and face that are free of hair—such as the forehead, eyes, nose, nostrils, and even the part in the hair—represent open paths for the flow of divine bounty. The hairs themselves are a physical representation of channels, streams, or conduits that regulate the current of light and being from deep within the divine brain.

Arikh Anpin is effectively described as a combination of face and hair, which together provide a fantastical language to describe processes of transmission. Here, the face stretches from the scalp to the nose, while the beard is described separately and encompasses the mouth and cheeks. The hairless features of the face are also developed and expounded upon by Rabbi Shim'on, but a significant portion of the Idra is devoted to the hair, and in particular the beards, of *Arikh Anpin* and *Ze'eir Anpin*.

Hillel Zeitlin, a great lover and scholar of the Zohar, describes the hair of *Arikh Anpin* as follows:

> The powers that are drawn from the supernal lights to act within the lower worlds are described as hairs. Just as hairs emerge from the head, cover it, and are attached to it, but are nonetheless external to it, and when they are shaved off, [the head] lacks nothing, these powers are drawn from *'Attiqa*, enclothe him, derive life from him and cleave to him—but nonetheless, it is as if they are external to him. If the wellspring from which they grow is disrupted, they will vanish entirely. But the wellspring remains one, [unchanged] whether they draw from it or not.[1]

The Idra Rabba's intensive preoccupation with the divine hair might also explain why the Idra is incorporated into the Zohar on the Torah portion (*parashah*) of Naso, which discusses the Nazirite, whose sacred devotion is expressed by growing his hair long and wild. Both in the printed versions of the Zohar and in various manuscripts, the passage immediately preceding the Idra includes a scriptural interpretation whose language is a foretaste of the Idra's language, drawing an association between the Nazirite and the long-haired divine *Adam*.[2] The Zohar claims that the Nazirite—who seeks to sanctify himself to the Divine—grows his hair in order to mirror or become a representation of God as the Ancient of Days, as described in the Book of Daniel, with hair "like pure wool" (Daniel 7:9). It emphasizes that the Nazirite's holiness is expressed specifically in the hair, rather than any other part of the body.

Regulation and Flow: The Hair and the Path

After being introduced to concealed Wisdom, enclosed and encased in its membrane, we encounter a description of the facial features. First appears an account of the white hairs of the head, straight and soft, streams of divine bounty. The hair falls to the shoulders, covers the back of the neck, and leaves the ears free so that they may remain "open."[3] This face exists in a perpetually open gaze; it is never closed or obstructed.

After this initial account, and before the face is further configured, Rabbi Shim'on makes the following comment, noting the difference between this head and any other and providing some orientation for how it might be "seen":

> "There is no left in this Ancient One; all is right. He is seen and not seen, concealed and not concealed. This pertains to His enhancements (*tiqqunoy*), all the more so to Him." (Zohar 3:129a; trans. Matt 8:334)

This is a highly paradoxical formulation. This is a head without distinct sides; it does not accommodate dualistic perception. This aspect of the Divine possesses no "left"—a representation of Judgment (*Din*); it is entirely composed of "right"—Compassion or Love (*Ḥesed*). This face, radiating love-filled oneness, is seen but not seen, concealed but not concealed. That is to say, that a mind that contemplates it cannot perceive it directly or constantly. To avoid any illusion concerning discursive perception of this face, Rabbi Shim'on emphasizes that this sublime paradox applies to the face, which is merely a *tiqqun* or enclothement of *'Attiqa*; and if such perception of the *enclothement* (that is, the face) is impossible, this must be all the more true of its divine essence.

Such statements, appearing again and again throughout the Idra, might be viewed as signals, warning the reader not to be fooled into approaching these faces through the lens of conventional perception, or to imagine them with the familiar imagery of the human face.

To the account of the hair on top of *ʿAttiqa*'s head, the Idra adds a surrealistic close-up depiction of the "path" through the middle of it. This is a part in the hair, forming an open and exposed stream of light, emerging and drawing a flow of divine bounty down into the parallel "path" through the middle of *Zeʿeir Anpin*'s hair:

> "In the parting of the hair, one path proceeds, illuminating 270 worlds; and from it shines a path by which the righteous are illuminated in the world that is coming, as is written: *The path of the righteous is like gleaming light, shining ever brighter until full day* (Proverbs 4:18). From here, the path branches into 613 paths, diverging in *Zeʿeir Anpin*, of which is written *All the paths of YHVH are kindness and truth, for the keepers of His covenant and His precepts* (Psalms 25:10)." (Zohar 3:129a; trans. Matt 8:334–335)

This passage, along with its parallel in the *tiqqunim* of *Zeʿeir Anpin*, describes a pathway that creates a visual and conceptual connection between the highest point of divinity on *Arikh Anpin*'s head, and the world of human beings who live according to the divine precepts and commandments.[4] The discussion of *ʿAttiqa*'s luminous "path" is not merely theoretical. The mystics are the "righteous" mentioned in the biblical verse, and they know how to attain conjunction with the Divine and live in a manner that will ensure that their path will become increasingly filled with light as they progress. Their mode of living leads them from the terrestrial path to that within YHVH, within which shines the path of *Arikh Anpin*. It is tempting to ask how the connection between the part in the hair of *ʿAttiqa* and the path of the righteous was drawn: was the author focused on the biblical account of the increasingly luminous way of the righteous, projecting it thereafter onto the motif of the pathway through *ʿAttiqa*'s hair? Or perhaps the author wished to emphasize that the path of the righteous mystics on earth, those who contemplate the mysteries of the Godhead, leads them to recognize and know the river of light flowing forth from the wellsprings of the Divine, and to follow it? Or maybe the mystic was looking for words to express some ecstatic contemplative experience, in which a flow of unique and strange light flowed through a field of vision that was entirely white—and the verse from Proverbs seemed to provide a fitting biblical image?

The River of *Ratson* (Will)

From the path of light through the middle of the hair, Rabbi Shim'on moves on to a description of *Arikh Anpin*'s forehead. As mentioned, the Idra divides *'Attiqa*'s head into the face and the beard. The forehead thus represents a broad expanse of the face, characterized by a lack of both hair and orifices.[5]

> "Forehead of the skull—Will of Wills (*Rava d'ravin*). The will of *Ze'eir Anpin* faces that will, as it is written: *It shall be upon his forehead perpetually* לרצון (*le-ratson*), *toward the will* [. . .] (Exodus 28:38). That forehead is called *Ratson*, Will, since it reveals the entire head and skull. [. . .]
>
> "[It] is revealed at that moment, so wrath subsides and prayer is accepted. [. . .]
>
> "[W]hen the forehead is revealed, desire and complete favor prevail, and all wrath subsides, overwhelmed by it. [. . .]
>
> "It has been taught: Hair does not exist in this place because it is revealed and not covered, so that Masters of Judgment will gaze and subside and [Judgment] will not be executed.
>
> "It has been taught: This forehead extends through 270,000 illuminating lamps from supernal Eden." (Zohar 3:129a–b; trans. Matt 8:335–336)

'Attiqa's forehead is described here as a tremendous expanse of light whose presence is Love and Will, a calming presence that makes all Judgment subside. The forehead is called the "Will of Wills" (*Rava d'ravin*). The word *ratson* carries two different associations in Hebrew. One is "will" as volition, determination, and desire, and the other evokes a sense of love and appeasement. This forehead, shining with so many thousands of lights, represents *'Attiqa*'s mode of providence: without judgment, simply acceptance and soothing. The forehead of *'Attiqa*'s Will is parallel to the forehead of the high priest, on whose brow is the golden frontlet, the *tsits*. In the Hebrew Bible, this represents appeasement of God, who forgives Israel and bears their iniquity: *It shall*

be upon his forehead perpetually so that they are accepted by YHVH (*le-ratson lahem lifnei YHVH*) (Exodus 28:38). The Idra reads this verse hyperliterally, understanding it to express an alignment between the wills (or foreheads) of *Ze'eir Anpin* and *'Attiqa*.

The forehead of *'Attiqa* is also understood as a barrier or a screen upon which the substance within the skull is represented, and through which it flows.[6] The forehead expresses what is occurring deep within the head, and in *'Attiqa*'s case it radiates soothing and appeasing love, the substance that flows eternally from the recesses of his being.

Providence in the Undifferentiated Dimension: Eyes

'Attiqa's eyes receive a more detailed description than any other feature of his face. The eyes express a connection to that which lies within; they thus constitute a central link between the various divine faces, and between God and humans. Indeed, the bulk of this account treats the relationship between *'Attiqa*'s eyes and those of *Ze'eir Anpin*. The description is structured as a series of citations from ancient traditions, related one after another, integrated with passages written in a deeply moving, hymn-like, ecstatic mode. The opening formula—"It has been taught"—is repeated, lending the entire passage a distinctive rhythm and an air of solemnity:

> "Eyes of the White Head are different from other eyes. There is no lid over the eye, nor any eyebrows. Why? Because it is written: *Behold, He neither slumbers nor sleeps, the Guardian of Israel* (Psalms 121:4)—Israel above.[7] And it is written: *that Your eyes may be open* (1 Kings 8:52). And it has been taught: Whatever comes in Compassion has no lid over the eye, nor any eyebrows. All the more so, the White Head, which has no need. [. . .]
>
> "It has also been taught: White within white, and a white including all whites. [. . .]
>
> "It has been taught: This eye is not closed, and they are two, turning into one. All is right, there is no left. It neither slumbers nor sleeps, needs no protection. No one protects it; it protects all, watches over all. From the watching of this eye, all are nourished.
>
> "It has been taught: If this eye closed for one moment, none could endure. Therefore it is called open eye, supernal eye, holy eye, eye of

> watchfulness, eye that neither sleeps nor slumbers, eye that is protector of all, eye sustaining all. Of this is written *He that has a good eye* יבורך (*yevorakh*), *will be blessed* (Proverbs 22:9). Do not read *yevorakh, will be blessed*, but rather יברך (*yevarekh*), *will bless*. For this is called *He that has a good eye*, through which He blesses all." (Zohar 3:129b–130a; trans. Matt 8:337–339)

The description opens by asserting the uniqueness of *'Attiqa*'s eyes: They have no eyelids or eyebrows. The reason soon becomes clear. Closing the eyes is a response to danger, creating a boundary or defense. But in the realm of *'Attiqa* there is no danger, no need for protection. All is safe, open, awake.

Open eyes are also associated with the Compassion that perpetually flows from *'Attiqa*. We emerge from Love and Compassion with our eyes open, not narrowed, hidden, or closed: "Whatever comes in Compassion has no lid over the eye, nor any eyebrows. All the more so, the White Head, which has no need." The eyes are open in a sure and trusting expression, open and flowing, without any defense mechanism. They watch over everything, exuding a bounteous flow that sustains all things. The face as a whole is an expression of divine providence, and this is all the more true of the forehead and the eyes. *'Attiqa*'s providence is unique insofar as it entails no scrutiny: it does not search the inner recesses of the human heart, accept or reject; it is simply love.

A unique and surprising image associated with this account is conjured by Rabbi Abba, in his response to Rabbi Shim'on asking to what eyes without eyelids might be likened:

> He replied, "To fish, fish of the sea, whose eyes have neither lids nor brows, and they do not sleep and need no protection for the eye. All the more so, the Ancient of Ancients—who needs no protection; and all the more so, since He watches over all, and all is nourished by Him, and He does not sleep." (Zohar 3:129b; trans. Matt 8:338)

The similarity between *'Attiqa*'s eyes and those of fish highlights the quality of the archaic. Fish live in the depths of the sea, cloaked in primordiality, as if in a state of perpetual wakefulness since the creation. Here, fish are depicted almost as part of the sea, without any need for protection or any barrier between their eyes and the world in which they live.

In the passage cited previously, Rabbi Shim'on emphasizes another aspect of *'Attiqa*'s eyes, bringing their otherness into still sharper relief: his two eyes appear as, or become, *one eye*. This strange image may emerge from the lack of distinction between the sides of *'Attiqa*'s head and face. As we have seen, here there is also no distinction between right and left: the eyes are absolutely identical, appearing as one. In the theological terminology of the Idra, we might say that while the eyes of *Ze'eir Anpin* express his two aspects—Love and Judgment, right and left—within *'Attiqa* there is only Love, the right side. Thus, even though there are two eyes, they really represent a single eye:

> "It is written: *He that has a good eye will be blessed* (Proverbs 22:9). Why is it referred to as one? Come and see: In the eyes of the one below [*Ze'eir Anpin*] there is a right eye and a left eye; there are two, in two colors. However, here [within *'Attiqa*] there is no left eye; both of them attain a single rung, and all is right. Therefore, *eye*—one, and not two." (Zohar 3:130a; trans. Matt 8:340–341)

We might liken the perception of the two eyes as one to the experience of looking at an object from a very close distance. Just as a baby gazes into her mother's face as she suckles, *Ze'eir Anpin*'s gaze locks with that of *'Attiqa*, causing *'Attiqa*'s two eyes to appear as one.

Either way, the image of the single eye emphasizes that all is white. As the Idra states, this is "white within white, and a white including all whites." The Idra goes on to describe the different kinds of white that issue from this eye: three rays of white that beget seven lights, or seven eyes. The whiteness goes through a process of differentiation and refinement. There are many types of white, prototypes of the *sefirot*, their initial pattern before they are flooded with colors. The whiteness does indeed become differentiated, but the providence issuing from *'Attiqa*'s eyes remains singular: it is entirely Love, nourishing all being.

As elsewhere in the account of *'Attiqa*'s face, here too are his eyes contrasted with those of *Ze'eir Anpin*, and here too this serves the Idra's central purpose: distinguishing between the various divine faces, while attempting to bring them together in alignment in order to heal *Ze'eir Anpin*. Thus, the whiteness gushing from *'Attiqa*'s eyes kindles all of the luminaries below, in the dualistic world of *Ze'eir Anpin*, so full of Judgment. We are told that one can bathe in the whiteness flowing from *'Attiqa*'s eyes, one can wash in it and be cleansed, perfumed. When *Ze'eir Anpin*'s eyes meet those of *'Attiqa*, they bathe in their soothing whiteness, and they are rinsed of their redness—of Judgment, constriction, and anger:[8]

> "It has been taught: There is no illumination for the lower eye, to be washed of its redness and blackness, except when it is bathed by the white light of the supernal eye called *He that has a good eye*. No one knows when this supernal holy eye illumines and bathes the lower eye. And the supremely righteous are destined to see this through wisdom, as is it written: *For eye-to-eye they will see*. When? *When YHVH returns to Zion* (Isaiah 52:8). And it is written: *For eye-to-eye You are seen, YHVH* (Numbers 14:14). Were it not for the supernal eye gazing upon and bathing the lower eye, the world could not endure for a single moment. [. . .]
>
> "It has been taught: This eye, the eye of watchfulness, is constantly open, constantly smiling, constantly joyous—which is not so with those below, mingled of red, black, and green: three colors. They are not constantly open, for they have a lid, a fold, over the eye. Thus it is written *Awake! Why do You sleep, O YHVH? Rouse Yourself!* (Psalms 44:24); *Open Your eyes* (Daniel 9:18).
>
> "When they are opened, on some they are opened for good, and on some they are not opened for good. Woe to him upon whom they are opened and the eye is mingled with red, and red confronts him, covering the eye! Who can be saved from it?
>
> "As for the Ancient of Days, a good eye—white within white, a white including all whites. Happy is the share of one upon whom He gazes with one of these whites! Surely it is written: *He that has a good eye will be blessed* (Proverbs 22:9); and it is written: *O House of Jacob! Come, let us walk in the light of YHVH* (Isaiah 2:5)." (Zohar 3:130a; trans. Matt 8:340–341)

The Idra draws a sharp distinction between the constant and all-encompassing love issuing from *'Attiqa*'s eye, and the threatening and frightening providence of the aspect of Divinity that manifests as *Ze'eir Anpin* or *YHVH*. The eyes of *Ze'eir Anpin*, and his mode of providence, are reflected in (and reflect in turn) the human mode of vision: both in human vision and that of *Ze'eir Anpin*, reality is perceived in a dualistic and ever-changing fashion, inviting various responses from the observer. Just like human eyes, *Ze'eir Anpin*'s eyes may be either open or closed, rendering the gaze—even the entire face—present or absent. The Idra observes that sometimes an absent or sleeping deity—with eyes shut tight—might even be preferable to an encounter with his open eyes, when they are full of judgment and anger.

In harmony with the Idra's overall agenda, which combines a consciousness of the Ancient Divine with the project of drawing light from that figure into human religious life, here too the description of *'Attiqa*'s eye is no mere theory. This eye is bound to our world and shapes it. First of all, when the whiteness of *'Attiqa*'s eye shines within *Ze'eir Anpin*'s eyes, this enables the existence of dualistic reality. For the latter cannot endure without an unconditional flow of bounteous love from the God of absolute Compassion. Furthermore, human beings can meet *'Attiqa*'s gaze. This encounter does not take place with the physical eye, but with the spiritual "eye of wisdom." *'Attiqa*'s eye is experienced—*eye-to-eye*—by human beings through the illumination of *Ze'eir Anpin*, occurring *when YHVH returns to Zion* (Isaiah 52:8). This expression describes both the messianic age, and a situation in which the divine Male and Female are in a state of coupling. One of the Idra's aims is to attain a situation in which the divine Male—*YHVH*—once again unites and couples with *Zion*, representing the *Shekhinah* in general and the divine Female's genitalia in particular. *'Attiqa*'s eyesight is thus linked to coupling, and to the encounter between several aspects of reality: *'Attiqa*, the Male and the Female, and Adam. The Sabbath is that auspicious time, when the light of *'Attiqa*'s providence illuminates *Ze'eir Anpin* and those human beings who are mentally aligned with him, as expressed by Isaac Luria in his poem "Benei Hekhala" (Children of the Palace), composed for the Sabbath afternoon.[9]

'Attiqa's eyes thus invoke a deeply archaic experience: a white, life-giving light, shining eternally out of an open eye—gushing Love. The image evokes primal experiences of life and nourishment—suckling milk from the breast, or the flow of semen from the phallus.

The power of the description lies in the fact that *'Attiqa*'s eyes (or eye) are so different from our own, while retaining distinct characteristics of the human gaze: emotional nourishment, wakeful vitality, the possibility of meeting that gaze directly, validation of life, and the promise and enduring presence that are expressed in the eyes.

However, it must be emphasized that the enduring steadiness of *'Attiqa*'s gaze does not imply apathy or stasis. On the contrary, "the eye of watchfulness is constantly open, constantly smiling, constantly joyous." Here we hear an echo of that most primal of experiences, that of an infant staring into a mother's eyes. The eye of *'Attiqa* is not closed in within itself, smiling and joyful always, always saying "yes." *'Attiqa*'s gaze is as nourishing as a mother's breastmilk, like a sweet dish that cannot be spoiled with salt, sustenance that is always available and always satisfying. In the Zohar, the teachings of Rabbi Shim'on are described in similar terms, as is their transmission to his disciples: He nourishes them with the sweetness of honey and milk issuing from under his tongue, and his Torah is openly equated with that of *'Attiqa*.

> Rabbi Yose said: "These matters—take them up to the Holy Lamp [Rabbi Shim'on], for he prepares sweet dishes, as prepared by the Holy Ancient One, Concealed of all concealed, and he prepares dishes that leave no room for another to come and throw in salt. Further, one can eat and drink and fill his belly from all the delights of the world and still have some left over. In him is fulfilled *He set it before them, and they ate and had some left over, according to the word of* YHVH (2 Kings 4:44)." (Zohar 2:149a; trans. Matt 5:366–367)

Rabbi Shim'on is the one who knows how to communicate the Torah of *'Attiqa* to his disciples, and to the world.

Patience: The Nose

The nose is the final facial feature to be configured and expounded before the *tiqqun* of *'Attiqa*'s beard. The *tiqqun* of the nose opens with a declaration that "by the nose, the face is recognized." This statement echoes classical rabbinic literature, emphasizing the dominance of the nose as an identifying marker of the human face.[10] "Nose," in Hebrew *af*, is the facial feature associated with temper and temperament. As noted earlier, the term *appin* or *anpin* is used in the Zohar to mean "face," "spirit," "breath," "nose," and "temperament." Here, *'Attiqa*'s nose reflects the totality of his being, which consists entirely of patience, forbearance, and forgiveness, as is made clear in the Idra Zuṭa: "The nose of the Holy Ancient One is אריך (*arikh*), long, and extended, so He is called ארך אפים (*erekh appayim*), Long-nosed, Long-suffering."[11]—meaning "the Patient One" in biblical idiom. This draws a link between the quality of patience and the physical nose, the latter symbolizing the former. *'Attiqa*'s nose issues a breath of pure calm and forgiveness, which are the essential qualities of *Erekh Appayim*.

"By the nose, the face is recognized.

"Come and see: What is the difference between the Ancient One, and *Ze'eir Anpin*? The former is Master of the Nose. From one nostril, life; from the other, life of life.

"This nose is an armoire,[12] through which blows breath to *Ze'eir Anpin*. We call it Forgiveness, tranquil pleasure of spirit. For the breath issuing from here, from those nostrils—one breath streams to *Ze'eir Anpin*, to arouse in the Garden of Eden. And one is a breath of life, by which the son of David will be welcomed to know wisdom.[13] From that nostril a breath is aroused, issuing from the concealed brain, destined to settle upon King Messiah, as is written: *The breath of YHVH will alight upon him: a breath of wisdom and understanding, a breath of counsel and power, a breath of knowledge and awe of YHVH* (Isaiah 11:2). [. . .]

"In the days of King Messiah no one will need to teach another, for their breath, encompassing all breaths, will know everything: *wisdom and understanding, counsel and power, knowledge and awe of YHVH*, because of the breath comprised of all breaths. [. . .]

"And it has been taught: All of them are included in this breath of the Ancient of Ancients, issuing from the concealed brain to the nostril of the nose." (Zohar 3:130a–b; trans. Matt 8:343–345)

The Idra apparently prefers the term *ḥotem* (nose) to *af* or *appayim*: the former explicitly refers to the physical feature of the face, while the latter may be understood to refer to the face, or as a symbol for the emotional state or attribute. Furthermore, the Idra focuses on the nostrils, described as passages for the breath issuing from *'Attiqa*'s brain. This is a breath of life, breathing all things into being by exhaling through the nose. The nose thus functions as a sort of bellows, conveying the life-breath that emerges from the depths of *'Attiqa*, as described in the narrative of Adam's creation: *He blew into his nostrils the breath of life* (Genesis 2:7).

In this case, the duality of *'Attiqa*'s nostrils does not lead to a dualistic interpretation—for example, associating each nostril with Compassion or Judgment—but is interpreted as an augmentation or amplification of the life-force surging out of *'Attiqa* and into the world: From one nostril issues "life," from the other "life of life." The twofold nature of the nostrils is also interpreted in a messianic vein. While the breath emerging from one nostril arouses *Ze'eir Anpin*, that which issues from the other will in the future accompany and inspire the Messiah.[14] This latter breath announces an epoch in which humans will perceive the Divine directly, without any need for study or instruction, as stated by Jeremiah: *Behold, the days are coming,* [. . .] *and every man shall no longer teach his neighbor, and every man his brother, saying: 'Know YHVH!" For they shall all know Me, from the least of them to the greatest of them, says YHVH; for I will forgive their iniquity, and their sin will I remember no more* (Jeremiah 31:30–33). *'Attiqa*'s patience—his Long Nose—and his spirit of forgiveness, are what enable this profound transformation in human consciousness.

From the description of the nose, the Idra moves to the *tiqqunim* of *'Attiqa*'s beard.[15] Transitioning to this topic, Rabbi Shim'on makes a paradoxical statement:

> "This is the praise of the configuration of His nose. This and all the configurations of the Ancient of Days are seen and not seen—seen by Masters of Qualities, yet not seen by all." (Zohar 3:130b; trans. Matt 8:346)

This pronouncement jolts the consciousness, preventing it from becoming too comfortable with the face's physicality. The assertion that "the configurations of the Ancient of Days are seen and not seen" expresses a deep awareness that *'Attiqa*'s face is not visible to physical eyes. It cannot be perceived through a normal state of consciousness, only through one that is more subtle and refined. The only people who can grasp *ʿAttiqa*'s face and see it are the "Masters of Qualities" (*marei middin*). These are the kabbalists who safeguard the esoteric knowledge of the divine "qualities," *middin*—here referring both to the "dimensions" (*middot*) of the *corpus dei*, the divine body, and to the ten *sefirot*.[16]

Arikh Anpin: An Overview

The configuration of *Arikh Anpin* in the early passages of the Idra Rabba is a skillful synthesis of intellectual conceptualization, mythical imagination, and emotional articulation. On the one hand, the Idra repeatedly emphasizes the existence of a face, even at the highest and most undifferentiated level of divine being. It goes still further, explicitly stating that the configuration of this face is a necessary condition for the creation of any stable and enduring existence. On the other hand, the Idra describes *ʿAttiqa*'s face in terms that emphasize the dialectic tension between familiarity and total otherness. When describing *ʿAttiqa*'s face, the authors thus deliberately abandon central characteristics of the human face as we know it: symmetry, color, motion, changing expressions, and emotions. At the same time, they emphasize the qualities of nourishment, attentiveness, love, compassion, forgiveness, and enduring presence.

The facial features of *ʿArikh Anpin*—the forehead, eyes, and nose—are no mere metaphors, born of the limitations of human speech to describe the Divine, as Maimonides understood anthropomorphic language employed in the Hebrew Bible. Nor are they a schematic illustration of abstract qualities. When speaking of God, the Idra offers an entirely different way of approaching visuality, language, and abstraction. It is a solution that demonstrates an ability to experience various aspects of the divine presence simultaneously: in a mythical dimension, the undifferentiated Divine has a head, with eyes and a nose; at the very same time, these features express distinct facets of the divine presence in the world. A case in point is *ʿAttiqa*'s forehead: Just as it represents divine Will and favor in the context of an undifferentiated Divinity, Will itself is an expression of *Arikh Anpin*'s forehead.

To conclude this chapter, it seems appropriate and informative to compare the Idra's *tiqqunim* of *ʿAttiqa*'s face with the parallel account in Sifra di-Tsniʿutaʿ,

which employs even more archaic imagery than the Idra in its portrayal of the emergence of the primordial divine face. While the Idra describes this face in terms of its features—the forehead, eyes, nose, beard—Sifra di-Tsni'uta' resorts to primal and primordial imagery, a language that is prior to the formation of a face or the conventions of corporeal terminology:

> Secrecy within secrecy was prepared and arranged in a single skull filled with crystalline dew. Membrane of air, purified and sealed; those strands of clean fleece hanging evenly. Will of Wills is revealed through prayer of those below. Open-eyed watching, never sleeping, ever vigilant; supervision below by supervision of radiance above, in whom are two holes of an armoire arousing breath for all." (Zohar 2:176b; trans. Matt 5:535)

Dew, membrane, wool, will, watchfulness, a breath. In the Idra, these are woven into the features of the face and skull. Thus, the dew is identified with the contents of the brain, the membrane with the boundaries of concealed consciousness, wool with the hair, Will with the forehead, watchfulness with the eyes, and the breath with the nose and nostrils. The account in Sifra di-Tsni'uta captures these qualities at the very boundary of language, before they are assembled, before they materialize into a face. Here, we are able to glimpse the most elemental qualities, which will be cast in the detailed mold of a face in the Idra: Life, Consciousness, Will, Watchfulness, Forgiveness.

12

Arraying *Arikh Anpin*'s Beard

Up until this point, we have been becoming acquainted with the divine face of *Arikh Anpin*, as the Idra Rabba presents it in its unique and wondrous mode of expression. We have entered the pathways of light: the divine influx flowing from the head, forehead, eyes, and nose. The primordial quality of the white face's expression and features brings the reader to the very edge of the conscious mind, poised to plunge into the great ocean of the unconscious. But despite the otherness of the account, the reader's mind is able to contain the description of God's face, supported as it is by biblical verses that describe facial features, such as the eyes and nose.[1]

Now the Idra transitions to a new stage. The thirteen *tiqqunim* of *'Attiqa*'s beard cover ten complete pages of printed text, far more space than is devoted to the facial features. This is a work of true artistry that weaves the various parts of *'Attiqa*'s beard—the curls of the cheeks, the hair over the lips, the beard itself[2]—with his Attributes of Mercy (*raḥamim*). These Attributes of Mercy are derived from the Book of Micah: *Who is a God like You, removing iniquity and passing over the transgression of the remnant of His people? He does not retain His wrath forever, for He delights in love. He will return and have compassion upon us; He will subdue our iniquities; and You will cast all their sins into the depths of the sea. You will grant truth to Jacob, love to Abraham, as You swore to our fathers from days of old* (Micah 7:18–20). Each part of the beard expresses one of the attributes mentioned in these verses. Thus is a zoharic puzzle assembled—pieced together from ideas, images, face and hair, fragments of verses, interpretive and psychedelic imagination. It is the crowning achievement of a synthesis—fraught with tension and barely communicable through language—between, on the one hand, the concrete surrealism and hyperrealism of close-up images of the different parts of the beard and, on the other, an abstract account of the divine Attributes of Mercy.

The thirteen sections of the beard, defined precisely and in detail according to its concrete representation at the outset of the *tiqqunim*, are as follows:

> The first *tiqqun*: The contour of the edge of the beard, emerging from beside the ear and reaching the upper lip.
>
> The second and fourth *tiqqunim* are parallel to one another: The hair above the mouth, and below it.
>
> The third and fifth *tiqqunim* are also parallel to one another: The hairless path that passes from below the nostrils to the upper lip, and that which stretches from the lower lip to the center of the chin.
>
> The sixth *tiqqun*: The hairy cheeks. This portion of the beard is described as emerging from the upper lip, covering the cheeks, and descending to beneath the mouth. This *tiqqun* may be understood in relation to the contour traced in the first *tiqqun*, effectively filling it in with hair.
>
> The seventh *tiqqun*: The "apples of the cheeks," the hairless rounded surfaces under the eyes.
>
> The eighth *tiqqun*: The contour of the beard falling to the navel. The *tiqqun* traces the borders outside of which the beard itself does not go.
>
> The ninth *tiqqun*: The head and beard hairs that mingle with one another.
>
> The tenth *tiqqun*: The hairs of the neck, enclosed within the beard.
>
> The eleventh *tiqqun*: The hairs of the beard itself, which are all of equal length, and which exist independently of one another.
>
> The twelfth *tiqqun*: The hairless mouth.

> The thirteenth *tiqqun*: The volume of the beard, hidden beneath those hairs that are visible from in front.

During the *tiqqunim* of the beard, the dynamic of the Idra shifts. Until now, Rabbi Shim'on was the main speaker, configuring and interpreting *'Attiqa*'s facial features. The disciples listened, and the master only rarely turned to them with questions. Now begins a process of examination for the disciples, constituting a part of their initiation and dedication. The nine students will be summoned to rise, each in turn, and to expound one of the *tiqqunim* of the beard. They will present longer and shorter interpretations, both visionary and exegetical, discursive and ecstatic—and the teacher will respond to them, and bless each presenter. The scene grows progressively, filling with dramatic and mystical tension.

When configuring the divine face, Rabbi Shim'on had at his disposal a wide array of verses that alluded to God's eyes, forehead, and nose. Here, all the disciples must pass a more difficult test. Each must draw a connection between an abstract attribute—for example, *removing iniquity* or *delighting in love*—and a specific section of *Arikh Anpin*'s beard. Each must find a way to expound the amorphous form of the segment of beard that he has been summoned to configure. He must draw a creative connection between its form, volume, contours, coarseness, or softness and a specific divine attribute. The teacher's own interpretations, beyond their content, model for the disciples the modes of *tiqqun* and exegesis suitable for the occasion. Through them, the teacher clarifies the "rules of the game" for configuring the divine face; now the disciples must take the plunge themselves. Now they must demonstrate their ability to—with creativity and virtuosity—weave the Attributes of Mercy together with the various parts of the beard, and to do so from a place of deep intent, resilience, and courage. Here, the test of initiation is determined by individual expression, bold and personal.

The Beard in the Zohar and in the Idra Literature

Our everyday consciousness screams with discomfort: What is God's beard?! And what can we make of the efforts of the Idra's authors, so wildly audacious, to delve so deeply into the minute details of the hairs of the most sublime divine beard?

In order to find an answer, we must identify the peculiar role of the beard in the Zohar, and in the Idra in particular, as well as the scriptural passages on which this conception is based. However, I must state at the outset that even with all of these explanations, the beard's centrality in the Zohar remains enchanting yet opaque, and perhaps a final and complete resolution to this riddle will remain out of reach. The Zohar's interest is all the more striking given that no Jewish text other than the Zohar accords the beard such a central place. On the contrary, it would seem that the very absence of biblical and rabbinic treatments of the beard provided the zoharic exegete with tremendous freedom to venture into unknown territory, evoking mysterious and primordial associations.

In order to develop a sense of the beard's meaning in the Idra, we must first consider Psalm 133. This text, more than any other, serves as a reservoir of sounds and images that perfuse the Idra Rabba and Idra Zuṭa.

> A Song of Ascents of David: Look, how good and how pleasant is the dwelling of brothers fully together. It is like fine oil on the head, running down upon the beard, the beard of Aaron, descending over the collar of his robes (*middotav*); like the dew of Hermon that descends upon the mountains of Zion. For there YHVH ordained the blessing, life forevermore.

This psalm describes the delight of friends sitting together, employing two similes. The first relates to the Temple and recalls the fragrant anointing oil that trickles from the priest's head down onto his beard and garments. The second simile is drawn from the natural environment of the Land of Israel and depicts the trickling of icy water from Mount Hermon to the Jerusalem Hills. The sweet, erotic, and fluid imagery of abundance and pleasure serves to illustrate the psalmist's sense of "dwelling fully together."

The three verses of this short psalm comprise imagery and principles that become foundational to zoharic discourse around the Divine and also to the language of the Idra. For example, the dynamic of perpetual divine vitality flowing from its unified source into our world is represented in the image of precious oil flowing from Aaron the priest's head onto his beard, and trickling from his beard onto his garments.[3]

In one particular scriptural interpretation, the Zohar draws a connection between the flowing oil described in Psalm 133 and Genesis 2:10—*A river issues from Eden to water the garden*.[4] These three accounts—the river flowing from Eden, the dew descending from Mount Hermon, and the oil trickling upon the beard—are foundational representations of the flow of being within the ten *sefirot* in the divine realm, and from them into the world. The image of precious oil trickling from *'Attiqa*'s head onto his beard and onto his garments or attributes (*middot*) is a personal-symbolic reflection of the natural-mythic description of divine emanation emerging from *Edenic* Wisdom (*Ḥokhmah*) and flowing through the sefirotic *river* to irrigate the *garden* of Sovereignty (*Malkhut*). The pleasantness and delight, represented by the oil, is also likened to dew descending from the whiteness of Hermon—the heights of the *sefirah* of Crown (*Keter*), or the beard of *'Attiqa*. It flows forth, filling *Ze'eir Anpin*'s beard with precious bounteous flux, reaching the hills of Zion, which represent the body of the Female (the *sefirah* of *Malkhut*). Zion, the Female's vagina, is the final destination of the flow of dew—the purpose of the divine flow being to enable the coupling of the Male and the Female in the divine world, and between that realm and the human realm.

In other places in the Zohar, the verses of Psalm 133 are interpreted in distinctly Idra-esque terms, combined with the language of the main body of the Zohar:

> "*Like fine oil on the head* (Psalms 133:2). What is *fine oil*? Oil of holy anointing, issuing and flowing from the Holy Ancient One, found in that supernal river suckling the children, to kindle lamps. That oil flows upon the head of the King, and from His head to the glory of the holy beard, flowing from there onto all those splendid garments in which the King is arrayed, as is written: *descending* על פי מדותיו (*al pi middotav*), *over the collar of his robes* (*ibid.*), literally! These are the crowns of the King, whose name appears in them.
>
> "Come and see: All the flow, all the radiance, and all the joy of the worlds descend to bless only through these holy crowns, which are the name of the Holy King. Thus, *descending al pi middotav, according to his attributes* [. . .] it descends and flows upon all the worlds, providing blessings for all." (Zohar 3:7b; trans. Matt 7:34)

Apart from the Psalm 133 verses used to describe processes in the supernal realms, the final verse of that psalm—*For there YHVH ordained the blessing, life forevermore*—is particularly important in the Idra literature. At the end of the Idra Zuṭa, Rabbi Shim'on's soul departs in erotic ecstasy as he recites this verse, as his lips utter the word *life*. This psalm therefore weaves the two Idra works together exquisitely, from the beginning of the Idra Rabba to the final words of the Idra Zuṭa. The Companions, enclosed in their ring of vows, on their mission to configure the divine faces and stimulate the flow of divine bounty, may indeed perceive themselves to be the subject of this psalm.

Another perspective on the beard in Jewish literature may be revealed in its relationship to the phallus. The ancient rabbis make a connection between the beard and the penis: Although the penis is hidden modestly within one's clothing, its existence and potency may be ascertained through the beard, displayed proudly on the face. Both attest to sexual maturity, and both are deficient in eunuchs.[5]

In the Zohar, the beard is indeed connected to the attribute of Foundation (*Yesod*), representing the phallus. Both the beard and the penis are called "splendor of the body" and "completion of the body" in the Zohar, and the dialectic of revelation and concealment applies in connection to both.

Thus, the Zohar perceives the magnificence of the masculine body in the *sefirah* of Foundation, the phallus. However, it must be concealed, not exposed. Thus, the most magnificent part of the body is also the most hidden:

> הוד (*Hod*), *Splendor, and majesty before Him* (Psalms 96:6). Why is it called *majestic*, and who is *majestic*? Righteous One. Why is He called *majestic*, when it is a concealed place, which is not to be revealed and must always be covered, whereas *majestic* applies only to one who is revealed and seen? Well, although it is a concealed rung, it is the majesty of the whole body, and there is no majesty to the body except for this. Why? One who lacks this rung lacks the majesty to associate with people: he lacks a masculine voice, and the majesty of voice has been seized from him; he lacks a beard and the majesty of a beard. So although that rung is covered, all majesty of the body depends upon it; it is covered and revealed." (Zohar 2:186b; trans. Matt 6:49–50)

This is also the case in the *tiqqunim* of the beard in the Idra. *'Attiqa*'s beard may be hidden from the revealed stratum of reality; however, according to the Zohar's logic—prioritizing the concealed and the mysterious—his beard is most glorious and unique precisely due to its hiddenness. Furthermore, this is the reason that the Idra identifies the absence of the beard from the revealed surface of the Written Torah—it is not mentioned even in the accounts of the beloved in the Song of Songs, upon which the *Shi'ur Qomah* literature is based, describing the figure of God.[6]

In addition to the beard's literary contexts—Psalm 133 and the rabbinic association of the beard with the phallus—one might also propose a historical and social background to the emphasis placed on the beard in the Zohar. Yehuda Liebes has suggested that a historical figure with a striking appearance and long beard was active in or around the circle that produced the Zohar. He even suggested that this elderly figure might have served as inspiration for the character of Rav Hamnuna Saba, who is identified to a large extent with *'Attiqa Qaddisha* at the outset of the Idra Zuṭa.[7]

But these associations with the beard from Jewish literature and the social context in which the Zohar was composed do not explain the tremendous meaning that the Idra literature attributes to it. The beard's exceptional importance stems from the role that it plays in these works: within the figurative framework of the wellspring from which divine emanation flows, the beard is understood as a means to convey and regulate the flow of oil. It is a kind of active organ of the face, whose role is to flow outward, to vivify and give birth, and it joins *Arikh Anpin* to *Ze'eir Anpin*.

In other words, the beard is a personified expression of the figures of rivers, streams, channels, and rapids that transmit the divine flow from its source into external reality. We can think of the beard as a primordial mode of transmission, a kind of nervous or electrical system that conveys and regulates the flow, full of Love, from *'Attiqa*'s brain into the cosmos. *'Attiqa*'s brain—enclosed—enters the cosmos through countless capillaries, channels of emanative flow that communicate life, forgiveness, and love. These capillaries represent an aura of strength, life, and light that envelops *'Attiqa*'s head.

Furthermore, the beard is to some degree a representation of the divine personality. It is associated with the sublime visage of God, the glory (*kavod, yaqqiruta*) that adorns his face and shines forth from it.[8] Like the facial features, the beard provides a means to know something of the concealed nature of the Divine and to connect to it. According to the Idras, this nature is the none other than the divine Attributes of Mercy. As we shall see later, at some length, thirteen modes of Mercy and Love are refracted in the beard, becoming many and diversifying, and these sustain all being.

Perhaps most of all, the beard's centrality in the Idra literature is expressed in the hymn that Rabbi Shim'on recites at the outset of the beard's *tiqqunim*. Here, the beard receives lavish praise, unlike anything else in the Idra. This praise is connected to the idea that the white beard on *'Attiqa*'s face is more concealed and exalted than any conception humans can attain by discursive means; in addition, it depicts majestic beauty, the Glory adorning the face of *'Attiqa*:

> Rabbi Shim'on opened, saying, "Woe to one who extends his hand into the glorious supernal beard of the holy Elder, hidden and concealed of all—the beard that is most concealed and precious of all His array, the beard not known by those above or those below, the beard that is praise of all praises, the beard that no human prophet or saint has ever approached to see, the beard that hangs by its hair to the navel of the heart, white as snow, most glorious of all, concealed of all, faith of all faith!" (Zohar 3:130b; trans. Matt 8:346)

Just as we saw at the beginning of the Idra Rabba, here too, Rabbi Shim'on begins the process of the *tiqqunim* of *'Attiqa*'s beard with a warning: "Woe to one who extends his hand into the glorious supernal beard of the holy Elder." In what follows, Rabbi Shim'on repeats this formulation: "Whoever extends his hand to swear is as if he swears by the thirteen enhancements of the beard."[9] Grasping the beard becomes akin to taking hold of an object while swearing by God's name, an act that imbues the oath with authority and force. The source of this gesture appears to be in the biblical narrative of Abraham asking his servant to place his hand beneath his thigh while adjuring him (Genesis 24:2), apparently alluding to the phallus.[10]

Tiqqunim of the Beard: The Opening Passage

In the opening passage of the *tiqqunim* of the beard, we find the first description of its various parts. Rabbi Shim'on quotes from Sifra di-Tsni'uta concerning *'Attiqa*'s beard, as if he were citing an ancient rabbinic tradition, not yet explained or elucidated.[11]

> "It has been taught in the Concealment of the Book: This beard, faith of all, proceeds from His ears—descending and ascending around the holy mouth; descending, ascending, and covering the abundant offering of spice; great white of the glorious, descending evenly and covering to the navel.
>
> This is the glorious beard, perfect faith, within which stream thirteen flows—springs of fine anointing oil, arranged in thirteen enhancements." (Zohar 3:130b–131a; trans. Matt 8:347)

Here, Rabbi Shim'on scans the parts of the beard in a single glance, tracing its physical contours without providing any further interpretation or detail. The opening of the account is a naturalistic portrayal of a beard: sprouting beside the ears, descending and surrounding the mouth, ascending and covering the cheeks, and hanging evenly to the navel. Overlaid on the image of the beard in Psalm 133, the beard that Rabbi Shim'on is describing now takes on cosmic dimensions, and it is described as the source of thirteen wellsprings of precious anointing oil. This account resonates with the thirteen rivers of pure persimmon oil that are mentioned in classical rabbinic literature as the future reward of the righteous.[12] These wellsprings correspond with God's Thirteen Attributes of Mercy, which will be expounded throughout this section of the Idra as they relate to each part of the beard.

Immediately after this succinct opening passage, Rabbi Shim'on enumerates the thirteen distinct sections of the beard in fine detail and with close scrutiny, as well as the various divine qualities that are revealed in them and spring from them. Thereafter appears another passage that is important for a finely grained characterization of the beard and its *tiqqunim*:

> "Through these thirteen enhancements flow forth thirteen springs of anointing oil, streaming to all those below, who glow from that oil

> and are anointed by that oil. By these thirteen enhancements is distinguished the glorious beard, concealed of all, that of the Ancient of Ancients. [. . .]
>
> "These thirteen enhancements appear in the beard, and with the perfection of the beard by its enhancements a person is called faithful, for whoever sees his beard attributes faithfulness to him.
>
> "It has been taught in the Concealment of the Book: Of these thirteen enhancements dependent upon the glorious beard, some are manifested on the seventh in the world and thirteen gates of Compassion are opened." (Zohar 3:131a; trans. Matt 8:349, emended)

Following Sifra di-Tsni'uta, the Idra asserts that the time at which the reserves of precious oil will be released upon the beard and will flow into the human realm is in the seventh month (Tishrei).[13] In Jewish liturgy, during the High Holy Days of Tishrei, Thirteen Attributes of Mercy are repeated again and again. These Thirteen Attributes, derived from Exodus 34:6–7, are distinct from the Thirteen Attributes of Mercy associated with *'Attiqa*, which are those of Micah 7:18–19. As we shall see in greater detail in a later chapter, reflecting the theurgical approach taken in Sifra di-Tsni'uta and the Idra Rabba, the Rosh ha-Shanah and Yom Kippur prayers—using the Thirteen Attributes of Exodus—invoke *'Attiqa*'s Attributes of Mercy, summoning them to soothe the excess Judgment (*Din*) that dominates in the world during that period. Therefore, during the period between Rosh ha-Shanah and Yom Kippur, the white Mercy of *'Attiqa*'s beard gradually floods *Ze'eir Anpin*'s excessive Judgment. Configuring the various parts of the beard, invoking and summoning them, is a theurgical act that brings these channels into the forefront of human consciousness, actively opening the flow of divine bounty into them.

Similarly, in this passage, the beard is associated with faith. The beard is in fact referred to as "faith of all," rendering one who perceives or grasps it "faithful." The term *faithful* carries an additional association in the Zohar: one who knows the secret, who is resilient, steadfast, and possessed of a settled mind. We saw this in the opening passages of the Idra, where those who are worthy of the divine secrets are called "faithful of spirit," possessed of *qiyyuma de-ruḥa*—a stable spirit that remains steady and firm.

Following this introductory passage appear a series of compelling scriptural interpretations, broadly elucidating the thirteen *tiqqunim* of the beard. Rather than treating each and every *tiqqun*, here we shall focus on a narrower selection. First, I present an overview of the first *tiqqun*, while the analysis that follows is devoted to four *tiqqunim*: the second, eighth, twelfth, and thirteenth.[14]

The Power of Mercy: The First *Tiqqun*

Rabbi Shim'on summons Rabbi Yitsḥak to begin the *tiqqunim* of the beard, which he will do by connecting the first Attribute of Mercy—*Who is El, a God, like You?*—to the hair at the temples and the edges of the cheeks, emerging at the ears and descending to the mouth. The first *tiqqun* is particularly long. Indeed, from a literary perspective it appears to be a collection of beginnings of interpretations, also comprising statements of a general nature. Perhaps Rabbi Yitsḥak, as the first speaker, has discovered that beginning an interpretation always requires further introductions, before one comes to the specific content of this particular interpretation.

Thus, by way of introduction to Rabbi Yitsḥak's interpretation, I must mention a surprising and informative idraic understanding of the relationship between love and strength in the Idra Rabba. Contrary to what our assumptions may be, in the Idra, Mercy (*raḥamim*) and Love (*Ḥesed*) are not understood merely in terms of bounteousness and gentleness. *'Attiqa* may fundamentally exist as a wellspring of Love, but at the same time, he suppresses Judgment. We must keep in mind that while *'Attiqa* himself is white radiating whiteness, he is seated on the fiery redness of Judgment.[15] Similarly, *'Attiqa*'s beard—gushing with Love—also holds within it tremendous power, a strength that has the purpose of suppressing the redness of the primordial forces of Judgment. As we shall see at a later stage in the Idra, *'Attiqa*'s beard illuminates *Ze'eir Anpin* in order to confront, counterbalance, and even suppress the Judgment that inheres within this *partsuf*. In order for the Attributes of Mercy to reach *Ze'eir Anpin* and flow into him, they must be extremely powerful, for without the requisite strength, they will never succeed in overcoming Judgment.

"First enhancement—enhancement beginning from the start of the hair of the head. [. . .]

"The beginning of the first enhancement is thirty-one even locks, extending to the top of the mouth. [. . .] The thirty-one even locks within the first enhancement are strong, to subdue below, numerically equivalent to אל (*El*). What is meant by *El*? Strong, able.

"Within each lock branch out thirty-one worlds, powerful and dominating, to scrutinize—thirty-one on this side and thirty-one on that side. [. . .] All is concealed in the top of the beard, embracing strength, and they are included in this *El*. Even so, this *El* is overwhelmed by the Compassion of the Ancient of Days—sweetened, absorbed, and diffused within it.

"Why to the mouth? Because it is written *Judgment sat* (Daniel 7:10). What is meant by *Judgment sat*? It sat in its place, not prevailing. [. . .] *El* who is mighty, yet He is assuaged by the holy beard of the Ancient of Days. And the mystery written—*Who is El, a God, like You?* (Micah 7:18)—refers to the Ancient of Days, to the enhancement of the holy supernal beard." (Zohar 3:132a; trans. Matt 8:354–355)

The nature of the first attribute, *Who is a God like You*, is understood here by reading *El* (God) in its sense as power or strength.[16] This attribute thus represents the ability of God's tremendous Mercy to suppress the forces of primordial Judgment, thus generating a different reality. These forces of Judgment, here called "wailers" and "howlers," are a manifestation of the kings of Edom—entities encountered and confronted in the first *tiqqun*. The bristly, white hairs of the temples and cheeks, representing the first attribute within *'Attiqa*'s beard, are likened to spears possessing the necessary power to confront Judgment, to subdue it and drive it far away. It should be noted that according to the account in this *tiqqun*, the forces of Judgment are not destroyed, but rather infused with fragrance (*bissum*) and refined in the Great Sea: "By this enhancement all of them are subdued and assuaged, like the bitterness of tears sweetened in the Great Sea."[17] *Bissum* as a way of confronting Judgment, and the desire to transform Judgment into a force that might encourage and stimulate life and being, are themes that will appear again and again throughout the Idra Rabba.

It becomes clear from Rabbi Yitsḥak's words that this part of the beard also plays a role in configuring *Ze'eir Anpin*'s face and beard: the hairs of the temples and cheeks signify both the first emergence of the beard, and the initial penetration of the attributes of *'Attiqa*'s beard into the realm of *Ze'eir Anpin*. Thus they must possess enormous strength, the essence of which is not rooted in Judgment. At the same time, these spear-like hairs must not be allowed to rule or dominate *'Attiqa*'s face; they therefore end when they reach the mouth, and they do not interfere with the breath of eternal forgiveness that is exhaled from there.

The first *tiqqun* thus creates a boundary, defining a space or expanse within *'Attiqa*'s face. More than any other *tiqqun*, it depicts the power that inheres in the Attributes of Mercy.

Rabbi Yitsḥak concludes the first *tiqqun* in exalted and ecstatic fashion:

> "Who can behold this enhancement of the whole supernal glorious beard and not be put to shame? Who can behold the secrecy of locks of hair hanging from this elder, sitting adorned with a crown of crowns—crown of all crowns, crowns to which crowns below are linked. Therefore to these enhancements are linked those enhancements below.
>
> "Enhancements were arranged because it is necessary to bless whoever requires a blessing. For corresponding to all enhancements that are arranged, blessings appear, and whatever is enacted is enacted. All is encompassed by these enhancements. All rise toward the enhancements of the King, the Ancient One, concealed of all, and all are sweetened by these enhancements of the Ancient King.
>
> "It has been taught: If the Ancient of Ancients, Holy of Holies, were not arrayed in these enhancements, those above and those below would not exist, and all would be as if it were not." (Zohar 3:132a; trans. Matt 8:356–357)

These words express amazed astonishment at the sight of *'Attiqa* and the locks of his beard. Rabbi Yitsḥak asks in ecstatic wonderment: Who can behold this *tiqqun*, this exalted vision of the "crown of all crowns"? But his very words reveal the image, testifying to his own perception of it. The lingering, the languages of paradox, repetition, and hyperbole in his account of this mysterious vision contribute a sense of exaltedness to the image, and to the conceptual and abstract aspects of the beard. However, from an experiential point of view, the very same characteristics amplify the mythical presence of the beard.

The image conjured by Rabbi Yitsḥak turns our consciousness all the way back to the "crown of all crowns."[18] These crowns transcend the *sefirot*—they are prior to the latter and, indeed, appear to be their source. The *tiqqunim* of the beard thus constitute a stage prior to existence itself; indeed, they represent a necessary condition for that existence to emerge. Rabbi Yitsḥak's concluding oration also implies that the *tiqqunim* are configured for the sake of those who need blessing: "Enhancements were arranged because it is necessary to bless whoever requires a blessing." The connection between the hidden *tiqqunim* and our world lies in the profound need of all existence for a blessing.

Bearing Iniquity: The Second *Tiqqun*

Some of the Idra's most climactic revelatory moments occur in the second *tiqqun*. Rabbi Shim'on summons Rabbi Ḥizkiyah to accept the honor, and configure the portion of beard above the upper lip—that is, the moustache. The building blocks at Rabbi Ḥizkiyah's disposal are the image of the hair above the upper lip and the second attribute in the verse from Micah: *removing* or *bearing iniquity*, describing God's ability to bear or tolerate human misdeeds, and to forgive them. Rabbi Ḥizkiyah's mission is to draw a connection between these two elements with creative originality.

A reader who is familiar with the end of the Idra knows that before it is over Rabbi Ḥizkiyah, along with two other Companions, will die an ecstatic death. This adds a tremulous undercurrent to the events as they unfold.

> "Second enhancement: Hair is arranged from the top of the mouth, ascending to the other top in symmetrical array." [. . .]
>
> "Rise, Rabbi Ḥizkiyah! Stand erect and celebrate the glory of the enhancements of the holy beard!"
>
> Rabbi Ḥizkiyah rose. He began, saying, "*I am my beloved's, and his desire is upon me* (Song of Songs 7:11). What brought about that *I am my beloved's*? Because *his desire is upon me*.
>
> "I was contemplating, and behold, I saw a precious light of super-

> nal lamps, shining and ascending in 325 directions. One darkness was bathing in that light, like someone washing off what is coating him in a deep river whose branching waters stream and flow in every direction. That light rose to the shore of the supernal deep sea, by whose opening all fine and precious openings are released.
>
> "I asked, 'What is the meaning of that which I saw?'
>
> "They opened, saying, 'You have seen *removing iniquity* (Micah 7:18).'"
>
> He said, "This is the second enhancement." He sat down. (Zohar 3:131a; trans. Matt 8:348; and Zohar 3:132b; trans. Matt 8:358–359).

This is the most terse, dense, and visionary of the *tiqqunim* in the Idra Rabba. It comprises an introductory midrashic interpretation on the topic of love; a sublime vision; and finally, a few words of elucidation from the mouths of speakers knowing yet unknown.

Rabbi Ḥizkiyah begins with a verse from the Song of Songs, in which the female lover addresses her beloved with words of love and desire: *I am my beloved's, and his desire is upon me.* He interprets the verse in the first person, as if it is speaking specifically of him, in what amounts to a mystical prelude, articulating his own state of consciousness at that moment. *I am my beloved's*—I am now experiencing a connection with my beloved, God, for his desire is upon me. Desire here appears as a thirst for the potion, the kiss that unites lovers. Rabbi Ḥizkiyah is in an ecstatic state, in which he surrenders to desire for the Divine that has seized him. His reference to God's desire *for him* may even allude suggestively to his own rapturous death.

It should be noted that this verse from the Song of Songs is interpreted elsewhere in the Idra literature in the first person, in the opening passages of the Idra Zuṭa, which describes the events surrounding Rabbi Shim'on's death.[19] There, Rabbi Shim'on expounds the verse in reverse order: Because *I am my beloved's*—all my days I shared an intimate bond with him—therefore, now *his desire is upon me.* That is, Rabbi Shim'on declares that all his days have been in preparation, orienting him toward his encounter with his beloved God, and that his lifelong arousal of the divine realms from below has now, at the end of his days, led to God's arousal and desire for him from above.[20] It thus seems that the verse from the Song of Songs serves to introduce ecstatic death, in the Idra Zuṭa and in Rabbi Ḥizkiyah's presentation alike.

After this highly personal and emotional introduction, Rabbi Ḥizkiyah continues his interpretation in a unique vein. Instead of weaving together a virtuosic exegesis, drawing associations between the literary building blocks through scriptural wordplay, as is the case in most of the Idra's *tiqqunim*, he rises and offers a description of a vision. His vision is devoid of biblical citations, comprising instead a series of surrealistic images, lying at the very boundary of that which can be uttered in words. The vision itself is the *tiqqun* that brings the Attributes of Mercy together with the portion of the beard that has been allocated to Rabbi Ḥizkiyah. The wondrous vision conveys within it the physical, sensory, and fantastical dimensions of this part of *'Attiqa Qaddisha*'s beard, alongside the conceptual and experiential profundity of God as the "remover of iniquity."

Employing a visionary formulation appropriated from the Book of Daniel—*I was contemplating, and behold, I saw*[21]—Rabbi Ḥizkiyah describes a source of light resembling a deep river, its waters gushing in hundreds of directions. Deep within it, a shadowy fluctuation becomes visible, a single dark current in the heart of the river of light. This darkness is carried within the current, washes in it. The river of light flows, reaching the shore of the supernal sea.

As the vision progresses, Rabbi Ḥizkiyah cannot grasp its meaning: "I asked, 'What is the meaning of that which I saw?'" And from somewhere unseen and unknown, the reply is heard: "They opened, saying, 'You have seen *removing iniquity* (Micah 7:18).'"

Now Rabbi Ḥizkiyah, as if returning to the Companions from far away, concludes: "This is the second enhancement." He takes his seat, perhaps exhausted. His presentation is complete.

How might we decipher the great enigma of Rabbi Ḥizkiyah's presentation? And what is the connection between, on the one hand, this vision and God's beard and, on the other, the attribute of *removing iniquity*? Rabbi Ḥizkiyah's vision is a testament to the Zohar's gift for creating a sense of multiple layers and simultaneity that might seem to us to be inexpressible in words: visually, we have an image of close contemplation, almost without any distance, of the face. It is a nearness that does not allow one to see the face as a whole, and the focus is thus upon one small part of it, perhaps like the stare of a newborn or a child into the face of an elder, gazing into surrealistic vistas that emerge from the contours of the face before one must close one's eyes due to the sheer closeness. The image is essentially a close-up of the hair of the beard descending and surrounding the upper lip (blending with the hair that extends from the temples to the corners of the mouth). Within the hair, luminous in its whiteness and cascading like a river, there is some darkness—perhaps a single dark hair—sunken deep within the whiteness: "One darkness was bathing in that light." The hair reaches the hairless lip, like the shore of a deep ocean: "That light rose to the shore of the supernal deep sea."

From a theological point of view, Rabbi Ḥizkiyah's imagery speaks of an aspect of the Divine that is so luminous and forgiving it can bear and cleanse any iniquity. It is an experiential and visionary account of God as one who tolerates and *removes iniquity*. God is a tremendous river of light; no sin is too great for him to bear and cleanse. The infinite divine river carries and washes within it the blemish of human error.[22]

We might also interpret the vision as a personal account: Rabbi Ḥizkiyah may see himself as the strand of darkness, perhaps due to some past sin that he carries inside. It may be a subjective experience, beyond his conscious mind, in which he is carried within the river of light and cleaned of his sense of sin. It is thus possible that his soul is gradually cleansed within the river, eventually reaching the great sea of forgiveness, and that the account alludes to the release of that soul, which is soon to come.[23]

How strikingly different is this image of being borne along in an expanse of light from parallel accounts that discuss the Divine as *removing iniquity*: the scapegoat carrying Israel's sins into the desert on Yom Kippur; the image of God's suffering servant in the Book of Isaiah; or the description of Jesus as *agnus dei*, the lamb of God, taking on and bearing the world's sins.

Our understanding of Rabbi Ḥizkiyah's vision might become yet clearer in light of the process of repentance and forgiveness as it is described in various passages in the Zohar. In the Zohar, repentance (*teshuvah*) and forgiveness are understood as a dynamic process that includes explicit confession of one's sin and a willingness to receive one's punishment. Confession takes place both in the presence of human beings and in the presence of various aspects of the Divine: the Mother (the *sefirah* of *Malkhut*), the divine dimension that represents human desire (*Yesod*), and the divine Judge (*Tif'eret*). After confessing, the final stage entails giving the sin over to the divine attribute of *bearing iniquity*. Deep within the Divine, no sin is too heavy to bear, for God can carry it in his capacity as the wellspring of bounty and being.[24]

One possible meaning of this transmission of iniquity to the Divine may be that, after confession and accepting the judgment, we should no longer carry the guilt of the sin. We entrust the sin to God in order to attain forgiveness, to be freed from the sense of alienation and distance that accompanies transgression, and to find ourselves once more in the river of life. A "milder," more moderate interpretation of the Zohar might be that we now no longer bear the guilt *alone*, in existential isolation, and we are not rejected. The Divine carries our transgression within, in its compassionate, ancient, integrated face—like a single dark strand in a great sea of white.

Rabbi Shim'on's dramatic response to Rabbi Ḥizkiyah's *tiqqun* launches the discussion into new expanses of consciousness:

> Rabbi Shim'on said, "Now the world is bound together.[25] Blessed are you, Rabbi Ḥizkiyah, by the Ancient of Ancients!"
>
> Rabbi Shim'on said, "All lamps—you Companions, who are in this holy ring—I call the highest heaven and the highest holy earth as witnesses that I see now what no human has seen since the day that Moses ascended Mount Sinai the second time. I see my face shining like the light of the powerful sun that is destined to radiate healing for the world, as is written: *For you who revere My name the sun of righteousness will shine, with healing in its wings* (Malachi 3:20).
>
> "Furthermore, I know that my face is shining, whereas Moses did not know or see, as is written: *Moses did not know that the skin of his face was radiant* (Exodus 34:29).
>
> "Furthermore, I see with my own eyes these thirteen engraved before me, shining like lamps. When each one of them is elucidated, issuing from your mouths, it ascends and is crowned and arrayed, concealed within recesses of the enhancements of the beard, while all the

> others remain. As each one is elucidated, issuing from your mouths, it shines and is crowned, sitting like a king among his legions. When the elucidation is completed, it ascends and is adorned with a holy crown, arranged and concealed, taking its place among the enhancements of the holy beard. And so with every single one.
>
> "Gird yourselves, holy Companions, for there will never be a monumental event like this until King Messiah appears!" (Zohar 3:132b; trans. Matt 8:359–361, emended)

Much has been written about this passage, and its importance for understanding the character of Rabbi Shim'on and his self-perception.[26] What are we to make of his personal, emotional, even ecstatic response?

Rabbi Shim'on begins with the dramatic assertion that the world is now "bound together." That is to say that something in Rabbi Ḥizkiyah's *tiqqun* generated some fundamental repair in real time, "Now," also elevating the Idra assembly to a new mode of consciousness. The *tiqqun* is not theoretical; it generates reality. Rabbi Ḥizkiyah's words have invoked this reality of streaming divine light from *'Attiqa*; they have made it immediately and directly present.

In what follows, Rabbi Shim'on makes it clear that his participation in Rabbi Ḥizkiyah's visionary and visual experience has suddenly enabled him to perceive the events unfolding in a manner spanning worlds. In response, he offers his disciple a unique blessing. Instead of a familiar formulation such as "blessed are you to YHVH," Rabbi Shim'on formulates a new blessing that draws a link with *'Attiqa*: "Blessed are you, Rabbi Ḥizkiyah, by the Ancient of Ancients!"

Rabbi Ḥizkiyah's vision thus seems to kindle a flame within Rabbi Shim'on, connecting him to a visual mode of consciousness and inspiring him to speak in visionary language himself. The vision described by Rabbi Shim'on articulates a transformative experience: he recounts that he can see, using a spiritual sense of sight that he had not attained until now, his own face radiating cosmic, messianic, healing light. This spiritual perception crosses into temporal and spatial dimensions that are closed to our normal mode of vision. A barrier that separates the divine and human realms has been removed.[27]

This is a moment of shocking personal revelation. This illuminating insight, born of independent introspection, accords Rabbi Shim'on a higher rank than Moses himself. Both Moses and Rabbi Shim'on attained the supreme experience of a luminous face; however, while Moses was unaware that the skin of his face was radiating light, Rabbi Shim'on shines spectacularly and, while doing so, is aware of his own experience and its messianic implications. This reflective quality—the ability both to be within an experience and to be conscious of it at the same time—is what here and in many passages in the Zohar places Rabbi Shim'on at a level higher than Moses who brings down the written Torah.[28] In psychoanalytic terminology, it might be said that the conscious and self-contemplating ego is understood here as more developed than the ego that experiences events without self-awareness or self-consciousness. In the Idra's own terminology, another advantage over Moses is implied here: whereas the aspect of God that Moses encountered "face to face" was YHVH, whom the Idra identifies with *Ze'eir Anpin*, Rabbi Shim'on's face is described as glowing from within with the light of *'Attiqa*. Also in contrast with Moses, Rabbi Shim'on does not cover his face with a veil. Indeed, his radiant face is a healing presence for the world, just like the sun described by the prophet Malachi when foreseeing the messianic age: *the sun of righteousness will shine, with healing in its wings* (Malachi 3:20). This is a face-to-face experience, with the various faces of the Divine meeting the human face: Rabbi Shim'on's radiant face is like that of *Ze'eir Anpin* when the light of *'Attiqa* shines through it.

Reading this passage out of context may shock the reader, who might see Rabbi Shim'on's statement as haughty or arrogant. Indeed, we must recall that the Zohar constructs Rabbi Shim'on as a character who exemplifies freedom and boldness. Rabbi Shim'on is a king, a free man who speaks his mind without fear. He is a roaring lion, shaking the earth and all the upper and lower worlds. Rabbi Shim'on is the luminary of Torah in all worlds; he is at once terrestrial and divine. His character is replete with all the qualities attributed to him in classical rabbinic literature: when we meet him in the Talmud, he is utterly convinced of his own uniqueness; he is described as having perceived "through a luminous lens" like Moses; he sees himself as the most elite human being alive, and declares that he can acquit the world from divine judgment.[29] The Zohar also makes use of aspects of other great figures from early rabbinic literature when constructing Rabbi Shim'on, in particular Rabbi Eliezer b. Hyrcanos and Rabbi Akiva. To this assemblage of rabbinic materials the Zohar adds erotic, messianic, and cosmic qualities.[30]

Apart from the general characteristics of the figure of Rabbi Shimʿon in the Zohar, we must keep in mind that the words spoken here are uttered in the unique context of the closed circle of the Companions. In such a situation, concealment is inappropriate, not to mention adopting a posture of false modesty.

As has been said, there is a distinctly messianic dimension to Rabbi Shimʿon's experience: with the help of the visionary power aroused by Rabbi Ḥizkiyah, Rabbi Shimʿon attains a mental expansion into new horizons that enable a glimpse of the future messianic state of the world. The messianic state is expressed in Rabbi Shimʿon's identification—as part of the alignment of the Companions' faces with *ʿAttiqa*—with *the sun of righteousness*, here representing *Zeʿeir Anpin*. His radiant face mediates between the undifferentiated Divine and the world. He is able to contain the tremendous light and transmit it to the world in a manner that heals and does not destroy. At this moment, the future world's potential is revealed, and Rabbi Shimʿon takes on the role of the perfect or whole human being who clears the path toward messianic consciousness.[31] Rabbi Shimʿon realizes in the present the messianic ideal stated in the Book of Daniel: *The enlightened will shine like the radiance of the sky* (Daniel 12:3). These words are something of a byword for zoharic literature, and here Rabbi Shimʿon does indeed shine like the radiance of the sky, like a luminous sun.[32]

The messianic character of this experience is also connected to time, and the way in which it is it conceived or constructed. Within the intimate context of this unique gathering, time collapses, and for a moment one can experience something of existence in a paradigm that the world is not yet ready for. Rabbi Shimʿon emphasizes that this is a moment that must be savored, for it presents an opportunity to taste of that which will come to pass in the generation of the Messiah, at the End of Days. Just as this moment has arrived, it will soon pass: "Gird yourselves, holy Companions, for there will never be a monumental event like this until King Messiah appears!"

Another significant aspect of Rabbi Shimʿon's visionary perception touches upon the gathering of the Companions itself. The phenomenon of the *tiqqun* of the divine Attributes of Mercy appears before his eyes as a whole:

the Thirteen Attributes shine like lamps, and whenever one of the disciples elucidates one of them as part of his *tiqqun*, it lights up and radiates more brightly than the others. When the speaker concludes the *tiqqun* that has been allocated to him, that attribute ascends from among the other attributes to the sacred crown, taking its place within the *tiqqunim* of the beard while the others remain in their place. This is therefore both a coronation ceremony for each and every attribute and an initiation rite for each of the speakers.

Throughout the Idra's narrative, Rabbi Shim'on plays the role of the great master who is able to expand the consciousness of his disciples, providing a cosmic and divine perspective on the event. A similar scene will take place as the Idra continues, before the Companions begin the *tiqqunim* of *Ze'eir Anpin*'s beard.[33]

Rabbi Shim'on's ecstatic excitement leads him to invite Rabbi Ḥizkiyah to accept the honor of expounding the third *tiqqun* of the beard: "Rise, Rabbi Ḥizkiyah, a second time!" But a divine voice is suddenly heard, stopping him:

> It has been taught: Before Rabbi Ḥizkiyah could stand, a voice issued, declaring, "One messenger does not perform two missions."
>
> Rabbi Shim'on trembled, and said, "Each and every one in his place. Yet through me and Rabbi El'azar, my son, and Rabbi Abba, perfection will alight upon us." (Zohar 3:132b; trans. Matt 8:361)

The divine voice reveals that there is another presence surrounding the intimate terrestrial circle of the Companions. Here in the field, among the trees, Rabbi Shim'on is the director—but from above a divine voice is attentively present, perhaps the veiled voice of the Idra's author, functioning as the scene's celestial choreographer.

The voice's reproving words and Rabbi Shim'on's response require some explanation. Indeed, thirteen parts of the beard need to be configured, and the Companions number only ten. We may thus presume that Rabbi Shim'on had intended for Rabbi Ḥizkiyah to be one of those who expounds more than one *tiqqun*, completing the number of the beard's configurations. However, the celestial voice is suddenly heard, stopping him in his tracks. Rabbi Shim'on himself is presented here as a teacher who is affected, ready to change his position or admit error—and he accepts the judgment concerning the correct sequence of speakers and configurations: he, Rabbi El'azar his son, and Rabbi Abba the most advanced student will complete the *tiqqunim*. This decision highlights the special status of these three sages in the hierarchy of the group, also infusing the unfolding human drama with tension.

Reading with hindsight, taking into account Rabbi Ḥizkiyah's death at the end of the Idra, it may be that the divine voice is aware that Rabbi Ḥizkiyah's soul—which, as we have seen, is desired by God—could not endure another *tiqqun*, and would immediately depart from his body were he to attempt it. It seems that Rabbi Ḥizkiyah's presence is necessary for the event to proceed, and the voice thus forbids him from taking on the additional mission. A hint at this interpretation may be found in the voice's reference to Rabbi Ḥizkiyah as an angel (Hebrew *mal'akh*, also meaning "messenger"). Under normal circumstances this might be construed as a compliment, but here in the Idra, human beings are indeed permitted to perform two missions. Human beings, not angels, configure the face of God![34] It may thus be that Rabbi Ḥizkiyah has broken out of the realm of humanity, to which the other Companions belong, and that he occupies a liminal state between this life and the hereafter. Rabbi Ḥizkiyah's *tiqqun* and death echo the narrative of Nadab and Abihu, the sons of Aaron, who (according to classical interpretations) sacrifice themselves, thereby establishing the Tabernacle service on the day of its dedication (Leviticus 10:1–3). Rabbi Ḥizkiyah's expansion beyond the boundaries of human consciousness for the sake of the Companions initiates or stabilizes the Idra, but at the cost of his life in this world. In contrast, Rabbi Shim'on represents the ultimate High Priest, entering the Holy of Holies and emerging in peace, unharmed.[35]

There is no doubt that Rabbi Ḥizkiyah's *tiqqun* and Rabbi Shim'on's response constitute a climactic moment in the Idra. As Rabbi Ḥizkiyah summons and invokes *'Arikh Anpin*'s quality of *bearing iniquity*, it seems that he and all the participants are granted the privilege of bathing in the luminous river of *'Attiqa*. Next, the third *tiqqun* is recited by Rabbi Ḥiyya, and it is an exegetical masterpiece. In this *tiqqun* (which will not be discussed here), as in those that follow, one may detect an effort to cool down the intensity ignited by Rabbi Ḥizkiyah, and to return the assembly to its more familiar modes of visually descriptive, but not ecstatic, exegesis.[36]

Flowing Bounty: The Eighth *Tiqqun*

The eighth *tiqqun* of the beard—presented by Rabbi El'azar, Rabbi Shim'on's son—traces the border of the beard, almost as though an imaginary hair were marking its outline.[37] In this *tiqqun* we contemplate, for the first time, the entire beard: hanging from the face down to the navel, an imagined navel belonging to a body never described. The divine attribute associated with the *tiqqun* is *He will subdue our iniquities*—describing God's suppression of sins. In this passage, the outline of the beard is called *mazzal*—in reference not to the stars and constellations (*mazzalot*) but rather to the fluid (*nazel*) quality of the oil flowing over the entire beard. The eighth *tiqqun* is similar to the thirteenth (discussed later), insofar as they both treat the beard and its meaning for the world and human beings as a whole:

> "Eighth enhancement: One cord of hairs emerges around the beard and hangs evenly to the navel.
>
> "Rise, El'azar, my son, array this enhancement!"
>
> Rabbi El'azar rose. He opened, saying, "All depends upon מזל (*mazzal*),[38] even the Torah scroll in the ark.
>
> "This statement has been established in the Concealment of the Book, and so it says. But does all depend upon *mazzal*? We have learned: The Torah scroll is holy, its case is holy, the ark is holy. [. . .] All depends upon the Torah scroll, yet it depends on *mazzal*? It is written: *By signs in the heavens do not be dismayed* (Jeremiah 10:2). Should that which exists in such a state of holiness be dependent upon מזלא (*mazzala*)?
>
> "Well, it has been established as follows in the Concealment of the Book: This precious holy cord, upon which all hairs of the beard depend, is called *mazzal*. Why? Because all the holiest of holies depend upon this *mazzala*. [. . .]
>
> "Why *mazzal*? Because מזלי (*mazzalei*), signs of the zodiac, are suspended from it, and those above and those below נזלי (*nazlei*), flow, from it. Therefore it hangs, and upon it depend all things of the world and those above and below. Even the Torah scroll in the ark, adorned

> with ten types of holiness, is not exempt from this principle—along with all other holy things, all of which depend on this.
>
> "Whoever sees this enhancement, their iniquities are subdued and pressed down by it, as is written: *He will subdue our iniquities* (Micah 7:19)."
>
> Rabbi Shim'on said to him, "You are blessed, my son, by the Holy of Holies, most Ancient of all!" (Zohar 3:134a; trans. Matt 8:370–372, emended)

In this *tiqqun*, the Idra steps back from the fine details of the beard and views it as a whole. This perspective conjures three interrelated images: the magnificent white beard upon an elderly face; oil trickling down Aaron's beard, and the pleasure associated with it (Psalm 133); and a more cosmic and fantastical image—that of a tremendous luminous flow, emerging from a single source, flowing through myriad channels.

The configuration begins with a rhetorical process that is aimed at freeing the term *mazzal* from its astrological sense (as a constellation of celestial bodies), as well as its sense as "fortune," "fate," or "luck."[39] The new meaning that Rabbi El'azar accords to it is that of flowing (the usual sense of Hebrew *nazal*). The *mazzal* is the flowing stream of cosmic divine bounty issuing from *'Attiqa*. At the same time, the association between the *mazzal* and astrology is not entirely absent, for this beard, from which all the upper and lower worlds are suspended, is also the source of the heavenly firmament in which the stars and constellations hang. This *tiqqun* thus implies that the astrological dimension depends upon something higher than it: the undifferentiated Divine, from which all flows, and upon which all depends.[40]

This matter is linked to the theological or mystical-experiential insight that accompanies this *tiqqun*: all existence depends upon the bounteous flow emerging from various channels and from its source within the primordial divine brain. This river-beard, with all of its parts, is a pathway for the Divine to overflow from within itself. It all flows, gushing, hanging from the beard. Religious symbols, such as the scroll of the Torah, are also caught up in this *mazzal*, this flow—they are suspended within it, and they emerge from it.

The *mazzal* is also the source of *Ze'eir Anpin*'s power, as is stated in the

Idra Zuṭa:

> "*Now, please, let the power of YHVH be great* (Numbers 14:17)—the one who is called Holy *Mazzala*, concealed of all concealed. For this power and this radiance derive from *mazzala*." (Zohar 3:295b; trans. Matt 9:835)

The power of this *tiqqun* thus applies to the entire realm of religion. We learn that the initial building blocks of religion—the Holy of Holies, the Torah, and even YHVH—are not the most elevated instance of religion; rather, they derive their sanctity from *'Attiqa*. Implicit here is a demand to summon the presence of *'Attiqa* (not only *Ze'eir Anpin*) into religious consciousness, while affirming a profound theological position: just as astrology is a misguided form of divine service, aimed at too low an aspect of the divine, so too is divine service that is aimed at *Ze'eir Anpin* in isolation from *'Attiqa*. To put it boldly: normative Jewish religious practice, which worships YHVH as its supreme divine persona without acknowledging *'Attiqa*, is disconnected from its supernal source.

The *tiqqun* concludes thus: "Whoever sees this enhancement, their iniquities are subdued and pressed down by it, as is written: *He will subdue our iniquities* (Micah 7:19)." Whoever expands their religious consciousness to include the perspective of *'Attiqa*, and an awareness of the eternal flow of Mercy, merits to have their sins subdued within the great current of Mercy. Beneath the tremendous pressure of the *mazzal*, a person's sins become less absolute, and their volume changes. From the formulation—"whoever sees this enhancement"—it emerges that this deep perspective on reality is possible even for us, human beings in the present. Further evidence for this may be found in Rabbi Shim'on's blessing for his son at the conclusion of the *tiqqun*, a blessing that summons the presence of *'Attiqa* in our world: "You are blessed, my son, by the Holy of Holies, most Ancient of all!"

Eternal Forgiveness: The Twelfth *Tiqqun*

The twelfth *tiqqun* focuses on *'Attiqa*'s mouth, and on the meaning of the fact that it is hairless yet surrounded by hair. The Idra does not disclose the identity of the speaker of this *tiqqun*, nor does Rabbi Shim'on offer a blessing at its conclusion. It is thus implicit that the speaker may be Rabbi

Shim'on himself.

This *tiqqun* is surprising in two ways. The first is its conception of the mouth as part of the beard, a sort of hairless orifice within it, rather than classifying it with the features of the head—the forehead, the eyes, and the nose. The second is its description of the mouth more as an opening than as a distinct and expressive facial feature. There is no description of the lips or of the tongue, palate, or teeth within the divine mouth, nor any account of the mouth opening and closing.[41] What is invoked in this *tiqqun* is the mouth as an unobstructed aperture through which a river of life-breath and forgiveness flow, emerging from deep within the undifferentiated Divine, without any interference or impediment whatsoever:

> "Twelfth enhancement: No hair overhangs the mouth, and the mouth is clear on all sides, with lovely hair all around.
>
> "This enhancement—that they [the hairs] are all eliminated from the mouth—is so that there will be no trouble. [. . .]
>
> "From this holy supernal mouth, Holy of Holies, blows a breath. What breath? A breath pouring into *Ze'eir Anpin*, enveloping Him, and by this breath are enveloped all those below. [. . .]
>
> "This [mouth] is hiddenness of all, grasped neither above nor below—concealed with utmost concealment, unknown. This is the one unadorned, having no enhancement." (Zohar 3:134a–b; trans. Matt 8:374)

In the course of this section of the Idra Rabba, the reader has already encountered hairless expanses within the beard, such as the pathway from the nostrils to the lips and the rounded cheeks. The uniqueness of these parts of the beard lies in their role as pathways of divine bounty that remain unregulated by the hair, flowing instead from the inner reaches of *'Attiqa*'s brain, through a wide-open channel. Thus, for example, the rounded surfaces emerging from the *fragrant flowerbeds* (that is, the cheeks) are described as the source of life, light, and joy for all worlds.[42] The mouth is the largest of all the hairless areas. Since the nose and mouth are the apparatuses for breathing, the mouth's hairlessness enables the breath—which emerges from it and breathes life into *Ze'eir Anpin*—to flow without effort or hindrance. Here, *'Attiqa*'s mouth is called "hiddenness of all"—it is the secret, remaining utterly mysterious due to the absence of any barrier that might "translate" it. It is "unadorned, having no enhancement," in the sense that it is neither enclothed nor covered.

'Attiqa's mouth does not speak, and does not establish any existence through speech or make pronouncements of Judgment or Mercy. The only expression that might be heard from the mouth of the Lord of Forgiveness, were he to speak in a manner that we were able to hear, is *I have forgiven*. Thus do we find in the third *tiqqun* of the beard, describing the hairless passageway from the nostrils to the lips:

> "[*P*]*assing over transgression*—providing passage to the holy mouth, so that it may say, *I have forgiven* (Numbers 14:20).
>
> "It has been taught: Numerous registrars await that mouth, but it is not revealed to any of them, for it ascends and is crowned and concealed—known and unknown." (Zohar 3:133a; trans. Matt 8:362–363)

The Idra emphasizes that any speech or vision that can be described verbally already belongs to the realm of *Ze'eir Anpin*, rather than *'Attiqa*. At the same time, the breath issuing from *'Attiqa* enclothes *Ze'eir Anpin*, and is a source of his own breath, a speaking breath, a breath that pronounces and enacts. Through *Ze'eir Anpin*, the prophets are also enclothed in breath—as in the biblical expression, *the spirit of God clothed itself in Zechariah* (2 Chronicles 24:20)—and they in turn give expression to *the mouth of YHVH*, that is, of *Ze'eir Anpin*, the External One:

> "Consequently, the breath proceeding [from the one that is] outside [that is, *Ze'eir Anpin*], enveloping the faithful prophets, is called 'the mouth of *YHVH*,' but in this Ancient of Ancients it is not expressed, and there is no one who knows His breath beside Himself. Therefore its hairs lie symmetrically around the mouth, which is clear on all sides.
>
> "In this the patriarchs trusted, to be enveloped by this breath spreading in so many directions from the place surrounded symmetrically by all the hair, as is written: *as You swore to our fathers* (Micah 7:20)." (Zohar 3:134b; trans. Matt 8:374–375)

From the way that *Ze'eir Anpin* is clothed in the breath of *'Attiqa*'s mouth, we learn that *ʿAttiqa*'s breath lies deep within the spirit of human prophecy and inspiration. This is the reason that the *tiqqun* of the mouth is such a profound mystery: it expresses the fundamental root of existence through the breath. The breath of *ʿAttiqa* does not merely dwell in far-off and transcendent dimensions but reaches the human realm and acts within it. The prophets, the exegete tells us (possibly also alluding to the Companions), live, create, and prophesy through the breath of *Zeʿeir Anpin*—and through it, they are bound to *ʿAttiqa*, the Holy Ancient One.

In the present *tiqqun*, *ʿAttiqa*'s mouth receives the distinction of being called the "Holy of Holies"—a term also used to refer to the female genitalia in the Idra Zuṭa's account of the divine Female's body.[43] They are in fact parallel to each other: the upper and lower mouth; the locus of kissing and the locus of coupling; the site of the birth of language and speech and the site of the birth of human beings. But while the Female's vagina is treated at length, the twelfth *tiqqun* depicts the mouth as a mysterious aperture through which life-breath flows, out of the depths of *ʿAttiqa*.

As I have stated, there is no mention whatsoever of *ʿAttiqa*'s lips in this *tiqqun*—even if we can find a poetic allusion to their existence in Rabbi Ḥizkiyah's vision, which describes the gushing light reaching "the shore [lit., lip] of the supernal deep sea."[44] The absence of the lips from the passage treating the divine mouth is particularly striking when we compare it with other images employed in the Idra literature. A first example may be drawn from Sifra di-Tsniʿuta, which describes both *ʿAttiqa*'s lips and the miraculous possibility of a kiss between divine and human lips: "Lips are free from all sides. Happy is one who is kissed by those kisses!"[45] We encounter a second example in the sensuous account of *Zeʿeir Anpin*'s lips, both in the Idra Rabba and the Idra Zuṭa: "*His lips are roses* (Song of Songs 5:13), red as roses; [*dripping*] *liquid myrrh* (*ibid.*), intensely red";[46] and "[T]he lips are entirely red as a rose [. . .] lips murmuring *Gevurah*, Power, murmuring *Ḥokhmeta*, Wisdom. Upon those lips depend good and evil, life and death."[47]

Perhaps the reason for the absence of lips from the description of *ʿAttiqa*'s mouth is that there are two of them, whereas the Idra Rabba seeks to emphasize the unified aspect of this *partsuf*. Thus, *ʿAttiqa*'s two eyes become as one, and his two nostrils perform a similar task, effectively doubling the flow of life-giving breath issuing from them, virtually unifying them. (This is in contrast with *Ze'eir Anpin*, in whose face each nostril performs a distinct role.) The account of the eternally open mouth "by whose opening all fine and precious openings are released"[48] may also explain the absence of lips, the role of which is to cover or close the mouth.

In concluding this *tiqqun*, the question remains: What is the connection between the mouth and the Attribute of Mercy, *as You swore to our fathers*. The connection does not emerge explicitly from the scriptural interpretations in this *tiqqun* but from an association between the similar sounds of *You swore* (*nishba'ta*) and *you breathed* (*nashabta*)—the latter referring to the life-breath issuing from *'Attiqa*'s mouth and reaching the patriarchs, or *sefirot*, which are enclothed in this breath. On another level, the connection is anchored in the fact that the mouth, breathing the life-breath, provides human beings with the sense of trust that they are not disconnected from the flow of the life-breath of God. In this sense, the connection to this divine attribute enables faith in the perpetuity of the oath from days of old and faith in the infinitude of the breath issuing from *'Attiqa*'s mouth.

The Greater Perspective: The Thirteenth *Tiqqun*

The thirteenth *tiqqun* is the last of those of *Arikh Anpin*'s beard, and it is presented by Rabbi Shim'on. Its topic is a broad and inclusive view of *'Attiqa*'s face, adorned with a beard that extends to the navel, and it corresponds with the phrase *from days of old* that concludes the Thirteen Attributes of Mercy enumerated in the verses from Micah. This *tiqqun* contains within it all the other *tiqqunim* of the beard, summarizing and synthesizing them into a single coherent portrait. Thus, even more than in the eighth *tiqqun* (discussed earlier), there is a generalizing aspect to this configuration—the noble beauty of the entire flowing beard.

> "Thirteenth enhancement: Hair hangs beneath the beard on either side in fine glory, in beautiful glory, covering to the navel. None of the face of the fragrant offering is seen except for those beautiful white apples."
>
> Rabbi Shim'on said: "Happy is the share of whoever is present in this holy supernal assembly of ours! Happy is his share in this world

> and in the world that is coming! For we are sitting amid supernal fire surrounding us. Behold, all the sublime enhancements of the holy beard have been arrayed and adorned, encircling their places.
>
> "This thirteenth enhancement—this fine enhancement, to which they are joined! What yearning to raise the head toward it! From it dangle all those joined to *Ze'eir Anpin*; from it dangle those above and those below. This is the perfect enhancement, completing all enhancements, consummating all." (Zohar 3:134b; trans. Matt 8:375)

Rabbi Shim'on begins the thirteenth *tiqqun* with a summary of the preceding *tiqqunim* of *'Attiqa*'s beard, and his discourse lends the scene a revelatory quality. A supernal fire descends, surrounding the Companions, like the fire that surrounds the rabbis of classical talmudic literature when they expound the esoteric secrets of the Work of the Chariot, or when they creatively string together the words of Scripture like pearls. This celestial fire—explains the early sage ben 'Azzai—is an expression of Torah in its primordial and fiery state, before contracting and being translated into letters.[49] The supernal fire surrounds the Companions, and Rabbi Shim'on's discourse makes it clear to the participants that they are no longer within the temporal dimension but rather dwelling in supernal holiness.

With his spiritual vision, Rabbi Shim'on perceives the *tiqqunim* as adorned entities, ascending from the mouths of the Companions and taking their place within *'Attiqa*'s beard. As in the eighth *tiqqun*, the beard is here described from a distant perspective that deemphasizes details and enables a broad view of the glorious flowing beard as a whole. The sight of the entire beard, hanging evenly like a white river, covering the navel, is splendorous. Rightly is the beard called *mazzal*, for the precious oil descending upon it is a river that flows, *nazel*, carrying with it the elixir of life from deep within the divine Eden.

This complete image of the beard is the ultimate desire of all reality, which seeks to orient itself, align itself, and direct its vision toward this beard. Seeing the beard is essentially a metonymic or modest expression for contemplating the face of *'Attiqa*, for it enables one to perceive the flowing and vibrant aura that surrounds the face.

Furthermore, spiritual perception of the beard as a whole is satisfying, nourishing. It is reminiscent of Nahmanides' account of the mystics who refine themselves spiritually to the point that the very experience of cleaving to the Divine satisfies their hunger. In this context, Nahmanides cites the verses, *In the light of the king's countenance is life* (Proverbs 16:15), and *I shall be satisfied, when I awake, with Your likeness* (Psalms 17:15). In the Idra, these verses will be interpreted mystically and hyperliterally—God's face is the sustenance of all things.[50]

> "It has been taught: These enhancements are called *days of old* (Micah 7:20), days most ancient of all. Those appearing in *Ze'eir Anpin* are called *days of the world* (Isaiah 63:9).
>
> "It has been taught: These *days of old* are all arranged in the enhancements of the beard of the Ancient of Ancients, and this thirteenth one includes them. All hidden treasures above and below are included in this *mazzala*, from which all flows, as has been said. This day is not included among them; rather it includes all.
>
> "At the time when the Ancient of Days is aroused, that enhancement will be called יום אחד (*yom eḥad*), *one day*, in which He intends to glorify His beard, as is written: *He will be known to YHVH* (Zechariah 14:7)—*He* alone, more than all; *He*, encompassing all; *He*, not called by any known name.
>
> "For we have learned: Wherever there is day, there is night, since there is no day without night. Because that time will be the beard's glory and *He* alone will exist, it will be called neither day nor night. For day is only called so from our perspective, and night is only called so from our perspective." (Zohar 3:134b; trans. Matt 8:375–376)

The thirteenth *tiqqun* is the totality of the *tiqqunim*, the glory of the entire beard. It unites the preceding *tiqqunim*, called *days of old* or *primordial years*: that is, the attributes of God, or proto-*sefirot* in their inchoate and primordial state as they are manifest within *'Attiqa*. A distinction is drawn between the primordial days and *days of the world* (*yemei 'olam*),[51] which are the attributes or *sefirot* as expressed in the dimension of *Ze'eir Anpin*.[52] The *tiqqunim* of *Arikh Anpin* are archaic, primordial, while those of *Ze'eir Anpin* already pertain to the world (*'olam*)—time, space, and language as we know them. The possibility of grasping or experiencing something of the *days of old* grants human beings the privilege of participating in a dimension of being that bears no connection to time in its usual sense, or to life as we know it. Thus, in a famous zoharic passage, several of Rabbi Shimʿon's disciples encounter Rav Hamnuna Saba, who reflects some of *Arikh Anpin*'s qualities. The elderly figure says to them: "Whoever is bound to those primordial years, life is bound to him."[53]

Indeed, *Arikh Anpin*'s beard is not a part of the world in terms of time and space. Therefore, the possibility of attaining some perception of it is connected to a reality beyond time, to "one day" (*yom eḥad*) which is "neither day nor night." It is not counted among the days, but rather encompasses them. The glory of the flowing beard can be manifest only in a state of unity and expansiveness, both cosmic and psychic, and there is no doubt that the Idra represents such a moment.

Notwithstanding this quality of being beyond time and space, the Idra goes on to pose the question of the connection between *ʿAttiqa* and human beings in the real world. Rabbi Shimʿon describes how the entirety of *ʿAttiqa*'s beard causes thirteen mysterious wellsprings to flow forth with divine bounty, gushing with divine anointing oil. These wellsprings link *ʿAttiqa* to the terrestrial realm of humanity:[54]

> "Since this enhancement encompasses all, it is not known or seen. From it flows anointing oil in thirteen directions—springs for all those below, who glow from that oil.
>
> "Thirteen enhancements of the holy supernal beard are arrayed, and these enhancements of the beard descend in countless directions. How they spread and how they radiate cannot be seen; they are hidden from all, concealed from all. No one knows a bodily place in this Ancient One. In their expansion, all are included, as has been said.
>
> "He is known and unknown, concealed and not concealed. Of Him is proclaimed *I am YHVH*, הוא (*hu*), *He, is my name; My glory I will not yield to another* (Isaiah 42:8); and it is written: *Know that YHVH is God, Hu, He, made us, and not we ourselves* (Psalms 100:3). It is also written: *The Ancient of Days sat* (Daniel 7:9)—*sat*, surely: *sat* in His place, unknown to anyone; *sat*, not to be found. And it is written: *I praise You, for*

> *awesomely and wondrously I am made; wondrous are Your works,* [*my soul knows well*] (Psalms 139:14)." (Zohar 3:134b; trans. Matt 8:377)

'Attiqa's transcendence and sublimeness thus do not imply that he is disconnected from humanity. The language here is distinctly paradoxical: *'Attiqa* is not only hidden, he is "known and unknown, concealed and not concealed." *'Attiqa* is wondrous, and despite the fact that he does not exist in the sense that other entities exist, part of the human psyche knows him, for *He made us.* The glorious wonder of human existence is that, within ourselves, we recognize some subtle aspect of *'Attiqa* despite his transcendence. Even if he does not fit within the boundaries of discursive knowledge, our *soul knows well.*

A Summary of the *Tiqqunim* of the Beard

The *tiqqunim* of *'Attiqa*'s beard are complete. One by one, the Companions have risen, weaving the segments of the beard together with the Attributes of Mercy.

This section of the Idra is constructed in a unique fashion: it begins with a schematic overview of the *tiqqunim* of the beard, then moves to a series of scriptural interpretations presented by the Companions, each exegesis "filling in" the contours defined at the outset, producing a multidimensional image. Each *tiqqun* evokes and configures the hairs of the beard, like canals conveying vital substance from the brain, oil that illuminates and anoints. Once the *tiqqunim* are complete, all is aflow, rivers of precious oil pour mellifluously into reality, causing it to become iridescent and luminous.

On the one hand, the collaborative effort of the Companions leads to a concentrated concretization of the beard. The reader enters a realm filled with accounts of hair: straight hair, coarse hair, evenly hanging hair, hair of the temples, the moustache, the cheeks, beard hair falling to the navel of the heart. All is white, flowing, no strand is entangled with another. On the other hand, this concretization is presented with fantastical resolution. We do indeed begin with an account of some detail of the beard, evoking a human face, even if it is in a schematic fashion—but at some point, through reflection, each detail takes on new and giant proportions, becoming a quality, a flow, of cosmic dimensions. Each *tiqqun* constitutes a visual and conceptual space. Sometimes it is terse and enigmatic; sometimes brimming, bursting. From up close, it is difficult not to drown in the beard.

And so, the concrete becomes an abstract quality; at the very same time, the abstract is given form, and takes its place within the face. The Idra gives a face to the attributes, but the experience is not one of static iconization of the face. From a distance, the entire vista is one of mighty and radiant abundance, emphasizing the tremendous resplendence emanating from this primordial head.

The wondrous white beard of *'Attiqa* was internalized, deeply etched into post-zoharic Jewish consciousness. We may find an enchanting example of this in the dream diary of Moshe Ḥayyim Ephraim of Sudilkov (1742–1800), a grandson of Israel Ba'al Shem Tov (the Besht), found at the end of his book *Degel Maḥaneh Efrayim*:

> In a dream, I saw that I adhered to him—my body to his holy body, within his beard, the Holy Beard. Afterwards, I heard the congregation reciting the Thirteen Attributes—*YHVH, Merciful,* and so on—and I too began to recite within the mouth, without articulation of the lips. For I thought: Are these not the very Thirteen Attributes, whose Holy Beard I am within?[55]

In this mystical dream, the author does not need to articulate the Attributes of Mercy with his lips, for he is within them, clinging to them, resting as he is within the holy beard—the beard of *'Attiqa*. Of course, it is possible that this image stems from the author's childhood memory of being draped in his grandfather's white beard, or alternatively, that it represents his desire to connect and cleave to his grandfather, the Besht, whom his grandson sees as representing *'Attiqa*, full of love.

The Ceremonial Closing of the *Tiqqunim* of *'Attiqa*

Once this section of the work has drawn to a close, the *tiqqunim* of the beard having been configured and arrayed, Rabbi Shim'on offers a visionary and revelatory description of them. The vision demonstrates that the *tiqqunim* arrayed by Rabbi Shim'on and the Companions actually set the divine and human realms into motion, thus giving full expression to the Idra's theurgic aspect:

> Rabbi Shim'on said to the Companions, "When this canopy that you see over us was spread, I saw all these enhancements descending within it, illumining this place—and one curtain, a vestment of holiness, spread over four columns in four directions.
>
> "I saw these enhancements shining upon it, awaiting the words of our mouths—to be crowned, each ascending to its place. [. . .] As each of us opened his mouth to arrange a certain enhancement, that enhancement sat waiting for the word to issue from your mouth, and then it was crowned, ascending to its place to be adorned.
>
> "All the columns on either side rejoice upon hearing what they do not know and they listen to your voices. How many chariots appear here for your sake! Happy are you in the world that is coming, for all these words issuing from your mouths are holy words, worthy words, not deviating to the right or the left.
>
> "The blessed Holy One delights in hearing and listening to these words, eventually decreeing that in the world that is coming you will utter all these holy words a second time. Of you is written *Your palate is like fine wine—flowing to my beloved smoothly, stirring the lips of sleepers* (Song of Songs 7:10). What is meant by *stirring the lips of sleepers*? Even in the world that is coming your lips will be astir in His presence.
>
> "Now focus your minds to arrange the enhancements of *Ze'eir Anpin*—how He is arrayed and how He is clothed in His enhancements by the enhancements of the Ancient of Days, Holy of Holies, Concealed of the Concealed, concealed from all. Now it is incumbent upon you to decree a true, fine, and beautiful judgment, and to arrange all enhancements thoroughly." (Zohar 3:134b–135a; trans. Matt 8:377–379)

Rabbi Shim'on describes the curtain draped over them—a screen, veil, a canopy, or a celestial firmament—in which the face of *'Attiqa* appears with its luminous *tiqqunim*. This curtain takes the reader back to the initial account of *'Attiqa*'s *tiqqunim*, at the outset of the Idra Rabba. As the reader recalls, before the divine face is configured, *'Attiqa* spreads a curtain before him upon which he engraves engravings—the source of the primordial kings that did not endure. By the Torah's wise counsel, he then enters that curtain and is himself configured through his *tiqqunim* within it. This is the beginning of an enduring existence, a mode of being that does not fade.[56] It seems that now, after completing the configurations of *'Attiqa*'s beard, the face of the ancient Deity is manifest within or upon the curtain—configured, luminous with the radiance of the *tiqqunim* that emerge from the mouths of the Companions, like stars shining in the heavens. Above the Companions, *'Attiqa*'s curtain is spread like a wedding canopy, and the *tiqqunim* that have been arrayed enable him to descend and shine from within it. As the Idra continues, the figure of *Ze'eir Anpin* will also take shape within that canopy, and thereafter the divine Male and Female as one.

The entire narrative might thus be conceived as an initialization, with the aim of coronating *'Attiqa*. But why is it necessary? Why do the Companions again have to perform the *tiqqunim* through which the Holy Ancient One has already been configured? The speech of the Companions seems to summon the face, to evoke its presence and renew it. In the Zohar, the idea that human speech, like divine speech, establishes reality is articulated again and again. This is particularly true of innovative interpretations of Torah.[57] The Companions' *tiqqunim* are an example of such innovative interpretation, generating proper "maintenance" for the figure of *'Attiqa*. *'Attiqa* would, of course, endure without innovative exegesis, but the latter enables the presence of his face and its renewal within the human realm. It might be said that the channels of communication exist, but the flow of bounty within them is amplified when they are vivified within the human consciousness.

Furthermore, as in other passages throughout the Zohar, in which creative human speech in the process of Torah study brings joy and comfort to God in the celestial realm, here too the interpretations offered by the Companions bring joy to God, who announces that these words, the words of the Idra, will never fade or vanish. Rabbi Shim'on declares that even in "the world that is coming" these discourses will be heard—these interpretations flowing from the palate like fine wine, guiding the Divine surely, from within the depths of himself and into our world. Like the ancient sages, whose teachings in Torah do not perish when they die—for, when their words are studied, their lips move in the grave[58]—the Companions (and the authors of the Idra) are assured that their words will live on, even in the world that is coming, even at other times.

In his account of his vision, Rabbi Shim'on provides a sublime description of the tension of mutual desire between the *tiqqunim* in their archetypical state within the divine realm and the words issuing from the Companions' mouths in this world. The *tiqqunim* await the words of the human beings with anticipation. For their part, the words themselves crave to ascend, to crown and be crowned, and to fill the *tiqqun* above with new-ancient substance. The palpable, luminous yearning of the words and the *tiqqunim* to attain union generates a unique image, at once encompassing the supernal and lower realms in an account of life and emotion pulsating through the humans and the *tiqqunim* themselves. Rabbi Shim'on perceives the event within the curtain, as well as the power and energy of the *tiqqunim* in the world below: "awaiting the words of our mouths—to be crowned, each ascending to its place. [. . .] As each of us opened his mouth to arrange a certain enhancement, that enhancement sat waiting for the word to issue from your mouth, and then it was crowned, ascending to its place to be adorned."

This visionary portrayal, whose literary formulations allude to the biblical accounts of the curtain (*parokhet*) in the Tabernacle,[59] also depicts how the four pillars—perhaps representing the *sefirot*, perhaps the patriarchs and King David, or perhaps Rabbi Shim'on, Rabbi El'azar, Rabbi Abba, and the Messiah—hold the curtain within which the configured face of *'Attiqa* may be seen, lowering it down to our world.

Finally, the vision of the canopy descending upon the Companions also represents separation. *'Attiqa* remains set apart from our everyday consciousness, the curtain being a semipermeable fabric separating the realm of *'Attiqa* from that of the Companions even as it joins them together. The canopy is draped upon the celebration, enveloping it, and simultaneously bringing the first episode of the Idra to a close, enabling us to turn to the next chapter.

Indeed, Rabbi Shim'on's words in concluding this section of the Idra are also the master's words to his disciples on the occasion of their initiation. They allude to and illumine all that has occurred until this point, complimenting the Companions on their active and effectual part in completing the *tiqqunim* of *'Attiqa*, and encouraging them to direct their minds toward the journey ahead. Now the mission presented to them is that of configuring *Ze'eir Anpin* from within the *tiqqunim* of *'Attiqa*, emphasizing the relationship between the two divine faces. This connection ensures that *Ze'eir Anpin* will not be understood as a distinct entity, external and strange, rootless and without origin. Rather, he is an image drawn from the supernal image of the Holy Ancient One.

13

The Kings of Edom

The Second Appearance

The *tiqqunim* of *Ze'eir Anpin* begin with a glorious hymn that honors him as the Divine in human likeness. But following the hymn, which I discuss later, Rabbi Shim'on does not proceed directly to the configuration of *Ze'eir Anpin*. First, the primordial kings of Edom erupt into the narrative once again. Having already encountered the kings of Edom in the opening passages of the Idra Rabba, before the configuration of *'Attiqa*; we now meet them again in the context of and in relation to *Ze'eir Anpin*.

In the initial reality of *'Attiqa*, the primordial kings were a first expression of the will to become distinct and separate from the uniting and undifferentiated quality of infinitude; in a sense, they were at first conjectures within the undifferentiated divine mind— unripe thoughts, perhaps powerful and beautiful, but without enduring existence. In contrast, at the outset of the *tiqqun* of *Ze'eir Anpin*, the myth of the kings speaks of a later stage in the emergence of reality from its primordial state of unity. Now the kings of Edom are identified with initial attempts to become actualized, to take on form. They are now built and destroyed in actuality; they do not reside merely in the consciousness of *'Attiqa* but also outside it, in the Land of Edom. (This mirrors *Ze'eir Anpin* himself, who is called "the exterior one."[1]) It seems that even now, the Divine has not attained the degree of maturity that would enable the kings to manifest in a balanced and durable fashion. On a psychological level, they represent one-dimensional structures, lacking some component that would balance and stabilize them. On a physiological level, the manifestation of the kings is connected here to birth––the stage at which one emerges from within—as opposed to conception, which occurs hidden deep within the inner reaches of *'Attiqa*.

Avishar Har-Shefi, who has analyzed all the references to the Death of the Kings in the Idra literature, points out that at the outset of the *tiqqunim* of *Ze'eir Anpin*, we may identify an attempt to understand what went wrong during the initial attempt to emerge into existence, and how this might be rectified. According to him, the failure is rooted in an excess of Judgment (*Din*). Judgment is indeed necessary for existence to emerge, become distinct, and come into the fullness of being. However, the kings possess no quality that might balance out Judgment, and the latter is thus so powerful that it allows for no resistance:[2]

> "It has been taught in the Concealment of the Book: The Ancient of Ancients, before preparing His enhancements, fashioned kings and gauged kings, but they did not endure; so He eventually put them aside and concealed them for a later time, as is written: *These are the kings who reigned in the land of Edom before a king reigned over the Children of Israel* (Genesis 36:31). *In the land of Edom*—in the place where all judgments exist. None of them endured until the White Head, Ancient of Ancients, was arrayed. [. . .]
>
> "[. . .] [F]or until He Himself was arrayed in His enhancements, all those that He intended to arrange did not endure, and all those worlds were destroyed, as is written: *There reigned in Edom Bela son of Beor* (Genesis 36:32). *There reigned in Edom*—a precious secret: the place where all judgments cluster, from where they dangle.
>
> "*Bela son of Beor*—it has been taught: He is the harshest of all decrees of Judgment, through whom band together one million wailers and howlers.
>
> "*And the name of his city was Dinhabah* (Genesis 36:32). What is דנהבה (*Dinhavah*)? That is to say, דין הב (*Din hav*), Give judgment—as is said: *The leech has two daughters*—הב הב (*Hav, hav*), *'Give!' 'Give!'* (Proverbs 30:15).

> "As soon as he ascended to settle, he did not endure, nor could he. Why? Because *Adam* had not been arranged. Why? Because the arrangement of *Adam* and His image comprise all, and all can settle in Him." (Zohar 3:135a–b; trans. Matt 8:380–381)

Bela son of Beor, whose name is reminiscent of the prophet and sorcerer Balaam son of Beor, is a powerful force with whom formidable entities of Judgment are associated. His city is Dinhabah, here understood as a force of Judgment that hungers for ever more Judgment. Similarly, the land over which he rules is Edom, the locus of all Judgment. Bela's desire to enter Dinhabah in Edom and to reign within it results in an amplification of redness and Judgment, without being balanced by any other mode of being. Therefore, he cannot endure.

When the kings first appeared, they were unable to exist, for the White Head had not yet been configured, and the face of *Arikh Anpin* had not yet emerged. However, here, Rabbi Shim'on declares that the kings cannot endure due to the absence of a complex framework called *Adam*, which could configure and array them, contain and settle them.

> "[S]ince this arrangement of *Adam* did not exist, they could not endure or settle, and they were nullified.
>
> "Would you ever imagine that they were nullified? Look, they are all included in *Adam*! Rather, they were nullified and removed from that arrangement, until the image of *Adam* appeared. When this image appeared they were all engraved and transformed into another existence. Some of them became fragrantly firm, some of them not entirely so, and some of them not at all.
>
> "Now, you might say, 'But it is written *He died* [. . .] *he died* (Genesis 36:33–39)—implying that they were nullified completely.' Not so! Rather, anyone who descends from his original rung of existence is said to have died, as is written: *The king of Egypt died* (Exodus 2:23)—meaning that he descended from the rung that he occupied. Once *Adam* was arrayed, they were called by different names and became fragrantly firm through existing in him, enduring in their places." (Zohar 3:135b; trans. Matt 8:381–382)

This interpretation delves into the mystical meaning of the death or nullification of the kings, claiming that it does not refer to their total disappearance or annihilation. Because the kings are forces too primal, exclusively anchored in Judgment, they must be set aside and hidden away until a mode of existence is established that can contain them, withstand them. Their death does not signify complete eradication but rather a descent from their original rung of existence. They depart from center stage, where existence is taking shape, and await such time as they will be able to be included and find their place in the emerging cosmos.

Here *Ze'eir Anpin*'s role becomes clear: *Adam* is the representation that contains all, and so long as divine existence is not configured into a human likeness, the kings will not be able to endure. Configuring *Ze'eir Anpin*'s face—and at a later stage, shaping his body and that of his female counterpart—enables the gradual emergence of the kings from their concealment, reviving them from their deathly state and finding them a place in the personality of God in human likeness as it continues to take shape.

How might one understand the restoration of the kings through the figure of *Adam*? From a mythical and psychological point of view, we might suggest that there is a danger in the existence of forces that orbit the outer reaches of the cosmos in eternal exile, without ever becoming part of the Divine in human likeness, as *Adam does*. The figure of *Adam* balances, and indeed is comprised of, both Judgment (*Din*) and Compassion (*raḥamim*). The sheer intensity of Judgment within the kings is unsuited to the figure of *Adam*. This intensity of judgment transforms the kings into shadow forces in relation to unfolding existence. The power of these shadow forces becomes terrifying, and the kings grow to seem ever more immense and dangerous, and perhaps this is actually the case. Without place, definition, or name within the human realm, the realm of *Adam*, they become an enemy or a threat. According to the profound interpretation of the Death of the Kings offered by Isaac Luria, who understood it to be a foundational myth, the ultimate telos of human history is the increasing integration of fragments of the kings into the figure of *Adam*. The more that human beings are able to discover, recognize, and illuminate these fragments, and the more that they succeed in containing them, finding them a place, and renaming them, the more perfected humanity will become.[3]

The psychoanalytic language of Wilfred Bion comes to our aid in trying to understand this complicated myth. In Bion's understanding, the infant's experiences, which he calls "beta elements," are inchoate, raw, unthinkable, inflexible, and uncontained. Held within the caring container of the parent's gaze, these beta elements can be named and made meaningful, transformed into "alpha elements," which may be thought and contained and allow for the healthy development of the child.[4] In Bion's language, the suppressed fragments of the dead kings of Edom are beta elements that are transformed into thinkable, usable alpha elements only when contained in the figure of *Adam*.[5]

Indeed, the Idra prefigures a future time in which some of the kings will move on from the nonverbal dimension of primordiality, and take their place within the wonderfully complex structure of the divine *Adam*, comprising both masculine and feminine. They will settle and endure, and perhaps even constitute a necessary element in the figure of *Adam*. Other parts of the kings will also endure, but in an unsettled and impermanent way. Their presence within the divine personality, and within the human being patterned upon it, is characterized by a dynamic similar to the rising and falling tides: sometimes they are present, and one can even point to them and name them; and sometimes they sink deep into the divine depths, beyond the boundaries of the conscious mind. Rabbi Shim'on even notes that some of the kings never become "fragrantly firm": they are never refined, they cannot attain a different name or mode of being, and they have not yet been integrated into the figure of *Adam* and perhaps never will be. One may view them as waste, chaff, remains that have no place within the structure. But perhaps they too play an important role as sparks of being that define that which is not part of the increasingly balanced cosmos. They are the fragments of being that forever remain beyond the boundary, beyond the horizon of consciousness, form, and language. We might understand this through Julia Kristeva's language of the *abject*; these rejected residual elements help define who *Adam* is by clarifying who he is not.[6]

Before we part from the kings and turn to the *tiqqunim* of *Ze'eir Anpin*, the Idra makes an important observation about the kings, pointing out that one of them is exceptional. Concerning this one, it is written: *Hadar reigned in his stead; and the name of his city was Pau, and the name of his wife was*

Mehetabel, the daughter of Matred, the daughter of Me-zahab (Genesis 36:39). Unlike the other kings, this one's wife is named alongside him; in addition, his death is never mentioned.

> "All of them were called by different names, except for the one of whom is written *The name of his wife was Mehetabel daughter of Matred daughter of Me-zahab* (Genesis 36:39). Why? Because these were not nullified like the others. Why? Because they were male and female—like a palm tree, which flourishes only when it is male and female. So now they were male and female, and death is not applied to them as it is to the others, and they endured, though they did not settle. Once the image of *Adam* was established, they were transformed into another existence, settling securely." (Zohar 3:135b; trans. Matt 8:382)

Hadar and Mehetabel were thus not nullified, for they were stabilized by a balance between masculinity and femininity that provided enduring existence. They are not nullified, but neither are they settled in any kind of reality until the fully developed figure of *Adam* comes into being. It seems that their significance at this point in the Idra lies in their function as a preliminary archetype for *Ze'eir Anpin* and his female counterpart, who will be configured subsequently, immediately following the configuration of *Ze'eir Anpin*'s face.

14

Ze'eir Anpin Comes into Being

In the first part of the Idra Rabba, the Companions configured God's most ancient face, *Arikh Anpin*, the Source of all being. The configuration of this face is indispensable to the beginning of orientation, of *facing*, and it is a necessary condition of the establishment of any distinct mode of existence. From this point onward, the Divine is no longer an undifferentiated infinite light: God now has a face. Once the face of *Arikh Anpin* is arrayed, the Companions begin the *tiqqunim* of *Ze'eir Anpin*, summoning his presence. As the process of his configuration and refinement progresses, *Ze'eir Anpin* will develop into a human likeness, Male and Female. In the pages that follow, as *Ze'eir Anpin* unfolds before the reader, we come to know the glorious and splendid face of the divine king, which seems familiar, human, and more variegated than the primordial white face of *'Attiqa*, the Ancient One.

The mission that lies ahead is a highly complex one. In the case of *Arikh Anpin*, the goal of the *tiqqunim* was to summon that aspect of the Divine as a face, to invoke its presence. Here, the purpose is different: *Ze'eir Anpin*, the Small-Faced One, the Impatient One, requires rectification and healing in addition to configuration. For *Ze'eir Anpin* reveals a duality that is not expressed in a beautiful and glorious balance, a perfect comingling of opposites; rather, it is framed primarily in stark dichotomies between his various attributes, which in turn reflect the distinctions between himself and *Arikh Anpin*. Rabbi Shim'on and his Companions must therefore rectify and heal *Ze'eir Anpin*, making him whole. Furthermore, the *tiqqun* of *Ze'eir Anpin* treats not only the head, as in the case of *'Attiqa*, but also includes the configuration of the divine body as a complete figure, unfolding and particularizing as it does into the Male and the Female.

A Hymn to God in Human Likeness

The opening lines of the *tiqqun* of *Ze'eir Anpin* also mark the conclusion of the section in which *Arikh Anpin* is configured, appearing as they do before our second encounter with the kings of Edom. In an opening similar to that of the Idra Rabba, Rabbi Shim'on begins with a grand and momentous call to the Companions, summoning them to prepare for the mission ahead:

> "Now focus your minds to arrange the enhancements of *Ze'eir Anpin*—how He is arrayed and how He is clothed in His enhancements by the enhancements of the Ancient of Days, Holy of Holies, Concealed of the Concealed, concealed from all. Now it is incumbent upon you to decree a true, fine, and beautiful judgment, and to arrange all enhancements thoroughly.
>
> "The enhancements of *Ze'eir Anpin* were arrayed by the enhancements of *Arikh Anpin*, and His enhancements spread on this side and on that, like the appearance of a human being—to draw in a breath of the Concealed One on all sides, in order to sit upon the Throne, as is written: *Upon the image of a throne, an image like the appearance of a human being upon it above* (Ezekiel 1:26).
>
> *Like the appearance of* אדם (*adam*), *a human being*—including all images.
>
> *Like the appearance of adam*—in whom are concealed all worlds above and below.
>
> *Like the appearance of adam*—including all secrets uttered and prepared before the world was created, even if they did not endure." (Zohar 3:135a; trans. Matt 8:379)

This passage places at its center the *Adam*ness, the humanness, of the Divine as *Ze'eir Anpin*. Thus we readers, whose consciousness carries the baggage of abstract and transcendental theology, must make room in our minds for the powerfully personal and distinctly anthropomorphic language that Rabbi Shimʿon employs in speaking about God.

This section of the Idra is focused on establishing and configuring the figure of *Zeʿeir Anpin* in the likeness of *Adam*, into whom the breath of *Arikh Anpin* can be blown. This breath that is blown into the figure of *Adam* enables him to reign, as is represented by his installment on the throne.

A guiding principle of this passage is that the "enhancements of *Zeʿeir Anpin* were arrayed by the enhancements of *Arikh Anpin*." That is to say that the source of the *tiqqunim* of *Zeʿeir Anpin*, his fundamental components, lie within *Arikh Anpin*. The smaller, constricted, younger figure is derived from the great, expansive, ancient figure of *Arikh Anpin*, and is defined in relation to that figure. That is to say, despite *Zeʿeir Anpin* appearing to be distinct, his very existence depends upon that of *Arikh Anpin*.

Another fundamental principle in defining *Zeʿeir Anpin* as *Adam* lies in the figure's androgyny, comprising Male and Female. As we shall see, the account of the processes of *Zeʿeir Anpin*'s emanation and development is deeply bound up and interwoven with the biblical and midrashic narratives of Adam's creation in chapters 1 and 2 of Genesis, in addition to Ezekiel's vision of God in human likeness.

The conclusion of Rabbi Shimʿon's call is rhythmic and hymn-like, and it is entirely devoted to praising the divine figure in human likeness. This human figure, this *Adam*, contains within itself in a unified manner that which is separate and distinct in humanity. It would seem that *Zeʿeir Anpin*, the divine *anthropos*, is a kind of prototype for terrestrial human beings, and that every human being—though having a distinct name, personality and image—is but one iteration of the infinite images and names contained within the divine *Adam*. What we have here is a paraphrase of the rabbinic teaching on the uniqueness of God as an artisan, as compared to artisans of flesh and blood:

> Therefore, Adam was created alone [. . .] to proclaim the greatness of the blessed Holy One. For a human being mints many coins in a single mold, and they all resemble one another. But the King, the King of Kings, the blessed Holy One, mints each person in the mold of Adam, and none is similar to another.[1]

However, in the Idra, the image upon which all images are patterned is not Adam, the first terrestrial human being, but God himself—who constitutes a kind of archetype of the earthly Adam. The source of the infinite diversification of human beings is rooted in this aspect of the Divine, called "the image that includes all images," and the uniqueness of each and every human being is a result of its being minted in this all-inclusive image.[2] Furthermore, Liebes notes that the severe proscription against making a graven image that appears in the opening passage of the Idra Rabba is connected to the Divine's existing in a human likeness that contains all likenesses. Since this likeness is universal and all-encompassing, there is a severe prohibition against limiting God by representing any particular iconic likeness.[3]

This discussion of the likeness of Adam, as it is near the end of the Idra Rabba, is a glorious hymn to the concept of humanity. As the Idra progresses, the concept of Adam, of humanity as we usually understand it, gradually transforms. Adam is amplified and becomes divine.

The Emergence of *Ze'eir Anpin*

The account of *Ze'eir Anpin*'s emergence begins as follows: "When an impulse arose in the will of the White Head to enhance His glory [. . .]" *'Attiqa*, the White Head, wishes to be revealed, to spread out, perhaps to be known—and he requires a reality that will enable his revelation. The configuration of *Ze'eir Anpin* is thus a realization of this divine will. The description of the will to spread forth, in the expression "to enhance His glory" (or more literally, "to render glory for His glory"), is reminiscent of the beginning of emanation and of the manifestation of the *sefirot* of Wisdom (*Ḥokhmah*) and Understanding (*Binah*)—the former as a seed, or as a point that weaves the palace of Understanding around itself for its own honor or glory, like a silkworm weaving a cocoon.[4] Indeed, from this point of view *Ze'eir Anpin* is like *'Attiqa*'s body, his home or world, hidden away within himself. Just as the point of Wisdom requires the palace of Understanding in order to develop and unfold within it, and just as semen requires a womb, so *'Attiqa* needs a body.

But how, and out of what, does *Ze'eir Anpin* come into being? In order to respond to this question, the Idra draws on elements of the narrative of Adam's creation in the second chapter of Genesis, reworking them in order to fit this account of the beginning of all beginnings, before the emergence of the cosmos itself. According to the creation story of Genesis 2, Adam emerges from a combination or coupling of two elements: the dust of the earth and the divine breath that is breathed into him. Similarly, *Ze'eir Anpin* is brought into being through a combination of the primordial Divine, who is pure whiteness, and the mode of being that exists outside the boundaries of this whiteness—the redness upon which *'Attiqa* is seated, thereby suppressing it.

The Formation of *Ze'eir Anpin*'s Skull

Alongside *'Attiqa*'s whiteness, there exists another primordial entity known as the Lamp of Adamantine Darkness[5] (*botsina de-qardinuta*), which constitutes a basic tool of the Divine in bringing any mode of existence into being. The Lamp of Adamantine Darkness is a catalyst, setting in motion the processes of creation and differentiation that enable the emergence of any distinction. The Idra describes the Lamp of Adamantine Darkness in terms of fire, redness, judgment, and forcefulness. *Ze'eir Anpin* emerges from a conjunction between this entity and the "pure ether" (*aveira dakhya*) that emerges from the depths of *'Attiqa*. Out of these two elements—the primal creative force associated with fire, and the pure ether associated with air or wind—*Ze'eir Anpin* is formed, as described in the following primordial and abstract account:

> "It has been taught: When an impulse arose in the will of the White Head to enhance His glory, He arranged, prepared, and generated from the Lamp of Adamantine Darkness a single spark. He breathed upon it and it flamed; His will arose and it scattered in 370 directions. Then the spark stood still, and pure air began to issue, whirling and expanding, and a single mighty skull emanated in four directions.
>
> "Within this pure air, the spark was absorbed, grasped, and enveloped. Would you ever imagine 'within it'? Rather, concealed within it, and so this skull expanded in its directions, while this air is secreted in the secrecies of the Ancient of Days, in the breath that it treasures away.
>
> "In this skull, fire spread on one side and air on the other, with pure air presiding over this side and pure fire presiding over the other. What is fire doing here? Well, it is not fire, but rather this spark enveloped

> in the pure air, illuminating 270 worlds, and from its side stems Judgment. Therefore this skull is called 'the mighty skull.'" (Zohar 3:135b; trans. Matt 8:383)

Unlike emanations as they are described in the Neoplatonic tradition, *Ze'eir Anpin* is actively shaped by the primordial Deity. However, the divine act is tremendously primal and subtle, a mere breath of ether from within *'Attiqa*. It is worth recalling that from a visual point of view, *Arikh Anpin* is only a beginning, a head—without hands with which to shape anything. In place of limbs, he must use his breath like a glassblower, exhaling in order to create. *Arikh Anpin* generates a spark from the Lamp of Adamantine Darkness—apparently by exhaling—and it spreads, grows, and continues to glimmer without fading.[6] The White Head then makes the pure ether blow; it swells and increases in volume, becoming a great ball. At this point, the ball of ether exists alongside the spark from the Lamp of Adamantine Darkness. A mysterious proto-physical force of attraction draws the spark into the ball of ether, and it is absorbed into it. Within the ball, which is itself a kind of germinal skull, the ether and the spark are united, setting in motion a process of evolution and variegation. Indeed, the spark from the Lamp of Adamantine Darkness will continue to be an active force within *Ze'eir Anpin*'s skull, ultimately serving as a catalyst for additional functions within his dimension of being. The Idra describes how primordial forces surround the pure ether and fire, encircling the skull, which in turn contains both fire and ether.

This is an initial account of a particularly fruitful coupling: that of the circle and the point within it.[7] It is particularly interesting that within this primordial coupling, male and female roles are reversed. In most zoharic accounts, the seed is presented as a masculine element that encounters a feminine element—spherical or uterine in quality—and is received by it, evolving within it. Here, however, the spark is connected to the feminine element of fire, and it plays the role of the seed, while the male skull becomes the womb that contains the spark and the ether as they are united. This account echoes myths of the birth of consciousness or the intellect from within the head or brain, understood as a reproductive organ or male womb, such as the narrative of the birth of Athena (the goddess of wisdom) from Zeus' head.

Another association that arises from this passage is that of the smith, plying his craft with fire and bellows: the fire burns, and transforms the elements, while the flow of air regulates the process and ensures the final creation. In the process of forming *Zeʿeir Anpin*'s skull, the elemental fire emerges from the Lamp of Adamantine Darkness, while *ʿAttiqa*'s nose and mouth play the role of the bellows. The production of a sphere of ether is also reminiscent of the similar act of inflation performed by the glassblower.

It is noteworthy that in contradistinction to *ʿAttiqa*, who sits *upon* the element of fire—representing, as we have seen, ancient forces of Judgment, perhaps remnants of the dead kings—here, the spark of the most primordial fire exists *within Zeʿeir Anpin*'s skull. According to this account, Judgment (*Din*) is immanent in *Zeʿeir Anpin*, existing within him from the moment of his inception. It is from within *Zeʿeir Anpin*'s head that Judgment emerges into the cosmos, manifesting within it. Judgment also constitutes the basis for this skull's name, "the mighty skull." Another name for Judgment is *Gevurah*, a word that also means "Power" or "Might."

> "Into this skull trickles dew from the White Head, filling it constantly, and from this dew the dead are destined to be revived.
>
> "That dew comprises two colors. From the aspect of the White Head, its color is white, including all whites, entirely white; but when it settles in this head of *Zeʿeir Anpin*, red appears in it—like a crystal, which is white, yet the color red appears within the color white.
>
> "Therefore it is written: *Many of those who sleep in the dust of the earth will awake—these to eternal life, those to shame and eternal contempt* (Daniel 12:2). *To eternal life*—because they are seen by that white, coming from the aspect of the Ancient of Days, *Arikha de-Anpin*, Elongated Countenance. *To shame and eternal contempt*—because they are seen by that red of *Zeʿeir Anpin*. All is included in that dew, as is written: *For Your dew is a dew of lights* (Isaiah 26:19)—two!" (Zohar 3:135b; trans. Matt 8:384, emended)

From within *Arikh Anpin*'s white head life-giving dew drips semen-like, filling the head of *Zeʿeir Anpin*, which here plays the role of a receptacle.[8] The dripping dew is pure white, but once it enters *Zeʿeir Anpin*, it becomes a crystalline blend of white and red, drawn both from *ʿAttiqa* and from

Judgment (*Din*). Here, the red *Din* is an elemental feature of *Ze'eir Anpin*. At this point, when the crystalline dew produces hues of white and red, duality emerges: the striking and sometimes terrifying dichotomy that characterizes the Divine as the *partsuf* of *Ze'eir Anpin*. Following this moment, reality is configured in harshly polarized terms. Accordingly, the human realm is sometimes opened up to the white Compassion that inheres within the personality of *Ze'eir Anpin*, while at other times it is—terrifyingly—governed by the redness within the same *partsuf*. This sharp polarization within *Ze'eir Anpin* is softened so long as the connection between him and *'Attiqa* remains vital and vibrant.

> "And that dew drips every day to the Apple Orchard, colored white and red.
>
> "This skull shines in two colors, on this side and on that. Some of the pure air expands from the skull to His face into 1,500,000 worlds, and therefore He is called *Ze'eir Anpin*, Small Countenance. When the need arises, His face expands and lengthens, for He gazes upon the face of the Ancient of Ancients, and He has compassion on the world." (Zohar 3:135b; trans. Matt 8:384–385)

Just as the dew drips constantly from the White Head to *Ze'eir Anpin*, once it has received its red and white hues within *Ze'eir Anpin*, it trickles unceasingly into the Apple Orchard. Throughout the Zohar, the Apple Orchard, or the Orchard of Holy Apples, represents the *sefirah* of Sovereignty (*Malkhut*); in the Idra, it also corresponds with the body of the divine Female. It is a field with curved, rounded limbs; the mystics must maintain and cultivate it. Apart from being a divine body and *partsuf*, this Orchard also constitutes the matrix, the fundamental structure, of the world. For while the divine Female is called the "supernal Orchard," human beings exist within the terrestrial orchard.[9]

The evocative and enchanting image that is now conjured before the reader is that of *'Attiqa*, *Ze'eir Anpin*, and the Apple Orchard, all joined together by the dew that perpetually trickles from one to the other. This description does not merely account for the emergence of existence, but for the way in which it is sustained at each and every moment. The liquid essence of the worlds, red-white dew, daily flows into the Apple Orchard.

The pure ether within the skull of *Ze'eir Anpin* generates one million and five hundred thousand worlds.[10] All the worlds that emanate from *Ze'eir Anpin* stand in a mysterious relationship of appearing both in front of and within the white light that radiates directly from *'Attiqa*, as well as making an offering of sorts in return for the privilege of being seen by him.

This passage presents a delicate and subtle sketch of the particular relationship between *'Attiqa*, *Ze'eir Anpin*, and the Apple Orchard. *Ze'eir Anpin*—smaller, younger, and impatient—does not gaze upon *Arikh Anpin* at all times but only when necessary. In general, his face is turned toward the Apple Orchard below, and toward the world that he governs. But when his gaze shifts from the world and turns back to *'Attiqa*, he receives bounteous sustenance and healing, enabling him to return once more to a more balanced stance toward the world. Turning toward *'Attiqa* is the mechanism through which *Ze'eir Anpin* becomes more expansive and is healed.

Brain

Once the *tiqqunim* of *Ze'eir Anpin* have been introduced and his skull has been configured, the focus of the account shifts inward, toward the skull's interior and its content. *Ze'eir Anpin*'s skull is divided into three distinct cavities called ventricles (*rahaṭei moḥa*), in which the brain sits. The substance of *Ze'eir Anpin*'s brain is similar or even identical to that of *'Attiqa*; however, while the latter's brain is calm and enclosed, not spreading out, *Ze'eir Anpin*'s brain is in a state ripe for expansion. The distinction between the two brains reflects the difference in their cranial cavities. Each cavity shapes the way in which the brain within it spreads out, and each cavity bestows upon the brain within it a particular character. This is expressed primarily in the structure of the cranial membrane: while that of *'Attiqa* is hard and hermetically sealed, that of *Ze'eir Anpin* is fine and permeable.

From *Ze'eir Anpin*'s first cranial cavity emanate thirty-two paths of divine flux.[11] These paths are generated by penetrating the cranial membrane, breaking forth like a spring might burst forth from a sealed pool. Thus does *Ze'eir Anpin*'s brain begin to spread forth and illuminate; his consciousness opening up. It is in light of this process that the Idra interprets the verse *A river flows from Eden to water the garden* (Genesis 2:10). This verse, which becomes something of a code verse in the Zohar, carries a rich set of conceptual and visual associations. Indeed, it serves as a visual epitome of the work's account of the various divine worlds, or of the *sefirot*, and their relationships with one another.[12] In the context of the Idra Rabba, the threefold structure—a stream from Eden, through the river, into the garden—perfectly fits the Idra's own scheme of three *partsufim* and their relationships with one another: *Arikh Anpin*, *Ze'eir Anpin*, and the Female. Here, the term *Eden* is indeed interpreted as a reference to *Arikh Anpin*'s brain, calm and still within itself. *Ze'eir Anpin*'s brain emerges like a river and waters the garden, bursting forth and flowing into the canals and rivulets that lead out of him. The garden is the Apple Orchard, the divine Female. It is also the world in which human beings live, the human consciousness that seeks to be irrigated, drenched by the gushing river of divine bounty.

From the second cranial cavity emerge fifty "gates," fifty "years," and fifty "generations." All of these multiples of fifty will return to their source at some stage, just as exhaled air is subsequently inhaled again. These accounts of return are bound up with the symbolism of the *sefirah* of Understanding (*Binah*) as the cosmic womb; as the symbol of *teshuvah* (repentance, return to the Divine), from which all emerges and to which it returns; and as the Jubilee, the cycle of fifty years at the end of which everything returns to its source.

From the third cranial cavity, located between the first and the second, emerge one million chambers that fill with the knowledge that flows into them from the other two cavities. This is in fulfillment of the scriptural verse *And by knowledge, rooms are filled* (Proverbs 24:4).[13]

After the account of the three segments of the brain, an important detail is mentioned, introducing the continuation of the Idra's treatment of *Ze'eir Anpin*:

> "These three cavities permeate the whole body on one side and the other. The entire body is linked with them, intermingling with them in all aspects; throughout the whole body they spread." (Zohar 3:136a; trans. Matt 8:387)

Whereas *Arikh Anpin* is described as a head only, as one might expect in connection with the first stage of creation, in this account of *Ze'eir Anpin*'s brain we encounter the first reference to the divine body, the brain spreading from *Ze'eir Anpin*'s head into all parts of his body. In light of the fact that *Ze'eir Anpin*'s body develops initially from the head, and that this head itself emerges from that of *'Attiqa*, one might consider *Ze'eir Anpin* to be akin to *'Attiqa*'s body. Perhaps this is also one way of understanding the references to *Ze'eir Anpin* as "the exterior one": He is external to *'Attiqa*, like a garment; their relationship is one of interiority versus exteriority.

Now, having moved outward, *Ze'eir Anpin* begins to take on the form of a majestic young man, a warrior modeled on the male lover of the Song of Songs.[14]

15

Ze'eir Anpin's Head and Its Features

Hairs as Channels of Transmission

From within the skull, and the pathways that open up in it, emerge countless hairs, like channels that allow the outward flow of the precious essence of the divine brain. The hairs are described, in terminology drawn from the Song of Songs, as the beloved's raven-black curls. Viewed in psychedelic high resolution, it becomes clear that they are entangled and enmeshed. Millions of hairs, the ringlets on *Ze'eir Anpin*'s head, represent the duality, plurality, and variegation in *Ze'eir Anpin*'s consciousness: right and left, Compassion and Judgment, pure and impure.

> "It has been taught: From the skull of the head hang ten billion and one hundred million locks of black hair, interwoven and mingling with one another. [. . .]
>
> "On all aspects that are pure and on all aspects that are impure lie locks interwoven and coarse—some of them smooth and some of them coarse. In every single lock, strands appear in heaps of wavy curls, glistening and dangling—like a mighty hero victorious in battles—arranged beautifully and powerfully, distinguished as grand and mighty cedars, as is written: *distinguished as the cedars* (Song of Songs 5:15). Locks arranged in dangling curls, from one side to the other upon the skull, as it is written: *his locks, wavy, black as a raven* (Song of Songs 5:11).

> "It has been taught: They appear in heaps of wavy curls because they flow from many springs of the three channels of the brain. [. . .]
>
> "All the flows drawn from the three cavities of the skull's brain, and all those locks, hang down and cover the sides of the ears. Therefore it is written: *Incline Your ear, O YHVH, and hear* (2 Kings 19:16).
>
> "Upon this depend right and left, radiance and darkness, Compassion and Judgment. All right and left depend upon this, not upon the Ancient One." (Zohar 3:136a; trans. Matt 8:387–388, emended)

In these accounts of *Ze'eir Anpin*—his head, face, and beard—we see that the binarity and polarity of his character, and his responses to the reality that exists outside of himself, are repeatedly emphasized. The hairs present a particularly striking example of this.

The account of *Ze'eir Anpin*'s hair invites discussion of both the difference in the qualities of the hair of *'Attiqa* and *Ze'eir Anpin* as well as the connection between these two divine *partsufim*. Thus, in the *tiqqunim* of *'Attiqa*'s head, we read as follows:

> "Why are the strands of the beard, which are not so long, coarse, whereas those of the head are not coarse?
>
> "Well, all strands of the head and beard are evenly balanced. Those of the head extend to the shoulders to reach the head of *Ze'eir Anpin*, from the flow of the brain to His brain. Therefore, they are not coarse, and should not be so.
>
> "For we have learned as follows: Why is it written *Wisdoms cry aloud outside, in the squares she lifts her voice* (Proverbs 1:20)? [. . .] *Wisdoms cry out in the streets*—when it flows from the concealed brain of *Arikh Anpin* to the brain of *Ze'eir Anpin* through those strands, it is as if two brains join outside, becoming one brain, for the lower brain has no existence without the existence of the upper brain. And when there is flow from one to the other, it is written *she lifts her voice*—in the singular.
>
> "Because of the flow from brain to brain through those strands, they are not coarse. Why? Because if they were coarse, nothing could flow through them to the brain. Thus, no wisdom emerges from a person who is coarse and angry, as is written: *Words of the wise said gently are heard* (Ecclesiastes 9:17). [. . .]

> "And it has been taught: Those of the beard are all coarse. Why? Because they are strongest of the strong, to bequeath thirteen attributes that are bestowed below." (Zohar 3:131b; trans. Matt 8:351–352)

'Attiqa's hair is soft and smooth, as befits its function: drawing the content of the enclosed brain into that of *Ze'eir Anpin*, in order to give him life. In contrast, the hair of *'Attiqa*'s white beard is coarse, as its role is to subdue Judgment by issuing forth the Thirteen Attributes of Mercy. Therefore, the beard hairs must be strong and sturdy.

Through the cerebral content flowing through *'Attiqa*'s hair into *Ze'eir Anpin*, an encounter between the two brains takes place; indeed, the two brains are perceived and experienced as one, on account of the sheer abundance of hair. This unity is not merely perceived—it is fundamental, essential. For *Ze'eir Anpin*'s brain cannot exist without that of *'Attiqa*, from which it is drawn. The connection between the two brains is expressed in an exegesis of the verse *Wisdoms cry aloud outside, in the square she lifts her voice* (Proverbs 1:20). The tension between the plural subject *wisdoms* (*ḥokhmot*) and the singular formulation *she lifts her voice* facilitates a creative interpretation: the *wisdoms* are the two brains, flowing into one another and thus appearing to be one, a single consciousness raising its voice. The expression *outside* refers to the occurrence of the encounter between the brains via contact between the hairs externally, not within the confines of the skull. The hairs might be likened to external nerve endings, axons, and synapses. They constitute a kind of brain that extends beyond the confines of the skull.

The hairs of *Ze'eir Anpin*—long, curled, coarse, entangled—direct the content of his three cranial ventricles outward. The fluctuating nature of the hairs is bound up in their role as modes of transmission between the supernal brain of *'Attiqa* and the lower brain of *Ze'eir Anpin*. As in the case of *'Attiqa*, *Ze'eir Anpin*'s hair will determine the nature of the connections—bonds of love, defense, or battle—between this figure and the worlds emerging from him and beyond him.

The Pathway: Marking Binary Existence

In the case of *Arikh Anpin*, the pathway, the part through the middle of *'Attiqa*'s hair, represents an expanse of unregulated divine flow, which can be experienced by the righteous, whose way of life represents the ever-increasing illumination of the divine presence. Not so the pathway through the middle of *Ze'eir Anpin*'s hair. Its purpose is to mark a distinction, a separation between left and right within this figure, representing his binary mode of existence. As we shall see, the *tiqqunim* of *Ze'eir Anpin*'s forehead, eyes, nose, and ears are expressions of his various modes of relation and reaction to the reality around him, and in particular to the human realm. In each of his facial features there inheres the possibility of expressing Judgment (*Din*) alongside the possibility of expressing Love (*Ḥesed*). Usually, the righteous experience *Ze'eir Anpin*'s Love, while the sinners and Gentiles who oppress Israel are given portions of destructive Judgment.

Ze'eir Anpin's face does indeed contain both Love and Judgment, but most accounts of this *partsuf* present it as full of Judgment rather than as illuminated by Love. And while the modes of his Love are understood to be determined by *'Attiqa*'s illumination, the Judgment that issues from *Ze'eir Anpin*'s face is his alone. Many readers, certainly all those who seek justice, can identify with this Judgment; its purpose is to call oppressors and the wicked to account. But there is no doubt that *Ze'eir Anpin*'s face, which is now being configured, primarily arouses fear, even terror.

The Forehead: A Searchlight of Providential Justice

Ze'eir Anpin's forehead is the external expression of his consciousness. It is understood as a distinct region of the face, without orifices or hair, and it serves as a window of sorts, a screen upon which the internal brain is projected. As we have seen, in *'Attiqa* these properties of the forehead facilitate the flow of Love, forgiveness, and life; the forehead represents a positive *facing* toward all existence, full of appeasement and good will, enduringly and eternally. In contrast, *Ze'eir Anpin*'s forehead sends forth red and deadly denizens of *Din*. While *Arikh Anpin*'s forehead is called Will of Wills (*Rava d'ravin*), *Ze'eir Anpin*'s forehead is called "scrutinizing providence" (*ashgaḥuta de-ashgaḥuta*; lit., "providence of providence"). *Ze'eir Anpin*'s forehead becomes manifest when the time comes to punish the wicked; at such a time, the whole world is in a state of Judgment. Or to put it differently, at that time the forces of Judgment that inhere in *Ze'eir Anpin* are given license to go forth and wreak destruction.

> "Forehead of the skull—scrutinizing providence, not revealed except when the wicked must be called to account and their deeds examined.
>
> "It has been taught: When this forehead is revealed, all Masters of Judgment are aroused, and the whole world is delivered to Judgment. [. . .]
>
> "It has been taught: This forehead expands into two hundred thousand reddest of the red, adhering to it, included in it. When it is revealed, they are all empowered to destroy—were it not for the revealing of the forehead of the Will of Wills, which shines upon this forehead and upon all of them, and then all are assuaged." (Zohar 3:136a–b; trans. Matt 8:389–390)

For the wicked, *Ze'eir Anpin*'s forehead is providence in the sense of judgment, surveillance, enforcement, and punishment. For the righteous, however, it is primarily connected with the experience of Love, in the context of its illumination by *'Attiqa*'s own forehead.

What emerges from the study of *Ze'eir Anpin*'s forehead is a theological drama framed in mythical and anthropomorphic terms, revealing a fundamental insight into the relational triangle of *'Attiqa*, *Ze'eir Anpin*, and human beings. According to this account, when the presence of *Ze'eir Anpin*'s forehead becomes too much to bear, and when the Judgment spilling forth from it threatens to consume everything in its path, Israel's prayers ascend heavenward, imploring the Divine for mercy. Alternatively, a will arises in *'Attiqa* to deal mercifully with his children, human beings, to deliver them from the destructive Judgment of *Ze'eir Anpin*. In this state of deep distress, *'Attiqa* reveals his radiant forehead, illuminating that of *Ze'eir Anpin* and calming his raging Judgment. Surprisingly, these accounts of *'Attiqa* present him as a caring and active figure, which is unusual, considering the Idra's dominant portrayal of this *partsuf* as a figure more associated with *being* than *doing*:[1]

> "It has been taught: When this forehead is revealed, all Masters of Judgment are aroused, and the whole world is delivered to Judgment—except at the time when prayers of Israel ascend before the Ancient of Days, and He wishes to have compassion upon His children: He reveals the forehead of the Will of Wills and illumines that of *Ze'eir Anpin*, and Judgment is soothed. [. . .]

"And it has been taught: Hair does not exist in this place on the forehead, so that it can be revealed to those who are impudent in their sins.

"When the blessed Holy One is aroused to delight with the righteous, the face of the Ancient of Days shines upon the face of the Youthful of Days, and His forehead is revealed and illumines this forehead. Then it is called *a time of favor* (Psalms 69:14). Whenever Judgment looms, and this forehead of *Ze'eir Anpin* is revealed, the forehead of the Ancient of Ancients is revealed, and Judgment is soothed and not enacted." (Zohar 3:136a–b; trans. Matt 8:389–390)

The relationships described here are a source of fear and trembling: human beings are described as *'Attiqa*'s children, who stand in need of mercy before the mighty Judgment of *Ze'eir Anpin*, YHVH, the God who sits at the center of the Jewish religious imagination, of traditional Jewish discourse. In other words, *Ze'eir Anpin*, the God of Israel, is here described as an intermediary figure that conjoins Israel to *'Attiqa* or, alternatively, separates them. This relationship could easily be defined as a kind of Gnostic dualism in which *'Attiqa*, the supernal good God, is distinguished from *Ze'eir Anpin*, the demiurge, full of Judgment, and perhaps even lacking love and care for his creatures. Indeed, in certain anti-Jewish Gnostic texts, the despised demiurge is identified with the God of Israel. But in contrast with these conceptions, the Idra maintains that *Ze'eir Anpin*, the God of Israel, is a God of Judgment, justice, and righteousness.[2]

At the center of this drama sits the question of the relationship between Judgment or justice, on the one hand, and Mercy, on the other. To beseech *'Attiqa* in prayer essentially means circumventing the verdict of the divine Judge. Here, an awareness—prevalent throughout the Zohar—is expressed that the world cannot endure divine Judgment (or justice) in its purity, cannot survive it: divine Mercy must be invoked and aroused in order to neutralize or temper Judgment. Of course, the roots of this conception lie in rabbinic thought, where we encounter the desire to regulate the balance of divine anger by arousing and amplifying divine Mercy. The rabbinic interpretation of the liturgical recitation God's Thirteen Attributes of Mercy—"it is a sealed covenant that the Thirteen Attributes do not return empty-handed"[3]—is a striking example of this process of regulation and mediation of divine

Judgment, and takes on major importance in the Idra Rabba. Yet these rabbinic formulations speak of *attributes*, which may have some autonomous dimension, but remain the attributes of a single deity. The splitting of the two divine faces is what lends a Gnostic hue to the Idra's account. The Idra goes to great lengths to limit and qualify this split, and to describe it as a mere perception of human consciousness rather than a reflection of the divine mode of being in any true sense. But these efforts do not dispel the distinct sense of a sharp divide between two aspects of the Divine that emerges from a reading of these passages.[4]

Between the Forehead and the Human Figure, Adam

In the course of configuring the forehead, an exceptional psychological reflection is revealed concerning the relationship between the brain, head, and body, through contemplation of the relationship between *Ze'eir Anpin*'s forehead (*mitsḥa*, *metsaḥ*) and his *netsaḥ* (eternal one, eternity, victory, as well as brain matter).[5] The forehead is an external, skeletal aspect of *Ze'eir Anpin*, which contains the *netsaḥ*, his brain in a concentrated state before it expands and emanates forth. It is a harsh force of Judgment that does not soften or change.[6] When a face and body emerge from *Ze'eir Anpin*'s brain, they become the "figure of Adam":

> "It has been taught: Twenty-four supernal judgments appear, all of them called נצחים (*Netsaḥim*), each one called נצח (*Netsaḥ*). [. . .]
>
> "It has been taught: What is meant by, *Moreover,* נצח (*Netsaḥ*), *the Eternal One of, Israel does not lie and does not regret, for He is not a human to have regret* (1 Samuel 15:29). This mystery we have established: All that *Netsaḥ* spreading through the body sometimes looms over the world to execute Judgment—and it turns back in regret, not enacting Judgment, if they turn back in repentance. Why? Because the matter pertains to the place called *Adam*, *human*, and He can regret. But if this *Netsaḥ* appears revealed in the place called Head—in this *mitsḥa*, forehead—then it is neither the time nor the place to regret. Why? Because it does not pertain to the place called *Adam*, *human*, since neither the face nor the nose is revealed, just the forehead alone; and wherever the face does not appear, it is not called *Adam*, *human*. Thus, *for He is*

> *not adam, a human, to have regret*—as with *Netsaḥ* in the other arrangements of the body." (Zohar 3:136b; trans. Matt 8:391)

It is only when the *netsaḥ* spreads throughout the face and body that the possibility of change arises within this divine figure. Now God can be comforted, can experience regret for the sheer force of Judgment within him, and can fill himself with Mercy. In contrast, when Judgment is still concentrated only within his brain and forehead, there is no such possibility. We therefore have here a mythical-physiological account of the movement of Judgment from its concentrated state within the brain and the forehead to a more tolerable state of diffusion, spread throughout the face and body. It is significant that the forehead is conceived of here as an entity that is not yet part of the representation of the human figure, the figure of Adam. Only when the eyes and nose are configured will *Ze'eir Anpin* be considered to have a face; then it may be called *Adam*.

From an exegetical point of view, this entire passage is constructed as a visually evocative interpretation of the verse *Moreover, the Eternal One of Israel does not lie and does not regret, for He is not a human to have regret* (1 Samuel 15:29). In this midrashic interpretation, *the Eternal One of Israel* represents the Judgmental consciousness of Israel (that is, *Ze'eir Anpin*), concentrated within his brain and forehead. This aspect of *Ze'eir Anpin* is incapable of regret. He *does not regret*, for he is not yet configured as Adam, *for He is not a human* (*adam*). But when God *does* take on the form of Adam, he will be able to regret and forgive.

Several surprising insights emerge from an analysis of this passage. First of all, the face and body define humans as human, not merely the mind or brain alone. Another defining aspect of human beings is the ability to regret. Instead of considering the ability to change to be an imperfection or blemish in the Divine—as opposed to the stability and fixity of a perfect and unchanging God—here, God learns from Adam how to forgive.[7] God must evolve into this human image in order to come to know regret and forgiveness. Similarly, we learn that the body, by virtue of its complexity and expansiveness, tempers and regulates the strength of Judgment. The encounter between *netsaḥ* and the body softens its rigid force and enables the development of Mercy. It is the body that enables God to change.

The Eyes: Divine Providence in the Dual Dimension

The sense of sight occupies a central place in zoharic literature. The Zohar regularly addresses its reader with the call, "Come and see!" It identifies and maps out various degrees and kinds of physical and spiritual-mystical sight. A notable expression of this may be found in the Idra's particular care in describing the eyes of *Ze'eir Anpin*, the God in whose image and likeness humans are created, and in exploring the similarities and differences between the eyes of *Ze'eir Anpin*, *'Attiqa*, and human beings. In contradistinction to the hair and forehead, which are understood to be secondary to the account of the face, the eyes are of central importance in their expressive capacity and as channels of communication. It is through them that one comes to know an identity, a personality. Indeed, this is one of the broadest and most colorful and varied of *Ze'eir Anpin*'s *tiqqunim*.

The *tiqqun* of the eyes is woven like a tapestry of biblical interpretations, providing a physical, mythical, and conceptual expression of the idea of divine providence in a world of duality.[8] As we have seen, the forehead also contains some dimension of providence; but while the forehead is an expression of providence in general—the fundamental fact of the Divine turning toward reality—the eyes express the modes of providence of both *partsufim* in much greater detail. As in the case of the forehead, the descriptions of *Ze'eir Anpin*'s eyes emphasize the difference between *Arikh Anpin*'s providence, full of Love, and that of *Ze'eir Anpin*. In the latter, there is an active foundation of discernment, surveillance, enforcement, and reactivity that can be either benevolent or vengeful. As we have seen, the eyes of *Arikh Anpin* are described in the Idra as smiling, unguarded by eyelids, and they appear as a single eye. From them issues the white stream of life; Love's providential governance of the world depends on them. Thus, the presence or absence of *'Attiqa*'s gaze into *Ze'eir Anpin*'s eyes carries dramatic implications for the state of *Ze'eir Anpin* and the human world.

> "Eyes of the head are different from other eyes. The painting of the eyebrows above the eyes is colored black. Heaps of hair hang. [. . .] Adhering to both of them are seven hundred thousand masters of watchfulness, above the eyelashes.

"In the cover of the eyes flash fourteen million, adhering to the eyelids, which are the cover, and the providential eye of the Ancient One is above them.

"When that cover lifts, He appears as one who awakens from sleep. His eyes open and see the open eye, and are bathed in one whiteness of the good eye, as is written: *bathing in milk* (Song of Songs 5:12). What is meant by *in milk*? In the white of the primordial eye. During that time compassionate providence prevails. Therefore Israel prays that He may open His eyes, to be bathed in this whiteness, as is written: *Awake! Why do You sleep, O YHVH? Rouse Yourself!* (Psalms 44:24). Whenever His eyes are not open, all Masters of Judgment subjugate Israel, and other nations rule over them. But when He opens His eyes, they are bathed in the good eye, and there is Compassion upon Israel; and the eye revolves, wreaking vengeance upon the other nations. [. . .]

"When His eyes open, they are beautiful to behold, like doves—red, black, and green. White does not appear except when He gazes into the good eye and all those colors are bathed in that white. [. . .]

"Therefore it is written: *Awake! Why do you sleep, O YHVH? Rouse Yourself!* (Psalms 44:24). *Awake* and *Rouse Yourself*—two supervisions, two openings, two benefits: compassion and vengeance." (Zohar 3:136b–137a; trans. Matt 8:392–393)

In contrast with *'Attiqa*'s white eyes, *Ze'eir Anpin*'s eyes have eyebrows, eyelids, and eyelashes, emphasized as if with kohl. Three hues are manifest in his eyes, each relating to a different quality of providence: the black of the eye is encircled by red, which is in turn surrounded by green.

The open or closed state of the eyes expresses the different ways in which human beings experience their presence before the Divine. A depiction of *Ze'eir Anpin* with closed eyes represents human terror. The absence of any gaze expresses God's turning away from the world and its needs. It is as if God is sleeping, as if he has cast care for the world and Israel out of his conscious mind. The result is suffering and oppression.[9]

In contrast, when *Ze'eir Anpin*'s eyes are open, the world is exposed to the great drama of the divine gaze, whether that means punishment or loving affection. On the one hand, the opening of the divine eyes could mark the advent of burning fury. This situation is navigated by seeking to turn the raging Judgment of those eyes toward Israel's enemies. On the other hand, when the eyes are washed in *'Attiqa*'s whiteness, loving providence may be discovered in *Ze'eir Anpin*'s eyes. Then the forces of Judgment that inhere in *Ze'eir Anpin*'s providence are removed, and the colors in his eyes settle down. At this point, the dual is flooded in oneness, the hues melt away before the whiteness of the merciful and loving gaze of *'Attiqa*. The emotional force embedded in the Idra's accounts testifies to a great yearning for such moments filled with love and mercy in the human-Divine relationship, just as it testifies to their rarity.

In the framework of the biblical interpretations concerning *Ze'eir Anpin*'s eyes, there is a paraphrase of a talmudic narrative that speaks of two tears that fall from the eyes of the blessed Holy One into the Great Sea, expressing his great pain at the fate of his children. These tears cause an earthquake and turmoil—representing divine grief.[10] Here, the rabbinic motif is reworked in the Idra's unique voice, now describing the healing process that *Ze'eir Anpin*'s powers of Judgment undergo, by means of the whiteness of *'Attiqa*'s Mercy:

> "It has been taught: In these eyes—in two of its colors: red and black—dwell two tears. When the Holy of Holies wishes to have compassion upon Israel, He sheds two tears to be sweetened in the great sea. Who is the great sea? The sea of supernal Wisdom. That is to say, they are bathed in the whiteness of the wellspring issuing from great Wisdom, and He has compassion upon Israel." (Zohar 137b; trans. Matt 8:396, emended)

Within *Ze'eir Anpin*'s eyes inheres a primordial presence of Judgment, black and red, and the tears are the way in which to drain and expel it. When *Ze'eir Anpin* seeks to deal mercifully with Israel, he cries, allowing two tears—black and red, the distilled powers of Judgment—to be washed, aromatized, and sweetened in the Great Sea, the Sea of Wisdom, and in the river of whiteness that emerges from it.[11] The tears descend into the very depths of Divinity, into the Sea of Supernal Wisdom. Judgment does not vanish; instead, it is sweetened. The great enveloping sea transforms the tears that bathe within it; they absorb supernal whiteness and fill with Mercy. From this description, we get the impression that if the tears fell upon the earth, it would be utterly destroyed. It is their containment within the sea that enables Mercy and ensures that these tears do not fall destructively. The account of sweetening the tears is a metonym for the Idra's overarching *tiqqun*, which seeks to turn *Ze'eir Anpin*'s face toward that of *Arikh Anpin*.

In the discussion of *'Attiqa*'s eyes, we read an account of the relationship between the lower eyes of *Ze'eir Anpin* and the higher eye of *Arikh Anpin*. It is fitting to revisit the passage here and consider it closely:

> "It has been taught: There is no illumination for the lower eye, to be washed of its redness and blackness, except when it is bathed by the white light of the supernal eye called *He that has a good eye*. No one knows when this supernal holy eye illumines and bathes the lower eye. And the supremely righteous are destined to see this through wisdom, as is it written: *For eye-to-eye they will see*. When? *When YHVH returns to Zion* (Isaiah 52:8). And it is written: *For eye-to-eye You are seen, YHVH* (Numbers 14:14). Were it not for the supernal eye gazing upon and bathing the lower eye, the world could not endure for a single moment." (Zohar 130a; trans. Matt 8:340)

The statement is decisive. *Ze'eir Anpin*'s eyes are unable to be cleansed of Judgment without first establishing a connection with the stream of whiteness gushing from *'Attiqa*'s eyes. Finding that connection and summoning it is a precondition for calming Judgment. Judgment cannot be softened or calmed from within itself alone. From a psychological point of view, this is a fascinating statement. The dual consciousness requires an open path that connects it to the undifferentiated, unified consciousness; indeed, its very existence depends upon it. "No one [but him] knows when this supernal holy eye illumines"—the knowledge spoken of here, of calming, softening, and nourishment, is experiential and intimate. It is known only by one who has this experience of immersive cleansing.

> "When the white revolves and the eyes are bathed, all those colors subside and sink below, and none are seen except that white, shining from the Ancient of Days, and all those below shine from it. No color is visible except that white alone, and consequently all masters of red and

> black vanish. [. . .] [T]heir whiteness is like the white of the eyes when they are bathed in the white of the supernal eye.
>
> "This the righteous are destined to see in the spirit of wisdom, as is said: *For eye-to-eye they will see.* When? *When YHVH returns to Zion* (Isaiah 52:8). And it is written: *For eye-to-eye You are seen, YHVH* (Numbers 14:14).
>
> "Then, opening of the eyes for the good and opening of the eyes for evil. [. . .] [S]ince one is not performed without the other." (Zohar 137a–b; trans. Matt 8:394–395)

The Idra Rabba imagines a future state in which all the hues of judgmental providence will be eliminated, and dualistic existence will be filled with *'Attiqa's* white love. This state is possible only through aligning aspects of the world and the Divine with one another. Only then will human beings be able to see eye to eye with *'Attiqa's* good eye, glowing luminous within that of *Ze'eir Anpin*. As we shall see in coming chapters, the coupling of the Male and the Female, and the possibility of an eye-to-eye encounter, allow for the experience of the manifestation of *'Attiqa* in the human realm without its immediately dissolving back into its oneness.

The ideal future described here emerges from a combination of three images, each drawn from different rungs of reality. The image of the Male and Female coupling is placed upon that of the future state of redeemed consciousness in perceiving eye to eye, and upon this is superimposed the national-messianic-mythical image that emerges from the verse *When YHVH returns to Zion* (Isaiah 52:8). Here, cosmic coupling receives a national-mythical garment, and in parallel, according to the Zohar's hermeneutical method, biblical verses describing a future state of perfection receive erotic kabbalistic interpretation.[12] The Land of Israel and Jerusalem, full of Judgment, represent the Female who requires her Judgment to be sweetened and aromatized with the Male's Mercy, while the formulation *When YHVH returns to Zion* is understood to refer to the state of coupling and alignment of divine faces with one another. In this state, humans can experience *'Attiqa's* light in reality.

It seems to me that by projecting these images, the authors of the Idra reveal something about their visual perception and contemplative abilities. The mode of being that they seek is not merely located in the future, deferred to the End of Days. They are describing a state that one can actually experience in this world, the state in which the kabbalist experiences *ʿAttiqa* consciousness by way of its illumination through *Zeʿeir Anpin*—for example, on the Sabbath and on Yom Kippur.[13] The Idra Rabba even makes this explicit, claiming that the consciousness of the righteous in this world is to be identified with that of *Zeʿeir Anpin*; it is therefore able to connect to the *tiqqunim* of *ʿAttiqa*.[14] Following in the wake of this zoharic conception, Isaac Luria composed Sabbath hymns that frame the revelation of *ʿAttiqa*'s light on that holy day in poetic terms.[15]

Furthermore, it seems that the Idra Rabba and the Idra Zuṭa describe moments of such an alignment of divine faces, during which the face of the deepest aspect of the Divine shines forth within human existence. At the same time, the Idras emphasize that a continuous experience of such perfection and delight is impossible; for within a dualistic mode of human existence, we do not experience the undifferentiated gaze of *ʿAttiqa* directly but as it is reflected through the dualistic eyes of *Zeʿeir Anpin*. We encounter something of the profound desire to experience the future providence of *ʿAttiqa*'s singular eye in the stirring image that emerges from interpreting Isaiah's verses of consolation. This image communicates the calm stillness that may be found in dwelling under the gaze of this compassionate eye:

> "What is the meaning of *Your eyes will see Jerusalem a tranquil abode*? [. . .] For He is a serene and *tranquil* eye, an eye of Compassion, an eye that does not move from one watchfulness to another. [. . .]
>
> "In the time to come, one eye of Compassion will be upon Her—the eye of the Ancient of Ancients—as is written: *With great compassion will I gather you* (Isaiah 54:7)." (Zohar 137a–b; trans. Matt 8:395–396)

The Nose: The Flaring of Divine Wrath

Zeʿeir Anpin's very name makes reference to his nose, literally meaning "Short Nosed." Having a short nose is in turn linked, in Hebrew, to shortness of breath and shortness of patience, to anger or even rage. Its configuration thus invites terrifying descriptions of divine wrath. Since the nose is also the most prominent feature of the human face, it serves as a distinguishing identifier, as noted in classical rabbinic literature.[16]

From an acquaintance with the dualistic qualities of *Ze'eir Anpin*, we might have imagined that one nostril would emit fire and the other would flow with forgiveness or Mercy. But this is not the case. Just as both nostrils of *Arikh Anpin* represent a doubling of the quality of life that is exhaled by them, the nostrils of *Ze'eir Anpin* augment each other, amplifying the force of Judgment. One nostril exhales scorching smoke, while the other blasts raging fire. The account of *Ze'eir Anpin*'s nose thus presents a concentrated image of divine rage as an essential state of this *partsuf*.

The nose blasts smoke, embers, and fire—in red and black hues. These are the forces of the nose, of the anger and destruction wrought by God as manifest in the figure of *Ze'eir Anpin*. The five Powers (*Gevuran*) of *Ze'eir Anpin*, spread throughout his body, are concentrated and focused into a unified force of Power (*Gevurah*) within his nose. This state resembles preparation for battle:

> "It has been taught: There are five *Gevuran*, Powers, in this *Ze'eir Anpin* [. . .] spreading through His nose, the mouth, the arm, the hand, the fingers. [. . .] When all those *Gevuran* unite, they are called one *Gevurah*.
>
> "All those *Gevuran* begin descending from the nose [. . .] and from this smoke that He spews from His nose dangle 10,000,000,405, from the side of this *Gevurah*." (Zohar 137b; trans. Matt 8:397–398)

Arikh Anpin's infinite patience offers a remedy for *Ze'eir Anpin*'s fire and anger. When *'Attiqa*'s light illumines within *Ze'eir Anpin*, the anger, fire, and smoke settle down, and he attains a measure of *Arikh Anpin*'s breath—full of forgiveness, satisfaction, and sweetness. By drawing the attributes of *Arikh Anpin* into himself, *Ze'eir Anpin* can breathe deeply and find patience. As we read previously, in the account of *'Attiqa*'s nose:

> "Come and see: What is the difference between the Ancient One and *Ze'eir Anpin*? The former is Master of the Nose. From one nostril, life; from the other, life of life.
>
> "This nose is an armoire, through which blows breath to *Ze'eir Anpin*. We call it Forgiveness, tranquil pleasure of spirit." (Zohar 130a–b; trans. Matt 8:343)

Who might be able to appease divine fury, to calm the rage? According to the Idra, the perfect human being, the *tsaddiq*, is able to transform the situation. In the Hebrew Bible, Moses is the exemplary human who can stand between the world and divine wrath. When divine rage threatens to annihilate the Israelites, Moses draws the Attributes of Mercy from *'Attiqa* to *Ze'eir Anpin*. When *Ze'eir Anpin* fills with whiteness and Love, he finds respite from his anger:

> "Moses spoke in a place of Judgment, to bring them from the Holy Ancient One down to *Ze'eir Anpin*. For we have learned as follows: 'How great is the power of Moses, who conveyed the attributes of Compassion below!'
>
> "When the Holy Ancient One is revealed to *Ze'eir Anpin*, all appear in Compassion; the nose is assuaged, and no smoke emerges, as we have learned, for it is written: *For the sake of My name, I delay My wrath* [lengthen My nose], *and for My praise*, אחטם (*eḥetom*), *I restrain* [the nose] *for you, so as not to cut you off* [. . .] (Isaiah 48:9)."[17] (Zohar 138a; trans. Matt 8:402, emended)

In the conceptual world of the Zohar, Rabbi Shim'on bar Yoḥai is Moses' heir.[18] Rabbi Shim'on convenes the Idra's assembly precisely in order to draw the forces of Mercy into *Ze'eir Anpin*, so that he will attain a greater balance, containing Love alongside anger.

Another way for humans to appease divine anger is to offer a sacrifice. *Ze'eir Anpin*'s anger is expressed in a sharp exhalation of blazing fury. The fiery breath must be calmed, cooled by inhaling, imparting patience to *Ze'eir Anpin*. In human experience, inhaling a pleasant fragrance calms and settles the mind; in the context of the Divine, it is the fragrance of incense and sacrifices that sweetens celestial wrath. This is the case in the biblical account of Noah appeasing God after the flood, as well as in the Zohar's understanding of sacrifices in general: the smoke of the incense and the sacrifices rises, engulfing the smoke of divine anger, while the red fire of the burning offerings sweetens the flames of celestial fury.[19] Scent is thus the subtle link between the human and divine realms, or more precisely, between the human realm and the realm of divine breathing.

What replaces sacrifices in the absence of the Temple? In the spirit of the rabbinic interpretation of the biblical verse *In place of bulls, we will pay [the offering of] our lips* (Hosea 14:3), the Zohar responds that words may replace sacrifices. Prayer and Torah study perform the theurgical function of the smoke, carrying a sweet scent to the Divine. In the Zohar, there are many accounts of the pleasure that God takes in smelling the words of Torah issuing from human beings, when he enjoys them in the company of the righteous in the Garden of Eden after midnight.[20] In addition, words of love also possess a fragrance. For example, in relation to Adam's first words to Eve in the Garden of Eden, the Zohar describes "the fragrance of words." The emotion accompanying the spoken word imparts its sweetness.[21]

Alongside words of Torah, prayer, and love, in the Idra—as in the Zohar in general—the appeasing sacrifice can also signify death. For example, in various accounts of the deaths of the righteous (*tsaddiqim*) throughout the Zohar, death is understood as a sacrifice of atonement. This applies in the zoharic narrative of the Ten Martyrs put to death by the Romans, as it does in the Idra Rabba's account of the deaths of three of the Companions at the conclusion of the assembly.[22] The Zohar thus relates to sacrifice in a range of ways, on a spectrum from a spiritualized and subtle sweetening and softening of divine anger to the ancient and mythical conception of human sacrifice as a fitting offering for God.

From a theological and psychological perspective, we may observe that two competing responses for confronting the existential and religious experience of divine anger are operating here. These two possibilities are strikingly reminiscent of responses to anger in human relationships, whether parent-child or within a couple. The first recognizes that within and beyond God's anger exists a divine dimension of Mercy and Love. The praxis based on this insight is to redirect the consciousness from anger to the undifferentiated Divine, with the intention of drawing its soothing light into the consciousness of *Ze'eir Anpin*. The second possible response is the human attempt to appease *Ze'eir Anpin* himself. Through sacrifice, humans attempt to break the strength of divine anger, arousing divine memory, Mercy, and Love anew. These two modes of response inhere in the deepest and most primal reaches of religious experience, and they are also expressed in the Temple's sacrificial system. In the *tiqqun* of *Ze'eir Anpin*'s nose the Idra presents these two possibilities alongside each other:

> "It has been taught: This nose is small, and when smoke begins to emerge, it comes out hurriedly and Judgment is executed. Who prevents this nose from spewing smoke? The nose of the Holy Ancient One, who is called ארך אפים (*Erekh Appayim*), Long-nosed, Long-suffering, of all. [. . .]
>
> "When the Holy Ancient One is revealed to *Ze'eir Anpin*, all appear in Compassion; the nose is assuaged, and no smoke emerges. [. . .]
>
> "This fire cannot be assuaged except by sacrificial smoke of the altar.
>
> "All depends upon the nose. Thus it is written *YHVH smelled the pleasing aroma* (Genesis 8:21), for all depends on the nose—that this nose may smell the smoke and red fire, whereby the offering is accepted with favor." (Zohar 137b–138a; trans. Matt 8:399–403)

'Attiqa's Responsibility for Divine Anger

In describing the *tiqqun* of *Ze'eir Anpin*'s nose, the Idra Rabba presents a biblical interpretation that discusses the relationship between *Ze'eir Anpin* and *Arikh Anpin* at a time when the world is flooded with Judgment. The question of which aspect of the Divine is responsible for this situation arises: Is it *Ze'eir Anpin* alone, or does *'Attiqa Qaddisha*, the Holy Ancient One, share in the responsibility? Here, the authors of the Idra are confronting the question of how to explain the sense that *'Attiqa*'s face is hidden, that the Mercy flowing from him is absent from the world. Remaining true to their commitment to refrain from attributing actions or change to *'Attiqa* himself, they assert that he does not actually conceal himself, but rather his face is obscured by a barrier that comes between the human realm and *'Attiqa*'s Mercy, a barrier resulting from human misdeeds:

> "[I]t has been taught as follows: It is not enough for the wicked that they fail to turn the Attribute of Judgment into the Attribute of Compassion, but they turn the Attribute of Compassion into the Attribute of Judgment!
>
> "How can they do so, when it is written *I am YHVH—I have not changed* (Malachi 3:6)? Well, whenever the Ancient of Ancients, the

White Head, is revealed—Will of Wills—great Compassion pervades all. And when He is not revealed, all judgments of *Ze'eir Anpin* lie in wait, and if one may say so, this Compassion executes that Judgment—most Ancient of all.

"It has been taught: When the Ancient of Ancients, Will of Wills, is revealed, all the lamps called by this Name shine and Compassion exists for all. But when the Concealed of the Concealed is not revealed, and these lamps do not shine, judgments are aroused and Judgment is enacted. Who causes this Judgment? The Will of Wills, who is not revealed. Thus, the wicked turn Compassion into Judgment." (Zohar 137b; trans. Matt 8:398–399)

This passage complicates the theological picture by delineating two distinct axes: the dynamic from below to above is that human beings are conducting themselves wickedly, causing *Ze'eir Anpin* to fill with Judgment and *'Attiqa*'s face to be hidden from the world. But following this, an additional dynamic is described, moving from above to below: the absence of any revelation of *'Attiqa* arouses Judgment, and even causes the wicked to invert Mercy and transform it into Judgment.[23]

The answer to the question of who is the primary cause of darkness and Judgment in the world becomes clear: it is *'Attiqa*, for he does not disclose himself. That is to say that alongside blaming the wicked as the cause of evil in the world, a serious claim is being made here against *'Attiqa* himself for failing to subdue the forces of Judgment. This account sits in tension with the way in which *'Attiqa* is constructed throughout the Idra Rabba. Like the Neoplatonic conception of the One, and like the Buddhist conception of the higher and undifferentiated consciousness, the Idra's account of *'Attiqa* up until this point has been as an entity whose essence is simply being. As we have seen, he does not suppress the forces of Judgment actively, as a result of some conscious decision; he achieves this merely by *being*, rather than by *doing*. In this sense, the account just cited, attributing the spread of Judgment in the world to *'Attiqa*'s inaction, is a theological and philosophical "misstep." However, emotionally, the account is deeply compelling. Although, formally speaking, the self-concealment of *'Attiqa* is not active, this does not exempt *'Attiqa* from the accusation, or from vicarious liability for the existence of

Judgment in the world. From the point of view of division of powers, actualization and application of the forces of Judgment is entirely in the hands of *Ze'eir Anpin*, while *'Attiqa* is simply *existence*, unchanging and closed within itself—*For I am YHVH—I have not changed* (Malachi 3:6). But from a human perspective, *'Attiqa* bears responsibility for his self-concealment, for it enables the deployment of the forces of Judgment and evil in the world.

The human desire for *'Attiqa* to reveal himself in a more active manner allows us a glimpse into the moment at which the mythical aspect of the Idra is weighed, figuratively speaking, against the metaphysical and philosophical—and the scales tip toward the mythical and the emotional. The Idra's spirit does not allow formal theology to gain the upper hand.

The Ears: Attentiveness, Discernment, Mechanisms of Delay

After we have observed the short breath, the divine wrath concentrated at the front of the face and in the nose at its center, the ears of *Ze'eir Anpin* are now configured. The ears located on the sides of the head are receptive organs. They are also analytical, discerning and processing the sound that enters them: *The ear tests arguments as the palate tastes food* (Job 34:3). According to the Idra, the impressions entering the ears arouse the brain:

> "The ear is for hearing, and it is formed by designs engraved within—like someone digging a winding stairway, from one direction to another. Why winding? In order to hear good and evil. [. . .]
>
> "Within this ear drips a trickle from the three cavities of the brain to the hollow of the ears. By means of that trickling, the voice enters that winding and is tested in the trickling as either good or evil. Good, as is written: *For YHVH hears the needy* (Psalms 69:34); evil, as is written: *YHVH heard and His nose flared, and the fire of YHVH blazed against them* (Numbers 11:1). (Zohar 138a; trans. Matt 8:403–404)

In configuring *Ze'eir Anpin*'s ears, the Idra focuses upon their internal spiral structure, as well as the wax secreted within. This structure creates a slowing in divine auditory perception, ensuring deep listening, enabling close examination, and providing time for the maturation of a response.[24]

The sound that enters the divine ears also stimulates a response from the nose and eyes. In an account that is shocking in its physicality and hyper-anthropomorphism, the Idra depicts the way in which hearing is translated into expressions of pain, suffering, and rage, and describes the tears, sobs, and sheer anger that burst forth from the divine face:

> "It has been taught: When [Israel] cries out in distress, and hair is withdrawn from over the ears, the voice enters the ears, into that hollow of trickling from the brain, and it strikes the brain, and then emerges through the nostrils. The nose contracts and heats up, fire and smoke spew from those nostrils, and all the *Gevuran*, Powers, are aroused to wreak vengeance.
>
> "Before fire and smoke emerge from those nostrils, that voice ascends, striking the top of the brain, and two tears flow from the eyes; then from His nostrils issue smoke and fire, by that voice conducting them outside.
>
> "By that voice entering the ears, all these are drawn and aroused. Thus it is written *YHVH heard and His nose flared, and the fire of YHVH blazed against them* [Numbers 11:1]. By that hearing of the voice, all is aroused." (Zohar 138a–b; trans. Matt 8:404–405)

The divine response to the sound that enters the ears is raging fury, which could be directed against Israel's enemies, or against Israel itself. Here, the ambivalent stance toward *Ze'eir Anpin* is once again modeled: on the one hand, the fear when divine fury is directed toward Israel; on the other hand, the desire for its manifestation when, as the God of Israel, he hears the distress of his children and responds with angry vengeance, poured out upon the heads of their oppressors.

The ear, as I have mentioned, is connected to the brain; the two ears—associated with reception and examination—emphasize the fundamental duality inherent in *Ze'eir Anpin*. This duality—and the oscillation between right and left, and good and evil, which are the distinctive qualities of *Ze'eir Anpin*—is described in the following highly condensed account:

> "Just as this ear tests to distinguish between good and evil, so it is entirely. For in *Ze'eir Anpin* there is a side of good and of evil, right and left, Compassion and Judgment. This ear is included in the brain, and because it is included there—in one particular cavity—it is included with the voice entering there. 'Hearing' is attributed to the ear, and included with hearing

> is *Binah*, Understanding—'Hear!' implies 'Understand!' Contemplate that all is evenly balanced. These words have been given to Masters of Qualities, to hear, to contemplate, and to know." (Zohar 138b; trans. Matt 8:405)

Anyone familiar with the discourse of the main body of the Zohar will identify the language used to describe the *sefirah* of Sovereignty (*Malkhut*) in the formulaic account of "a side of good and of evil, right and left, Compassion and Judgment." Such a reader will also sense the difference between this account and that of Beauty (*Tif'eret*)—the blessed Holy One—who is described as stable, fixed, transcending time.[25] This carries great significance in relation to the tantalizing suggestion that at the outset, during the developmental stages of the Idra literature, the relationship between the larger and smaller divine faces—*Arikh Anpin* and *Ze'eir Anpin*—was precisely the relationship between the Male and Female aspects of the Godhead, and the masculinity of these two *partsufim* was established only at a later date.[26] This doubtlessly raises the question of *Ze'eir Anpin*'s androgyny. That having been said, a comparison between Sovereignty's qualities of movement and duality in the main body of the Zohar and accounts of *Ze'eir Anpin* in the Idra points to Sovereignty's manifestation as a rounded, many-faced, whole, and balanced personality—more so than *Ze'eir Anpin*, who tends overwhelmingly toward Judgment.

Another important matter that arises from this passage is the positive and affirming description of the ability to distinguish, recognize, and discern—necessary tools in the dualistic dimension of *Ze'eir Anpin*. For the sake of comparison, in the realm of *Arikh Anpin* ears have no meaning, for his mode of interacting with the world requires no distinction, no determination regarding any particular kind of action—only a constant emotional state of tremendous Mercy and Love. Indeed, the Idra Rabba devotes no distinct *tiqqun* to *Arikh Anpin*'s ears. The sense of hearing, discernment, and examination that is centered upon *Ze'eir Anpin*'s ears is a paradigm for the self-conduct of the kabbalists within the human realm, which requires making distinctions at every moment. The kabbalists—the Masters of the Attributes—have been granted an attentive ear and a discerning heart.[27]

The *tiqqunim* of *Ze'eir Anpin*'s facial features conclude with the ear, and the *tiqqunim* of the beard now begin.

16

The *Tiqqunim of Ze'eir Anpin*

The Language of Flowing Bounty

The *tiqqunim* of *Ze'eir Anpin*'s beard begin with an account of the oil that flows from *'Attiqa*'s beard onto that of *Ze'eir Anpin*. *'Attiqa*'s precious oil—coming down upon the beard, Aaron's beard, "that cometh down upon the collar of his garments" (Psalms 133:2)—adorns and configures *Ze'eir Anpin*'s beard into nine *tiqqunim*. At propitious times or during periods of great distress, the light emanating from *'Attiqa*'s white beard illuminates and radiates through the face and beard of *Ze'eir Anpin*. When the hairs of the two divine beards make contact like cosmic synapses, the nine *tiqqunim* of *Ze'eir Anpin*'s beard join with the thirteen of *'Attiqa*'s. The total number of the *tiqqunim* of the beard now comes to twenty-two, constituting a point of origin for the twenty-two letters of the Hebrew alphabet. Thus, a language is generated in which one can speak about the Divine. According to the account in Sifra di-Tsni'uta, the letters transition from an undifferentiated state within the Divine to a more solid and constricted state as concrete letters. From these letters, the divine name is constructed (or according to other versions, the divine Torah, which is in turn the name of God).[1]

> "It has been taught: When the holy anointing oil descends from the precious supernal holy beard, hidden and concealed from all, to the beard of *Ze'eir Anpin* [. . .]
>
> "This beard—perfection of the face, beauty of *Ze'eir Anpin*—is arrayed in nine enhancements. When the precious beard of the Ancient

> of Ancients shines upon this beard of *Ze'eir Anpin*, thirteen springs of supernal oil flow into this beard, and twenty-two enhancements appear within it, from which stream the twenty-two letters of the holy Torah." (Zohar 3:139a; trans. Matt 8:408)

Introduction to the *Tiqqunim* of the Beard: The Teacher Awakens Consciousness

Throughout the Idra Rabba there are passages in which Rabbi Shim'on points to a new mode of consciousness or to shifting horizons of existence that affect the Companions, or that are affected by them. Thus, during the *tiqqunim* of *'Attiqa* and his beard, Rabbi Shim'on informs his disciples that they are surrounded by divine fire, and describes to them the vitality of their own words as they ascend and take their place within the face and beard of *'Attiqa*.[2] Similarly, at the conclusion of the *tiqqun* of *Ze'eir Anpin*'s ears, he presents a moving scriptural interpretation, one that is deeply revealing concerning the relationship between the mystic and the figure of *Ze'eir Anpin*.[3]

Now, before beginning the *tiqqunim* of *Ze'eir Anpin*'s beard, the great teacher Rabbi Shim'on declares as follows:

> "It has been taught": Rabbi Shim'on said, "I call as witnesses all those who stand over us, that these words rejoice in all worlds, and the words rejoice in my heart. Within the supernal curtained canopy they are concealed, ascending, and the Ancient of All—hidden and concealed from all—treasures them away.
>
> "When I began to speak, the Companions did not know that all these words would arouse here. Happy is your share, O Companions who are here! Happy is my share along with you in this world and in the world that is coming!" (Zohar 3:138b; trans. Matt 8:407)

Within the grandeur and fear, the urgency and the strangeness of the event, emerges the divine and human joy that marks the processes set in motion by the Idra's participants. The master facilitates the expansion of the disciples' consciousness by pointing to the rousing quality of their words. In so doing he emphasizes the theurgic aspect of the gathering, bringing it into sharper focus. The holy words, representing the divine realm itself, are awakened by the speech of terrestrial human beings. Human *speech* arouses the divine realms.

As we saw in the thirteenth *tiqqun* of *'Attiqa*'s beard, the Idra's account of the joyful words and speech clearly echoes classical rabbinic tradition. In several rabbinic sources, we find descriptions of divine fire descending from heaven and surrounding a figure who presents novel interpretations of the secrets of Torah. These narratives present joy in the words of Torah as the source of this divine fire. When one weaves together and expounds the words of Torah creatively, the words themselves are joyous, and they return to their primal and elemental state as divine fire, representing the divine Torah before it was contracted into human speech, narrative, and law.[4]

Rabbi Shim'on describes a vision that is visible to his eyes only, concealed from the disciples, in which the joyous words ascend through all supernal worlds. The higher they ascend, the more concealed they become, until they are finally hidden away within the most ancient and concealed aspect of God. The sheer bounty, the multiplicity, and the innovation of the Companions' discourses returns to deep within the hidden recesses of the Divine. This motion completes the primary trajectory of the Idra, which configures and describes the emanation of the faces of God, beginning with the loftiest, most hidden and undifferentiated mode of being, and moving toward a distinct and complex mode of existence. According to the zoharic conception, as expressed in the Idra, the words of the Companions constitute an "arousal below" (*it'aruta di-ltata*), which reaches from the world below into the heights of the divine realm. This arousal in turn causes an "arousal above" (*it'aruta di-l'eila*), drawing a bountiful flux of divine blessing from the celestial realms into our world. This state of affairs—in which the lower arouses the upper, the Female arouses the Male, and the human arouses the Divine—is one of the foundational tenets of the Zohar's view of the cosmos, describing the very structure and functioning of existence.

An additional comment offered by Rabbi Shim'on—"When I began to speak, the Companions did not know that all these words would arouse here"—carries significance both for his disciples and the reader. It emphasizes that the teacher is the one who is aware of the occasion's potency, and it is based on this knowledge that he issued the call, full of pathos, to convene the assembly. In contrast, the disciples are not aware of this. Their minds cannot comprehend the event from the grand perspective of the divine realms. They begin to speak without any consciousness of the vital potency of their words, of their ability to arouse the divine realm. The teacher's role is to expand the boundaries of the disciples' insight and consciousness, to awaken their own awareness of the greatness of the event taking place, their growing intimacy with the Divine, and thereby to amplify their creative power.

Between *'Attiqa*'s Beard and *Ze'eir Anpin*'s Beard

Before discussing the *tiqqunim* of *Ze'eir Anpin*'s beard, it is worth noting some of the inherent differences between that beard and *'Attiqa*'s beard. Indeed, it is clear that *Ze'eir Anpin*'s beard is configured in conscious comparison and (especially) contrast with that of *'Attiqa*.

First of all, it is striking that the *tiqqunim* of *Ze'eir Anpin* lack the literary, narrative, and exegetical force that we find in those of *'Attiqa*. They are also considerably shorter in length. On a more fundamental level, the *tiqqunim* of both beards construct a visual and conceptual language to discuss God's attributes and their manifestation in the world, and to sharpen the distinction between the experience of an undifferentiated manifestation of Divinity and the experience of a dualistic one. A foundational principle that differentiates the two modes of Divinity is that "in *Ze'eir Anpin* there is a side of good and of evil, right and left, Compassion and Judgment."[5] The left and right sides of his face and beard reflect his dual mode of existence, distinct from the unity that characterizes *'Attiqa*.

The striking differences between the two beards are bound up with the distinct quality of their hair: the coarseness of *Ze'eir Anpin*'s beard hairs, versus the softness of those of *'Attiqa*; and the mottled quality of *Ze'eir Anpin*'s beard, which has black and white hairs, versus the pure white of *'Attiqa*'s beard. Apart from representing a distinction between Judgment and Compassion, the difference between the respective colors of the beards also visually signifies the priority and primordiality of white over black in the Idra as cosmic modes of being. Moreover, it reflects the midrashic account of the Torah given at Mount Sinai as being written in black fire upon white fire, reformulated and represented in the context of a face.[6] The backdrop to the laws of the Torah, to its instruction written in black, is the whiteness of *'Attiqa*'s pure Compassion:

> "Now, you might say, 'If so, look, the hairs below are black! Why aren't these like those?' Because it has been taught: It is written *his locks wavy, black as a raven* (Song of Songs 5:11) and it is written *the hair of his head*

like clean fleece (Daniel 7:9)—there is no contradiction. One refers to the upper beard and the other to the lower beard, and therefore when Torah was given to Israel it was given as black fire upon white fire." (Zohar 3:132a; trans. Matt. 8:353, emended)[7]

Another important distinction between the two beards lies in the scriptural verses in which they are anchored. While *'Attiqa*'s beard is evoked and configured using verses from Micah, which praise God's attributes, the *tiqqunim* of *Ze'eir Anpin* are formulated through an interpretation of Psalm 118:5–14. The verses begin as a cry to God, from a state of danger and threat, before shifting to a hymn of salvation for God's defeat of the forces of oppression.

In distress I called on YHVH;
He answered me and brought me relief.
YHVH is on my side, I have no fear;
What can human beings do to me?
With YHVH on my side as my helper,
I will see the downfall of my foes.
It is better to take refuge in YHVH
Than to trust in man.
It is better to take refuge in YHVH
Than to trust in princes.
All nations have beset me;
By the name of YHVH I will surely cut them down.
They beset me, they surround me;
By the name of YHVH I will surely cut them down.
They have beset me like bees;
They shall be extinguished like burning thorns;
By the name of YHVH I will surely cut them down.
You pressed me hard, I nearly fell;
But YHVH helped me.
YHVH is my strength and might;
He has become my deliverance.

The narrator of this psalm is David, the warrior who invokes God—the ultimate warrior—to aid him in the battle against his enemies. David cries out to his Deity in a state of constriction and oppression, surrounded and besieged by his enemies. As the psalm proceeds, the narrow place widens, opening into an expanse in which God responds to the psalmist's call. The Idra understands David's cry to be addressed to *Ze'eir Anpin*, the God of Israel, who is summoned to battle, to free his servant at a time of distress. *Ze'eir Anpin*'s weapons—which are necessary when waging war against his enemies—are the *tiqqunim* of the beard. Thus, while the *tiqqunim* of *'Attiqa*'s beard represent a confrontation with the forces of Judgment and chaos, played out in his suppression and subjugation of those forces, the *tiqqunim* of *Ze'eir Anpin*'s beard actively and aggressively participate in the defense of human beings from Judgment.

According to the Idra, Psalm 118 describes a visionary event. King David, the warrior, sees *Ze'eir Anpin*'s beard configured and arrayed in its *tiqqunim*, and his hairy cheeks, and while contemplating the hair of the beard descending, he seizes it as if it were a shield: "YHVH is on my side, I have no fear!" David's cry to the Divine is an invocation; it seeks to make YHVH present. What is unique here is how we enter the imagistic and mythical aspect of these words: a human being seeks strength in the face of YHVH, and in the hairs of his beard.

The nine *tiqqunim* of *Ze'eir Anpin*'s beard are exegetically derived from verses 5 to 9 of this psalm, modeled on nine references to God in these verses. The first six are explicit instances of the divine name (*Yah*, *YHVH*). The three that remain are identified, somewhat surprisingly, in the terms *Adam* and *princes*—which are interpreted as references to *Ze'eir Anpin*![8]

The configuration of the nine *tiqqunim*—rather than *'Attiqa*'s thirteen—is linked to *Ze'eir Anpin*'s role as the mighty, heroic, masculine, reactive, and judging God. Humanity does not always need the dimension of God that flows forth with Thirteen Attributes of Mercy. At times of emergency and suffering, humans might precisely need a contraction and limitation of divine Compassion and an amplification or intensification of the forces of Judgment, in order to protect them from their enemies. Only when this *partsuf* is overly full of Judgment, thereby posing a threat to humanity, is there a need for the theurgical act of reciting the Thirteen Attributes of Mercy. It is at such times that the nine *tiqqunim* of *Ze'eir Anpin* fill with the Thirteen Attributes of Mercy flowing forth from *'Attiqa*'s beard, and *Ze'eir Anpin*'s beard radiates with twenty-two Attributes of Mercy. His face relaxes, softens, and he has mercy on the world.

The Thirteen Attributes of Mercy that are summoned to flow into *Ze'eir Anpin*, flooding him with mercy, are not those derived from the Book of Micah. In the Idra, the latter specifically represent the *tiqqunim* of *'Attiqa*'s beard. Rather, in the context of *Ze'eir Anpin*, the Thirteen Attributes of Mercy refer specifically to the attributes recited by Moses after the sin of the Golden Calf, which aroused God's deadly fury (Exodus 34:6–7). Moses attempts to soothe God's angry countenance by reciting his Attributes of Mercy. Indeed, it was the attributes recited by Moses, focused as they are on relief from suffering, that became established in the exegetical and liturgical tradition, rather than those in the Book of Micah—which are instead a hymn of praise to God's greatness, lacking any association with divine wrath. Moses, not Micah, becomes the exemplary human being who models the theurgical possibility of drawing the Attributes of Mercy from *'Attiqa*'s beard into the agitated and raging consciousness of *Ze'eir Anpin*, thereby appeasing and calming him. The Idra explains this as follows:

> "[W]e have learned: *Who is a God like You* (Micah 7:18–20). [. . .] Corresponding to this: *A Compassionate and gracious God* [. . .] (Exodus 34:6–7), and those are below.
>
> "Now, you might say, 'How could Moses not utter those supernal ones?' Well, Moses needed only the place where Judgment prevails, and where Judgment prevails, one must speak as he did. And Moses spoke only at a time when Israel had sinned and Judgment was looming, so Moses spoke only in a place where Judgment is found." (Zohar 3:131b; trans. Matt 8: 352–353)

The attributes enumerated in Micah are "supernal," above, while those recited by Moses are "below." Summoning the Attributes of Mercy into the Golden Calf's dimension of Judgment demands tremendous power and authority. The force of Mercy must be stronger than that of Judgment; thus, in contradistinction to the focus on the pure white of *'Attiqa*'s beard associated with the verses from Micah, Moses emphasizes the tremendous power of *Ze'eir Anpin*'s beard.[9]

In the *tiqqunim* of *Ze'eir Anpin*'s beard, the emotional ambivalence in addressing this aspect of the Divine is particularly emphasized. On the one hand, the depiction of God as a warrior defending his people and wreaking vengeance on their enemies is comforting. On the other hand, this figure's fury inspires fear, particularly when that fury is directed at Israel, his very own children.

Despite the fear inherent in *Ze'eir Anpin*'s manifestation, the process of configuring his beard begins with an emphasis on this figure's beauty, might, and perhaps even youth:

> "This beard—perfection of the face, beauty of *Ze'eir Anpin* [. . .] proceeds from His ears, descending and ascending, and covers an offering of spices. What is 'an offering of spices'? As is said: *like a bed of spices* (Song of Songs 5:13). [. . .]
>
> "This beard of *Ze'eir Anpin* is arrayed in nine enhancements, with black hair, beautifully arranged like a handsome man, of whom it is written *distinguished as the cedars* (Song of Songs 5:15)." (Zohar 3:139a; trans. Matt 8:408–409)

Beginning the *Tiqqunim* of the Beard

Before presenting the *tiqqunim* of the beard, Rabbi Shim'on enumerates the nine sections of the beard that are about to be configured by the Companions:

> "First enhancement: Hair is arranged from above. That spark—Scintilla of Adamantine Darkness—escapes the realm of pure air and strikes below the hair of the head, beneath the locks over the ears. It descends in front of the opening of the ears, strand by strand, until the top of the mouth.
>
> "Second enhancement: Hair emerges, ascending from the top of the mouth to the other top of the mouth's opening; and descending beneath the mouth to the other top, strand by strand, beautifully arranged.
>
> "Third enhancement: From the middle, beneath the nose, beneath the two nostrils, emerges a single path. Tiny coarse hairs fill that path, with other hair filling each side around the path. A path does not appear below at all, only that path above, descending to the top of the lips, where it is submerged.
>
> "Fourth enhancement: Hair emerges and is arranged, ascending and covering His Jowls—the offering of spices—as with the Ancient One.

"Fifth enhancement: Hair stops, and two apples appear, one on each side—red as a red rose, glowing in 270 worlds flashing from them.

"Sixth enhancement: Hair emerges as one cord around the beard and hangs down to the top of the belly, not descending to the navel.

"Seventh enhancement: No hair overhangs the mouth, and the mouth is clear on all sides, with hair set perfectly all around.

"Eighth enhancement: Hair descends beneath the beard, covering the neck so that it is not seen. All those hairs are thin, strand upon strand, full on all sides.

"Ninth enhancement: Hairs join, all evenly, until the hair that hangs—all in beautiful symmetry, like a mighty hero victorious in battles.

"By these nine enhancements flow forth nine springs of anointing oil from that anointing oil above, flowing on to all those below." (Zohar 3:139a; trans. Matt 8:409–411)

The *tiqqunim* of *Ze'eir Anpin*'s beard are not set out as painstakingly and impressively as those of *'Attiqa*'s beard. One might take this as an indication that the Idra Rabba was produced in an eclectic manner. According to such a view, the literary variation came about because the *tiqqunim* of *Ze'eir Anpin* were not edited as meticulously as those of *'Attiqa*, being a collection of scattered traditions that treat a range of subjects.[10] However, I am of the opinion that the *tiqqunim* are arranged according to a definite structure: the first four focus primarily on a comparison between the Attributes of Mercy of *Arikh Anpin* and those of *Ze'eir Anpin*, comparing scriptural verses and the names of their respective attributes; thereafter, from the fifth *tiqqun* onward, the focus shifts toward the specific nature of the portion of the beard being configured, and the attribute associated with it.

The next two sections briefly discuss the first, third, and fifth *tiqqunim* of *Ze'eir Anpin*'s beard, treating this figure's temples, nostrils, lips, and rounded cheeks. The chapter concludes with the ninth and final *tiqqun*, which includes all of those preceding it. These *tiqqunim* illustrate the manner in which the Idra Rabba discusses *Ze'eir Anpin*'s duality, modeling and sharpening that duality in the process.

The First *Tiqqun*

Rabbi El'azar is invited by his father to array the first of the *tiqqunim* of *Ze'eir Anpin*'s beard, relating to the hair that emerges in front of the opening of the ear and extends to the mouth. This hair occasions another encounter with the Lamp of Adamantine Darkness (*botsina de-qardinuta*), which formed *Ze'eir Anpin*'s skull in conjunction with the pure ether, as discussed earlier. This spark is embedded and concealed within the skull, and here too it continues to generate entities: it strikes the insides of the temples, which function as wellsprings from which the hairs of the beard emerge.

Considering this image and the coarseness of the beard hairs, Rabbi El'azar discusses the nature of divine governance of the cosmos, oscillating as it does between Judgment and Compassion:

> "[I]t has been taught: All these hairs of the beard are rough. Why? All those of Compassion must be rough in order to subdue Judgment, and all those that are Judgment are surely rough. In either case, they must be rough, from two aspects. When the world needs Compassion, Compassion intensifies and triumphs over Judgment. And when it needs Judgment, Judgment intensifies and triumphs over Compassion. [. . .] All is based on the beard." (Zohar 3:140a; trans. Matt 8:417)

Rabbi El'azar emphasizes that the coarseness of the hairs does not stem from their association with Judgment. The divine attributes that flow within *Ze'eir Anpin*'s beard may be of either Judgment or Compassion, and the hair must be coarse in order to conduct both modalities at once. When the hairs channel Compassion, this Compassion must be strong enough to subdue Judgment; when they flow with Judgment, it must be harsh enough to overpower Compassion. In this context, we come to a stunning account of the moment of divine favor, when the wellsprings of *'Attiqa*'s beard flow down to *Ze'eir Anpin*, bathing the Judgment and Compassion within his beard in pure white:

> "When the holy white beard is revealed, all of these and all of those are illumined and bathed—like someone bathing in a deep river from what was coating him. All of them are established in Compassion, and

Judgment is nowhere to be found. When all these nine shine as one, all are bathed in Compassion." (Zohar 3:140a; trans. Matt 8:418)

Judgment in Duality, Blushing Red: A Path, Lips, and Rounded Cheeks in the Third and Fifth *Tiqqunim*

Beneath the orifices in the nose, flaring with rage, is a path that passes from the nostrils to the upper lip. This path is described in the third *tiqqun* of *Ze'eir Anpin*'s beard. We are not told which of the Companions presents this interpretation.

As we have seen, in the context of *'Attiqa*'s beard, this hairless path represents the Attribute of Mercy referred to as *passing over transgression*. It facilitates the smooth flow of Compassion, which washes away sin, preventing it from becoming caught up in the hair of Judgment. Transgressions thus glide down this path to the mouth, which emits a breath of forgiveness. However, in *Ze'eir Anpin* the path is a precise inversion of this attribute. Already, in the *tiqqunim* of *'Attiqa*, a comparison was made between these two paths, from which we learn that one who finds oneself under the flaring and flaming nostrils of *Ze'eir Anpin* is doomed to destruction:

> "In *Ze'eir Anpin*, when that path descends from beneath His nostrils, it is written *The nose of YHVH flared against them*, וילך (*va-yelakh*), *and he went* (Numbers 12:9). What is meant by *and he went*? That a breath of wrath shoots forth from those nostrils, and whoever is found there is 'gone' and no longer exists—as is written: *For the breath of YHVH blows upon him* [*and he is gone*] (Isaiah 40:7).
>
> "Of Arikh Anpin is written *passing over* [*transgression*], and it is written: *A breath passes, purifying them* (Job 37:21). Here is written *and passing over transgression*—by that path. There, *YHVH will pass to strike Egypt* (Exodus 12:23).
>
> "Happy is the share of one who is worthy of this!" (Zohar 3:133a; trans. Matt 8:363–364)

Here, in the context of the *tiqqunim* of *Ze'eir Anpin*'s beard, we find another depiction of the path, full of tiny hairs. The anonymous exegete states that this locus within the Divine cannot indeed be called *passing over transgression*, for two reasons: first, it is difficult to *pass* through the path's tangled hairs, and second, one who actually makes the journey reaches *Ze'eir Anpin*'s lips, which, despite their beauty, do not represent a merciful God. Here, the erotic description in Song of Songs 5:13—*His lips are roses, dripping liquid myrrh*—is boldly interpreted as an account of lips blushing with anger, full of Judgment, dripping with bitterness and rage:

> "It has been taught: This path descending beneath two nostrils, with tiny hairs filling that path, is not called *passing over transgression*, since there is no place for passing over, from two aspects. One, because of the hairs occupying that path, making it difficult to pass. And the other, because that path descends to the top of the lips, and it is written *His lips are roses* (Song of Songs 5:13), red as roses; [*dripping*] *liquid myrrh* (*ibid.*), intensely red. This path here, in two hues, threatens and shows no mercy. Consequently, one who wishes to threaten strikes twice with his hand on that path." (Zohar 3:140b; trans. Matt 8:421)

This *tiqqun* depicts the copious Judgment that fills and crowds *Ze'eir Anpin*'s face. One might expect that the duality of the lips—like the duality of the nostrils—could in turn enable a dualistic interpretation. In such a scenario, those who find themselves upon *Ze'eir Anpin*'s lips might sometimes encounter Judgment and sometimes encounter Compassion. But such is not the case. Both lips represent the deep and harsh redness of Judgment. The image of sinking into the entanglement of hairs, full of furious breath, and lips shining with the redness of fearsome Judgment, is nightmarish—and full of theological and psychological significance.[11]

An additional expression of the alignment of *Ze'eir Anpin* with divine Judgment may be found in the fifth *tiqqun*, which addresses the rounded cheeks, the hairless portion of the beard. The rounded cheeks are red as roses, burning with the flame of Judgment, and only *'Attiqa*'s illumination within them can wash away their redness and enable them to shine forth with life for the world:

> "Fifth enhancement: Hair stops, and two apples appear, one on each side—red as a red rose, glowing in 270 worlds.

"When these two apples [of *Ze'eir Anpin*] shine on both sides from the radiance of two apples [of *'Attiqa*], red is withdrawn and white appears. Of this is written, *May YHVH shine His face upon you and be gracious to you* (Numbers 6:25), for when they shine, the world is blessed. And as red disappears, it is written *May YHVH lift up His face to you* (*ibid.*, 26), meaning: 'May wrath be removed, vanishing from the world.'" (Zohar 3:141a; trans. Matt 8:423)

The Priestly Blessing, with its allusions to the divine face, is here interpreted in an exceptional manner. According to the Idra, the verse *May YHVH shine His face upon you* describes a state in which *'Attiqa*'s face floods *Ze'eir Anpin* with luminous Compassion, causing the world to become blessed. In the subsequent verse, *May YHVH lift up His face to you*, the face represents divine wrath, as in other biblical passages such as *I will set my face against that man* (Leviticus 20:3), and *My face will pass, and I shall give you rest* (Exodus 33:14). We can understand this passage as a cry to *Ze'eir Anpin*, beseeching him to turn his furious face away from human beings, or alternatively, as a human prayer to *'Attiqa* for *Ze'eir Anpin* to turn toward him in order to be illuminated by the Ancient One.[12]

It is difficult to overstate the innovative quality of this interpretation of the Priestly Blessing. It is not addressed to the one God who has multiple attributes, but rather is a call for one divine face to be illuminated by another, and a plea to reduce or remove the presence of *Ze'eir Anpin*'s Judgment in the world.[13]

The Warrior's Mercy, *Tif'eret* (Beauty): The Ninth *Tiqqun*

The ninth and final *tiqqun* of the beard constitutes a complete picture of *Ze'eir Anpin*'s face, crowned with an abundance of curled black locks, like a warrior. This image is symbolized by Beauty (*Tif'eret*). Beauty is the force that measures out and configures the Male and Female bodies, functioning somewhat like the Lamp of Adamantine Darkness (*botsina de-qardinuta*) on a lower and more differentiated plane of existence. This Beauty should not be equated with the *sefirah* of Beauty (*Tif'eret*) and its corresponding qualities as they are familiar to us from the vast majority of the zoharic corpus, even though they do overlap to some degree (as will be discussed shortly).[14]

> "Ninth enhancement: Hairs join, all evenly, until the hair that hangs—all in beautiful symmetry, like a mighty hero victorious in battles. For all those hairs follow those that hang, and the consummation of them all is those hanging ones. All is drawn to this, as it is written: תפארת (*Tif'eret*), *The beauty of young men is their strength* (Proverbs 20:29). He appeared at the Sea like a fine young man,[15] as is written: *a young man like the cedars* (Song of Songs 5:15)—like a hero performing mighty deeds. This is *Tif'eret*, Beauty—power, might, and compassion."[16] (Zohar 3:141a; trans. Matt 8:425)

As we have seen, the discussions of *Ze'eir Anpin*—like many passages that treat *Arikh Anpin*—present a comparison between the two divine *partsufim*, which the Idra seeks to bring into a closer and more vital relationship. In concluding the discussion of *Ze'eir Anpin*'s beard, we shall examine the difference between the quality of Beauty within *Arikh Anpin*'s face and its manifestation within *Ze'eir Anpin*. Such a comparison will bring the distinctions between the two divine faces into sharper relief.

Tif'eret (Beauty), appears in the third *tiqqun* of *'Attiqa*'s beard, which treats the hairless path below the nostrils. The divine attribute from Micah that corresponds with this *tiqqun* is *passing over transgression*. However, the Idra recruits another verse in its account of this feature of *'Attiqa*'s face: *It is a person's intelligence to be slow to anger* (*he'erikh appo*)*; his beauty* (*ve-tif'arto*) *is passing over transgression* (Proverbs 19:11).[17] Therefore, *'Attiqa*'s Beauty, his *Tif'eret*, is a divine dimension without hair, enclothement, or configuration; it is a path of light and forgiveness that is free of all Judgment. On a theological level, this is the divine attribute that forgives all transgression, and therein lies his beauty: *his beauty is passing over transgression*.

Tif'eret as it is manifest in the concluding passages of the *tiqqunim* of *Ze'eir Anpin*'s beard is entirely different. It is an abundance of cascading black hair, framing *Ze'eir Anpin*'s face, thereby emphasizing it. The glorious beard that adorns this face is masculine beauty, the beauty of a young warrior. Indeed, this is how the term *Tif'eret* is interpreted in the context of the biblical verse *The beauty of young men is their strength* (Proverbs 20:29). The beauty of young men is their strength, and this strength is expressed in the beard. Beauty is characterized as a blend of Might and Compassion, which constitutes an appropriate basis for the extension and emanation of reality.

Whereas "glory, magnificence" (*ḳavod, yaqqiruta*) is emphasized in the context of *'Attiqa*'s beard, it is the warrior's *might* that stands out in that of *Ze'eir Anpin.* In contradistinction to *'Attiqa*'s Beauty, which is the ability to forgive all sin, *Ze'eir Anpin*'s Beauty lies in a commingling of *ḳo'aḥ* (power), *gevurah* (might and judgment) and *raḥamim* (compassion). It seems that the emphasis upon judgment and might in the account of *Ze'eir Anpin*'s beard is motivated by a desire to highlight the role of this divine figure as a warrior and defender. Rather than the mercy of a king upon a royal throne or a judge in a court, *Ze'eir Anpin*'s Attributes of Mercy most closely resemble those of a warrior in battle.

17

The Ancient of Ancients and *Ze'eir Anpin*

All Is One

Complex Unity

After configuring and adorning the two male *partsufim*, and emphasizing the differences between them, Rabbi Shim'on pauses to expound upon some intellectually demanding and paradoxical matters that rank among the foundations of the Idra Rabba's mystical theology.

Before presenting his insights, Rabbi Shim'on again emphasizes that his words are meant only for those who meet certain strict conditions: those who have been "weighed in the balance," who have "entered and emerged":

> It has been taught: Rabbi Shim'on said, "All these enhancements and all these matters I wish to reveal to Masters of Qualities, masters who have been weighed in the balance—not to those who have entered and not emerged, but to those who have entered and emerged. For whoever has entered and not emerged, better for him if he had never been created!"[1] (Zohar 3:141a; trans. Matt 8:425, emended)

For whom are these words intended? First of all, they are addressed to the inner circle of the Companions, the participants in the event: they must be aware that if they have in the past entered the divine Orchard but failed to emerge from it in peace, they are not worthy of participation in the assembly. The Idra's readers make up a broader audience, to whom the warning is also addressed. Its performative power lies in creating a sense of fear or dread in the reader, focused on that person's own worthiness to continue reading the mysteries contained within the Idra. At the same time, such a warning arouses curiosity, attracting and beckoning the reader to continue—indeed, the very fact that one is a reader, rather than a participant in the event, provides a sense of protection.

> "The principle of all: The Ancient of Ancients and *Ze'eir Anpin* are all one—He was all, is all, will be all; He did not change, will not change, does not change. He is arrayed in these enhancements—an image comprising all images, an image comprising all names. The image appearing in its facets in this image is not actually in this image, but rather resembles this image, when diadems and crowns conjoin in total perfection.
>
> "Therefore the image of *Adam* is the image of those above and those below, who are included in him. Since this image includes above and below, the Holy Ancient One arrayed His adornments and those of *Ze'eir Anpin* in this image.
>
> "Now, you might say, 'What is the difference between one and the other?' Well, all is evenly balanced—but by us paths are separated, by us Judgment comes into being, and from our perspective they differ from one another. These mysteries are transmitted only to the Reapers of the Field, and it is written: *The secret of YHVH is for those who revere Him* (Psalms 25:14)." (Zohar 3:141a–b; trans. Matt 8:426)

Rabbi Shim'on's statement that *'Attiqa* and *Ze'eir Anpin* "are all one" is nothing short of astonishing. How can we reconcile this declaration of unity with the significant differences between *'Attiqa* and *Ze'eir Anpin* that the Idra has emphasized again and again until this point?

The statement that these aspects of the Divine "are all one" points to an affirmation of monotheism, to some degree calming the reader's fear that there may exist, heaven forfend, distinct or competing deities. The formulation is reminiscent of the biblical verse that begins *Sh'ma Yisrael* (*Hear O Israel*) and declares that *YHVH is our God, YHVH is one*. Let us note, however, that in the case of the Idra Rabba, the divine unity that is affirmed is neither simple nor monolithic. Here we find one of the great ideas that emerges from the discourse of theosophical Kabbalah as a whole, whether it is framed in terms of the ten *sefirot* or the divine *partsufim*: unity is highly complex.

Here, divine unity is stated with dramatic effect: "He was all, is all, will be all; He did not change, will not change, does not change." Liebes has shown that these words appear to affirm a medieval philosophical theology.[2] But in my opinion, the use of philosophical terms here is more ecstatic than discursive. Throughout the Idra, the Divine has been configured, adorned, and arrayed; it has been enclothed in images, described with expressions that draw distinctions, at the very least on the level of human language and consciousness. But now the Idra emphasizes that divine unity exists, transcending time, beyond the boundaries of a consciousness that distinguishes, divides, and defines. It takes great emotional strength to redirect one's mind from thinking about details and distinctions, and then to affirm a conception of unity that transcends all differences and distinctions.

Rabbi Shim'on continues, drawing a connection between this divine unity and the image of *Adam*, through whom the divine *tiqqunim* are configured. The figure of *Adam* is completed only "when diadems and crowns conjoin"—that is, when *'Attiqa* and *Ze'eir Anpin* connect to one another, their gazes meeting as one.

Before us we find an unprecedented amplification of the figure of *Adam*. Here, this figure is understood to be the fundamental and ideal representation through which the Divine manifests itself. It becomes the supreme principle, containing everything within it and conveying and embodying all accounts of the Divine, in both the supernal and terrestrial realms. Here Rabbi Shim'on praises the figure of *Adam*, present as it is throughout every stage of existence, from the highest heights to the lowest rungs of being.

It is worth noting that the dramatic declaration that the figure of *Adam* is the likeness of the higher and lower worlds weaves the entire Idra together. *Adam* is tangibly present throughout the *tiqqun* of *Ze'eir Anpin*, and even more so in the Idra's account of the coupling of the divine Male and Female. But already, at the very outset of the Idra, *'Attiqa* chooses to be configured as a face—the clearest distinguishing feature of a human being, of Adam. Indeed, however strange and pure white *'Attiqa*'s face may be, human beings relate to it more as they would to the face of a fellow human being than they would, for example, to the "face" of the sun.

How might we relate, then, to the fact that, throughout the Idra, the differences between *Ze'eir Anpin* and *Arikh Anpin* have been emphasized, while here Rabbi Shim'on affirms the unity of the two *partsufim*? It seems that the apparent contradiction is anchored in the difference between essence and consciousness, between divine existence and the boundaries of the human mind: "all is evenly balanced—but by us paths are separated."

From the point of view of divine essence, *Arikh Anpin* and *Ze'eir Anpin* are equal. It is true that Compassion emanates from *Arikh Anpin* and Judgment issues from *Ze'eir Anpin*—but in truth, they are a single unity. In contrast, from a human perspective, *Arikh Anpin* and *Ze'eir Anpin* are conceived of as distinct from one another. Binary human consciousness struggles to contain the complexity and strangeness of such a unity, so ultimately, it must split it in two.

Rabbi Shim'on again emphasizes to the Companions, those who have earned the privilege of counting as Reapers of the Field, that they must cultivate a consciousness able to contain *Arikh Anpin* and *Ze'eir Anpin* as a unity, with all the distinctions between them. The Companions are summoned to experience the unity that dwells within the depths of difference, by finding the single scale upon which *Arikh Anpin* and *Ze'eir Anpin* are weighed.

Already, in classical rabbinic literature, there had been an attempt to grasp the relationship between the essential oneness of the Divine and its various manifestations in the world:

> The Blessed Holy One appeared to them at the sea as a warrior in battle, at Sinai as a scribe providing instruction, in the days of Daniel as an elder teaching Torah, in the days of Solomon as a young lad. The blessed Holy One said: Despite the fact that you see many likenesses, I am the one at the sea, I am the one at Sinai.[3]

According to this passage, God adopts different personae. The divine essence is one, but its manifestations differ according to the nature of the event. To adopt Franz Rosenzweig's formulation, we might say that the circumstances of the encounter between God and human beings are experienced in various ways, but this does not point to multiplicity of essence.[4] In the Idra, the paradoxical tension that arises from this pattern is all the greater because the work itself focuses so intensively on the differences between the two *partsufim*. In order to recognize an underlying unity for even a few moments, we must access new conceptual horizons.

A Figure within a Figure: The Structure of Reality

The Idra Rabba presents a structural account of the divine and human realms, a description that enables our consciousness to contain and hold their various dimensions as one. Rather than thinking of *'Attiqa*, *Ze'eir Anpin*, and *Adam* as facing one another in space, or consecutively in time, the Idra offers a new structural paradigm: form within form. The various levels of reality—Divine, Adamic, and human—stand in a relationship of internality and externality, content and garment.

Immediately following the hymn of praise for the figure of *Adam*, we find one of the most spectacular biblical interpretations in the entire Idra Rabba. This passage seeks a language to express the Idra's conception of the structure of reality. It is woven around a verse from Genesis that describes the creation of Adam and his transformation into a living being: *YHVH Elohim formed the human, dust from the earth; He blew into his nostrils the breath of life, and the human became a living soul* (Genesis 2:7).

> "It is written: וייצר יהוה אלהים (*Va-yiytser YHVH Elohim*), *YHVH Elohim formed, the human* (Genesis 2:7). וייצר (*Va-yiytser*), *Formed*—with two *yods*, completing an arrangement within an arrangement. Why two *yods*? Mystery of the Holy Ancient One and mystery of *Ze'eir Anpin*—י' י' צר (*yod yod tsar*), *yod, yod, formed*.
>
> "What did He form? He formed a form within a form, and this is *va-yiytser, formed*. And what is 'a form within a form'? Two names, called 'the complete name': *YHVH Elohim*. This is the mystery of the two *yods*—forming a form within a form, arrayal of the complete name: *YHVH Elohim*.
>
> "In what were they included? In this supernal image called *Adam*—*Adam*, comprising male and female.
>
> "את האדם (*Et HaAdam*) (Genesis 2:7)—amplifying the meaning to include generating and proliferating the species issuing from Him, from male and female.

"עפר מן האדמה (*Afar min Ha-Adama*) *Dust from the earth* (*ibid.*)—a figure within a figure.

He blew into his nostrils נשמת חיים (*nishmat ḥayyim*), *the breath of life* (Genesis 2:7), dazzling topaz of a signet ring, deep within.

"Why all this? In order to draw forth and infuse within Him concealed of concealed, consummation of all concealed, as is written: *He blew into his nostrils* נשמת חיים (*nishmat ḥayyim*), *the breath of life* (Genesis 2:7)—נשמתא (*nishmeta*), the soul-breath, upon which all *life* of those above and below depends, and by which it is sustained.

"*And the human became* נפש חיה (*nefesh ḥaya*) *a living soul* (Genesis 2:7)—pouring forth, entering the adornments in this manner; drawing forth that *nishmeta* from rung to rung to the end of all rungs, so that the *nishmeta* will manifest in all and spread through all, nothing else existing.

"Whoever separates this from the world is like one who separates this *nishmeta*, making it seem that there is some *nishmeta* other than this. Consequently, he and his memory will be eradicated for generations upon generations." (Zohar 3:141b; trans. Matt 8:427–428)

This passage depicts a chain of forms within forms. Its particular beauty lies in the fact that the various elements of the verse are presented as interconnected pairs, in developmental sequence. Each pair is constructed from one entity that is contained within another:

1. *Formed* (*va-yiytser*): The two *yods* in this word refer to *'Attiqa* and *Ze'eir Anpin*. *'Attiqa* is the first *yod*, while *Ze'eir Anpin* is the second.[5]
2. *YHVH Elohim*: Here too, we find a form within a form: *YHVH* is located within *Elohim*. Together, these two divine personae generate humanity.
3. *The human* (*et ha-adam*): Male and Female and their generations, their descendants, represented by the word *et*. The source of this multiplicity, this reading of many-ness within the text, lies in the definite article: *ha-adam*, *the* Adam. *Et* thus represents the generations of human beings that inhere within the archetypical Adam.
4. *Dust from the earth*: Dust is the inner form that lies within the earth.
5. *He blew into his nostrils the breath of life*: Adam is dust of the earth, matter awaiting molding, within which the Divine impresses the soul, as

> with the seal of a signet ring. The supernal form is thus exhaled into the form of Adam; it is the most subtle and sublime of all, the soul that issues from the Holy Ancient One. Here, the concentric structure of form within form attains its most sophisticated and complete expression: the most sublime soul is exhaled into the *human* Adam, both Male and Female, who is a form within a form within a form. It is the completion of this physical and material form that enables the loftiest spirit, the divine breath, to penetrate all rungs of being.

At the center of all of the concentric circles, deep within them, is the soul of the Infinite (*Ein Sof*). It enclothes itself in *'Attiqa*, then *Ze'eir Anpin*, in the divine names, in the dust of the earth, and finally in the all-inclusive figure of all of these things—*Adam*, Male and Female. The unity of the most hidden divine soul is by no means disconnected from the complex, variegated, and embodied human being.

The unfurling and unfolding of reality from the Concealed of the Concealed to the body of the terrestrial Adam reflects the great Neoplatonic chain of being, which was deeply internalized in zoharic thought.[6] According to this conception, all existence comprises a single chain; nothing is disconnected in even the slightest way from the Divine. All creation remains connected to its source, so that even the most physical phenomenon is a manifestation—crude and coarse though it may be—of the divine light, the Source of all being. According to the Idra, only the establishment of such a concentric structure can allow the soul of the most hidden Infinite to penetrate and extend all the way to human beings. Yehuda Liebes, even more radically, has noted that this passage presents "an extreme anthropomorphic ideology [. . .] the unity and completeness of the divinity is expressed in that it assumes the most complete form possible: the form of *Adam*."[7]

The Idra's interpretation concludes with a threat directed against whoever does not choose to establish future generations through the coupling of male and female: "Whoever separates this from the world is like one who separates this *nishmeta* [soul-breath]." According to the Idra, when human beings come together to reproduce, they ensure that the supernal divine spirit is drawn into the world. This is a reworking, a paraphrase of sorts, of classical rabbinic texts that emphasize the importance of the commandment to "be fruitful and multiply," as it ensures that the divine image continues to grow and spread throughout the world.[8]

In another passage in the concluding sections of the Idra, we again encounter an account of a structure of form within form, now with an even more far-reaching statement: only when the form of the whole *Adam* is completed—that is, when the Male and the Female are in a state of coupling—can the subtle and sublime divine spirit make itself known. *'Attiqa*'s breath awaits, as it were, the necessary and appropriate human manifestation before it is able to enter and dwell within it, as in a sanctuary. This is a case of mutual dependence: *Adam* is incomplete without the life-breath of *'Attiqa*; and the most primordial divine spirit is unable to be manifest if the Male-Female figure of *Adam* is not properly established, in a state of coupling.

To summarize my interpretation[9] of this important passage: we encounter a series of pairs of forms or elements, that exist in a relationship of a form within a form—two *yods*, *'Attiqa* and *Ze'eir Anpin*, *YHVH* and *Elohim*, Male and Female, dust and earth, and so on, as discussed earlier. The ultimate completion of this model is reached with the inclusion of the Male and the Female in a state of coupling. In light of this reading, we may better understand Rabbi El'azar's discourse, presented at the outset of the *tiqqunim* of *Ze'eir Anpin*'s beard:

> "Come and see mystery of the matter: Wherever אדם (*adam*), *human*, is mentioned here, it is mentioned only together with the Holy Name, as is fitting; for *adam* exists only with what befits Him. And what befits Him? The Holy Name, as is written: *YHVH Elohim formed* האדם (*ha-adam*), *the human* (Genesis 2:7)—by the complete Name, which is *YHVH Elohim*. [. . .]
>
> "For it has been taught: All those holy crowns of the King, when he is arrayed in his adornments, are called *Adam*, the image comprising all. What is infused into them is called the Holy Name, whereas the sheath and what it contains is called *YHVH*, is called *Adam*—all-inclusive, the sheath along with its contents." (Zohar 3:139b; trans. Matt 8:412–413)

When all of the King's crowns and adornments are arrayed—and here the reference appears to be to the *sefirot*—he is called *Adam*. The name YHVH penetrates deep into this *Adam*. But now the Idra Rabba makes an even more far-reaching claim about the human-Divine relationship: Both humans and God are called *Adam*. Furthermore, they are both called *YHVH*. The human *Adam* is called *YHVH*, for—when coupled together Male and Female—they serve as a receptacle for the supernal soul of *'Attiqa*, the divine name. Accordingly, *Adam* is called by the divine name—as the Zohar states elsewhere, even a lion's tail is called a "lion."[10] At the same time, God is called *Adam*, and the combination *YHVH Adam* that emerges from the Idra is yet another form of the full name of God, similar to *YHVH Elohim* (YHVH God, or The Lord God).[11] The Idra's stance regarding the divine *Adam* and the Adamic God represents a tremendously bold statement of similitude between YHVH and the human beings created in the divine image. In this sense, the Idra's interpretation of the term *He formed* (*va-yiytser*) and the hymn to *Adam* that appears at the outset of the *tiqqunim* of *Ze'eir Anpin* are climactic points within the Idra Rabba, amplifying and intensifying the figure of *Adam*.[12]

18

Forming the Male and Female Body

The passages of the Idra Rabba discussed in the previous chapters focus primarily on configuring the divine *faces*: first that of *Arikh Anpin*, with his white beard, and subsequently that of the black-bearded *Ze'eir Anpin*. Each stage has also presented us with some new variation on the theme of the primordial kings of Edom. Now that the faces have been configured and arrayed, the Idra describes the formation of *Ze'eir Anpin*'s body. If, at this point, the reader's mind has already expanded to contain the divine heads, along with detailed accounts of their various parts and organs, now it must stretch once again to comprehend the intensive treatment of the emergence of the divine body. Indeed, here the challenge is even greater, because the body is both male and female. Our consciousness must overcome the profound contradiction between the Idra's language and the language of Jewish theologies that negate any ascription of corporeality to the Divine. We are about to encounter a theology in which the imagination of a sexualized divine body is a necessary stage in the development of the Godhead.

The Idra Rabba presents an account of the complex process through which the body of *Ze'eir Anpin* is formed. He first emerges as an androgynous figure, comprising two bodies, male and female, joined back to back. These two bodies become increasingly distinct and refined, each one developing genitals, male and female, respectively. Upon their attaining sexual maturity, *'Attiqa* separates the two back-to-back bodies, and then brings them together face to face so that they may engage in sexual coupling. The coupling of the Male and the Female aspects of the Godhead marks a transition to a new relationship within the divine realm: after having focused on the configuration of the divine *partsufim* and the alignment of their gazes, associated with calming, patience, and compassion, the Idra now shifts to an account of erotic and sexual relations between the Male and the Female, bound up in great desire, attraction, complementariness, and fragrant sweetening.[1]

From the moment of their separation, the two figures are called Male and Female (*Dekhura* and *Nuqba*) or King and Queen (*Malka* and *Maṭronita*). The name *Ze'eir Anpin* is thus reserved as an appellation for the figure of *Adam* that precedes the distinction between Male and Female (even though, in accordance with grammatical convention, this figure continues to be referred to with masculine pronouns).

The coupling of the Male and the Female, body to body and face to face, is considered to be the climax and *telos*, the end goal, of the complex process in which the Divine moves from unity to multiplicity, oneness to distinctness. This coupling is described in extremely positive terms. Within and from it emerge wholeness, goodness, harmony, blessing, desire, and joy; it is the condition for the presence of *'Attiqa* within humanity.

So that we can understand the profound meaning of this passage in the Idra Rabba, I shall briefly present some of its background, and identify some sources for the myth of coupling between the Male and the Female as it appears in the Idra.

Sexuality and the Body in the Divine

The Hebrew Bible differs markedly from other ancient Near Eastern mythologies in its total rejection of any ascription of sexual reproduction to its Deity. The Hebrew Bible does not describe the birth of the Deity, or of a pantheon. Nor does this God have a female consort with whom to have intercourse, thereby ensuring the fertility and flourishing of the world.[2] However, it is clear from archaeological finds that during the biblical period and thereafter, there were Israelites who believed that Asherah was the consort of YHVH, the God of Israel, despite the fierce biblical battle against this belief.[3] And indeed, in biblical prophecy we learn that YHVH *does* have a consort: Israel. In the prophetic books, the relationship between God and Israel is described in romantic and erotic terms.[4]

Rabbinic literature charged the relationship between God and Israel with further eroticism through its allegorical or symbolic interpretation of the Song of Songs. The rabbis thus produced a discourse of erotic partnership between the male God, the blessed Holy One, and his female beloved, the Community of Israel.[5] In a different but contemporaneous stream of thought, the ancient *Shiʿur Qomah* literature does ascribe a physical body of cosmic dimensions to God, but without eroticism or any female consort.[6]

A significant change in this context came with the emergence of Jewish philosophy in the medieval period, which proposed an abstract and transcendent conception of the Divine. In a radical exegetical move, it firmly rejected efforts to describe a mythical divine figure with a body, emotions, and impulses. Jewish philosophical trends in the medieval period were deeply shaped by a Greek philosophical paradigm, to which they had been exposed in Arabic translation and transmission. These paradigms emphasized the absolute otherness of God, and the Deity's distance from any form, physical or anthropomorphic. Of course, this gives rise to a total rejection of any mode of binarity, any possibility of sexual coupling, or any eroticism or sexuality within the Divine.[7]

Viewed alongside this trend, one of the boldest innovations of kabbalistic thought is undoubtedly the identification of feminine and masculine aspects within the Godhead, the sexualization and eroticization of those aspects, and the intensive exploration of intra-divine erotic dynamics and their interplay with human beings.[8] The importance of eros, sex, and coupling within zoharic literature is impossible to overstate. Liebes puts this in pointed terms:

> In Jewish literature, there is no book as erotic as the Zohar, the Book of Eros, which does not lack eros even on a single page. The aspiration for erotic union is the foundation of the book, an aspiration that quenches the thirst of the entire earth, for the purpose of all existence is harmony and coupling between the cosmic Male and Female. Coupling is also the purpose of human beings and religion, and the ultimate mystery.[9]

So fresh and unapologetic is the Zohar's discourse around the body, sexuality, and genitals in the context of religious experience and the Divine, that it is sometimes difficult for the reader to come to terms with this aspect of the work. Even seasoned readers of the Zohar sometimes fall into this trap, reading bold and straightforward statements in a metaphorical or spiritualizing manner.

In the period of the Zohar's composition, broad and sophisticated conceptions of a feminine, sexual, and erotic divine entity—the *sefirah* of Sovereignty (*Malkhut*), the *Shekhinah*, or Queen (*Maṭronita*)—had already developed. This entity plays numerous roles in the human and divine realms. The *Shekhinah* is the last *sefirah* in the supernal world; she is the Queen who governs the worlds below her with integrity and justice. She maintains a relationship with the *sefirah* of Beauty (*Tif'eret*) that is framed in mythical terms as the romantic, erotic, and sexual drama of a couple. The existence of the People of Israel on the plane of human history is understood to be a reflection of the relationship between the divine Male and Female.[10] When they are alienated from one another, we suffer in exile. In the Zohar—and continuing in *Tiqqunei ha-Zohar* with even greater force, and reaching its climax with 16th-century Kabbalah—we see a deep fascination with femininity in the Divine and the world, an identification with this aspect of God, an enchantment with and attraction to its beneficent and terrifying manifestations, and a curiosity to discover further layers within this female entity.[11]

The Idra's Myth of the Male and Female, and Its Sources

The Idra's concern with sexuality, framed in direct and striking mythical terms, distinguishes it from the Zohar's symbolic and poetic treatment of the same theme. For example, where we find discussions of female sexuality in the Zohar that evoke the rose, or accounts of male sexuality that dwell upon the tree or pillar, in the Idra Rabba we encounter highly realistic physiological descriptions of the genitals and sexual intercourse. As in other cases, it is difficult to determine precisely when the Idra's mode of discourse developed or why it did, but we can identify biblical and rabbinic sources for its vivid myth of coupling between Male and Female.

The Idra Rabba's description of the formation of the Male and Female reworks and reframes two biblical accounts of the creation of Adam, appearing in Genesis, chapters 1 and 2. The Idra explores and expounds Genesis 1:27, which provides a visual and linguistic background for the Idra's narrative: *God created Adam in his image, in the image of God did he create him; male and female he created them.*[12] In this verse, the Idra finds evidence for a number of radical insights. The first is connected to the relationship between the terms *Adam* and *male and female*, and the grammatical contradiction in the verse, which employs the singular form (*did he create him*) immediately before adopting the plural (*male and female he created them*). As the Zohar and the Idra understand it, the biblical verse is not referring to humanity as a species (*adam*), which is further divided into men and women; rather, the name *Adam* is applied to the male and female when they are coupled as one. A further insight is that the Divine itself contains a Male and a Female, for *Adam* is created in a divine image that is both male and female, as is explicitly stated in the verse. Furthermore, the Idra understands the term *Adam* to refer not only to men and women of flesh and blood, but first and foremost to the Divine. Finally, even the simultaneity of the creation of the male body and female body in the Idra is faithful to the language of the biblical verse *male and female he created them*—at the same time, as it were, and not one after the other.[13]

The Idra also richly reworks the narrative of the creation of human beings in chapter 2 of Genesis. In this version of the creation narrative, the male Adam is created by God from the dust of the earth, while the female is taken from his side while he sleeps and is constructed into a woman, so that she may solve the problem of Adam's loneliness and become *a helper alongside him* (Genesis 2:18). This biblical myth describes a state of solitariness and aloneness as loneliness: *It is not good for Adam to be alon*e (ibid.). This value judgment obviously stands in some tension with the striking uniqueness and aloneness of the biblical Creator. Indeed, in rabbinic midrashim, the statement that *It is not good for Adam to be alone* is grounded in the danger of Adam's competition with the lone God if he remains alone.[14] That is to say that it may be appropriate for God to remain one and alone, but not for human beings. In the continuation of the biblical account, the etiological aspect is particularly pronounced: it is a narrative that explains why a man leaves his mother and father, cleaves to his wife, and becomes a single flesh with her in sexual coupling. The fundamental image of chapter 2—God's creation of the woman out of the body of the man, their stimulus to unite as a couple, and the positive perception of mutual attachment—provides a basis for the Idra's accounts, and shapes a considerable portion of the work's renewed myth of the *Adam*-God.

The myth of the evolution of the Male and Female figures in the Idra draws even more deeply from the conceptual and mythical heritage of rabbinic midrash than it does from the biblical sources themselves. In classical rabbinic literature, *Adam* is described as having been created as androgynous, double-faced:

> *God said, "Let us make humanity (adam) in our image, after our likeness* (Genesis 1:26).
>
> Rabbi Jeremiah b. Eleazar said: When the Blessed Holy One created Adam the First, He created him an androgyne. This is as it is written: *male and female He created them* (Genesis 5:2).
>
> Rabbi Samuel b. Naḥman said: When the Blessed Holy One created Adam the First, He created him double-faced. Then He sawed [Adam] in two, and made him into two bodies [lit., two backs]—one here and one here.[15]

Here, two mythical motifs are juxtaposed. According to Rabbi Jeremiah's interpretation, the primordial human being was androgynous, presenting physically as both male and female. In contrast, Rabbi Samuel b. Naḥman portrays *Adam* as double-faced (*diprosopon/du partsufin*; Greek *diprosōpon*). *Adam* is both male and female, here created simultaneously and joined together as one. According to this myth, God then saws through the back and sides of these conjoined figures, separating them into two distinct beings. As opposed to Plato's *Symposium*, in which we encounter the myth of the separation of the original androgyne as a punishment, separation in the Idra is apparently understood to be positive, as it transforms the childless androgynous or double-faced figure into two beings that can now mate, reproduce, and establish subsequent generations.[16] The Idra's creative use of all these sources, as we shall see, is breathtaking.

It is difficult to describe the Idra Rabba's account of the emergence of these bodies and their sexual organs adequately, to find the appropriate words. The passages are simultaneously laden with developmental thinking, mythical visuality, physiological curiosity, and cosmic, surrealistic, erotic imagination. It would seem that at the very foundation of these descriptions lies an extreme sense of inquisitiveness, driving a pursuit of the most primal images and metaphors of masculinity and femininity as the fundamental framework of differentiated existence. This investigation, undertaken with mythical and exegetical tools, produces the fundamental images of the male and female sexual organs, which wondrously enable the two separated bodies to reunite.

From a stylistic point of view, the Idra's account of the formation of the Male and the Female evokes the art of William Blake, or dance choreography that leads again and again from formlessness to varicolored vitality, from opacity to erotic radiance, from frozenness to living movement. As is only appropriate when discussing the mythical realm of the Godhead, all of this takes place in dizzying, close-up images of cosmic proportions.

It seems to me that a Jungian approach, drawing on the study of myth and dreams, is more helpful in deciphering these idraic texts on sexuality than an approach that draws from the fields of sociology or gender studies—at least in the beginning stages of the analysis. The Idra is not concerned with a flesh-and-blood man and woman, but with the initial emergence of the distinction between the masculine and feminine as divine principles that shape reality. The images that arise from the Idra refer to the primordiality of sexuality: the phallus extends, expands, and becomes a cosmic axis and a channel that flows with supernal love, the liquid semen establishing life itself. The Idra describes a mythical process of an increasingly configured and refined feminine sexuality, beginning with its strikingly primal and evocative portrayal as the Land of Edom, and concluding with the image of the Holy of Holies or the "point of Zion." A comparison might be drawn between this myth and that of the Hindu deity Shiva, depicted as the phallus (*lingam*), while his consort, Shakti, is depicted as the vagina (*yoni*). This deity is worshipped in its representation as the *lingam* and the *yoni* throughout the Indian subcontinent, to this day.[17] A comparison with the Hindu myth may sensitize us to the deeper aspects of the Idra's account.

Configuring the Male and Female Body

At this stage, we have not yet encountered a distinctly female aspect of the Divine. *'Attiqa*'s face radiates a love-filled and ever-present oneness, and admits no duality. *Ze'eir Anpin* is described as the head of a masculine figure, a valiant male warrior, without any female element to it. The Idra does indeed emphasize the multiplicity and duality of *Ze'eir Anpin*, in contradistinction to *'Attiqa*: the whiteness that flows into him from *'Attiqa* coexists with redness and Judgment, which are strongly associated in kabbalistic thought with the feminine *sefirot* within the Godhead. However, there is no independent manifestation of a feminine mode of being within *Ze'eir Anpin*, only an initial intimation of it. Perhaps the feminine is entirely latent in *Ze'eir Anpin* at this stage, like the woman contained within the man's side in the Garden of Eden, before God brought a deep slumber upon him.

Furthermore, the Idra has so far presented us only with accounts of divine *faces*—faces without a *body*. All of the qualities and attributes ascribed to God have emerged from a deep contemplation of the fine details of the face and head. Now a new stage begins, describing the formation of the male and female bodies of the Divine, including their sexual organs.

The head of the Male has already been configured—namely, *Ze'eir Anpin*, with his finely detailed face and beard. Perhaps the contours of his body already exist as a sort of schematic sketch, colorless and without content. Now the body will develop, drawn from *Ze'eir Anpin*'s head; and in parallel, behind him, the head and body of the Female take shape:

> "In this *Adam* the entirety of male and female begins to be arranged. Once the beard is arrayed in its enhancements, this begins from His chest, between the two arms, in the place where the hairs of the beard hang, called *Tif'eret*. This *Tif'eret* expands, arranging two chests, and is drawn backward, forming the skull of the Female." (Zohar 3:141b; trans. Matt 8:428–429)

The divine force responsible for creating *Ze'eir Anpin*'s body, and for weaving both the male and female body, is called *Tif'eret* (Beauty). *Tif'eret* is also the subject of the final *tiqqun* of *Ze'eir Anpin*'s beard, which describes the black hair of the head and beard adorning and framing his figure as a whole.[18] This refers to a force composed of Judgment and Compassion, representing balanced and measured relations between them. *Tif'eret* overlaps to some degree with the qualities of the *sefirah* of the same name that appears in other strata of zoharic literature—sitting at the center of the *sefirot*, mediating between Judgment (Din) and Love (Ḥesed)—yet it is not identical with it. *Tif'eret*, here, is a divine force that measures, creates, and animates. In these capacities, it is similar to the dynamic and creative measuring instrument that appears in the Zohar's accounts of the initial emergence of being, called the Line of Measure (*qav ha-middah*) or Lamp of Adamantine Darkness (*botsina de-qardinuta*).[19] The configuration and arrayal of *Tif'eret* is therefore what brings the image of *Ze'eir Anpin*'s face to completion. From this state of wholeness, *Tif'eret* emerges as an active and creative force in the next stage, in which the bodies of the Male and the Female are created.

The reader will recall that this is the third appearance of *Tif'eret* in the Idra Rabba. In the context of *Arikh Anpin*, *Tif'eret* is identified with Compassion, forgiveness, and whiteness: *his beauty (ve-tif'arto) is passing over transgression* (Proverbs 19:11). In the case of *Ze'eir Anpin*, it is associated with the valiant young God's strength and the balance of Judgment and Love or Compassion within him: *The beauty of young men is their strength* (Proverbs 20:29). Here, Adam's *Tif'eret* is associated with sexual coupling between the Male and the Female: *Like the beauty of a human (ke-tif'eret adam) to dwell in a house* (Isaiah 44:13). The Hebrew for "to dwell in a house" has resonances of sexual intercourse.[20]

Tif'eret begins its activity where *Ze'eir Anpin*'s beard ends, spreading from there, between his arms, where the upper torso will take shape. It configures two chests, a male and female torso, from which the full bodies will subsequently be formed. Following the double-formation of the torso, *Tif'eret* penetrates the male body, is withdrawn from it, and returns to its back in order to configure the skull of the Female. From this point, the alternating description of the generation of the male and female bodies proceeds from top to bottom. The Female is located behind the Male, with her head at the height between his chest and his navel.

The Female's skull initially exists in an unformed state—hidden and concealed, her face invisible. She has not yet awoken to life. She begins to fill with vitality when a lock of hair from the Male's head comes in contact with her own hair. Her hair now fills with reddish hues:

> "[The skull of the Female is] totally concealed on all sides by the hair, by the face of the head. [. . .]
>
> "When the face of the head of the Female was created, one lock of hair hung behind *Ze'eir Anpin*, hanging over the head of the Female, and hairs were aroused in Her head—all of them red, mingled with various colors, as is written: *The dangling locks of your head like purple*

(Song of Songs 7:6). What is meant by *purple*? Colors blended with colors." (Zohar 3:141b; trans. Matt 8:429)

The image combines what may look to us like a biological, almost neurological, account of the beginning of life—of nerves communicating, pulsating along axons and across synapses—with descriptions originating in the archetypical world of legend and myth. The latter speak of the magical touch of a man, arousing a woman to life. It is worth recalling that *Ze'eir Anpin* too is brought to life through the power of the hair on the head and in the beard of *Arikh Anpin*, as the flow of divine bounty is conducted through this hair to him.

In contrast with the extensive descriptions provided for the faces of *'Attiqa* and *Ze'eir Anpin*, the lack of a detailed description for the Female's face is striking indeed. It is even more notable in light of the Song of Songs, where many verses are devoted to the beautiful facial features of the female lover. The minimal and undeveloped treatment of the Female's face bears painful testimony to the lesser status of women, who were understood across patriarchal cultures to be "derived" from men and to be their property for thousands of years.[21] However, the absence of a description of the Female's face in the Idra does not mean that the Idra's authors did not believe her to have a face. As we shall see, in the account of the separation between the Male and the Female, the glowing illumination of the Male and the Female as they reunite face to face will be described.

After the Female's head is configured, *Tif'eret* once again enters the body, returning to the side of the Male, configuring and filling his loins with Compassion and Love. The loins, which are the lower belly, include the sexual organs. They are the seat of strength, emotion, and desire within the body.[22] Now, *Tif'eret* once again penetrates the body, crossing backward from the Male side to the Female, and configuring her loins: her lower torso and genitals. Thus are these two figures created, alternately, in a manner that emphasizes their interdependence and their nature as two aspects of a single whole. However, in each case a different aspect of *Tif'eret* (which contains both Compassion and Judgment) is employed: in the formation of the Male, the quality of Mercy is dominant; while in the Female, Judgment is dominant. As the Male and Female become increasingly distinct from one another, the qualities of Judgment drain into the Male's back and pass into the Female:

> "It has been taught: This *Tif'eret* is comprised of both Compassion and Judgment. Compassion spreads through the Male, passing through and penetrating to the other side and arranging the innards of the Female, on the side of Judgment, and her innards are arranged.
>
> "It has been taught: The Male is arrayed on His side in 248 enhancements included in Him, some internal and some external, some of Compassion and some of Judgment. All those of Judgment cling to His back, from where the Female extends, and they adhere to Her sides, spreading." (Zohar 3:141b–142a; trans. Matt 8:429–430)[23]

After the initial formation of the masculine and feminine bodies, we now find a more nuanced description of the organs that define the Female's distinctness and separateness: namely, the five modes of *'ervah* (nakedness) that are gradually revealed in her body. We are now deep within the most primordial processes of the divine realm, long before the existence of human beings and prior to any distinction between good and evil. Nevertheless, in a fascinating anachronism, the five modes of nakedness in this description are based on a pseudo-tannaitic tradition that enumerates the types of nakedness of a flesh-and-blood woman:[24]

> "It has been taught: Five types of nakedness (*'eryata*) are revealed in Her from the aspect of five judgments, and five judgments spread through 248 paths. We have learned as follows: 'A woman's voice is nakedness (*'ervah*); a woman's hair is nakedness; a woman's leg is nakedness; a woman's hand is nakedness; a woman's foot is nakedness.'" (Zohar 3:142a; trans. Matt 8:430, emended)[25]

Here an important question arises: How are we to understand the term *'ervah* in this mythic description? Here, the forces of nakedness are free of any context of good or evil, and must be understood in more primal terms as manifestations of Judgment (*Din*) or Strength (*Gevurah*), which are the elements within the Female that attract and draw in the masculine. It would be a mistake to flatten our understanding of these entities, to reduce them to negative or offensive forces. The concept of *Din* here includes the qualities of fire, heatedness, and arousal: qualities absolutely necessary for coupling.

It seems that *'ervah* is employed to some degree in complementary opposition to the concept of *tiqqun* in the Idra. Whereas *tiqqun* implies a dressing or enclothing of a particular aspect or organ of the Divine, in a manner that enables connection and communication, *'ervah* refers to exposure or nakedness that is the thing in and of itself, without garment or filter.

In the dimension of Male and Female becoming distinct from one another, the Female's nakedness refers to the lack of any covering. In other words, the relationship between *'ervah* and *tiqqun* might be described as being between the primordial organs and dimensions that possess a raw, vital, and dynamic aspect (*'ervah*), and the *tiqqunim*, which are more refined and cultivated both in consciousness and reality. In general, in the Idra's conception of the dynamic of creation, indistinct and primordial raw material is processed and refined, yet a continuous and vital connection with some aspect of that initial and primordial state is retained.

The central aspect in the process of establishing the body of the Female in the Idra is grounded in the sexual connection between her and the Male. The body is the living ground that enables and supports sexual union, which is the purpose of the entire process of *tiqqun*. This union is attained through sexual intercourse, or coupling, which supports the complete form of the Adamic figure: the Male and Female conjoined.

The Idra presents two major forms of relationship: one that occurs between the faces of *Arikh Anpin* and *Ze'eir Anpin* and the other that is the sexual relationship between the masculine and feminine. In the *tiqqunim* of *Arikh Anpin* and *Ze'eir Anpin*, the central enabling factors in the relationship between them are the face, beard, and gaze. Here, in the context of the distinction between the Male and Female, it is the very difference between the masculine and feminine sexual organs that enables the sexual union between the two bodies, a union that sustains the world, ensuring sweetness, joy, and balance.

As part of its account of the development of the Male and the Female into erotic and sexual maturity, the Idra presents a fascinating mythic description of the emergence of the sexual organs. These are now configured in preparation for the future sexual coupling between these figures, which will occur after their separation. First, the formation of the divine phallus is described. It is of cosmic proportions, and the description echoes the ancient *Shi'ur Qomah* literature, in which the divine limbs are described and measured (although this particular organ is not mentioned). At the mouth of the phallus—that is to say, at the urethral opening—the letter *yod* appears during erection.[26] At this stage of sexual development and ripeness, the phallus is ready for its cosmic purpose, which is to transmit divine Compassion and Love (*Ḥesed*) into the Female's vagina through sexual union. According to this conception, the phallus' purpose is of inestimable importance, for it draws supernal Love from *'Attiqa*, embodying it within the dual dimension of Male and Female. The emergence and expansion of the phallus in the Male's body enables the continuation of the configuration of reality, which needs Love if it is to endure.

In the Idra, the Male's phallus is understood in some sense to be a *tiqqun* of his nose. Physically speaking, their similarity is simple: the phallus protrudes from the body and the nose protrudes from the face. However, the need to provide a rectification for the nose of *Ze'eir Anpin* arises from its description as an organ filled with wrath and violence. The phallus could also have been a violent organ, were it not for the droplets of Love that flow within it, and were it not for the letter *yod* that is revealed in it—the seal of the Divine Name. The Male's phallus thus directs a flow of Love, becoming an organ that sweetens Judgment. In other words, the formation of the body and its accompanying sexuality enable a moderation and softening of Judgment within *Ze'eir Anpin*; they allow his Love to emerge victorious.

Throughout the creation of the distinct bodies of the Male and the Female, the two remain connected to one another back to back, and the processes affecting one thus influence the other. For example, when the Male's phallus grows larger and extends, the equivalent area in the Female is drawn inward and becomes progressively more concave, forming a deep indentation—the vagina. The term "covering" (*kesut*) here refers to the genitals of both the Male and Female. Naming masculine and feminine genitals as "covering" would seem to be a euphemistic inversion.[27]

> "It has been taught in the Concealment of the Book: The Male extended and was arrayed in His enhancements. The enhancement of His covering was arrayed, and this is His phallus. The length of

> that phallus is 248 worlds, all of them suspended from the mouth of the phallus, called י (*yod*). As soon as *yod* is revealed—mouth of the phallus—supernal *Ḥesed* is revealed. [. . .]
>
> "Once this phallus extended, the side of *Gevurah* extended, from those *Gevuran*, Powers, on the left side of the Female. It sank into the Female in a certain place and was designated as nakedness—it is the 'covering' of the whole Female body. That place is considered total nakedness—to conceal the site of that phallus called *Ḥesed*, in order to assuage this *Gevurah* comprising five *Gevuran*. And this *Ḥesed* comprises five types of *Ḥesed*. *Ḥesed*, right; *Gevurah*, left. One is assuaged by the other, and it is called *Adam*—comprised of two sides." (Zohar 3:142a; trans. Matt 8:430–432, emended)

The indentation in the Female's body is created by a concentration of powers of Judgment in the genital region of her body. This becomes a locus in which the Male phallus may be secreted away during their future sexual coupling, so that Love might sweeten those forces of Judgment. Thus, the formation of the sexual organs is completed in full accord with their future purpose: namely, union and coupling. Only through the varied, sweetened, and balanced coupling of Male and Female does the Godhead truly attain the title of *Adam*.

But now that the Male and the Female have been configured with their sexual organs, and as the tension grows in anticipation of the dramatic moment of sexual union between them, the Idra Rabba interrupts the narrative flow. Now, during this moment of tremendous suspense and expectation, we encounter, for the third time, a familiar mythic motif: the Death of the Kings.

19

The Kings of Edom

The Third Appearance

In the preceding chapters, at each stage of the configuration and adornment of the divine faces in the Idra Rabba, we encountered a tradition that describes entities that strove to emerge into being but faded away. This tradition informs and is shaped by the Idra's reading of Genesis 36:31–39, a passage that presents a list of the Edomite kings. Before each successive stage in the process of emanation, the Idra returns to the myth of the kings of Edom in order to highlight the particular imbalance or unripeness that is in need of rectification in the coming stage of the manifestation of the Divine faces. In the present formulation of this mythical motif, there is an effort to interpret it in terms relating to the figure of the divine Female (*Nuqba*), expressed in starkly sexual imagery, corresponding with the aspect of existence that the Idra is now discussing.

In the previous formulations of the Death of the Kings, the Land of Edom and the period *before a king reigned* were interpreted as references to the undifferentiated realm of *'Attiqa*, or as *Ze'eir Anpin*'s state of Judgment (*Din*). In contrast, here, the formulation *before a king reigned* is interpreted as a reference to the time preceding the configuration of the Divine as the Male and the Female, while the Land of Edom represents the Female's red vagina. The Hebrew for "red" is *adom*, and here the "Land of Edom" is being read as "Land of Redness." The Land of Edom is thus a mythical rendering of the primordial vagina before engaging in sexual coupling with the Male's phallus, which sweetens Judgment and directs a flow of loving whiteness (*Ḥesed*) into her.

> "Therefore, among those crowns—before the Ancient of Ancients prepared adornments of the King, built worlds, and established arrangements enduringly—that Female was not sweetened and they did not endure, until supernal *Ḥesed* descended and they did endure and the enhancements of the Female were sweetened by this phallus called *Ḥesed*. As is written: *These are the kings who reigned in the land of Edom* (Genesis 36:31)—the place where all judgments are found, namely the adornments of the Woman." (Zohar 3:142a; trans. Matt 8:432)

The kings struggle to exist in the feminine Land of Edom, and perhaps even to establish and sustain it. However, since they are forces of unadulterated Judgment, they cannot endure, and they die. The divine mode of being known as *Adam* enables lasting life. Without an environment that blends Judgment and Mercy, the kings try in vain to become realized, to endure in an atmosphere that is ablaze with fiery Judgment.

His study of manuscript and print zoharic sources has led Avishar Har-Shefi to propose an alternative version of this opening passage: "Before preparing the adornments of the King, the Ancient of Ancients, and building worlds, establishing arrangements enduringly for that Female to be sweetened and they did not endure."[1] According to this version, the sweetening of the Female is the conclusion, the *telos*, of the entire process of configuring and arraying all being, from *'Attiqa* downward. The Supernal King constructs worlds precisely in order to sweeten the Female. Even according to the standard edition of the Zohar, the Female is the final link in the chain of the Godhead; she binds it together, completing it. The existence of the whole structure depends upon the possibility of stabilizing, aromatizing, and sweetening the Female.

Whatever the case may be, the kings who were nullified may only reappear once the bodies of the Male and the Female, with their sexual organs, have been configured. Only then are the circumstances right for the Love (whiteness, semen) of the Male to flow into the red vagina of the Female; now the kings can be comprised of Love and Judgment intermingled. In the biblical passage listing the kings, this stage is represented by the final king, Hadar, who is the only figure whose female companion is mentioned, and the only one who is not described formulaically as having died. The royal couple—Hadar and Mehetabel, the daughter of Matred, the daughter of Me-zahab—form the prototype of the Godhead in its masculine and feminine aspects. They no longer represent a pairing of Judgment with Judgment, but rather a more enduring blend, which entails within it an element of divine Love:

> "As is written: *He died, he died* (Genesis 36:33–39), for they did not endure—Judgment was not sweetened by Judgment. [. . .]
>
> "None of them endured. Do not say that they were nullified, rather they did not endure in that kingdom of the Female side until this last one of all was aroused and emanated, as is written: *Hadar reigned in his stead* (Genesis 36:39). What is meant by הדר (*Hadar*), Majesty? Supernal *Ḥesed*.
>
> "*The name of his city was Pau* (*ibid.*). What is meant by פעו (*Pa'u*), *Pau*? By this a person who attains the Holy Spirit פעי (*pa'ei*), exclaims.
>
> "*And the name of his wife was Mehetabel* (*ibid.*)—here they were sweetened by one another, and she is called his wife, which is not written about any of the others.
>
> "מהיטבאל (*Meheitav'el*), *Mehetabel*—one sweetening another.
>
> "*Daughter of* מטרד (*Matred*), *Matred* (*ibid.*)—restorations from the side of *Gevurah*.
>
> "*Daughter of* מי זהב (*Mei zahav*), *Me-zahab*—one sweetening the other, intermingling; *Mei zahav*, Waters of Gold, Compassion and Judgment." (Zohar 3:142a; trans. Matt 8:432–434)

This passage is a dense interpretation of a single biblical verse: *Hadar reigned in his stead; the name of his city was Pau, and the name of his wife was Mehetabel, the daughter of Matred, the daughter of Me-zahab* (Genesis 36:39). Hadar is the last of the kings, the archetypal representation of the phallus itself, or alternatively, of a king whose penis the Zohar names *the end of the body or the glory* (*hadar*) *of the body*. This Hadar inaugurates a possibility that has not heretofore existed, of directing the flow of divine Love into reality, into the world. King Hadar has an aspect of femininity with which he can connect: a city, and a wife. His city, Pau, is the space within which he acts, and it is associated with the Holy Spirit, with prophecy, and not with the depths of

Judgment. The city is not one of silence, but there is not yet speech within it: As indicated by its name (*Pa'u*), it is associated with vocalizing, making a sound (*pa'ei*). Hadar has a wife called Mehetabel. In Hebrew, the name carries connotations of beneficence or intoxication (*tov, tovim*),[2] with the suffix *-el* evoking the Deity. The Zohar picks up on this meaning, reading it as a reference to the mutual sweetening of these figures, their balancing out of one another, perhaps even mutual intoxication. Mehetabel originates in the realm of Judgment—*daughter of Matred*, a reference to disturbance and dislocation—but within her genealogical tree we also find Me-zahab, Waters of Gold, referring to a primordial intermingling of the waters of Compassion with golden Judgment. Hadar and Mehetabel are the apex of the evolution of the kings. They exist in a state of sexual coupling, mutual aromatizing and sweetening, and as such they are archetypes of the Divine as Male and Female, and of course, human beings in a state of sexual coupling.

Here, the myth of the kings thus focuses upon the possibility, indeed the need, to sweeten the Female through sexual coupling. The focal point of the account is the mythical description of the most archaic state of the Female's sexuality, within which destructive forces of Judgment are active. This state cannot endure, for burning within it is the flame of life, the will to realize itself, desire, fire and Judgment, raging without any hope of being calmed or tempered. However, we also find an account of *tiqqun* here: Hadar and Mehetabel represent the primordial and primal conjoining and coupling of male and female. From this point of view, the third appearance of the myth of the Death of the Kings of Edom tells the story of the emergence of sexuality, the sexual organs, and primordial sexual coupling, which together enable existence and life to prevail, rather than death and negation.[3]

Within the narrative flow of the Idra Rabba, this version of the mythical motif is located between the configuration of the sexual organs of the Male and Female and the separation of the Male and the Female from one another in order to reunite face to face. In this sense, it represents a draft of sorts for what follows, in which the coupling of the Male and the Female sweetens both figures together, and completes the Godhead in its manifestation as *Adam*.

After this final delving into the myth of the Death of the Kings, the Idra returns to the process of *tiqqun*—to a reality in which two fully formed bodies already exist, Male and Female conjoined. The next phase will be their separation and the creation of the conditions necessary for them to reunite face to face in sexual coupling.

20

Separation and Coupling

Even as the male and female bodies begin to emerge, while they are still connected to one another back to back, the polarization between the Male's dominant Love (*Ḥesed*) and the Female's dominant Judgment (*Din*) becomes apparent. But more than this will be required to enable them to couple: they must be separated from one another, and an opposition, a tension, must be generated—ensuring mutual attraction. This is achieved through an extreme polarization of their qualities: red drains entirely into the Female, while white is concentrated in the Male, so that when they are separated the Female remains completely red and the Male completely white. Thus, an opposition between them is created, one that will result in the attraction of each figure to that which will complete it. Neither can exist without the other; they are mutually dependent in the most profound sense.[1]

The Idra explains the need to separate the Male and Female using another image:

> "It has been taught in the Concealment of the Book: All judgments deriving from the Male are harsh at the beginning and calm at the end, whereas all those deriving from the Female are calm at the beginning and harsh at the end. If they had not been formed as one, the world would be unable to bear it. Finally, the Ancient of Ancients, concealed of all, separated one from the other, and united them to be sweetened as one." (Zohar 3:142b; trans. Matt 8:438)

This description, which draws upon Sifra di-Tsni'uta,[2] does not view the Male as pure Love and the Female as complete Judgment. Rather, it distinguishes between the nature of the Judgment in each of them: the Male's Judgment is stronger at the outset and calmer in the end, while the reverse is true of the Judgment of the Female.[3] "Beginning" and "end" may be used to describe a temporal process in two distinct senses. The first relates to the dynamic of arousal to anger. In the case of the Male, Judgment and anger rage mightily at the outset but subsequently calm. The process is reversed in the Female—Judgment begins softly and gradually grows stronger.[4]

The second sense pertains to the strength of Judgment while the Male and Female are emerging into being. Within the Male, Judgment is concentrated within the head before the formation of the body; afterward, when the bodies are generated and Judgment flows into the Female, the Male's Judgment spreads out, becomes diffuse and more calm. The process that occurs within the Female is the precise opposite; at the outset, she exists in potential in *Ze'eir Anpin*'s head, but once the bodies emerge and are separated, Judgment drains into her and becomes harsh.

A final possibility is that "beginning" (*resha*, head) and "end" do not refer to time at all, but rather the body: in the Male, harsh Judgment exists in the head, and Love is associated with the phallus; while in the Female, the powerful aspects of Judgment are associated with her sexuality and become manifest in the "end" of her body, that is, her vagina.

Were the Male and Female to remain conjoined back to back, never being separated and never reuniting face to face, the world could not endure the sheer force of Judgment emanating from them—for there would be no relief from the constant presence of harsh Judgment. Their separation and subsequent reconnection results in their Judgment being tempered and sweetened, which in turn allows the world to exist. Reunion does not *nullify* the forces of Judgment but rather *softens* them. Now, commensurate with each powerful element of Judgment in the Female, there exists a gentle or soft aspect of Judgment in the Male, and vice versa.

In some ways, this account stands in opposition to another myth that appears both in classical rabbinic literature and the Zohar and concerns the creation of the great serpents in Genesis 1:21. According to the rabbinic narrative,

God created two primordial serpents—a male and a female. Were they to mate, they would destroy the world. In order to prevent this, God killed the female and castrated the male.[5] The power of the serpents' attraction to one another is thus a reason to prevent them from mating. In this mythical narrative, the world's survival is ensured through separation, killing, and castration. In contrast, in the Idra Rabba's myth, the union of the Male and Female safeguards life itself. The sexuality of the chaotic primordial serpents is so great that it threatens to destroy the world; the sexuality of the idraic Male and Female in a state of coupling sustains all existence.

The idraic account of the separation between the Male and the Female is constructed via a bold interpretation of a biblical verse: *YHVH Elohim cast a deep slumber on the Adam, and he slept; and He took one of his sides, and closed the flesh of her place* (Genesis 2:21). The Idra describes *'Attiqa* putting *Ze'eir Anpin* into a deep sleep in order to separate the Female from the Male:

> "When He separated them, He cast *dormita*, deep slumber, upon *Ze'eir Anpin* and separated the Female from His back, arraying all Her adornments and concealing Her for His day, to bring Her to the Male. As is written: *YHVH Elohim cast a deep slumber on the Adam, and he slept* (Genesis 2:21). What is meant by *and he slept*? As is written of Him: *Awake! Why do You sleep, O YHVH?* (Psalms 44:24).
>
> "*And He took one of his sides* (Genesis 2:21). What is meant by *one*? This is the Female. As it is written: *She is one, my dove, my perfect one; one she is to her mother* (Song of Songs 6:9). She ascended and was adorned, while in Her place were embedded Compassion and Kindness, as is written: *and closed the flesh of her place* (*ibid.*)—and it is written: *I will remove the heart of stone from your flesh and give you a heart of flesh* (Ezekiel 36:26)." (Zohar 3:142b; trans. Matt 8:438–439, emended)

The cut that divides the Male and the Female occurs deep in the Male's back. The forces of Judgment that had previously drained into his back now pass through the surgical incision into the Female. *'Attiqa* injects divine *Ḥesed* into the site of the incision, filling the space left by the now-absent forces of Judgment. This imagery is structured as a commentary upon two verses: the verse from Genesis, *He took one of his sides, and closed the flesh of her place* (*taḥtennah*), where the phrase *taḥtennah* is understood to mean *in its/her stead*; and the verse from Ezekiel, from which the Idra derives that *flesh* represents *Ḥesed*, since the prophet opposes it to the *heart of stone*. At this stage in the mythical narrative, the monochrome one-dimensionality of the Male and Female is striking—she is entirely red and he is entirely white—and creates an attraction of opposites.

As we have noted, separation only increases the interdependence of the Male and Female—from the moment that the androgynous divine figure is split in two, both the Male and Female are merely halves. The separation increases the desire between the two, and ensures the *telos* of the entire event: the Male's phallus entering the Female's vagina.

Here, the supreme and central importance that the Zohar attributes to *eros* reaches its climax. Sexual coupling sustains the world and configures reality. The Idra is not satisfied with a balance between Judgment and Compassion, which we encountered throughout the *tiqqun* of *Ze'eir Anpin*. There is a need for one last *tiqqun*, and that is *zivvug*, sexual coupling.

One segment of the account of separation and coupling between the Male and the Female is written in a style atypical of the Idra and more characteristic of the main body of the Zohar. It is one of the few passages in which the couple appear as King and Queen, *Malka* and *Maṭronita*, as opposed to Male and Female:

> "As Sabbath was about to enter, He was creating spirits, demons, and whirlwinds, and before He completed them, *Matronita* came in her adornments and sat before Him. When She did so, He left those creatures and they were not completed. Since *Matronita* was sitting with the King, and they joined face-to-face, who would dare to come between them? Who would approach them?
>
> "Accordingly, secret of the matter: The conjugal duty of disciples of the wise who know this mystery is from Sabbath to Sabbath.
>
> "When they united, they were sweetened by one another—a day on which all are sweetened. Consequently, judgments were sweetened by one another, and those above and those below were harmoniously arranged." (Zohar 3:142b–143a; trans. Matt 8:440)

This magnificent passage focuses on the sixth day of creation. The King, cast in the role of Creator as in Genesis 1, is busy creating demons and spirits. The first Sabbath is about to begin. Suddenly, the Queen appears in her regalia, and sits before the King. The King immediately abandons his creative efforts, leaving the demons incomplete, and directs his attention entirely toward the Queen. This passage is a remarkable reformulation of a rabbinic narrative according to which the cessation of divine labor at the beginning of the Sabbath resulted in the incomplete state of the demons and spirits.[6] In the midrashic narrative, the interruption is occasioned by the proscription of labor on the Sabbath. However, in the Idra Rabba, the reason is sheer erotic amazement, powerful attraction. The King abandons his work because the Queen has arrived and is sitting in his presence. From the moment that they sit face to face, there is no room for anything or anyone else in their enchanted gaze. Here, the Zohar alludes to a visually evocative rabbinic formulation: "Who would cast their garment between a lion and a lioness while they are mating?"[7] An erotic circle closes around the King and Queen, the Lion and the Lioness, the Male and the Female. There is no danger, the world around them seems to melt away, now all of the energy of existence is encapsulated within the gaze and in the attraction that brings them together in sexual union.[8] When the King and Queen couple, they become Creators together. The human Adam is created in their image: male and female. From this point onward, human beings will be created through coupling and childbirth.

Notably, throughout the account of the separation of the Male and Female, the figure of *'Attiqa* differs from its appearances elsewhere in the Idra. He is described here in active terms, as an active God, not as a figure who shapes all existence merely *by being*. Here, he is more like the mythical Creator God of the Hebrew Bible, the King, associated with the figure of the Blessed Holy One as he appears throughout the Zohar.[9] This narrative thus represents a synthesis of distinct mythical registers: biblical, midrashic, zoharic, and idraic. In each register, the Deity adopts an active posture toward the Male and the Female, but the identity of these divine figures shifts from one mythical narrative to the next.

The growing erotic tension between the Male and the Female in preparation for sexual coupling will remain at the center of the narrative from this point onward. As we have seen, during the process of the Male body's emergence into being, the letter *yod* at the tip of his phallus was described. The letter is revealed when the phallus is erect, and concentrated within it are the five Powers of *Ḥesed*, divine Love. Similarly, during the emergence of the Female's body, the five "nakednesses" (*'eryata*) were described as they were revealed within her. Now, the Female undergoes a process similar to the Male's: the sexual potency within her becomes concentrated in a single locus, and intensifies. In the great desire to connect anew—a direct result of the separation itself—the Female's erogeneity begins to migrate. The previously distinct nakednesses become increasingly concentrated in this desirous concavity, the female genitalia, which is called "total nakedness," or "the Bride's nakedness."

The concentration of the Female's five Powers (*Gevuran*) into a single Power is reminiscent of a description that we have already encountered in the Idra Rabba. In the *tiqqun* of *Ze'eir Anpin*'s nose, there is an account of the migration of five Powers from his body into his nose. They there become a single Power, concentrating the divine rage, activating it as it blasts from his nose.[10] Here, as the Powers are concentrated in the Female's vagina, we find a rectification of the Judgment-filled head of *Ze'eir Anpin*. For the concentration of Judgment within the Female is not for the sake of war but in order to arouse the desire to couple. This account echoes a statement from the Idra that we encountered earlier, according to which the Male's forces of Judgment are powerful in his head, while the Female's are powerful "at the end"—that is, at the end of her body.

The divine powers are thus concentrated within the sexual organs in a polarized fashion: The forces of divine Judgment and the Powers (*Dinim*, *Gevuran*) within the Female, and the forces of Love (*Ḥasadim*) within the Male. The proper configuration and healing for this polarized state will be attained by the penetration of the Male's phallus into the Female's "nakedness." The tension between Male and Female, Love and Judgment, white and red, arouses the erotic motion of sexual coupling.

It is important to note that the divine Love (*Ḥesed)* that flows from the Male into the Female during coupling is not essential to the Male; rather, it is supernal Love that originates in *'Attiqa*. It is this sublime whiteness that exists within the phallus, this droplet of *'Attiqa*'s essence, that sweetens the two figures, cooling the Female's burning Judgment. It might be said that the desirous Female, burning with Judgment, attracts the droplet from within *'Attiqa*'s brain down toward her. This follows the all-encompassing zoharic logic according to which "arousal below" (*it'aruta di-ltata*) stimulates "arousal above" (*it'aruta di-l'eila*), activating the intertwined structure of reality at every level. Thus, perhaps, within the depths of human erotic desire, there is a hidden yearning to experience the Love (*Ḥesed*) of *'Attiqa* within our own world.

Reading the process of the separation between the divine Male and Female, we run the risk of getting stuck on the text's seemingly polarized description of male and female. The Female is described as full of Judgment, entirely red. Whereas the Judgment, the anger and terrifying redness, of *Ze'eir Anpin* is entirely siphoned into the body of the Female, the Male remains white and full of divine Love.[11] However, even though Judgment is seen as inherent to the Female, we must recall that the draining of the forces of Judgment into her body and her appearance as full of redness are merely stages in the entire mythical process, which reaches its conclusion and ultimate purpose in sexual coupling and sweetening. In addition, we must make a distinction between various qualities of Judgment within the body of the divine Female. During the phase in which she has been separated from the Male, and before reuniting with him in coupling, she is filled with threatening, dangerous Judgment. However, as the process continues, a new quality of Judgment emerges: Judgment (*Din*) as an arousing and erotic quality, vital for the act of coupling and sweetening. This is absent from the Male.

Beyond this, in general, we must be wary of an oversimplified translation of the myth of the divine Male and Female into insights regarding gender in relation to men and women in our world. The Idra should be understood in the category of myths of origination and myths of primary processes. This understanding allows us to access the myth's grand questions: How does individuation occur in a mythical register? How does archetypal separation create the very possibility of connection? How do boundaries allow for relationships? How do difference and variety emerge and persist in the world? What is the role, and the destiny, of opposites in creation? How does reunion happen? The Idra presents a myth about the initial emergence of Male and Female as divine forces who act within the world, and we should not read it with a reductionist lens as prescribing particular understandings of gender and sexuality in our day.

An additional question arises from these passages: namely, what is the relationship between the Female in the Idra Rabba and the feminine aspect of the Divine called *Shekhinah* or Sovereignty (*Malkhut*) as depicted in the main body of the Zohar. The divine Female in the Idra is similar to the Zohar's *Shekhinah* in a number of ways: in her desire for an encounter, in her delight in sexual coupling with the divine Male, and in her more dangerous and frightening manifestation when she acts alone in the world, without any connection to the Male. However, there is no doubt that the emphasis in the Idra Rabba is quite different. The mythical-archaic accounts in this work focus on the process of the Female's emergence into being: the creation of her body, her attainment of sexual maturity, the pooling of Judgment within her, her separation from the Male, and finally her ever-sweetening coupling with the Male. In the background to these accounts sits the question of processing, restraining, and draining Judgment, and how these forces might be integrated into reality. This is not so in the main body of the Zohar, which does not discuss the formation of the *Shekhinah* so much as it does the mature and complex feminine entity through whose image and constancy the human realm endures. Her many-colored figure is beloved as the female Divinity that dwells in the world, in nature, in time, in the body, and in human emotions.

21

Sweetening Judgment

The Idra Rabba, as we have seen, describes the most primordial processes of configuring and arraying *'Attiqa*'s face and the face of *Ze'eir Anpin*. After these *partsufim* are configured, the work describes the way in which the bodies of the divine Male and Female are constructed, their separation, and finally, their reunion in sexual coupling. The formation of the various manifestations of the Divine, and their interrelationships with one another, also express a range of ways in which Judgment (*Din*) is processed. From the beginning of the Idra, *Arikh Anpin* is described as subduing Judgment merely by being seated upon a throne of flames associated with Judgment; next, the dynamic between the redness and whiteness within *Ze'eir Anpin* is recounted; later still, when the Divine is described as taking on the image of *Adam*, Male and Female, Judgment is processed through *bissum*—sweetening and aromatizing.

This chapter will discuss the continuation of the narrative of the divine Male and Female, following their first act of coupling, as described in the Idra. The narrative is constructed as a running mythical commentary on the biblical verses about Adam and Eve in the Garden of Eden, the encounter with the Serpent, Adam and Eve's expulsion from Eden, and the birth of their children: Cain, Abel, and Seth. The biblical narrative is interpreted as an account of the drawn-out and obstacle-ridden process of draining harsh Judgment from the Female, in preparation for her continued sweetening.

Only sweet coupling will enable the creation of future generations of humanity, allowing human beings to continue to exist.

Before discussing the details of this section of the Idra, we should note the centrality of the notion of *bissum* (sweetening and aromatizing). The term appears throughout the Idra's descriptions of coupling between the Male and Female. Again and again, the Idra repeats its definition of coupling and reunion as *bissum*. Sweetening, aromatizing, and tempering the aspects of Judgment within the Female, and the Male along with the Female, grants them the title *Adam*, sweetening all levels of reality: "When they united, they were sweetened by one another—a day on which all are sweetened. Consequently, judgments were sweetened by one another, and those above and those below were harmoniously arranged."[1]

Before entering into a deeper discussion of the concept, we must ask why this ephemeral and airy verbal root *b-s-m*, usually referring to fragrance or scent, took on such a central role in the process of *tiqqun*?[2] A close reading of the Idra suggests a few possible answers:

First of all, *bissum* in the Idra is associated with softening, attraction, and calm. It does not transform or dispel Judgment, for the latter is not essentially negative—indeed, it is vital for any act of creation. Judgment continues to exist after it is sweetened, but something is added to it: its effects soften and transform Judgment; awe turns to fragrance.

Bissum is also associated with erotic and sexual experiences, in which the frightening and strange becomes fragrant and attractive. Coupling gives off a pleasing scent, its fragrance is healing, a kind of aromatherapy.

In a different setting, it seems that *bissum* also brings God or humans back to themselves. *Bissum* soothes the anger that grips the soul, returning it to its natural state. For example, fragrance calmed God after the Flood—*YHVH smelled the pleasing odor* (Genesis 8:21). We also see this phenomenon in a human context—*Ah, the smell of my son is like the smell of the fields* (Genesis 27:27); *Your ointment yields a sweet fragrance* (Song of Songs 1:3). Fire and wrath blast out of the nose, whereas *bissum* is attained by inhalation: breathing in calm, patience, and forbearance. This is how the Temple incense works, for example, as it envelops God's smoking and smoldering Judgment.

In rabbinic terminology, the verbal root *b-s-m* can also refer to intoxication.[3] As Nahum Bronznick has demonstrated, another sense of the term in its rabbinic context is anchored in the association between the verbal roots *b-s-m* and *b-s-s* (base, stability).[4] Alongside its reference to intoxication, ecstasy, calm, and sweetness, the zoharic term *b-s-m* thus carries associations of stability and strength as well.

As we shall see throughout the present chapter, the Idra does not understand *bissum* as a singular event, but rather as an ongoing process that is not completed in the first act of coupling between the Male and the Female.

At this point, after the initial coupling of the divine Male and Female, *'Attiqa* suddenly reappears. And once again, he is described in atypically active terms. In a scene reminiscent of the biblical God's search for Adam and Eve in the Garden of Eden after they consumed the fruit of the Tree of Knowledge, *'Attiqa* seeks to test the developments in the great process of confronting and processing Judgment: "The Holy Ancient One wished to see if judgments had been assuaged."[5] Indeed, it seems that despite the fact that the Judgment concentrated in the Female *has begun* to sweeten, she remains full of Judgment. The primordial Serpent penetrates into their union, once more bringing about a surplus of harsh Judgment. A new character thus enters the narrative: the Serpent, who represents these forces of harsh Judgment. The appearance of the Serpent and its association with the Female disrupt the simple possibility of balancing Judgment in preparation for ideal coupling between the Male and Female, which would sweeten the world.

The myth of the Serpent penetrating the Female, and its association with the birth of Cain, is described in the following brief and dense passage:

> "It has been taught in the Concealment of the Book: The Holy Ancient One wished to see if judgments had been assuaged. These two cleaved to one another, and from the side of the Female issued harsh Judgment, which the world could not endure. As is written: *The Adam knew Eve his wife, and she conceived and bore* קין (*Qayin*), *Cain, and she said,* ` (*qaniti*), *I have acquired, a man with YHVH* (Genesis 4:1)—but it was not so, because She had not been sweetened, and the potently harsh Serpent

> had injected Her with the slime of harsh Judgment, so She could not be assuaged." (Zohar 3:143a; trans. Matt 8:441)

In rabbinic literature, one can find mythical narratives that speak of the Serpent having sex with Eve, and injecting a dangerous substance into her—a "slime" that continues to be transmitted among human beings.[6] Within the Idra Rabba's spiritual worldview, it seems that the Serpent is the archetype of all that is not comprised in the figure of *Adam*. It is a force of Judgment in which remnants of the kings are trapped, fragments that were never sweetened, that never found their place within the image of *Adam*.[7] The Serpent's powerful force of Judgment draws in other aspects of Judgment, which explains the mutual attraction of the Serpent and the Female, who remains in a state of concentrated Judgment after her separation from the Male. In addition, it should be recalled that in the Zohar's archetypical conception, the Female is characterized by the ability to connect. She is constructed to receive the other into her during coupling, and if the penetrator is not the appropriate partner it will be another, one from outside the realm of order and holiness.[8] In the rabbinic and zoharic myths, Eve has sexual intercourse with both the Serpent and Adam, conceiving by both of them.[9] She now contains Adam's semen, which will generate a body, and a considerable quantity of semen from the Serpent, which prevents her from becoming properly sweetened. She becomes a battlefield upon which violent struggles between competing forces of Judgment take place, even as she strives to expel Judgment from herself and be cleansed of it.

It is difficult to determine whether the Serpent's involvement is meant to represent an error in the process of creation, some kind of unforeseen mishap, or an inherent aspect of the evolution and differentiation of existence. In any case, the Female approaches the act of coupling with the Male saturated with her own Judgment that she has absorbed from the Male and also the "slime" deposited in her by the Serpent. The Serpent, with its ability to penetrate into the world, therefore eliminates the possibility of bringing the divine configuration to its completion.

At this point, searching for a solution to the problem, the Idra draws a link between the myth of the Serpent and the continuation of the biblical narrative that follows the expulsion from Eden: the birth of Cain and Abel, Cain's murder of Abel, and the third coupling of Adam and Eve, which leads to the birth of Seth. Drawing on these three stories, the Idra Rabba unveils a series of models for sweetening Judgment, which we trace in the present chapter.[10]

The Birth of Cain and Abel, and Their Archetypical Fate

The first solution that the Idra Rabba offers for this critical situation is to drain the Judgment and the Serpent's "slime" from the Female through the birth of Cain and Abel, each birth freeing her of yet more Judgment:

> "When this Cain emerged from the side of the Female, he emerged potently harsh—potent in his judgments, harsh in his judgments. Once he had emerged, She was soon weakened and assuaged, and She brought forth another, sweeter one. The first one prevailed, since he was potently harsh and all judgments had aroused with him." (Zohar 3:143a; trans. Matt 8:441)

The Female's excess Judgment is balanced by giving birth, for this weakens and sweetens her, softening her in the process.[11] Cain, the firstborn, represents harsh and unrefined Judgment. His birth siphons the destructive excess of Judgment—introduced into her by the Serpent—from his mother, continuing the process of sweetening.[12] Next, Abel is born. Even though he shares a greater portion in the figure of the divine *Adam* than his brother, he is still dominated by Judgment, albeit a milder form of it than that of his brother.

Cain's murder of Abel is the next step in the mythical narrative:

> "Come and see what is written: *When they were in the field* (Genesis 4:8)—*in the field* that is known above, *in the field* called Field of Apple Trees. This Judgment defeated his brother, for he was harsher than him; he overwhelmed him and concealed him beneath himself." (Ibid.)

According to the Idra, the field in which the murder is set is the Supernal Field, the *sefirah* of Sovereignty (*Malkhut*)—called the Field of Holy Apples in zoharic literature. This understanding of the narrative as an event that occurs *within* the Divine reveals that harsh Judgment threatens the Godhead itself, and teaches the reader about the need to confront it and be cleansed of it. The mother with her two sons together create an intensity of Judgment that is unbearable. The struggle between Cain and Abel is a battle between Judgment and Judgment, between two male serpents without consorts. Indeed, there is a dimension of coupling here, a desire to conjoin coercively. Cain, the force of pure Judgment, draws on his superior and mightier force of Judgment, arises against Abel, subdues him, and buries him beneath himself.[13]

From a literary point of view, it is unclear whether the narrator of this passage is drawn along by the biblical verses, or whether he draws them along with him. Are the goals and ends of the Idra Rabba at the center of the exegesis? Or is it that once the commentator begins to expound upon the story of Adam and Eve, he finds that he must interpret each and every verse until the end of the story? In any case, the interpretation transforms the biblical narrative into a foundational myth concerning the sweetening of Judgment at all levels of existence:

> "Until the blessed Holy One was aroused by this, and He removed [Cain] from His presence, sinking him into the hollow of the Great Abyss, and He immersed his brother in the depth of the Great Sea, which sweetens supernal tears.
>
> "From them, souls descend into the world, according to the way of each person. Although they are concealed, they expand toward one another, forming one body, and from this body descend souls of the wicked—brazen sinners. Do you imagine from both of them together? Rather, one on his side, and one on the other." (Zohar 3:143a; trans. Matt 8:441–442)

God, who here takes on the responsibility for the degree to which Judgment is tempered, sinks the two powers of Judgment—Cain and Abel—deep within the vast pools of femininity. Cain, absolute and completely unsweetened Judgment, is hidden away within *nikbat tehom rabba*, the Great Abyss that from time immemorial has been associated with the dark side of the primordial feminine, a place of demons and evil powers. His brother Abel is sunk deep in the Great Sea, which sweetens Judgment—apparently a symbol for the *sefirah* of Sovereignty.

Now, as is so often the case with archetypes, their expulsion and concealment in the depths does not mean that Cain and Abel have died. They expand, meet, and become a single body—the source of all of the souls of the wicked. At the heart of this myth, which has discernible Gnostic and dualistic overtones, is a chilling psychological intuition concerning the archetypical correlation of murderer and victim, with human evil emerging from the victim as well as the murderer, from the threatening and provocative association between them.

As we see in other parts of the Zohar, the Idra appears to be shocked by its own choice to turn the murderer and the victim into a single body. It seems to recoil from the dualistic force of this solution to the question of the source of the souls of the wicked, which appears to deny them free choice, and denies that all souls originate in a pure divine source. Thus, the Idra provides a moderating caveat, drawing a distinction between the souls that emanate from Cain and those that originate in Abel: "Do you imagine from both of them together? Rather, one on his side, and one on the other." From the side of Cain emerge purely wicked souls, while from the side of Abel come souls that might be described as "the sweetened wicked."

Despite this distinction between Cain and Abel, this expelled "body of impurity" is the generator in which the souls of the brazen-faced sinners of each generation take shape—those individuals who sin without shame. In contrast, the source of the righteous lies in the sacred body, the bond of life, in which all qualities are comprised:[14]

> "Happy are the righteous, who draw their souls from this holy body called *Adam*, comprising all, a place where holy diadems and crowns conjoin in the bundle of a cluster." (Ibid.)

Apart from being the source of the souls of the wicked, Cain and Abel's body of impurity is the source of disembodied demonic forces that crowd the cosmos. Here too, the Idra draws a distinction between those beings who originate in Cain and those that originate in Abel:

> "It has been taught: All those crowns that are not included in the body are loathsome and impure, defiling anyone who approaches them to gain information from them. [. . .]
>
> "It has been taught: All of them derive from the spirit of the left, which was not assuaged in *Adam*. They were excluded from the realm of the holy body, not cleaving to it. So all of them are impure—

> wandering and roaming through the world, entering the Hollow of the Great Abyss to cling to that primordial Judgment who emerged in the category of 'body'—called Cain, below. They roam through the whole world, fluttering, unable to cling to the realm of the body. [. . .]
>
> "With the spirit called Abel—who was somewhat assuaged, in the realm of the holy body—others emerge, who are somewhat assuaged, and they cling to the body, yet do not cling." (Zohar 3:143a–b; trans. Matt 8:444–445)

The forces originating in Cain are associated only with that source, and they have the quality of pure Judgment. They have no part whatsoever in the body of holiness. In contrast, the forces (or "crowns") associated with Abel have a partial connection to the holy body. As a manifestation of more sweetened Judgment, Abel is the source of spirits and demons that transmit messages from other worlds to our own. Thus, on one level we have an etiological myth about the origins of disembodied entities—spirits, shades, demonic forces—along with both the danger and the usefulness associated with them. On another level, this is a story about all the inhabitants of the abyss of the human subconscious mind, which emerge from the process of sweetening Judgment during the fateful encounter with the Serpent.

This myth of Cain and Abel emphasizes the tremendous value that the Idra Rabba ascribes to *Adam* and the *body*. One who is included in the figure of *Adam*, who finds oneself in the Adamic body, has found the possibility of being settled, enduring. Those who do not attain this become demonic, dangerous, impure. The source of demonic forces lies in the entities that did not succeed in becoming integrated into the holy body during the stage of emanation of the Left Side—the aspect of harsh Judgment within the Divine that remains unsweetened. Uprooted, expelled, disembodied, these forces wander about, as if possessed of an insatiable hunger, in desperate search of a body to which they might attach themselves. In this myth, the body in which Cain and Abel are imprisoned and bound, the body of impurity, becomes a focus of attraction for such forces. In the Idra's midrashic poetics, the Cain (*Qayin*) sunken within the womb of the Great Abyss becomes a nest (*qinna*, *qen*), a dwelling place for those beings that wander about without any body-home.[15]

Reading this myth against the background of the Idra Rabba as a whole, it seems that the story of Cain and Abel, so full of Judgment and unable to endure, is yet another expression of the myth of the Death of the Kings, occurring at other points in the emergence of being. There is a conceptual and mythical similarity between these two motifs. Both embody the conception that in any process of creation, configuration, and enclothement of various levels of being, there are impurities mixed in—chaff, or waste, or unworkable drafts. Another principle in both myths is that states of Judgment, even evil itself, precede refinement, sweetening, aromatizing, and goodness. This conception, according to which "the shell precedes the fruit," has many sources in kabbalistic literature.[16]

At this stage in the development of reality, the kings of Edom are replaced by Cain and Abel, the murderer and the victim, the first offspring of the coupling of the Male and the Female. They represent an imbalanced prototype of human beings, a model that cannot provide lasting stability for the cosmos. Both lose their place in the body of holiness, and become associated with the demonic realm of entities that have no share in the divine figure of *Adam*.[17] They are expelled from the process of cosmic *tiqqun* that follows, and continue to exist as a menacing force submerged deep in the abyss, ultimately becoming the source of evil in the human world.

If the kings represented unconfigured forces of Judgment in the more archaic stages of the emergence of being, at this stage, the narratives of Eve and the Serpent and of Cain and Abel become the central motifs employed by the Zohar in its descriptions of evil. Indeed, in many passages throughout the Zohar, the mythical motif of the primordial Serpent appears, along with its connection with the realm of holiness, the figure of *Adam*, and the Female. The Serpent does not vanish, but continues to lie in wait for opportunities to penetrate, to destroy, at every stage of the emergence of being. The zoharic corpus presents a wide range of ways to confront this entity. Its connection with the Female is a central aspect of the zoharic myth concerning the association between the *Shekhinah* and the forces of harsh Judgment and evil.[18]

The location of the mythical motif of the primordial Serpent within the Idra's creation narrative emphasizes this figure's destructive influence. Its venomous power prevents the sweetening of Judgment through the coupling of the divine Male and Female, thereby delaying the completion of the configuration of the divine *partsufim*. Only when Cain and Abel are buried in the body of impurity, deep within the abyss, and only when the cosmic cooling-off period of the separation of the Male and the Female is complete, can the ideal coupling take place, from which the generations of the configured Adam will arise.

All is Sweetened: Establishing the World with Seth

After the creation, the story of the Garden of Eden, the expulsion, the birth of Cain and Abel, and the murder of Abel, the time comes for a third coupling between Adam and Eve. From this union, Seth is born: *Adam knew his wife again, and she bore a son and named him Seth, meaning, "God has provided me with another offspring in place of Abel," for Cain had killed him. And to Seth, in turn, a son was born, and he named him Enosh. It was then that men began to invoke YHVH by name* (Genesis 4:25–26). This coupling brings the Idra to one of its great climactic moments: the sweetening of all things. The connection between the Female and the Serpent was one of like and like: Judgment with Judgment. In that sense, it was typical of the failed drafts of reality. Now, the conditions are right for a different kind of coupling, one between differing and complementary aspects: the Male and the Female. In this act of coupling, the processing of the forces of Judgment is harmoniously completed. The Judgment drained when Cain and Abel were born is now outside the holy body, and the Judgment of the Female is moderated and modified, matching the Male's aspects of Love (*Ḥesed*); they are now in harmonious alignment. The Female concentrates her Judgment so that it functions as a power of attraction, drawing in the quality that completes it, her partner the Male, and the *Ḥesed* that will enter her as they couple. The love game between *Ḥesed* and *Din*, sustaining all existence, is described here in terms of integration, connection, completion—and most of all, *bissum*:

> "It has been taught in the Concealment of the Book: Once the totality of *Adam* had been sweetened above—the holy body, male and female—they united a third time, and sweetness of all emerged and worlds above and below were assuaged. From here, the world above

> and below was completed, from the aspect of the holy body. Worlds embrace, merging with one another, becoming one body. Since they are all one body—*Shekhinah* above, *Shekhinah* below; the blessed Holy One above, the blessed Holy One below. Spirit is drawn forth, entering one body, and throughout all of them nothing is seen except one—*Holy, holy, holy is YHVH of Hosts; the whole earth is full of His glory* (Isaiah 6:3), for all is one body." (Zohar 3:143b; trans. Matt 8:446)

Here we have a song of praise to the Divine in its manifestation in the figure of *Adam*, once that figure has attained equilibrium and become sweetened. The account is extraordinary in its sensuousness. Rather than being visual, it is fragrant and subtle, exuding sweetness. The statements of this hymn-like passage convey a quality of totality. The upper and lower realms, all of the worlds that are bound to the divine body, are infused with this *bissum*.

Coupling, and the ensuing process of *bissum*, is like a honeyed glue that binds all the facets of reality to one another. For a single cosmic moment, all worlds are aligned, they are bound to one another and touch, as if mimicking the erotic embrace of the Male and the Female. This is the great *tiqqun*: no more does the world rest upon a single pillar but rather upon two who are interconnected, face to face.

Perhaps the most interesting aspect of all this is that the coupling between the Male and the Female generates a renewed theological meaning for the concept of unity and oneness, one that the Idra wishes to invoke in language and reality. It is not a rigid and primitive mode of unity but rather reflects the dynamism of two bodies that have become one. It is not static but rather in motion, and dependent upon a range of processes.

Only in this state, when multiplicity becomes complex unity, can the breath of *'Attiqa Qaddisha*, the Holy Ancient One, begin to waft through all worlds—from divine oneness down to the deepest recess of the figure of *Adam*, who is the Male and the Female united in sweet coupling. This is the moment in which the unity within all plurality is revealed, the moment in which there is no longer above and below, inner and outer, depth and surface. Plurality in all realms realizes the presence of the oneness within. Here, the Zohar's positive attitude toward corporeality receives its most perfect expression.

The account of coupling is ecstatic. All becomes connected and unified,[19] the focus of the gaze shifts, and from within unified multiplicity, one now only sees the oneness pervading all things. Only this mode of existence or consciousness is worthy of the praise of the celestial beings: *Holy, holy, holy is YHVH of Hosts; the whole earth is full of His glory* (Isaiah 6:3). All reality appears unified at the moment of coupling, the spirit of the Ancient of Days growing luminous deep within it.

The biblical verses about Adam and Eve are "projected" heavenward, and understood to describe divine processes. They are charged with tremendous power that also reflects the Idra's approach to human sexual coupling. Through its analogy with such a critical event in the divine realm, human sexuality receives unprecedented amplification. In the context of such an approach, sex between human beings occupies a supreme place: it is a sacred and cosmic event.

It is significant that the focus of the Idra's account is the act of coupling itself, rather than its fruit, the formation of a child. However, the work does describe the human being formed through the coupling of the Male and the Female, and it views this figure as enduring and stable, with a capacity to become still more refined. In the Hebrew Bible, the progeny of this relationship is Seth, the first individual who is said to be born in Adam's image and likeness (Genesis 5:3), and the figure from whom humanity was constructed.[20] Seth's son is Enosh, from whom all human beings descend. Seth's familial line amplifies the congruence between the image of God and its presence within human beings. Alongside such biblical figures as Abraham and Moses, the Zohar includes Rabbi Shim'on bar Yoḥai in the ever-evolving line of Adam, in addition to the Messiah. The Messiah brings the process of human perfection to an end. Indeed, the Idra Rabba concludes with an invocation of the Messiah.

The Aromatized Female

The most perfect and whole coupling is one in which the Male and Female are mutually sweetened in the intoxicating erotic awakening of lovemaking. Sweetening the forces of Judgment within the divine Female is one of the Idra's purposes; the work's effort is to not leave the Female wallowing in Judgment. This process is given a sublime description in an exegesis of a passage from the Song of Songs: *Lovely are your cheeks in bangles, your neck in strings of beads. Bangles of gold we will make for you, with spangles of silver* (Song of Songs 1:10–11). These are the words of the male lover to the female lover, in which he expresses how beautiful she is in her jewelry, and speaks of the precious ornament that he intends to make for her. The Idra understands these words to be a description of the erotic and fragrantly sweet state of Judgment into which divine Compassion has been mingled. Sexual coupling does not remove Judgment from the Female. Indeed, her Judgment is fitting, even beautiful: it is *bangles of gold*, adorning her. With the act of coupling, she is granted *strings of beads*, associated with the *spangles of silver*, studs of Love and Compassion that highlight the grace of golden Judgment, rendering her beauty many-colored:[21]

> "It has been taught: Once they were sweetened by one another—it is written: *Bangles of gold we will make for you, with spangles of silver* (Song of Songs 1:11)—Judgment was bound with Compassion, and She was sweetened by the Male. Thus one does not rise without the other, like a palm tree, in which one does not flourish without the other. Concerning this we have learned: One who excludes himself in this world from the realm of *Adam* cannot later—when he departs this world—enter the realm of *Adam*, called 'the holy body.' Rather, he enters those who are not called *Adam* and who are excluded from the realm of the body.
>
> "It has been taught: *Bangles of gold we will make for you, with spangles of silver*—for Judgments have been assuaged by Compassion, and there is no Judgment that does not contain Compassion. Of this it is written *Lovely are your cheeks in bangles, your neck in strings of beads* (Song of Songs 1:10). *In bangles*—as it is said: *bangles of gold.*
>
> "*In strings of beads*—as is written: *spangles of silver.*
>
> "*Your neck*—in the realm of Female, *Matronita*." (Zohar 3:143b; trans. Matt 8:447–448

By placing this passage immediately after the exclamation *Holy, Holy, Holy*—bursting forth as it does from the ecstatic force of the unification of all worlds, limbs, and modes of being—the Idra subtly suggests that a marvelous description of sexual coupling is insufficient. The Female's sweetening, and the highly visual account of this process, the beauty of her cheeks and neck after coupling, render the full figure of Adam whole. The enchanting pairing of gold and silver, red and white, Judgment and Compassion, represents the completion of the Female's configuration, adornment, *tiqqun*. To my mind, the Female's *tiqqunim* parallel those of the beard in the higher *partsufim*: just as the beard represents the final adornment that completes the face of the Male, the bangles and beads upon the Shulamite's neck represent the *tiqqunim* of the sweetened and fragrant Female.[22] It is worth noting that this description does not apply to any specific part of the Female: rather, her entire figure is adorned. The interpretation expands the sense of *neck* in the verse, taking it to apply to the entire figure of the Female.

The Female's aromatic sweetening transforms her from red, blazing, and primal into a regal figure. Just as *'Attiqa* subdues redness, and *Ze'eir Anpin* balances his redness with *'Attiqa*'s whiteness, the act of coupling transforms the *Nuqba* into crimson flecked with white, golden with silver studs. This account echoes the zoharic interpretation of another biblical verse: *I am a rose of Sharon, a lily of the valleys* (Song of Songs 2:1). The Zohar's interpretation describes the metamorphosis of feminine *eros* as it passes from the unripe, verdant desire of virginity into roselike red-white variegation following the act of coupling.[23]

> ". . . in the realm of Female, *Matronita*. So, the Temple above, Jerusalem, and the Temple.
>
> "All this, once She is sweetened by the Male and the totality of Adam is formed—totality of Faith. Why Faith? Because within Him is found all faith." (Zohar 3:143b; trans. Matt 8:448, emended)

The process of aromatic sweetening that the Female undergoes also enables the text to discuss "the totality of *Adam*," that is, the Male and Female sweetened in sexual union. This mode of being, "totality of *Adam*," establishes a correspondence or symmetry between the heavenly Temple, the lofty divine realm, and terrestrial Jerusalem with its Temple. This alignment or conjunction completes and comprises the human figure with all of its qualities. Here it is called "totality of Faith."

The description of the figure of the conjoined Male and Female as "totality of faith" has a power that cannot be understated. It is a reworking of a rabbinic narrative that describes the priests drawing back the curtain of the

Holy of Holies before the pilgrims, showing them the figures of the cherubs entwined in embrace:

> "When Israel ascended [to Jerusalem] for the Festival, the curtain would be rolled open for them and the cherubim revealed, their bodies intertwined. They [the people] would be addressed: 'Look! God's love for you resembles the love of male and female.'"[24]

According to this account, the sight conveys the content of faith, the act of coupling supplies experiential meaning to the connection between God and humans. The Idra presents a kabbalistic variation on this image of the cherubs on the Ark of the Covenant. Now, the united representation of the male and the female conjoined in mutual embrace becomes a representation of the Divine itself. It is not merely a term, an abstraction, a sense, or an idea, but an image of the act of love between the Male and the Female. This too is the "totality of Faith" according to the Idra: Faith is not some mode of theoretical knowledge, but the unified state of Adam, the human, contained and coupled.[25] This image of faith conveys the theological awareness that in this structure, containing the conjoined Male and Female and the divine faces above them, inhere all divine dimensions and qualities, including Judgment and Compassion.

In this section of the Idra, we find a paean to sexual coupling, the Male and the Female conjoined into a single body, the body of *Adam*:

> "It has been taught: All those arrangements above in the holy body, male and female—totality of *Adam*—are drawn from one another, joined to each other. They saturate one another, like blood flowing through a cluster of veins, here and there, this way and that, from one place to another, saturating the body and each other. Similarly, all the holy crowns in the body saturate one another, illuminating each other, until all worlds are illumined and blessed by them." (Zohar 3:143a; trans. Matt 8:444)

These words describe the moments of coupling in which all is blessed and illuminated. The Male and the Female become not only "one flesh" but an entity in which all the *tiqqunim*, the sacred adornments and divine qualities of the body, open up into a network of mutual nourishment, irrigation, and illumination—sweetening all worlds, making them fragrant.

Sweetening the Powers of Judgment Continues: The Conclusion of the Idra Rabba

Even in the wake of this sublime account of the divine body in its state of irrigation, satiation, and illumination, we discover that the process of sweetening Judgment has not yet come to an end. The Idra continues to follow the verses of Genesis, and thus treats the encounter between the daughters of *Adam* and the sons of *Elohim* (Genesis 6:2). The Idra understands this episode as a description of an abominable admixture of the forces of Judgment that emerge from the conjoined body of Cain and Abel, on the one hand, and the daughters of *Adam*, that is, those born of the divine figure now called *Adam*, on the other. This event threatens the process of clarifying and sweetening Judgment, and its descendants are the mighty warriors of the world and disembodied demons, who have no share in the figure of *Ze'eir Anpin*. Then, once the earth has become corrupted, once that which had been pure and refined has once again become adulterated, God comes to regret the very project of creating Adam: *YHVH regretted having made the human on earth, and He was pained, to His heart* (Genesis 6:6).

> "*YHVH regretted having made* האדם *(ha-adam), the human, on earth* (Genesis 6:6)—excluding *Adam* above, who was not *on earth. YHVH regretted*—referring to *Ze'eir Anpin.*
>
> "ויתעצב *(va-yit'atsev), And He was pained, to His heart* (*ibid.*)—it is not said, ויעצב *(va-ye'atsev), And He pained*, but rather *va-yit'atsev, And He pained Himself*, for the matter depended on Him, excluding the one who is not pained.
>
> "*To His heart*—it is not written *in His heart* but rather *to His heart*, like someone expressing his pain and complaining to his master; for He displayed this to the heart of all hearts." (Zohar 3:144a; trans. Matt 8:450)

The picture that emerges here is attentive to the mythical account of the personal God of the Hebrew Bible, expressing himself internally and to himself. At the same time it overflows, with its own gushing idraic mystical-theological conception. In a process typical of the Idra, the mythical moment of divine regret becomes a drama unfolding between the various aspects of the Godhead: *Ze'eir Anpin*, the Creator God, despairs of the deeds of human beings upon the earth, regretting the entire project of creating Adam. The Idra emphasizes that it is referring to human beings, not the divine figure of *Adam*. The biblical formulation *He was pained* expresses God's inner emotional utterance, addressed to himself. In contrast, in the Idra, God's heart transforms from an emotional representation of his personality into *Ze'eir Anpin*'s addressee in his hour of distress. *Ze'eir Anpin* turns to the heart, "the heart of all hearts," meaning *'Attiqa Qaddisha*, the Holy Ancient One—the deeper, concealed aspect of the Divine. The deeper essence of *Ze'eir Anpin* is *'Attiqa*; it is only to *'Attiqa* that he can turn in his anguish.

However, *Ze'eir Anpin* is reflexive, and his self-contemplation surfaces the profound interdependence between the divine *Adam* and the human being. For what would become of the supernal *Adam* if the earthly Adam were utterly annihilated? Earthly human beings are an extension and embodiment of the divine *Adam* in this world; thus, wiping them out would be an admission of profound, inherent failure. Furthermore, if earthly human beings were to be completely destroyed, the supernal *Adam* would perish along with them:

> "*YHVH said, 'I will wipe out* האדם (*ha-adam*), *humankind, whom I created, from the face of the earth'* (Genesis 6:7)—excluding *Adam* above. But if you say, '*Adam* below, alone'—not to exclude at all, since one cannot exist without the other." (Ibid.)

The Idra again asserts that the biblical verse that speaks of wiping out human beings is *not* referring to the divine *Adam*. However, we discover that one cannot distinguish between the divine and terrestrial Adams, and one cannot destroy only the latter, for the two figures are dependent upon one another: "one cannot exist without the other." From this perspective, there is something suicidal about divine regret. The total obliteration of human beings would mean drawing the manifestation of the Divine as *Adam* back into its source, harming the archetype of *Adam* itself. The Idra enlarges upon the rabbinic conception of interdependence between God and humans and comes to a disturbing conclusion: the destruction of human beings means the disappearance of a particular face of the Godhead, for humans on earth draw the Divine from the infinite and abstract plane into the very fabric of reality and humanity.

From a certain perspective, the great story of the Idra Rabba is that of the "totality of *Adam*," the divine figure drawn out from itself, taking shape and variegating, and ultimately reaching completion in the figure of *Adam*. But God as *Adam* is sustained through human effort, which ensures the direction of flow: from the abstract to the figure of *Adam* to this world. If human beings do not hold on tight to the cord of divinity in our world, the kite of the Divine will lift off, disappearing into the sky of the Infinite. So *Ze'eir Anpin* turns to *'Attiqa*, knowing deep down that the latter will not allow the project of humanity to be destroyed, for the spirit of *'Attiqa* abides in the inner depths of human beings.

A mere moment before humanity is destroyed, before the Idra concludes, concealed Wisdom is revealed, offering a solution to the critical state of affairs:

> "Were it not for Wisdom, concealed of all, all would have been rearranged as in the beginning, as is written: *I am Wisdom. I dwell in shrewdness* (Proverbs 8:12)—do not read שכנתי (*shakhanti*), *I dwell*, but rather שיכנתי (*shikkanti*), *I cause to dwell*. Were it not for this, the world would not exist, as is written: *YHVH by wisdom established the earth* (*ibid.*, 3:19); and it is written: *And Noah found favor in the eyes of YHVH* (Genesis 6:8).
>
> "It has been taught: All brains depend upon this brain. Wisdom is totality of all, and this concealed Wisdom empowered and ordained the arrayal of *Adam*, stabilizing it, as is written: *Wisdom strengthens the wise by ten rulers* (Ecclesiastes 7:19)—who are the complete array of *Adam*." (Zohar 3:144a; trans. Matt 8:450–451)

The concealed divine Wisdom discussed here is that of *'Attiqa*, existing before creation, the beginning of every creative process. Concealed Wisdom acts *in shrewdness* (as stated in Proverbs 8:12), behind closed doors: it dissuades *Ze'eir Anpin* from wiping out humanity by planting its counsel in his heart, without his knowing who or what is behind the notion. The counsel itself is shrewd indeed, accepting *Ze'eir Anpin*'s plan to a limited degree, advising him to destroy humanity—but not entirely. Primordial Wisdom plants affection toward Noah in *Ze'eir Anpin*—*And Noah found favor in the eyes of YHVH*

(Genesis 6:8). *Ze'eir Anpin*'s enraged, blazing eyes now flood with affection and forgiveness. Affection for Noah replaces God's regret, overwhelming the impulse toward total destruction and enabling the deliverance of humanity from annihilation. It is notable that affection saves humanity, rather than justice, compassion, or honor. It would seem that affection is a generally positive feeling, intuitive and difficult to explain. It is similar to *bissum*: one may find favor with us without our really understanding why this is so.

Concealed Wisdom's counsel brings us back to the beginning of the Idra, where the Torah appears in the role of *'Attiqa*'s advisor. Two moments of counsel thus set the unfolding of the Divine in motion. At the beginning of the work, when the divine mind conjectures kings into being out of itself, beings that glimmer and die, primordial Torah advises the Divine to configure itself, to manifest as a face; now, approaching the end of the work, *'Attiqa*'s Concealed Wisdom counsels *Ze'eir Anpin* not to wipe out humanity. Concealed Wisdom regulates deadly divine wrath; it ensures divine sobriety and the continued existence of human beings. It weaves the Idra Rabba together: first as primordial Torah, then as *'Attiqa*'s Concealed Wisdom.

Wisdom's second counsel concludes the sequence of biblical passages expounded by the Idra in generating its myth. The Creation narrative, the Garden of Eden, Cain and Abel, the sons of *Elohim* and daughters of *Adam*, divine regret, the primordial kings of Edom—all represent cosmic processes of generation, a draft, destruction, and the configuration of existence. The creation of the cosmos and humanity are read as inner-divine events, within the framework of divine self-differentiation, as God emerges from mysterious oneness.

An interpretation of the narratives of Eden and of Noah and the flood as drafts, or failed attempts, in the repeatedly disrupted process of creating a stable and enduring world has precedents in rabbinic thought. Midrashic literature describes how the world remained unstable, becoming fixed in place only after its creation, and how there was a need for the presence of a unique human being for the sake of whom creation might endure. Adam was selected for this role, but the sin of eating from the Tree of Knowledge disrupted the equilibrium of the entire world. Noah was next in line, and he did indeed ensure the continuation of humanity, but his intoxication and the subsequent exposure of his nakedness after emerging from the ark disqualified him from occupying such a rank. Abraham was then chosen, and his love for God and the covenant of circumcision etched into his flesh finally placed the world upon a solid foundation.[26] Indeed, many passages in the Zohar discuss Abraham's place as the pinnacle of the lineage of human beings who firmly establish the cosmos.[27]

In light of this, it is notable that the Idra does not portray Abraham as a stabilizer or founder of the world, stopping instead at Noah. The character whom it portrays as ensuring the endurance of the world is Moses, who invokes *'Attiqa*'s Attributes of Mercy and summons them to appear within the enraged *Ze'eir Anpin*. Another such figure is Rabbi Shim'on himself, the Idra's protagonist and hero, and the single pillar upon whom the world rests. Finally, a messianic Adamic figure joins the Idra's line of world founders:

> "*Adam* is the arrangement, and within exists the spirit. [. . .]
>
> "In this array appears perfection, faith of all, poised upon the Throne. [. . .] [A]nd it is written: *Behold, with the clouds of heaven came one like a human being; he reached the Ancient of Days and was brought before Him* (Daniel 7:13)." (Zohar 3:144a; trans. Matt 8:451)

The Idra concludes with a verse from Daniel, interpreted in Jewish tradition as a reference to the Messiah.[28] Indeed, as the work draws to a close, we can see that the assembly described therein possesses a distinctly messianic aspect, as Yehuda Liebes has demonstrated.[29] It seeks to ensure an open and continuous path between Adam, Moses, Rabbi Shim'on, and the future Messiah. It would seem that the appearance of the Messiah in the concluding lines of the Idra represents his completion of this work's great project: establishing an intimate and unobstructed connection between human beings and the deepest reaches of the Ancient One.

22

Emerging from the Idra Rabba

We have come to the end of the Idra Rabba. Rabbi Shim'on's discourses and the *tiqqunim* presented by the Companions have established a mode of religious discourse that is rich and complex, in which we can perceive an ongoing dynamic between various dimensions of the Divine: the undifferentiated, the dual, the Male and Female.

The divine faces have been configured. Even the most sublime and primordial aspects of the Godhead have been given a face. *Ze'eir Anpin*, God of the World and of Israel, has been configured and adorned. By aligning *Ze'eir Anpin*'s face with that of *Arikh Anpin*, the dual face of God is repaired and healed. God's body has been restored.

Adam is present in every dimension of existence. The eroticization and sexualization of the divine Male and Female have been rendered appropriate, even sacred, modes of discourse through which to discuss processes of divine unification. The coupling of the Male and Female is recognized as a paradigmatic event, enabling *bissum*, blessing, and birth. The parallels of the coupling in "what is above" with that in "what is below" have been accentuated.

The minds of the Idra's characters and readers have been expanded, opening up to new horizons. Their consciousness can now contain new and complex images of the Divine, conceiving of multiple dimensions that exist simultaneously.

Existence itself has been configured, no longer resting upon a single pillar. Rabbi Shim'on, the great master and teacher, has initiated the Companions. They too have become pillars upon which the world may rest.

Now, the question arises: How do we emerge unharmed from the Idra Rabba, from such an intense encounter with the sacred? This question is at least as important as the question of how to enter, perhaps even more critical.[1]

Just as an array of opening sequences mark the entry into the Idra, the emergence represents a synthesis of midrashic narratives and motifs that together conclude the work, each contributing in a distinct way. In the following pages, we will trace these various ending passages closely, and I will present a reading of the components that draw the work to a fitting close.[2]

Ending 1: Concealment and Clarity

> "*Adam* is the arrangement, and within exists the spirit, as is written: *For* האדם *(ha-adam), the human, sees what is visible, but YHVH sees into the heart* (1 Samuel 16:7).
>
> "In this array of *Adam* appears perfection, faith of all, poised upon the Throne, as is written: *an image like the appearance of a human being upon it above* (Ezekiel 1:26), and it is written: *Behold, with the clouds of heaven came one like a human being; he reached the Ancient of Days and was brought before Him* (Daniel 7:13).
>
> "Until here, words are concealed and meanings are clear." (Zohar 3:144a; trans. Matt 8:451–452, emended)

Following the Idra's usual method, one could interpret 1 Samuel 16:7—*For (ha-adam), the human, sees what is visible, but YHVH sees into the heart*—as drawing a distinction between terrestrial human beings and God: human beings understand matters as they appear to the eyes, while YHVH, *Ze'eir Anpin*, perceives with his heart, that is, *'Attiqa*. But in this case, the verse is understood to set up a dichotomy between *Ze'eir Anpin* and *Arikh Anpin*. On one hand, *Adam* (*Ze'eir Anpin*) sees what transpires with his eyes, and from this follows the blazing quality of his providence, to the point that in his fury he seeks to annihilate his own creation, humanity. On the other hand, *'Attiqa* (here called YHVH) sees into the heart, that which exists deep within.[3]

This zoharic passage, along with the verse from Daniel that bookends it, constitutes the climax and conclusion of the Idra's disclosure of its mysteries. Here we have a succinct conclusion of the Idra Rabba: the complete human being, *Adam*, and the Ancient of Days, are conjoined. "In this array of *Adam* appears perfection, faith of all." The life-breath of *'Attiqa* can now dwell in the heart of hearts of the *Adam*—Male and Female, united in coupling.

This account encapsulates the Idra Rabba's far-reaching amplification of the concept of *Adam*. The *Adam* depicted at the end of the Idra is actually one of the "states" of the Divine (as water and ice are two states of the same substance). The locus of the connection of divine and human is not merely the intellect, as some medieval philosophers held, but the structure of the human body, its sexuality, and the life-breath and spirit that dwell deep within. God is actually *Adam* par excellence—the prototype for every human being. God is the totality of every human being, male or female; God comprises all past and future generations in human history.[4]

In effect, the Idra amplifies the concept of *Adam* to such a degree that it applies it even to the most undifferentiated and abstract aspect of the Divine. The Ancient of Days too is a figure seated upon a throne. His body is not described, but his face is—and despite all of its strangeness, it is human. The Idra's radical trajectory comes to its conclusion with a return to the verses from Ezekiel and Daniel upon which the discussion is based. It is as if the work is returning to its foundations, to scriptural discourse, and asserting that at the great moments of divine self-disclosure, in waking or sleeping visions, God is manifest in human form and humans in divine form.

There is tremendous significance in the choice to conclude the Idra with this verse from the Book of Daniel, a work that sits on the boundary between wisdom and prophecy. This is also a world to which the authors of the Zohar self-consciously belong.[5] The Zohar is deeply nourished by the images and vocabulary of the Book of Daniel. Indeed, the Zohar's very title is drawn from Daniel: *The enlightened will shine like the radiance* [*zohar*] *of the sky, and those who lead many to righteousness like the stars forever and ever* (Daniel 12:3). The Zohar interprets this verse in a number of ways. The Book of Daniel carries even greater significance for the Idra Rabba than it does for the main body of the Zohar. The Idra begins with an image appropriated from Daniel—the Ancient of Days seated on a throne of flames—and concludes with the human figure standing near the Ancient of Days. Daniel is granted a fleeting vision, a moment in which he looks deep into time itself, and perceives a different possibility for the world. Something like this also occurs in the Idra Rabba, which enables its readers to dive into the deepest reaches of another time and space.

Another verse from Daniel that is not explicitly cited in this context, but which is also of significance for the conclusion of the Idra, introduces the account of the Ancient of Days: *As I watched, thrones were placed* (or *cast*), *and the Ancient of Days sat—His garment like white snow, the hair of His head like clean fleece, His throne flames of fire, its wheels blazing fire* (Daniel 7:9). In the Talmud, Rabbi Akiva interprets this verse, imbuing it with theological, mystical, and messianic tension. His interpretation points out that the verse uses the plural form of thrones (*khorsavan*), and he asserts that there are in fact two: "One for him, and one for David." Rabbi Yose the Galilean rebukes him: "Akiva, how long will you treat the *Shekhinah* as profane?"[6] Rabbi Akiva's interpretation is controversial, scandalously equating the human with the Divine. He understands the two thrones as a representation of future sovereignty, with God sitting upon one and David (or the Messiah) upon the other. As Rabbi Yose forcefully asserts, Rabbi Akiva's exegesis profanes the *Shekhinah*, for it supposes that the human can dwell with God, and thereby negates divine transcendence and remoteness. However, it seems that Rabbi Akiva's conception of divine and human existence is entirely different: rather than profaning the sacred, he draws humanity near to the Divine.[7] The Idra, like the Zohar in general, is an heir to the spiritual and exegetical tradition of Rabbi Akiva. It places Daniel's vision at its very conclusion, a vision in which a human figure standing near the Ancient of Days is granted glory and sovereignty over the entire world.

Rabbi Shimʿon's concluding words—"Until here, words are concealed (*setiman millin*) and meanings are clear"—also correspond with a verse from Daniel: *I heard and did not understand, so I said, "My lord, what will be the outcome of these things?" He said, "Go, Daniel, for these words are secret and sealed (setumim va-ḥatumim) to the time of the end"* (Daniel 12:8–9). These verses describe a vision that remains undeciphered. The divine voice of the man dressed in linen determines that these matters are "secret and sealed" until the End of Days. But the subsequent verse asserts that, as time progresses, esoteric knowledge may become more accessible to those who are of the requisite moral standing: *None of the wicked will understand, but the enlightened will understand* (Daniel 12:10). These words bring us back to the world of the Zohar. The Companions are the enlightened; thus, despite the concealment of the words communicated, they are able to understand them.

Rabbi Shim'on's assertion that "words are concealed and meanings are clear" reflects a profound insight regarding the Idra Rabba. Indeed, the words discussed in the work remain inaccessible and enigmatic, even bizarre. But the meaning of the Idra as a whole has become clear. One who has traversed the work's thousands of words, and attempted to enter into its images and illuminate them, knows that what we have here is not chaos, nor some idiosyncratic hallucination. Beyond all the images, verses, midrashic interpretations, and narratives, one recognizes a coherence—even if it is not linear or logical in its progression. The components of the Idra Rabba all coalesce in its fundamental program, which becomes increasingly clear as the work progresses, beginning with the call *Time to act for YHVH!* at the outset of the work, and concluding with the description of the human figure drawing near to the Ancient of Days.

Ending 2: Fear of Revelation and the Death of the Companions

> "Happy is the share of one who knows and examines them, and does not err in them! For these words have been given only to Masters of Qualities, Reapers of the Field, who have entered and emerged. It is written: *For the ways of YHVH are right; the righteous walk in them, [while transgressors stumble in them]* (Hosea 14:10)."

> It has been taught: Rabbi Shim'on wept. He raised his voice, saying, "If by these words revealed here, the Companions are hidden away in the chamber of the world that is coming and they depart from this world, that would be fitting and fine, so that these words will not be revealed to any inhabitant of the world."

> Then he said, "I retract! For it is revealed before the Ancient of Ancients, Concealed of all Concealed, that I have not acted for my own glory, nor for the glory of my father's house, nor for the glory of these Companions—but rather so that they not err in His ways, nor enter the gates of His palace in shame, nor be hindered. Happy is my share with them in the world that is coming!" (Zohar 3:144a; trans. Matt 8:452, emended)

Rabbi Shimʿon blesses the Companions—those who know to safeguard the profound, esoteric insights that have now been divulged to them—with the Zohar's favorite formulation: "Happy is the share [. . .]"[8] He calls those who are able to internalize such matters "Masters of Qualities, Reapers of the Field, who have entered and emerged." When Rabbi Shimʿon convened the assembly at the outset of the work, he gathered the Companions and described them as the few, scattered Reapers of the Field. When Rabbi Abba sought to encourage Rabbi Shimʿon to divulge mysteries to those who are worthy, he described the Companions as having among them those who have entered and emerged. In discussions of these passages, we have noted that throughout zoharic literature, "entering and emerging" becomes something of a definition of the adept mystic. We also explored a number of ways to understand the state of consciousness of an individual who enters but does not emerge.[9]

Paying close attention to the rhythm of Rabbi Shimʿon's words, we are able to hear the tension building, nearly to the point of eruption. Rabbi Shimʿon weeps, and shockingly suggests that it might be better if all of the participants, so full of divine revelations, were now to die, to be sequestered away in another world along with all of their mysteries. That way, the esoteric content of the assembly would not be compromised, would not leak and be improperly circulated.[10] Surely, an enthusiasm for secrecy and an anxiety about improper revelation are characteristic of the Zohar as a whole. However, this formulation is more extreme, and it raises discomfort and tension in the reader. On the one hand, the passage exhibits an awareness that layers of mysteries have been unearthed here that have never before been seen; on the other hand, Rabbi Shimʿon's words, as well as his tears, express a deep anxiety that perhaps too much has been revealed. The teaching that has been unveiled in the course of this work is creatively potent but also, it would seem, very dangerous. Indeed, Rabbi Shim'on's statement in this passage has informed how the Idra's content has been used throughout history. For example, some halakhic authorities have forbidden the translation of the Idra literature from Aramaic, fearing that people would not properly understand its images, and that they would make incorrect use of it.[11]

Attentiveness to the tone of Rabbi Shim'on's statement, however, may lead us to a different interpretation. It may be that Rabbi Shim'on means to say that, now that the Companions have attained such a rank, they can die in peace, without a sense of having missed out, for this event represents a climax that will never again be reached. Indeed, the Companions make such a statement elsewhere in the Zohar, in *Rav Metivta*, a narrative that describes a collective mystical experience in which they cross the usual boundaries of space and time, arriving in the mythical realm of the Dead of the Desert.[12] Upon awakening in another world and discovering that they have entered a new mode of consciousness, they say to one another: "Since we are here and have seen all this, if we die here, we will certainly enter the world that is coming!"[13]

In any case, Rabbi Shim'on immediately recoils from entertaining (or wishing for) the death of the Companions following the conclusion of the event. He asserts—as if engaged in both an internal dialogue with himself and a testimony to the whole world—that the assembly was not summoned in his honor, nor that of the Companions. As we saw in the opening passages of the Idra Rabba, Rabbi Shim'on summoned the Companions in response to his awareness that the world can no longer rest upon a single pillar and his understanding that, in order to remedy this situation, the deep well of profound secrets must be opened, despite the dangers inherent in divulging such matters. He states that such an act of revelation is necessary, so that the disciples may "not err in His ways, nor enter the gates of His palace in shame, nor be hindered." That is, so they do not err in central matters of religion and mysticism: the essence of the Divine, the human, and the connection between them.[14] Those Who Know, according to the Zohar, are the members of the Royal Palace, the mystics who realize their goals in contemplating the figure of the Divine. From the point of view of *ars poetica*, reading between the lines of Rabbi Shim'on's words, we might perceive a careful introduction to the very project of the Idra, for those who seek to know the ways of God, those who desire to enter the King's palace without shame, in all generations.

While we are still under the strong impression of Rabbi Shimʿon's statements, simultaneously expressing his desire for the mystical death of the Companions and recoiling from that desire, we are told that three of the Companions have in fact died before emerging:

> It has been taught: Before these Companions emerged from that threshing chamber, Rabbi Yose son of Yaʿakov, Rabbi Ḥizkiyah, and Rabbi Yeisa died, and the Companions saw holy angels carrying them in that canopy.
>
> Rabbi Shimʿon uttered a word, and they settled down. He cried out, saying, "Perhaps, heaven forbid, a decree of punishment has been issued against us, for by our hand has been revealed what has not been revealed since the day that Moses stood on Mount Sinai, as is written: *He was there with YHVH forty days and forty nights* (Exodus 34:28). What am I doing here if they were punished because of this?"
>
> He heard a voice: "Happy are you, Rabbi Shimʿon! Happy is your share—and these Companions standing with you! For to you have been revealed what has not been revealed to all the powers above. But come and see, for it is written: *At the cost of his firstborn he shall lay its foundation, and at the cost of his youngest he shall set up its gates* (Joshua 6:26). All the more so, for—by great, intense desire—their souls cleaved [above] at the moment they were taken away. Happy is their share, for they departed in perfection—which is not so with those who preceded them!" (Zohar 3:144a–b; trans. Matt 8:452–453, emended)

Three of the Companions die, and those that remain watch in terror as angelic beings carry the dead off in a canopy. This is the very same curtain that we have encountered throughout the Idra, that formed a canopy over the heads of the Companions, in which all the *tiqqunim* presented by the Companions glimmered as if they were stars in the night sky. In horror, the reader now understands that the Idra does not have an entirely happy ending. Not all of those who enter emerge in peace. An atmosphere of terror permeates the entire passage, a fear that all is about to be destroyed: the Companions are disoriented; the upper worlds rage. Then Rabbi Shimʿon speaks, and it all stops. Rabbi Shimʿon, the man who shook the earth, now brings a moment of silence to a world that threatens to return to chaos. We now hear Rabbi Shim'on's cry, and we fear that he has lost control of the situation. It seems that this is not part of the plan, that Rabbi Shim'on, the commander who summoned his warriors to battle, is taken by surprise by the mission's casualties. His initial response shatters the reader's trust in his self-confidence and stability, features that are so typical of Rabbi Shim'on's character: "Perhaps, heaven forbid, a decree of punishment has been issued against us, for by our hand has been revealed what has not been revealed since the day that Moses stood on Mount Sinai"? These words must be read carefully, as they carry a great deal of tension. On the one hand, they express the fear that the death of the Companions is a punishment for revealing too much, or for hubris. On the other hand, we discover that the Idra Rabba, now drawing to a close, occupies a status equal to the revelations attained by Moses at Mount Sinai, perhaps even more sublime.

Here Rabbi Shim'on appears in full glory as the archetypical hero. He is responsible for the assembly as a whole—he summoned it, and he demanded that the Companions reveal, and do not conceal. There is thus no justice in punishing his disciples for his own misguided decisions. He is the one who should be taken from the world: "What am I doing here if they were punished because of this?"

Alternatively, we could understand "What am I doing here?" as an expression of Rabbi Shim'on's bewilderment concerning his own role in the cosmos. According to this reading, it is as if he is asking: "What am I doing here if this is the punishment? Am I no longer the 'sign in the world'? The righteous one, in whose lifetime a rainbow was never seen? The one who decrees, and the blessed Holy One upholds? If I am the righteous one, the *tsaddiq*, the pillar upon whom the world rests—does my presence not protect us from death? Does it not ensure safe passage out of this assembly?"

The reader's confidence is now shaken. Suddenly, a *deus ex machina* intervenes: a divine voice authorizes the assembly and all the mysteries unveiled throughout its course. In explaining the deaths of the three Companions, the voice makes an astonishing proclamation:

> He heard a voice: "Happy are you, Rabbi Shim'on! Happy is your share—and these Companions standing with you! [. . .] But come and

> see, for it is written: *At the cost of his firstborn he shall lay its foundation, and at the cost of his youngest he shall set up its gates* (Joshua 6:26). All the more so, for—by great, intense desire—their souls cleaved [above] at the moment they were taken away. Happy is their share, for they departed in perfection—which is not so with those who preceded them!" (Ibid.)

There is something alarming about citing a verse that curses anyone who dares to rebuild the city of Jericho after its miraculous destruction.[15] The verse is dislocated here, removed from its context, and now it is interpreted as a confirmation that the process of cosmic foundation and configuration does indeed demand casualties. To some extent, the dead Companions are parallel to Aaron's sons, Nadab and Abihu, so beloved in the Zohar. Indeed, the Zohar states that "these two had no equal in all of Israel."[16] The Zohar understands Nadab and Abihu, who died in the process of establishing the Tabernacle in the desert camp of the Israelites, to be a sacrifice that inaugurated the institution within which God and human beings could establish a connection.

The passage that immediately follows seems to take a step back in time, again describing the final moments of the assembly, and the deaths of the three Companions as they occur:

> It has been taught: While words were being revealed, those above—who are in chariots—trembled, and a voice was aroused in 250 worlds, for ancient words were being revealed below. While the souls of these ones were being sweetened by those words, their souls departed by a kiss and were bound in that canopy and carried away by supernal angels.
>
> Why these ones? Because on a previous occasion they entered and did not emerge, whereas all the others entered and emerged.
>
> Rabbi Shim'on said, "How happy is the share of these three, and happy is our share on account of this!"
>
> The voice issued a second time, saying, "*You, cleaving to YHVH your God, are alive every one of you today!* (Deuteronomy 4:4)."
>
> They rose, and no place they looked at failed to exude fragrance. Rabbi Shim'on said, "From this you can infer that the world is blessed because of us."

Everyone's face shone so brightly that no one could look at them. (Zohar 3:144b; trans. Matt 8:454–455)

Divulging profound mysteries and aligning the divine faces with one another moves the upper and lower worlds. In this state of excitement and commotion, and as the Idra's secrets are being spoken, the souls of the three Companions are aromatized. In a state akin to intoxication, their souls slip away, carried upward by the angels.

Particularly interesting here is the discussion of why the three Companions died. These are the individuals who had, on an earlier occasion, "entered but not emerged." Emerging in peace, successfully returning to the world after attaining a mystical experience, is the completion of the sacred mission. Just as entering the sacred precinct potentially endangers one's life, so does emerging from it.[17] What is the Idra referring to here? As we saw at the beginning of the work, when Rabbi Abba argued that the Companions are worthy of these mysteries, he claimed that "they have already entered the Holy Assembly of the Dwelling, some of them entering and emerging."[18] This means that a gathering had already taken place at which divine mysteries were revealed, apparently regarding the meaning of the Tabernacle, at that event they entered in peace, but only some emerged in peace.[19]

We have no explicit zoharic account of the Holy Assembly of the Dwelling (Idra de-Vei Mashkena), but one alternative might be to gather other examples of questionable or inappropriate behavior on the part of these three Companions from elsewhere in the Zohar. The Zohar itself takes such a path by means of its scattered allusions to the Idra in a range of contexts. For example, we find one narrative in which Rabbi Yeisa is punished by Rabbi Shim'on for speaking in riddles rather than divulging a mystery clearly and directly, as would be appropriate in Rabbi Shim'on's presence. After he presents the riddle, which speaks of an egg abiding in fire that splits, Rabbi Shim'on responds: "Before the egg splits, you will depart from the world." The narrator adds: "And so it happened, in the Assembly of Rabbi Shim'on."[20] Rabbi Yeisa's fate is thus intimated even before the Idra begins, and it may perhaps be a result of his excessive esotericism that does not match the attitude of disclosure, of openness, required when standing in Rabbi Shim'on's presence.

A possible cause for Rabbi Ḥizkiyah's death might be found within the Idra Rabba itself. In discussing Rabbi Ḥizkiyah's presentation of the second *tiqqun* of *'Attiqa*'s beard, we noted that he had entered an ecstatic state that approached the departure of the soul from the body.[21] Furthermore, Shifra Asulin has suggested that Rabbi Ḥizkiyah's death may be the result of a theological shortcoming expressed figuratively in his vision. The dark spot that Rabbi Ḥizkiyah sees within the abundant flow of white may suggest an attribution of Judgment, evil, or sin to the absolute whiteness of *'Attiqa*'s Compassion.[22]

Perhaps the Idra also hints at a reason for Rabbi Yose's death. In the context of configuring and arraying *'Attiqa*'s nose, Rabbi Shim'on asks Rabbi Yose a complex question about the nostrils. Upon hearing Rabbi Yose's convoluted response, Rabbi Shim'on states: "Your breath will find rest in the world that is coming!"[23] Immediately, Rabbi Yose corrects himself and presents an appropriate answer. It may be that Rabbi Yose did not pass the interpretive test, and that Rabbi Shim'on's response foreshadows his death.

If we take these allusions into account, the three Companions did not die arbitrarily. Rather, their deaths were justified, as they did not attain the high rank of those who "enter and emerge in peace." In this context, perhaps it would not be out of place to draw an association with the myth of the Death of the Kings, echoing here for the last time in the Idra in this passage about the deaths of the Companions. As we have seen, wherever they appear, the kings do not represent merely a draft of reality but also a sacrifice that facilitates the establishment of reality. The three Companions are not associated with Judgment, as are the kings, but their failure to "enter and emerge" suggests a parallel: like the kings, they did not possess sufficient resilience to attain a stable and enduring existence; and also like the kings, they become something of a sacrifice. It may also be that the failure to enter and emerge refers to their not being balanced by a feminine aspect—either physically or spiritually—as they were unable to endure the power of the Idra's revelations.

Yet another way to understand the deaths of the three Companions suggests itself in light of the zoharic understanding that death may be the result of great spiritual effort, reaching its climax in the departure of the soul. According to this reading, death is not necessarily a punishment. We find some support for such an interpretation in another zoharic narrative about Rabbi

Yeisa, which presents him in a distinctly positive light. According to this story, as a reward for his helping a sick pauper who resided in his neighborhood, the heavenly beings state that "Rabbi Yeisa's spirit is destined to ascend and be bound in a certain holy chamber (*idra qaddisha*)." Moreover, three thrones have been allocated in heaven for Rabbi Yeisa and his colleagues.[24] The narrative thus anticipates Rabbi Yeisa's death in the Idra Rabba—as well as that of two of his friends—and informs us that his death is to be understood as a reward for his care for the pauper.

This reading is supported in the Idra Rabba passage itself, which states that the three Companions died "with a kiss." Death with a kiss is originally a rabbinic concept, referring to the departure of the soul with a kiss on the mouth from God. It is a loving kiss that draws the soul to God without suffering. The living thus yearn for such a death, hoping to attain it when their final moment arrives.[25] This would also seem to be the most straightforward way to understand Rabbi Shim'on's response: "How happy is the share of these three, and happy is our share on account of this!"

The account of the three Companions, with their intoxicated souls and rapturous deaths, echoes the classical rabbinic interpretation of the verse *My soul went out as he spoke* (Song of Songs 5:6). The Talmud transposes the intoxicated and erotic state of the female lover in the Song of Songs, projecting it onto the encounter between Israel and God at Sinai.[26] According to this interpretation, the sheer power of the divine voice causes the Israelites to swoon and their souls to depart. But in that narrative, God then rains the "Dew of the Resurrection" down upon Israel, restoring their souls. In the final passages of the Idra, the death of the Companions is final.

In this context, it is worth paying close attention to this verse called out by a divine voice: "*You, cleaving to YHVH your God, are alive every one of you today!* (Deuteronomy 4:4). Cleaving to the Divine is true life; perhaps this state is even intensified with the death of the body. These deaths are thus ecstatic, occurring in a vigorous state of attachment to God. We should also keep in mind that the next assembly of the Companions, the Idra Zuṭa, comes to its climax with the ecstatic death of Rabbi Shim'on bar Yoḥai.

Haviva Pedaya suggests that we understand the ten participants in the Idra to represent the ten *sefirot*. She reads the deaths of three of the Companions as a response to the group's decision to venture beyond expounding the secrets of the seven lower *sefirot*, stepping over the boundary into the realm of the three upper *sefirot*.[27]

Ultimately, as mentioned earlier, we may also view the deaths of the Companions as a sacrifice, an expiation for the fact that the entire Idra is, to some extent, a *violation of the Torah*, crossing the boundaries of any normative conception of Jewish religion. The "violation" may indeed involve *acting for the sake of YHVH* (*la'asot l'Adonai*), as explained in the opening lines of the Idra Rabba, but such radical activity cannot take place without casualties. The three Companions are those casualties.[28]

Ending 3: Validating the Assembly

The final scene is now narrated. The Companions emerge from the assembly:

> They rose, and no place they looked at failed to exude fragrance. Rabbi Shim'on said, "From this you can infer that the world is blessed because of us."
>
> Everyone's face shone so brightly that no one could look at them. (Zohar 3:144b; trans. Matt 8:454–455)

The Companions who have emerged whole from the Idra's Orchard bring blessed sweetening back with them into the world. They have undergone a transformation: not only do they look upon the world with generosity and love but their very gaze generates a deeply blessed change in the world, raising a sweet fragrance everywhere that their glance falls. How different this description is from the Talmudic account of Rabbi Shim'on bar Yoḥai, who emerges from the cave in which he had hidden only to burn everything that his eyes fall upon![29] The fragrances described in the Idra create an association with the Talmud's account of Rabbi Shim'on's second exit from the cave, after a period of thirteen years. This time, Rabbi Shim'on turns from world burner to world healer: "Everywhere that Rabbi Eli'ezer would afflict, Rabbi Shim'on would heal." The pleasant aromas spread by the presence of the Companions confirm to Rabbi Shim'on that the world has indeed been blessed by the assembly. The fragrances testify to a connection between the upper and lower worlds, and validate the activities of the Companions above and below.

The status of the Idra as revelation is also made clear in the description of the Companions emerging from the assembly in a state of illumination. Like Moses descending Mount Sinai, the Companions radiate light; just as the Israelites could not look at Moses owing to the intensity of the light, the people of the world cannot look upon the Companions. Divine authorization of the Idra Rabba is not communicated with earthquakes or fire, but through the more refined sensory experiences of smell and light emanating from the face.[30]

Throughout the Idra we encountered Rabbi Shimʿon alone as a luminous figure, radiating healing light; now the six remaining Companions that emerge from the assembly shine like the very heavens. They radiate a brilliant light that is not of this world. It would seem that Rabbi Shimʿon's concern at the outset of the work—namely, that the world rests only upon a single pillar—has finally been remedied.

Ending 4: Legitimizing a Smaller Circle of Companions

Even now, in the context of such a harmonious closing scene, the Idra does not shy away from its own tragedy. Just as any truly groundbreaking process in a culture, religion, science, or art carries a price, so too does the Idra. It is a tremendous sacrifice—close to a third of the participants do not come out alive. While exploring the grief of losing the three Companions, the work now steps out of the present time of the narrative and describes events occurring in the period following the assembly:

> It has been taught: Ten entered and seven emerged. Rabbi Shimʿon was happy, and Rabbi Abba was sad.
>
> One day Rabbi Shimʿon was sitting, and Rabbi Abba was with him. Rabbi Shimʿon said a word, and they saw these three being brought by supernal angels, who were showing them treasure chambers on high, due to their honor, and they entered mountains of pure balsam. Rabbi Abba's mind was eased. (Zohar 3:144b; trans. Matt 8:455)

Master and disciple emerge from the Idra in contrasting emotional states: while Rabbi Shimʿon is happy, Rabbi Abba, the most senior of the disciples, is distressed. We do not know how much time has lapsed between the assembly and the vision recounted here, but it seems that Rabbi Abba's pain has persisted throughout that period. This is an astute literary move, as the vision eases the reader's sorrow over the Companions' deaths. The divine voices that authorized and validated the Idra did not offer any cathartic closure, allowing the reader's pain and unease to linger. The reader might even entertain doubts about Rabbi Shim'on's mode of leadership. But now that Rabbi Abba's mind has been settled, perhaps the reader also finds some comfort.[31]

But even this may not seem to suffice, for the Idra remains focused on the drama of losing the three Companions:

> It has been taught: From that day on, the Companions did not leave Rabbi Shim'on's house; and when Rabbi Shim'on was revealing secrets, only they were present. Rabbi Shim'on would call out to them, "We seven are the eyes of *YHVH*, as is written: *Those seven are the eyes of YHVH* (Zechariah 4:10). This has been said for us!"
>
> Rabbi Abba said, "We are six lamps shining from the seventh, for you are seventh of all. Surely, the six exist only by the seventh, for all depends on the seventh!"
>
> Rabbi Yehudah called him "Sabbath of all those six," as is written: *Sabbath for YHVH, holy*. Just as *Sabbath for YHVH* is *holy*, so is Rabbi Shim'on *Sabbath for YHVH, holy*.[32] (Zohar 3:144b; trans. Matt 8:455–456)

The reduced size of the group has created a more intense bond between the teacher and his remaining disciples. They now accompany him constantly, and only they are privy to the mysteries that he discloses. Here we encounter three metaphors for the newly configured circle, each anchoring the group's authority in its own way.

Rabbi Shim'on provides the group with a new designation: *the eyes of YHVH*. Now, the master and his disciples together become the eyes of God in the world.

Rabbi Abba describes the circle in terms of the seven-branched *menorah* (candelabrum) in the Tabernacle, and the golden *menorah* perceived by the prophet Zechariah in his vision. Rabbi Shim'on, known as the Holy Lamp (*botsina qaddisha*), no longer shines alone. The world is now illuminated by a seven-branched *menorah*, each branch also constituting a pillar upon which the cosmos rests.[33] Rabbi Abba emphasizes that this is not an egalitarian association, with seven members of equal status, but rather a group of six disciples who are in turn illuminated and sustained by the seventh, Rabbi Shim'on. This, of course, follows the pattern of the *menorah*: a central branch with three more branches on either side.

Rabbi Yehudah employs a different symbol, calling his master "the Sabbath." The six disciples are then represented by the six weekdays, which receive their vital essence from the Sabbath—Rabbi Shim'on.

These three symbolic depictions, presented according to the position of the speaker in the circle's hierarchy, express a need for reorganization in the wake of the loss of the three Companions.

A Comic Interlude

Among the various elements that conclude the Idra Rabba is the following passage. It appears that its literary function is to relieve the mounting tension of the narrative:

> Rabbi Shim'on said, "I am surprised about that hairy one with girded loins—why was he absent from our threshing chamber while holy words were revealed?"
>
> Just then, Elijah arrived, with three diadems illuminating his face. Rabbi Shim'on said to him, "Ah, the one who was absent for the carved groat cake of his Lord on the day of the wedding celebration!"
>
> He replied, "By your life, Rabbi! Seven days before you entered the threshing chamber, all those who would come and appear with Him were selected by the blessed Holy One. And I pleaded before Him to be invited, clinging to His shoulders; but I couldn't be, because that same day He sent me to perform miracles for Rav Hamnuna Sava and his companions, who were imprisoned by edict of the royal crown. I brought about a miracle for them, casting down the rampart of the king's palace, and they were trapped in the magical entanglement, in which forty-five officers died. I extricated Rav Hamnuna and his companions and cast them into the valley of Ono, saving them. Then I prepared bread and water for them, since they hadn't eaten for three days, and that whole day I didn't part from them. (Zohar 3:144b; trans. Matt 8:455–456)

In the company of the Companions, Rabbi Shim'on expresses his amazement that Elijah the Prophet was absent from the assembly. In classical rabbinic literature and subsequent Jewish thought, Elijah is construed as an angelic human being who appears when the human and divine realms meet.[34] So how is it that Elijah was not present at such a momentous human-divine encounter as the Idra?

In a scene reminiscent of Indian myths, Elijah arrives in flight, with "three diadems illuminating his face," while Rabbi Shim'on is still speaking. Rabbi Shim'on inquires as to the reason for his absence, in a tone of complaint and in somewhat oblique language. Elijah's answer constitutes a comic interlude, providing the reader with a momentary escape from the Idra's heaviness and pathos.

Like the Greek Hermes or the Indian Narada, Elijah bursts into a humorous, even gossipy tale about the thronging crowds of venerable heavenly beings who tried to gain access to the Idra's guest list. Of course, Elijah wanted to participate, and responded to the call. But suddenly, as if in a comedy, he was thrown into a miraculous tale of heroism, in which he was sent by God to save Rav Hamnuna Sava, who no doubt should have been present at the Idra.[35] Miraculously, Elijah saves Rav Hamnuna and his companions, bringing them to safety in the Valley of Ono, where he provides for their every need.[36]

The Elijah story is amusing, even absurd. Why are we suddenly told about the earthly escapades of Rav Hamnuna Sava? And since when does this figure require food and protection? Perhaps the funniest aspect of this story is its apologetic tone, making the situation genuinely entertaining. It is as if Elijah is saying to Rabbi Shim'on: "You have no idea how hard I tried to attend, but my official position meant that I had no choice but to accept this extraordinary mission."

The comic relief allows the reader to let down her guard. Now, unexpectedly, Elijah brings us back to a point that evokes acute pain:

> "When I returned, I found the canopy carried by all those columns, with three of the Companions upon it. I asked them, and they told me, 'The share of the blessed Holy One from the wedding celebration of Rabbi Shim'on and his Companions.'" (Zohar 3:144b; trans. Matt 8: 456)

Elijah relates that, after completing his top-secret mission, and having already set off, flying, on the journey back from the Valley of Ono in the direction of the Idra, he encountered flying angelic beings bearing the souls of the three dead Companions in a curtain. In response to Elijah's question about the meaning of this sight, the angels respond with chilling brevity: "The share of the blessed Holy One from the wedding celebration of Rabbi Shim'on and his Companions." From their perspective, the three are an offering,[37] a payment or tax to which God has some right. God takes his portion, and rejoices over it. From the Zohar's perspective, from within its frame of consciousness, perhaps the souls themselves rejoice over their fate. For worthy souls continue to exist after death within the sublime and refined astral realm. Indeed, their existence is intensified upon their release from corporeality, as they draw nearer to the Life of Life, the Divine.

The mythical force here lies in the surprising way in which the blessed Holy One is depicted in this concluding passage of the work. The entire Idra has been devoted to the articulation and configuration of a complex and multifaceted, many-faced, Godhead—so different from the personal figure of "the blessed Holy One." This concluding narrative transports the reader out of the complex world of medieval thought and into a simpler religious context, pre-kabbalistic, in which humans understand their connection to the Divine in terms of sacrifice—perhaps even human sacrifice.[38]

After recounting his tale, Elijah goes on to describe the praise, delight, and mountains of pure balsam that await Rabbi Shim'on and the Companions in the World to Come: "How many rungs are arranged for you in the world that is coming! How many glowing lamps are destined to illumine you!"[39]

In a passage reminiscent of a later stratum of zoharic literature, *Tiqqunei ha-Zohar*, the dialogue between Rabbi Shim'on and Elijah continues:

> [Rabbi Shim'on] said to him, "Are the righteous bound in a cluster of crowns on festivals and Sabbaths more than of other days?"
>
> He replied, "And even all those outside, as is written: *From new moon to new moon and from Sabbath to Sabbath, all flesh shall come to bow down before Me—says YHVH* (Isaiah 66:23). If these come, how much more so the righteous!" (Zohar 3:144b–145a; trans. Matt 8:458)

Rabbi Shim'on asks Elijah, a visitor from the supernal realm, to clarify whether certain times of the year—the New Moon, festivals, and the Sabbath—are characterized by an intensification for those righteous souls that dwell in the Garden of Eden and are adorned with crowns in the presence of the Divine. Elijah responds that at such times, not only are the righteous present, but all souls are present, make an appearance before God, and prostrate themselves. The New Moon and Sabbath are particularly auspicious times for the adornment of souls: at the time of the former, the Patriarchs are crowned, whereas the Sabbath is the most blessed of all days. For a moment it seems that, in their discussion, Rabbi Shim'on—like so many other sages—is seeking to learn from Elijah about the workings of the World to Come, and receives a response. But here Elijah's discourse at last attains the momentum needed to bring the Idra to its final conclusion.

Ending 5: Amplifying the Figure of Rabbi Shim'on

> "You are Rabbi Shim'on, seventh of the six. You will be crowned and hallowed more than all! And because of you, three delights found on the seventh will be relished by the righteous in the world that is coming. It is written: *You will call the Sabbath 'delight,' the holy of YHVH 'honored'* (Isaiah 58:13). Who is *the holy of YHVH?* Rabbi Shim'on son of Yoḥai, who is called *honored* in this world and in the world that is coming." (Zohar 3:145a; trans. Matt 8:459)

We now learn that the crowned and adorned Sabbath in Elijah's account represents none other than Rabbi Shim'on himself, along with his six disciples. He tells us that "the righteous Companions"—apparently the three whose souls have already ascended into the heavenly realm—will enjoy the pleasures of the Sabbath by the merit of their master, holy and blessed like the Sabbath.[40] Elijah concludes by offering grand praise for Rabbi Shim'on, based on the verse *You will call the Sabbath "delight," the holy of YHVH "honored"* (Isaiah 58:13). The entire verse is applied to Rabbi Shim'on bar Yoḥai: He is the Sabbath; delight flows from him; he is "the Lord's holy one"; he is thus honored in all worlds. The praise offered to Rabbi Shim'on is thus situated within a tangle of the six Companions that remain and unsettling reflections on the three departed Companions.[41] Death underlies these words; it seems that even the promise of great future reward for the Companions' souls in the World to Come is evidence of an anxiety that must be calmed.

The circle of disciples has grown smaller. There are no longer nine Companions—nine lights emanating from the great luminary, *ʿAttiqa*, or perhaps Rabbi Shimʿon. In other words, the group no longer represents a cosmic structure of ten *sefirot*.[42] The new circle thus needs a new language, new symbols, a myth to bind them. Rabbi Shimʿon, Rabbi Abba, and Rabbi Yehudah have begun this process, while the divine figure of Elijah brings it to completion, authorizing Rabbi Shimʿon's status within the group as the Sabbath among the weekdays.

The sacred ceremony of the Idra Rabba is now complete. Despite the assertions of heavenly beings, the guarantees and the concluding discourses, the Idra ultimately leaves us with a sense of openness. Uncertainties hang in the air, remain in the reader's heart and mind, without a clear answer to restore balance and wholeness. The lack of catharsis may be deliberate. It leaves us holding our breaths, paving the way for the next assembly, the Idra Zuṭa.

We emerge from the Idra Rabba, our heads still spinning from the flood of images and light, from the grand drama, from the swift and sudden motion between cosmic dimensions. Our consciousness is slow to absorb all of this. Some episodes leave an indelible mark on our minds, while others sink, drowning in an ocean of details, fragments of biblical verses, and vast numbers. As readers, it is our duty to pay close attention to what is gained in the act of reading, what has happened to *us* in the course of being exposed to this magnificent work. The words must be allowed to settle, so we can detect which broad strokes, fundamental ideas, and overarching images remain with us from our encounter with the Idra Rabba.

It is now upon us to remember once more the call to gather together to *act for the sake of YHVH*, to seek the faces of God, to configure and heal them, to restore them to our consciousness, to transform and heal the face of religion. We are called to impress upon our consciousness the central significance of *Adam*, as the Idra presents it—a human likeness that spans all reality; to sense the fragments of the primordial kings scattered in the world, the forces of harsh Judgment at work throughout each and every aspect of divine and human life; to pay attention to divine and human consciousness, and its workings as articulated to us in this great work; to etch the Idra Rabba's narrative into our memories, and its heroes, living and departed; to allow our imagination to hold the faces, the body, the images; and to allow our awakened consciousness to preserve something of the sheer creative force of the Idra Rabba and its wonders.

Epilogue

"It is written: *When you come to appear before My face* [. . .] (Isaiah 1:12). [. . .] *When you come* לֵרָאוֹת פני *(le-ra'ot panai), to appear before My face,* [*who asked this of you, to trample My courts?*].

"The verse should read לִרְאוֹת *(lir'ot), to see.* Why לֵרָאוֹת *(le-ra'ot), to appear?* Well, all those faces of the King are concealed in the depth behind darkness, and all those who know how to unify the Holy Name fittingly split all those walls of darkness, and the faces of the King *appear,* illumining everything. When they appear and shine, all are blessed, those above and those below. Then blessings prevail in all the worlds; then, לֵרָאוֹת פני *(le-ra'ot panai), that My faces will appear.* (Zohar 2:57a; trans. Matt 4:300)

Deep, deep beyond the darkness, the faces of the Divine are found. The darkness that conceals these faces is itself multifaceted: it is the darkness of the depth of mystery in which Divinity resides; it is the darkness of the depths of the subconscious from which we must draw out and bring to light the faces of the Divine; this darkness is the dormant consciousness of suppression and repression; it is the darkness that is created from excessive veiling and from the fear of encountering more faces of the Divine; it is the darkness of violence and evil; and it is the darkness arising from ignorance and narrow-mindedness.

It is only human beings who know how to cause these faces to appear and be seen, that is, to cause them to be visible in the human and linguistic reality. Upon those who know how to unify the Holy Name lies the responsibility of discerning the different faces within Divinity and unifying them with one another.

There is no doubt that by means of this imagined narrative and its protagonists—Rabbi Shim'on and his Companions—the authors of the Idra Rabba delved into these depths, broke through the walls of darkness, and brought to light new-ancient faces of Divinity that were previously not visible due to a lack of language to describe them.

May these faces shine upon us and within us, and may more and more faces of the Divine appear and shine, bringing blessing to all worlds.

Amen.

Notes

Introduction

1. In this context, see Arthur Green's introduction to his book about neo-Hasidic theology, *Seek My Face, Speak My Name: A Contemporary Jewish Theology* (Northvale, NJ: Aronson, 1992).

2. On Agnon and the *Shekhinah*, see Tzahi Weiss, *Mot ha-Shekhinah be-Yeẓirat Sha"Y 'Agnon: Qeri'ah be-'Arba'ah Sippurim u-be-Mekorotehem* [Death of the Shekhina: Readings in four Agnon stories and in their sources] (Ramat Gan: Bar-Ilan University Press, 2009); on Bialik and the *Shekhinah*, see Weiss, *Mot ha-Shekhinah*, 42–45, 134–136; on Zeitlin and the *Shekhinah*, see Hillel Zeitlin, *'Al Gevul Shenei 'Olamot* [On the border between two worlds] (Tel Aviv: Yavneh, 1997), 113–126.

Chapter 1: Introduction to the Idra Rabba

1. In the world of Zohar scholarship, the last two decades have witnessed the emergence of a dynamic discussion about the manner in which the Zohar was composed, received, and transmitted. There are some scholars who prefer to speak about "zoharic literature," a category that includes the works and fragments that did not find their way into the printed editions of the Zohar; there are those who employ the expression "zoharic compilations"; and there are those who see the zoharic texts as "a family of textual phenomena." In using the term "the Book of the Zohar," or simply "the Zohar," I am referencing the zoharic literature that has been published and received under this heading. For an exhaustive overview and a critique of zoharic scholarship, see Daniel Abrams, *Kabbalistic Manuscripts and Textual Theory: Methodologies of Textual Scholarship and Editorial Practice in the Study of Jewish Mysticism* (Jerusalem: Hebrew University Magnes Press, 2010), 256–370; and Neta Sobol, *Transgression of the Torah and the Rectification of God: The Theosophy of Idra Rabba in the Zohar and Its Unique Status in Thirteenth-Century Spanish Kabbalah* [in Hebrew] (Los Angeles: Cherub Press, 2017), 129–142. Another concept that I employ throughout this book is "the body of the Zohar," which refers to the zoharic texts that constitute the majority of the Zohar's substance and structure, and in which the Godhead is described in terms of the ten *sefirot* (or in the Zohar's terminology, "levels," "lights," "crowns," and so on). The body of the Zohar is thus distinct from the Idras, which describe the Godhead using "face" terminology.

2. The Idra works belong to the *epic stratum* within the Zohar, a term coined and developed by Ronit Meroz. See "Der Aufbau des Buches Sohar," *PaRDeS: Zeitschrift der*

Vereinigung für Jüdische Studien 5, no. 2 (2005): 16–36. Recently, Meroz has sharpened this distinction by describing a limited collection of narratives within the epic stratum as the *epic section*, in which she includes the Idra Rabba and the Idra Zuṭa. See Ronit Meroz, "Maḥarozet Ha-Sippurim 'Ḥayyei RaShB"I' ve-ha- Shikhvah ha-Epit ba-Zohar" ["RaShB"I's Biography" as a Zoharic unit and the epic layer of the Zohar], in *Ha-Sipur ha-Zohari* [The zoharic story], ed. Yehuda Liebes, Jonatan Benarroch, and Melila Hellner-Eshed, 1:63–96 (Jerusalem: Ben-Zvi Institute, 2017).

3. Yehuda Liebes has explored all possible etymologies of the word *idra*, showing that it designates a room, a gathering, or a threshing floor. See Yehuda Liebes, *Studies in the Zohar* (Albany: State University of New York Press, 1993), 164n6. On the possible connections between the Idra Rabba and *tiqqun leil shavu'ot*, see ibid., 74–84. The word *idra* may also be alluding to the threshing floor as described in the Book of Ruth, which is read on Shavuot.

4. Yehuda Liebes, "Peraqim be-Milon Sefer ha-Zohar" [Sections of the zohar lexicon] (PhD diss., Hebrew University, 1976), 93–106.

5. The term *appin*, or *anpin*, is used in the Zohar to mean "face," "spirit," "breath," "nose," and "temperament." "Nose," in Hebrew *af*, is the facial feature associated with temper and temperament. For example, *Arikh Anpin* is the Aramaic and personalized version of the biblical Hebrew term *erekh appaim*, which is one of God's Attributes of Mercy and means "Slow to Anger" or "Patient" and also "Long-Nosed." *Ze'eir Anpin* means "Small-Faced" or "Young-Faced," as well as "Short-Nosed" and "Short-Tempered." For a discussion of the face in classical rabbinic literature and Kabbalah, see Moshe Idel, "Panim: On Facial Re-Presentations in Jewish Thought: Some Correlational Instances," in *On Interpretation in the Arts: Interdisciplinary Studies in Honor of Moshe Lazar*, ed. Nurit Yaari, 21–56 (Tel-Aviv: Yolanda and David Katz Faculty of the Arts, Tel Aviv University, 2000).

6. On mysticism as vocation, see Erich Neumann, *Ha-Adam ha-Misṭi* (Tel Aviv: Resling, 2007), published in English as "Mystical Man," in *The Mystic Vision*, Papers from the Eranos Yearbooks: Eranos 6, edited by Joseph Campbell, 375–415 (Princeton, NJ: Princeton University Press, 1968).

7. For different possibilities for the identity of the Idra de-Vei Mashkena, see Liebes, "Peraqim be-Milon Sefer ha-Zohar," 101–102; Liebes, "The Messiah of the Zohar," in *Studies in the Zohar*, 35n109; Elliot R. Wolfson, "Forms of Visionary Ascent as Ecstatic Experience in the Zoharic Literature," in *Gershom Scholem's Major Trends in Jewish Mysticism 50 Years After: Proceedings of the Sixth International Conference on the History of Jewish Mysticism*, ed. Peter Schäfer and Joseph Dan (Tübingen: J.C.B. Mohr, 1993), 212; Elliot R. Wolfson, *Luminal Darkness: Imaginal Gleanings from Zoharic Literature* (Oxford: Oneworld, 2007), 135; Shifra Asulin, "Qomatah Shel ha-Shekhinah: Mekomo Shel ha-Parẓuf ha-Elohi ha-Niqbi Ben Ha-'Idra Raba' Le-'Idra Zuṭa'" [The stature of the Shekhinah: The place of the feminine divine countenance (*partsuf*) in Idra Rabba and Idra Zuṭa], in *Samkhut Ruḥanit: Ma'avaqim 'Al Koaḥ Tarbuti Be-Hegut Ha-Yehudit* [Spiritual authority: Struggles over cultural power in Jewish thought], ed. Howard Kreisel, Boaz Huss, and Uri Ehrlich (Beer Sheva: Ben-Gurion University of the Negev Press, 2009), 131–135; Shifra Asulin, "Ha-Pegam ve-Tiquno: Nidah, Levanah, ve-Shekhinah: 'Iyun Murḥav Be-Daf 'Et

Be-Zohar 'Aḥarei Mot" [The flaw and its correction: Impurity, the moon and the Shekhinah—A broad inquiry into Zohar 3:79 (Aharei Mot)], *Kabbalah* 22 (2010): 221–224; and Sobol, *Transgression*, 129–142.

8. In addition to all these works, zoharic literature contains additional narrative and exegetical fragments that bear an obvious relationship with the conceptual and literary world of the Idras by virtue of their terminology and style. One important fragment of this type—interpreting the verse *For YHVH is righteous, loving righteous deeds, the upright behold His face* (Psalms 11:7)—appears in the Zohar in Parashat Vayyiqra (3:15a). Additional fragments that appear to be selections from an incomplete Idra appear in Parashat Mishpaṭim (2:122a–123b).

9. However, there are sections of Sifra di-Tsni'uta that are not reflected at all in the Idra Rabba. Moreover, in light of the way in which Sifra di-Tsni'uta is interpreted in the Idras, Liebes suggests it is possible that "the last members of the Zoharic circle no longer clearly understood the whole of this cryptic work." Yehuda Liebes, *Torat ha-Yeẓirah Shel Sefer Yeẓirah* [Ars poetica in Sefer Yetzirah] (Jerusalem: Schocken Books, 2000), 128.

10. For preliminary studies on this topic, see Liebes, *Studies in the Zohar*, 85–138; and Sobol, *Transgression*, 29–36, 175–180, 116–180.

11. On R. Joseph of Hamadan, see Iris Felix, "Te'urgiah, Magiah, ve-Mistiqah be-Qabalato Shel Rabi Yosef ha-ba'me-Shushan ha-birah" [Theurgy, magic, and mysticism in the Kabbalah of R. Joseph of Shushan] (PhD Diss., Hebrew University, 2005), especially the overview of scholarly literature on pp. 5–10. See also, Leore Sachs Shmueli, "The Rationale of the Negative Commandments by R. Joseph Hamadan: A Critical Edition and Study of Taboo in the Time of the Composition of the Zohar" [in Hebrew] (PhD diss., Bar Ilan University, 2019). On R. David b. Judah he-Ḥasid, see Amos Goldreich, "Sefer ha-Gevul le-Rabi David Ben Yehudah ha-Ḥasid: Darkei 'Ibud Shel Tekst Zohari 'Aḥrei Hofa'at ha-Zohar" [The book of the boundary by Rabbi David ben Judah ha-Ḥasid: Forms of adaptation of a zoharic text after the appearance of the Zohar] (master's thesis, Tel Aviv University, 1972); Daniel C. Matt, ed., *The Book of Mirrors: Sefer Mar'ot ha-Zove'ot by R. David ben Yehudah he-Hasid* (Chico, CA: Scholars Press, 1982); and Moshe Idel, "The Image of Man above the Sefirot: R. David ben Yehudah ha-Hasid's Theosophy of Ten Supernal Shasahot and Its Reverberations," *Kabbalah* 20 (2009), 181–212. For treatments of the complex and fascinating topic of the qualities that distinguish the language of the Idras from that of these works, see Liebes, "How the Zohar Was Written," in *Studies in the Zohar*, 95–110; and Sobol, *Transgression*, 116–142.

12. As described in Micah 7:18–19. Not be confused with the Thirteen Attributes derived from Exodus 34:6–7 and more widely known from the important role they have in Jewish liturgy and midrashic imagination.

13. Throughout this work, the term *Ḥesed* is translated interchangeably as Love or Compassion.

14. Bracha Sack has devoted a number of important studies to Cordovero's kabbalistic thought, including his treatment of the Idra literature. See, in particular, Bracha Sack, *Be-Sha'arei ha-Qabalah Shel Rabi Mosheh Qordovero* [The Kabbalah of R. Moshe Cordovero] (Beer Sheva: Ben-Gurion University of the Negev Press, 1995); Bracha Sack, *Ma'ayan 'Ein*

Ya'aqov le-Rabi Mosheh Qordovero [The 'Ein Ya'aqov Spring of Rabbi Moses Cordovero] (Beer Sheva: Ben Gurion University of the Negev, 2008); and Bracha Sack, *Me-Ma'ayyanot Sefer 'Alimah le-R. Mosheh Qordovero ve- Meḥqarim be-Qabalato* [*From the Fountains of Sefer Elimah* by R. Moshe Cordovero and studies in his Kabbalah] (Beer Sheva: Ben-Gurion University of the Negev Press, 2013).

15. On this event, see Meir Benayahu, *Sefer Toldot ha-Ari: gilgule nusḥa'otav ve-'erko mi-beḥinah hisṭorit, nosfu 'alav hanhagot ha-An ve-azkarot rishonot* [The Life of the Ari: Its various recensions and its historical value] (Jerusalem: Ben-Zvi Institute, 1967), 178–181. The scholarly literature on Luria and his kabbalistic teachings is vast and beyond the scope of the present discussion. Yet, few have discussed Luria's relation to the Idras. For examples of the latter, see Liebes, *Studies in the Zohar*, 107–110 (where he also discusses Cordovero and Moses Ḥayyim Luzzatto); Joseph Avivi, *Qabalat ha-AR"I* [Kabbala Luriana] (Jerusalem: Ben-Zvi Institute, 2008), 3:1444–1452 (see also, Avivi's editions of Luria's commentary on Sifra di-Tsni'uta and the Idra Zuṭa, ibid., 2:947–1016); Idel, "The Image of Man"; and Lawrence Fine, *Physician of the Soul, Healer of the Cosmos: Isaac Luria and his Kabbalistic Fellowship* (Stanford, CA: Stanford University Press, 2003), 300–304.

16. Moshe Ḥayyim Luzzatto, *Sefer Adir Ba-Marom* (Jerusalem: Yosef Spiner, 1990), 3a.

17. For up-to-date and comprehensive scholarship on Luzzatto and his circle, see Jonathan Garb, *Mequbal be-Lev ha-Se'arah: R. Mosheh Ḥayyim Luẓ'ato* [Kabbalist in the heart of the storm: R. Moses Ḥayyim Luzzatto] (Tel Aviv: Tel Aviv University Press, 2014). On *Adir Ba-Marom*, see ibid., 217–228.

18. Gershom Scholem, *On the Mystical Shape of the Godhead: Basic Concepts in the Kabbalah* (New York: Schocken Books, 1991), 15–55.

19. See Gershom Scholem, *Kabbalah* (New York: New York Times Book Company, 1974), 220.

20. Liebes, *Studies in the Zohar*, 1–84.

21. Liebes, *Studies in the Zohar*, 85–138.

22. Liebes had initially proposed this view in his doctoral dissertation, in which he suggested seeing the Idras as an early stratum in zoharic literature. See Liebes, "Peraqim be-Milon Sefer ha-Zohar," 95–96. Liebes points out that Moses de León does not employ the religious terminology of Sifra di-Tsni'uta or the Idras at all in his Hebrew works, whereas the Idras clearly bear an affinity with the works of kabbalists contemporary with de León.

23. Moshe Idel, "'Ha-Maḥshavah ha-Ra'ah' Shel ha-'El" ["The evil thought" of the Deity], *Tarbiz* 49, no. 3/4 (1980): 356–364; Idel, "The Image of Man"; Moshe Idel, "'Od 'Al Rabi David Ben Yehudah ha-Ḥasid ve-ha-'AR"I" [Once More about R. David Ben Yehudah ha-Ḥasid], *Daat* 7 (1981): 69–71; Moshe Idel, "Ha-Sefirot she-me-'Al ha-Sefirot: Le-Ḥeker Mekoroteihem Shel Rishonei ha-Mequbalim" [The sefirot above the sefirot: The history of the sources of the first kabbalists], *Tarbiz* 51, no. 2 (1981): 239–280.

24. Elliot R. Wolfson, "Dimui 'Antropomorfi ve-ha-Simboliqah Shel ha-'Otiyot be-Sefer ha-Zohar" [The anthropomorphic and symbolic image of the letters in the Zohar], *Jerusalem Studies in Jewish Thought* 8 (1989): 147–181; Elliot R. Wolfson, *Through a Speculum That Shines: Vision and Imagination in Medieval Jewish Mysticism* (Princeton, NJ: Princeton University Press, 1997); Elliot R. Wolfson, "Woman—the

Feminine as Other in Theosophic Kabbalah: Some Philosophical Observations on the Divine Androgyne," in *The Other in Jewish Thought and History: Constructions of Jewish Culture and Identity*, ed. Laurence J. Silberstein and Robert L. Cohn, 166–204 (New York: New York University Press, 1994); Elliot R. Wolfson, "Iconicity of the Text: Reification of Torah and the Idolatrous Impulse of Zoharic Kabbalah," in *Elliot R. Wolfson: Poetic Thinking*, ed. Elliot R. Wolfson, Hava Tirosh-Samuelson, and Aaron W. Hughes, 69–96 (Leiden: Brill, 2015); Elliot R. Wolfson, "Sacred Space and Mental Iconography: Imago Templi and Contemplation in Rhineland Jewish Pietism," in *Ki Baruch Hu: Ancient Near Eastern, Biblical, and Judaic Studies in Honor of Baruch A. Levine*, ed. R. Chazan, W. W, Hallo, and L. H. Schiffman, 593–634 (Winona Lake, IN: Eisenbrauns, 1999); Elliot R. Wolfson, "Murmuring Secrets: Eroticism and Esotericism in Medieval Kabbalah," in *Hidden Intercourse: Eros and Sexuality in the History of Western Esotericism*, ed. Wouter J. Hanegraff and Jeffrey J. Kripal, 65–109 (New York: Fordham University Press, 2011).

25. Sobol, *Transgression.*

26. Asulin, "Qomatah"; Shifra Asulin, "Ha-Havnayah ha-Kefulah Shel Demut ha-Shekhinah be-Ma'yan 'Ein Ya'aqov ve-Zeqatah le-Sifrut ha-'Idrot" [The double construct of the image of the Shekhinah in *Ma'ayan 'Ein Ya'aqov* and its relation to the Idra Literature], in *Ma'ayan 'Ein Ya'aqov le-R. Mosheh Qordovero* [The *'Ein Ya'aqov* Spring of Rabbi Moses Cordovero], ed. Bracha Sack, 61–111 (Beer Sheva: Ben-Gurion University of the Negev Press, 2008); Asulin, "Ha-Pegam." Asulin also discusses the role of verses from the Song of Songs in the Idra literature, in "Ha-Parshanut ha-Mistit le-Shir ha-Shirim be-Sefer ha-Zohar ve-Req'ah" [The mystical commentary of the Song of Songs in the Zohar and its background] (PhD diss., Hebrew University, 2006).

27. Avishar Har-Shefi, *Malkhin Qadma'in: Ha-beri'ah ve-ha-Hitgalut be-Sifrut ha-'Idrot Shel ha-Zohar* [The myth of the Edomite kings in zoharic literature: Creation and revelation in the Idrot texts of the Zohar] (Los Angeles: Cherub Press, 2014).

28. Avishar Har-Shefi, "Kamah Shan'ay Sha'ata' Da' me-'Idra': Ha-'Idra' Zuṭa'—Mivneh ve-Mashma'ut" [How different is this time from the Idra: The Idra Zuṭa—structure and meaning], *Kabbalah* 26 (2012): 203–228.

29. Pinchas Giller, *Reading the Zohar: The Sacred Text of the Kabbalah* (Oxford: Oxford University Press, 2001), 89–158.

30. Daniel Matt, *The Zohar: Pritzker Edition*, vol. 8 (Stanford, CA: Stanford University Press, 2014), 318–459.

31. In addition to these studies, see Boaz Huss, *The Zohar: Reception and Impact* (Oxford: Littman Library of Jewish Civilization in association with Liverpool University Press, 2016).

Chapter 2: The Language of Divine Faces

1. For "the body of the Zohar," see note 1 in Chapter 1.

2. The term appears in the well-known midrash on the creation of Adam: "R. Samuel b. Naḥmani said: When the Holy Blessed One created Adam the First, He created him

double-faced (*du partsufin/diprosopon*)" (Genesis Rabbah 8:1). It also appears in the Talmud: "One who sees large populations of Israelites recites: *Blessed is He who is Wise of all Secrets*. For neither their minds nor their faces (*partsufehen*) are similar to one another." BT Berakhot 58a.

3. See note 5 in Chapter 1.

4. During a moment of sensitive introspection concerning his earlier work, Moses Cordovero states that in *Pardes Rimmonim* he was entirely focused on the ten *sefirot*, while face terminology and considering the Divine in human form only came later: "The existence of the ten *sefirot* in the mystical sense of ten levels emanating from one another is not likened to a human [i.e., Adamic] figure. This is the sense in which we studied the Zohar according to the method that we employed in our first work, *Sefer Pardes Rimmonim*; namely, the ten *sefirot*. [. . .] It is very difficult to ascribe a human likeness to this figure. [. . .] The only figure that can contain all figures, so that in that figure and in that seal they can all be inscribed, is that of the human likeness. Thus, this figure was implanted in its likeness, in the mystery of the configurations of *Arikh Anpin*." Moshe Cordovero, *Sefer ha-Zohar im Perush Or Yaqar* [The Zohar with the Or Yaqar commentary] (Jerusalem: Ahuzat Yisrael, 1972–1990), 23:31–32; hereinafter *Or Yaqar*. My thanks to Bracha Sack, who pointed me to this passage. See Liebes' discussion on this point, in Yehuda Liebes, "Shablonizaẓiah Ve-Heḥiyy'atah Be-Mitos Ha-Zohari" [Shablonization and its revival of Jewish myth], lecture presented at the conference "Kenes Sifrut Ha-Zohar ve-Dorah" [The literature of the Zohar and its generation], Beer Sheva, Israel, June 12, 2014. The Hebrew text is available at https://liebes.huji.ac.il/files/shablonization.pdf. In Lurianic Kabbalah, which developed the discourse of the Idras in exceptional ways, we find a formulation that accurately pinpoints the difference between the two approaches: sefirotic discourse presents a series of points or dots (*nekudot*) that hold the unrealized potential to be connected to form a face, while the discourse of faces broadens and deepens the points into a complete and whole *partsuf*. See, for example, Luria's *Sefer 'Ets Ḥayyim*, 28:1, 18a.

5. See Melila Hellner-Eshed, *A River Flows from Eden* (Stanford, CA: Stanford University Press, 2009), 229–251.

6. Neta Sobol presented a fresh analysis of the relationship between the *partsufim* and the *sefirot* in the Idras, in order to address the question of whether the two sets of terminology that describe the Divine are parallel in terms of chronological development, or whether it is possible to determine which one developed first. In this context, she points to the fact that in the Idra Rabba, the *sefirot* are joined to one another at certain parts of the faces, but their usual names are not mentioned. Sobol also notes the great difference in this respect between the Idra Rabba and the Idra Zuṭa, in which there is indeed an identification of the *partsufim* with the *sefirot* (in particular in the second part of that work). See Sobol, *Transgression*, 19–29.

7. While the Zohar's resonances with Christianity are not a focal point of this study, there is a growing body of research on the dialectic relationship between Judaism and Christianity that plays out in the Zohar. See Ellen Haskell, *Mystical Resistance: Uncovering the Zohar's Conversations with Christianity* (Oxford: Oxford University Press, 2016); Jonatan M. Benarroch, "God and his Son: Christian Affinities in the Shaping of the

Sava and Yanuka Figures in the Zohar," *Jewish Quarterly Review* 107, no.1 (2017), 38–65; Jonatan M. Benarroch, "'Son of an Israelite Woman and an Egyptian Man'; Jesus as the Blasphemer (Lev. 24:10–23): An Anti-Gospel Polemic in the Zohar," *Harvard Theological Review* 110, no. 1 (2017), 100–124; Jonatan M. Benarroch, "A Medieval Kabbalistic Response to the Patristic Exegesis on Exodus 23:19," *Journal of Religion* 99, no. 3 (2019), 263–287.

8. See Har-Shefi, "Kamah Shan'ay." For more on the differences between the Idra Rabba and the Idra Zuṭa, see Asulin, "Qomatah shel ha-Shekhinah"; Sobol, *Transgression*, 19; on additional implications of the difference between the Idras, see the section "A Song of Praise to Adam: Humanity, the Body, and Eros," in Chapter 7.

9. This topic—in particular facial expressions and their qualities—is discussed further in Chapter 3, which is entirely devoted to the divine countenance.

10. See Elliot Wolfson's intriguing articles "Iconicity of the Text" and "Sacred Space," treating the tension between anthropomorphism or the construction of an idol and the exaltation of God in one's consciousness and discourse through human likeness.

11. Yehuda Liebes, *'Alilot 'Elohim: Ha-Mitos ha-Yehudi—Masot ve-Meḥqarim* [God's story: Collected essays on the Jewish myth] (Jerusalem: Carmel Press, 2008), 193.

12. Jean-Luc Marion, *God without Being* (Chicago: University of Chicago Press, 1995), 11–24.

13. Yehuda Liebes, "Zohar ve-'Eros" [Zohar and eros], *Alpayyim* 9 (1994): 112–113.

14. For a discussion of this passage in its broader context, see the section "The Ceremonial Closing of the *Tiqqunim* of *'Attiqa*," in Chapter 12.

15. For example, see Idel, "Panim"; Wolfson, *Through a Speculum*; Elliot R. Wolfson, "The Image of Jacob Engraved upon the Throne," in *Along the Path: Studies in Kabbalistic Myth, Symbolism, and Hermeneutics*, 1–62 (Albany: State University of New York Press, 1995); Michael Fishbane, "Some Forms of Divine Appearance in Ancient Jewish Thought," in *From Ancient Israel to Modern Judaism: Intellect in Quest of Understanding: Essays in Honor of Marvin Fox*, ed. Jacob Neusner, Ernest S. Frerichs, and Nahum Sarna, 2:261–270 (Atlanta, GA: Scholars Press, 1989); Shama Friedman, "Graven Images," *Graven Images* 1 (1994): 233–238; and Daniel Abrams, "The Boundaries of Divine Ontology: The Inclusion and Exclusion of Meṭaṭron in the Godhead," *Harvard Theological Review* 87, no. 3 (1994): 291–321.

16. Enoch 1, 71:9–17; Enoch 2, 13:48.

17. Pesiqta de-Rav Kahana 12:24. See also the midrashic collection on the face of God in Yalquṭ Shim'oni, Shemot [Exodus] 286. A fuller discussion of this series of midrashim can be found in Arthur Green, "The Children in Egypt and the Theophany at the Sea," *Judaism* 24, no. 3 (Fall 1975): 446–456.

18. BT Yoma 54a. See Moshe Idel, *Kabbalah and Eros* (New Haven, CT: Yale University Press, 2005), 31–32, 58–59. The terms "large face and small face" (*appei ravrevei ve-appei zuṭra*) that serve as a source for describing the two *partsufim* in the Idra—*Arikh Anpin* and *Ze'eir Anpin*—are present in the talmudic account of the cherubs' faces. See BT Sukkah 5b.

19. See Idel, *Kabbalah and Eros*, 35–38; Haviva Pedaya, "Re'iyyah, Nefilah, Shirah; Hishtoqequt Re'iyyat ha-'El ve-ha-Yesod ha-Ruḥi be-Mistorin ha-Yehudi ha-Qadum"

[Sight, fall, song: The desire to see God and the spiritual element in ancient Jewish mysticism], *Asufot* 9 (1995): 237–277.

20. Hekhalot Rabbati, sec. 163–164, lines 24–43. For Elliot Wolfson's treatment of this passage, see Wolfson, "The Image of Jacob."

21. Wolfson, "The Image of Jacob."

22. On the *Shi'ur Qomah* literature and its connections with the Song of Songs, and on the exegesis of Song of Songs in the Idras, see the thorough analysis of Asulin, "Ha-Parshanut ha-Mistit le-Shir ha-Shirim," 99–150.

23. On anthropomorphism in the circles of Ḥaside Ashkenaz, see Joseph Dan, *'Iyunim be-Sifrut Ḥasidut 'Ashkenaz* [Studies in Ashkenazi Hasidic literature] (Ramat Gan: Masada, 1975), 118, 128–138; Idel, *Kabbalah and Eros*, 38–39; Elliot R. Wolfson, "Images of God's Feet: Some Observations on the Divine Body in Judaism," in *People of the Body: Jews and Judaism from an Embodied Perspective*, ed. H. Eilberg-Schwartz (Albany: State University of New York Press, 1992), 156–160; Wolfson, *Through a Speculum*, 192–296.

24. Arthur Green, *Keter: The Crown of God in Early Jewish Mysticism* (Princeton, NJ: Princeton University Press, 1997), 106–120. This infatuation with God's face, which Green analyzes, is a very interesting precursor to what we find in the Idra Rabba.

25. Pesiqta Rabbati, *parashah* 21.

26. Gershom Scholem, "'Iqvotaw shel Gabirol ba-Qabbalah" [The imprint of Gabirol in the Qabbalah], in *Ma'asef Sofrey Eretz Yisra'el* [Anthology of the authors of the Land of Israel], 160–178 (Tel Aviv: Aggudat ha-Sofrim, 1940).

27. Plotinus, *Enneads*, trans. A. H. Armstrong (Cambridge, MA: Harvard University Press, 1969), 7:137.

28. For example, see the description of *Arikh Anpin* and its connections with Neoplatonic terminology later in this chapter, and throughout the book. On the impact of Neoplatonic elements on Jewish thought, see Yehuda Liebes, "Zohar and Iamblichus," *Journal for the Study of Religions and Ideologies* 6, no. 18 (2007), 95–100.

29. Moshe Halbertal, *Maimonides: Life and Thought* (Princeton, NJ: Princeton University Press, 2014), 288–296. See also his description of Maimonides' overarching project: "The biblical and midrashic opposition to the worship of idols was directed toward external, plastic representation of the divinity, but Maimonides redirected it toward mental representation; henceforth, it would be necessary to shatter the internal idol" (290–291).

30. Yehuda Liebes, "Le-Haḥzir le-'El Et Panav" [Returning God's face], *Dimmuy* 25 (2005): 50–53. Liebes also expressed his own identification with this religious agenda, and its role in the emotional motivations that led him to research the Kabbalah.

31. Wolfson, "Dimui 'Antropomorfi," 179.

32. In this context, see Liebes' instructive comment, in which he locates a source for the identification of *'Attiqa Qaddisha*'s eyes with providence in Maimonides' *Guide* (1:44), where the "eye" attributed to God in the Bible is identified with divine providence, and also possibly in the Arabic term *'ināya* (providence; cf. Hebrew *'eynayim*). Liebes, "Peraqim be-Milon Sefer ha-Zohar," 369–370.

33. Cordovero, *Or Yaqar*, 21:196 (introduction to *Ḥeleq Shi'ur Qomah*).

34. Ibn al-ʿArabī, *Fuṣūṣ al-Ḥikam* [Bezels of wisdom], trans. Sara Sviri (personal correspondence with the author).

35. As noted above, the Aramaic term *appin* denotes both the face and the nose in the Zohar (and thus also breath or breathing).

36. For more on the name *Arikh Anpin* and its connection to Erikapaios in Orphic mythology, see Yehuda Liebes, "Ha-Mitos ha-Qabali she-be-Fi ʾOrfiʾus" [The kabbalistic myth of Orpheus], *Jerusalem Studies in Jewish Thought* 7 (1988): 425–459.

37. For a more detailed discussion of this passage, see the section "Skull and Brain," in Chapter 10.

38. I wish to thank Raphael Dascalu, the translator of this work; editor Minna Bromberg; and my teacher Art Green for their thoughtful insights on this matter.

39. Plotinus, *Enneads*, 5:59.

40. See Karen L. King, *The Secret Revelation of John* (Cambridge, MA: Harvard University Press, 2006), 28–32. For further comparisons and contrasts between the discourse of the Idras and that of Gnostic works from the second and third centuries CE, expressed in a synthesis of abstraction with the personal, see the sections "Zeʿeir Anpin and Gnosticism" and "A Prayer for *Zeʿeir Anpin*'s Life," in Chapter 4.

41. For more on the Idra Rabba's conception of the beard and its earlier sources, along with further discussion of this hymn of praise to the beard, see the section "The Beard in the Zohar and in the Idra Literature," in Chapter 12.

42. This is informed by rabbinic usage. Cf. the expression "styling his hair" (*metaqqen bi-seʿaro*) in Bereshit Rabbah 22:6.

43. Zohar 3:131a; trans. Matt 8:346.

44. For more on this relationship, see the opening paragraphs of Chapter 3.

45. For more on the differentiation in *Zeʿeir Anpin*'s face, see Chapter 15, especially the first section, "Hairs as Channels of Transmission."

46. For more on *Zeʿeir Anpin*'s nose, see the section "The Nose: The Flaring of Divine Wrath," in Chapter 15.

47. For more on this topic, see the section "*Zeʿeir Anpin* and Gnosticism: Between Splitting and Healing," in Chapter 4.

48. For more on the ideas in this passage, see the section "The Warrior's Mercy," in Chapter 16.

49. For a discussion of the sources for the Idra's terminology in its account of the divine body, including a discussion of this midrash and the divine body in pre-zoharic sources, see the section "The Idra's Myth of the Male and Female, and Its Sources," in Chapter 18.

50. Bereshit Rabbah 8:1.

51. *Kesut* is the general term for genitalia in the Idra Rabba. See the extensive treatment of this point in the discussion of this passage in Chapter 18 and especially the section "Configuring the Male and Female Body" and related notes.

52. The ancient mythical territory ruled by the kings of Edom is here read as wordplay on the word *adom*, meaning "red" and referring to the vagina.

53. For example, see the discussion of the red and judgmental figure of the female Divine, and gendered aspects of this figure, in Chapter 20.

54. For more on this *tiqqun*, see Chapter 20, "Separation and Coupling."

55. For a discussion of the partial and inferior status of the feminine in theosophical Kabbalah, see Wolfson, "Woman—The Feminine as Other." The question of the Idra Rabba's stance toward the body of the feminine Divine is discussed extensively by Shifra Asulin in "Qomatah Shel ha-Shekhinah," where she investigates the depiction of the feminine figure in both the Idra Rabba and the Idra Zuṭa and notes differences between them, pointing to a lack of detail in the description of the female body and its organs and raising possible reasons for this (such as a concern with concealment or modesty, possible influences of different kabbalistic schools upon the Idras, etc.). For a summary of earlier scholarship on this topic, see ibid., 122–123n60. It is worth noting that to some degree, lacunae in the Idra's account of the feminine body are filled in by *Tiqqunei ha-Zohar* and by Moses Cordovero. On *Tiqqunei ha-Zohar*, see Biti Roi, *Love of the Shekhina: Mysticism and Poetics in Tiqqunei ha-Zohar* [in Hebrew] (Ramat Gan: Bar Ilan University, 2017), 311–400; and on Cordovero, see Asulin, "Ha-Havnayah ha-Kefulah Shel Demut ha-Shekhinah."

56. On this return to the relationship between the *partsufim*, see the section "Sweetening the Powers of Judgment Continues," in Chapter 21.

57. Manna appears in the Zohar as the spiritual food that sustains the mystics, with the jar containing a full *omer* of manna (Exodus 16:33; and cf. BT Yoma 52b; and Horayot 12a) representing the Zohar itself (Zohar 1:217a). Also see Liebes, *Studies in the Zohar*, 200n58; and Hellner-Eshed, *A River Flows from Eden*, 368–370.

58. For more on this point, see the section "A Figure within a Figure: The Structure of Reality," in Chapter 17.

Chapter 3: The Gaze

1. See Michael Eigen, "On the Significance of the Face," *Psychoanalytic Review* 67, no. 4 (1980–1981): 425. This topic has also been studied in carer-patient relationships in a therapeutic context. See, for example, Edward Emery, "Facing 'O': Wilfred Bion, Emmanuel Levinas, and the Face of the Other," *Psychoanalytic Review* 87, no. 6 (2000): 799–840.

2. Eigen, *Significance of the Face*, 435–437. Eigen is also of the opinion that at deeper levels of the personality, the human face possesses a luminosity or radiance that authorizes, restores, and enables the existence of the contemplating subject.

3. Zohar 3:130a; trans. Matt 8:341.

4. This characterization is similar in many respects to Maimonides' account of divine providence in the *Guide for the Perplexed*. Maimonides does not make a connection between providence and divine intervention in the world, but rather describes a mode of contemplative providence. See Halbertal, *Maimonides*, 335–341; Micah Goodman, *Sodotav Shel Moreh ha-Nevukhim* [Maimonides and the book that changed Judaism: Secrets of *The Guide for the Perplexed*] (Or Yehudah: Dvir, 2010), 116–118. There is a similar account in Plotinus, in his description of the One's providence over its creatures. For example, see *Enneads*, 6:7.1.

5. A wonderful portrayal of this is found in the Idra Zuṭa, in a passage interpreting this verse from 1 Samuel 2:3: *For a God of knowledge* (*de'ot*; lit., "knowledges") *is YHVH, and by Him actions are determined*. The biblical text retains two options for reading the

verse, referred to as the *ketiv* (the way the verse is written) and the *qeri* (the way the verse is traditionally read). Here the *qeri*, is *lo* (spelled lamed-vav, ולו, "by Him") and is seen as referring to *Ze'eir Anpin*, the God by whom actions and plurality are determined. The *ketiv* is *lo'* (spelled lamed-aleph, לא, "no") and is interpreted as alluding to *'Attiqa*, for whom there are no actions:

> *For a God of knowledges is YHVH, and by Him actions are determined* (1 Samuel 2:3)—because He has two colors, *by Him actions are determined*. However, for the Holy Ancient Concealed One, *[actions] have no place*—they do not befit Him, for all exists as one, a joy for all, life for all. (Zohar 3:292b; trans. with reference to Matt 9:812)

6. Neumann distinguishes between various stages within the feminine archetype. It seems that the archetypal aspect connected to the accounts in the Idra is that of the Uroboric Great Mother. See Erich Neumann, *The Great Mother* (Princeton, NJ: Princeton University Press), 18–23, 120–146.

7. On the relationship between the mother's breasts and her face, see Renato J. Almansi, "The Face-Breast Equation," *Journal of the American Psychoanalytic Association* 8 (1960): 65: "[C]linical experience indicates unequivocally that on a primitive perceptual level the face may be equated with the breasts, and that there is a particularly strong correlation between the nipples and the eyes."

8. On Great Space and limited space in Tibetan Buddhism, see Tarthang Tulku, *Time, Space and Knowledge: A New Vision of Reality* (Emeryville, CA: Dharma Publishing Bookstore, 1977). This description of a state of consciousness in spatial terms is reminiscent of the Lurianic distinction between *moḥin de-gadlut* and *moḥin de-qaṭnut*. Also potentially useful in understanding *Arikh Anpin* is the Tibetan Buddhist account of another state of consciousness, *Bhavanga*. This is an expansive and radiant state of mind, forming the basis of the various other modes of consciousness and connected among other things with compassion. See B. Alan Wallace, "Intersubjectivity in Indo-Tibetan Buddhism," *Journal of Consciousness Studies* 8 (5–7) (2001): 212–213.

9. This appears, for example, in the account of Joseph of Hamadan. See Alexander Altmann, "Le-She'elat Ba'aluto Shel Sefer Ta'amei ha-Miẓvot ha-Meyuḥas le-Rabi Yiẓḥaq Ibn Parḥi" [On the question of the authorship of the book Ta'amei ha-Miẓvot attributed to Rabbi Isaac Ibn Parhi], *Kiryat Sefer* 40, no. 2 (1965): 274–275; Liebes, *Studies in the Zohar*, 104–107; Moshe Idel, *Kabbalah: New Perspectives* (New Haven, CT: Yale University Press, 1990), 134–135, 118–120; and Sobol, *Transgression*, 14–18, 124–127.

10. Cf., however, the remarks of Wolfson, who understands *'Attiqa*'s illumination of *Ze'eir Anpin* in homoerotic terms. See Elliot R. Wolfson, *Language, Eros, Being: Kabbalistic Hermeneutics and Poetic Imagination* (New York: Fordham University Press, 2005), 368–370.

11. See also, Hana Rippel-Kleiman, "Mel'ai 'Einayyim: 'Al 'Einayyim ve-Re'iyyah be-Sefer ha-Zohar" [Full of eyes: On eyes and vision in the Zohar] (master's thesis, Hebrew University, 2009), 20–21.

12. Erich Neumann, *The Origins and History of Consciousness* (Princeton, NJ: Princeton University Press, 1995), 411; Neumann, *Ha-Adam ha-Misṭi* ["Mystical Man"].

13. For more on this point, see the section "Ze'eir Anpin and Gnosticism," in Chapter 4.

14. Zohar, 3:135b; trans. Matt 8:385.

15. See mainly Zohar 3:136b–137a.

16. As mentioned previously, in note 4 for this chapter, Plotinus' description of the One's providence over its creatures bears a resemblance to *'Attiqa*'s gaze.

17. For more on this passage, see the section "The Eyes: Divine Providence in the Dual Dimension," in Chapter 15.

Chapter 4: Reflections on *Ze'eir Anpin*

1. On these two archetypes in a zoharic context, see Jonatan M. Benarroch, "'Ha-Sava'-Yanuqa' ve-Ḥanokh-Metatron ke-'Arkhitip Senex-Puer (Zaqen-Na'ar): Qeri'ah Post-Yungi'anit be-Sifrut ha-Zoharit (Al Pi James Hilm'an)" [Sava-Yanuka and Enoch-Metatron as James Hillman's *senex-puer* archetype: A post-Jungian inquiry to a zoharic myth], in *Ha-Dimyon ha-Parshani: Dat ve-'Emunot be-Tarbut ha-Yehudit be-Heqsherehah* [The exegetic imagination: Relationships between religion and art in Jewish culture], ed. Ruth Hacohen et al., 46–71 (Jerusalem: Hebrew University Magnes Press, 2016).

2. I thank my friend Ayelet Naeh for this observation. Indeed, it should be pointed out that in the Idra Zuṭa this binary tension is softened by deploying a more diverse range of divine personas. In that work, five *partsufim* appear as a family of sorts, with an additional male figure of God as Father (*Abba*) appearing between *Arikh Anpin* and *Ze'eir Anpin*, alongside the divine Mother (*Imma*). This series of figures tempers the emotional tension and significantly moderates the work's presentation of the Divine and the world, in contradistinction to the Idra Rabba, which bases its entire theological discourse upon three elemental figures. I hope to explore the absence of the father figure from the Idra Rabba further in the future.

3. See, for example, Zohar 1:221a; and on this passage, see Hellner-Eshed, *A River Flows from Eden*, 340–351.

4. As discussed further in Chapter 11, Hebrew *ratson* has two valences: one is "will" as volition, determination, and desire; the other evokes love and appeasement.

5. For general treatments of Gnosticism, see Hans Jonas, *The Gnostic Religion: The Message of the Alien God & the Beginnings of Christianity* (Boston: Beacon Press, 1968); and Karen L. King, *What Is Gnosticism?* (Cambridge, MA: Harvard University Press, 2005).

6. For example, see Gershom Scholem, *On the Kabbalah and Its Symbolism* (New York: Schocken Books, 1969), 96–100; and Gilles Quispel, "Ezekiel 1:26 in Jewish Mysticism and Gnosis," *Vigilia Christianae* 34, no. 1 (January 1980): 1–13.

7. Idel summarizes Scholem's understanding of the relationship between Gnosticism and Kabbalah, presenting a detailed critique: see Idel, *Kabbalah: New Perspectives*, 30–32. See also, Fishbane, "Some Forms of Divine Appearance"; and Elliot R. Wolfson, "The Tree That Is All: Jewish-Christian Roots of a Kabbalistic Symbol in *Sefer ha-Bahir*," in *Along the Path: Studies in Kabbalistic Myth, Symbolism, and Hermeneutics*, 63–88 (Albany: State University of New York Press, 1995).

8. Similar examples of division as a mode of coping with ambivalence appear elsewhere

in the Zohar, the most striking of which is that between good and evil—between the *Siṭra di-Qedushah* (the Side of Holiness) and *Siṭra Aḥra* (the Other Side). This distinction is the central tool the Zohar uses to construct the evil demonic realm. See Nathaniel Berman, *Divine and Demonic in the Poetic Mythology of the Zohar: The "Other Side" of Kabbalah* (Boston: Brill, 2018), 37–44, and in particular his discussion of Freud's concept of the splitting between the father figure and the divine figure.

9. Zohar 3:141a; trans. Matt 8:426.

10. For a broad discussion of the unity of the various aspects of the Divine, see the section "Complex Unity," in Chapter 17.

11. On ancient theurgy and Kabbalah, see Idel, *Kabbalah: New Perspectives*, 176–199.

12. As Matt notes at this point, "Habbakuk perceives the entire auditory process of *Ze'eir Anpin*, he understands how this arouses forces of Judgment so he was fittingly afraid."

13. Zohar, trans. Matt 8:406n301. The ears of *Ze'eir Anpin* are understood as taking in the voice rising from humanity and discerning whether to react with love or wrath.

14. Thus the expression *yemot 'olam* appears in the biblical Song of Moses (*ha'azinu*), in the call to Israel to recall their history, albeit in a slightly varied grammatical form (*yemot 'olam*): "Remember the days of old (*yemot 'olam*), / Consider the years of ages past" (Deuteronomy 32:7).

15. The *days of old* (*yemei qedem*) appears at the end of the account of God's Attributes of Mercy in Micah, which constitutes the basis of the primary exegesis of the Idra Rabba, by means of which the *tiqqunim* of *Arikh Anpin*'s beard are described: "Who is a God like You, forgiving iniquity and remitting transgression. [. . .] You will keep faith with Jacob, loyalty to Abraham, as you promised on oath to our fathers in days gone by (*mi-yme qedem*)" (Micah 7:18–20).

16. R. Naḥman of Breslov employed this exegesis from the Idra, and the division between Primordial Years (*shanim qadmoniyyot*) and *days of the world* (*yemei 'olam*), with stunning creativity, in a teaching that formed the conceptual basis of his own choice to tell the members of his community stories rather than only expounding his convoluted and profound teachings to them. He distinguishes between the teachings of *yemei 'olam*, which are connected to the Jewish culture and religion, and the legends that come from the archaic realm of *'Attiqa* of *shanim qadmoniyyot*. See *Liqquṭe Moharan* 1:60, #6.

17. BT Berakhot 7a.

18. Earlier on this page in the Talmud, the same formulation appears as God's prayer to Himself: "R. Yoḥannan says in the name of R. Yose: How do we know that the Blessed Holy One prays? [. . .] What does He pray? Said R. Zuṭra b. Ṭubiah, said Rab: 'May it be My will that My mercy will overcome My anger, and may My mercy prevail over My attributes, and may I conduct Myself toward My children with the attribute of mercy, and may I enter before them [in Judgment] while stopping short of strict Justice.'"

19. Allen Afterman, *Kabbalah and Consciousness* (New York: Sheep Meadow Press, 1992), 113.

Chapter 5: Literature, Mysticism, Praxis

1. On the relationship between the scriptural interpretations and the narrative frame in the Idra, see Sobol, *Transgression*, 29–36, 125–127. This literary genre, combining intellectual discourse with narrative, has received particular attention from the French thinker Jacques Derrida, who noted the special quality of Plato's Socratic dialogues, in which philosophy is interwoven with narrative and interpersonal narratives without distinction or separation, with the former being built upon the latter. See Jacques Derrida, *Dissemination* (Chicago: University of Chicago Press, 2017), 69–73. A particularly striking example of this approach is Plato's *Symposium*. See Liebes' discussion of the Idra and the *Symposium*, in Liebes, "Zohar ve-'Eros," 112–117.

2. On the commentaries penned by Cordovero and Luria, see the section "Interpreters of the Idra," in Chapter 1.

3. On this point, Derrida again contributes to our understanding of the Idra with his insights on the relationship between orality with a speaker, voice, presence, and control on the one hand and writing on the other. He points to the uniqueness of Platonic philosophy in its orality, its wandering, and its interpersonal explication. Derrida devotes a fascinating discussion to the deep ambivalence that accompanies Western thought in its transition from oral culture to literary culture, focusing on an interpretation of the myth of the origins of writing as presented in Plato's *Phaedrus*. See Derrida, *Dissemination*, 73–80.

4. Liebes, *Studies in the Zohar*, 60–61. Yehuda Liebes also suggests that the Idra Rabba itself is convened as a *tiqqun leil shavu'ot* (ibid., 74–82).

5. For a broad discussion of this passage, see the section "The Adjuration and the Curse," in Chapter 8.

6. See Ruth Kara-Ivanov Kaniel, "Likhtov 'O Lo' Likhtov: Mitos ha-Ketivah be-Sefer ha-Zohar" [To write or not to write: The myth of writing in the Zohar], in *Ha-Sipur ha-Zohari* [The zoharic story], ed. Yehuda Liebes, Melila Hellner-Eshed, and Jonatan Benarroch, 1:238–306 (Jerusalem: Ben-Zvi Institute, 2017).

7. See Liebes, *'Alilot 'Elohim*, 137n51.

8. In this context, see Haviva Pedaya's deep study of the representation of images as a central aspect of mythical-mystical consciousness: Haviva Pedaya, *Ha-Mar'eh ve-ha-Dibur: 'Iyun be-Tiv'ah Shel Ḥavva'yat ha-Hitgalut be-Mistorin ha-Yehudi* [Vision and speech: Models of revelatory experience in Jewish mysticism] (Los Angeles: Cherub Press, 2002), esp. 31–42.

9. Haviva Pedaya richly describes the quality of revelatory imagery: "Simultaneous expression is part of the essence of visual transmission in kabbalistic revelation. We do not merely find a plot, but often a moving picture. One always finds in this image a powerful unifying element, uniting all of the details; one might say that it is precisely through the power of its movement, simultaneity, multilocality, and polymorphism that the revelatory image occurs, and demands actualization and its mode of evocation." Pedaya, *Ha-Mar'eh ve-ha-Dibur*, 33.

10. Other narratives in the Zohar begin with the same phrase (see Zohar 1:223a, 3:56b). It should be noted that the Idra Rabba is indeed understood to be a hallowed traditional text, recited ritually on Shavuot. On the source of the custom to recite the Idra Rabba on

Shavuot, see Liebes, *Studies in the Zohar*, 74–82 and related notes.

11. Liebes, *Studies in Zohar*, 11–12, 95–138; Asulin, "Qomatah Shel ha-Shekhinah," 120–138, 152–154. Asulin's suggestions are an important contribution to the attempt to describe the way in which the various drafts of the Idra were synthesized into a complete and closed work. Also see Sobol, *Transgression*, 19–36.

12. Moshe Idel, "Leviyatan u-Vat Zugo" [Leviathan and its consort], in *Ha-Mitos be-Yahadut: Historiah, Hegut, Sifrut* [Myths in Judaism: History, thought, literature], ed. Moshe Idel and Ithamar Gruenwald, 145–189 (Jerusalem: Zalman Shazar Center for Jewish History, 2004), esp. 157.

13. Zohar 3:128a; trans. Matt 8: 322. This is the verse that takes the reader into the Idra Rabba, as described in Chapter 8.

14. An example of this is the verses that treat the divine eyes. Verses containing the word "eye," in the singular, are applied to *'Attiqa*, while those containing "eyes" (*'eynayim*), the dual form, are interpreted as referring to *Ze'eir Anpin*. See Zohar 3:137a–b.

15. On the characteristics of Zoharic midrash, see Hellner-Eshed, *A River Flows from Eden*, 189–203.

16. See, for example, Zohar 3:138b.

17. See Hellner-Eshed, *A River Flows from Eden*, 202–203.

18. See Hellner-Eshed, *A River Flows from Eden*, 341–343.

19. Zohar 3:130b; trans. Matt 8:346. On "seen and not seen," see the section "Patience: The Nose," in Chapter 11.

20. Zohar 3:130b.

21. Zohar 1:94a, 2:15a, and elsewhere. On the loss of the experience of time, also see Hellner-Eshed, *A River Flows from Eden*, 300–302; and Omri Shasha, "'Milin La' 'Itgalyan 'Ela' Beinena": 'Al Sipur Kefar Tarsha' ve-'Ibudo" ['Words are revealed only among us': On the story of Kfar Tasha and its adaptation], in *Ha-Sipur ha-Zohari* [The zoharic story], ed. Yehuda Liebes, Jonatan M. Benarroch, and Melila Hellner-Eshed, 2:463–514 (Jerusalem: Ben-Zvi Institute, 2017).

22. Yehuda Liebes, "Myth vs. Symbolism in the Zohar and in Lurianic Kabbalah," in *Essential Papers on Kabbalah*, ed. Lawrence Fine (New York: New York University Press, 1995), 213.

23. Luzzatto, *Sefer Adir Ba-Marom*, 15a–b.

24. Cordovero, *Or Yaqar*, 21:28–30. See also his additional comments on the terrestrial Garden of Eden and the possibility of entering it in *Or Yaqar*, 11:65–66.

25. See BT Ḥagigah 14b–16a; and Song of Songs Rabbah 1:27.

26. For example, in his *Meccan Openings* (3:177), Ibn al-'Arabī says: "The *barzakh*-imagination is the cornerstone. The senses ascend to it, and spiritual essences descend to it [. . .] the *barzakh* [. . .] is the place between this world and the hereafter, this being the imaginal world. [. . .] In the imaginal realm of being, the imagination brings God into existence," quoted in Sara Sviri, *Ha-Sufim* [The Sufis: An anthology] (Tel Aviv: Tel Aviv University, 2008), 531–532 and related notes.

27. Ibn al-'Arabī, *Meccan Openings*, quoted in Henry Corbin, *Spiritual Body and Celestial Earth* (Princeton, NJ: Princeton University Press, 1989), 137.

28. Corbin, *Spiritual Body*, vii–xix; Henry Corbin, *Mundus Imaginalis, or the Imaginary and the Imaginal* (Ipswich: Golgonooza Press, 1976).

29. On the depiction of the Divine in human form in the imagination as a method of connecting and attaining union, and on the sacred imagination in Henry Corbin's thought, see Wolfson, "Sacred Space."

30. The Persian name of this medial dimension is *na-ḳoja-abad* or No-Where-Land. In Arabic, it is called *ʿālam al-mithāl*, the World of Likeness (or Image). See Moshe Idel, *Peraqim be-Qabalah Nevu'it* [Studies in ecstatic Kabbalah] (Jerusalem: Academon, 1990), 87–89, 107–109. As pointed out to me by Yehuda Liebes, the term *mithāl* also refers to the Platonic idea.

31. This mingling of dimensions occurs explicitly or implicitly in many other zoharic narratives. The words spoken by the Companions as they walk along the path, or during their gatherings by night, drive reality, setting it in motion in some mystical sense. See, for example, the story that occurs on the banks of the lake at Ginosar (Zohar 2:127–145b), or the story of Rav Hamnuna the Elder, told in the section of the Zohar called *Saba de-Mishpaṭim* (Zohar 2:94b–114a). For more on this topic, see Hellner-Eshed, *A River Flows from Eden*, 105–120, 321–326.

32. In a psychoanalytic context, this medial realm is similar to a degree to Winnicott's "potential space." In an infant's world, this is the imaginary playful space between union with the mother and the child's own separateness. This zone is perhaps the ground upon which something like the events of the Idra can be constructed. D. W. Winnicott, *Playing and Reality* (London: Routledge, 2017), 55, 128–139.

33. Chapter 8 presents a broad and detailed analysis of this scene and its various gestures.

34. Hellner-Eshed, *A River Flows from Eden*, 321–339. Indeed, in these stories, there are sublime moments that endanger the soul's continued existence within the body, sometimes necessitating the tempering or conclusion of a strong spiritual experience—as in the story of R. Eleazar and R. Abba (Zohar 1:5a–7b); the story of Kefar Ṭarsha (Zohar 1:92b–96b); and the story of bringing down rain (Zohar 3:59b–62b). But usually, summoning a different state of consciousness is achieved in a subtle and sometimes solemn way.

35. See the section "Ending 2: Fear of Revelation and the Deaths of the Companions," in Chapter 22.

36. For a broad discussion of this passage, see the section "Bearing Iniquity: The Second *Tiqqun*," in Chapter 12.

37. See the discussion of this passage in its broader context in the section "The Ceremonial Closing of the *Tiqqunim* of *ʿAttiqa*," in Chapter 12.

38. On the complex questions of the initiation aspect of the Idra, see the section "Ending 3: Validating the Assembly," in Chapter 22.

39. Zohar 3:129a; trans. Matt 8:336.

40. Zohar 3:129b; trans. Mat 8:339.

41. Zohar 3:132b; trans. Matt 8:358. See also the blessing addressed to Rabbi Yose after the *tiqqun* of *Ariḳh Anpin*'s nose, which treats the life-breath that emerges from it: "Your breath will find rest in the world that is coming!" (Zohar 3:130b; trans. Matt 8:344); the

blessing after the second *tiqqun* of *'Attiqa*'s beard: "Now the world is rendered fit. Blessed are you, Rabbi Ḥizkiyah, by the Ancient of Ancients!" (Zohar 3:132b; trans. Matt 8:359); and the blessing after the *tiqqun* of *'Attiq Yomin*'s throne, enacted by Rabbi Judah: "Your path and your seating are prepared by the Ancient of Days!" (Zohar 3:130a; trans. Matt 8:342).

42. In this context, we should note other places in the Zohar in which the Idra's theology is translated into religious praxis. An example is the request for an individual praying to direct the mind beyond the Divine King, into the Depths, the Source of all, the Wellspring (Zohar 2:63a, 3:69b–70a).

43. Ḥayyim Vital, *Sha'ar HaKavvanot*, Drushei Rosh HaShana, introduction.

44. An example that models this well is the important kabbalistic liturgical formulation, apparently originating in 16th-century Safed, recited before performing *mitsvot*: "In order to unify the Blessed Holy One and his *Shekhinah*, for the sake of the Hidden and Concealed One, in the name of all of Israel." The obvious meaning of this formulation is to evoke and connect the divine figures within the realm of daily religious discourse, before each and every *mitsvah*. But the fate of this formulation today is that most of those who recite it know only the beginning, and not the end "the Hidden and Concealed One." *'Attiqa Qaddisha* has been largely removed from this religious practice. See Moshe Hallamish, *Ha-Qabalah ba-tefila, be-halakha, u-v'minhag* [The Qabalah in prayer, law, and custom]. Ramat Gan: Bar Ilan University, 2002, 51–52, 58; and see Sack, *Me-Ma'ayyanot Sefer 'Alimah*, 70–72.

Chapter 6: Overarching Themes in the Idra Rabba

1. This was suggested by my teacher Moshe Idel, and I thank him for this insight.

2. This is in contradistinction to the Idra Zuṭa, which describes the affairs of the divine realm within time. Thus, at the climax of the Idra Zuṭa, Rabbi Shim'on transforms into a transpersonal figure of the High Priest, the human being who is adorned with the crowns of the *sefirah* of Foundation (*Yesod*). He is characterized by the phallus, which enacts the sexual coupling of the divine Male and Female, and of the Divine and the human.

3. BT Ḥagigah 13a.

4. Mishnah Ḥagigah 2:1.

5. Saying, for example, "By these words you will attain the world that is coming" (Zohar 3:143a; trans. Matt 8:442).

6. Zohar 3:143a; trans. Matt 8:441.

7. However, note this important difference between the Idra Rabba and the Idra Zuṭa: whereas the Idra Rabba focuses on describing the initial processes, the establishment and installation, of coming-into-being, the Idra Zuṭa tends to focus on the activation and maintenance of the system that has been installed.

8. On this myth, its various attestations, and their purposes throughout the Idra, see Chapters 9, 13, and 19.

9. For more on this topic, see Chapter 21, which is devoted to the process of sweetening Judgment as described in the concluding passages of the Idra.

10. On evil and the construction of evil in zoharic literature, see Berman's wonderful study, *Divine and Demonic in the Poetic Mythology of the Zohar*.

11. Zohar 3:128b; trans. Matt 8:329.

12. Hellner-Eshed, *A River Flows from Eden*, 340–351.

13. This point is further sharpened in light of the kabbalistic tradition in which the two divine faces appear as Male and Female. See Chapter 3. The Idra also differs from the main body of the Zohar in its characterization of masculine consciousness. *Ze'eir Anpin* is presented as more full of *Din* than the figures of the blessed Holy One or YHVH in the main body of the Zohar.

14. "Death will take the spectacular difference / between fire and water / and cast it to the abyss." Zelda, *The Spectacular Difference: Selected Poems of Zelda*, trans. Marcia Falk (Cincinnati, OH: Hebrew Union College Press, 2004), 221.

15. On *hieros gamos* between the *anima* and *animus*, see Carl Gustav Jung, *Symbols of Transformation: An Analysis of the Prelude to a Case of Schizophrenia* (New York: Pantheon Books, 1956), 243–244, 341–343. It should be noted that while in the Idra the separation occurs between the couple themselves, the process of individuation described by Jung and Neumann occurs between the child and mother or parent. See Erich Neumann, *Ha-Yeled: ha-'Ishiyut be-Shaḥar Hitpatḥutah*, trans. Yael Treiber (Beit Yehoshua: Hasinut, 2011), 33–66, originally published as *Das Kind: Struktur und Dynamik der werdenden Persönlichkeit*; and Neumann, *Ha-Adam ha-Misṭi* ["Mystical Man"].

Chapter 7: What Is the Idra Rabba Trying to Communicate?

1. On the relationship between the development of Kabbalah and earlier Jewish philosophy, see Idel, *Kabbalah: New Perspectives*.

2. For medieval attitudes toward the corporeality of the Divine, see Green, *Keter*, 88–105.

3. See Isadore Twersky, *Rabad of Posquières: A 12th Century Talmudist* (Cambridge, MA: Harvard University Press, 1962), 282–286.

4. Hassagah on Mishneh Torah, Hilchot Teshuvah 3:7, quoted in Twersky, *Rabad of Posquières*, 282.

5. See Gershom Scholem, "Shekhinah: The Feminine Element in Divinity," in *On the Mystical Shape of the Godhead*, 140–196 (New York: Schocken Books, 1991); Isaiah Tishby, *The Wisdom of the Zohar: An Anthology of Texts* (Oxford: Published for the Littman Library by Oxford University Press, 1989), 1:371–387; Arthur Green, "Bride, Spouse, Daughter: Images of the Feminine in the Classical Jewish Sources," in *The Heart of the Matter: Studies in Jewish Mysticism and Theology* (Philadelphia, PA: Jewish Publication Society, 2015), 75–86; Idel, *Kabbalah and Eros*; and Elliot Wolfson, *Circle in the Square: Studies in the Use of Gender in Kabbalistic Symbolism* (Albany: State University of New York Press, 1995.

6. See also, Zohar 3:137a; trans Matt 8:394–395: "[The whiteness] is like the white of the eyes when they are bathed in the white of the supernal eye. This the righteous are destined to see in the spirit of wisdom, as it is said: *For eye-to-eye they will see*."

7. See Chapter 3, "The Gaze."

8. The exaltation of the human form receives a picturesque articulation in the *tiqqun* of *Arikh Anpin*'s nose. From the nostrils of this nose, the world receives the breath of life. From one nostril, the breath enters *Ze'eir Anpin*, the divine "Adam"; from the other, it

enters the Messiah—the most perfect and whole human being. See Zohar 3:130b.

9. On this work by Cordovero, see Sack, *Be-Sha'arei ha-Qabalah*, 214–229; and Sack, *Me-Ma'ayyanot Sefer 'Alimah*, 203–213.

Chapter 8: Entering the Idra Rabba

1. My teacher Yehuda Liebes' seminal article *Ha-Mashiaḥ Shel ha-Zohar* (part of which has been translated as "The Messiah of the Zohar," in Liebes, *Studies in the Zohar*, 1–84) is primarily concerned with the messianic dimensions of Rabbi Shim'on bar Yoḥai and the Idra Rabba, but it is also a broad and penetrating commentary on this entire opening scene. Liebes' article models the many ways in which the opening passages of the Idra may be interpreted.

2. This verse has been included in keeping with the version of the Idra Rabba in Rabbi Moshe Cordovero's *Or Yaḳar*, 13:254.

3. On Rabbi Shim'on's opening statement, and in particular on the words "pillar" (*qayma*) and "base" (*samḳha*), see Liebes, *Studies in the Zohar,* 12–21. Liebes proposes several possible translations: "How long will we sit upon a single-based/pillared place (or position, situation, reality, mode of being, world, or foundation)." He also enumerates ten ways in which to understand this mode of being that is supported upon a single pillar. Recently, Liebes has offered another interpretation, according to which a "single pillar" refers to the conventional structure of the ten *sefirot*, from which Rabbi Shim'on sought to free himself by revealing divine mysteries of the Idra. See Liebes, "Shablonizaẓiah Ve-Heḥiyy'atah," 4.

4. In classical rabbinic literature, the expression "pillars of the world" may refer to the biblical patriarchs, teachers, and sages. See, for example, *Pirqe de-Rabbi Eli'ezer*, chap. 47; and *Yalquṭ Shim'oni*, Ruth 4:606. In the Zohar, the disciples are called "pillars" who must be erected or supported; see, for example, the narrative of R. Ḥiyya's initiation (Zohar 2:13a).

5. See BT Sukkah 45b; and BT Sanhedrin 97b. For the singular and unique character of Rabbi Shim'on in the Zohar, see Liebes, *Studies in the Zohar*, 12–19; Yehuda Liebes, "Mar'ish ha-Areẓ: Yeḥiduto Shel RaSHB"I" [Earth shaker: RaShBY's aloneness], in *Yahadut: Sugiyot, Qeta'im, Panim, Zehuyot* [Judaism, topics, fragments, faces, identities.], ed. Haviva Pedaya and Ephraim Meir, 337–357 (Beer Sheva: Ben-Gurion University of the Negev Press, 2007); Huss, *Zohar: Reception and Impact*; and Hellner-Eshed, *A River Flows from Eden*, 31–61.

6. BT Ḥagigah 12b.

7. *Sefer ha-Bahir*, 102.

8. For examples, see Zohar 1:186a. On the *tsaddiq*/pillar, see Joseph Gikatilla *Gates of Light: Sha'are Orah*, trans. Avi Weinstein (Walnut Creek, CA: Altamira Press), 55–114. See also, Arthur Green, "The Zaddiq as *Axis Mundi* in Later Judaism," in *The Heart of the Matter: Studies in Jewish Mysticism and Theology*, 204–222 (Philadelphia, PA: Jewish Publication Society, 2015). See also, Scholem, *On the Mystical Shape of the Godhead*, 89–115.

9. For example, see Zohar 1:225a; 3:9a; 3:62a–b. See also, Liebes, *Studies in the Zohar*, 12–19; and Hellner-Eshed, *A River Flows from Eden*, 37–51, 245–249.

10. These two interpretive possibilities are placed side by side in the Babylonian Talmud (Berakhot 63a). For the interpretation of the verse in the various places that it is cited

in the Idra, see Liebes, *Studies in the Zohar,* 175n99; and Liebes, "Zohar ve-'Eros," 72n34.

11. A clear example of such a violation for religious motivations (*for YHVH*) was the decision to record the Oral Torah in writing, an act motivated by a fear of forgetting, despite the traditional proscription against the practice. See BT Giṭṭin 60a.

12. BT Berakhot 63a. See also the subsequent discussion of Hillel's words and Rabbi Shim'on bar Yoḥai's reference to them in the Palestinian Talmud. In this context, also consider the talmudic account of the emergency gathering in Yavneh after the destruction of the Temple, at which the sages are terrified that the Torah will be forgotten. In response, Rabbi Shim'on bar Yoḥai expresses his trust in the eternal bond between Israel and the Torah. See BT Shabbat 138b: "When our rabbis entered the Vineyard at Yavneh they said: The Torah will be forgotten by Israel! Rabbi Shim'on b. Yoḥai says: God forfend that the Torah will be forgotten by Israel, as it is written: *For it shall never be forgotten from his seed's mouth* (Deut. 31:21)."

13. For a discussion of the additional interpretation of this verse in the Idra as well as its use in the works of Maimonides and other sections of the Zohar, see the section "Time to Act for YHVH—Deepening the Interpretation," later in this chapter.

14. Mishnah Avot 2:15 reads as follows: "Rabbi Tarfon says: The day is short, the work is much, the laborers are slothful, the reward is great, and the Master of the house is pressing." Cf. the similar formulation that appears in the New Testament, in Jesus' statement to seventy emissaries before they depart on their mission (Luke, 10:2). Similarly, Rabbi Shim'on's reference to the herald corresponds with Mishnah Avot 6:2: "Rabbi Joshua b. Levi says: Each and every day, a heavenly voice [*bat qol*] goes forth from Mount Horeb, and proclaims as follows: *Woe to the creatures* [i.e., human beings], *due to the humiliation of the Torah!*"

15. For the various voices in the Zohar, alluded to here in the Idra, see Hellner-Eshed, *A River Flows from Eden*, 204–217.

16. Liebes, *Studies in the Zohar*, 175n99.

17. For example, see BT Ḥagigah 14a; BT Qiddushin 30b; Be-Midbar Rabbah 11:3; and so on.

18. For example, see Zohar 2:51a, 3:59b. Cf., in particular, with Rabbi Shim'on's call to gather the great scholars of the Hebrew Bible to arise and go to battle for the *Sheḵhinah*: *Tiqqunei Zohar* 61a (*tiqqun* 21). On this, see Roi, *Love of the Sheḵhina*, 137–308.

19. Proverbs 18:21: *Death and life are in the power of the tongue.*

20. See BT 'Arakhin 15b; Kaplan, *Sefer Yetzirah* 6:8; Liebes, "Zohar ve-'Eros," 71–72; and Liebes, *Torat ha-Yeẓirah*, 144–148.

21. PT Berakhot 68a. Also see the parallel in the Tosefta Berakhot 6:30.

22. The source of this formulation is Rabbi Yoḥannan b. Zakkai's statement (in Hebrew) in the Mishnah Kelim 17:16: "Woe if I say! Woe if I do not say!" On crying in the Zohar, see Eitan Fishbane, "Tears of Disclosure: The Role of Weeping in Zoharic Narrative," *Journal of Jewish Thought & Philosophy* 11, no. 1 (2002): 25–47; and Oded Yisraeli, *Parshanut ha-Sod ve-Sod ha-Parshanut: Megamot Midrashiot ve-Hermenuitiot be-'Sava de-Mishpatim' she-be-Zohar* [The interpretation of secrets and the secret of interpretation: Midrashic and hermeneutic strategies in Sabba de-Mishpatim of the Zohar] (Los Angeles: Cherub Press, 2005), 52–54, 97–105.

23. On the dialectic between revelation and concealment of secrets in the context of the Idra, see, for example, Liebes, *Studies in the Zohar*, 26–30. On *eros* and esotericism in general, see Wolfson's fascinating article "Murmuring Secrets," which also addresses this particular passage in the Idra, 91–92; and Hellner-Eshed, *A River Flows from Eden*, 155–188.

24. See Idel, *Kabbalah: New Perspectives*, 210–215, 250–256; Moshe Idel, *Shelemuyot Bol'ot: Qabalah ve-Parshanut* [Absorbing perfections: Kabbalah and interpretation] (Tel Aviv: Yediot Aharonot, 2012), 396–417; Halbertal, *Seter ve-Gilluy*, esp. 63–69; Haviva Pedaya, "Zeman Ma'agali ve-Zeman Qavvi: Ha-'Em ha-Gedolah ve-ha-'Em ha-Qetanah, ha-Shekhinah; Ben Ḥug ha-RaMBa"N le-Ḥug ha-Zohar" [Circular time and linear time: The Great Mother and the Small Mother, the Shekhinah in the circle of Nahmanides and the circle of the Zohar], in *Shedamot ve-Ruaḥ: Maḥavvat Hoqarah ve-Yedidut le-'Avraham Shapira'* [Fields in the wind: A tribute to Avraham Shapira, in friendship and appreciation], ed. Avihu Zakai, Paul Mendes-Flohr, and Zeev Gries, 322–337 (Jerusalem: Carmel Press, 2015); and Daniel Matt, "New/Ancient Words: The Aura of Secrecy in the Zohar," in *Gershom Scholem's Major Trends in Jewish Mysticism 50 Years After: Proceedings of the Sixth International Conference on the History of Jewish Mysticism*, ed. Peter Schäfer and Joseph Dan, 181–207 (Tübingen: J.C.B. Mohr, 1993); and Huss, *Zohar: Reception and Impact.*

25. Genesis 45:1–4.

26. See the series of interpretations of the verse *Joseph could no longer restrain himself* (Genesis 45:1) in Zohar 1:208a.

27. See BT Ḥagigah 3b; and BT Soṭah 4b. On the use of this verse, see Liebes, *Studies in the Zohar*, 34–37 and related notes.

28. See Liebes, *Studies in the Zohar*, 34–37 and related notes; and Hellner-Eshed, *A River Flows from Eden*, 63–67.

29. BT Ḥagigah 14b.

30. For a discussion of Rabbi Shim'on's statements, see the section "Ending 4: Legitimizing a Smaller Circle of Companions," in Chapter 22.

31. On various possibilities concerning the location and identification of the Idra de-Vei Mashkena (Assembly of the Dwelling [i.e., the Tabernacle]), see the section "Idra Literature in the Zohar," in Chapter 1, n7.

32. Zohar 3:144b; trans. Matt 8:454.

33. This interpretation may possibly explain the condition of Ben Zoma, one of the four who entered the Orchard, about whom it is said "he glimpsed and was harmed." See Yehuda Liebes, *Ḥet'o Shel 'Elisha': 'Arba'ah she-Nikhnesu le-Pardes ve-Tiv'ah Shel ha-Mistiqah ha-Talmudit* [The sin of Elisha: Four entered the orchard and the nature of talmudic mysticism] (Jerusalem: Academon, 1990), 111–129.

34. For a broad discussion of the deaths of the Companions at the end of the Idra, see the section "Ending 2: Fear of Revelation and the Deaths of the Companions," in Chapter 22.

35. Rabbi Moses Ḥayyim Luzzatto, the 18th-century Italian kabbalist, exhibits tremendous mystical sensitivity in his attempt to diagnose "entering but not emerging" as a state of consciousness, distinguishing it from the consciousness of one who has "entered and emerged." In his opinion, "emerging in peace" refers to an individual who exits the consciousness of the Orchard in the appropriate manner—through the portal through which

the individual entered: i.e., *Shekhinah*, the *sefirah* of Sovereignty (*Malkhut*). In contrast, the soul of one who "enters but does not emerge" remains within the Garden, Orchard, or divine psychic dimension, but as a result loses its spiritual inspiration. In such a case, one finds oneself spiritually excluded from the Orchard, without actually having exited it through the entryway. The loss of inspiration in the course of the process is that which precludes the appropriate and necessary emergence. See Luzzatto, *Sefer Adir Ba-Marom*, 21a–b. See also Erich Neumann's distinction between disintegrative mystical experience, which tears a person away from the human, and transformative mysticism, which entails entering into divine emptiness but also *returning* from this state that validates and affirms the world. See Neumann, *Ha-Adam ha-Misṭi* ["Mystical Man"], 50–54.

36. See Jonathan Z. Smith, *Map Is Not Territory* (Chicago: University of Chicago Press, 1978).

37. On gestures and their role in Zoharic literature, see Eitan Fishbane, *The Art of Mystical Narrative: A Poetics of the Zohar* (Oxford: Oxford University Press, 2018), 54–127.

38. See Hellner-Eshed, *A River Flows from Eden*, 111–120.

39. For more on the various appearances of the field in the Idra, both in the narrative frame and in the *tiqqunim* themselves, see Sobol, *Transgression*, 100–103.

40. See BT Yevamot 34b.

41. In his commentary on the Idra Rabba, R. Moses Ḥayyim Luzzatto develops this theme with great profundity. In his opinion, since the time was not yet ripe for bringing the potent divine influx down from the upper realms, the Companions had to gather and ascend together in their minds to the place that opens into the expanses of the divine world. Foundation (*Yesod*) of the Female, the sexual organ of the *Shekhinah*, the Garden of Eden—this is the place from which the *tiqqun* must begin, and it is symbolized by the field in which the Companions gather. See Luzzatto, *Sefer Adir Ba-Marom*, 15a–b.

42. So read most of the manuscripts. According to a variant that appears in the printed editions, Rabbi Shim'on asks those present to place their hand upon their own breast.

43. See Rashi's commentary on Genesis 24:2: "*Under my thigh*—for one who makes an oath must take a sacred object in one's hand, such as a scroll of the Torah or phylacteries, and circumcision was [Abraham's] first *mitsvah*, was attained at the cost of great pain, and was very dear to him, so [his servant] took it [in his hand]." In the account of the adjuration in the Idra, one might interpret the term *toqpoi* not in its usual sense in Aramaic as "breast," but rather as a reference to the organ in which a man's strength and might (*toqef, toqpo*) resides.

44. *Sefer HaZohar* (Jerusalem: Hotza'at Mossad haRav Kook, 1984), 3:127b.

45. In a somewhat similar fashion, Shifra Asulin has suggested that here we see a polemic against other works that are close to the Idra in spirit but in which an anthropomorphic conception prevails, such as those of Joseph of Hamadan. See Asulin, "Ha-Havnayah ha-Kefulah Shel Demut ha-Shekhinah"; and Asulin, "Ha-Pegam ve-Tiquno," 223.

46. On the tense and dialectical relationship between the Zohar's understanding that conceiving the Divine in personal and corporeal likeness is the apogee of religious and spiritual activity, and its contrasting position that one must beware of depicting this likeness physically, see Wolfson, "Iconicity of the Text," 232–234.

47. Liebes, *Studies in the Zohar*, 23–26. Liebes notes that innovative interpretations lacking a proper source are also linked to sexual transgressions. See also, Liebes, "Zohar ve-'Eros," 88–89; and Matt, "New/Ancient Words."

48. Sobol, "Ḥativat ha-'Idrot be-Sifrut ha-Zohar" [The Idra stratum in Zoharic literature] (PhD diss., Tel Aviv University, 2011), 132–134.

49. See the discussion in the section "The Idra Rabba's Manifesto: A Call to Heal and Renew the Face of Jewish Religion," in Chapter 7.

50. Tosefta Ḥagigah 2:2.

51. This is how Elliot Wolfson understands the passage. See Wolfson, *Iconicity of the Text*, 232–242.

52. See *Guide for the Perplexed*, prologue to part I. Also see, Halbertal, *Maimonides*, 286–288; and Goodman, *Sodotav Shel Moreh ha-Nevukhim*, 21–23.

53. For example, see Zohar 1:116a and 2:155b. For a similar interpretation, see Gikatilla, *Gates of Light: Sha'are Orah*, 60–63.

54. This account is based on the midrashic motif of the primordial Torah, or Wisdom, that preceded the world, and into which the holy Ancient One gazed before creating the world. See Bereshit Rabbah 1:1.

55. Liebes, "Zohar ve-'Eros," 72.

56. Zohar 3:138b–139a; trans. Matt 8:407–408.

57. On the relationship between Rabbi Shim'on, Rabbi El'azar, and Rabbi Abba and the three divine *partsufim*, and also the three *sefirot* of Wisdom (*Ḥokhmah*), Understanding (*Binah*), and Knowledge (*da'at*), see Liebes, *Studies in the Zohar*, 19–22 and related notes (where he also discusses the connection to the Christian Trinity).

58. For various aspects of love (*ḥavivuta*) in the Idra Rabba, see Liebes, *Studies in the Zohar*, 37–43.

59. Rudolf Otto, *The Idea of the Holy: An Inquiry into the Non-rational Factor in the Idea of the Divine and Its Relation to the Rational* (New York: Oxford University Press, 1958).

60. For the figure of Habakkuk in the Zohar, see Melila Hellner-Eshed, "Ha-Meqane' le-Brit ve-Ba'al ha-Shigyonot; 'Eliyahu ve-Ḥabaquq be-Zohar: 'Al ha-Zikhri ve-ha-Niqbi be-Nefesh ha-'Adam" [The zealot of the covenant and the ecstatic Elijah and Habakkuk in the Zohar: On the masculine and feminine in the human psyche], *Kabbalah* 22 (2011): 169–180, 189–192. On the verse from Habakkuk and its various interpretations, see Liebes, *Studies in the Zohar*, 34–37.

61. This interpretation appears in the context of the *tiqqun* of *Ze'eir Anpin*'s ears (Zohar 3:138b, section 30). For the interpretation, see the section "A Prayer for Ze'eir Anpin's Life," in Chapter 4.

62. Yehuda Liebes devotes an entire article to the theme of *eros* in zoharic literature. See Liebes, "Zohar ve-'Eros."

63. See Hellner-Eshed, *A River Flows from Eden*, 107–110.

64. On this zoharic narrative, see Hellner-Eshed, *A River Flows from Eden*, 245–247; and Ronit Meroz, "Reqimato Shel Mitos: Diyun be-Shenei Sipurim ba-Zohar" [The weaving of a myth: The analysis of two zoharic homilies on the Shekhina and their narrative context], in *Limud ve-Da'at be-Maḥshavah Yehudit* [Study and knowledge in Jewish

thought], ed. Howard Kreisel, 2:167–205 (Beer Sheva: Ben-Gurion University of the Negev Press, 2006).

65. In the Pritzker edition of the Zohar (3:128a; trans. Matt 8:323), we see only two verses:, one expressing God's love for humans, and the second expressing humanity's love for God.

66. Cordovero, *Or Yaqar*, 13:254.

67. On the *faithful of spirit*, see Liebes, *Studies in the Zohar*, 25–26. More recently, Liebes has suggested that the tension between the *faithful of spirit* and *one who goes about gossiping* reflects the author's critique of the free and associative style of the *tiqqunim* stratum within the Zohar. See Liebes, "Shablonizaẓiah Ve-Heḥiyy'atah," 5.

68. On the secret in late antiquity and medieval thought, see Moshe Halbertal, *Concealment and Revelation: Esotericism in Jewish Thought and Its Philosophical Implications* (Princeton, NJ: Princeton University Press, 2007). On the secret and esotericism in Kabbalah, see Scholem, *Reshit ha-Qabbalah*, 18–24; Gershom Scholem, *Major Trends in Jewish Mysticism* (New York: Schocken Books, 1991), 20–23; Idel, *Kabbalah: New Perspectives*, 253–256; Elliot R. Wolfson, "Occultation of the Feminine and the Body of Secrecy in Medieval Kabbalah," in *Rending the Veil: Concealment and Revelation of Secrets in the History of Religions*, ed. Elliot R. Wolfson, 113–154 (New York: Seven Bridges Press, 1999); and Wolfson, "Murmuring Secrets," 65–77. On the secret in the Zohar, see Liebes, *Studies in the Zohar*, 23–37; and Hellner-Eshed, *A River Flows from Eden*, 155–188.

69. Gikatilla, *Gates of Light: Sha'are Orah*, second gate, ninth sphere 129; translation by Avi Weinstein.

70. This observation was made by Yehuda Liebes, and I thank him for this insight.

71. At times the Zohar even emphasizes that heaven and earth, invoked by Moses as the foundations of the world, are themselves supported by that Covenant. For example, see Zohar 1:32b.

72. Liebes, *Studies in the Zohar*, 4; Liebes, "Ha-Mashiaḥ Shel ha-Zohar" [The Messiah of the Zohar], in *The Messianic Idea in Israel* (Jerusalem: National Israeli Academy of Sciences, 1982), 105–107; Hellner-Eshed, *A River Flows from Eden*, 37–41, 44–48; Huss, *Zohar: Reception and Impact*.

73. Corresponding with the Work of Creation (*Ma'aseh Bereshit*).

74. Corresponding with the Work of the Chariot (*Ma'aseh Merkavah*).

75. On transformation mysticism, and on the processes of training and initiation that enable a person to come into contact with the numinous, see Neumann, *Ha-Adam ha-Misṭi* ["Mystical Man"], 60.

Chapter 9: The Kings of Edom: The First Appearance

1. I am referring to Jorge Luis Borges' story "Tlön, Uqbar, Orbis Tertius," in *Ficciones*, ed. Anthony Kerrigan, trans. Alastair Reed, 17–35 (New York, Grove Press: 1962).

2. On the myth of the kings of Edom, see Liebes, *Ha-Mashiah shel HaZohar*, 219–221; and Liebes, *Studies in the Zohar*, 65–67, 134–135; Liebes, *Torat ha-Yeẓirah*, 136–140; Yose Yarḥi, "Ma'amar 'Aseret Harugei Malkhut ve-Mot ha-Melakhim she-me-Ketivat Yad ha-'AR"I; Hebetim Shel Torat ha-Gilgul be-Me'ot ha-Shelosh Esrei la-Shesh Esrei" [The

exegesis on the Ten Martyrs and the death of the kings from the original writings of the Ari: Aspects of the theory of Gilgul between the 14th and the 16th centuries] (master's thesis, Hebrew University, 1995); Har-Shefi, *Malkhin Qadma'in*; and Giller, *Reading the Zohar*, 89–158. On this myth in pre-zoharic literature, see Idel, *Ha-Maḥshavah ha-Ra'ah shel ha-El*; and Har-Shefi, *Malkhin Qadma'in*, 225–227. For the relationship between the Death of the Kings and the question of the origins of evil in early Kabbalah, see Asi Farber-Ginat, "Qelipah Qodemet le-Peri" [The husk precedes the fruit], in *Ha-Mitos be-Yahadut* [Mythos in Judaism], ed. Haviva Pedaya, 118–142 (Jerusalem: Bialik Institute, 1996).

3. Chapters 13 and 19 of this book are dedicated to the additional attestations of this myth within the Idra.

4. Har-Shefi, *Malkhin Qadma'in*. For critique of the cathartic conception that was dominant in Kabbalah scholarship in general, and for a new inquiry into the construction of evil in the Zohar, see Berman, *Divine and Demonic*.

5. Alongside this curiosity about beginnings, we find in post-biblical literature (as, for example, in the book of *Ben Sira*) and midrash a growing tendency to create boundaries attempting to limit the human impulse to explore the origins of creation and human existence.

6. Zohar 3:292b; trans. Matt 9:809.

7. This passage is cited, along with a thorough discussion (comparing it with the motif of the Death of the Kings, among other things), in Farber-Ginat, "Qelipah Qodemet le-Peri," 133–138. For more on this passage, see Haviva Pedaya, *Ha-RaMBa"N: Hit'alut: Zeman Maḥzori ve-Teqst Qadosh* [Nahmanides: Cyclical time and holy text] (Tel Aviv: Am Oved, 2003), 417.

8. BT Bava Batra 74b. On the evolution of this myth, see Idel, "Leviyatan u-Vat Zugo"; Esther Liebes, "Qordovero ve-ha-'AR"I: Beḥinah Meḥudeshet Shel Mitos Mot Malkhei 'Edom" [Cordovero and Luria], in *Ma'ayan 'Ein Ya'aqov le-R. Mosheh Qordovero* [The *'Ein Ya'aqov* Spring of Rabbi Moses Cordovero], ed. Bracha Sack (Beer Sheva: Ben-Gurion University of the Negev Press, 2008), 41–43; Michael Fishbane, *Biblical Myth and Rabbinic Mythmaking* (Oxford: Oxford University Press, 2005), 115–116; and Pedaya, *Ha-RaMBa"N*, 291–296. Note that Sifra di-Tsni'uta itself draws a connection between the kings of Edom and the mythic creatures—the great reptiles and sea serpents—whose power lies in their opposition to cosmic order.

9. Several studies have been written on the myth of the kings of Edom in the works of Cordovero and Luria. See Liebes, "Qordovero ve-ha-'AR"I," and the extensive review of earlier research therein; and Fine, *Physician of the Soul*, 131–138.

10. Isaiah Tishby, *Paths of Faith and Heresy* [in Hebrew] (Jerusalem: Hebrew University Magnes Press, 1982).

11. For an analysis of the myth of the kings in Sifra di-Tsni'uta, see Har-Shefi, *Malkhin Qadma'in*, 230–232.

12. Scholem, *On the Mystical Shape of the Godhead*, 48–49. See also his illuminating observations on the motif of the scales in the works of Dionysius the Areopagite.

13. Liebes, *Torat ha-Yeẓirah*, 134.

14. Liebes, *Torat ha-Yeẓirah*, 136–137.

15. Liebes, *Torat ha-Yeẓirah*, 137: "These 'kings,' thoughts that never became actions, were indeed nullified, but they did not disappear entirely from the world. After the Creator was 'configured' [or 'adorned,' *nitqan*], he himself configures and heals them, finding a place for them within established existence. Into those scales [. . .] come the kings who died to be weighed, all of those ideas that arose in [the Creator's] mind and never became actions [lit., weighed upon it were those who did not exist], some of which will ultimately become actions and be integrated into the created world, and some of which will remain as empty thoughts: 'Upon it rose and upon it rise those who were not, and who were, and who will be'" (citing Sifra di-Tsni'uta, Zohar 2:176b; trans. Matt 5:535).

16. It should be noted that Liebes showed that the interpretations that develop the myth of the kings in the Idra *Rabba* are entirely unattested in the works of Moses de León. Nor do they stem from the works of other kabbalists in the Zohar circle, in particular David ben Judah he-Ḥasid's *Sefer ha-Gevul*, a Hebrew reworking of the Idra. Given this finding, he concluded that the interpretations concerning the kings of Edom were interpolated into the Idra only in the final stages of its redaction. See Liebes, *Studies in the Zohar*, 127–129; and Yehuda Liebes, "Shenat Petirato Shel R. Mosheh De Li'on," in *Sefer ha-Zikaron le-Me'ir Benayahu* [Meir Benayahu—Memorial volume], ed. Moshe Bar-Asher et al., 745–750 (Jerusalem: Carmel Press, 2019).

17. See Haviva Pedaya's discussion of the veil and the screen in Jewish esotericism. Pedaya, *Ha-Mar'eh ve-ha-Dibur*, 245–255.

18. See Chapter 13.

Chapter 10: *Arikh Anpin*: Origins

1. For more on the face of God in pre-kabbalistic Jewish sources, see Chapter 2.

2. For example, see the Song of Songs Rabbah (5:10): "R. Ḥunia in the name of Resh Laqish: By two thousand years did the Torah precede the creation of the world. What is the basis [of this position]? *I was with Him, as a nursling; daily (yom yom) did I delight* (Proverbs 8:30). The day (*yom*) of the blessed Holy One is one thousand years, as it is said: *A thousand years in Your sight is like a passing day* [. . .] (Psalms 90:4)." See also, Genesis Rabbah 1:1.

3. See Zohar 3:20b.

4. The text is here presented as two separate teachings ("it has been taught"). Thus, despite the fact that the teaching that refers to *'Attiqa*'s ascent into the curtain precedes the teaching that recounts the Torah's counsel, one can understand the advice to have come before the ascent and thus to have initiated the ascent.

5. Ronit Meroz has noted the connections between the zoharic corpus and formulations for the Book of Daniel. See Ronit Meroz, *Yuvalei Zohar: Meḥqar u-Mahadurot Shel Zohar, Parashat Shemot* [Headwaters of the Zohar: Analysis & annotated critical edition of Parashat Exodus of the Zohar] (Tel Aviv: Tel Aviv University Press, 2019).

6. Scholem, *On the Mystical Shape of the Godhead*, 45–46.

7. The detail and fantastic numerosity we find here is also found in an earlier strata of Jewish mysticism in the Hekhalot literature and is ubiquitous in the ancient writings of Hinduism and Buddhism.

8. Mishnah Avot 2:6.

9. Joseph ben Abraham Gikatilla, *Sha'arei Tsedeq*, sec. 10, 104b.

10. Entities external to *'Attiqa* are also described as "skulls" (*gulgoltin*), perhaps also conveying the sense of "spheres" (*galgalim*): "From this skull emerges one white route to the skull of *Ze'eir Anpin*, enhancing the head, and from here to other skulls of those below without number. Each skull offers a payment of tribute to the Ancient of Days as they come to be numbered under the scepter. Corresponding to this, *a beqa per skull* (Exodus 38:26) below when they come to be numbered" (Zohar 3:128b; trans. Matt 8:330).

11. Plotinus, *Enneads*, 5:117.

Chapter 11: *Arikh Anpin*: Features of the Face

1. Hillel Zeitlin, *Be-Pardes ha-Qabalah ve-ha-Ḥasidut* [In the orchard of Qabalah and Ḥasidut] (Tel Aviv: Yavneh, 1982), 211.

2. Zohar 3:127a–b. So it appears in MS Escorial G-1-15, MS Vatican 186 (though it is not included in the portion of *Naso*), and other manuscript sources. I thank my friend Merav Carmeli for this information. For this entire zoharic passage, possible interpretations of it, and its relationship to the Idra Rabba, see Liebes, *Studies in the Zohar*, 119–126.

3. The Idra states: "as is written: *so that Your ears may be open*" (Zohar 3:129a; trans. Matt 8:333). There is no such verse in the Hebrew Bible, and this seems to be a paraphrase (or "correction") of 1 Kings 8:52: *May Your eyes be open to the supplication of Your servant, and to the supplication of Your people Israel, to listen to them whensoever they cry unto You.* This may have been conflated with another verse: *YHVH, hear my voice, let Your ears be attentive to the voice of my supplications* (Psalms 130:2); or alternatively: *My God, incline Your ear and hear, open Your eyes, and behold* [. . .] (Daniel 9:18).

4. For a discussion of the passage on the path on *Ze'eir Anpin*'s head (Zohar 3:136a), see the section "The Pathway: Marking Binary Existence," in Chapter 15.

5. In the Idra, the term "face" (*appayim*) itself sometimes refers more narrowly to the forehead, as in the verses, *By the sweat of your brow* (*appekha*) *shalt thou eat bread* (Genesis 3:19); and *he fell down with his brow* (*appayim*) *to the earth* (Genesis 19:1).

6. This substance is called *netsaḥ* (eternity, victory, lifeblood), following biblical usage. See Isaiah 63:3–6. See also, Zohar 3:136b for further idraic interpretations concerning *Ze'eir Anpin*'s forehead.

7. "Israel above" is *Ze'eir Anpin*, and *Arikh Anpin* is his guardian.

8. In another passage in the Zohar that bears a strong affinity with the Idra (Zohar 2:122b), the cleansing of *Ze'eir Anpin*'s eyes is described as bathing in milk, flowing from the breasts of the Mother, who is illuminated by *'Attiqa*. See the section "The Face's Healing," in Chapter 3.

9. Yehuda Liebes, "Zemirot le-Se'udot Shabat she-Yasad ha-'AR"I ha-Qadosh" [The Sabbath table songs established by R. Isaac Luria], *Molad* 4, no. 23 (1972): 540–555.

10. See Mishnah Yevamot 16:3; BT Bekhorot 46b; and BT Yevamot 120a, with Rashi's commentary. See also, Nahmanides' commentary on Leviticus 21:18.

11. Zohar 3:294a; trans. Matt 9:824.

12. In Aramaic *pardashqa*, apparently derived from the rabbinic term *pardesqin*

(Mishnah Oholot 6:7; and Ovadiah of Bertinoro's commentary: "Hollow columns placed in the house walls").

13. See Zohar 3:289a (Idra Zuṭa).

14. This echoes the interpretation attributed to Rabbi Akiva, focused on the plurality of thrones mentioned in the verses describing God in the Book of Daniel 7:9. Rabbi Akiva interprets the plural form as a reference to two thrones: one connected to the divine realm, and the other for King David, the Messiah. This exegesis aroused the ire of Rabbi Yose, who objected that this inappropriately blurs the boundaries between the human and the Divine. See BT Ḥagigah 14a. Without doubt, the Idra here aligns itself with Rabbi Akiva and develops upon his position. See Liebes, *'Alilot 'Elohim*, 143.

15. The Idra appears to omit the mouth, which we might have expected here after the descriptions (moving down the face) of the forehead, eyes, and nose. However, the mouth is still to come, for the Idra considers it to be part of the beard.

16. See Zohar 2:34a.

Chapter 12: Arraying *Arikh Anpin's* Beard

1. A testament to the fact that the biblical accounts of a divine face had become etched in the minds of Jewish readers is Maimonides' program, spanning many pages of his *Guide for the Perplexed*, to provide a new and innovative interpretation of these biblical descriptions, freeing them of their physical sense and replacing it with a metaphorical understanding.

2. In the Idra, the beard encompasses all of the hair-covered parts of the lower portion of the face.

3. The good and pleasant quality of the Companions' dwelling together also arises from the flow of oil—the bounteous flow reaches them after emerging from *'Attiqa*'s head, passing over his garments or attributes (*middot*; i.e., the divine *sefirot* or *partsufim*). For the important role of this chapter of the Psalms in the zoharic narrative of bringing rain (Zohar 3:59b–64b), which focuses strikingly on the theme of communal dwelling and love among the Companions, see Meroz, "Reqimato Shel Mitos," 174 and notes. In that narrative, the account of "brethren dwelling together in unity" represents both the coupling of the divine Male and Female, and the coupling of the cherubs in the Holy of Holies.

4. "'[*A*] *good name from fine oil* (Ecclesiastes 7:1)! For the Holy Name issues from oil, kindling holy lamps. What is this oil? As is written: *A river issues from Eden to water the garden* (Genesis 2:10).' Rabbi Yitsḥak said, 'As is written: *like precious oil on the head* [. . .] (Psalms 133:2).' Rabbi El'azar said: 'These are mountains of pure balsam.' Rabbi Shim'on said, '*A good name* (Ecclesiastes 7:1)—how good is the supernal Name of holy lamps, all of which glow *from fine oil*, as I have said'" (Zohar 2:87b; trans. Matt 4:496). See also, Hellner-Eshed, *A River Flows from Eden*, 229–251.

5. See, for example, BT Yevamot 80b; BT Shabbat 152a; and Rashi on BT Shabbat 50b, among other instances.

6. "Now, you might say, 'The beard is nowhere to be found, and Solomon said only *his cheeks* (Song of Songs 5:13), never mentioning a beard.' However, we have learned as follows in the Concealment of the Book: All that is concealed and hidden away—not

mentioned or revealed—is most sublime and precious of all, precisely because it is concealed and hidden. Since the beard is the praise and precious perfection of the face, Scripture treasured it away, and it remains unrevealed" (Zohar 3:139a; trans. Matt 8:408). Also, an awareness of this absence is already evident in Sifra di-Tsni'uta: "The beard of faith is not mentioned for it is Glory of all" (Zohar 2:177a; trans. Matt 5:537).

7. See Liebes, *Studies in the Zohar*, 62–63 and related notes.

8. As stated by the rabbis: "Glory of the face—a beard; joy of the heart—a wife; YHVH's portion—children." BT Shabbat 152a.

9. Zohar 3:131a. This statement is presented as a citation from Sifra di-Tsni'uta, but it does not appear in that work in its present form. See Liebes, *Studies in the Zohar*, 187n176. In a personal conversation with the author, Liebes noted an interesting parallel between extending the hand into the beard in the Idra, and the account of the *Iliad*'s warriors who, when captured during war, touch the beard of their captor while pleading for their lives. See, for example, *Iliad*, 10.454–455.

10. See Targum Pseudo-Jonathan, Rashi, and Ibn Ezra on Genesis 24:2, and Genesis 47:29 with its commentators. See also the section "The Adjuration and the Curse" and note 43, in Chapter 8.

11. There is indeed a similar formulation in Sifra di-Tsni'uta (Zohar 2:177a).

12. See PT Avodah Zarah 18b; Bereshit Rabbah 62:2; and BT Ta'anit 25a.

13. The formulation "some are manifested on the seventh in the world," brought in our Idra Rabba text as a citation from Sifra di-Tsni'uta, refers to the seventh month, Tishrei. This is made explicit in Sifra di-Tsni'uta following the thirteen *tiqqunim*: "When Tishrei, the seventh month, arrives, these thirteen appear in the supernal world and thirteen gates of Compassion open" (Zohar 2:177a; trans. Matt 5:537, emended).

14. In the discussion of the third *tiqqun* of *Ze'eir Anpin*'s beard, I also briefly discuss the third *tiqqun* of *'Attiqa*'s beard. See the section "Judgment in Duality, Blushing Red: A Path, Lips, and Rounded Cheeks in the Third and Fifth *Tiqqunim*," in Chapter 16.

15. See the section "The Ancient of Days," in Chapter 10.

16. This is indeed one of the basic meanings of the term *el* in biblical Hebrew. Cf. Deuteronomy 28:32.

17. Zohar 3:132a; trans. Matt 8:356.

18. As Art Green has pointed out, the early kabbalistic designation of ןוילע רתכ (*Keter 'Elyon*, Supernal Crown) as the first *sefirah* meant that it was higher than all the other crowns (personal correspondence with the author). See also, Green, *Keter*, 151–165.

19. Zohar 3:288a.

20. See Liebes, *Studies in the Zohar*, 100–103. There is some resemblance between this episode and the narrative of Ben Zoma, one of the four who entered the Orchard (*ha-pardes*), who "glimpsed and was harmed." The Talmud relates that, after emerging from the Orchard, his teacher Rabbi Yehoshua found him contemplating the second day of creation, sinking deep into a vision of the work of creation. See BT Ḥagigah 15a. Ben Zoma contemplates the work of creation in the Talmud, while in the Zohar Rabbi Ḥizkiyah's vision focuses on the Work of the Chariot. Perhaps their unmediated contact with the depths of the divine realms alludes to their inevitably impending deaths.

21. See Daniel 7, throughout.

22. Neta Sobol has offered an alternative interpretation of Rabbi Ḥizkiyah's vision, understanding the darkness cleansed in the river of light as *Ze'eir Anpin* being washed in the whiteness of *'Attiqa*, or alternatively, as the black orifice of the mouth surrounded by white. See Neta Sobol, "'En Mal'akh 'Eḥad 'Oseh Shetei Sheliḥuyot: 'Al Rega' Dramati ba-'Idra' Raba'" [No angel performs two missions: On one dramatic moment in Idra Rabba], *Kabbalah* 22 (2010): 288–289; Sobol, *Transgression*, 153–154.

23. See Mary Oliver's resonant description of death in her beautiful poem "White Owl Flies Into and Out of the Field," in Mary Oliver, *New and Selected Poems* (Boston: Beacon Press, 1992), 99–100.

24. Zohar 3:20a.

25. The text of the Zohar established by Matt has a different spelling of one word, which renders the translation "Now the world is rendered fit."

26. See, for example, Liebes, *Studies in the Zohar*, 26–31; Huss, *Zohar: Reception and Impact*, 23–24; and Hellner-Eshed, *A River Flows from Eden*, 42–51.

27. The Idra is aware that the ability to perceive subtle strata of reality is not available to all, but is rather the peculiar lot of the Companions, mystics, those who know the divine attributes. For example, see Zohar 3:130b, and the discussion of this passage in the section "The Figure of the Master and the Purpose of the Circle of Companions," in Chapter 5.

28. On the superiority of Rabbi Shim'on over Moses in the Zohar, see: Zohar 3:15a, 3:149a, and others. For more on this matter, see Liebes, *Studies in the Zohar*, 106; Yehuda Liebes, "Ha-Zohar ve-ha-Tiqunim: Me-Renesans la-Mahapekhah" [Zohar and *tiqqunei* Zohar: From renaissance to revolution], *Te'uda: New Developments in Zohar Studies* 21/22, no. 2 (2007): 251–301; Huss, *Zohar: Reception and Impact*, 11–42; and Hellner-Eshed, *A River Flows from Eden*, 44–48. On this special state of consciousness that combines the visual with a discursive and reflective quality, see Ibn Arabi's fascinating discussion in his book *The Meccan Revelations*, quoted in Corbin, *Spiritual Body*, 135–143.

29. See BT Yevamot 49b; and BT Sukkah 45b.

30. On Rabbi Shim'on's character, see Liebes, *Studies in the Zohar*, 4–12, 14–19; Hellner-Eshed, *A River Flows from Eden*, 29–53; and Huss, *Zohar: Reception and Impact*, 11–42.

31. On Rabbi Shim'on as the announcer of the Messiah, and on his messianic traits, see Liebes, *Studies in the Zohar*, 1–12.

32. For this verse in zoharic literature, see Liebes, "Zohar ve-'Eros," 73–76; Liebes, "Ha-Zohar ve-ha-Tiqunim," 264–268; and Hellner-Eshed, *A River Flows from Eden*, 75–80.

33. See the section "Introduction to the Tiqqunim of the Beard: The Teacher Awakens Consciousness," in Chapter 16.

34. For the formula, "One messenger does not perform two missions," see Bereshit Rabbah 50:2.

35. On the story of Nadab and Abihu and its interpretation in Kabbalah, see Hellner-Eshed, "Ha-Meqane' le-Brit"; Yehuda Liebes, "Ha-'Erom ha-Melubash: 'Avodat ha-Qodesh ha-Sodit ve-ha-'Ezoteriut 'Eẓel Filon ha-'Aleksandroni" [Clothed nudity: The esoteric cult of Philo], *Jerusalem Studies in Jewish Thought* 24 (2015): 9–28; and Ruth Kara-Ivanov Kaniel, "Liv'or me-Ahavah: Ma'aseh Nadav ve-'Avihu ke-Ritu'al 'Eroti 'Unio

Misti" [Consumed by love: The death of Nadav and Avihu as a ritual of erotic mystical union], *Te'uda* 26 (2014): 585–653.

36. This is the opinion of Neta Sobol, who has analyzed the second and third *tiqqunim* in great depth, and compared them side by side. Sobol, "'En Mal'akh 'Eḥad," 293–300. This suggestion is in harmony with her general interpretation of the second *tiqqun*, which differs from that which I have presented here. According to Sobol, Rabbi Ḥizkiyah's *tiqqun* is subversive, putting the rest of the gathering at risk. Rabbi Ḥizkiyah's decision to recount a vision rather than presenting an exegesis crosses boundaries and violates the Idra's norm of scriptural interpretation, built as it is upon drawing connections between the parts of the beard and the Attributes of Mercy by means of expounding biblical verses. In the process, the necessary stability for the gathering to continue is disrupted, returning to equilibrium only as the normative exegetical *tiqqunim* progress.

37. This resembles the first *tiqqun*, in which a single line descends to the mouth, but in reference to the contour of the hair, rather than an actual hair. See Zohar 3:131a.

38. "The term *mazzal* has a wide range of meaning: constellation, planet, planetary or astrological influence, zodiacal sign, destiny, fortune, guardian angel" (Zohar 3:1344; trans. Matt 8:370–371n179).

39. See BT Moed Katan 28a.

40. See Yehuda Liebes, *Pulḥan ha-Shaḥar: Yaḥas ha-Zohar le-'Avodah Zarah* [The cult of the dawn: The attitude of the Zohar toward idolatry] (Jerusalem: Carmel Press, 2011), 16–30, and his associated references to classical rabbinic and kabbalistic literature.

41. For other zoharic accounts of the divine mouth, see Zohar 1:74a; 2:3a; 2:123a; 3:295b (Idra Zuṭa).

42. On the rounded cheeks of both *Arikh Anpin* and *Ze'eir Anpin*, see Liebes, *Studies in the Zohar*, 31 and note. On *Ze'eir Anpin*'s cheeks as a field with apples, see Sobol, "Ḥativat ha-'Idrot," 178–181

43. Zohar 3:296b.

44. Zohar 3:132b.

45. Zohar 2:177a.

46. Zohar 3:140b; trans. Matt 8:421.

47. Zohar 3:295b (Idra Zuṭa).

48. Zohar 3:132b.

49. See BT Ḥagigah 14b; Vayyiqra Rabbah 16:4; and Ruth Rabbah 6:4. Torah as fire comes also from the reading of the verse in Deuteronomy 33 of the words מימינו אשדת למו (*mimino eshdat lamo*)—"from His right hand the fire of law."

50. Moses ben Naḥman, *Kitvei ha-Ramban* [The works of Nahmanides], ed. Charles B. Chavel (Jerusalem: Mossad HaRav Kook, 1968), 2:303–304.

51. Here *'olam* means the physical and temporal world. In contrast, in biblical usage, *'olam* means "eternity."

52. Indeed, in Parashat Vayyiqra of the Zohar, in a passage with a clear affinity with the Idras, *'Attiqa* is called *days of old* (*yemei qedem*), while *Ze'eir Anpin* is called *days of the world* (*yemei 'olam*). See Zohar 3:15a–b. See also my discussion in the section "A Prayer for Ze'eir Anpin's Life," in Chapter 4.

53. Zohar 1:7b; trans. Matt 1:49.

54. These wellsprings are also described by the kabbalist Joseph Gikatilla in his work *Sod YG Middot ha-Nove'ot min ha-Keter 'Elyon ve-Niqra'im Ma'yenei ha-Yeshu'ah* [The secret of the thirteen attributes that flow from the upper crown and are called wellsprings of redemption], in *Kitve Yad ba-Qabbalah* [Manuscripts of Qabbalah], ed. Gershom Scholem (Jerusalem: Hebrew University Press, 1930), 219–225. However, in Gikatilla's work, the anthropomorphic elements—the beard and its *tiqqunim*—are absent.

55. Moshe Ḥayyim Ephraim, *Degel Maḥaneh Efrayim* [The flag of the camp of Ephrayim] (Jerusalem, 1963), 110b. Cf. also the dream in which Ḥayyim Vital attains a vision of the Ancient of Days, and "his snow-white beard, infinitely glorious." See Idel, *Kabbalah: New Perspectives*, 81.

56. See the section "Origins," in Chapter 10.

57. On this point, see Liebes, "Zohar ve-'Eros," 71–72.

58. See BT Yevamot 97a.

59. See Exodus 26:30–33: "You shall make a curtain . . . and the curtain shall divide for you between the holy place and the Holy of Holies."

Chapter 13: The Kings of Edom: The Second Appearance

1. Zohar 3:128b.

2. Har-Shefi, *Malkhin Qadma'in*, 86–111.

3. On Luria's interpretation of the Myth of the Kings, and on the processes that it treats, see the section "The Kings of Edom in the Works of Cordovero and Luria," in Chapter 9.

4. Wilfred R. Bion, *Second Thoughts: Selected Papers on Psycho-analysis* (London: Heinemann, 1967), chap. 9; and Wilfred R. Bion, *Learning from Experience* (London: Maresfield Library, 1991).

5. Melila Hellner-Eshed, "Malkhei Edom v'Ḥomrei Beta: K'she-safot Nifgashot" [The Kings of Edom and beta elements: When two languages meet], lecture presented at the Tel Aviv Psychoanalytic Institute, December 2018).

6. Julia Kristeva, *Powers of Horror: An Essay on Abjection* (New York: Columbia University Press, 1982). Also see Berman, *Divine and Demonic*, 275–283.

Chapter 14: *Ze'eir Anpin* Comes into Being

1. Mishnah Sanhedrin 4:5.

2. *Ze'eir Anpin* also comprises all possible worlds: those that came into being, and those that did not. (Or as the Idra puts it here, "including all secrets uttered and prepared before the world was created, even if they did not endure.") Here, this seems to refer specifically to the primordial kings of Edom, who are themselves included in the figure of Adam, although their mode of existence was not rectified and healed in the present reality.

3. Liebes, "Le-Haḥzir le-'El Et Panav"; Liebes, "Peraqim be-Milon Sefer ha-Zohar," 50–51.

4. See Zohar 1:15a.

5. This is how this phrase is translated by Matt. The difficult and paradoxical name of this force has been creatively translated many times. Other renderings include Matt's "Spark of Impenetrable Darkness" and Wolfson's "Luminal Darkness" as well as "Dark Luminescence," and "Joy of the Heart." On different translations and their origins see Zohar, Matt, 1:107–108n4. See also, Liebes, "Peraqim be-Milon Sefer ha-Zohar," 145–151, 161–164; Yehuda Liebes, "Ha-Sipur ha-Zohari bi-Khelal ve-Gilgulei Hormenuta' ve-Semitra'" [The zoharic story in general, and the development of the ideas of "Hormenuta" and "Semitra"], in *Ha-Sipur ha-Zohari* [The zoharic story], ed. Yehuda Liebes, Jonatan Benarroch, and Melila Hellner-Eshed, 1:14–60 (Jerusalem: Ben-Zvi Institute, 2017); Liebes, *Torat ha-Yeẓirah*, 135, 166; and Har-Shefi, *Malkhin Qadma'in*, 86–104.

6. The motif of the ever-glimmering spark is highly significant, for the Idra Zuṭa does not describe the primordial entities that did not endure as *kings*, but rather as *sparks* that glimmered and immediately faded into nothingness. In contrast, the spark ignited by the Lamp of Adamantine Darkness glimmers and endures.

7. Isaac Luria identified the image of sexual coupling implicit in this imagery, and considered it to be a supernal coupling in the divine realm, arising from the supernal will and unrelated to human activity. See *Sefer 'Ets Ḥayyim*, 39:2.

8. Both in Sifra di-Tsni'uta and here in the Idra, the question arises as to whether the dew is dripping from *'Attiqa* into *Ze'eir Anpin*'s skull or upon the latter's head and hair. It seems to me that the primary account describes *Ze'eir Anpin*'s skull being constantly filled with *'Attiqa*'s dew; divine bounty then emanates from *Ze'eir Anpin*'s skull into the entire cosmos via his hair and face. This is reflected in the description of "the flow from brain to brain" in several places in the Idra Rabba (Zohar 3:131b).

9. The Apple Orchard is mentioned repeatedly in the zoharic accounts of Cain and Abel (Zohar 3:123, as discussed later). Neta Sobol has dedicated considerable attention to the Apple Orchard, comparing and contrasting its various appearances in the Idra. In her view, when the motif appears in the *tiqqunim* of *'Attiqa* and *Ze'eir Anpin* it represents the cheeks rather than the Female. See Sobol, "Ḥativat ha-'Idrot," 179–182. However, it is worth noting that outside the Idra, it represents the Female or the *Shekhinah*. See Zohar 1:143b; 2:61b.

10. This huge number is still less than half of the 3,700,000 worlds of the face of *Arikh Anpin*, hence the name "Small-Faced." See Zohar 3:128b, trans. Matt, 385n230.

11. Thirty-two paths are mentioned in the opening passage of Sefer Yetzirah, which describes how God created the world "by means of thirty-two wondrous paths of wisdom," comprising "twenty-two letters, and ten foundational *sefirot* (or: *sefirot* of nothingness)." See Aryeh Kaplan, *Sefer Yetzirah: The Book of Creation* (York Beach, ME: Weiser, 1997), 19–22; A. Peter Hayman, *Sefer Yeṣira: Edition, Translation and Text-Critical Commentary* (Tübingen: Mohr Siebeck, 2004), 64–66; and Liebes, *Torat ha-Yeẓirah*, 31–34.

12. Hellner-Eshed, *A River Flows from Eden*, 229–251.

13. See also the Idra Zuṭa, Zohar 3:289b, 291a, 296a. My teacher Yehuda Liebes pointed out to me that this account is reminiscent of the structure of the upper and lower brain, the latter extending into the spinal cord.

14. An account of God drawing on this figure may be found in rabbinic midrashim that discuss the divine tendency to tailor theophanies to the nature of the event. Among other figures, the divine warrior is the one who frees Israel from Egyptian bondage and splits the sea before them (Pesiqta de-Rav Kahana 12:24).

Chapter 15: *Ze'eir Anpin's* Head and Its Features

1. A similar example in which *'Attiqa* is described in interventionist terms appears in the *tiqqun* of *Ze'eir Anpin*'s nose, described later in this chapter.

2. There is another layer of complexity in this text: alongside *'Attiqa* and *Ze'eir Anpin* also appears "the Blessed Holy One"—the anthropomorphic "traditional" figure of the God of Israel, who is identified in the main body of the Zohar with the *sefirah* of Beauty (*Tif'eret*). It is the Blessed Holy One who seeks to delight with the righteous, not *Ze'eir Anpin* or *'Attiqa*. Thus, what we have here is a combination of two mythical languages that are not in the same "register"—the rabbinic-zoharic myth of the Blessed Holy One who takes pleasure, and the Idra's myth of the illumination of the forehead.

3. BT Rosh ha-Shanah 17b.

4. For more on the tension between Gnosticism and the unity of the divine *partsufim*, see the section "Ze'eir Anpin and Gnosticism: Between Splitting and Healing," in Chapter 4.

5. For *Netsaḥ* as "brain matter" in biblical Hebrew, see Isaiah 63:3–6. *Netsaḥ* as it is used here is not to be confused with the *sefirah* of the same name as commonly used in kabbalistic language.

6. The distinction is, of course, also rooted in the similarity of the terms *metsaḥ* and *netsaḥ*, which are differentiated by only a single letter: *mem* or *nun* (the subsequent letter in the Hebrew alphabet). See further in the same passage in the Idra on 3:136b.

7. As Art Green has noted (personal communication with the author), already in midrash we might find the basis for the idea of God learning from human beings how to forgive. See BT Rosh HaShana 17b.

8. The association of the eyes with providence is attested as far back as the Hebrew Bible, which describes God's supervision and governance of the world in terms of the eyes and gaze. Maimonides too identified God's eyes as a metaphor for divine providence. See *Guide for the Perplexed*, 1:44.

9. As we saw, in the Idra Rabba *Ze'eir Anpin*'s eyes are compared with doves. In the Idra Zuṭa, however, the term *doves* (*yonim*) is also interpreted as being derived from *ona'ah* (cheating, oppression). See Zohar 3:293b.

10. BT Berakhot 59a: "When the blessed Holy One recalls his children, immersed in suffering among the nations of the world, he lets two tears drop into the Great Sea, and the sound is heard from one end of the earth to the other."

11. Indeed, in the first *tiqqun* of the beard there is a description of the forces of Judgment becoming sweetened from the sweetened bitterness of the tears that dwell in the Great Sea. See Zohar 3:132a.

12. On hermeneutic methods in theosophical Kabbalah and the eroticization of biblical verses, see Idel, *Kabbalah: New Perspectives*, 218–234, esp. 223–224.

13. For the Sabbath, see Zohar 2:88b; for Yom Kippur, see Zohar 3:214b.

14. Zohar 3:129a. See also the section "The Human Gaze," in Chapter 3.

15. See Liebes, "Zemirot le-Se'udot Shabat."

16. See the section "Patience: The Nose," in Chapter 11.

17. For more on this verse and the linguistic connection between "nose" and "restraint," see Zohar 138a; trans. Matt 8:402n288.

18. See the section "Heaven and Earth," in Chapter 8.

19. See Zohar 2:20a–b.

20. On smell in the context of innovative Torah study, cf. Zohar 1:4b. See also, Hellner-Eshed, *A River Flows from Eden*, 302–304.

21. See Zohar 1:49b.

22. On the possibility that the three Companions who die in the Idra constitute a sacrifice, see the section "Ending 2: Fear of Revelation and the Deaths of the Companions," in Chapter 22.

23. Cf. Bereshit Rabbah 33:3: "Woe to the wicked, who turn the Attribute of Mercy into the Attribute of Judgment"; BT Yoma 87a: "Woe to the wicked! Is it not sufficient that they condemn themselves? But they condemn their children and their children's children until the end of all generations."

24. In some printed editions of the Zohar, this version of the description appears: "so that the sound may linger in its entering the brain, and be discerned by the brain, and not hurriedly."

25. See Hellner-Eshed, *A River Flows from Eden*, 340–348.

26. See the section "'*Attiqa*'s Gaze," in Chapter 3.

27. Another scriptural interpretation that appears in the Idra here, in the framework of the discussion of *Ze'eir Anpin*'s ears, is focused on the verse *O YHVH! I have heard Your renown; I am awed, O YHVH, by Your deeds—renew them in these years; oh, make them known in these years! Though angry, may You remember compassion* (Habakkuk 3:1–2). This is discussed in the section "A Prayer for Ze'eir Anpin's Life," in Chapter 4.

Chapter 16: The *Tiqqunim* of *Ze'eir Anpin* : The Language of Flowing Bounty

1. On the Torah as a divine name, see the introduction to Moses ben Naḥman [Nahmanides], *Commentary on the Torah*, ed Charles Ber Chavel (New York: Shilo, 1971).

2. See the section "The Greater Perspective: The Thirteenth *Tiqqun*," in Chapter 12.

3. See the section "A Prayer for *Ze'eir Anpin*'s Life," in Chapter 4.

4. See the section "Flowing Bounty: The Eighth *Tiqqun*," in Chapter 12, and the accompanying references to rabbinic sources.

5. Zohar 3:138b; trans. Matt 8:405.

6. See Song of Songs Rabbah 5:15; and Rashi's commentary on Deuteronomy 33:2.

7. Matt's edition of the Aramaic of the Zohar varies here considerably from the Mossad HaRav Kook edition of the Sefer HaZohar. His choice is attested to in numerous reliable manuscripts that state that the Torah was given as white fire upon black fire—the reverse of the rabbinic saying "black fire upon white fire." See Matt, Zohar, 8:353–354.

8. In Sifra di-Tsni'uta, precisely how the nine *tiqqunim* are derived from the psalm is not explicitly stated (Zohar 2:177b). Here, the Idra Rabba presents an extensive solution to this riddle.

9. In the Idra Zuṭa, an additional scriptural interpretation concerning *Ze'eir Anpin*'s nine *tiqqunim* provides more clarification for their number (Zohar 3:295b). According to this interpretation, the nine *tiqqunim* are also those which Moses recites to God in the passage in which he beseeches God not to destroy his people in the desert after the sin of the spies (Numbers 14:18). The Idra Zuṭa's interpretation emphasizes *Ze'eir Anpin*'s dependence on *'Attiqa*'s beard; he can manifest as a mighty warrior only when *'Attiqa*'s beard shines within him. Yehuda Liebes discusses this interpretation at length, raising various interpretive possibilities concerning the "contraction" of thirteen attributes into nine. See Yehuda Liebes, "Ko'aḥ ha-Milah ke-Yesod Mashma'utah be-Sifrut ha-Qabalah" [The power of a word as the basis for its meaning in Kabbalah], in *Devar Devor 'Al 'Ofanav: Meḥqarim be-Parshanut ha-Miqra' ve-ha-Qur'an be-Yemei ha-benayyim Mugashim le-Ḥagai Ben-Sham'ai* [A word fitly spoken: Studies in medieval exegesis of the Hebrew Bible and the Qur'ān: Presented to Haggai Ben-Shammai], ed. Meir M. Bar-Asher et al., (Jerusalem: Ben-Zvi Institute, 2007), 163–177.

10. This argument is presented by Neta Sobol. See Sobol, "Ḥativat ha-'Idrot," 23–25, 194.

11. See the section "A Prayer for *Ze'eir Anpin*'s Life," in Chapter 4.

12. The verb *yissa* (lift) in the Priestly Blessing had already been interpreted in terms of "removal," in Midrash Be-Midbar Rabbah 11:7: "*May YHVH lift up His face to you*—may he remove his anger from you. *Lift* (*yissa*) means none other than *removal* (*hasarah*)." Cf. also Targum Onqelos on this verse: "May the Lord remove his anger (lit. 'face') from you (lit. 'to you' or 'in relation to you')." See also, Zohar 3:147a.

13. The connection between the cheeks and the Priestly Blessing is also made in the seventh *tiqqun* of *'Attiqa*'s beard (describing the cheeks of that *partsuf*). These white cheeks grow luminous within the face of *Ze'eir Anpin*, causing blessing to flow into the world: "From these apples issues life to the world, and they manifest joy to *Ze'eir Anpin*. [. . .] *May YHVH shine His face upon you* (Numbers 6:25)—the outer face, which, when it shines, brings blessing to the world" (Zohar 3:134a; trans. Matt 8:369). Note that in this interpretation, the tetragrammaton represents *'Attiqa* rather than *Ze'eir Anpin*.

14. Also see, the section "Configuring the Male and Female Body," in Chapter 18.

15. For the appearance of God as a fine young man, see Song of Songs Rabbah 1:2. See also, Green, "The Children in Egypt."

16. Yehuda Liebes suggests that Beauty, *Tif'eret*, is a mingling of two powers: "This is *Tif'eret*, Beauty—power *of* might and compassion."

17. Zohar 3:141a. Here, the Idra Rabba (Zohar 3:141a; trans. Matt 8:425) cites Sifra di-Tsni'uta (Zohar 2:177a): "A path emerging below two holes of an armoire to eliminate sin, as is written: *His splendor is forgiving transgression* (Proverbs 19:11)."

Chapter 17: The Ancient of Ancients and *Ze'eir Anpin*: All Is One

1. See Mishnah Ḥagigah 2:1: "Whoever considers four things, it would have been better had they never come into the world: What is above, what is below, what is before, and

what is after. And whoever has no regard for his Creator's honor, it would have been better had he never come into the world." For a discussion of these conditions for participating in the Idra, see the section "The Unfolding of Existence," in Chapter 6.

2. Liebes, *Studies in the Zohar*, 110–112.

3. Pesiqta de-Rav Kahana 12:24.

4. Franz Rosenzweig, *Naharayyim: Mivḥar Ketavim* [A land of two rivers: Selected works], ed. and trans. Yehoshua Amir (Jerusalem: Bialik Institute, 1977), 35. See also, Green, "The Children in Egypt."

5. In the background to this interpretation sit rabbinic sources that inquire into the significance of the two *yods* in the phrase *He formed* (*va-yiytser*): "*He formed* (*va-yiyitser*)—why two *yods*? One for the Good Inclination, and one for the Evil Inclination. Another interpretation [. . .] One for the creation of Adam, and one for the creation of Eve. Another interpretation [. . .] One for face in front (*partsuf shel panav*), and one for the face behind (*partsuf shel aḥarav*)." Otiyyot de-Rabbi 'Aqiva, 412. Also see Liebes, *Studies in the Zohar*, 110–114. The responses seek out something that necessitates binarity, and ask what is gained in this duality. The answers are that the ethical sphere is maintained through a distinction between good and evil; the realm of sexual reproduction is maintained through the distinction between a male and a female sex or gender; and the spatial dimension of the world and human beings, perhaps even the soul, is based upon the existence of a front and a back. In contradistinction to the rabbinic interpretation here, the Idra does not see the two *yods* as an expression of difference or binarity, but rather as a graphic representation of the paradigmatic structure of "form within form."

6. On the great chain of being and its profound presence throughout the world of Kabbalah, see Moshe Idel, *Enchanted Chains: Techniques and Rituals in Jewish Mysticism*. Los Angeles: Cherub Press, 2005.

7. Liebes, *Studies in the Zohar*, 112 (emended).

8. On the rabbinic conception of *imago dei*, which is the foundation for the kabbalistic interpretation, see Yair Lorberbaum, *In God's Image: Myth, Theology, and Law in Classical Judaism* (New York: Cambridge University Press, 2015).

9. Yehuda Liebes presented a different reading of this Idraic passage, reading it as standing in opposition to the theology of the rest of the work. See Liebes, *Studies in the Zohar*, 110–119. See also, Asulin, "Qomatah Shel ha-Shekhinah," 119. According to Liebes, these differences point to the possible existence of literary sources that antedated the circle of kabbalists associated with the Zohar, and that discussed the divine face and the Thirteen Attributes of Mercy. The participants in this scholarly and mystical circle reworked these sources, each in their own way, as is attested in various works by the Castilian kabbalists. In his view, within the Idra itself we may find a collection of scriptural interpretations that were apparently produced by different authors—interpretations that exhibit a range of sometimes contradictory theologies.(For further discussion, see above, Part I, p. .)

10. Zohar 2:147b.

11. We have already encountered the close affinity between *Adam* and the divine name, in the *tiqqunim* of *Ze'eir Anpin*'s beard, in an interpretation that was presented for

the terms *Adam* and *Nedivim* (princes or nobles) in Psalm 118. See the section "Between *'Attiqa*'s Beard and *Ze'eir Anpin*'s Beard," in Chapter 16.

12. See the section "A Hymn to God in Human Likeness," in Chapter 14.

Chapter 18: Forming the Male and Female Body

1. On the construction of the Male and Female in the Idra Rabba, see also, Asulin, "Ha-Parshanut ha-Mistit le-Shir ha-Shirim," 112–115; Asulin, "Qomatah Shel ha-Shekhinah," 120–129; and Har-Shefi, *Malkhin Qadma'in*, 142–157.

2. Yehezkel Kaufmann, *Toldot ha-'Emunah ha-Yisra'elit: me-Yemei Qedem 'Ad Sof Bayit Sheni* [The history of the Israelite faith: From antiquity to the end of the Second Commonwealth] (Jerusalem: Bialik Institute, 1965), 244–245, 298–300; Israel Knohl, *'Emunot ha-Miqra': Gevulot ha-Mahapekhah ha-Miqra'it* [Biblical beliefs: The borders of the biblical revolution] (Jerusalem: Hebrew University Magnes Press, 2007), 24–39.

3. Shmuel Aḥituv, *'Asufat Ketuvot 'Ivri'ot me-Yemei Bayit Rishon ve-Reshit Bayit Sheni* [Handbook of ancient Hebrew inscriptions from the period of the First Commonwealth and the beginning of the Second Commonwealth] (Jerusalem: Bialik Institute, 1992, 111–112, 152–162.

4. Knohl, *'Emunot ha-Miqra'*, 24–27, 54–57.

5. On the Song of Songs in rabbinic literature, see Michael Fishbane, "The Song of Songs and Ancient Jewish Religiosity: Between Eros and History," in *Von Enoch bis Kafka: Festschrift für Karl E. Grözinger zum* 60. *Geburtstag*, ed. K. E. Grözinger, M. Voigts, and F. Battenberg, 69–81 (Wiesbaden: Harrassowitz, 2002); Idel, *Kabbalah and Eros*, 22–38.

6. Saul Lieberman, "Mishnat Shir ha-Shirim," in *Jewish Gnosticism: Merkabah Mysticism and Talmudic Tradition*, by Gershom Scholem (New York: Jewish Theological Seminary Press, 1960), 118–126; Rachel Elior, "Yehudah Shel ha-Tofa'ah ha-Datit be-Sifrut ha-Hekhalot: Demut ha-'El ve-Harḥavat Gevulot ha-Hasagah" [The concept of God in Hekhalot mysticism], *Jerusalem Studies in Jewish Thought* 6, no. 1/2 (1987): 13–64; Joseph Dan, *Ha-Mistiqah ha-'Ivrit ha-Qedumah* [The ancient Jewish mysticism] (Tel Aviv: Modan, 1989), 48–58.

7. Of course, a primary representative of these trends is Maimonides. On his theology, see Halbertal, *Maimonides*, 288–296; and Menachem Lorberbaum, *Nuzaḥnu be-Ne'imuto: Torat ha-'Elohut ke-Po'etiqah be-Yeẓirah ha-Yehudit ha-'Andalusit* [Dazzled by beauty: Theology as poetic in medieval Jewish thought] (Jerusalem: Ben-Zvi Institute, 2011), 72–121.

8. For discussions of Kabbalah and *eros* and their trends, see Idel, *Kabbalah and Eros*, 11–12; and Arthur Green, "The Song of Songs in Early Jewish Mysticism," *Orim* 2 (1987): 49–63.

9. Liebes, Zohar ve-'Eros," 99–103. For more on *eros* in Kabbalah in general, see Scholem, *Major Trends*, 225–229; Tishby, *The Wisdom of the Zohar*, 3:1355–1372; Idel, *Kabbalah and Eros*, 1–12, 202–250; and Wolfson, *Language, Eros, Being*.

10. See Scholem, *On the Mystical Shape of the Godhead*, 140–196; Tishby, *The Wisdom of the Zohar*, 1:298–302; Idel, *Kabbalah and Eros*, 59–73; Daniel Abrams, *Ha-Guf ha-'Elohi ha-Nashi ba-Qabalah* [The female body of God in kabbalistic literature] (Jerusalem: Hebrew University Magnes Press, 2004), 180–181; Haviva Pedaya, "'Ve-Hashta' 'Ima' Let Lan':

Qavvim le-Geni'ologiah Shel ha-Shekhinah ve-ha-'Em" [And now we have no mother: Toward a genealogy of the Shekhinah and the mother], in *As a Perennial Spring: A Festschrift Honoring Rabbi Dr. Norman Lamm*, ed. Bentsi Cohen, 87–151 (New York: Downhill 2013).

11. See Scholem, ibid.; Tishby, *The Wisdom of the Zohar*, 1:371–385; Green, "The Song of Songs"; Biti Roi, "Mitos ha-Shekhinah be-Sifrut Tiqunei ha-Zohar: Hebetim Po'etim, Parshani'im, ve-Misti'im" [The myth of the Shekhinah in tiqunei Zohar literature: Poetic, hermeneutic, and mystical aspects] (PhD diss., Bar-Ilan University, 2012); and Sarah Schneider, *Kabbalistic Writings on the Nature of Masculine and Feminine* (Northvale, NJ: Aronson, 2001). See also, Sack, *Ma'ayan 'Ein Ya'aqov*, 11–188.

12. The Idra also interprets the verses that appear at a later point in connection to the creation of human beings: *This is the book of the generations of Adam, on the day that God created Adam, in the image of God did he make him. Male and female, he created them. He blessed them and called them Adam, on the day that they were created* (Genesis 5:1–2).

13. There is debate among scholars as to whether the Male and Female emanate simultaneously, or whether the Male precedes the Female. For a discussion, see Asulin, "Qomatah Shel ha-Shekhinah," 122–128; and for a summary of the literature on this point, see ibid., 122–123n60.

14. For example, see *Pirqe de-Rabbi Eli'ezer*, chap. 12: "Said the blessed Holy One: I am alone in my world, and this one is alone in his world; I have no fruitfulness and reproduction, and this one has no fruitfulness and reproduction. Later, the creatures will say, 'Since he has no fruitfulness and reproduction, he must be the one who created us!' *It is not good for Adam to be alone, I shall create an aide alongside him.*" See also the discussion of these midrashim in Yehuda Liebes, "Golem be-Gimatria' Ḥokhmah [Golem in numerology is Ḥokhmah]," *Kiryat Sefer* 63, no. 4 (1989): 1309–1311.

15. Bereshit Rabbah 8:1.

16. See Plato's *Symposium*. On androgyny and double-facedness in the midrash and Kabbalah, see Idel, *Kabbalah and Eros*, 53–97; and Elliot R. Wolfson, "Re/membering the Covenant: Memory, Forgetfulness, and History in the Zohar," in *Jewish History and Jewish Memory: Essays in Honor of Yosef Hayim Yerushalmi*, ed. Elisheva Carlebach, John M. Efron, and David N. Myers, 214–246 (Hanover, NH: University Press of New England for Brandeis University Press, 1998). See also the discussion in Asulin, "Qomatah Shel ha-Shekhinah," 122–129; and the summary of scholarship in ibid., 122n59. It is interesting that the term "sawing" (*n-s-r*), used in the accounts of Adam and Eve's creation in both the midrashic passage and the Zohar, is absent from the accounts of the separation of the divine Male and Female bodies in the Idra literature. In contrast, in later kabbalistic works, such as those of Lurianic Kabbalah, *n-s-r* is the most frequently used term for this process.

17. See Wendy Doniger, "When a Lingam Is Just a Good Cigar: Psychoanalysis and Hindu Sexual Fantasies," in *The Psychoanalytic Study of Society: Essays in Honor of Alan Dundes*, ed. L. Bryce Boyer et al. (Hillside, NJ: Analytic Press, 1993), 81–104.

18. See the section "The Warrior's Mercy, *Tif'eret* (Beauty): The Ninth *Tiqqun*," in Chapter 16.

19. For example, consider Sifra di-Tsni'uta's identification of the Lamp of Adamantine Darkness with the letter *vav*, which is the standard signifier for *Tif'eret* in the Zohar (2:177a). It also should be noted that the Lamp of Adamantine Darkness possesses a distinctly feminine aspect. See the section "The Formation of *Ze'eir Anpin*'s Skull," in Chapter 14.

20. See BT Shabbat 118b for language identifying "woman" with "house."

21. The author of *Tiqqunei ha-Zohar* provided an admirable remedy for this in a beautiful description of the *Shekhinah*'s head, as did Moses Cordovero in his detailed account of the *Shekhinah*'s body in his work *Elimah*. On the account in *Tiqqunei ha-Zohar*, see Roi, "Mitos ha-Shekhinah," 234–304. On Cordovero's account, see Shifra Asulin, "Ha-Havnayah ha-Kefulah Shel Demut ha-Shekhinah be-Ma'yan 'Ein Ya'aqov ve-Zeqatah le-Sifrut ha-'Idrot" [The double construct of the image of the Shekhinah in *Ma'ayan 'Ein Ya'aqov* and its relation to the 'Idra' literature], in *Ma'ayan 'Ein Ya'aqov le-R. Mosheh Qordovero* [The *'Ein Ya'aqov* Spring of Rabbi Moses Cordovero], edited by Bracha Sack (Beer Sheva: Ben-Gurion University of the Negev Press, 2008), 61–111. On the lack of detail in the description of the Female body in the Idra, see the section "The Divine Body: Male and Female," in Chapter 2.

22. In the Hebrew Bible, the loins (*me'ayim*) are understood to be a locus of the emotions. See, for example, Jeremiah 31:20: *My loins* (*me'ay*) *yearn for him*. From a physical point of view, they refer to the belly, both inside and out. See Song of Songs 5:14: *his belly* (*me'av*) *is a tablet of ivory, adorned with sapphires*.

23. Avishar Har-Shefi offered a precise description of this: "*Tif'eret* (when it is one of *Ze'eir Anpin*'s *tiqqunim*) includes both Mercy and forces of Judgment, and when it constructs *Ze'eir Anpin* and *Nuqba* it divides so that its Mercy constructs *Ze'eir Anpin* while its Judgment constructs *Nuqba*. If we pay close attention to the portrayal, in the case of each body part discussed, that of *Ze'eir Anpin* is constructed first, and thereafter the Mercy remains within him while the forces of Judgment are transferred to *Nuqba*, and it is they that construct that body part within her." Har-Shefi, *Malkhin Qadma'in*, 147.

24. On the female *'ervot*, see BT Berakhot 24a. The Talmud lists three areas of nakedness, to which the Idra adds two.

25. Matt chooses to translate *'ervah* as "lewdness," which, for our purposes, has overly negative connotations.

26. The impression of the letter *yod*, part of the divine name, is considered to be a seal and sign of the covenant upon the circumcised penis. See, for example, Zohar 1:95a. From this point of view, the Idra's description of the divine Male's phallus is of a circumcised penis.

27. On the terms *'ervah* and *kesut*, see the notes to Matt 8:430–431.

Chapter 19: The Kings of Edom: The Third Appearance

1. Har-Shefi, *Malkhin Qadma'in*, 142 and notes.

2. In Biblical Hebrew, *tovim* also means "intoxicating," as in Song of Songs 1:2.

3. Avishar Har-Shefi has summarized the distinctive quality of this instance of the mythical motif of the kings of Edom, comparing it with its other appearances. See Har-Shefi, *Malkhin Qadma'in*, 142–157; and cf. Asulin, "Qomatah Shel ha-Shekhinah," 116.

Chapter 20: Separation and Coupling

1. See the RaBad's comments and Idel's discussion in Idel, *Kabbalah and Eros*, 62–69.

2. The formulation in Sifra di-Tsni'uta is as follows: "The male extended and was arrayed with His enhancements, with the phallus, with the mouth of the phallus. Kings who were nullified were here established. Judgments of the male are harsh at the beginning, at the end calm. Of the female, the reverse" (Zohar 2:178a; trans. Matt 5:540).

3. This account contradicts the imagery discussed previously, in which Judgment is concentrated in the Female alone, and the Male remains filled with white Love. However, the imagery of the Male's Judgment as "harsh at the beginning" is reconcilable with the earlier account if we view the divine Male as expanding from *Ze'eir Anpin*'s head, which comprises both Compassion and Judgment.

4. This was Moses Cordovero's interpretation. See Melila Hellner-Eshed, "Temunot me-Ḥayyei Mishpaḥah: Mitosim 'Al ha-Shekhinah Metokh "Ein Ya'aqov' le-R. Mosheh Qordovero [Domestic troubles: Family myths in Moshe Cordovero's book *'Eilima*]," *Te'uda* 21/22, no. 3 (2007): 427–435.

5. See BT Bava Batra, 74b. For the myth of the serpents, see the section "Pre-Creation Processes," in Chapter 9 and related notes therein.

6. Genesis Rabbah 7:5: "These are the demons whose souls the blessed Holy One created, but before he could create their bodies the Sabbath began—and he did not create them. This instructs you in proper conduct, based on [the creation of] the demons. For if a person is holding a precious object or jewel at the beginning of the Sabbath, around the time of dusk, he will be told: Cast it away! For the One who spoke and brought the world into being was busy creating the world, and he had created their souls, but before he could create their bodies the Sabbath began—and he did not create them."

7. BT Sanhedrin 106a.

8. This aromatized coupling is highly reminiscent of the accounts of the erotic encounter and preparation for coupling between the King and Queen on the Sabbath eve that we find throughout the Zohar. The most famous is "The Secret of the Sabbath" (*raza de-shabbat*), which appears in some prayer books at the conclusion of the service inaugurating the Sabbath (*qabbalat shabbat*). See Zohar 2:135b.

9. For another active portrayal of *'Attiqa*, see the section, "*'Attiqa*'s Responsibility for Divine Anger," in Chapter 15.

10. Zohar 3:137b.

11. Avishar Har-Shefi has noted that while *Ze'eir Anpin* is rooted in Judgment, he is constructed from both Judgment and Love together, and there is thus a *tiqqun* in his very creation. In contrast, the Female is entirely red, and constructed entirely from Judgment. Her sweetening occurs only after she is constructed, and it too fails to liberate her entirely from the side of Judgment. See Har-Shefi, *Malkhin Qadma'in*, 145–146.

Chapter 21: Sweetening Judgment

1. Zohar 3:143a; trans. Matt 8:440.

2. Interestingly, in the course of the history of Kabbalah and Hasidism, this concept—so central in the Zohar and Idras—became interchangeable in its meaning with the verbal

root *m-t-q* (sweet). On scents and fragrances as arousing, see Zohar 3:191a. On *bissum* as sweetening, see Scholem, *Major Trends in Jewish Mysticism*, 388n44; and Liebes, "Peraqim be-Milon Sefer ha-Zohar," 55 (entry 149), 243 (entry 323). On "olfactory symbolism" in Kabbalah, see Elliot K. Ginsburg, *The Sabbath in the Classical Kabbalah* (Albany: State University of New York Press, 1989), 129, 262. On fragrance and the mystical experience, see Hellner-Eshed, *A River Flows from Eden*, 302–304.

3. See BT Megillah 7b.

4. Nahum Bronznick, "L'hora'ato shel haShoresh *b-s-m*" [To the understanding of the root *b-s-m*], *Sinai* 63 (1968), 81–85. In a conversation, Yehuda Liebes also pointed out to me a possible connection with the Arabic verb *basama* (smile).

5. Zohar 3:143a; trans. Matt 8:441.

6. BT Yevamot 103b.

7. From a literary point of view, it would seem that during the configuration and completion of the divine faces, and with the configuration of Adam, primordial Edom becomes increasingly marginalized, and the forces of Judgment are no longer described in the primordial and archetypical terminology of "the kings of Edom," but rather with the names of figures from the Genesis narratives.

8. This conception appears several times in the main body of the Zohar: when the Female is not sustained by the wellsprings of divine bounty, she becomes attached to the Other Side (*Siṭra Aḥra*) and suckles from it. See, among other passages, Zohar 1:35a; 1:92b.

9. In *Pirqe de-Rabbi Eli'ezer* (chap. 21), the Serpent even precedes Adam in seducing Eve—but the Idra provides no details on this matter.

10. It should be noted that the solution put forward by the Idra Rabba—namely, to include and balance Judgment and Compassion through coupling—is different from that of Sifra di-Tsni'uta. In the latter, it appears to be achieved through the internal split between the human and animal aspects of a person's soul, meaning that now a person is disconnected from their evil aspect. Part of the animal soul extends outside the body and becomes foreign to it, and these elements that should have been part of the human are no longer contained within him. The human being thus continues to exist, and to "serve," in a proper fashion, but the price is an inability to contain and integrate evil.

11. Elsewhere in the Zohar, there is a parallel statement that is important in this context, providing an account of the formation of Adam (Zohar 2:167b–168a). The passage implies that the Serpent's force is present in Eve's first two births, but its power diminishes with each subsequent birth. It is only with the birth of Seth that a human likeness is achieved that balances Judgment, a likeness that corresponds with Adam's image.

12. According to Sifra di-Tsni'uta, the Serpent created a space within the Female when he copulated with her, "a nest of slime," in which all the unsweetened disembodied forces may dwell. Cain (*Qayin*) is the physical representation of that nest (*qinna*) of pollution (Zohar 2:178a).

13. On the myth of Cain and Abel in the Idra, see Gershom Scholem, *Qabalot R. Ya'aqov v'R. Yiẓḥaq Benei Ya'aqov Ha-Kohen* [The Qabala of Rabbis Jacob and Isaac, sons of Jacob the Cohen] (Jerusalem: Hamadpis, 1923), 75; Liebes, "Peraqim be-Milon Sefer ha-Zohar," 180; and Neta Sobol, "Sipur Qayin ve-Hevel ke-Pereq Siyum le-Mitos Mot

ha-Melkhim ba-'Idra' Raba" [The story of Cain and Abel as a closing chapter for the myth of the death of the kings in the Idra], in *Ha-Sipur ha-Zohari* [The zoharic story], ed. Yehuda Liebes, Jonatan Benarroch, and Melila Hellner-Eshed, 2:564–585 (Jerusalem: Ben-Zvi Institute, 2017). For the major sources for this myth, see Zohar 3:76b, 1:36b.

14. See Tishby, *Wisdom of the Zohar*, vol. 2, 692-731 and 749-761. In contrast with this conception, which distances the souls of Cain and Abel from the existing Adamic figure, R. Isaac Luria was of the opinion that Cain and Abel represent the source of most souls (referring, for example, to "all of the sparks of the souls from the roots of Cain and Abel, the sons of First Adam, whence most human souls derive"), with very few new souls originating in Seth (such as that of Rabbi Israel Baal Shem, the Besht, according to Hasidic tradition). R. Ḥayyim Vital, *Sha'ar HaKavvanot* [The gate of intentions], in vol. 11 of *Kitve ha-Ari* [The works of the Ari], (Jerusalem, 1988).

15. See Sifra di-Tsni'uta (Zohar 2:178a).

16. See Farber-Ginat, "Qelipah Qodemet le-Peri"; and see Berman, *Divine and Demonic*, 136–224. On the mythic body of impurity, see Sobol, "Sipur Qayin ve-Hevel," 2:564–585.

17. On the divinity of the body in the Zohar, see Liebes, "Zohar ve-'Eros," 99. It is worth noting that the concept of *Adam* here is not one of a physical body, for incorporeal angels are holy and yet they are considered to be part of Adam (as opposed to demons).

18. For example, the cycle of the emergence, waxing, waning, and concealment of the moon every month becomes a symbol of the cyclic relations between the sacred and the demonic, the association between holiness and evil in the human soul. On another zoharic reworking of the narrative of the Serpent injecting its venom into the feminine Divine, see Asulin's extensive study "Ha-Pegam ve-Tiquno."

19. This view of sexual coupling as ecstatic abounds throughout the Zohar. See the discussion in Chapter 18.

20. For example, see Numbers Rabbah 14:11: "*He named him Seth* (*Shet*) (Genesis 5:3)—for it was from him that the world was established (*hushtat*)."

21. The very decision to employ verses from the Song of Songs, praising as they do the beauty of the female lover bedecked in gold, is powerful evidence that the Idra does not understand Judgment (*Din*) to be purely evil, polluting, or demonic, and that the work's stance toward *Din* also entails love and admiration.

22. See Zohar 1:209b; trans. Matt 3:286: "As all of a woman's adornments suspend from her neck [. . .]"

23. Zohar 3:107a–b. On the difference between Jewish and Christian views of virginity and sexuality, see Arthur Green, "Shekhina, the Virgin Mary and the Song of Songs," *AJS Review* 26, no. 1 (2002): 1–52.

24. BT Yoma, 54a.

25. This sits in some tension with the main body of the Zohar, in which the "Mystery of Faith" (*raza di-mehemnuta*) refers to theoretical and experiential knowledge of the process by which divine bounty and being emanates, flowing from its source through all of the *sefirot* and into the *sefirah* of Sovereignty (*Malkhut*), which is connected to the potencies of the Male in the *sefirot* above her. The Mystery of Faith also comprises the virtuosic theurgical

knowledge required to expound scriptural verses in such a way that the interpretation stimulates the flow of divine bounty to the interpreters, bringing blessing to the world. See Jonathan Garb, "Sodot ha-'Emunah be-Sefer ha-Zohar" [The "secrets of faith" in the Zohar], in *'Al ha-'Emunah u-be-Toldotav be-Mesoret ha-Yehudit* [On faith: Studies in the concept of faith and its history in the Jewish tradition], ed. Moshe Halbertal, David Kurzweil, and Avi Sagi, 294–311 (Jerusalem: Keter, 2005).

26. BT Ḥullin 60b; *Tanḥuma*, Genesis 11; Genesis Rabbah 12:9. There is a similar account in Sefer Yetzirah, for which see the extensive discussion in Liebes, *Torat ha-Yeẓirah*, 73–105.

27. See, for example, Zohar 1:97a–b.

28. BT Sanhedrin 98a. In his notes to the conclusion of the Idra, Daniel Matt interprets this verse not in a messianic vein, but as an account of *Ze'eir Anpin*, God as a human figure (*ke-bar enash*), approaching the Ancient of Days. See Zohar, trans. Matt 8:451 and related notes.

29. Liebes, *Studies in the Zohar*.

Chapter 22: Emerging from the Idra Rabba

1. On emerging from mystical states of consciousness, see Idel, *Enchanted Chains*, 69–75. See also Isaac of Acre's discussion of exiting such states, in note 17 of this chapter. For a discussion of entering the Orchard (*pardes*) at the outset of the Idra, see the section "Those Who Enter and Emerge," in Chapter 8.

2. In order to understand the many-layered and eclectic processes that characterize the Idra's composition, Neta Sobol has studied its concluding passages from a stylistic and conceptual perspective, while paying close attention to manuscript evidence. See Sobol, *Transgression*, 34–36.

3. There are other cases in the Idra Rabba in which YHVH appears as a name of *'Attiqa* (see, for example, Zohar 3:138b). Daniel Matt offers an additional interpretive possibility, suggesting that the term *sees* (*yir'eh*) be vocalized passively, *is seen* (*yera'eh*). That is: *Adam is seen by the eyes, but YHVH [Ze'eir Anpin] is seen by the heart ['Attiqa]*. See Zohar, trans. Matt 8:451n457.

4. Indeed, this verse is understood to describe the figure of the Messiah, the perfected human being. For example, see BT Sanhedrin 98a; Rashi on Daniel 7:13; Nahmanides commentary on Genesis 2:3; and others. In 1 Enoch 46–48, there is an account of the connection between the Ancient of Days and the human figure of the Messiah, the chosen one.

5. See Boaz Huss, *Zohar: Reception and Impact*, esp. the chapter "The Depiction of R. Shimon bar Yohai and Moses," 9–35.

6. BT Ḥagigah 14a.

7. On this interpretation, see Liebes, *'Alilot 'Elohim*, 143.

8. On this zoharic blessing, see Yehuda Liebes, "'Zaka'in 'Inun Yisra'el': Berakhah be-Lashon ha-Zohar ve-Riq'ah ha-Yehudi-Noẓri" ["Happy are Israel": A blessing in the language of the Zohar and its Jewish-Christian background], *Iggud* 14, no. 3 (2005): 85–94.

9. See the section "Those Who Enter and Emerge," in Chapter 8.

10. See Sobol, *Transgression*, 132–136.

11. See, for example, this 19th-century instance: R. Joseph Ḥayyim [Ben Ish Ḥai], *She'elot u-Teshuvot Rav Pe'alim* [Responsa of Rav Pe'alim], vol. 1, *Yoreh De'ah*, 56, ed. Salah Mansour. Jerusalem, 1970.

12. Zohar 3:161b–174a. On this stratum of the Zohar, see Hellner-Eshed, *A River Flows from Eden*, 86–89; Nathan Wolski and Merav Carmeli, "Those Who Know Have Wings: Celestial Journeys with the Masters of the Academy," *Kabbalah* 16 (2007): 83–115; Jonatan M. Benarroch, *Sava and Yanuḳa: God, the Son, and the Messiah in Zoharic Narratives* [in Hebrew] (Jerusalem: Hebrew University Magnes Press, 2018), 3–6, 44–48, 103–111, 138–141, 155–163, 410, 451–455; and Kara-Ivanov Kaniel, "Likhtov 'O Lo' Likhtov."

13. Zohar 3:161b; trans. Matt 9:54.

14. For more on those admitted to the King's palace without opposition, see Zohar 3:22a; 2:128b.

15. Joshua 6:26: *At that time Joshua pronounced this oath: "Cursed of YHVH be the man who shall undertake to fortify this city of Jericho. He shall lay its foundations at the cost of his first-born, and set up its gates at the cost of his youngest.*

16. Zohar 3:56b; trans. Matt 7:361. This statement is based on Vayiqra Rabbah 12:2.

17. Such a concept was well articulated by Isaac of Acre, who was active in the Land of Israel and in Spain in the late 13th and early 14th centuries. In his work "Otsar Ḥayyim," a contemplative and mystical diary of sorts, he writes about the dangers of entering and emerging from a mystical state of consciousness: "One who fails in the Work of the Chariot, abandoning the spiritual beings with which his soul has enclothed itself, and exiting the abode of his aloneness/meditation to strip it from his soul, [instead] enclothing his soul in sensory things. Anybody who does such a thing is liable with his life, and will not escape punishment." Isaac of Acre, "Otsar Ḥayyim," Manuscript, Günzburg Collection, ms. 1062 [775], Russian State Library, Moscow, 44a, and also, for example, 174b–175a, 182a.

18. Zohar 3:127b; trans. Matt 8:321.

19. See the section "Idra Literature in the Zohar," in Chapter 1, esp. note 7, referring to the non-extant work Idra de-Vei Mashkena and controversies about defining it. For more on the deaths of the Companions, and on the meaning of their description as those who "entered but did not emerge," see Sobol, "'En Mal'akh 'Eḥad," 300–303.

20. Zohar 3:79a; trans. Matt 7:540. On this narrative, and on the riddle in particular, see Asulin, "Qomatah Shel ha-Shekhinah," 234–236; and Asulin, "Ha-Pegam ve-Tiquno," 224–236.

21. See the section "Bearing Iniquity: The Second *Tiqqun*," in Chapter 12.

22. See Asulin, "Qomatah Shel ha-Shekhinah," 229n139.

23. Zohar 3:130b; trans. Matt 8:344.

24. Zohar 2:61b; trans. Matt 4:330.

25. See BT Bava Batra 17a; Song of Songs Rabbah 1:16. Death is a major theme in the Zohar in general, leading Isaiah Tishby to devote a complete chapter to it in his *Wisdom of the Zohar*, 2:831–863. Also see Michael Fishbane's monograph on the place of death and "death with a kiss" in Jewish spiritual and mystical discourse. Michael Fishbane, *The Kiss of God: Spiritual and Mystical Death in Judaism* (Seattle: University of Washington Press, 1996).

26. BT Shabbat 88b.

27. Pedaya, "Zeman Ma'agali."

28. On the deaths of the three Companions as "death with a kiss" and as a sacrifice that enables the rebuilding of Jericho (representing the *Shekhinah*), see Liebes, *Studies in the Zohar*, 51–55.

29. BT Shabbat 33b.

30. On fragrant scents and illumination of the face as an authorization of mystical experience, see Hellner-Eshed, *A River Flows from Eden*, 302–304. A testimony to the deeply personal ways in which the Idra has been internalized throughout the generations, and to experiences of identification with the Companions as they leave the assembly in a state of illumination and radiance, may be found in an account of Rabbi Nathan of Nemirov, Rabbi Nachman of Bratslav's close disciple. In a letter in which Rabbi Nachman's final days are described, the people of Bratslav testified: "[Rabbi Nathan] then related a tremendous tale about the book that was burnt [. . .] and that he wrote the book in three and a half hours, 'and afterwards I emerged as if from the Idra.'" Cited in Joseph G. Weiss, *Meḥqarim be-Sifrut Breslav* [Studies in Breslav Hassidism] (Jerusalem: Bialik Institute, 1974), 242 n78.

31. There are other zoharic narratives in which the reader identifies specifically with Rabbi Abba. This is also linked to the perspective from which the events are narrated. For example, see Shasha, "'Milin La' 'Itgalyan."

32. Here, the Zohar appears to conflate Exodus 16:23 with Exodus 20:10. See Zohar, trans. Matt 8:456n474.

33. It is notable that the figure employed by Rabbi Shim'on, *the eyes of YHVH*, also originates in Zechariah's vision (Zechariah 4:10). Indeed, the candelabra of the Temple and of Zechariah's vision are mentioned in the *tiqqunim* of *'Attiqa* as symbols of the channels of divine bounty that lead from *'Attiqa* to *Ze'eir Anpin*, and they are associated with God's eyes (Zohar 3:129b).

34. Hellner-Eshed, "Ha-Meqane' le-Brit," 156–169; Oded Yisraeli, *Pitḥei Hekhal: 'Iyunei 'Agadah ve-Midrah be-Sefer ha-Zohar* [Temple portals: Studies in Aggadah and Midrash in the Zohar] (Jerusalem: Hebrew University Magnes Press, 2013), 290–309.

35. The heavenly figure of Rav Hamnuna the Elder is analogous to Rabbi Shim'on on earth. His absence from the Idra Rabba appears to be of great significance, for in the Idra Zuṭa Rabbi Shim'on emphasizes that he is present with seventy elders who radiate with the glory of *'Attiqa* in order to hear Rabbi Shim'on's words. See Zohar 3:288a.

36. Some of the details of this narrative appear to have been inspired by the story in 1 Kings 20:28–30.

37. As with Nadab and Abihu, as mentioned earlier.

38. Paralleling this, the absence of any reference here to the *Siṭra Aḥra* is notable. This is in contradistinction to many other passages throughout the Zohar, in which it is stated that every sacrifice (except for the burnt offering) contains a portion that is offered to the *Siṭra Aḥra*, or Azazel. (This is also true of the zoharic narrative about that other case of human sacrifice, the Ten Martyrs. See Zohar 2:254b.)

39. Zohar 3:144b; trans. Matt 8:457.

40. Since the three Companions have been liberated from their bodies, it is possible that the three Sabbath delights set aside for them represent the spiritual bliss in the encounter with the three *partsufim* at the three Sabbath meals (cf. Zohar 2:88b). Another possible interpretation is that the reference to three delights that inhere in the seventh is an allusion to the three Patriarchs that exist within the seventh *sefirah*, Sovereignty (*Malkhut*).

41. In this context, it is notable that while Rabbi Shim'on inaugurates the Idra by declaring that "I will not tell the heavens to listen, nor will I tell the earth to hear, for we sustain the worlds" (Zohar 3:128a; trans. Matt 8:325), it is not he who concludes the work, but rather the heavenly and divine figure of Elijah the Prophet.

42. The three departed Companions might also be interpreted as a representation of the upper *sefirot* (Crown-Wisdom-Understanding/*Keter-Ḥokhmah-Binah*) that ascended, leaving the seven lower ones—associated to a greater degree with a discursive mode of being—on earth.

Bibliography

Primary Sources

Classical rabbinic sources (such as Talmud, midrash, and Torah commentaries) are cited according to their traditional ordering systems. Where a specific edition was consulted, it is included here.

Zohars and Commentaries (in chronological order)

Sefer HaZohar. Jerusalem: Hotza'at Mossad haRav Kook, 1984.

Cordovero, Moshe. *Sefer ha-Zohar im Perush Or Yaqar* [The Zohar with the Or Yaqar commentary]. Vols. 11, 13, 21, 22, 23. Jerusalem: Ahuzat Yisrael, 1972–1990.

Matt, Daniel. *The Zohar: Pritzker Edition: Aramaic Texts*. Available online at Stanford University Press, last updated 2020, https://www.sup.org/zohar/?d=Aramaic%20Texts&f=index.

Matt, Daniel, trans. *The Zohar: Pritzker Edition*. Vols. 1–9. Stanford, CA: Stanford University Press, 2003–2016.

Hecker, Joel, trans. *The Zohar: Pritzker Edition*. Vol. 11. Stanford, CA: Stanford University Press, 2016.

Wolski, Natan, and Joel Hecker, trans. *The Zohar: Pritzker Edition*. Vol. 12. Stanford, CA: Stanford University Press, 2017.

Other Primary Sources (in chronological order)

Plotinus. *Enneads*. Vols. 5, 6, and 7. Translated by A. H. Armstrong. Cambridge, MA: Harvard University Press, 1969.

Sefer ha-Bahir. Jerusalem: Mossad HaRav Kook, 1994.

Maimonides, Moses. *The Guide of the Perplexed*. Translated by Shlomo Pines. Chicago: University of Chicago Press, 1963.

Naḥman, Moses ben [Nahmanides]. *Commentary on the Torah*. Edited by Charles Ber Chavel. New York: Shilo, 1971.

Naḥman, Moses ben. *Kitvei ha-Ramban* [The works of Nahmanides]. Edited by Charles B. Chavel. Jerusalem: Mossad HaRav Kook, 1968.

Gikatilla, Joseph ben Abraham. *Gates of Light: Sha'are Orah*. Translated by Avi Weinstein. Walnut Creek, CA: Altamira Press, 1994.

Gikatilla, Joseph ben Abraham. *Sha'arei Tsedeq* [*Gates of justice*]. Warsaw, 1883.

Gikatilla, Joseph ben Abraham. *Sod YG Middot ha-Nove'ot min ha-Keter 'Elyon ve-Niqra'im Ma'yenei ha-Yeshu'ah* [The secret of the thirteen attributes that flow from the upper crown and are called wellsprings of redemption]. In *Kitve Yad ba-Qabbalah* [Manuscripts of Qabbalah]. Edited by Gershom Scholem, 219–225. Jerusalem: Hebrew University Press, 1930.

Isaac of Acre. "Otsar Ḥayyim," Manuscript. Günzburg Collection, ms. 1062 [775], Russian State Library, Moscow.

Vital, Ḥayyim. *Sefer 'Ets Ḥayyim*. Warsaw, 1891.

Vital, Ḥayyim. *Sha'ar HaKavvanot* [The gate of intentions]. Vol. 11 of *Kitve ha-Ari* [The works of the Ari]. Jerusalem, 1988.

Luzzatto, Moshe Ḥayyim. *Sefer Adir Ba-Marom* [Mighty on high]. Jerusalem: Yosef Spiner, 1990.

Ephraim, Moshe Ḥayyim. *Degel Maḥaneh Efrayim* [The flag of the camp of Ephrayim]. Jerusalem, 1963.

Naḥman of Breslov, Rabbi. *Liqquṭe Moharan* [The gleanings of MoHaRan]. Breslov: Bnei Brak 1966.

Ḥayyim, R. Joseph [Ben Ish Ḥai]. *She'elot u-Teshuvot Rav Pe'alim* [Responsa of Rav Pe'alim]. Vol. 1. *Yoreh De'ah*, 56. Edited by Salah Mansour. Jerusalem, 1970.

Secondary Sources

Abrams, Daniel. "The Boundaries of Divine Ontology: The Inclusion and Exclusion of Meṭaṭron in the Godhead." *Harvard Theological Review* 87, no. 3 (1994): 291–321.

Abrams, Daniel. *Ha-Guf ha-'Elohi ha-Nashi ba-Qabalah* [The female body of God in Kabbalistic literature]. Jerusalem: Hebrew University Magnes Press, 2004.

Abrams, Daniel. *Kabbalistic Manuscripts and Textual Theory: Methodologies of Textual Scholarship and Editorial Practice in the Study of Jewish Mysticism*. Jerusalem: Hebrew University Magnes Press, 2010.

Afterman, Allen. *Kabbalah and Consciousness*. New York: Sheep Meadow Press, 1992.

Aḥituv, Shmuel. *'Asufat Ketuvot 'Ivri'ot me-Yemei Bayit Rishon ve-Reshit Bayit Sheni* [Handbook of ancient Hebrew inscriptions from the period of the First Commonwealth and the beginning of the Second Commonwealth]. Jerusalem: Bialik Institute, 1992.

Almansi, Renato J. "The Face-Breast Equation." *Journal of the American Psychoanalytic Association* 8 (1960): 43–70.

Altmann, Alexander. "Le-She'elat Ba'aluto Shel Sefer Ta'amei ha-Miẓvot ha-Meyuḥas le-Rabi Yiẓḥaq Ibn Parḥi" [On the question of the authorship of the book Ta'amei ha-Miẓvot attributed to Rabbi Yiẓḥaq Ibn Parḥi]. *Kiryat Sefer* 40, no. 2 (1965): 256–276.

Asulin, Shifra. "Ha-Havnayah ha-Kefulah Shel Demut ha-Shekhinah be-Ma'yan 'Ein Ya'aqov ve-Zeqatah le-Sifrut ha-'Idrot" [The double construct of the image of the Shekhinah in *Ma'ayan 'Ein Ya'aqov* and its relation to the 'Idra' literature]. In *Ma'ayan 'Ein Ya'aqov le-R. Mosheh Qordovero* [The *'Ein Ya'aqov* Spring of Rabbi Moses Cordovero], edited by Bracha Sack, 61–111. Beer Sheva: Ben-Gurion University of the Negev Press, 2008.

Asulin, Shifra. "Ha-Parshanut ha-Mistit le-Shir ha-Shirim be-Sefer ha-Zohar ve-Req'ah" [The mystical commentary of the Song of Songs in the Zohar and its background]. PhD Diss., Hebrew University, 2006.

Asulin, Shifra. "Ha-Pegam ve-Tiquno: Nidah, Levanah, ve-Shekhinah; 'Iyun Murḥav Be-Daf 'Et Be-Zohar 'Aḥarei Mot" [The flaw and its correction: Impurity, the moon and the Shekhinah—A broad inquiry into Zohar 3:79 (Aharei Mot)]. *Kabbalah: Journal for the Study of Jewish Mystical Texts* 22 (2010): 193–251.

Asulin, Shifra. "Qomatah Shel ha-Shekhinah: Mekomo Shel ha-Parẓuf ha-Elohi ha-Niqbi Ben Ha-'Idra Raba' Le-'Idra Zuṭa'" [The stature of the Shekhina: The place of the feminine Divine countenance (*parzuf*) in Idra Rabba and Idra Zuṭa]. In *Samkhut Ruḥanit: Ma'avaqim 'Al Koaḥ Tarbuti Be-Hegut Ha-Yehudit* [Spiritual authority: Struggles over cultural power in Jewish thought], edited by Howard Kreisel, Boaz Huss, and Uri Ehrlich, 103–82. Beer Sheva: Ben-Gurion University of the Negev Press, 2009.

Avivi, Joseph. *Qabalat ha-AR"I* [Kabbala Luriana]. Vols. 2 and 3. Jerusalem: Ben-Zvi Institute, 2008.

Benarroch, Jonatan M. "God and his Son: Christian Affinities in the Shaping of the Sava and Yanuka Figures in the Zohar." *Jewish Quarterly Review* 107, no. 1 (2017), 38–65.

Benarroch, Jonatan. "'Ha-Sava'-Yanuqa' ve-Ḥanokh-Metatron ke-'Arkhitip Senex-Puer (Zaqen-Na'ar): Qeri'ah Post-Yungi'anit be-Sifrut ha-Zoharit (Al Pi James Hilm'an)" [Sava-Yanuka and Enoch-Metatron as James Hillman's senex-puer archetype: A post-Jungian inquiry to a zoharic myth]. In *Ha-Dimyon ha-Parshani: Dat ve-'Emunot be-Tarbut ha-Yehudit be-Heqsherehah* [The exegetic imagination: Relationships between religion and art in Jewish culture], edited by Ruth Hacohen, Galit Hasan-Rokem, Richard Cohen, and Ilana Pardes, 46–71. Jerusalem: Hebrew University Magnes Press, 2016.

Benarroch, Jonatan M. "A Medieval Kabbalistic Response to the Patristic Exegesis on Exodus 23:19." *Journal of Religion* 99, no. 3 (2019), 263–287.

Benarroch, Jonatan M. *Sava and Yanuka: God, the Son, and the Messiah in Zoharic Narratives*. [In Hebrew]. Jerusalem: Hebrew University Magnes Press, 2018.

Benarroch, Jonatan M. "'Son of an Israelite Woman and an Egyptian Man'; Jesus as the Blasphemer (Lev. 24:10–23): An Anti-Gospel Polemic in the Zohar." *Harvard Theological Review* 110, no. 1 (2017), 100–124.

Benayahu, Meir. *Sefer Toldot ha-Ari: gilgule nusḥa'otav ve-'erko mi-beḥinah hisṭorit, nosfu 'alav hanhagot ha-An ve-azkarot rishonot* [The life of the Ari: Its various recensions and its historical value]. Jerusalem: Ben-Zvi Institute, 1967.

Berman, Nathaniel. *Divine and Demonic in the Poetic Mythology of the Zohar: The "Other Side" of Kabbalah*. Boston: Brill, 2018.

Bion, Wilfred R. *Learning from Experience*. London: Maresfield Library, 1991.

Bion, Wilfred R. *Second Thoughts: Selected Papers on Psycho-analysis*. London: Heinemann, 1967.

Bronznick, Nahum. "L'hora'ato shel haShoresh *b-s-m*" [To the understanding of the root *b-s-m*]. *Sinai* 63 (1968), 81–85.

Corbin, Henry. *Mundus Imaginalis, or the Imaginary and the Imaginal*. Ipswich: Golgonooza Press, 1976.

Corbin, Henry. *Spiritual Body and Celestial Earth*. Princeton, NJ: Princeton University Press, 1989.

Dan, Joseph. *Ha-Mistiqah ha-ʿIvrit ha-Qedumah* [The ancient Jewish mysticism]. Tel Aviv: Modan, 1989.

Dan, Joseph. *ʿIyunim be-Sifrut Ḥasidut ʾAshkenaz* [Studies in Ashkenazi Hasidic literature]. Ramat Gan: Masada, 1975.

Derrida, Jacques. *Dissemination*. Chicago: University of Chicago Press, 2017.

Doniger, Wendy. "When a Lingam Is Just a Good Cigar: Psychoanalysis and Hindu Sexual Fantasies." In *The Psychoanalytic Study of Society: Essays in Honor of Alan Dundes*, edited by L. Bryce Boyer, Ruth M. Boyer, and Stephen M. Sonnenberg, 81–104. Hillside, NJ: Analytic Press, 1993.

Eigen, Michael. "On the Significance of the Face." *Psychoanalytic Review* 67, no. 4 (1980–1981): 425–439.

Elior, Rachel. "Yeḥudah Shel ha-Tofaʿah ha-Datit be-Sifrut ha-Hekhalot: Demut ha-ʾEl ve-Harḥavat Gevulot ha-Hasagah" [The concept of God in Hekhalot mysticism]. *Jerusalem Studies in Jewish Thought* 6, no. 1/2 (1987): 13–64.

Emery, Edward. "Facing 'O': Wilfred Bion, Emmanuel Levinas, and the Face of the Other." *Psychoanalytic Review* 87, no. 6 (2000): 799–840.

Farber-Ginat, Asi. "Qelipah Qodemet le-Peri" [The husk precedes the fruit]. In *Ha-Mitos be-Yahadut* [Mythos in Judaism], edited by Haviva Pedaya, 118–142. Jerusalem: Bialik Institute, 1996.

Felix, Iris. "Te'urgiah, Magiah, ve-Mistiqah be-Qabalato Shel Rabi Yosef ha-Ba'me-Shushan ha-Birah" [Theurgy, magic, and mysticism in the Kabbalah of R. Joseph of Shushan]. PhD Diss., Hebrew University, 2005.

Fine, Lawrence. *Physician of the Soul, Healer of the Cosmos: Isaac Luria and His Kabbalistic Fellowship*. Stanford, CA: Stanford University Press, 2003.

Fishbane, Eitan. *The Art of Mystical Narrative: A Poetics of the Zohar*. Oxford: Oxford University Press, 2018.

Fishbane, Eitan. "Tears of Disclosure: The Role of Weeping in Zoharic Narrative." *Journal of Jewish Thought & Philosophy* 11, no. 1 (2002): 25–47.

Fishbane, Michael. *Biblical Myth and Rabbinic Mythmaking*. Oxford: Oxford University Press, 2005.

Fishbane, Michael. *The Kiss of God: Spiritual and Mystical Death in Judaism*. Seattle: University of Washington Press, 1996.

Fishbane, Michael. "Some Forms of Divine Appearance in Ancient Jewish Thought." In *From Ancient Israel to Modern Judaism: Intellect in Quest of Understanding: Essays in Honor of Marvin Fox*, vol. 2, edited by Jacob Neusner, Ernest S. Frerichs, and Nahum M. Sarna, 261–270. Atlanta, GA: Scholars Press, 1989.

Fishbane, Michael, "The Song of Songs and Ancient Jewish Religiosity: Between Eros and History." In *Von Enoch bis Kafka: Festschrift für Karl E. Grözinger zum 60. Geburtstag*, edited by

K. E. Grözinger, M. Voigts, and F. Battenberg, 69–81. Wiesbaden: Harrassowitz, 2002.

Friedman, Shama. "Graven Images." *Graven Images: A Journal of culture, Law, and the Sacred* 1 (1994): 233–238.

Garb, Jonathan. *Mequbal be-Lev ha-Se'arah: R. Mosheh Ḥayyim Luz'ato* [Kabbalist in the heart of the storm: R. Moses Ḥayyim Luzzatto]. Tel Aviv: Tel Aviv University Press, 2014.

Garb, Jonathan. "Sodot ha-'Emunah be-Sefer ha-Zohar" [The "secrets of faith" in the Zohar]. In *'Al ha-'Emunah u-be-Toldotav be-Mesoret ha-Yehudit* [On faith: Studies in the concept of faith and its history in the Jewish tradition], edited by Moshe Halbertal, David Kurzweil, and Avi Sagi, 294–311. Jerusalem: Keter, 2005.

Giller, Pinchas. *Reading the Zohar: The Sacred Text of the Kabbalah*. Oxford: Oxford University Press, 2001.

Ginsburg, Elliot K. *The Sabbath in the Classical Kabbalah*. Albany: State University of New York Press, 1989.

Goldreich, Amos. "Sefer ha-Gevul le-Rabi David Ben Yehudah ha-Ḥasid: Darkei 'Ibud Shel Tekst Zohari 'Aḥrei Hofa'at ha-Zohar" [The book of the boundary by Rabbi David ben Judah ha-Ḥasid: Forms of adaptation of a zoharic text after the appearance of the Zohar]. Master's thesis, Tel Aviv University, 1972.

Goodman, Micah. *Sodotav Shel Moreh ha-Nevukhim* [Maimonides and the book that changed Judaism: Secrets of *The Guide for the Perplexed*]. Or Yehudah: Dvir, 2010.

Green, Arthur. "The Children in Egypt and the Theophany at the Sea." *Judaism* 24:3 (Fall 1975): 446–456.

Green, Arthur. *Keter: The Crown of God in Early Jewish Mysticism*. Princeton, NJ: Princeton University Press, 1997.

Green, Arthur. *Seek My Face, Speak My Name: A Contemporary Jewish Theology*. Northvale, NJ: Aronson, 1992.

Green, Arthur. "Shekhina, the Virgin Mary and the Song of Songs." *AJS Review* 26, no. 1 (2002): 1–52.

Green, Arthur. "The Song of Songs in Early Jewish Mysticism." *Orim: A Jewish Journal at Yale* 2 (1987): 49–63.

Green, Arthur. "The Zaddiq as *Axis Mundi* in Later Judaism." In *The Heart of the Matter: Studies in Jewish Mysticism and Theology*, 204–222. Philadelphia, PA: Jewish Publication Society, 2015.

Halbertal, Moshe. *Concealment and Revelation: Esotericism in Jewish Thought and Its Philosophical Implications*. Princeton, NJ: Princeton University Press, 2007. Originally published as *Seter ve-Galui: Ha-Sod ve-Gevulotav be-Mesoret ha-Yehudit be-Yemei ha-Bena'im*. Jerusalem: Arna Hess, 2001.

Halbertal, Moshe. *Maimonides: Life and Thought*. Princeton, NJ: Princeton University Press, 2014.

Hallamish, Moshe. *Ha-Qabalah ba-tefila, be-halakha, u-v'minhag* [The Qabalah in prayer, law, and custom]. Ramat Gan: Bar Ilan University, 2002.

Har-Shefi, Avishar. "Kamah Shan'ay Sha'ata' Da' me-'Idra': Ha-'Idra' Zuṭa'—Mivneh ve-Mashma'ut" [How different is this time from the Idra: The Idra Zuṭa—structure and meaning]. *Kabbalah: Journal for the Study of Jewish Mystical Texts* 26 (2012): 203–228.

Har-Shefi, Avishar. *Malkhin Qadma'in: Ha-Beri'ah ve-ha-Hitgalut be-Sifrut ha-'Idrot Shel ha-Zohar* [The myth of the Edomite kings in zoharic literature: Creation and revelation in the Idrot texts of the Zohar]. Los Angeles: Cherub Press, 2014.

Haskell, Ellen. *Mystical Resistance: Uncovering the Zohar's Conversations with Christianity*. Oxford: Oxford University Press. 2016.

Hayman, A. Peter. *Sefer Yeṣira: Edition, Translation and Text-Critical Commentary*. Tübingen: Mohr Siebeck, 2004.

Hellner-Eshed, Melila. "Ha-Meqane' le-Brit ve-Ba'al ha-Shigyonot; 'Eliyahu ve-Ḥabaquq be-Zohar: 'Al ha-Zikhri ve-ha-Niqbi be-Nefesh ha-'Adam" [The zealot of the covenant and the ecstatic Elijah and Habakkuk in the Zohar: On the masculine and feminine in the human psyche]. *Kabbalah: Journal for the Study of Jewish Mystical Texts* 22 (2011): 149–192.

Hellner-Eshed, Melila. "Malkhei Edom v'Ḥomrei Beta: K'she-safot Nifgashot" [The Kings of Edom and beta elements: When two languages meet]. Lecture presented at the Tel Aviv Psychoanalytic Institute, December 2018.

Hellner-Eshed, Melila. *A River Flows from Eden*. Stanford, CA: Stanford University Press, 2009.

Hellner-Eshed, Melila. "Temunot me-Ḥayyei Mishpaḥah: Mitosim 'Al ha-Shekhinah Metokh "Ein Ya'aqov' le-R. Mosheh Qordovero" [Domestic troubles: Family myths in Moshe Cordovero's book *'Eilima*]. *Te'uda* 21/22, no. 3 (2007): 419–448.

Huss, Boaz. *The Zohar: Reception and Impact*. Oxford: Littman Library of Jewish Civilization in association with Liverpool University Press, 2016.

Idel, Moshe. *Enchanted Chains: Techniques and Rituals in Jewish Mysticism*. Los Angeles: Cherub Press, 2005.

Idel, Moshe. "'Ha-Maḥshavah ha-Ra'ah' Shel ha-'El" ["The evil thought" of the Deity]. *Tarbiz* 49, no. 3/4 (1980): 356–364.

Idel, Moshe. "Ha-Sefirot she-me-'Al ha-Sefirot: Le-Ḥeker Mekoroteihem Shel Rishonei ha-Mequbalim" [The sefirot above the sefirot: The history of the sources of the first kabbalists]. *Tarbiz* 51, no. 2 (1981): 239–280.

Idel, Moshe. "The Image of Man above the Sefirot: R. David ben Yehuda ha-Hasid's Theosophy of Ten Supernal Shasahot and Its Reverberations" [in Hebrew]. *Kabbalah* 20 (2009): 181–212.

Idel, Moshe. *Kabbalah and Eros*. New Haven, CT: Yale University Press, 2005.

Idel, Moshe. *Kabbalah: New Perspectives*. New Haven, CT: Yale University Press, 1990.

Idel, Moshe. "Leviyatan u-Vat Zugo" [Leviathan and its consort]. In *Ha-Mitos be-Yahadut: Historiah, Hegut, Sifrut* [Myths in Judaism: History, thought, literature], edited by Moshe Idel and Ithamar Gruenwald, 145–189. Jerusalem: Zalman Shazar Center for Jewish History, 2004.

Idel, Moshe. "'Od 'Al Rabi David Ben Yehudah ha-Ḥasid ve-ha-'AR"I" [Once more about R. David Ben Yehudah ha-Ḥasid]. *Daat: A Journal of Jewish Philosophy & Kabbalah* 7 (1981): 69–71.

Idel, Moshe. "Panim: On Facial Re-Presentations in Jewish Thought: Some Correlational

Instances." In *On Interpretation in the Arts: Interdisciplinary Studies in Honor of Moshe Lazar*, edited by Nurit Yaari, 21–56. Tel-Aviv: Yolanda and David Katz Faculty of the Arts, Tel Aviv University, 2000.

Idel, Moshe. *Peraqim be-Qabalah Nevu'it* [Studies in ecstatic Kabbalah]. Jerusalem: Academon, 1990.

Idel, Moshe. *Shelemuyot Bol'ot: Qabalah ve-Parshanut* [Absorbing perfections: Kabbalah and interpretation]. Tel Aviv: Yediot Aharonot, 2012.

Jonas, Hans. *The Gnostic Religion: The Message of the Alien God & the Beginnings of Christianity*. Boston: Beacon Press, 1968.

Jung, Carl Gustav. *Symbols of Transformation: An Analysis of the Prelude to a Case of Schizophrenia*. New York: Pantheon Books, 1956.

Kaplan, Aryeh. *Sefer Yetzirah: The Book of Creation*. York Beach, ME: Weiser, 1997.

Kara-Ivanov Kaniel, Ruth. "Likhtov 'O Lo' Likhtov: Mitos ha-Ketivah be-Sefer ha-Zohar" [To write or not to write: The myth of writing in the Zohar]. In *Ha-Sipur ha-Zohari* [The zoharic story], edited by Yehuda Liebes, Melila Hellner-Eshed, and Jonatan Benarroch, 1:238–306. Jerusalem: Ben-Zvi Institute, 2017.

Kara-Ivanov Kaniel, Ruth. "Liv'or me-Ahavah: Ma'aseh Nadav ve-'Avihu ke-Ritu'al 'Eroti 'Unio Misti" [Consumed by love: The death of Nadav and Avihu as a ritual of erotic mystical union]. *Te'uda* 26 (2014): 585–653.

Kaufmann, Yehezkel. *Toldot ha-'Emunah ha-Yisra'elit: me-Yemei Qedem 'Ad Sof Bayit Sheni* [The history of the Israelite faith: From antiquity to the end of the Second Commonwealth]. Jerusalem: Bialik Institute, 1965.

King, Karen L. *The Secret Revelation of John*. Cambridge, MA: Harvard University Press, 2006.

King, Karen L. *What Is Gnosticism?* Cambridge, MA: Harvard University Press, 2005.

Knohl, Israel. *'Emunot ha-Miqra': Gevulot ha-Mahapekhah ha-Miqra'it* [Biblical beliefs: The borders of the biblical revolution]. Jerusalem: Hebrew University Magnes Press, 2007.

Kristeva, Julia. *Powers of Horror: An Essay on Abjection*. New York: Columbia University Press, 1982.

Lieberman, Saul. "Mishnat Shir ha-Shirim." In *Jewish Gnosticism: Merkabah Mysticism and Talmudic Tradition*, by Gershom Scholem, 118–126. New York: Jewish Theological Seminary Press, 1960.

Liebes, Esther. "Qordovero ve-ha-'AR"I: Beḥinah Meḥudeshet Shel Mitos Mot Malkhei 'Edom" [Cordovero and Luria]. In *Ma'ayan 'Ein Ya'aqov le-R. Mosheh Qordovero* [The *'Ein Ya'aqov* Spring of Rabbi Moses Cordovero], edited by Bracha Sack, 32–60. Beer Sheva: Ben-Gurion University of the Negev Press, 2008.

Liebes, Yehuda. *'Alilot 'Elohim: Ha-Mitos ha-Yehudi—Masot ve-Meḥqarim* [God's story: Collected essays on the Jewish myth]. Jerusalem: Carmel Press, 2008.

Liebes, Yehuda. "Golem be-Gimatria' Ḥokhmah" [Golem in numerology is Ḥokhmah]. *Kiryat Sefer* 63, no. 4 (1989): 1305–1322.

Liebes, Yehuda. "Ha-'Erom ha-Melubash: 'Avodat ha-Qodesh ha-Sodit ve-ha-'Ezoteriut 'Ezel Filon ha-'Aleksandroni" [Clothed nudity: The esoteric cult of Philo]. *Jerusalem*

Studies in Jewish Thought 24 (2015): 9–28.

Liebes, Yehuda. "Ha-Mashiaḥ Shel ha-Zohar" [The messiah of the Zohar]. In *The Messianic Idea in Israel*, 87–236. Jerusalem: National Israeli Academy of Sciences, 1982.

Liebes, Yehuda. "Ha-Mitos ha-Qabali she-be-Fi 'Orfi'us" [The Kabbalistic myth of Orpheus]. *Jerusalem Studies in Jewish Thought* 7 (1988): 425–59.

Liebes, Yehuda. "Ha-Sipur ha-Zohari bi-Khelal ve-Gilgulei Hormenuta' ve-Semitra'" [The zoharic story in general, and the development of the ideas of "Hormenuta" and "Semitra"]. In *Ha-Sipur ha-Zohari* [The zoharic story], edited by Yehuda Liebes, Jonatan Benarroch, and Melila Hellner-Eshed, 1:14–60. Jerusalem: Ben-Zvi Institute, 2017.

Liebes, Yehuda. "Ha-Zohar ve-ha-Tiqunim: Me-Renesans la-Mahapekhah" [Zohar and tiqqunei Zohar: From renaissance to revolution]. *Te'uda* 21/22, no. 2 (2007): 251–301.

Liebes, Yehuda. *Ḥet'o Shel 'Elisha': 'Arba'ah she-Nikhnesu le-Pardes ve-Tiv'ah Shel ha-Mistiqah ha-Talmudit* [The sin of Elisha: Four entered the Orchard and the nature of talmudic mysticism]. Jerusalem: Academon, 1990.

Liebes, Yehuda. "Ko'aḥ ha-Milah ke-Yesod Mashma'utah be-Sifrut ha-Qabalah" [The power of a word as the basis for its meaning in Kabbalah]. In *Devar Devor 'Al 'Ofanav: Meḥqarim be-Parshanut ha-Miqra' ve-ha-Qur'an be-Yemei ha-Benayyim Mugashim le-Ḥagai Ben-Sham'ai* [A word fitly spoken: Studies in medieval exegesis of the Hebrew Bible and the Qur'ān: Presented to Haggai Ben-Shammai], edited by Meir M. Bar-Asher, Simon Hopkins, Sarah Stroumsa, and Bruno Chiesa, 163–177. Jerusalem: Ben-Zvi Institute, 2007.

Liebes, Yehuda. "Le-Haḥzir le-'El Et Panav." [Returning God's face]. *Dimmuy* 25 (2005): 50–53.

Liebes, Yehuda. "Mar'ish ha-Areẓ: Yeḥiduto Shel RaSHB"I" [Earth shaker: RaShBY's aloneness]. In *Yahadut: Sugiyot, Qeta'im, Panim, Zehuyot* [Judaism, topics, fragments, faces, identities], edited by Haviva Pedaya and Ephraim Meir, 337–357. Beer Sheva: Ben-Gurion University of the Negev Press, 2007.

Liebes, Yehuda. "Myth vs. Symbolism in the Zohar and in Lurianic Kabbalah." In *Essential Papers on Kabbalah*, edited by Lawrence Fine, 212–242. New York: New York University Press, 1995.

Liebes, Yehuda. "Peraqim be-Milon Sefer ha-Zohar" [Sections of the Zohar lexicon]. PhD diss., Hebrew University, 1976.

Liebes, Yehuda. *Pulḥan ha-Shaḥar: Yaḥas ha-Zohar le-'Avodah Zarah* [The cult of the dawn: The attitude of the Zohar toward idolatry]. Jerusalem: Carmel Press, 2011.

Liebes, Yehuda. "Shablonizaẓiah Ve-Heḥiyy'atah Be-Mitos Ha-Zohari" [Shablonization and its revival of Jewish myth]. Lecture presented at the conference "Kenes Sifrut Ha-Zohar ve-Dorah" [The literature of the Zohar and its generation], Beer Sheva, Israel, June 12, 2014.

Liebes, Yehuda. "Shenat Petirato Shel R. Mosheh De Li'on." In *Sefer ha-Zikaron le-Me'ir Benayahu* [Meir Benayahu—memorial volume], edited by Moshe Bar-Asher, Yehuda Liebes, Moshe Assis, and Yosef Kaplan, 745–750. Jerusalem: Carmel Press, 2019.

Liebes, Yehuda. *Studies in the Zohar*. Albany: State University of New York Press, 1993.

Liebes, Yehuda. *Torat ha-Yeẓirah Shel Sefer Yeẓirah* [Ars poetica in Sefer Yetzirah]. Jerusalem: Schocken Books, 2000.

Liebes, Yehuda. "'Zaka'in 'Inun Yisra'el': Berakhah be-Lashon ha-Zohar ve-Riq'ah ha-Yehudi-Noẓri" ["Happy are Israel": A blessing in the language of the Zohar and its Jewish-Christian background]. *Iggud: Selected Essays in Jewish Studies* 14, no. 3 (2005): 85–94.

Liebes, Yehuda. "Zemirot le-Se'udot Shabat she-Yasad ha-'AR"I ha-Qadosh" [The Sabbath table songs established by R. Isaac Luria]. *Molad* 4, no. 23 (1972): 540–555.

Liebes, Yehuda. "Zohar and Iamblichus." *Journal for the Study of Religions and Ideologies* 6, no. 18 (2007): 95–100.

Liebes, Yehuda. "Zohar ve-'Eros" [Zohar and eros]. *Alpayyim* 9 (1994): 67–115.

Lorberbaum, Menachem. *Nuẓaḥnu be-Ne'imuto: Torat ha-'Elohut ḳe-Po'etiqah be-Yeẓirah ha-Yehudit ha-'Andalusit* [Dazzled by beauty: Theology as poetic in medieval Jewish thought]. Jerusalem: Ben-Zvi Institute, 2011.

Lorberbaum, Yair. *In God's Image: Myth, Theology, and Law in Classical Judaism*. New York: Cambridge University Press, 2015.

Marion, Jean-Luc. *God without Being*. Chicago: University of Chicago Press, 1995.

Matt, Daniel C., ed. *The Boọk of Mirrors: Sefer Mar'ot ha-Zove'ot by R. David ben Yehudah he-Hasid*. Chico, CA: Scholars Press, 1982.

Matt, Daniel. "New/Ancient Words: The Aura of Secrecy in the Zohar." In *Gershom Scholem's Major Trends in Jewish Mysticism 50 Years After: Proceedings of the Sixth International Conference on the History of Jewish Mysticism*, edited by Peter Schäfer and Joseph Dan, 181–207. Tübingen: J.C.B. Mohr, 1993.

Meroz, Ronit. "Der Aufbau des Buches Sohar." *PaRDeS* (Zeitschrift der Vereinigung für Jüdische Studien) 5, no. 2 (2005), 16–36.

Meroz, Ronit. "Maḥarozet Ha-Sippurim 'Ḥayyei RaShB"I' ve-ha- Shikhvah ha-Epit ba-Zohar" ["RaShB"I's biography" as a zoharic unit and the epic layer of the Zohar]. In *Ha-Sipur ha-Zohari* [The zoharic story], edited by Yehuda Liebes, Jonatan Benarroch, and Melila Hellner-Eshed, 1:63–96. Jerusalem: Ben-Zvi Institute, 2017.

Meroz, Ronit. "Reqimato Shel Mitos: Diyun be-Shenei Sipurim ba-Zohar" [The weaving of a myth: The analysis of two zoharic homilies on the Shekhina and their narrative context]. In *Limud ve-Da'at be-Maḥshavah Yehudit* [Study and knowledge in Jewish thought], edited by Howard Kreisel, 2:167–205. Beer Sheva: Ben-Gurion University of the Negev Press, 2006.

Meroz, Ronit. *Yuvalei Zohar: Meḥqar u-Mahadurot Shel Zohar, Parashat Shemot* [Headwaters of the Zohar: Analysis & annotated critical edition of Parashat Exodus of the Zohar]. Tel Aviv: Tel Aviv University Press, 2019.

Neumann, Erich. *The Great Mother*. Princeton, NJ: Princeton University Press, 1991.

Neumann, Erich. *Ha-Adam ha-Misṭi*. Tel Aviv: Resling, 2007. Published in English as "Mystical Man." In *The Mystic Vision*, Papers from the Eranos Yearbooks: Eranos 6, edited by Joseph Campbell, 375–415. Princeton, NJ: Princeton University Press, 1968.

Neumann, Erich. *Ha-Yeled: ha-'Ishiyut be-Shaḥar Hitpatḥutah*. Translated by Yael

Treiber. Beit Yehoshua: Hasinut, 2011. Originally published as *Das Kind: Struktur und Dynamik der werdenden Persönlichkeit*.

Neumann, Erich. *The Origins and History of Consciousness*. Princeton, NJ: Princeton University Press, 1995.

Oliver, Mary. *New and Selected Poems*. Boston: Beacon Press, 1992.

Otto, Rudolf. *The Idea of the Holy: An Inquiry into the Non-rational Factor in the Idea of the Divine and Its Relation to the Rational*. New York: Oxford University Press, 1958.

Pedaya, Haviva. *Ha-Mar'eh ve-ha-Dibur: 'Iyun be-Tiv'ah Shel Ḥavva'yat ha-Hitgalut be-Mistorin ha-Yehudi* [Vision and speech: Models of revelatory experience in Jewish mysticism]. Los Angeles: Cherub Press, 2002.

Pedaya, Haviva. *Ha-RaMBa"N: Hit'alut: Zeman Maḥzori ve-Teqst Qadosh* [Nahmanides: Cyclical time and holy text]. Tel Aviv: Am Oved, 2003.

Pedaya, Haviva. "Re'iyyah, Nefilah, Shirah: Hishtoqequt Re'iyyat ha-'El ve-ha-Yesod ha-Ruḥi be-Mistorin ha-Yehudi ha-Qadum" [Sight, fall, song: The desire to see God and the spiritual element in ancient Jewish mysticism]. *Asufot* 9 (1995): 237–277.

Pedaya, Haviva. "'Ve-Hashta' 'Ima' Let Lan': Qavvim le-Geni'ologiah Shel ha-Shekhinah ve-ha-'Em" [And now we have no mother: Toward a genealogy of the Shekhinah and the mother]. In *As a Perennial Spring: A Festschrift Honoring Rabbi Dr. Norman Lamm*, edited by Bentsi Cohen, 87–151. New York: Downhill, 2013.

Pedaya, Haviva. "Zeman Ma'agali ve-Zeman Qavvi: Ha-'Em ha-Gedolah ve-ha-'Em ha-Qetanah, ha-Shekhinah; Ben Ḥug ha-RaMBa"N le-Ḥug ha-Zohar" [Circular time and linear time: The Great Mother and the Small Mother, the Shekhinah in the circle of Nahmanides and the circle of the Zohar]. In *Shedamot ve-Ruaḥ: Maḥavvat Hoqarah ve-Yedidut le-'Avraham Shapira'* [Fields in the wind: A tribute to Avraham Shapira, in friendship and appreciation], edited by Avihu Zakai, Paul Mendes-Flohr, and Zeev Gries, 322–337. Jerusalem: Carmel Press, 2015.

Quispel, Gilles. "Ezekiel 1:26 in Jewish Mysticism and Gnosis." *Vigilia Christianae* 34, no. 1 (January 1980): 1–13.

Rippel-Kleiman, Hana. "Mel'ai 'Einayyim: 'Al 'Einayyim ve-Re'iyyah be-Sefer ha-Zohar" [Full of eyes: On eyes and vision in the Zohar]. Master's thesis, Hebrew University, 2009.

Roi, Biti. *Love of the Shekhina: Mysticism and Poetics in Tiqqunei ha-Zohar*. [In Hebrew.] Ramat Gan: Bar Ilan University, 2017.

Roi, Biti. "Mitos ha-Shekhinah be-Sifrut Tiqunei ha-Zohar: Hebetim Po'etim, Parshani'im, ve-Misti'im" [The myth of the Shekhinah in tiqunei Zohar literature: Poetic, hermeneutic, and mystical aspects]. PhD diss., Bar-Ilan University, 2012.

Rosenzweig, Franz. *Naharayyim: Mivḥar Ketavim* [A land of two rivers: Selected works]. Edited and translated by Yehoshua Amir. Jerusalem: Bialik Institute, 1977.

Sachs Shmueli, Leore. "The Rationale of the Negative Commandments by R. Joseph Hamadan: A Critical Edition and Study of Taboo in the Time of the Composition of the Zohar." [In Hebrew.] PhD diss., Bar Ilan University, 2019.

Sack, Bracha. *Be-Sha'arei ha-Qabalah Shel Rabi Mosheh Qordovero* [The Kabbalah of R. Moshe Cordovero]. Beer Sheva: Ben-Gurion University of the Negev Press, 1995.

Sack, Bracha. *Ma'ayan 'Ein Ya'aqov le-Rabi Mosheh Qordovero* [The *'Ein Ya'aqov* Spring of Rabbi Moses Cordovero]. Beer Sheva: Ben Gurion University of the Negev, 2008.

Sack, Bracha. *Me-Ma'ayyanot Sefer 'Alimah le-R. Mosheh Qordovero ve- Meḥqarim be-Qabalato* [*From the Fountains of Sefer Elimah* by R. Moshe Cordovero and studies in his Kabbalah]. Beer Sheva: Ben-Gurion University of the Negev Press, 2013.

Schneider, Sarah, ed. *Nefilatah Ve-'Aliyyatah Shel ha-Shekhinah: Ketavim Qabali'im 'Al Nashiut ve-Gavriut* [Kabbalistic writings on the nature of masculine and feminine]. Jerusalem: Reuven Mas, 2008.

Scholem, Gershom. "'Iqvotaw shel Gabirol ba-Qabbalah." [The imprint of Gabirol in the Qabbalah]. In *Ma'asef Sofrey Eretz Yisra'el* [Anthology of the authors of the Land of Israel], 160–178. Tel Aviv: Aggudat ha-Sofrim, 1940.

Scholem, Gershom. *Kabbalah*. New York: New York Times Book Company, 1974.

Scholem, Gershom. *Major Trends in Jewish Mysticism*. New York: Schocken Books, 1991.

Scholem, Gershom. *On the Kabbalah and Its Symbolism*. New York: Schocken Books, 1969.

Scholem, Gershom. *On the Mystical Shape of the Godhead: Basic Concepts in the Kabbalah*. New York: Schocken Books, 1991.

Scholem, Gershom. *Qabalot R. Ya'aqov v'R. Yiẓḥaq Benei Ya'aqov Ha-Kohen* [The Qabala of Rabbis Jacob and Isaac, sons of Jacob the Cohen]. Jerusalem: Hamadpis, 1923.

Scholem, Gershom. "Shekhinah: The Feminine Element in Divinity." In *On the Mystical Shape of the Godhead: Basic Concepts in the Kabbalah*, 140–196. New York: Schocken Books, 1991.

Shasha, Omri. "'Milin La' 'Itgalyan 'Ela' Beinena'': 'Al Sipur Kefar Tarsha' ve-'Ibudo" ["Words are revealed only among us": On the story of Kfar Tasha and its adaptation]. In *Ha-Sipur ha-Zohari* [The zoharic story], edited by Yehuda Liebes, Jonatan M. Benarroch, and Melila Hellner-Eshed, 2:463–514. Jerusalem: Ben-Zvi Institute, 2017.

Smith, Jonathan Z. *Map Is Not Territory*. Chicago: University of Chicago Press, 1978.

Sobol, Neta. "'En Mal'akh 'Eḥad 'Oseh Shetei Sheliḥuyot: 'Al Rega' Dramati ba-'Idra' Raba'" [No angel performs two missions: On one dramatic moment in Idra Rabba]. *Kabbalah: Journal for the Study of Jewish Mystical Texts* 22 (2010): 282–303.

Sobol, Neta. "Ḥativat ha-'Idrot be-Sifrut ha-Zohar" [The Idra stratum in Zoharic literature]. PhD diss., Tel Aviv University, 2011.

Sobol, Neta. "Sipur Qayin ve-Hevel ke-Pereq Siyum le-Mitos Mot ha-Melkhim ba-'Idra' Raba" [The story of Cain and Abel as a closing chapter for the myth of the death of the kings in the Idra]. In *Ha-Sipur ha-Zohari* [The zoharic story], ed. Yehuda Liebes, Jonatan Benarroch, and Melila Hellner-Eshed, 2:564–585. Jerusalem: Ben-Zvi Institute, 2017.

Sobol, Neta. *Transgression of the Torah and the Rectification of God: The Theosophy of Idra Rabba in the Zohar and Its Unique Status in Thirteenth-Century Spanish Kabbalah*. [In Hebrew.] Los Angeles: Cherub Press, 2017.

Sviri, Sara. *Ha-Sufim* [The Sufis: An anthology]. Tel Aviv: Tel Aviv University, 2008.

Tishby, Isaiah. *Paths of Faith and Heresy*. [In Hebrew.] Jerusalem: Hebrew University Magnes Press, 1982.

Tishby, Isaiah. *The Wisdom of the Zohar: An Anthology of Texts*. 3 vols. Oxford: Published for the Littman Library by Oxford University Press, 1989.

Tulku, Tarthang. *Time, Space and Knowledge: A New Vision of Reality*. Emeryville, CA: Dharma Publishing Bookstore, 1977.

Twersky, Isadore. *Rabad of Posquières: A 12th-Century Talmudist*. Cambridge, MA: Harvard University Press, 1962.

Wallace, B. Alan. "Intersubjectivity in Indo-Tibetan Buddhism." *Journal of Consciousness Studies* 8 (5–7) (2001): 209–230.

Weiss, Joseph G. *Meḥqarim be-Sifrut Breslav* [Studies in Breslav Hassidism]. Jerusalem: Bialik Institute, 1974.

Weiss, Tzahi. *Mot ha-Shekhinah be-Yeẓirat Sha"Y 'Agnon: Qeri'ah be-'Arba'ah Sippurim u-be-Mekorotehem* [Death of the Shekhina: Readings in four Agnon stories and in their sources]. Ramat Gan: Bar-Ilan University Press, 2009.

Winnicott, D. W. *Playing and Reality*. London: Routledge, 2017.

Wolfson, Elliot R. *Along the Path: Studies in Kabbalistic Myth, Symbolism, and Hermeneutics*. Albany: State University of New York Press, 1995.

Wolfson, Elliot R. *Circle in the Square: Studies in the Use of Gender in Kabbalistic Symbolism*. Albany: State University of New York Press, 1995.

Wolfson, Elliot R. "Dimui 'Antropomorfi ve-ha-Simboliqah Shel ha-'Otiyot be-Sefer ha-Zohar" [The anthropomorphic and symbolic image of the letters in the Zohar]. *Jerusalem Studies in Jewish Thought* 8 (1989): 147–181.

Wolfson, Elliot R. "Forms of Visionary Ascent as Ecstatic Experience in the Zoharic Literature." In *Gershom Scholem's Major Trends in Jewish Mysticism* 50 *Years After: Proceedings of the Sixth International Conference on the History of Jewish Mysticism*, edited by Peter Schäfer and Joseph Dan. Tübingen: J.C.B. Mohr, 1993.

Wolfson, Elliot R. "Iconicity of the Text: Reification of Torah and the Idolatrous Impulse of Zoharic Kabbalah." In *Elliot R. Wolfson: Poetic Thinking*, edited by Elliot R. Wolfson, Hava Tirosh-Samuelson, and Aaron W. Hughes, 69–96. Leiden: Brill, 2015.

Wolfson, Elliot R. "The Image of Jacob Engraved upon the Throne." In *Along the Path: Studies in Kabbalistic Myth, Symbolism, and Hermeneutics*, 1–62. Albany: State University of New York Press, 1995.

Wolfson, Elliot R. "Images of God's Feet: Some Observations on the Divine Body in Judaism." In *People of the Body: Jews and Judaism from an Embodied Perspective*, edited by H. Eilberg-Schwartz, 143–181. Albany: State University of New York Press, 1992.

Wolfson, Elliot R. *Language, Eros, Being: Kabbalistic Hermeneutics and Poetic Imagination*. New York: Fordham University Press, 2005.

Wolfson, Elliot R. *Luminal Darkness: Imaginal Gleanings from Zoharic Literature*. Oxford: Oneworld, 2007.

Wolfson, Elliot R. "Murmuring Secrets: Eroticism and Esotericism in Medieval Kabbalah." In *Hidden Intercourse: Eros and Sexuality in the History of Western Esotericism*, edited by Wouter J. Hanegraff and Jeffrey J. Kripal, 65–109. New York: Fordham University Press, 2011.

Wolfson, Elliot R. "Occultation of the Feminine and the Body of Secrecy in Medieval

Kabbalah." In *Rending the Veil: Concealment and Revelation of Secrets in the History of Religions*, edited by Elliot R. Wolfson, 113–154. New York: Seven Bridges Press, 1999.

Wolfson, Elliot R. "Re/membering the Covenant: Memory, Forgetfulness, and History in the Zohar." In *Jewish History and Jewish Memory: Essays in Honor of Yosef Hayim Yerushalmi,* edited by Elisheva Carlebach, John M. Efron, and David N. Myers, 214–246. Hanover, NH: University Press of New England for Brandeis University Press, 1998.

Wolfson, Elliot R. "Sacred Space and Mental Iconography: Imago Templi and Contemplation in Rhineland Jewish Pietism." In *Ki Baruch Hu: Ancient Near Eastern, Biblical, and Judaic Studies in Honor of Baruch A. Levine*, edited by R. Chazan, W. W. Hallo, and L. H. Schiffman, 593–634. Winona Lake, IN: Eisenbrauns, 1999.

Wolfson, Elliot R. *Through a Speculum That Shines: Vision and Imagination in Medieval Jewish Mysticism.* Princeton, NJ: Princeton University Press, 1997.

Wolfson, Elliot. "The Tree That Is All: Jewish-Christian Roots of a Kabbalistic Symbol in *Sefer ha-Bahir*." In *Along the Path: Studies in Kabbalistic Myth, Symbolism, and Hermeneutics*, 63–88. Albany: State University of New York Press, 1995.

Wolfson, Elliot R. "Woman—the Feminine as Other in Theosophic Kabbalah: Some Philosophical Observations on the Divine Androgyne." In *The Other in Jewish Thought and History: Constructions of Jewish Culture and Identity*, edited by Laurence J. Silberstein and Robert L. Cohn, 166–204. New York: New York University Press, 1994.

Wolski, Nathan, and Merav Carmeli. "Those Who Know Have Wings: Celestial Journeys with the Masters of the Academy." *Kabbalah* 16 (2007): 83–115.

Yarḥi, Yose. "Ma'amar 'Aseret Harugei Malkhut ve-Mot ha-Melakhim she-me-Ketivat Yad ha-'AR"I; Hebetim Shel Torat ha-Gilgul be-Me'ot ha-Shelosh Esrei la-Shesh Esrei" [The exegesis on the Ten Martyrs and the death of the kings from the original writings of the Ari: Aspects of the theory of Gilgul between the 14th and the 16th centuries]. Master's thesis, Hebrew University, 1995.

Yisraeli, Oded. *Parshanut ha-Sod ve-Sod ha-Parshanut: Megamot Midrashiot ve-Hermenuitiot be-'Sava de-Mishpatim' she-be-Zohar* [The interpretation of secrets and the secret of interpretation: Midrashic and hermeneutic strategies in Sabba de-Mishpatim of the Zohar]. Los Angeles: Cherub Press, 2005.

Yisraeli, Oded. *Pitḥei Hekhal: 'Iyunei 'Agadah ve-Midrah Be-Sefer ha-Zohar* [Temple portals: Studies in Aggadah and Midrash in the Zohar]. Jerusalem: Hebrew University Magnes Press, 2013.

Zeitlin, Hillel. *'Al Gevul Shenei 'Olamot* [On the border between two worlds]. Tel Aviv: Yavneh, 1997.

Zeitlin, Hillel. *Be-Pardes ha-Qabalah ve-ha-Ḥasidut.* [In the orchard of Qabalah and *Ḥasidut*]. Tel Aviv: Yavneh, 1982.

Zelda. *The Spectacular Difference: Selected Poems of Zelda*. Translated by Marcia Falk. Cincinnati, OH: Hebrew Union College Press, 2004.

Index

Stanford Studies in Jewish Mysticism
Clémence Boulouque & Ariel Evan Mayse, EDITORS

Stanford Studies in Jewish Mysticism seeks to provide a prominent forum for pathbreaking academic scholarship that explores the multifaceted phenomena of Jewish mysticism spanning from late antiquity into the present from a variety of perspectives.

This new series is meant to serve as an intellectual meeting ground for scholars interested in the many worlds of Jewish mysticism. *Stanford Studies in Jewish Mysticism* welcomes innovative studies that draw upon textual, hermeneutical, historical, philosophical, sociological, anthropological, and cultural modes of analysis. The series also invites work that interrogates mysticism as a central category and thereby aims to apply new theoretical and methodological lenses; manuscripts that engage with broader issues and cut across disciplinary silos are particularly welcome. Further, the series will consider rigorous works of constructive theology that represent a sustained engagement with the writings and traditions of Jewish mysticism.

CPSIA information can be obtained
at www.ICGtesting.com
Printed in the USA
LVHW112114200721
693245LV00001B/1/J